LINES OF SUCCESSION

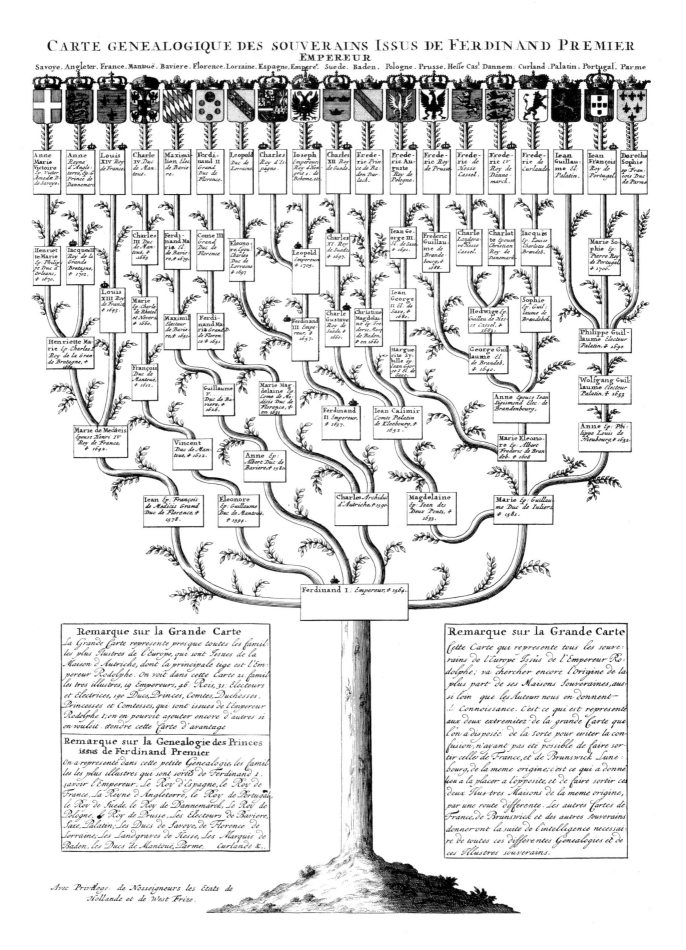

LINES OF SUCCESSION

HERALDRY OF THE ROYAL FAMILIES OF EUROPE

TABLES BY
JIŘÍ LOUDA

TEXT BY
MICHAEL MACLAGAN

MACMILLAN PUBLISHING COMPANY
NEW YORK

MAXWELL MACMILLAN CANADA
TORONTO

To my wife, Jára, for the countless silent evenings
and weekends during which this book was created

Jiří Louda

The publishers would like to thank the following for providing the illustrations on the pages listed below:

Ampliaciones Reproducciones Mas, Barcelona 66 (Museo del Prado,
Madrid), 90 (Patrimonio Nacional, Madrid); BBC Hulton Picture Li-
brary, London 82, 116, 136; Bibliotèque Nationale, Paris 13; Bibliotèque
Royale, Albert I, Brussels 226; Bildarchiv Preussischer Kulturbesitz, Ber-
lin 204 (Gemäldegalerie, Dresden), 215; British Library, London 28, 129,
146, 173, 232, 233, 249; Caisse Nationale des Monuments Historiques,
Paris 11; Collection Viollet, Paris 205 (Gemäldegalerie, Dresden);
Danish Ministry of Foreign Affairs, Copenhagen 48; Det Nationalhis-
toriske Museum, Frederiksborg 59; Giraudon, Paris 141 (Musée Condé,
Chantilly); I.G.D.A., Milan 257 (M. Carrieri); Kunsthistorisches
Museum, Vienna 154; Mansell Collection 103 (Museo del Prado), 122
top, 122 bottom, 244, 281, 296; Musée de l'Armée, Paris 143; Öster-
reichische Nationalbibliothek, Vienna 39; Popperfoto, London 35, 206;
Reproduced by gracious permission of Her Majesty the Queen 54, 198;
Rijksmuseum, Amsterdam 76; Sammlungen des Regierenden Fürsten
von Liechtenstein 112; Staatsarchiv Schwerin, Berlin 219; Statens Kon-
stmuseer, Stockholm 277; Svenska Porträttarkivet Nationalmuseum,
Stockholm 61; Universitätsbibliothek, Heidelberg 214.

Macmillan Publishing Company   Maxwell Macmillan Canada, Inc.
866 Third Avenue   1200 Eglington Avenue East
New York, NY 10022   Suite 200
                                      Don Mills, Ontario M3C

Macmillan Publishing Company is part of the Maxwell
Communication Group of Companies.

Printed in Czechoslovakia by Neografia, Martin

printing number
1 2 3 4 5 6 7 8 9 10

Library of Congress Number: 91-35681

ISBN 0-02-897255-4

CONTENTS

NOTES TO THE TABLES

Members of the reigning family of a country are given in capital letters, and on the Tables with general surveys the rulers' line of descent is indicated by a red line. Illegitimate descent is indicated by a wavy line. It should be noted that names have been anglicized except when they are better known in their original form (see p.8); a uniform style of spelling some names has therefore not been adopted.

Abbreviations and symbols

abdic.	abdicated
Abp.	Archbishop
AD.	Archduke, Archduchess
Alb.	Albert
Albr.	Albrecht
Alex.	Alexander
Anth.	Anthony
Aug.	Augustus
B.	Baron, Baroness
Bgv.	Burgrave
Bp.	Bishop
Bt.	Baronet
C.	Count, Countess
Christ.	Christian
cr.	created
Cr. Pr.	Crown Prince
d.	daughter
D.	Duke, Duchess
decl.	declared
div.	divorced
E.	Earl
El.	Elector
Eman.	Emanuel
Emp.	Emperor, Empress
ex.	executed
ext.	extinct
Ferd.	Ferdinand
Fred.	Frederick
gd.	granddaughter
Gd.	Grand
Gd. M.	Grand Master
GD.	Grand-Duke, Grand-Duchess
Gov.	Governor
gs.	grandson
Gust.	Gustavus
Her. Pr.	Hereditary Prince
illeg.	illegitimate
Jos.	Joseph
k.	killed
K.	King
L.	Lord
Lgv.	Landgrave
m.	married
M.	Marquis, Marquess
Magd.	Magdalen
Max.	Maximilian
Mgv.	Margrave
murd.	murdered
nat.	natural (illegitimate)
O.	Order
Palat.	Palatine
Patr.	Patriarch
Pgv.	Palsgrave
Pr.	Prince, Princess
procl.	proclaimed
Q.	Queen
res.	resigned
rest.	restored
Roman K.	King of the Romans
Roman Emp.	(Holy) Roman Emperor [the adjective 'Holy' was introduced by Barbarossa in 1157]
s.	son, sister
Salv.	Salvator
Sig.	Sigismund
suic.	suicide
Theod.	Theodore
tit.	titular
V.	Viscount
w.	widow
Wm.	William
♔	reigning sovereign
=	married
(1)	number of marriage
*	born
†	died
×	slain in battle

FOREWORD

Genealogy is perhaps as old as the history of the human race itself. Ever since the hazy beginnings of organized human society the powerful have kept records of their ancestors. The Bible contains a fine collection of lineal descents of several outstanding personages, even of Jesus Christ himself, and although they are now hardly regarded as indisputable historical evidence, they certainly prove that genealogy has always stood in the forefront of interest for many people, being for some a time-honoured science and for others an exciting pastime.

As soon as heredity in the leadership of human tribes became a more or less established principle, it was obviously of the utmost importance for the aspiring leader to show that he was lineally descended from the former leaders and rulers. It is true that originally many nations adopted their rulers on the basis of an election, but even then it was customary to elect to the supreme post someone who was related, however remotely, to the previous prince. Both England in Saxon times and Bohemia under the Přemyslids are excellent examples. To prove this records had to be kept, and often falsified. When primogeniture became an accepted method of succession to the thrones and crowns, it was even more important to maintain records and charts showing all the branches and members of the reigning House, often together with a very intricate relationship to other princely Houses. That such charts and records were often twisted and abused so that they would suit an ambitious pretender was of course the result of his ardent desire or the sycophancy of his servants.

These sycophantic record-keepers and chroniclers were often busy tracing the descent of their sovereigns beyond any purely human origin in order to show them not only as rulers 'by the grace of God' but even as actual demi-gods. This can be seen in the old pedigrees of the ancient Saxon Kings of Wessex, where the chroniclers were trying to prove that the Kings were descended from the pagan storm-god Woden. It may seem surprising that people in the early days of Christianity were impressed by the doubtful fact that their pious sovereign had for his ultimate ancestor a member of the numerous family of heathen gods, but we should realize that the mind of the common people was still under the spell of heathen legends and customs for centuries after their conversion to Christianity.

What is probably less surprising is the fact that sovereigns prided themselves upon the most illustrious of their ancestors. It became a fashion to show that everybody whose brow was adorned (or burdened, whichever you prefer) by a crown descended from a famous, potent and ever victorious monarch such as Charlemagne. One of the Tables in this book shows the descent of all the present European sovereigns from William the Conqueror, who before the conquest of England called himself defiantly 'the Bastard'. Yet exactly the same Table would also show that the crowned heads of Europe descend from a forgotten tanner of Falaise whose daughter had the historical good luck to have been seduced by Robert the Devil, Duke of Normandy.

Many a haughty sovereign in past centuries tried hard to forget about his less illustrious ancestors, and yet if even a single one of them, no matter how low his style, had not lived, the haughty sovereign himself would never have been born to sway his mighty sceptre. Even today historians often discuss the Hanoverian heritage, to good or bad effect, in Queen Victoria's blood while no one seems to take into consideration the fact that she was just as much a descendant of the Counts of Erbach, and their moods and spirits, as she was of the rulers of Hanover.

Nevertheless, the study of genealogy is inseparable from the study of history. While not denying that economic, national and other deep reasons were the cause of many an important and basic change in the history of mankind, we must also accept that genealogical background can and must be sought as an explanation of many medieval and even later wars and other events. This has always been an easy excuse and reason for publishing genealogical books and Tables all over the world.

The present book ranks itself with a large number of genealogical works and yet it is not simply a repetition of what has already been collected and printed. There are several genealogical books in which fuller dates, and as far as possible all the branches of the European princely Houses, are given. A good example of this is, among others, a German handbook, Prince von Isenburg's *Stammtafeln*. Such absolutely complete genealogical Tables have, however, a very serious disadvantage; they are invariably and unavoidably so complicated that they lose much of their instructiveness. Moreover, not everybody wants the Tables encumbered with the names of dozens of children who died in their early infancy, or women who died unmarried without ever achieving anything spectacular, except having been born with a princely coronet. Furthermore, these books usually show all the respective Houses without too clear a stress on their succession in various countries. Yet, apart from deposed dynasties, princely Houses have never lived in a territorial vacuum; they were closely tied to a certain country. I have also tried to distinguish whether a death was a natural one or whether the person in question was accidentally killed, murdered, slain in a battle or even executed; there were times in practically all countries when natural death was almost an exception among the princes. Precisely this distinction is often omitted in other genealogical works.

On the other hand, there are genealogical Tables and books which are clear enough, but which in their information omit not only many dates and titles but also even names of members of collateral branches in spite of their eventual importance.

I have tried to take a middle path. The Tables are arranged according to the individual countries, the existing monarchies taking precedence, and not according to dynasties, although they are always clearly marked. Some of the former minor principalities in Germany and elsewhere have not been included: it can hardly be argued that for example, the Princes of Schwarzburg, although no doubt sovereigns, ever played a big role, either militarily or genealogically, in the history of Europe. However, all the former kingdoms of Europe are treated in sufficient detail, while for all German and Italian grand-duchies, and some duchies, at least a general survey is given.

For several practical reasons the eleventh century has been taken as the earliest starting point. When necessary, the text gives an outline of the dynastic development prior to that dateline. The names given in the Tables are necessarily only a selection, but a much wider one than is usually found in historical handbooks. Omitted are those persons who played no important part in the history of Europe (i.e. most of the unmarried women) or persons who died very young without having been regarded as eventual heirs. Sometimes even women whose marriages were of no great importance or who remained without issue had to be excluded for lack of space or for the preservation of clarity. Children of married princesses are shown only when they played some role in the succession to the throne of the given country. The same ruling has been applied to natural children. The detailed Tables are preceded by Tables which give a general survey of practically all the male members of all the reigning Houses in each country, with an indication in which of the following Tables detailed information can be obtained. Lineal descent of the present sovereign or head of the House from the most remote ancestor is shown by a red line. Reigning sovereigns in each country are marked by a small crown next to their name (the actual crown used for this purpose having no other significance).

A word ought perhaps to be said about the spelling of names. The practice not only in Britain but in almost every other country is sadly confused. While some of the names are kept in their native form, such as the Carols of Rumania or Juans of Spain, others are 'translated' into English or the author's language. I have never in an English book read about a Johann or Karl in Germany, a Nikolai in Russia or a Georgios or Pavlos in Greece. In order to avoid what I have always felt to be a sort of discrimination, all the names in this book have been anglicized wherever it is possible. A compromise had, however, to be made for some names in some countries when the original name is too familiar to be dismissed – such as the Manuels in Portugal.

Apart from the usual type of genealogical Tables two other types are included. In one, a genealogical background is shown for various historical events, such as for the Wars of the Roses, the Union of Kalmar, or the Wars of the Spanish Succession. In the other, the descent from eight ancestors, called 'eight quarters' (i.e. three generations back), of some of the more outstanding or interesting princes is traced. This helps to show some of the little-known or even claimed forebears of the person in question.

In this the present book resembles other published works. There are, however, two features in which it differs considerably. Most people feel that genealogy and heraldry are two disciplines which are most closely related. Both the College of Arms in London and the Court of Lord Lyon in Edinburgh issue fine genealogies richly adorned and enlightened by coats-of-arms. Yet there has been no work to do the same for the whole of Europe, that is for the European reigning Houses. In this book I have considered heraldry to be an indispensable part of the genealogical Tables; the coats-of-arms illustrated here show the changes which went hand-in-hand with the various matrimonial alliances or territorial acquisitions or losses, or rise in rank.

Naturally it has not been possible to include the arms of all the persons listed in the Tables but only a relatively narrow selection. Nevertheless, the arms of almost all consorts of sovereigns have been illustrated, the arms of the sovereigns themselves being shown when they changed from the previously used form. I must, of course, warn the reader that in central Europe, and even elsewhere, several forms of arms were often in use by more than one person at the same time, in contrast with the one and only legal form used in Britain. In countries where differencing for cadets of the princely Houses is in practice, as wide a selection of the marks of cadency as possible has been made. It is in this sense that the book is a history of the regal heraldry of Europe.

The Tables with general surveys show two types of arms. On top, usually the original simple arms of the country or dynasty are reproduced, while below the latest form of the arms of the monarchy, with the proper crown and highest order of chivalry but without the supporters, is displayed. Supporters can, however, be seen in the line drawings at the chapter openings. The larger scale in which the arms accompanying the general survey Tables are drawn has enabled me to show the so-called 'greater' arms, with numerous quarterings (such as in Prussia, Naples etc.). Such complicated arms would be almost unreadable on the small shields in the detailed Tables, where a simpler form of arms is usually shown.

The other difference from any similar previous publication is the textual part. I have always felt that in spite of the fact that genealogical Tables speak for themselves, there are many facts which cannot find their way into the actual Tables and yet need to be mentioned and explained in one way or another. It can hardly be expected that by reading a haphazard historical book together with following a genealogical Table one would find all the explanations needed. In no history of Russia, for instance, can you find more than perhaps a mention of some of the several branches of the House of Rurik and their succession. A combination of genealogical Tables, illustrated with shields of arms and accompanied by a text which describes in words what the Tables leave untold, should fill a wide gap in literature of this sort.

Mr Michael Maclagan, CVO, Richmond Herald and Senior Fellow of Trinity College in Oxford, both an expert historian and a scholar in heraldry, who agreed to write such a text, has created a history book which makes fascinating reading in itself. I am very much indebted to him for his suggested corrections and amendments to my Tables. Without the close and friendly co-operation which has so happily existed between us I could hardly have hoped to see the book as it now is.

My gratitude goes, of course, to several people whose unselfish and untiring help enabled me to assemble all the material for such a vast enterprise. Years ago, Charles, Prince of Schwarzenberg, opened the treasures of both his library and knowledge to me, and most of the heraldry in these pages can really be traced to his friendly help. Nevertheless, when the actual work started, numerous question marks appeared, and if now few blank spaces remain in the following pages, it is due to the generous advice of the late M. Meurgey de Tupigny, President of the French Heraldic and Sigillographic Society, Mr G. Scheffer, Chamberlain and Herald of Sweden, M. Roger Harmignies, Mr Roger Pye of Oporto, expert in Portuguese heraldry, and many other scholars in different countries.

As for the section covering Britain, it is impossible not to mention the inexhaustible patience of the late Mr R.P. Graham-Vivian, MVO, MC, formerly Norroy and Ulster King of Arms, Mr J.P. Brooke-Little, CVO, the present Norroy and Ulster King of Arms, and the late Mr D. Pottinger, LVO, Islay Herald, who, in spite of their several and burdensome duties, have always found time to search for missing information and showed great interest in the progress of my work.

And last but not least, I am very much indebted to the skill of the publishers who have made it possible for such an extensive work to be produced at all, and I owe a special debt to Mr Martin Heller for his enthusiastic support throughout.

Finally, I should like to say that the study of history leads to the study of genealogy and heraldry and vice versa. When combined, no one of these three is a dull affair. The medieval battlefields of Europe were – in spite of all the savage slaughtering – grand scenes of heraldic display where gaily coloured banners, shields of arms and surcoats worn over the armour proudly announced their owners' might. No princely marriage would ever have been complete without pompous heraldic pageantry, and when the people laid their princely leaders to their final rest, heraldry again played, and still plays, an important part in the funeral rites. If this book helps to show that history, by means of genealogy and heraldry, can be made an interesting and even thrilling study, I shall be happy that I have not been working in vain.

Chapter 1

INTRODUCTION TO HERALDRY

The practice of heraldry, as we understand it, arose in western Europe in the middle of the twelfth century. It comprises the use on a shield of patterns which are definable, recognizable and hereditary. There were probably two principal causes for this development. In the first place, helmets were covering more and more of the wearer's face making his identification in battle difficult. Secondly, increasing employment of documents called for a visual means of authentication; in an age when literacy was almost confined to the clergy, a seal was more use than a signature. To reproduce on the seal the same pattern as that on the shield was commonplace.

Most of our early evidence of heraldry comes from seals. Several English heraldic seals survive from around 1140. The arms of Savoy (Table 120) are found in 1143, those of the Count of Provence, which were the same as Aragon (Table 45), in 1150, those of Henry the Lion, Duke of Saxony (Table 99), in 1144. Many other early seals must have perished, but these examples demonstrate that heraldry was already an international manifestation. One exciting testimony from France is earlier and not sigillary: the famous enamel preserved at Le Mans appears to show the blazon of Geoffrey Plantagenet (d.1151) (Table 2). It is quite clear that the growth of heraldry answered a general need in the feudal societies of the twelfth century. It is also at least possible that its similarity in different countries was furthered by encounters on the organized crusades or in the Holy Land. Certainly warfare in the heat of Palestine encouraged the wearing of a linen covering or surcoat over the chainmail of the day; it was an easy and an obvious step to repeat on this the pattern from the shield; and from this is derived the English phrase 'coat-of-arms'.

To write thus about the beginnings of heraldry is not to deny that seals with some sort of device had been in use for centuries and that emblems, often of an animal kind, had been associated with units or peoples – the lion of the tribe of Judah, the eagle of the Roman legion or the crescent of Islam. It is also the case that very soon after heraldry started – and it could not be said to be established until numerous families had used a distinctive blazon for several generations – men began to invent coats-of-arms for people who had lived long before, for biblical characters, for kings and saints like Edward the Confessor (Table 66), or heroes of romance like Arthur, Charlemagne or Godfrey de Bouillon.

Certain basic laws were common to all countries. The hues available were divided into two main classes. The 'metals' were gold and silver, often, as in this volume, portrayed by yellow and white; and the 'colours' were red, blue, black, green and purple, of which the first three were by far the most often used. A third, and scarcer, class were 'furs' of which ermine (Table 67: Brittany) was the commonest. If the background of the shield, called the 'field', was of a metal, then the objects thereon, known as 'charges', must be of one of the colours and vice-versa. Either colour or metal could be placed on a fur. This rule was not unbreakable: it was deliberately flouted in devising a blazon for the Kingdom of Jerusalem (Table 113 and elsewhere) as a tribute to the sanctity of the city. Other breaches are recorded, not least in eastern Europe (Table 137: Narishkin or Razumovski, or 118: Douglas). An early convention allowed a background of mixed colour and metal to count as either (Table 2: Marshal, or 86: Luxemburg). Not only individuals or families used coats-of-arms; they could be employed by countries, towns, bishoprics and, later on, by merchant companies, religious orders or any corporate body.

In England the upper classes spoke Norman-French at this time, and therefore the blazons were described in that tongue. As English developed into

The 12th-century enamel of Geoffrey of Anjou at Le Mans, one of the earliest pieces of heraldic evidence.

the national speech in the fourteenth and fifteenth centuries, the language of heraldry remained strongly infected with French terms and became increasingly esoteric. This tendency was fostered by the heralds in the sixteenth and seventeenth centuries, who were as anxious to have their own peculiar parlance, not easily comprehended by the layman, as the doctor, the lawyer or the parliamentary draftsman. As far as possible, this specialized terminology has been eschewed in the pages which follow; it has the advantage of being precise to the expert. As illustrations, two blazons follow for shields on Table 86, as they would be described in England today: Moravia – 'Azure, an eagle displayed checky argent and gules, beaked, membered and crowned or', and Bourbon –

'Azure, semé of lys or, a bend gules.' It will be seen that a 'bend' (French *bande*) is in fact a straight diagonal stripe; similarly an upright one is a 'pale' and transverse ones are 'bars'. In the other realms of western Europe, in Germany, France, Spain or Italy, the descriptions of heraldry are nearer to normal speech.

In many cases it is not known how a particular family acquired or chose its coat-of-arms; often it must have been by a whim or accident. A certain number of basic geometric patterns clearly reflect strips of wood or leather affixed to the shield to strengthen it. Such would be the bend of Baden (Table 106) or perhaps the bars of Oldenburg (Table 112). Many others represent a play upon words. Easy examples are the blazons of Bowes-Lyon (Table 9) or of Castile and Leon (Table 47). Yet others may indicate regional or feudal fashions; there is a strong concentration of coats-of-arms with lions on barry fields or barry lions in the old province of Lotharingia (Limburg, Luxemburg, Hesse and so on); the 'tressure' with its fleurs-de-lys is commoner in Scotland than elsewhere (Table 13). In the animal world the eagle and the lion were regarded as the kings of birds and beasts, and were accordingly popular. The eagle grew in esteem as it came to be associated with empire, but was also used by quite humble families. From the start, the lion was portrayed in two basic postures: he was 'rampant' as he rose on one foot to strike, he was 'passant' when he ran across the shield from left to right, most often in a group of three (Table 1: England, Table 15: Denmark). In the Middle Ages the upright beast was simply called a lion; when he ran, he was a 'leopard'. It must be emphasized that, in describing the right and the left of a shield, one speaks as though wearing it, not from the viewpoint of the beholder. An early variant form was the lion with two tails (Table 2: Montfort, Table 85: Bohemia).

DIVIDING THE SHIELD

Early in the story of heraldry, the problems posed by alliances, inheritance and large families began to make themselves felt. One pristine solution was dimidiation, that is to divide two shields vertically and unite half of each (Table 86: Děpolt, or Table 133: Kuiavia), but this could lead to bizarre results. Soon the simpler device of 'impalement' was evolved which represented the whole of each coat-of-arms on half a shield (Table 133: Hungary and Anjou); the arms of the husband were normally represented on the right, or 'dexter' side. This was particularly the case in England and France, where bishops also used to 'impale' the arms of their diocese; but in Germany impalement often indicates the union of two lordships rather than a definite marriage, and bishops more often quarter their own arms with those of their See. In fact, the arrangements for 'marshalling' more than one coat-of-arms are apt to differ from country to country. It was, however, general practice that, when a ruler inherited two territories, as it might be one from his father and another through his mother, he divided his shield into four and placed his paternal blazon in the first and fourth quarters while that of his mother decorated the second and third. The earliest known illustration of this idea occurs in the combined arms of Castile and Leon on Table 47.

As a family began to build up dynastic power, it probably made many profitable alliances and acquisitions. A shield of four sections was no longer enough. There is no limit to the number of divisions on a single shield; but in England it is normal to speak of 'quarterly of six', or eight, or sixty-eight, while on the Continent the nature of the divisions is specified. In England, also, representation of an heiress (that is, a woman without brothers) is common; in Scotland, and abroad, small attention was paid to her arms, unless she also brought land. In Germany, in particular, the extensive quartered coats tend to indicate a great aggregation of lordships (Table 95) with the actual family arms on a small shield in the middle, 'an escutcheon in pretence', or 'over all'. On the Continent, also, the terms 'sixteen quarterings', or 'thirty-two quarterings', had a specialized meaning. They did not signify that an individual represented that number of families or had acquired that number of fiefs, but that *all* his ancestors (male and female) for five or six generations backwards were of noble birth. Sets of eight shields, showing great-grandparents, are frequent in these Tables. The stern laws governing dynastic marriages in Germany and Austria (Chapter 30) made such a boast much more common than in England, where society was relatively fluid.

Naturally enough some form of control over the usages of a blazon became essential. This duty was assigned by a gradual process in the fourteenth and fifteenth centuries to the heralds, officers whose main functions hitherto had lain in the spheres of diplomacy and the tournament. Thus the general name 'heraldry' was born. One of their main duties was to avoid as far as possible the use by two different families of the same shield. In England a *cause célèbre* in the reign of Richard II concerned the rival claims of Scrope and Grosvenor to 'Azure, a bend or'. The fact that the Bohemian family of Count Thun of Hohenstein (Table 55) bore the same arms was as irrelevant as much of the other evidence offered. Rather more surprising is the fact that the important family of de Ligne in Hainault and the rulers of Baden (Table 106) both bore 'Or, a bend gules' from the Middle Ages to today without exciting conflict.

Different countries found different solutions for the

problems of the younger brother and the younger son. One charge, the 'label' (a narrow horizontal line across the top of the shield with three, four or five pendants dropping from it), was mostly confined to the shields of minor members of a family. It is relatively certain that it was originally a cord with tags which could be removed when necessary. In England (Table 3) and in Portugal (Table 116) labels became exceedingly elaborate. But other cadets of great families used a border (or 'bordure') and a small bend (or 'bendlet') as a mark of 'difference'. In France the bendlet was perhaps more popular than in England. Bastardy was sometimes signified by a bend from left to right, though this could be an innocent charge as in the Folkunga arms (Table 27). The French for a 'bend sinister' was *une barre*, which probably inspired the popular British myth of the '*bar* sinister', to mean illegitimacy.

ESSENTIAL DIFFERENCES

The heraldic connoisseur can often guess at the nationality of an unknown coat-of-arms, but may find his opinion no easier to explain than the difference between Claret and Burgundy. To indicate some possible characteristics is not to ignore the many common features in all realms or the incidence of migrants and 'rogues' in any grouping.

It is not easy to distinguish between the heraldry of France and England, which stemmed from a common root. French blazon did not pass through so marked a phase of complexity as did English in the sixteenth century, and never, perhaps, indulged in so lavish a display of quarterings. On the other hand the heraldry of the Bourbons was abruptly cut off by the Revolution, to be replaced by the orderly but artificial Napoleonic system (Chapter 17). Scotland boasts, it may be claimed, the most logical and systematic control of arms of any country and is still, heraldically, discrete from England. Great use is made of the bordure as a difference, often with many charges on it.

In the Iberian peninsula the shield itself is almost always drawn in a rather square shape. Hence it comes that a pattern of six charges will be arranged in three pairs (Table 115: Castro) and not in ranks of 3, 2 and 1 as is more usual (see Table 130: Parma). Considerable use is made of elaborate bordures (Table 47: Molina, Table 52: Moscoso) and also of letters (Table 118: Mendoça). The combination of two shields in one by a diagonal cross, or 'saltire', (Table 46: Sicily, Urgel) is usually Spanish. An interesting Hispanic charge is the cauldron (Table 48 or 119: Guzman) which appears in many noble blazons. In the first instance, this was a mark of nobility denoting the ability to feed a contingent. The animals which appear from the pot are today usually blazoned as serpents, but may have begun life as the more palatable eel. Another most distinctive Spanish charge (Table 48) is the bend issuing from two lions' mouths.

The early heraldry of Germany shows a certain predilection for bold geometric patterns (Table 91: Hohenzollern, Table 56: Liechtenstein, Table 96: Bavaria, Table 98: Preysing). The popularity of the eagle led to the development of the 'bearing', or device, called a *kleestengel* (clover-stalk), on its breast, which could itself have an addition made to it; it was in origin probably only an artistic definition of the breastbone of the eagle.

A feature of Teutonic heraldry is the display of a large number of quarterings representing the fiefs held by the family; normally they were those which gave the right to one vote in the Diet of the Empire. On a smaller shield in the centre would be placed the arms of the family itself (often the same as its oldest or original estate) though there are exceptions (Chapter 29: Mecklenburg). Among the quarterings is sometimes found one of plain red ('gules'); this is the 'Blut-Fahne' or 'Regalien' quartering (Table 101: Saxony) and was thought to indicate the ownership of royal prerogatives, personally bestowed by the emperor. It is a common artistic practice in Teutonic lands where there are lions disposed on both sides of the shield to make those on the 'dexter' or right, face inwards. This would not be done in France or Britain.

Italy was so fragmented that it is difficult to write cohesively of her heraldry. In Naples, Spanish influence not surprisingly made itself felt. The tree is perhaps more frequent than elsewhere; another highly typical charge is the mount, often triple, at the base of the shield, a feature which also occurs in the arms of Hungary 'modern' (Table 88). Italian families often added a 'chief' (the top slice of the shield) of the Empire or Anjou to display Guelph or Ghibelline sympathies. In Poland a number of original and unusual charges appear, which have sometimes been derived from Scandinavian runes: crosses and arrows spring from horseshoes or from geometrical shapes (Table 123: Krasiński, Table 131: Wiśniowiecki). Russian heraldry was not a natural growth, and shows signs of laboured invention: military emblems abound, as might be expected in an aristocracy which was originally one of service (Table 137: Apraxin or Razumovski).

The emphasis throughout these Tables is on the shield, for the shield with its blazon is the central

The King of Arms for Brittany in an ermine tabard (the blazon of his duke) presents a roll of arms to the Duke of Bourbon sitting on a mantle of his own arms. MS of c. 1460–5.

feature of heraldry. None the less from the earliest days knights also used, especially in tournaments, a 'crest', a single object bound to their helmets with a wreath of twisted silk. As the pageantry of heraldry developed, differing coronets and helmets were introduced for the varying degrees of rank, and 'supporters' to uphold the shield became common. Below the shield might appear a motto or *cri de guerre*. The whole assembly of heraldic pride is known as an 'achievement' and for reigning Houses is often backed by a mantle or pavilion. Illustrations of such achievements appear at the head of many of the chapters which follow. The 'boast of heraldry' was indeed part of the 'pomp of power', but it is also a vivid and illuminating shorthand to dynastic history.

Chapter 2

ENGLAND: MEDIEVAL

'What! will the line stretch out to the crack of doom?'
Macbeth IV:I

England and Scotland have known many dynasties of rulers. Table 1 shows in outline the descent of the present Queen from Duncan, King of Scotland, and William the Conqueror of England, and the union of the two countries in the person of James I. The Scottish kings on the left are derived from characters who figure in Shakespeare's *Macbeth*; the rulers of England stem from William, Duke of Normandy, who won the Crown and the country at the decisive Battle of Hastings in 1066. Neither Duncan nor William has left direct male descendants but their blood has reached Queen Elizabeth II through a number of female links, links which brought other families – Stuart, Plantagenet, Tudor and so on – to the thrones of one or both realms.

The history of England goes back far beyond the reign of William I. South of Hadrian's Wall, the island had formed part of the Roman Empire, and then had been largely overrun by Teutonic invaders from northern Germany. These Anglo-Saxon barbarians had driven many of the original Celtic inhabitants towards the west and had seized control of the flatter, richer lands of south and east England, lands which throughout our history have been a temptation to raiders from the Continent. At first there were a number of separate Anglo-Saxon kingdoms, but from time to time outstanding rulers gained a brief supremacy; of such were Ethelbert of Kent, the first Christian king, at the end of the sixth century, or Offa of Mercia at the end of the eighth. The unity of England was accelerated by the need to resist a fresh series of invasions, by the Vikings who sailed from their Scandinavian homes to plunder, and later to settle, along the coasts of England and France.

Resistance to these invaders was led by Alfred, King of Wessex – roughly the area south of the Thames – in fierce fighting at the end of the ninth century. For a hundred years his descendants were rulers of England. But troubled times came again at the beginning of the eleventh century; Danish and West Saxon kings both reigned, and there was no accepted system of succession. The death without children of the saintly but ineffectual Edward the Confessor left the way open for new contenders. At Hastings the Englishman Harold was defeated by the Duke of Normandy.

Since then England has been ruled by six families, not one of which could be called English by name. The Normans were succeeded by the Plantagenets who stemmed from Anjou, in central France. At the end of the Wars of the Roses the last Plantagenet king, Richard III, was overthrown by the Welshman, Henry Tudor. His family endured only for three generations; and Elizabeth I was followed by her Scottish cousin, James I and VI, in 1603. Thereafter England and Scotland shared the same ruler. Then, in 1714, George I, Elector of Hanover, arrived from Germany and the next five kings were of Teutonic stock. Queen Victoria married Prince Albert of Saxe-Coburg and Gotha, another German royal family; and our present Queen has married the Duke of Edinburgh who in male descent derives from the Danish dynasty (Table 143). Thus, the people of England early became used to the idea that the Crown could pass through a woman and that a queen could reign over them, ideas which have never been acceptable to (for example) the French.

The early history of Scotland is lost in mists of obscurity. The northern part of the country was inhabited by the Picts, whose origin is still debated. Much of the south was peopled by Celts, but to these were added Scandinavian and Anglo-Saxon settlers

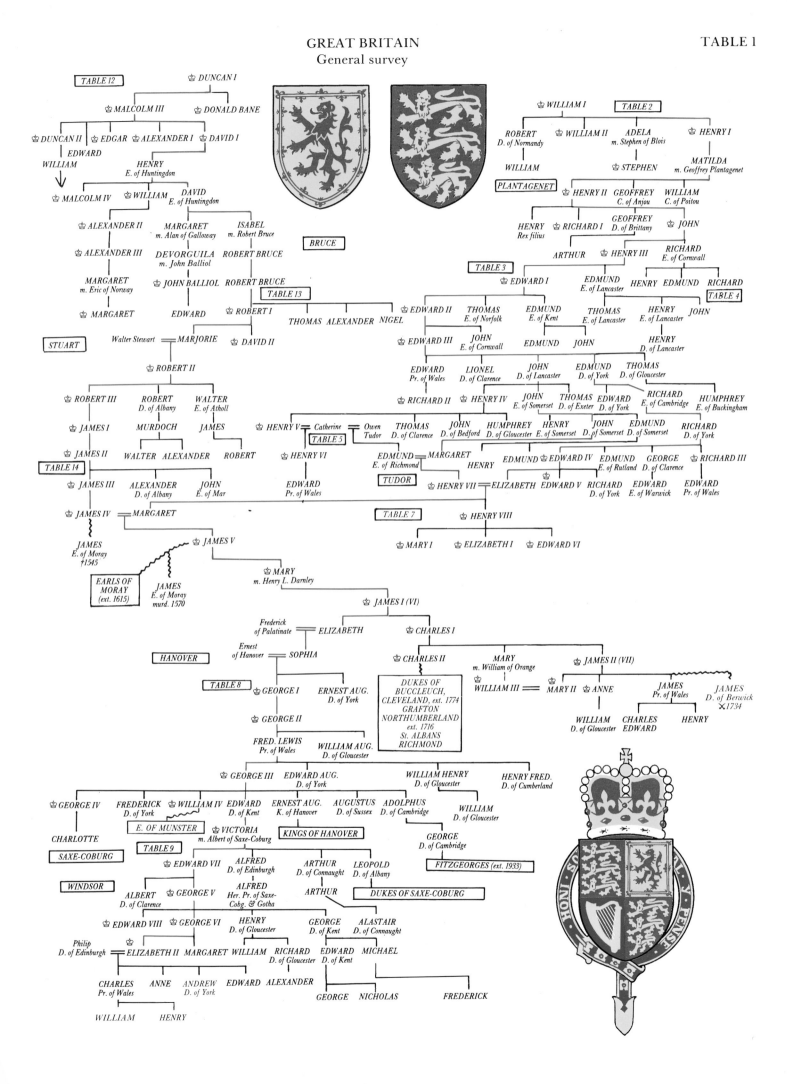

from the east and Irish from the west. It is one of the ironies of history that the very name 'Scot' is derived from a tribe originally settled in what today would be called Ulster.

At the head of Table 1 are the two shields of arms associated with Scotland and England; their story will be discussed in more detail later. They were not united until 1603, and even then were linked with the arms of France for another 200 years. It was also in 1603 that the harp, which symbolizes Ireland, was introduced into the royal arms, though the Kings of England had been Lords of Ireland since the twelfth century. Wales, which was conquered by Edward I of England, has never figured in the royal shield, though it appears in that of the Prince of Wales (Table 9). At the bottom of Table 1 are the arms of Queen Elizabeth II, encircled by the riband of the Garter, as they have been borne by every monarch since 1837. They are the arms of the country over which she reigns, rather than those of the Queen herself, and are flown wherever the Queen is in residence in England. In Scotland they appear in a different form; the upright lion of Scotland figures twice, in the first and fourth quarters, and the three running lions of England only feature once, in the second quarter.

THE NORMAN INVASION

In 1066 Duke William of Normandy conquered England. He claimed to be the heir to his cousin, Edward the Confessor, and regarded Harold as an usurper. In consequence there were two facets to his reign. He preserved much of what was best in former English government, including for example the shire system. But there was an almost complete change-over in the ownership of estates; the land-hungry followers of Duke William replaced the Anglo-Saxon or Danish proprietors. Two new features were at once apparent up and down the countryside, the mounted Norman knight and the Norman castle on its artificial hillock.

Who were these Normans? Their ducal family and most of their aristocracy were descended from Danes who settled near the mouth of the Seine under their leader Rollo in 911. It is probable that the stalwart resistance of Alfred deflected many Viking invaders from England to the less defended shores of France. In any case a substantial body of 'Northmen' soon gave their name to the district of Normandy, and rapidly acquired a polish of French chivalry and language.

William I made a stern and powerful king. He loved hunting and cleared part of Hampshire to make the New Forest. Rebellion in the north was savagely repressed, and the countryside devastated. Towards the end of his reign he carried out an exhaustive survey of his kingdom, village by village and

county by county. The result, the Domesday Book, is an authoritative record which has no parallel to this day. When he died, he bequeathed Normandy to his firstborn, Robert, and England to his second son, William Rufus, so-called from his red face.

As has been seen in Chapter I, heraldry was unknown at this time. The shield shown for William I (Table 2) was not actually used by him in his lifetime; that displayed for his wife, Matilda of Flanders, was associated later with her kinsfolk. No coat-of-arms is known for Henry I. That shown for his son-in-law Geoffrey Plantagenet, is based on the beautiful enamel at Le Mans. Part of the shield is here hidden from the viewer, and it is uncertain whether the number of lions was intended to be six or seven; it is suggestive that one of Henry II's illegitimate children used *six* similar lions.

Henry I, a vigorous and able monarch, succeeded in winning both England and Normandy to his rule. He did not, however, succeed in persuading his subjects to accept his daughter as his heiress after his only legitimate son had been drowned. Matilda was haughty and her second husband, Geoffrey of Anjou, was not popular. On the death of Henry I, the barons of England chose Stephen as their king in preference to Matilda; but much of Stephen's reign was consumed in civil warfare between them. Matilda was at one point proclaimed queen, but she was never crowned; eventually it was agreed that her son should succeed at the death of Stephen. It is from this juncture that the Crown of England begins to pass by hereditary descent.

Henry II, son of Matilda and acknowledged heir of Stephen, had a long and splendid reign. In England he was keenly interested in justice; and his legal reforms effectively established a common law throughout the length and breadth of the land, with judges going on circuit as they do today. But he governed a much wider area than England. He naturally inherited Anjou; he had won back Normandy before he came to England; he became the Lord of Ireland; in addition he made a splendid match by marrying the heiress of the Duke of Aquitaine. With her extensive lands in his control, his realm had its northern frontier on the Tweed and the southern at the Pyrenees; but for all his territory in France – Normandy, Anjou and Aquitaine – he was a subject of the French king and not an independent ruler. This position led to many complications and caused the fortunes of England to be closely entangled with those of France for 400 years.

It is during the reign of Richard I, a romantic figure but a feckless and absentee king, that the well-known arms of England appear. Richard's first seal only shows part of the king's shield on which is a single upright ('rampant') lion; the whole shield may have exhibited two such lions. However, on his second great seal (1198) the whole shield is clearly visible, portraying three running lions with their heads turned towards the beholder; this has been the blazon of England from that day to this.

At Richard's death his younger brother John seized the throne, though some would have preferred their nephew Arthur. John almost certainly had Arthur murdered. He had considerable ability but lacked any capacity to make himself liked; towards the end of his reign a group of the nobility, exacerbated by their sovereign's caprice and by heavy taxation, compelled John to seal Magna Carta, the most famous charter of liberties in the history of the English people.

John's son, Henry III, continued to use the three leopards as his coat-of-arms. His younger brother, Richard, Earl of Cornwall, was a rich and ambitious man who sought in vain to secure effective election as Emperor of Germany. He devised his own shield (Table 2) of a red lion rampant within a black border dotted with gold discs (*bezants*, so called from the coinage of Byzantium). The lion may refer back to the first seal of Richard I; the gold discs (*poix*) allude to his French county of Poitou. As has been suggested, many early shields were linked with a play upon words of this character.

Like his father, Henry III failed to keep on good terms with his subjects. The opposition to him, at the end of his very long reign, was led by his brother-in-law, Simon de Montfort. His shield shows a lion with two tails; the popularity of the lion as a charge was already leading to ingenious variations. The struggle was protracted, and towards the end of it (1265) Simon de Montfort caused to be assembled what was perhaps the first English Parliament.

The reign of Edward I (Table 3) was important for several reasons; he was one of the most robust and forceful of English rulers. He carried to conclusion the conquest of Wales; and then gave to the Welsh, as he is said to have promised, a prince who could speak no English – his infant son Edward, the first Prince of Wales. He attempted, but in vain, to conquer Scotland. He waged long wars against the King of France, seeking to recover the full inheritance of Henry II, of which John and Henry III had lost considerable portions. The King and his advisers carried through a great volume of legislation, an achievement which, coupled with his arduous campaigning, has caused him to be called the English Justinian. Of more lasting significance were the steps taken under his guidance in the evolution of Parliament. Here he learned from the ideas of his uncle Simon.

Edward II married Isabel, the only daughter of Philip IV of France. The shield of the latter shows an example of dimidiation. Philip had three sons, but no grandsons, and thus Isabel could be regarded as his heiress (Table 65). As her son, Edward III proceeded to claim the throne of France itself; this was a more thorough and drastic step than any attempt to regain the lost provinces of his ancestors. In 1340 he symbolized this claim by uniting the arms of France with those of England. As a compliment to France, he placed the gold lilies in a blue field in the first (and fourth) quarters of his new shield and the leopards of England in the second and third. From this date until 1801 the rulers of England continued to style themselves Kings of France and show the French lilies somewhere on their shield.

THE HUNDRED YEARS' WAR

At first Edward III's war went well. A great naval victory at Sluys (1340) was followed by triumphs on land at Crécy (1346) and Poitiers (1356). He founded the Order of the Garter, the greatest surviving order of chivalry in the world. Its motto *Honi soit qui mal y pense* (Ashamed be he who thinks ill of it) may refer to the legendary Countess of Salisbury – though at this date ladies did not usually wear garters – but may with greater likelihood allude to his claims on the French Crown. At almost the same time, the pestilential Black Death spread disaster over Europe. The heavy mortality (probably more than a third of the population of England perished) contributed to social disorder and the Peasants' Revolt in the next reign (1381). The campaigns in France languished, and the King, grown senile, died in an atmosphere of unrest after his long and at times glorious reign.

The problem of distinguishing cadet members of the royal family can easily be seen on Table 3. The label and the bordure were the devices mainly employed in England. Down to and including Edward III the eldest sons of the ruler seem to have used a blue label of three points. Accordingly a white (or silver) label could be used for another son, as it was for Thomas of Brotherton, Earl of Norfolk. Edward the Black Prince, eldest son of Edward III, changed to a white label in 1340, presumably because a blue label would not have shown up well over the blue arms of France. Ever since then the eldest son has used a white label during the lifetime of the sovereign (see the shield of Prince Charles at the bottom of Table 9). The Black Prince, so-called from the colour of his armour, never came to the throne. His original shield, helmet and surcoat can still be seen over his tomb at Canterbury, splendid examples of fourteenth-century craftsmanship.

His next three brothers all used labels of various designs, but the youngest, Thomas, Duke of Gloucester, used a plain bordure. Other royal princes had used bordures before; the shield of John of Eltham on his effigy in Westminster Abbey is one of the master-

TABLE 2

ENGLAND
Normans and early Plantagenets

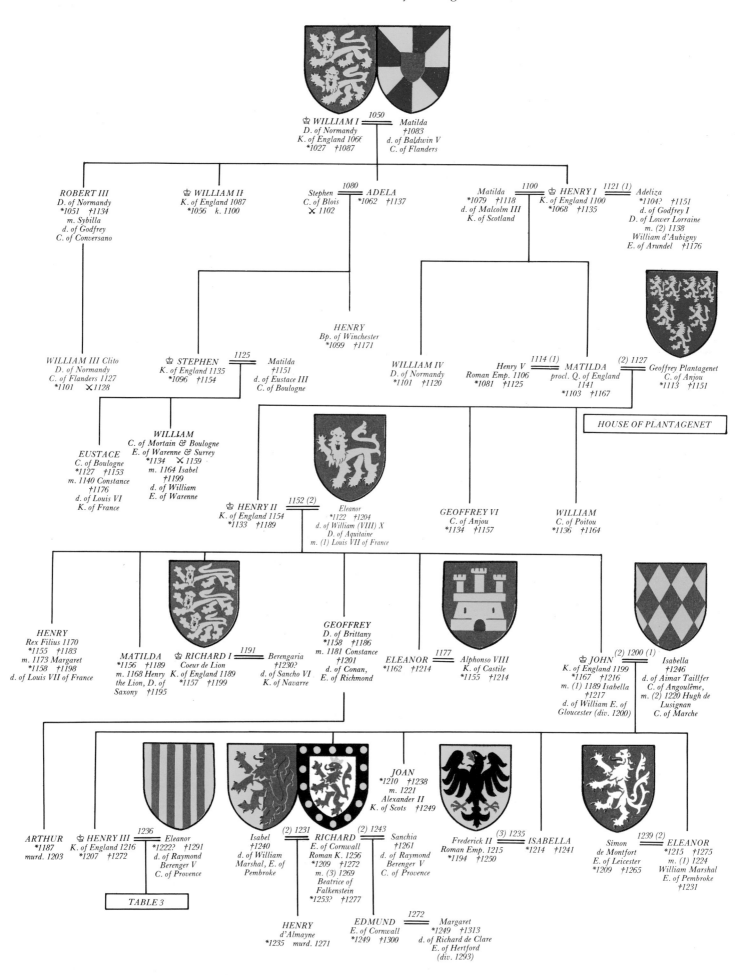

👑 **WILLIAM I** —1050— Matilda
D. of Normandy †1083
K. of England 1066 d. of Baldwin V
*1027 †1087 C. of Flanders

ROBERT III
D. of Normandy
*1051 †1134
m. Sybilla
d. of Godfrey
C. of Conversano

👑 **WILLIAM II**
K. of England 1087
*1056 k. 1100

Stephen —1080— **ADELA**
C. of Blois *1062 †1137
✕ 1102

Matilda —1100— 👑 **HENRY I** —1121 (1)— Adeliza
*1079 †1118 K. of England 1100 *1104? †1151
d. of Malcolm III *1068 †1135 d. of Godfrey I
K. of Scotland D. of Lower Lorraine
m. (2) 1138
William d'Aubigny
E. of Arundel †1176

HENRY
Bp. of Winchester
*1099 †1171

WILLIAM III Clito
D. of Normandy
C. of Flanders 1127
*1101 ✕ 1128

👑 **STEPHEN** —1125— Matilda
K. of England 1135 †1151
*1096 †1154 d. of Eustace III
C. of Boulogne

WILLIAM IV
D. of Normandy
*1101 †1120

Henry V —1114 (1)— **MATILDA** —(2) 1127— Geoffrey Plantagenet
Roman Emp. 1106 procl. Q. of England C. of Anjou
*1081 †1125 1141 *1113 †1151
*1103 †1167

HOUSE OF PLANTAGENET

EUSTACE
C. of Boulogne
*1127 †1153
m. 1140 Constance
†1176
d. of Louis VI
K. of France

WILLIAM
C. of Mortain & Boulogne
E. of Warenne & Surrey
*1134 ✕ 1159
m. 1164 Isabel
†1199
d. of William
E. of Warenne

👑 **HENRY II** —1152 (2)— Eleanor
K. of England 1154 *1122 †1204
*1133 †1189 d. of William (VIII) X
D. of Aquitaine
m. (1) Louis VII of France

GEOFFREY VI
C. of Anjou
*1134 †1157

WILLIAM
C. of Poitou
*1136 †1164

HENRY
Rex Filius 1170
*1155 †1183
m. 1173 Margaret
*1158 †1198
d. of Louis VII of France

MATILDA
*1156 †1189
m. 1168 Henry
the Lion, D. of
Saxony †1195

👑 **RICHARD I** —1191— Berengaria
Coeur de Lion †1230?
K. of England 1189 d. of Sancho VI
*1157 †1199 K. of Navarre

GEOFFREY
D. of Brittany
*1158 †1186
m. 1181 Constance
†1201
d. of Conan,
E. of Richmond

ELEANOR —1177— Alphonso VIII
*1162 †1214 K. of Castile
*1155 †1214

👑 **JOHN** —(2) 1200 (1)— Isabella
K. of England 1199 †1246
*1167 †1216 d. of Aimar Taillfer
m. (1) 1189 Isabella C. of Angoulême,
†1217 m. (2) 1220 Hugh de
d. of William E. of Lusignan
Gloucester (div. 1200) C. of Marche

ARTHUR
*1187
murd. 1203

👑 **HENRY III** —1236— Eleanor
K. of England 1216 *1222? †1291
*1207 †1272 d. of Raymond
Berenger V
C. of Provence

TABLE 3

Isabel —(2) 1231— **RICHARD** —(2) 1243— Sanchia
†1240 E. of Cornwall †1261
d. of William Roman K. 1256 d. of Raymond
Marshal, E. of *1209 †1272 Berenger V
Pembroke m. (3) 1269 C. of Provence
Beatrice of
Falkenstein
*1253? †1277

JOAN
*1210 †1238
m. 1221
Alexander II
K. of Scots †1249

Frederick II —(3) 1235— **ISABELLA**
Roman Emp. 1215 *1214 †1241
*1194 †1250

Simon —1239 (2)— **ELEANOR**
de Montfort *1215 †1275
E. of Leicester m. (1) 1224
*1209 †1265 William Marshal
E. of Pembroke
†1231

HENRY
d'Almayne
*1235 murd. 1271

EDMUND —1272— Margaret
E. of Cornwall *1249 †1313
*1249 †1300 d. of Richard de Clare
E. of Hertford
(div. 1293)

Plantagenets and the Hundred Years' War

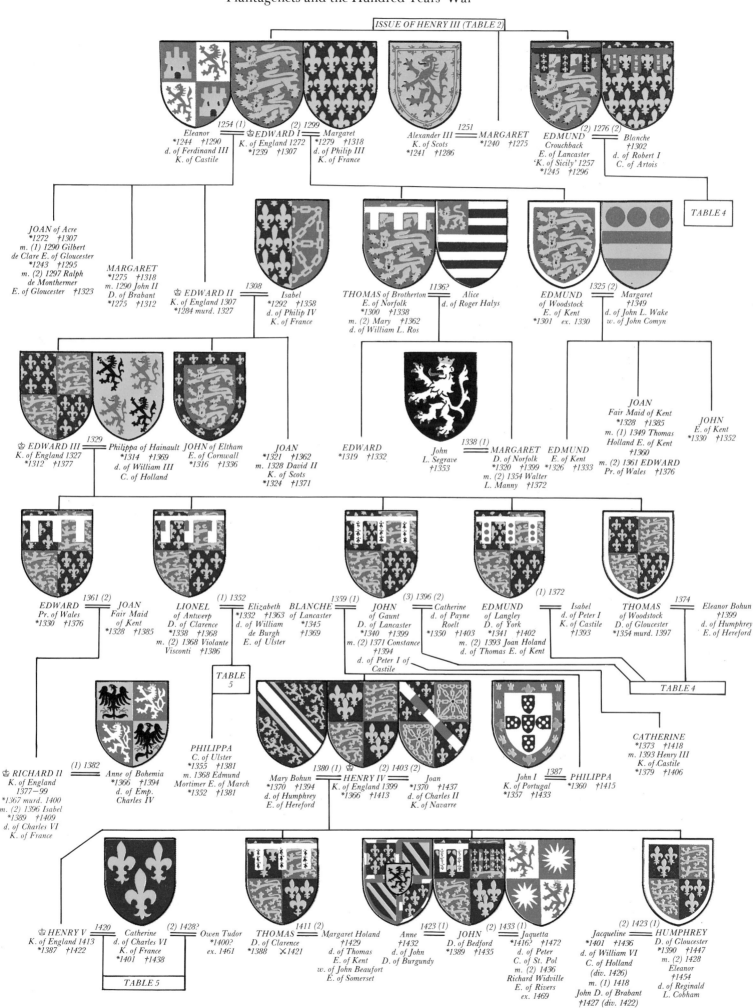

ISSUE OF HENRY III (TABLE 2)

Eleanor
*1244 †1290
d. of Ferdinand III
K. of Castile

1254 (1)

♚ **EDWARD I**
K. of England 1272
*1239 †1307

(2) 1299

Margaret
*1279 †1318
d. of Philip III
K. of France

Alexander III
K. of Scots
*1241 †1286

1251

MARGARET
*1240 †1275

(2) 1276

EDMUND
Crouchback
E. of Lancaster
'K. of Sicily' 1257
*1245 †1296

(2)

Blanche
†1302
d. of Robert I
C. of Artois

TABLE 4

JOAN of Acre
*1272 †1307
m. (1) 1290 Gilbert
de Clare E. of Gloucester
*1243 †1295
m. (2) 1297 Ralph
de Monthermer
E. of Gloucester †1323

MARGARET
*1275 †1318
m. 1290 John II
D. of Brabant
*1275 †1312

♚ **EDWARD II**
K. of England 1307
*1284 murd. 1327

1308

Isabel
*1292 †1358
d. of Philip IV
K. of France

THOMAS of Brotherton
E. of Norfolk
*1300 †1338
m. (2) Mary †1362
d. of William L. Ros

1136?

Alice
d. of Roger Halys

EDMUND
of Woodstock
E. of Kent
*1301 ex. 1330

1325 (2)

Margaret
d. of John L. Wake
w. of John Comyn

JOAN
Fair Maid of Kent
*1328 †1385
m. (1) 1349 Thomas
Holland E. of Kent
†1360
m. (2) 1361 EDWARD
Pr. of Wales †1376

JOHN
E. of Kent
*1330 †1352

♚ **EDWARD III**
K. of England 1327
*1312 †1377

1329

Philippa of Hainault
*1314 †1369
d. of William III
C. of Holland

JOHN of Eltham
E. of Cornwall
*1316 †1336

JOAN
*1321 †1362
m. 1328 David II
K. of Scots
*1324 †1371

EDWARD
*1319 †1332

MARGARET
D. of Norfolk
*1320 †1399
m. (2) 1354 Walter
L. Manny †1372

1338 (1)

John
L. Segrave
†1353

EDMUND
E. of Kent
*1326 †1333

EDWARD
Pr. of Wales
*1330 †1376

1361 (2)

JOAN
Fair Maid
of Kent
*1328 †1385

LIONEL
of Antwerp
D. of Clarence
*1338 †1368
m. (2) 1368 Violante
Visconti †1386

(1) 1352

Elizabeth
*1332 †1363
d. of William
de Burgh
E. of Ulster

BLANCHE
of Lancaster
*1345
†1369

1359 (1)

JOHN
of Gaunt
D. of Lancaster
*1340 †1399
m. (2) 1371 Constance
†1394
d. of Peter I of
Castile

(3) 1396 (2)

Catherine
d. of Payne
Roelt
*1350 †1403

EDMUND
of Langley
D. of York
*1341 †1402
m. (2) 1393 Joan Holand
d. of Thomas E. of Kent

(1) 1372

Isabel
d. of Peter I
K. of Castile
†1393

THOMAS
of Woodstock
D. of Gloucester
*1354 murd. 1397

1374

Eleanor Bohun
†1399
d. of Humphrey
E. of Hereford

TABLE 5

TABLE 4

♚ **RICHARD II**
K. of England
1377–99
*1367 murd. 1400
m. (2) 1396 Isabel
*1389 †1409
d. of Charles VI
K. of France

(1) 1382

Anne of Bohemia
*1366 †1394
d. of Emp.
Charles IV

PHILIPPA
C. of Ulster
*1355 †1381
m. 1368 Edmund
Mortimer E. of March
*1352 †1381

Mary Bohun
*1370 †1394
d. of Humphrey
E. of Hereford

1380 (1)

♚ **HENRY IV**
K. of England 1399
*1366 †1413

(2) 1403 (2)

Joan
*1370 †1437
d. of Charles II
K. of Navarre

John I
K. of Portugal
*1357 †1433

1387

PHILIPPA
*1360 †1415

CATHERINE
*1373 †1418
m. 1393 Henry III
K. of Castile
*1379 †1406

♚ **HENRY V**
K. of England 1413
*1387 †1422

1420

Catherine
d. of Charles VI
K. of France
*1401 †1438

(2) 1428?

Owen Tudor
*1400?
ex. 1461

THOMAS
D. of Clarence
*1388 ✕1421

1411 (2)

Margaret Holand
†1429
d. of Thomas
E. of Kent
w. of John Beaufort
E. of Somerset

Anne
†1432
d. of John
D. of Burgundy

1423 (1)

JOHN
D. of Bedford
*1389 †1435

(2) 1433 (1)

Jaquetta
*1416? †1472
d. of Peter
C. of St. Pol
m. (2) 1436
Richard Widville
E. of Rivers
ex. 1469

Jacqueline
*1401 †1436
d. of William VI
C. of Holland
(div. 1426)
m. (1) 1418
John D. of Brabant
†1427 (div. 1422)

(2) 1423 (1)

HUMPHREY
D. of Gloucester
*1390 †1447
m. (2) 1428
Eleanor
†1454
d. of Reginald
L. Cobham

TABLE 5

pieces of medieval art. Both a label and a bordure might be necessary, as in the case of Richard, Earl of Cambridge, younger son of the Duke of York (Table 4). It did not follow that a man would use the same arms all his life. John of Gaunt, in the latter part of his life, put forward a claim to the throne of Castile in right of his wife: he therefore abandoned his ermine label, and added the arms of Castile and Leon to his own. Richard II, son of the Black Prince, an artistic but on the whole unsuccessful monarch, had a more unusual whim; he impaled with his own arms the mythical blazon attributed to Edward the Confessor (who in fact lived and died before the age of heraldry), and allowed the same privilege to some of his kinsfolk, including Thomas Mowbray. Richard's composition can be seen on the Wilton Diptych in the National Gallery, London, and in Table 66. At the end of his reign, Richard, the reputed inventor of the handkerchief, showed signs of mental unbalance and tyranny. His cousin Henry invaded the country and was accepted as Henry IV.

This accession was, however, an act of violence. The descendants of Lionel of Clarence also had a claim; several of Edward III's sons had married wealthy English heiresses and established powerful families. Another future complication was caused by the private life of John of Gaunt. During the lifetime of his second wife he had several children by Catherine Roelt. Eventually he married her, but their offspring, who bore the name of Beaufort (Table 4), were not legitimate. They were later legitimized, but specifically not for the inheritance of the Crown. After their legitimation they bore the arms of England with a bordure of blue and white sections. Geoffrey Chaucer was a brother-in-law of Catherine Roelt. His greatest poem, the *Canterbury Tales*, written in the closing years of the fourteenth century, is a reminder that one of the results of the war against France was a gradual substitution of English for French as the language of the upper classes.

It will be noticed that where the arms of France appear in the lowest two ranks of Table 3, only three fleurs-de-lys are depicted. Henry IV, early in his reign, followed the example of Charles V (Table 66) in reducing the number shown; gradually other members of the English royal family copied him, so that the coat strewn with lilies (France ancient) disappeared.

Henry V re-opened the war with France, and won a sensational victory at Agincourt in 1415; the French nobility suffered hideous casualties from the English archers. Among the few English dead was Edward, Duke of York (Table 4). In 1420 Henry married the daughter of the French King and was proclaimed as his heir. The world seemed at his feet, but he died unexpectedly and prematurely of dysentery in 1422.

Henry's son was then less than one year old: minorities were always dangerous in the Middle Ages and that of Henry VI was no exception. Aristocratic factions began to compete for dominance. Prominent among them were the Beaufort descendants of John of Gaunt, and a group led by the Duke of Suffolk (his son's arms appear on Table 6). Gradually Richard, Duke of York, emerged as the most formidable critic of the Crown. He was himself descended from the fourth son of Edward III, but his mother, Anne Mortimer, had been the representative of Lionel, Duke of Clarence, the second son, a fact which gave him a better claim to the throne than the hapless Henry VI (Table 5). In 1454 Henry lost his reason and York was appointed Protector. However, in 1455 the King recovered his wits and York was expelled from office.

Gradually the situation deteriorated into civil war. After hesitation York bid for the Crown itself, but was slain before he could win it; it was his son who became Edward IV in 1461.

THE WARS OF THE ROSES

The struggles which are by custom called the Wars of the Roses were episodic and without principle, a contest of 'Outs' against 'Ins'. The Crown had not enough money or power; the aristocracy had too much. On the whole the wars had little effect on the life of the towns or the countryside, which were more conscious of lack of strong government and certain justice.

In 1471 Edward IV firmly defeated a coalition of his cousin Warwick, called the Kingmaker, and Margaret of Anjou, wife of Henry VI (Table 5); he reigned securely until his early death in 1483. But the battles, and the trials which followed them, did have a serious effect on the male descendants of Edward III; seven were killed and five more executed or murdered. After the death of Edward IV, his brother Richard seized the throne, prompted no doubt by ambition but also by fear of another minority. Allegedly, to safeguard his own position, he caused the death of his two nephews – the Princes in the Tower – a ruthless deed but in accord with the general spirit of a callous age. Two years later he was himself defeated and killed by Henry Tudor, Earl of Richmond, at Bosworth.

Nothing could be stronger evidence of the mortality among the Lancastrian party than the emergence of Henry VII; but he was the only adult male dimly connected with John of Gaunt or Henry V. It is true that his mother, Lady Margaret Beaufort, was the great-granddaughter of John of Gaunt; but the legitimation of the Beauforts expressly excluded any pretensions to the Crown. His father, Edmund Tudor, was the offspring of a curious alliance between Catherine of France and an obscure squire named Owen Tudor. It is usually accepted that they must have been married but no evidence survives of where, or when, the wedding took place. Henry VII proceeded to consolidate his position by marrying the eldest daughter of Edward IV. The red rose of Lancaster and the white rose of York were now symbolically united in the Tudor rose with petals of both colours.

None the less the Tudor rulers continued to be suspicious of anyone possessing Plantagenet blood, even by female descent. Table 6 demonstrates clearly the number of descendants of Edward III who perished, or nearly perished, on Tudor scaffolds. The last death shown, that of Thomas Howard in 1572, was for treason connected with Mary, Queen of Scots, but in the other eight cases Plantagenet ancestry was certainly a contributory cause. It was even alleged against the Earl of Surrey that he had used a coat-of-arms which laid stress on his kinship with Richard II and thus indicated his pretensions to the throne.

As can be seen the display of heraldry in this age was becoming more and more elaborate. In battle, men still used a simple shield – if they used one at all – for practical reasons. Richard Neville, the Kingmaker (Table 5), no doubt bore in action the simple blazon of his father, a white saltire on a red field, differenced with a label of blue and white, the colours of the bordure in his Beaufort mother's arms. But on his seal, in stained glass and elsewhere, he would add the proud quarterings of the families – Clare, Despencer, Montagu, Beauchamp and others – whose inherited lands made up his power and wealth.

The shields of two of the queens of this period illustrate this pattern of complexity. Margaret of Anjou (Table 5) was the daughter of King René (Chapter 28) who laid claim to the thrones of Hungary, Naples and Jerusalem, and to the Duchies of Lorraine and Bar. His six 'quarterings', including one for Anjou, make clear his pretensions; two of them call for comment. The third is for Jerusalem and seems to violate one of the basic laws of heraldry by having gold crosses on a silver field; this was a deliberate way of honouring the kingdom whose soil witnessed the life and death of Our Lord. The fifth section is for Bar and once again shows a play upon words, for the fish in it are barbels.

Elizabeth Widville (or Woodville) was the widow of a minor Lancastrian knight when she married the Yorkist King, Edward IV. Her mother was, however, a foreign lady of good birth. During her brief first marriage Elizabeth merely allied the simple arms of her father to those of her husband, John Grey. But when the attractive widow had captivated Edward

IV and become queen, this was not good enough. Accordingly the alien quarterings of her mother (to which she was not strictly entitled because her mother was in no sense an heiress) took pride of place and her paternal arms were relegated to the sixth quarter (Table 4). Study of the various royal differences will also suggest that certain marks were becoming associated with particular titles. Thus, Humphrey, Duke of Gloucester, echoed the silver bordure of his great-uncle Thomas, Duke of Gloucester (Table 3); this was possible since the latter died without a son. Similarly George, Duke of Clarence, younger brother of Edward IV (Table 4) employed the same label as Lionel, Duke of Clarence, the second son of Edward III.

More important things were happening in England in the fifteenth century than the disputes of factious nobles round an inane king (though Henry VI must be given credit for his foundation of Eton and his share in the soaring beauty of King's College, Cambridge). Gradually the influence of the Renaissance in Italy, with its humanist approach to art and letters, was reaching England. Magnificent, tall churches were being erected in the more prosperous parts of the country. Fortified castles were giving place to manor houses built for comfort rather than for defence. All our possessions in France, except Calais, had been lost before the accession of Edward IV, and England was thus freed of an inheritance which had become an entanglement. But of more consequence than all these was the return to England in 1476 of the artisan, William Caxton, who had learned his trade of printing abroad and now set up his press at Westminster. He was to introduce a revolution in communication more striking than the advent of television.

A revolution was also taking place in the practice of war. Gradually the use of fire-arms was increasing, both in the development of artillery and in weapons which could be operated by hand. The penetrating power of a bullet impelled by gunpowder was superior to that of the arrow, even if its accuracy was less. In consequence, the use of full body armour gradually diminished in the sixteenth century, and so did the wearing of a helmet which masked the owner's face. As a result the practical, military need for heraldry passed away, but it survived as a decorative facet of all the arts and can be found on textiles, on sculpture, on china, engraved on silver, and on book-stamps and book-plates.

Politically the end of the Yorkist dynasty and the coming of the Tudors was not very significant, least of all to those living at the time. But in the century and more of Tudor rule a great change took place; the Tudor sovereigns found a medieval kingdom, they left the beginnings of a modern one.

TABLE 4

ENGLAND
Last Plantagenets

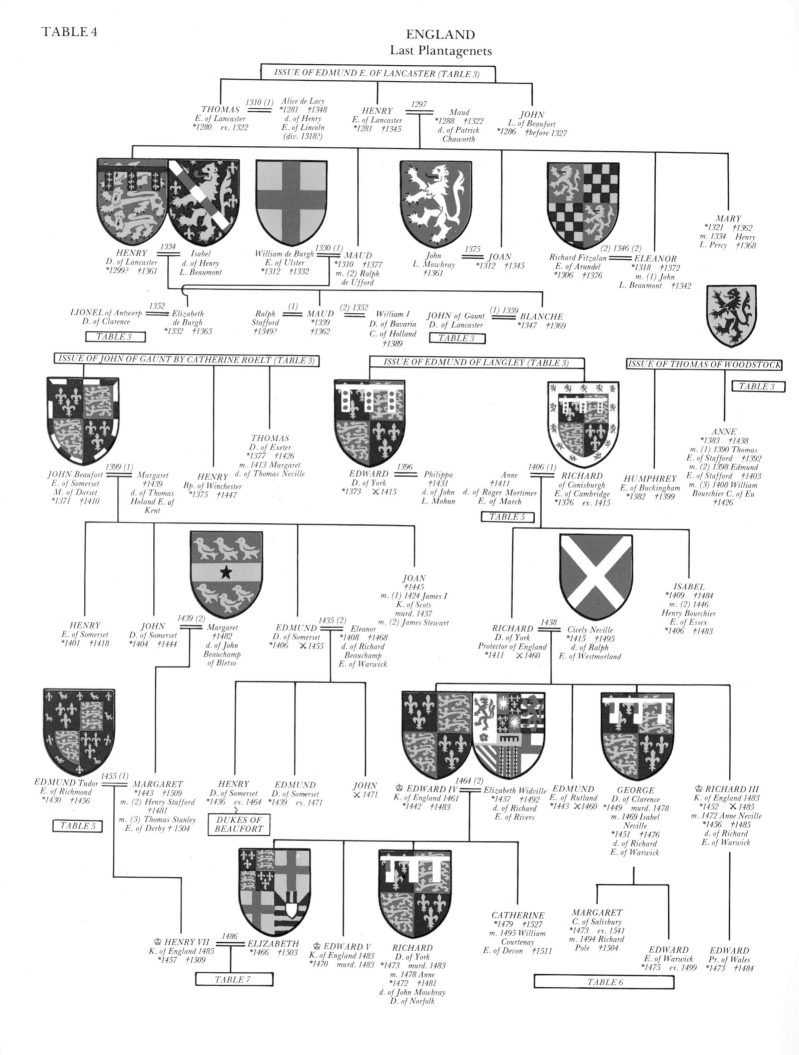

ISSUE OF EDMUND E. OF LANCASTER (TABLE 3)

THOMAS
E. of Lancaster
*1280 ex. 1322
— 1310 (1) —
Alice de Lacy
*1281 †1348
d. of Henry
E. of Lincoln
(div. 1318?)

HENRY
E. of Lancaster
*1281 †1345
— 1297 —
Maud
*1288 †1322
d. of Patrick
Chaworth

JOHN
L. of Beaufort
*1286 †before 1327

HENRY
D. of Lancaster
*1299? †1361
— 1334 —
Isabel
d. of Henry
L. Beaumont

William de Burgh
E. of Ulster
*1312 †1332
— 1330 (1) —
MAUD
*1310 †1377
m. (2) Ralph
de Ufford

John
L. Mowbray
†1361
— 1375 —
JOAN
*1312 †1345

Richard Fitzalan
E. of Arundel
*1306 †1376
— (2) 1346 (2) —
ELEANOR
*1318 †1372
m. (1) John
L. Beaumont †1342

MARY
*1321 †1362
m. 1334 Henry
L. Percy †1368

LIONEL of Antwerp
D. of Clarence
TABLE 3
— 1352 —
Elizabeth
de Burgh
*1332 †1363

Ralph
Stafford
†1349?
— (1) —
MAUD
*1339
†1362
— (2) 1352 —
William I
D. of Bavaria
C. of Holland
†1389

JOHN of Gaunt
D. of Lancaster
TABLE 3
— (1) 1359 —
BLANCHE
*1347 †1369

ISSUE OF JOHN OF GAUNT BY CATHERINE ROELT (TABLE 3)

ISSUE OF EDMUND OF LANGLEY (TABLE 3)

ISSUE OF THOMAS OF WOODSTOCK
TABLE 3

JOHN Beaufort
E. of Somerset
M. of Dorset
*1371 †1410
— 1399 (1) —
Margaret
†1439
d. of Thomas
Holand E. of
Kent

THOMAS
D. of Exeter
*1377 †1426
m. 1413 Margaret
d. of Thomas Neville

HENRY
Bp. of Winchester
*1375 †1447

EDWARD
D. of York
*1373 ✕1415
— 1396 —
Philippa
†1431
d. of John
L. Mohun

Anne
†1411
d. of Roger Mortimer
E. of March
— 1406 (1) —
RICHARD
of Conisburgh
E. of Cambridge
*1376 ex. 1415
TABLE 5

HUMPHREY
E. of Buckingham
*1382 †1399

ANNE
*1383 †1438
m. (1) 1390 Thomas
E. of Stafford †1392
m. (2) 1398 Edmund
E. of Stafford †1403
m. (3) 1408 William
Bourchier C. of Eu
†1426

HENRY
E. of Somerset
*1401 †1418

JOHN
D. of Somerset
*1404 †1444
— 1439 (2) —
Margaret
†1482
d. of John
Beauchamp
of Bletso

EDMUND
D. of Somerset
*1406 ✕1455
— 1435 (2) —
Eleanor
*1408 †1468
d. of Richard
Beauchamp
E. of Warwick

JOAN
†1445
m. (1) 1424 James I
K. of Scots
murd. 1437
m. (2) James Stewart

RICHARD
D. of York
Protector of England
*1411 ✕1460
— 1438 —
Cicely Neville
*1415 †1495
d. of Ralph
E. of Westmorland

ISABEL
*1409 †1484
m. (2) 1446
Henry Bourchier
E. of Essex
*1406 †1483

EDMUND Tudor
E. of Richmond
*1430 †1456
TABLE 5
— 1455 (1) —
MARGARET
*1443 †1509
m. (2) Henry
Stafford †1481
m. (3) Thomas Stanley
E. of Derby † 1504

HENRY
D. of Somerset
*1436 ex. 1464

EDMUND
D. of Somerset
*1439 ex. 1471
DUKES OF
BEAUFORT

JOHN
✕1471

EDWARD IV
K. of England 1461
*1442 †1483
— 1464 (2) —
Elizabeth Widville
*1437 †1492
d. of Richard
E. of Rivers

EDMUND
E. of Rutland
*1443 ✕1460

GEORGE
D. of Clarence
*1449 murd. 1478
m. 1469 Isabel
Neville
*1451 †1476
d. of Richard
E. of Warwick

RICHARD III
K. of England 1483
*1452 ✕1485
m. 1472 Anne Neville
*1456 †1485
d. of Richard
E. of Warwick

HENRY VII
K. of England 1485
*1457 †1509
— 1486 —
ELIZABETH
*1466 †1503
TABLE 7

EDWARD V
K. of England 1483
*1470 murd. 1483

RICHARD
D. of York
*1473 murd. 1483
m. 1478 Anne
*1472 †1481
d. of John Mowbray
D. of Norfolk

CATHERINE
*1479 †1527
m. 1495 William
Courtenay
E. of Devon †1511

MARGARET
C. of Salisbury
*1473 ex. 1541
m. 1494 Richard
Pole †1504

EDWARD
E. of Warwick
*1475 ex. 1499

EDWARD
Pr. of Wales
*1473 †1484

TABLE 6

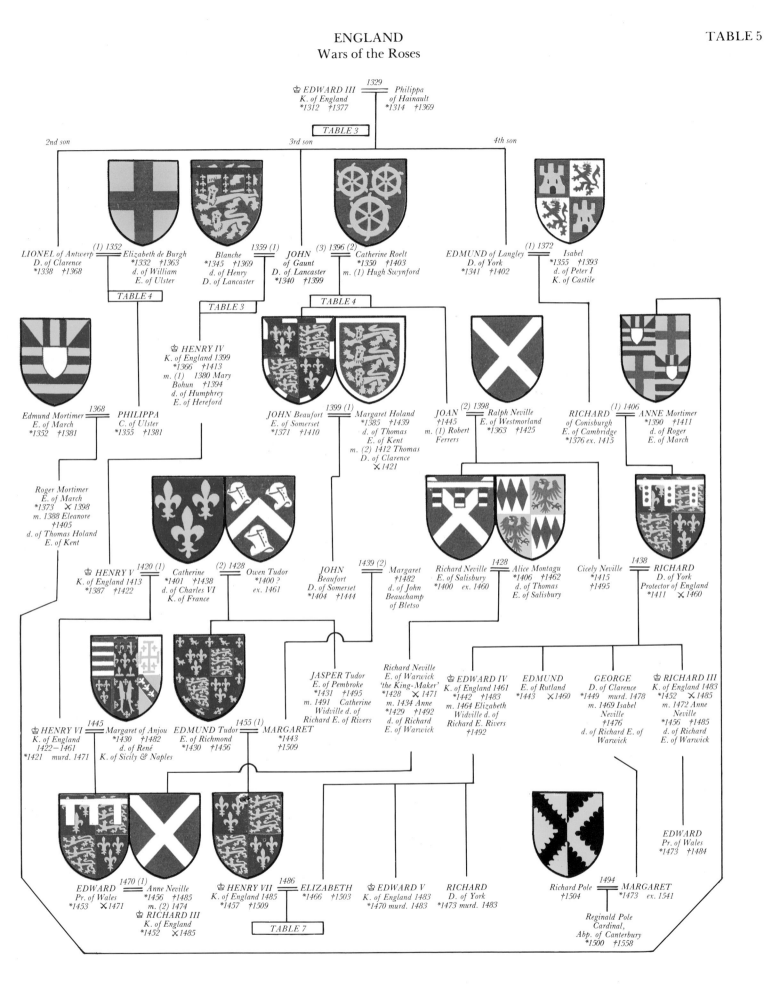

EDWARD III
K. of England
*1312 †1377

Philippa
of Hainault
*1314 †1369

1329

TABLE 3

2nd son

3rd son

4th son

LIONEL of Antwerp
D. of Clarence
*1338 †1368

Elizabeth de Burgh
*1332 †1363
d. of William
E. of Ulster

(1) 1352

TABLE 4

Blanche
*1345 †1369
d. of Henry
D. of Lancaster

1359 (1)

JOHN
of Gaunt
D. of Lancaster
*1340 †1399

Catherine Roelt
*1350 †1403
m. (1) Hugh Swynford

(3) 1396 (2)

TABLE 3

TABLE 4

EDMUND of Langley
D. of York
*1341 †1402

Isabel
*1355 †1393
d. of Peter I
K. of Castile

(1) 1372

👑 HENRY IV
K. of England 1399
*1366 †1413
m. (1) 1380 Mary
Bohun †1394
d. of Humphrey
E. of Hereford

Edmund Mortimer
E. of March
*1352 †1381

PHILIPPA
C. of Ulster
*1355 †1381

1368

JOHN Beaufort
E. of Somerset
*1371 †1410

Margaret Holand
*1385 †1439
d. of Thomas
E. of Kent
m. (2) 1412 Thomas
D. of Clarence
✕1421

1399 (1)

JOAN
*1445
m. (1) Robert
Ferrers

Ralph Neville
E. of Westmorland
*1363 †1425

(2) 1398

RICHARD
of Conisburgh
E. of Cambridge
*1376 ex. 1415

ANNE Mortimer
*1390 †1411
d. of Roger
E. of March

(1) 1406

Roger Mortimer
E. of March
*1373 ✕1398
m. 1388 Eleanore
†1405
d. of Thomas Holand
E. of Kent

👑 HENRY V
K. of England 1413
*1387 †1422

Catherine
*1401 †1438
d. of Charles VI
K. of France

1420 (1)

Owen Tudor
*1400 ?
ex. 1461

(2) 1428

JOHN
Beaufort
D. of Somerset
*1404 †1444

Margaret
*1482
d. of John
Beauchamp
of Bletso

1439 (2)

Richard Neville
E. of Salisbury
*1400 ex. 1460

Alice Montagu
*1406 †1462
d. of Thomas
E. of Salisbury

1428

Cicely Neville
*1415
†1495

RICHARD
D. of York
Protector of England
*1411 ✕1460

1438

JASPER Tudor
E. of Pembroke
*1431 †1495
m. 1491 Catherine
Widville d. of
Richard E. of Rivers

Richard Neville
E. of Warwick
'the King-Maker'
*1428 ✕1471
m. 1434 Anne
*1429 †1492
d. of Richard
E. of Warwick

👑 EDWARD IV
K. of England 1461
*1442 †1483
m. 1464 Elizabeth
Widville d. of
Richard E. Rivers
†1492

EDMUND
E. of Rutland
*1443 ✕1460

GEORGE
D. of Clarence
*1449 murd. 1478
m. 1469 Isabel
Neville
†1476
d. of Richard E. of
Warwick

👑 RICHARD III
K. of England 1483
*1452 ✕1485
m. 1472 Anne
Neville
*1456 †1485
d. of Richard
E. of Warwick

👑 HENRY VI
K. of England
1422–1461
*1421 murd. 1471

Margaret of Anjou
*1430 †1482
d. of René
K. of Sicily & Naples

1445

EDMUND Tudor
E. of Richmond
*1430 †1456

MARGARET
*1443
†1509

1455 (1)

EDWARD
Pr. of Wales
*1473 †1484

EDWARD
Pr. of Wales
*1453 ✕1471

Anne Neville
*1456 †1485
m. (2) 1474
👑 RICHARD III
K. of England
*1452 ✕1485

1470 (1)

👑 HENRY VII
K. of England 1485
*1457 †1509

ELIZABETH
*1466 †1503

1486

👑 EDWARD V
K. of England 1483
*1470 murd. 1483

RICHARD
D. of York
*1473 murd. 1483

Richard Pole
†1504

MARGARET
*1473 ex. 1541

1494

TABLE 7

Reginald Pole
Cardinal,
Abp. of Canterbury
*1500 †1558

Chapter 3

GREAT BRITAIN

At the end of the Battle of Bosworth (1485), after Richard III had died valiantly, sword in hand, the crown of England was found under a hawthorn bush and forthwith placed on the head of Henry VII. In a sense this acclamation was more valid than his tarnished descent from John of Gaunt or his later marriage. It remained to see how far Henry could make it good.

In the event the new King founded a great, though short-lived dynasty; his career was a remarkable achievement for the posthumous child of a thirteen-year-old widow with few expectations. His first aim was to establish his position at home and abroad. An early rising was defeated at Stoke in 1487 and the false pretender, Lambert Simnel, contemptuously dismissed to the royal kitchens; he claimed to be the Earl of Warwick, whom in truth Henry held in the Tower. A later insurgent, Perkin Warbeck, who had been accepted in Scotland as the Duke of York, son of Edward IV, was hanged after his defeat. And at the same time Henry put to death the real Earl of Warwick; thus perished unhappily the last descendant in male line of Geoffrey of Anjou, the sad and bloody sunset of the great Plantagenet family (Table 6). Henry VIII was more ruthless. At the beginning of his reign he beheaded the last Duke of Suffolk whose younger brother, doomed to exile, fell at the Battle of Pavia. In 1539 the Marquess of Exeter and Henry Pole, Lord Montagu, went to the block; and, more barbarously, the latter's mother was sent to the scaffold in 1541. The aged lady declined to lie down and the executioner had to attack her standing.

At the very end of his reign Henry VIII's fury blazed again. In 1521, on trumped-up charges, he had executed one of his greatest nobles, the Duke of Buckingham; now his suspicion fell on Buckingham's son-in-law and grandson, the Duke of Norfolk and the Earl of Surrey. The charge against Surrey was in part heraldic. It was alleged that he removed the silver label from the second quarter of his arms (which indicated his descent from Thomas of Brotherton, Table 3, younger son of Edward I) and thus displayed the pure blazon of England; furthermore, in virtue of his descent from the Mowbray family, to one of whom Richard II had accorded the privilege of the arms of Edward the Confessor, Lord Surrey had added the arms of the Confessor to his own. These heraldic actions were regarded as indicating a claim to the throne. Accordingly Surrey, a brave soldier and a talented poet, went to the block and only Henry's own death saved the aged Norfolk. Surrey's poetry included experiments in blank verse which foreshadowed the triumphs of Shakespeare and Milton in that metre.

Henry VII went cautiously in foreign affairs. He avoided trouble with France and sought peace with Scotland and an alliance with Spain. He married one daughter to the King of France and the other to the King of Scotland, an alliance from which stemmed the union of thrones in 1603. His elder son Arthur, Prince of Wales, was married to Katherine (usually called of Aragon) daughter of the King of Spain. Slowly and cautiously Henry VII moved towards stability and order. He preferred to punish by fine rather than by execution; he studiously fostered the royal revenues and encouraged commerce. John Cabot was allowed to sail under the English flag from Bristol to Newfoundland. When Henry died his fortune had reached the huge sum of £1,500,000; his subjects, looking back, could realize that the Wars of the Roses had ended at Stoke. Henry had proved himself a great king, prudent, parsimonious, peaceful, but above all successful.

Arthur had died in his father's lifetime, and his younger brother succeeded as Henry VIII, an equally outstanding ruler, but in different ways. The new

King began by marrying his brother's widow to preserve the Spanish alliance, an effort in diplomacy which produced unexpected consequences. The major event of his reign was the English Reformation, but this was political as well as religious, linked with the King's private life and the fate of his queens.

Henry was young, well-built, handsome and active, a good player of games, intelligent and ambitious to play his part in Europe. He spent his father's money freely on tournaments and displays, but also on ships and foreign expeditions. In 1513 his armies defeated France at the Battle of the Spurs, and Scotland, disastrously, at Flodden. Henry himself became increasingly concerned over the failure of his wife to produce a male heir and to safeguard the dynasty; only one daughter, Mary, born in 1516, had lived beyond birth. By about 1524 he was already in love with Anne Boleyn, but it was difficult to obtain permission for a divorce from the Pope. Failure to achieve this proved also to be failure for Cardinal Wolsey, the great minister on whom the King had relied in his early years. Wolsey fell from power in 1530, and in the next few years Henry broke away from the Papacy and in 1533 finally married Anne.

A Protestant reaction against orthodox Catholic religion and ritual was part of a European movement of ideas and revolt; but in England the rejection of the Pope's authority came in order to secure Henry's divorce. From the conversion in the seventh century, England had been part of the fabric of western Christendom owing loyalty to the Pope at Rome; now Henry declared himself supreme head of the Church of England. Gradually the liturgy was translated from Latin into English. By one of the ironies of history, the Pope had conferred on Henry only a few years before (1521) the title of Defender of the Faith, in reward for a tract composed by Henry against Luther. Unabashed, Henry continued to use the title; his successors followed him and it still appears on the English coinage today.

Queen Anne gave Henry one daughter, the future Queen Elizabeth; soon he began to look elsewhere in his search for a son. Anne was condemned on charges (probably fabricated) of adultery, and beheaded in 1536. In the same month the King married Jane Seymour; next year she produced the long-desired heir but died in doing so. She was the happiest of Henry's wives; his grief at her death kept him unmarried for two years.

To all his English wives he gave heraldic distinctions; two are shown at the head of Table 7. Anne Boleyn in youth used her father's simple coat with three bulls' heads (another punning coat: Table 10, top row); but this was not grand enough for Henry's Queen. A new shield of six proud quarterings was devised for her, stressing her devious descent from the Plantagenets through her Howard mother; by strict heraldic law, she was not entitled to one of them. Jane Seymour belonged to a more ancient family with lawful quarterings of their own. When she presented him with a son, the King added a new quartering (the first on her shield in Table 7) based on the lilies and leopards of the royal arms. The present Seymour family, descended from her brother, still use this augmentation.

On his death-bed Henry VIII probably still regarded himself as a Catholic who had quarrelled with the Pope. The forces of Protestantism had been growing, however, and took greater control in the short rule of his son, Edward VI. At Edward's death the Duke of Northumberland attempted to bring his daughter-in-law, Lady Jane Grey, to the throne. The coup enlisted no popular support and Mary, elder daughter of Henry VIII, became Queen. She was a resolute Catholic and married her cousin Philip II of Spain, who, though never crowned, was reckoned as King of England with her. The short reign saw a brief and violent Catholic reaction, including the burning of three Protestant bishops, but at Mary's death her half-sister succeeded without opposition.

Queen Elizabeth I was the third great Tudor sovereign. Her triumphs came slowly; had she died after, say, twenty years, she might have seemed less glorious. She achieved a religious settlement; England was firmly established in a Protestant and Episcopalian course, without yielding to extreme puritanism. The Queen dressed with great splendour, but conducted the national finances with prudence. Many of the great houses of England were rebuilt to entertain the royal retinue. Despite a number of suitors, she never married. Relations with Spain had worsened. In 1588 Drake and the English seamen defeated the great Armada which Philip II launched against England. Drake had already circumnavigated the globe in 1577 and had frequently plundered the Spanish colonies in the new world of America. Furthermore, the closing years of her long reign saw a ferment of literary activity which continued into the next century. Spenser, Marlowe, Raleigh, Sidney, Shakespeare and Bacon are only a few of the writers who were making their names known.

By the end of her life Elizabeth was indeed 'Gloriana' to many of her people; in fact her personal popularity, her combination of royal dignity and political circumspection, her proud if faded looks, concealed a series of problems which were to embarrass her successors. She was a true ruler of her realm and one of the most native-born in blood who ever held the throne. A glance at her ancestry in Table 10 reveals that six of her great-grandparents were English, one Welsh and one Irish. No other English or

TABLE 6

ENGLAND
Extirpation of Plantagenet blood under the Tudors

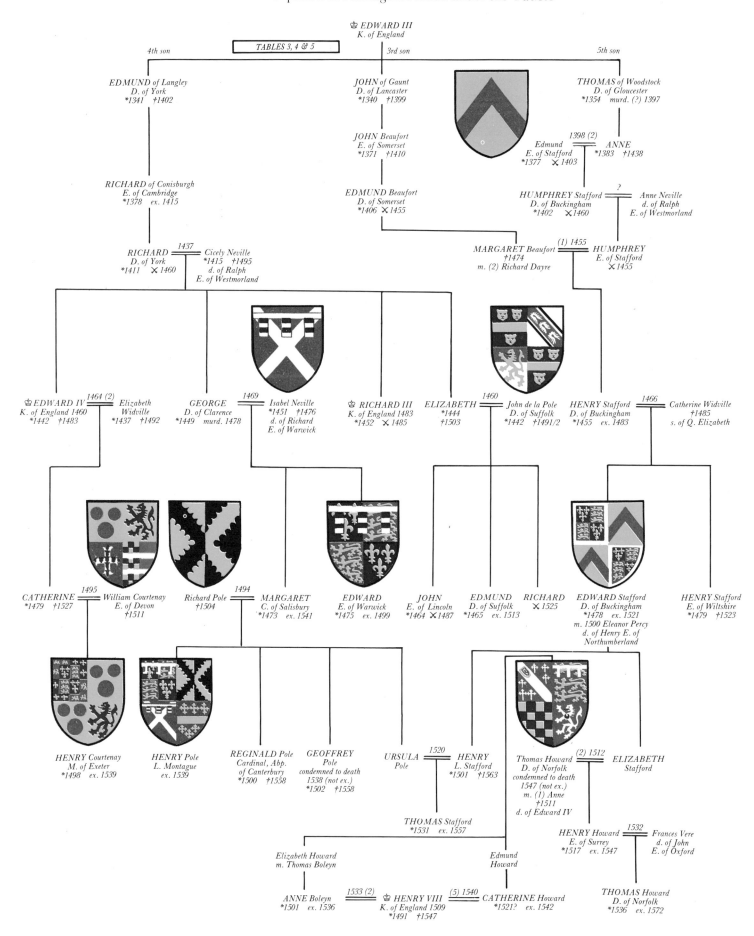

EDWARD III
K. of England

TABLES 3, 4 & 5

4th son — *3rd son* — *5th son*

EDMUND of Langley
D. of York
*1341 †1402

JOHN of Gaunt
D. of Lancaster
*1340 †1399

THOMAS of Woodstock
D. of Gloucester
*1354 murd. (?) 1397

JOHN Beaufort
E. of Somerset
*1371 †1410

1398 (2)
Edmund ═══ **ANNE**
E. of Stafford   *1383 †1438
*1377 ✕1403

RICHARD of Conisburgh
E. of Cambridge
*1378 ex. 1415

EDMUND Beaufort
D. of Somerset
*1406 ✕1455

HUMPHREY Stafford ═══ Anne Neville
D. of Buckingham   d. of Ralph
*1402 ✕1460   E. of Westmorland   ?

1437
RICHARD ═══ Cicely Neville
D. of York   *1415 †1495
*1411 ✕1460   d. of Ralph
E. of Westmorland

MARGARET Beaufort ═══ *(1) 1455* **HUMPHREY**
†1474   E. of Stafford
m. (2) Richard Dayre   ✕1455

1464 (2)
☙ **EDWARD IV** ═══ Elizabeth
K. of England 1460   Widville
*1442 †1483   *1437 †1492

1469
GEORGE ═══ Isabel Neville
D. of Clarence   *1451 †1476
*1449 murd. 1478   d. of Richard
E. of Warwick

☙ **RICHARD III**
K. of England 1483
*1452 ✕1485

ELIZABETH ═══ *1460* John de la Pole
*1444   D. of Suffolk
†1503   *1442 †1491/2

HENRY Stafford ═══ *1466* Catherine Widville
D. of Buckingham   †1485
*1455 ex. 1483   s. of Q. Elizabeth

1495
CATHERINE ═══ William Courtenay
*1479 †1527   E. of Devon
†1511

Richard Pole ═══ *1494* **MARGARET**
†1504   C. of Salisbury
*1473 ex. 1541

EDWARD
E. of Warwick
*1475 ex. 1499

JOHN
E. of Lincoln
*1464 ✕1487

EDMUND
D. of Suffolk
*1465 ex. 1513

RICHARD
✕1525

EDWARD Stafford
D. of Buckingham
*1478 ex. 1521
m. 1500 Eleanor Percy
d. of Henry E. of
Northumberland

HENRY Stafford
E. of Wiltshire
*1479 †1523

HENRY Courtenay
M. of Exeter
*1498 ex. 1539

HENRY Pole
L. Montague
ex. 1539

REGINALD Pole
Cardinal, Abp.
of Canterbury
*1500 †1558

GEOFFREY
Pole
condemned to death
1538 (not ex.)
*1502 †1558

URSULA ═══ *1520* **HENRY**
Pole   L. Stafford
*1501 †1563

Thomas Howard ═══ *(2) 1512* **ELIZABETH**
D. of Norfolk   Stafford
condemned to death
1547 (not ex.)
m. (1) Anne
†1511
d. of Edward IV

THOMAS Stafford
*1531 ex. 1557

Elizabeth Howard
m. Thomas Boleyn

Edmund
Howard

HENRY Howard ═══ *1532* Frances Vere
E. of Surrey   d. of John
*1517 ex. 1547   E. of Oxford

ANNE Boleyn ═══ *1533 (2)* ☙ **HENRY VIII** ═══ *(5) 1540* **CATHERINE** Howard
*1501 ex. 1536   K. of England 1509   *1521? ex. 1542
*1491 †1547

THOMAS Howard
D. of Norfolk
*1536 ex. 1572

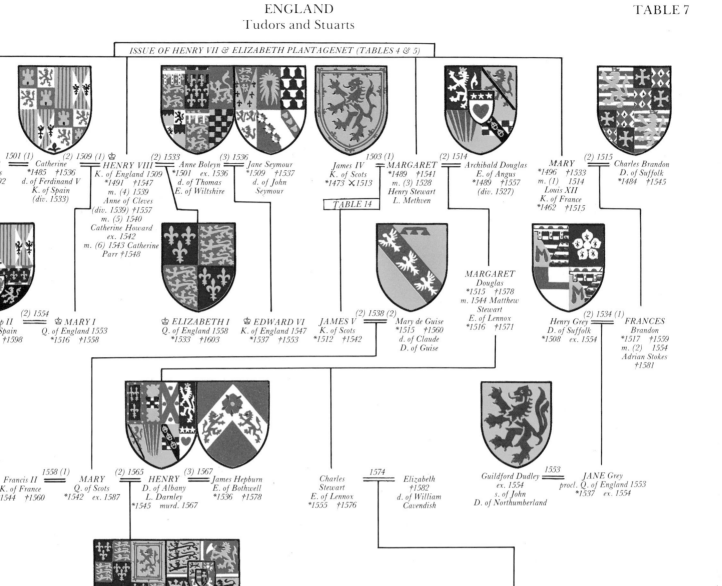

ISSUE OF HENRY VII & ELIZABETH PLANTAGENET (TABLES 4 & 5)

ARTHUR
Pr. of Wales
*1486 †1502

1501 (1)
Catherine
d. of Ferdinand V
K. of Spain
(div. 1533)

(2) 1509 (1) 👑
HENRY VIII
K. of England 1509
*1491 †1547
m. (4) 1539
Anne of Cleves
(div. 1539) †1557
m. (5) 1540
Catherine Howard
ex. 1542
m. (6) 1543 Catherine
Parr †1548

(2) 1533
Anne Boleyn
*1501 ex. 1536
d. of Thomas
E. of Wiltshire

(3) 1536
Jane Seymour
*1509 †1537
d. of John
Seymour

1503 (1)
James IV
K. of Scots
*1473 ✕1513

(2) 1514
MARGARET
*1489 †1541
m. (3) 1528
Henry Stewart
L. Methven

TABLE 14

Archibald Douglas
E. of Angus
*1489 †1557
(div. 1527)

MARY
*1496 †1533
m. (1) 1514
Louis XII
K. of France
*1462 †1515

(2) 1515
Charles Brandon
D. of Suffolk
*1484 †1545

Philip II
K. of Spain
*1527 †1598

(2) 1554
👑 MARY I
Q. of England 1553
*1516 †1558

👑 ELIZABETH I
Q. of England 1558
*1533 †1603

EDWARD VI
K. of England 1547
*1537 †1553

JAMES V
K. of Scots
*1512 †1542

(2) 1538 (2)
Mary de Guise
*1515 †1560
d. of Claude
D. of Guise

MARGARET
Douglas
*1515 †1578
m. 1544 Matthew
Stewart
E. of Lennox
*1516 †1571

Henry Grey
D. of Suffolk
*1508 ex. 1554

(2) 1534 (1)
FRANCES
Brandon
*1517 †1559
m. (2) 1554
Adrian Stokes
†1581

Francis II
K. of France
*1544 †1560

1558 (1)
MARY
Q. of Scots
*1542 ex. 1587

(2) 1565
HENRY
D. of Albany
L. Darnley
*1545 murd. 1567

(3) 1567
James Hepburn
E. of Bothwell
*1536 †1578

Charles
Stewart
E. of Lennox
*1555 †1576

1574
Elizabeth
†1582
d. of William
Cavendish

Guildford Dudley
ex. 1554
s. of John
D. of Northumberland

1553
JANE Grey
procl. Q. of England 1553
*1537 ex. 1554

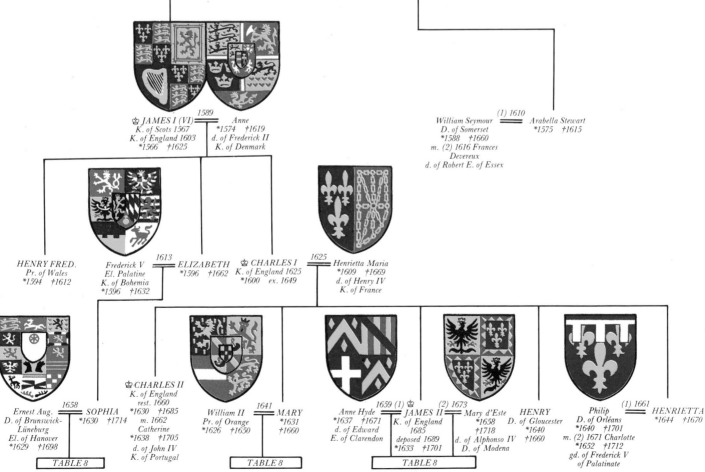

👑 JAMES I (VI)
K. of Scots 1567
K. of England 1603
*1566 †1625

1589
Anne
*1574 †1619
d. of Frederick II
K. of Denmark

William Seymour
D. of Somerset
*1588 †1660
m. (2) 1616 Frances
Devereux
d. of Robert E. of Essex

(1) 1610
Arabella Stewart
*1575 †1615

HENRY FRED.
Pr. of Wales
*1594 †1612

Frederick V
El. Palatine
K. of Bohemia
*1596 †1632

1613
ELIZABETH
*1596 †1662

👑 CHARLES I
K. of England 1625
*1600 ex. 1649

1625
Henrietta Maria
*1609 †1669
d. of Henry IV
K. of France

Ernest Aug.
D. of Brunswick-
Lüneburg
El. of Hanover
*1629 †1698

1658
SOPHIA
*1630 †1714

👑 CHARLES II
K. of England
rest. 1660
*1630 †1685
m. 1662
Catherine
*1638 †1705
d. of John IV
K. of Portugal

William II
Pr. of Orange
*1626 †1650

1641
MARY
*1631
†1660

Anne Hyde
*1637 †1671
d. of Edward
E. of Clarendon

1659 (1) 👑
JAMES II
K. of England
1685
deposed 1689
*1633 †1701

(2) 1673
Mary d'Este
*1658
†1718
d. of Alphonso IV
D. of Modena

HENRY
D. of Gloucester
*1640
†1660

Philip
D. of Orléans
*1640 †1701
m. (2) 1671 Charlotte
*1652 †1712
gd. of Frederick V
of Palatinate

(1) 1661
HENRIETTA
*1644 †1670

TABLE 8

TABLE 8

TABLE 8

The funeral procession of Queen Elizabeth I in 1603. Her funeral bier is surrounded by the twelve banners of her forebears, beginning with that of Henry II (upper left) and ending with that of her father, Henry VIII (lower right).

British ruler can show a similar absence of alien blood.

Her nearest kinsman, James VI of Scotland (Tables 7 and 14), succeeded without controversy as James I of England, first of the Stuart kings. He was a Protestant, had already been King of Scotland for 36 years, and was an odd mixture of wisdom and conceit, of learning in theory and tactlessness in practice, which justified his nickname 'the wisest fool in Christendom'. It must be stressed that the union was at this stage only one of crowns; England and Scotland each preserved their own separate parliaments, peerages, judicatures and customs. This was recognized in the new arrangement of the royal arms. The claim to France was maintained (though the last piece of French soil, Calais, had been lost by Mary) and since it was attached to the Crown of England, the lilies and leopards were placed in the first and fourth quarters; Scotland filled the second, while the harp of Ireland appeared, for the first time, in the third.

One feature of government under the Tudors had been an increasing consultation with Parliament. This in turn had led the House of Commons to seek greater powers and privileges, to aim indeed at control of the Crown. The contest between Crown and Parliament was to be the main theme of the seventeenth century; two subjects which invited conflict were finance and religion. Elizabeth had been short of money at the end of her reign; James I was no better off. There was still a substantial Catholic minority in England; it was a desperate clique of them who tried to blow up Parliament by the hand of Guy Fawkes in 1605. On the other flank of the Church of England a more radical Puritan or Nonconformist movement was manifesting itself in the country and in Parliament.

Charles I, short, stubborn and godly, was not the monarch to find an answer to these problems. The first phase of his reign saw a series of disputes with the House of Commons; then for eleven years (1629–40) he tried to manage without summoning a Parliament and by reviving obsolete medieval taxes. In 1642 civil war broke out. In general the nobility, the Catholics, the west and the north were for the King. London, East Anglia, the merchant classes and the Puritans supported the Parliament. Sometimes brother fought against brother. A Huntingdonshire squire of Nonconformist opinions, Oliver Cromwell, became the outstanding general of the war. Finally, Charles fell into the hands of his enemies; after much debate he was tried and condemned to death by a special court. The King, who behaved with massive dignity, was beheaded on a cold January day in 1649 'by no known law and an unknown executioner'.

A by-product of the troubled times was the growth of emigration to America. About 25,000 had settled in New England by 1640; later in the century colonies were established as refuges for specific faiths, Pennsylvania for Quakers or Maryland for Catholics. The life of the early colonists was hard, but they cultivated alike the rich soil of the New World and a sturdy independence of thought in political fields.

For eleven years after Charles I's execution England was a Commonwealth under Oliver Cromwell as Lord Protector. The Crown was offered to this plain, blunt, dour, religious man, who bade his portraitist depict him warts and all, but he resolutely refused it. Various constitutional schemes were put forward, but none found universal favour. When he died there was but a brief hesitation before the restoration of the Stuarts with the crowning of Charles II in 1660.

THE RESTORATION

Charles II was a very different man from his father. Tall, good-looking, amusing, a lover of women and something of a cynic, he was determined not to face again the bitterness of exile. Under the able guidance of his Chancellor, Lord Clarendon, a settlement was reached. Absolute monarchy was a thing of the past – but so was republicanism. Henceforth taxation had to be approved by Parliament. After the austerities of the Commonwealth, the English, led by their King, embarked upon an age of licence, the world of Pepys' diaries. All was not pleasure; the fearful Plague broke out in 1665, and was followed the next year by the Great Fire of London, which gave extensive opportunities to Sir Christopher Wren, the greatest of English architects. Charles was childless and his brother James a Catholic, a circumstance which produced political unrest.

James II was less intelligent than his brother, more bigoted and more tactless. He had first married a daughter of his brother's great minister, Lord Clarendon; Anne Hyde was a loyal Protestant and brought up her two daughters in that faith. His second wife, Mary of Modena, appeared barren. James left his subjects in no doubt that he aimed to restore the Roman Catholic religion and popular anxiety was already considerable when the Queen finally produced a son. Hope of a peaceful Protestant succession vanished: seven prominent figures drawn from both Whig and Tory parties (as left and right had begun to be called) sent an appeal to William of Orange, nephew and son-in-law of the King.

With remarkable courage William collected a force and landed in Devon in 1688. James II lost heart and fled, petulantly flinging the Great Seal into the Thames, whence a fisherman very shortly recovered it. William III and Mary were proclaimed joint sovereigns in February 1689. They were offered their common crown by Parliament. It was now clear, if it had not been before, that Parliament could control the succession. This process was carried a stage further in 1701 when the Act of Settlement laid down that William should be followed by Anne (his wife's sister) and after her by the nearest available Protestant – at that date the Electress Sophia of Hanover (Table 7: bottom row). The real triumph of William and his friends was two-fold: the Glorious Revolution of 1688–9 was bloodless in England, and the settlement which sprang from it has stood the test of time. During his reign he imposed on the royal arms a small escutcheon of his family shield of Nassau (Table 8: top row).

Queen Anne made a more significant alteration. In 1707 was brought about the Union with Scotland, which gave the two realms a common Parliament of Great Britain as well as a common Crown. The people of Scotland prized their independence, but the blunt truth is that they were being kept back by lack of resources and a still primitive agriculture. If the benefits for Scotland were mainly economic, in the form of expanded commerce and intercourse with England, those for England were largely political. Queen Anne could not live for ever; and a Stuart restoration was more plausible north of the Tweed than south of it. In the years that followed, Scots were able to share with English in overseas expansion; from Canada to Calcutta their names will be found among the great administrators and on the humblest tombstones. To symbolize the Act of Union Anne altered the royal arms. The closer intimacy of England and Scotland was reflected by joining them in the first and fourth quarters while France was promoted to the second and Ireland held the third (Table 8). William III had involved England in war against the ambitions of Louis XIV; strife with France was to continue intermittently for more than a century, but the conflict in Anne's reign was made glorious by Blenheim and the other great victories of the Duke of Marlborough, the first prepotent Churchill.

THE HANOVERIANS

When Anne died in 1714, the Electress Sophia was a few weeks dead and the next Protestant heir was her son George Louis, the Elector of Hanover (Table 99); accordingly he became King George I of Great Britain. Fifty-seven living men, women and children had a better genealogical right but all adhered to the Catholic faith. George, stout and Teutonic, was already in late middle age; he was a soldier with a good grip of politics and more ability than has generally been credited to him. His paternal coat-of-arms was of Germanic complexity as can be seen from the shields of his father (Table 7: bottom row) or his wife, who was also his first cousin (Table 8: top row). Fortunately, not all his many quarterings were incorporated in the arms of Great Britain: it was enough to take the two lions of Brunswick, the white horse of Westphalia and the blue lion and red hearts of Lüneburg and place them in the fourth quarter. Above them on a smaller shield was the crown of Charlemagne which represented George's position as Arch-Treasurer of the Holy Roman Empire. The new King's ancestry can be seen on Table 10; of the eight forebears shown, only James I came from within Great Britain.

George I, quite rightly, suspected many of the Tories of sympathy with the exiled son of James II (the

TABLE 8

GREAT BRITAIN
House of Hanover

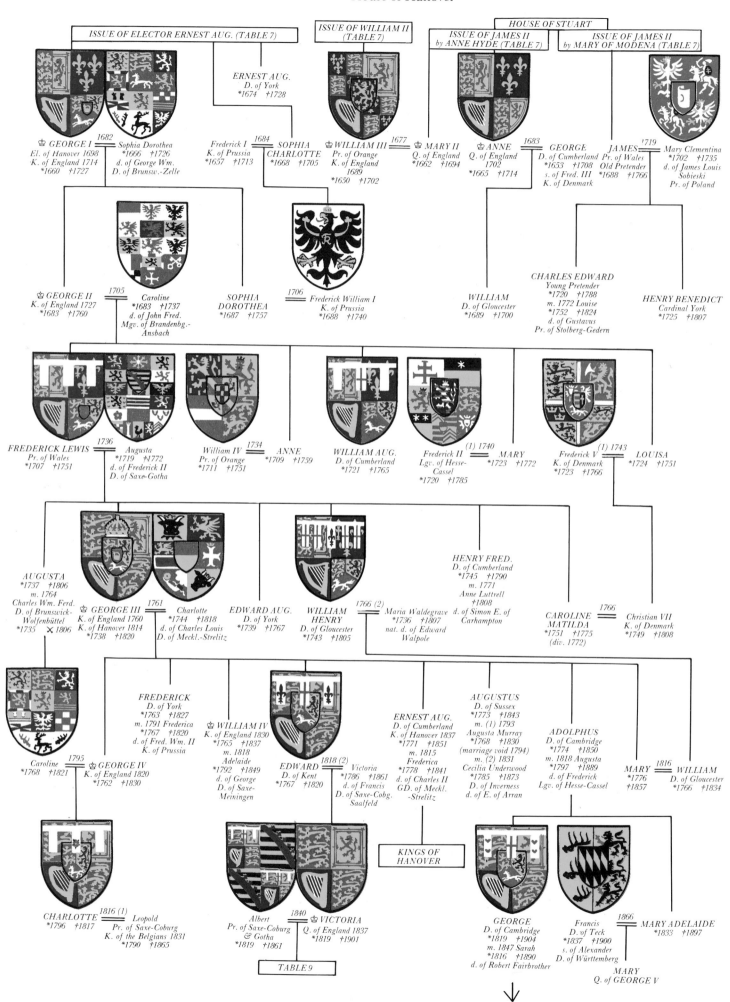

ISSUE OF ELECTOR ERNEST AUG. (TABLE 7)

ISSUE OF WILLIAM II (TABLE 7)

HOUSE OF STUART

ISSUE OF JAMES II by ANNE HYDE (TABLE 7)

ISSUE OF JAMES II by MARY OF MODENA (TABLE 7)

ERNEST AUG.
D. of York
*1674 †1728

♔ GEORGE I
El. of Hanover 1698
K. of England 1714
*1660 †1727

1682
Sophia Dorothea
*1666 †1726
d. of George Wm.
D. of Brunsw.-Zelle

Frederick I
K. of Prussia
*1657 †1713

1684
SOPHIA
CHARLOTTE
*1668 †1705

WILLIAM III
Pr. of Orange
K. of England
1689
*1650 †1702

1677
MARY II
Q. of England
*1662 †1694

ANNE
Q. of England
1702
*1665 †1714

1683
GEORGE
D. of Cumberland
*1653 †1708
s. of Fred. III
K. of Denmark

JAMES
Pr. of Wales
Old Pretender
*1688 †1766

1719
Mary Clementina
*1702 †1735
d. of James Louis
Sobieski
Pr. of Poland

♔ GEORGE II
K. of England 1727
*1683 †1760

1705
Caroline
*1683 †1737
d. of John Fred.
Mgv. of Brandenbg.-
Ansbach

SOPHIA
DOROTHEA
*1687 †1757

1706
Frederick William I
K. of Prussia
*1688 †1740

WILLIAM
D. of Gloucester
*1689 †1700

CHARLES EDWARD
Young Pretender
*1720 †1788
m. 1772 Louise
*1752 †1824
d. of Gustavus
Pr. of Stolberg-Gedern

HENRY BENEDICT
Cardinal York
*1725 †1807

FREDERICK LEWIS
Pr. of Wales
*1707 †1751

1736
Augusta
*1719 †1772
d. of Frederick II
D. of Saxe-Gotha

William IV
Pr. of Orange
*1711 †1751

1734
ANNE
*1709 †1759

WILLIAM AUG.
D. of Cumberland
*1721 †1765

Frederick II
Lgv. of Hesse-
Cassel
*1720 †1785

(1) 1740
MARY
*1723 †1772

Frederick V
K. of Denmark
*1723 †1766

(1) 1743
LOUISA
*1724 †1751

AUGUSTA
*1737 †1806
m. 1764
Charles Wm. Ferd.
D. of Brunswick-
Wolfenbüttel
*1735 ✕ 1806

♔ GEORGE III
K. of England 1760
K. of Hanover 1814
*1738 †1820

1761
Charlotte
*1744 †1818
d. of Charles Louis
D. of Meckl.-Strelitz

EDWARD AUG.
D. of York
*1739 †1767

WILLIAM
HENRY
D. of Gloucester
*1743 †1805

1766 (2)
Maria Waldegrave
*1736 †1807
nat. d. of Edward
Walpole

HENRY FRED.
D. of Cumberland
*1745 †1790
m. 1771
Anne Luttrell
†1808
d. of Simon E. of
Carhampton

CAROLINE
MATILDA
*1751 †1775
(div. 1772)

1766
Christian VII
K. of Denmark
*1749 †1808

FREDERICK
D. of York
*1763 †1827
m. 1791 Frederica
*1767 †1820
d. of Fred. Wm. II
K. of Prussia

♔ WILLIAM IV
K. of England 1830
*1765 †1837
m. 1818
Adelaide
*1792 †1849
d. of George
D. of Saxe-
Meiningen

EDWARD
D. of Kent
*1767 †1820

1818 (2)
Victoria
*1786 †1861
d. of Francis
D. of Saxe-Cobg.
Saalfeld

ERNEST AUG.
D. of Cumberland
K. of Hanover 1837
*1771 †1851
m. 1815
Frederica
*1778 †1841
d. of Charles II
GD. of Meckl.
-Strelitz

AUGUSTUS
D. of Sussex
*1773 †1843
m. (1) 1793
Augusta Murray
*1768 †1830
(marriage void 1794)
m. (2) 1831
Cecilia Underwood
*1785 †1873
D. of Inverness
d. of E. of Arran

ADOLPHUS
D. of Cambridge
*1774 †1850
m. 1818 Augusta
*1797 †1889
d. of Frederick
Lgv. of Hesse-Cassel

MARY
*1776
†1857

1816
WILLIAM
D. of Gloucester
*1766 †1834

Caroline
*1768 †1821

1795
♔ GEORGE IV
K. of England 1820
*1762 †1830

CHARLOTTE
*1796 †1817

1816 (1)
Leopold
Pr. of Saxe-Coburg
K. of the Belgians 1831
*1790 †1865

Albert
Pr. of Saxe-Coburg
& Gotha
*1819 †1861

1840
♔ VICTORIA
Q. of England 1837
*1819 †1901

KINGS OF
HANOVER

GEORGE
D. of Cambridge
*1819 †1904
m. 1847 Sarah
*1816 †1890
d. of Robert Fairbrother

Francis
D. of Teck
*1837 †1900
s. of Alexander
D. of Württemberg

1866
MARY ADELAIDE
*1833 †1897

MARY
Q. of GEORGE V

TABLE 9

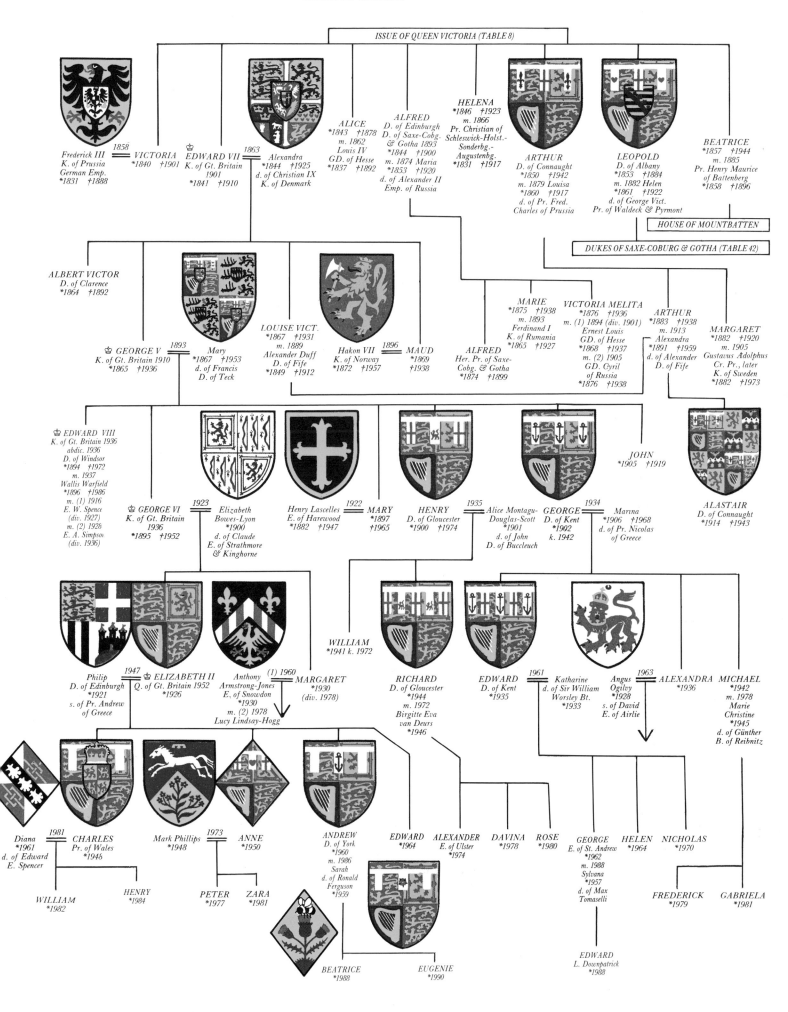

ISSUE OF QUEEN VICTORIA (TABLE 8)

Frederick III
K. of Prussia
German Emp.
*1831 †1888

— 1858 —

VICTORIA
*1840 †1901

♔ **EDWARD VII**
K. of Gt. Britain
1901
*1841 †1910

— 1863 —

Alexandra
*1844 †1925
d. of Christian IX
K. of Denmark

ALICE
*1843 †1878
m. 1862
Louis IV
GD. of Hesse
*1837 †1892

ALFRED
D. of Edinburgh
D. of Saxe-Cobg.
& Gotha 1893
*1844 †1900
m. 1874 Maria
*1853 †1920
d. of Alexander II
Emp. of Russia

HELENA
*1846 †1923
m. 1866
Pr. Christian of
Schleswick-Holst.-
Sonderbg.-
Augustenbg.
*1831 †1917

ARTHUR
D. of Connaught
*1850 †1942
m. 1879 Louisa
*1860 †1917
d. of Pr. Fred.
Charles of Prussia

LEOPOLD
D. of Albany
*1853 †1884
m. 1882 Helen
*1861 †1922
d. of George Vict.
Pr. of Waldeck & Pyrmont

BEATRICE
*1857 †1944
m. 1885
Pr. Henry Maurice
of Battenberg
*1858 †1896

HOUSE OF MOUNTBATTEN

DUKES OF SAXE-COBURG & GOTHA (TABLE 42)

ALBERT VICTOR
D. of Clarence
*1864 †1892

♔ **GEORGE V**
K. of Gt. Britain 1910
*1865 †1936

— 1893 —

Mary
*1867 †1953
d. of Francis
D. of Teck

LOUISE VICT.
*1867 †1931
m. 1889
Alexander Duff
D. of Fife
*1849 †1912

Hakon VII
K. of Norway
*1872 †1957

— 1896 —

MAUD
*1869
†1938

MARIE
*1875 †1938
m. 1893
Ferdinand I
K. of Rumania
*1865 †1927

ALFRED
Her. Pr. of Saxe-
Cobg. & Gotha
*1874 †1899

VICTORIA MELITA
*1876 †1936
m. (1) 1894 (div. 1901)
Ernest Louis
GD. of Hesse
*1868 †1937
m. (2) 1905
GD. Cyril
of Russia
*1876 †1938

ARTHUR
*1883 †1938
m. 1913
Alexandra
*1891 †1959
d. of Alexander
D. of Fife

MARGARET
*1882 †1920
m. 1905
Gustavus Adolphus
Cr. Pr., later
K. of Sweden
*1882 †1973

♔ **EDWARD VIII**
K. of Gt. Britain 1936
abdic. 1936
D. of Windsor
*1894 †1972
m. 1937
Wallis Warfield
*1896 †1986
m. (1) 1916
E. W. Spence
(div. 1927)
m. (2) 1928
E. A. Simpson
(div. 1936)

♔ **GEORGE VI**
K. of Gt. Britain
1936
*1895 †1952

— 1923 —

Elizabeth
Bowes-Lyon
*1900
d. of Claude
E. of Strathmore
& Kinghorne

Henry Lascelles
E. of Harewood
*1882 †1947

— 1922 —

MARY
*1897
†1965

HENRY
D. of Gloucester
*1900 †1974

— 1935 —

Alice Montagu-
Douglas-Scott
*1901
d. of John
D. of Buccleuch

GEORGE
D. of Kent
*1902
k. 1942

— 1934 —

Marina
*1906 †1968
d. of Pr. Nicolas
of Greece

JOHN
*1905 †1919

ALASTAIR
D. of Connaught
*1914 †1943

WILLIAM
*1941 k. 1972

Philip
D. of Edinburgh
*1921
s. of Pr. Andrew
of Greece

— 1947 —

♔ **ELIZABETH II**
Q. of Gt. Britain 1952
*1926

Anthony
Armstrong-Jones
E. of Snowdon
*1930
m. (2) 1978
Lucy Lindsay-Hogg

— (1) 1960 —

MARGARET
*1930
(div. 1978)

RICHARD
D. of Gloucester
*1944
m. 1972
Birgitte Eva
van Deurs
*1946

EDWARD
D. of Kent
*1935

— 1961 —

Katharine
d. of Sir William
Worsley Bt.
*1933

Angus
Ogilvy
*1928
s. of David
E. of Airlie

— 1963 —

ALEXANDRA
*1936

MICHAEL
*1942
m. 1978
Marie
Christine
*1945
d. of Günther
B. of Reibnitz

Diana
*1961
d. of Edward
E. Spencer

— 1981 —

CHARLES
Pr. of Wales
*1948

Mark Phillips
*1948

— 1973 —

ANNE
*1950

ANDREW
D. of York
*1960
m. 1986
Sarah
*1957
d. of Ronald
Ferguson
*1959

EDWARD
*1964

ALEXANDER
E. of Ulster
*1974

DAVINA
*1978

ROSE
*1980

GEORGE
E. of St. Andrew
*1962
m. 1988
Sylvana
*1957
d. of Max
Tomaselli

HELEN
*1964

NICHOLAS
*1970

FREDERICK
*1979

GABRIELA
*1981

WILLIAM
*1982

HENRY
*1984

PETER
*1977

ZARA
*1981

BEATRICE
*1988

EUGENIE
*1990

EDWARD
L. Downpatrick
*1988

Old Pretender) whose titular reign (1701–66) was longer even than that of Queen Victoria; he therefore relied on Whig ministers of whom the most distinguished was Sir Robert Walpole, a tough, coarse, Norfolk squire of immense political capacity. Under his guidance, and with the King often absent, the cabinet system and the leadership of the 'Prime' Minister began to evolve. The supporters of the Stuart dynasty – the Jacobites – made two vain attempts at restoration, in 1715 and 1745; the second was led by the glamorous figure of Prince Charles Edward (the Young Pretender) and came nearer to success.

George II spoke English, but not well. At the Battle of Dettingen (1743) he was the last British sovereign to lead his troops into battle. His own campaigns on the Continent were far less important than those being waged overseas at the end of his reign. During the Seven Years' War, the commanding genius of William Pitt, Earl of Chatham, directed the armies of Britain to victory in India and Canada and laid the foundations of the British Empire, a task which could not have been accomplished without mastery of the seas. In 1757 the Battle of Plassey marked the end of French rivalry in India; in 1759 British arms triumphed at Quebec in Canada, Minden in Germany and Quiberon Bay off Brittany. George II died at a glorious moment.

His son, Frederick, Prince of Wales, predeceased him. It will be noticed that the red escutcheon in the centre of his Hanover quartering is blank, because he never became the Treasurer of the Empire, and that he uses the conventional silver label of an eldest son. By that date it was established that sons of the sovereign had labels of three points, the younger sons marking one or more points with a sign of distinction (William, Duke of Cumberland, or George, Duke of Cambridge, on Table 8), while grandsons used a label of five points, again with appropriate differences (William Henry, Duke of Gloucester). The continuance of the practice can be observed on Table 9.

George III was much more English in his upbringing; his reign of sixty years – longer than that of Henry III – saw fantastic changes in his realms. It is impossible to outline more than the most significant. Saddest was the loss of the American colonies. Freed from all danger of French invasion, their independence became more manifest; their complaints were ill-handled at home; war broke out, and within a decade the Americans, under the talented leadership of George Washington, had gained their freedom. A more complex process transformed England, which in 1700 was still basically an agricultural nation, into an industrial people with rich resources in coal and iron. With the Industrial Revolution came a shift in population from south to north which is only being redressed in our own day.

A more political manoeuvre was the Act of Union with Ireland in 1800. By this measure the hitherto separate Irish Parliament was amalgamated with that of Great Britain; the United Kingdom was thus created. From 1801 a further change took place in the royal arms. The empty claim to France was at long last abandoned (partly perhaps because Napoleon was now in control there) after 461 years. England, now divorced from its link with Scotland, took the first and fourth quarters, Scotland the second and Ireland the third. Hanover, which was not represented at Westminster, was placed on a central escutcheon with above it the bonnet of an elector. In 1814 Hanover became a kingdom and the bonnet was replaced by a crown; the new shield is shown on Table 8 for George III. This promotion was one of the consequences of the great wars against Napoleon (Table 72). There are curious parallels between this grim conflict and the war against Hitler. In both, the United Kingdom stood awhile alone; in both, invasion of England was threatened but not achieved; in both, the enemy received a devastating blow amid the snows of Russia; in both, British armies ultimately invaded the homeland of the foe. When the Duke of Wellington finally triumphed at Waterloo (1815), George III was already old and senile.

Neither of his sons, George IV and William IV, produced an heir; accordingly in 1837 the throne passed to their niece, Queen Victoria. Hanover, however, was governed by the Salic Law, which forbade the accession of a female, and passed to another son of George III, Ernest, Duke of Cumberland (Table 100). As a result of this, the escutcheon of Hanover disappeared, and the royal arms of England assumed the form which they still exhibit today (Table 1: bottom, or Table 8: bottom row). Queen Victoria married her cousin, Albert of Saxe-Coburg and Gotha, who was given the style of Prince Consort and the arms shown at the base of Table 8; his family arms can be seen in the top rank of Table 11. Victoria was an essentially British queen, but it can be seen from Table 11 that her ancestors were almost exclusively Germanic.

Her reign, the longest in British history, was mainly one of peace and prosperity. At home Britain became the workshop of the world; overseas her dominions expanded, not least in Australia and New Zealand. To modern purses a striking feature of the period would be the general stability of prices; this was accompanied by a great growth in population. In the world of politics the rivalry of Liberals and Conservatives, replacing the old Whigs and Tories, saw such formidable figures as Peel and Palmerston, Disraeli and Gladstone locked in parliamentary battle. Bill by reform bill the suffrage was extended, though women did not obtain the vote until the present century. At

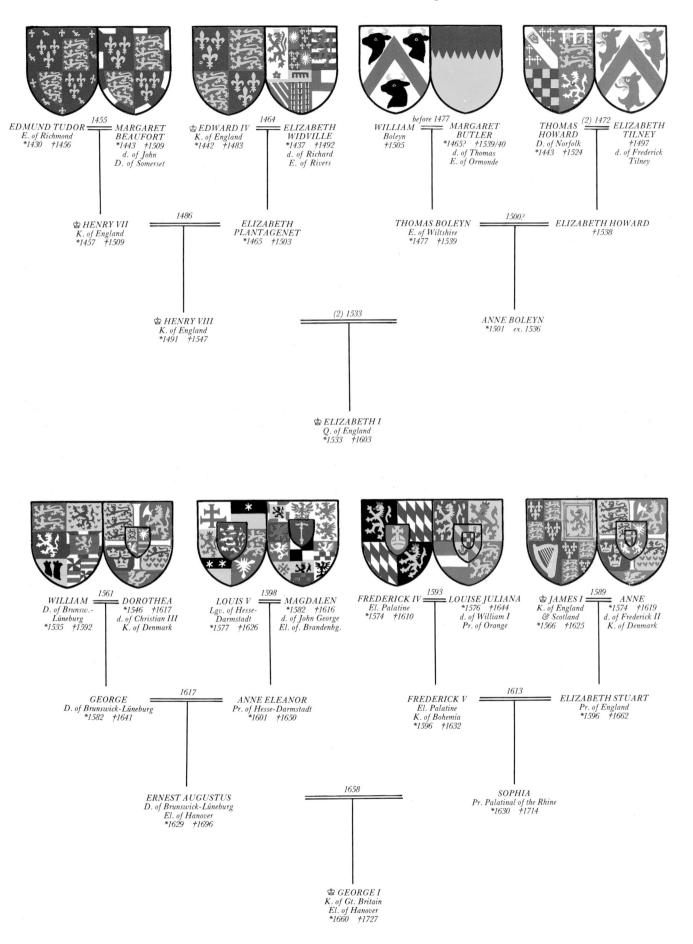

EDMUND TUDOR
E. of Richmond
*1430 †1456

— 1455 —

MARGARET
BEAUFORT
*1443 †1509
d. of John
D. of Somerset

♔ EDWARD IV
K. of England
*1442 †1483

— 1464 —

ELIZABETH
WIDVILLE
*1437 †1492
d. of Richard
E. of Rivers

WILLIAM
Boleyn
†1505

— before 1477 —

MARGARET
BUTLER
*1465? †1539/40
d. of Thomas
E. of Ormonde

THOMAS
HOWARD
D. of Norfolk
*1443 †1524

— (2) 1472 —

ELIZABETH
TILNEY
†1497
d. of Frederick
Tilney

♔ HENRY VII
K. of England
*1457 †1509

— 1486 —

ELIZABETH
PLANTAGENET
*1465 †1503

THOMAS BOLEYN
E. of Wiltshire
*1477 †1539

— 1500? —

ELIZABETH HOWARD
†1538

♔ HENRY VIII
K. of England
*1491 †1547

— (2) 1533 —

ANNE BOLEYN
*1501 ex. 1536

♔ ELIZABETH I
Q. of England
*1533 †1603

WILLIAM
D. of Brunsw.-
Lüneburg
*1535 †1592

— 1561 —

DOROTHEA
*1546 †1617
d. of Christian III
K. of Denmark

LOUIS V
Lgv. of Hesse-
Darmstadt
*1577 †1626

— 1598 —

MAGDALEN
*1582 †1616
d. of John George
El. of. Brandenbg.

FREDERICK IV
El. Palatine
*1574 †1610

— 1593 —

LOUISE JULIANA
*1576 †1644
d. of William I
Pr. of Orange

♔ JAMES I
K. of England
& Scotland
*1566 †1625

— 1589 —

ANNE
*1574 †1619
d. of Frederick II
K. of Denmark

GEORGE
D. of Brunswick-Lüneburg
*1582 †1641

— 1617 —

ANNE ELEANOR
Pr. of Hesse-Darmstadt
*1601 †1650

FREDERICK V
El. Palatine
K. of Bohemia
*1596 †1632

— 1613 —

ELIZABETH STUART
Pr. of England
*1596 †1662

ERNEST AUGUSTUS
D. of Brunswick-Lüneburg
El. of Hanover
*1629 †1696

— 1658 —

SOPHIA
Pr. Palatinal of the Rhine
*1630 †1714

♔ GEORGE I
K. of Gt. Britain
El. of Hanover
*1660 †1727

TABLE 11

GREAT BRITAIN
Ancestors of Queen Victoria, Elizabeth II and Prince Philip

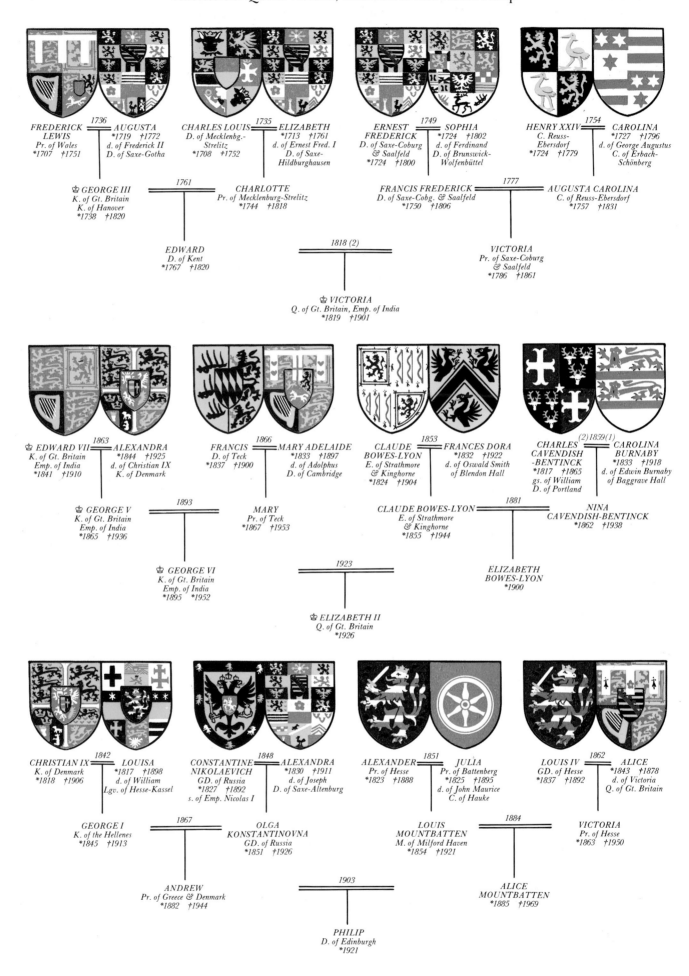

FREDERICK LEWIS — 1736 — **AUGUSTA**
Pr. of Wales *1719 †1772
*1707 †1751 d. of Frederick II
D. of Saxe-Gotha

CHARLES LOUIS — 1735 — **ELIZABETH**
D. of Mecklenbg.- *1713 †1761
Strelitz d. of Ernest Fred. I
*1708 †1752 D. of Saxe-Hildburghausen

ERNEST FREDERICK — 1749 — **SOPHIA**
D. of Saxe-Coburg *1724 †1802
& Saalfeld d. of Ferdinand
*1724 †1800 D. of Brunswick-Wolfenbüttel

HENRY XXIV — 1754 — **CAROLINA**
C. Reuss-Ebersdorf *1727 †1796
*1724 †1779 d. of George Augustus
C. of Erbach-Schönberg

♔ **GEORGE III** — 1761 — **CHARLOTTE**
K. of Gt. Britain Pr. of Mecklenburg-Strelitz
K. of Hanover *1744 †1818
*1738 †1820

FRANCIS FREDERICK — 1777 — **AUGUSTA CAROLINA**
D. of Saxe-Cobg. & Saalfeld C. of Reuss-Ebersdorf
*1750 †1806 *1757 †1831

EDWARD — 1818 (2)
D. of Kent
*1767 †1820

VICTORIA
Pr. of Saxe-Coburg
& Saalfeld
*1786 †1861

♔ **VICTORIA**
Q. of Gt. Britain, Emp. of India
*1819 †1901

♔ **EDWARD VII** — 1863 — **ALEXANDRA**
K. of Gt. Britain *1844 †1925
Emp. of India d. of Christian IX
*1841 †1910 K. of Denmark

FRANCIS — 1866 — **MARY ADELAIDE**
D. of Teck *1833 †1897
*1837 †1900 d. of Adolphus
D. of Cambridge

CLAUDE BOWES-LYON — 1853 — **FRANCES DORA**
E. of Strathmore *1832 †1922
& Kinghorne d. of Oswald Smith
*1824 †1904 of Blendon Hall

CHARLES CAVENDISH-BENTINCK — (2)1859(1) — **CAROLINA BURNABY**
*1817 †1865 *1833 †1918
gs. of William d. of Edwin Burnaby
D. of Portland of Baggrave Hall

♔ **GEORGE V** — 1893 — **MARY**
K. of Gt. Britain Pr. of Teck
Emp. of India *1867 †1953
*1865 †1936

CLAUDE BOWES-LYON — 1881 — **NINA CAVENDISH-BENTINCK**
E. of Strathmore *1862 †1938
& Kinghorne
*1855 †1944

♔ **GEORGE VI** — 1923
K. of Gt. Britain
Emp. of India
*1895 *1952

ELIZABETH BOWES-LYON
*1900

♔ **ELIZABETH II**
Q. of Gt. Britain
*1926

CHRISTIAN IX — 1842 — **LOUISA**
K. of Denmark *1817 †1898
*1818 †1906 d. of William
Lgv. of Hesse-Kassel

CONSTANTINE NIKOLAEVICH — 1848 — **ALEXANDRA**
GD. of Russia *1830 †1911
*1827 †1892 d. of Joseph
s. of Emp. Nicolas I D. of Saxe-Altenburg

ALEXANDER — 1851 — **JULIA**
Pr. of Hesse *1825 †1895
*1823 †1888 d. of John Maurice
C. of Hauke

LOUIS IV — 1862 — **ALICE**
GD. of Hesse *1843 †1878
*1837 †1892 d. of Victoria
Q. of Gt. Britain

GEORGE I — 1867 — **OLGA KONSTANTINOVNA**
K. of the Hellenes GD. of Russia
*1845 †1913 *1851 †1926

LOUIS MOUNTBATTEN — 1884 — **VICTORIA**
M. of Milford Haven Pr. of Hesse
*1854 †1921 *1863 †1950

ANDREW — 1903
Pr. of Greece & Denmark
*1882 †1944

ALICE MOUNTBATTEN
*1885 †1969

PHILIP
D. of Edinburgh
*1921

the end of her life the old Queen had done much to establish the role of a constitutional monarch, and had a memory and experience without parallel in Europe, not to mention her extensive kinship (Tables 59–60).

Her son Edward VII, genial and cosmopolitan, reigned only briefly in a splendid twilight of a now vanished age. To his son George V, straightforward and courageous, fell the crushing burden of leading his empire in the First World War (1914–18) and the troubled years which followed. The wealth and manpower of Britain had been sadly reduced by the war; unemployment rose; most of Ireland broke away from the United Kingdom. In all his tasks he was aided by his beloved wife, Queen Mary.

George V was followed by his eldest son, who had a brief reign. Even before he was crowned, he made known his desire to marry an American divorcée, Mrs Simpson. The sentiments of the country and the empire were resolutely opposed to the breach with tradition; at the end of 1936 he abdicated and was created Duke of Windsor.

George VI, like his father, had been trained as a sailor and had fought at Jutland. He had to lead his countrymen in the Second World War against the ambitions of Hitler, more sinister and more diseased than those of Louis XIV or Napoleon. Like many of his family in this century, George VI married outside the world of foreign princesses. As a consequence Table 11 reveals that the immediate ancestors of Queen Elizabeth II have more British blood than those of any sovereign since Elizabeth I. Similarly the arms of Lord Harewood, Angus Ogilvy and Lord Snowdon, of whom the first two belong to ancient families, have replaced the blazons of the Germanic princelings to whom the Hanoverian kings betrothed their daughters (Table 9).

The early death of King George VI brought the present Queen to the throne. Her husband, Prince Philip, Duke of Edinburgh, belongs to the royal

Queen Elizabeth II and Prince Philip on their wedding day in 1947, flanked by the then King George VI, the Queen Elizabeth and Mary the Queen mother.

family of Greece which is a branch of that of Denmark; his ancestors, as can be seen from Table 11, came mainly from Germany, but his mother was a Mountbatten and the prince had adopted that name before his marriage. The coat-of-arms devised for him refers in the four quarters to his Danish, Greek and Mountbatten ancestry and to the city of Edinburgh from which he takes his title. The arms of the royal issue exhibit some customary features. The Prince of Wales has a small escutcheon of the arms of Wales, surmounted by his coronet, in the centre of his shield. The blazons of Princess Anne and Lady Diana Spencer, now Princess of Wales, are shown upon lozenges, a custom for women which goes back at least to Tudor times. Even in heraldic display, the hopes of the future are mingled with the traditions of the past. For the sake of convenience, however, the practice has not been followed throughout this book.

Lady Diana's arms, used by her family since the end of the sixteenth century, are in fact a variant of the shield of the distinguished medieval family of Despencer. This is the first marriage of an heir to the throne to an Englishwoman since the future James II married Anne Hyde in 1659. Beside the lozenge of Princess Anne can be seen the blazon of her husband; this coat-of-arms was granted to the father of Captain Mark Phillips, who accordingly will use a label of three points during his father's lifetime. The Phillips arms reflect the family's equestrian interests. A second son, such as Angus Ogilvy, may similarly use a small crescent. Recent marriages of the royal family of the United Kingdom show a range of social standing and nationality which would have amazed, and certainly shocked, the Hanoverians of the eighteenth century with their rigid protocol.

Chapter 4

SCOTLAND

The earliest evidence of a cohesive northern kingdom is linked with the name of Kenneth MacAlpin and the period 843–50. He succeeded in uniting the four races which inhabited what today we call Scotland, the Picts in the north, the Celts in the South, the Angles in the southeast, and in the west the immigrants from Northern Ireland. It was to this group that Kenneth himself belonged, and their name, Scots, originally applied to the Irish, has come to be used for the northern Kingdom. The union of Scotland was made easier by attacks on the country from Scandinavia. Wide Norwegian settlement took place in the Orkneys, Shetlands and Western Isles and even in northeast Scotland. Orkney and Shetland did not finally become part of Scotland until 1468. The work of blending these various races, divided by mountains and seas, into a single nation was bound to be slow and laborious.

Kenneth MacAlpin died in 858. The Crown continued in his family but seldom directly from father to son; more normally a reigning King of Alba – as the realm was called – was succeeded by a brother or nephew. Gradually the kingship came to alternate between two branches of the descendants of Kenneth. This system avoided the peril of minorities, but substituted the temptation of anticipatory assassination. At the head of Table 12 is the name of Duncan I. He was murdered by Macbeth, a scion of the other line. Macbeth ruled for seventeen years before he was slain by Duncan's son, Malcolm III. This sort of thing had been going on for 200 years, but Shakespeare picked on a particular example to metamorphose into his powerful tragedy. Only with the descendants of David I does an hereditary descent begin to be visible.

Malcolm III married a remarkable woman, Margaret, who was a great-niece of the last Anglo-Saxon King, Edward the Confessor. Though saintly, she

was a significant figure. Under her influence there was an infiltration of clergy and others from the south, while the splendour of her court encouraged commerce in wine and other luxuries and lessened the isolation of Scotland. Her son, David, profited by the disorders in England during the reign of Stephen and managed to occupy Carlisle and Newcastle, thus bringing his frontier down to the Roman wall: his authority even reached into parts of Lancashire. In 1149 the lands between Tweed and Tyne were ceded to him 'for ever'. While he reigned, a substantial number of Norman families came north and settled in Scotland, and others intermarried with Scottish neighbours. With their advent Scotland moved from tribalism into the feudal pattern of western Europe.

In Scotland the powerful King David I was succeeded by the youthful Malcolm IV; in England the weak Stephen was followed by the powerful Henry II, who in 1157 compelled Malcolm to give back the northern counties and in 1174 captured William the Lion and extorted an oath of feudal homage from him. However, Richard I sold back this superiority for 10,000 marks towards his crusade; Scotland was free again, and there was warm friendship between the two chivalrous Kings. All his life William hoped to regain Northumberland, but in vain. In 1237 his son, Alexander II, finally accepted by treaty the frontier of Cheviot and Tweed, which lasted till 1603 and is still marked today.

The well-known arms of Scotland are depicted on Table 12 by the name of William the Lion. He may well have used the lion which was his nickname; there is no positive evidence that it was enclosed within the decorative double line of fleurs-de-lys ('a double tressure flory counterflory'). But this blazon certainly appears on the seal (1215) of his son, Alexander II, and may well have been used by William also. Established tradition maintains that the fleurs-de-lys

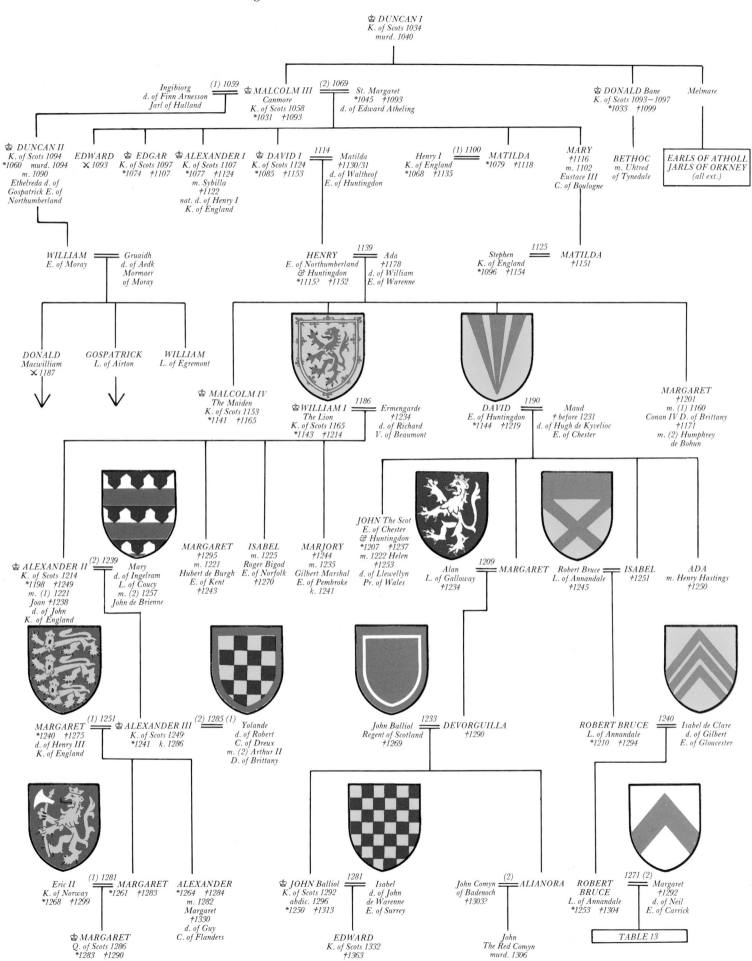

♔ DUNCAN I
K. of Scots 1034
murd. 1040

Ingibiorg   (1) 1059   ♔ MALCOLM III   (2) 1069   St. Margaret   ♔ DONALD Bane   Melmare
d. of Finn Arnesson   Canmore   *1045 †1093   K. of Scots 1093−1097
Jarl of Halland   K. of Scots 1058   d. of Edward Atheling   *1033 †1099
                               *1031 †1093

♔ DUNCAN II   EDWARD   ♔ EDGAR   ♔ ALEXANDER I   ♔ DAVID I   1114   Matilda   Henry I   (1) 1100   MATILDA   MARY   BETHOC   EARLS OF ATHOLL
K. of Scots 1094 ✕ 1093 K. of Scots 1097 K. of Scots 1107 K. of Scots 1124   †1130/31   K. of England   *1079 †1118   †1116   m. Uhtred   JARLS OF ORKNEY
*1060 murd. 1094 *1074 †1107 *1077 †1124 *1085 †1153   d. of Waltheof   *1068 †1135   m. 1102   of Tynedale   (all ext.)
m. 1090   m. Sybilla   E. of Huntingdon   Eustace III
Ethelreda d. of   †1122   C. of Boulogne
Gospatrick E. of   nat. d. of Henry I
Northumberland   K. of England

WILLIAM   Gruaidh   HENRY   1139   Ada   Stephen   1125   MATILDA
E. of Moray   d. of Aedk   E. of Northumberland   †1178   K. of England   †1151
              Mormaer   & Huntingdon   d. of William   *1096 †1154
              of Moray   *1115? †1152   E. of Warenne

DONALD   GOSPATRICK   WILLIAM   MARGARET
Macwilliam   L. of Airton   L. of Egremont   †1201
✕ 1187   m. (1) 1160
                                                                                                                           Conan IV D. of Brittany
                                                                                                                           †1171
                                                                                                                           m. (2) Humphrey
                                                                                                                           de Bohun

              ♔ MALCOLM IV   ♔ WILLIAM I   1186   Ermengarde   DAVID   1190   Maud   MARGARET
              The Maiden   The Lion   †1234   E. of Huntingdon   † before 1231
              K. of Scots 1153   K. of Scots 1165   d. of Richard   *1144 †1219   d. of Hugh de Kyvelioc
              *1141 †1165   *1143 †1214   V. of Beaumont   E. of Chester

♔ ALEXANDER II   (2) 1239   Mary   MARGARET   ISABEL   MARJORY   JOHN The Scot   Alan   1209   MARGARET   Robert Bruce   ISABEL   ADA
K. of Scots 1214   d. of Ingelram   †1295   m. 1225   †1244   E. of Chester   L. of Galloway   L. of Annandale   †1251   m. Henry Hastings
*1198 †1249   L. of Coucy   m. 1221   Roger Bigod   m. 1235   & Huntingdon   †1234   †1245   †1250
m. (1) 1221   m. (2) 1257   Hubert de Burgh   E. of Norfolk   Gilbert Marshal   *1207 †1237
Joan †1238   John de Brienne   E. of Kent   †1270   E. of Pembroke   m. 1222 Helen
d. of John   †1243   k. 1241   †1253
K. of England   d. of Llewellyn
                                                                                     Pr. of Wales

MARGARET   (1) 1251   ♔ ALEXANDER III   (2) 1285 (1)   Yolande   John Balliol   1233   DEVORGUILLA   ROBERT BRUCE   1240   Isabel de Clare
*1240 †1275   K. of Scots 1249   d. of Robert   Regent of Scotland   †1290   L. of Annandale   d. of Gilbert
d. of Henry III   *1241 k. 1286   C. of Dreux   †1269   *1210 †1294   E. of Gloucester
K. of England   m. (2) Arthur II
                                                     D. of Brittany

Eric II   (1) 1281   MARGARET   ALEXANDER   ♔ JOHN Balliol   1281   Isabel   John Comyn   (2)   ALIANORA   ROBERT   1271 (2)   Margaret
K. of Norway   *1261 †1283   *1264 †1284   K. of Scots 1292   d. of John   of Badenoch   BRUCE   †1292
*1268 †1299   m. 1282   abdic. 1296   de Warenne   †1303?   L. of Annandale   d. of Neil
                                  Margaret   *1250 †1313   E. of Surrey   *1253 †1304   E. of Carrick
                                  †1330
                                  d. of Guy
                                  C. of Flanders

♔ MARGARET   EDWARD   John   TABLE 13
Q. of Scots 1286   K. of Scots 1332   The Red Comyn
*1283 †1290   †1363   murd. 1306

symbolize the 'auld' alliance between France and Scotland: legends that this amity went back to the time of Charlemagne can be dismissed. It may be that the tressure was initially a device for strengthening the shield, or that the king wished for a distinctive and decorative difference from other members of the nobility using lions of various colours. In any case we may say as did the poet Dunbar of the Scottish lion:

In field of gold he stude full myghtely
With floure-de-lucis sirculit lustely.

UNIFICATION

Alexander II died in 1249 leaving an infant son of the same name, whose minority was overseen by a body of regents. Unluckily Alexander III was killed in a riding accident in 1286 while still only 44. His son and daughter were dead, and his only descendant was a distant baby granddaughter, the Fair Maid of Norway. The nobles of Scotland recognized her as the heiress of the throne and appointed six guardians: their action shows how fully the idea of hereditary succession had become accepted. By 1290 it had also been agreed with Edward I of England that his eldest son should marry the infant princess and thus unite the two Kingdoms. Most unhappily little Margaret did not survive the voyage from Norway and died in Orkney later in the year.

The succession to the Scottish throne was now wide open. Thirteen candidates presented themselves, many the issue of illegitimate children of William the Lion. The most prominent were two descendants of David, Earl of Huntingdon, John Balliol and Robert Bruce, and also John Comyn who was descended from Bethoc, son of Donald Bane, and was brother-in-law of Balliol. The magnates of Scotland asked the help of Edward I; when he met them he made clear that he had come to give his decision as overlord of Scotland. This was an unwarrantable claim, for if Edward had truly believed himself the feudal Lord of Scotland, he ought to have assumed the wardship of the Fair Maid of Norway from the moment of Alexander III's death. None the less Edward was supported by a considerable army; the realm of Scotland, though protesting, was disorganized and the main competitors accepted his arbitration on his own terms.

In effect two of the claimants led the field. John Balliol was the son of an elder John Balliol, a northern English baron, and his wife Devorguilla, a great Scottish heiress (it was they who founded Balliol, one of the earliest Oxford colleges). Through his mother the younger Balliol was the senior descendant of David, Earl of Huntingdon. Robert Bruce derived from a younger daughter of Huntingdon but was a genera-

tion nearer to him, a circumstance which counted for more in the Middle Ages than it would do today. At the end of 1292 Edward gave his verdict for Balliol, who became John I. Almost at once resistance in Scotland began to stiffen against Edward, regarded as a foreign tyrant, and Balliol, viewed as his puppet. The unification of the Scottish nation was undoubtedly advanced by Edward's aggression. In 1296 the hapless and spiritless King John abdicated and Edward took Scotland into his own hands.

For ten years Scotland had no king. At first, resistance crystallized round the heroic figure of Sir William Wallace; then Robert Bruce, Earl of Carrick, grandson of the competitor, took up the struggle. In 1306 he murdered John Comyn, the Red (son of the competitor, John the Black Comyn), a curious reversion to the dynastic rivalries of earlier centuries, and was crowned King of Scotland at Scone. Next year the aged Edward I died on his way to fight Bruce. The next King of England, Edward II, lacked both vigour and military capacity. Robert I (Table 13) was able to build up his forces and eventually to win a striking military triumph at Bannockburn in 1314; the English army was routed and many rich prisoners captured by the Scots while Edward fled southwards.

INDEPENDENCE

Before Bruce died in 1329, England had abandoned by treaty all claim to superiority over Scotland. Henceforward Scotland was free. David, King Robert's only son, was born late in life, and had a long minority; during this period Edward, son of John Balliol, landed with an army, contrived to be crowned but was soon driven out, only to be reinstated briefly by the forces of Edward III of England, to whom he proceeded to surrender the southern counties of Scotland. It was many years before the Scots recovered all that he had so improvidently given away. David II had been moved to France and soon after his return he was captured by the English at Neville's Cross (1346), and not released until 1357 when a heavy ransom was paid. The country had suffered severely from the constant wars, from the Black Death in 1349–50 (and again in 1361–2), and was now drastically taxed to free the King, who was only 46 when he died childless in 1371. During his reign we hear for the first time of the three estates of the Scottish Parliament – the prelates, the nobility and the burghs.

It had long been settled that Robert the Steward was heir to the throne. He belonged to a family, originally from Brittany, which had crossed to England where they became known as Fitzalan. A younger son, Walter, accompanied David I to Scotland and was appointed High Steward. Their coat-of-arms with its checkered fess may allude to the squared cloth spread in the Exchequer to aid counting; it is known from a seal dated 1190. Unluckily, Robert II came to the throne old and did not prove a vigorous king, nor did his son Robert III, who also became king at an advanced age. The nobility, strong in their own regions, began to usurp the power which ought to have belonged to the Crown. Ironically, after the death of Robert III in 1406, the problem of disorder and over-mighty subjects was complicated by a series of minorities resulting from violent deaths. James I was eleven, James II six, James III eight and James V and James VI each one year old at their accessions. Queen Mary was seven days old.

Scotland was normally allied to France; France and England were at war; there was intermittent fighting mingled with more serious campaigns. In the fifteenth century detachments of Scottish troops went to France and valiantly assisted the French in their battles with the English; indeed the French kings had a personal Scots Guard. Some Scottish nobles received French titles: Archibald Douglas, Earl of Douglas and Duke of Touraine (Table 13), is an example. His coat-of-arms with its red heart commemorates the mission of his ancestor, Sir James Douglas, who was charged to bear the heart of Robert Bruce to the Holy Land, but actually fell fighting the infidel in Spain. Another interesting shield is that of Sir John Lyon, son-in-law of Robert II: his original arms were simply a blue lion on a silver field, but he was granted on marriage the same tressure as appears in the royal arms. This blazon is still borne by his direct descendant, Elizabeth, the Queen Mother (Table 9).

For nearly fifty years Scottish history was dominated by the Dukes of Albany. Robert, brother of Robert III (who had been called John till he ascended the throne), was first regent in 1388 during the incapacity of his father and held the post for most of his brother's reign: his very title of Albany was derived from the old name for Scotland. In 1406 Robert III sent his infant son (James I to be) to France but he was captured by the English and kept prisoner till 1423 while the Albanys, father and son, continued as regents. James I was then in the prime of life and vigour; he passed a series of laws seeking to curb the disorders of the day and sought, though without success, to enlarge the Scottish Parliament rather on the lines of what he had seen in England. In private life he was musical and a writer of poetry; his murder in 1437 abruptly terminated the reign of one of the ablest Stuart kings. Disorder and lawlessness broke out again.

James II tried in the eleven years of his active reign to follow up the work of his father but was sadly slain by the explosion of one of his own guns at the

King James IV of Scotland (1473–1513) before an altar with the full achievement of Scotland. 16th-century MS.

siege of Roxburgh in 1460. Once again there was a minority; but when James III (Table 14) began to reign he proved a feckless ruler, interested in the arts but little concerned with government. The King continued to bicker with his nobility and was mysteriously murdered in 1488. It is fair to note that his reign saw widespread developments in architecture in Scotland and in general a higher standard of living. This was accompanied by inflation and debasement of the coinage; at this time four Scots pounds equalled one English.

James IV was a handsome, talented and industrious king. In his turn he attacked the problems of

TABLE 13

SCOTLAND
Houses of Bruce and Stuart

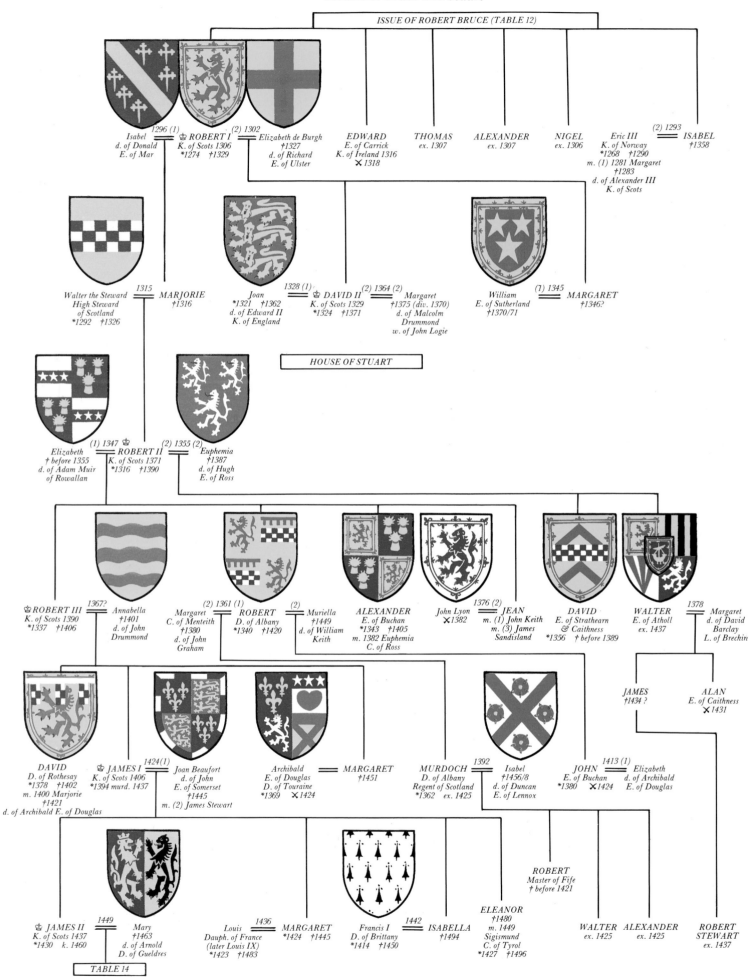

ISSUE OF ROBERT BRUCE (TABLE 12)

Isabel
d. of Donald
E. of Mar

1296 (1) ♔ **ROBERT I** *(2) 1302* ═══ *Elizabeth de Burgh*
K. of Scots 1306 *†1327*
*1274 †1329 *d. of Richard*
E. of Ulster

EDWARD
E. of Carrick
K. of Ireland 1316
✗ *1318*

THOMAS
ex. 1307

ALEXANDER
ex. 1307

NIGEL
ex. 1306

Eric III
K. of Norway
*1268 †1290
m. (1) 1281 Margaret
†1283
d. of Alexander III
K. of Scots

(2) 1293 ═══ **ISABEL**
†1358

Walter the Steward
High Steward
of Scotland
*1292 †1326

1315 ═══ **MARJORIE**
†1316

Joan
*1321 †1362
d. of Edward II
K. of England

1328 (1) ♔ **DAVID II** *(2) 1364 (2)* ═══ *Margaret*
K. of Scots 1329 *†1375 (div. 1370)*
*1324 †1371 *d. of Malcolm*
Drummond
w. of John Logie

William
E. of Sutherland
†1370/71

(1) 1345 ═══ **MARGARET**
†1346?

HOUSE OF STUART

Elizabeth
† before 1355
d. of Adam Muir
of Rowallan

(1) 1347 ♔ **ROBERT II** *(2) 1355 (2)* ═══ *Euphemia*
K. of Scots 1371 *†1387*
*1316 †1390 *d. of Hugh*
E. of Ross

♔ **ROBERT III** *1367?* ═══ *Annabella*
K. of Scots 1390 *†1401*
*1337 †1406 *d. of John*
Drummond

Margaret *(2) 1361 (1)* ═══ **ROBERT** *(2)* ═══ *Muriella*
C. of Menteith *D. of Albany* *†1449*
†1380 **1340 †1420* *d. of William*
d. of John *Keith*
Graham

ALEXANDER
E. of Buchan
*1343 †1405
m. 1382 Euphemia
C. of Ross

John Lyon *1376 (2)* ═══ **JEAN**
✗ *1382* *m. (1) John Keith*
m. (3) James
Sandisland

DAVID
E. of Strathearn
& Caithness
*1356 † before 1389

WALTER
E. of Atholl
ex. 1437

1378 ═══ *Margaret*
d. of David
Barclay
L. of Brechin

JAMES
†1434 ?

ALAN
E. of Caithness
✗ *1431*

DAVID
D. of Rothesay
*1378 †1402
m. 1400 Marjorie
†1421
d. of Archibald E. of Douglas

1424(1) ♔ **JAMES I** ═══ *Joan Beaufort*
K. of Scots 1406 *d. of John*
*1394 murd. 1437 *E. of Somerset*
†1445
m. (2) James Stewart

Archibald ═══ **MARGARET**
E. of Douglas *†1451*
D. of Touraine
*1369 ✗ *1424*

MURDOCH *1392* ═══ *Isabel*
D. of Albany *†1456/8*
Regent of Scotland *d. of Duncan*
*1362 ex. 1425 *E. of Lennox*

JOHN *1413 (1)* ═══ *Elizabeth*
E. of Buchan *d. of Archibald*
*1380 ✗ *1424* *E. of Douglas*

ROBERT
Master of Fife
† before 1421

♔ **JAMES II** *1449* ═══ *Mary*
K. of Scots 1437 *†1463*
*1430 k. 1460 *d. of Arnold*
D. of Gueldres

Louis *1436* ═══ **MARGARET**
Dauph. of France **1424 †1445*
(later Louis IX)
*1423 †1483

Francis I *1442* ═══ **ISABELLA**
D. of Brittany *†1494*
*1414 †1450

ELEANOR
†1480
m. 1449
Sigismund
C. of Tyrol
*1427 †1496

WALTER
ex. 1425

ALEXANDER
ex. 1425

ROBERT STEWART
ex. 1437

TABLE 14

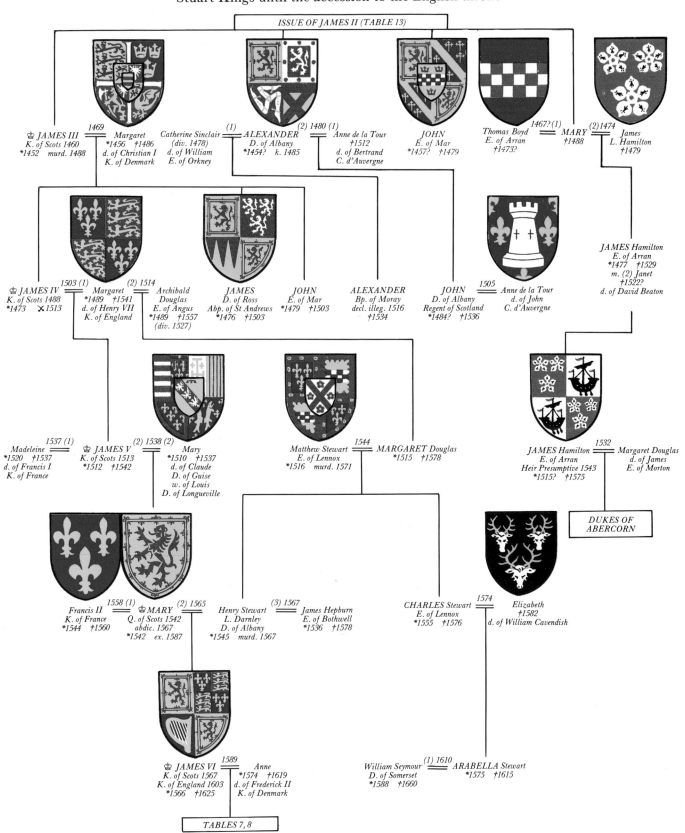

ISSUE OF JAMES II (TABLE 13)

♔ JAMES III
K. of Scots 1460
*1452   murd. 1488

1469
Margaret
*1456   †1486
d. of Christian I
K. of Denmark

Catherine Sinclair
(div. 1478)
d. of William
E. of Orkney

(1)   ALEXANDER   (2) 1480 (1)
D. of Albany
*1454?   k. 1485

Anne de la Tour
†1512
d. of Bertrand
C. d'Auvergne

JOHN
E. of Mar
*1457?   †1479

Thomas Boyd
E. of Arran
†1473?

1467? (1)
MARY   (2) 1474
†1488

James
L. Hamilton
†1479

♔ JAMES IV
K. of Scots 1488
*1473   ✕ 1513

1503 (1)
Margaret   (2) 1514
*1489   †1541
d. of Henry VII
K. of England

Archibald
Douglas
E. of Angus
*1489   †1557
(div. 1527)

JAMES
D. of Ross
Abp. of St Andrews
*1476   †1503

JOHN
E. of Mar
*1479   †1503

ALEXANDER
Bp. of Moray
decl. illeg. 1516
†1534

JOHN
D. of Albany
Regent of Scotland
*1484?   †1536

1505
Anne de la Tour
d. of John
C. d'Auvergne

JAMES Hamilton
E. of Arran
*1477   †1529
m. (2) Janet
†1522?
d. of David Beaton

Madeleine
*1520   †1537
d. of Francis I
K. of France

1537 (1)
♔ JAMES V   (2) 1538 (2)
K. of Scots 1513
*1512   †1542

Mary
*1510   †1537
d. of Claude
D. of Guise
w. of Louis
D. of Longueville

Matthew Stewart
E. of Lennox
*1516   murd. 1571

1544
MARGARET Douglas
*1515   †1578

JAMES Hamilton
E. of Arran
Heir Presumptive 1543
*1515?   †1575

1532
Margaret Douglas
d. of James
E. of Morton

DUKES OF
ABERCORN

Francis II
K. of France
*1544   †1560

1558 (1)
♔ MARY   (2) 1565
Q. of Scots 1542
abdic. 1567
*1542   ex. 1587

Henry Stewart   (3) 1567
L. Darnley
D. of Albany
*1545   murd. 1567

James Hepburn
E. of Bothwell
*1536   †1578

CHARLES Stewart
E. of Lennox
*1555   †1576

1574
Elizabeth
†1582
d. of William Cavendish

♔ JAMES VI
K. of Scots 1567
K. of England 1603
*1566   †1625

1589
Anne
*1574   †1619
d. of Frederick II
K. of Denmark

William Seymour
D. of Somerset
*1588   †1660

(1) 1610
ARABELLA Stewart
*1575   †1615

TABLES 7, 8

the turbulent and powerful aristocracy, vigorously moving round the country and holding courts of law. Printing came to Scotland. Edinburgh was established as the royal capital, and the palace of Holyroodhouse erected. But his relations with the Tudors deteriorated, and in 1513 he advanced into England only to be defeated catastrophically at Flodden. The King was killed and the Scottish nobility suffered fearful losses.

The long minority of James V was marked by a new fear of England and a lack of enthusiasm for the old alliance with France, but when James at last came of age he sought two French brides in succession. He also courted the favour of the Pope and was able to found the College of Justice, Scotland's highest court, with money from the Church. But he foolishly invaded England in 1542; his army was defeated at Solway Moss, and James died on hearing the news, leaving his new-born daughter Mary as his only heir.

QUEEN OF SCOTS

Mary, Queen of Scots, is one of the romantic and tragic figures of history. Tall—over 1.8m (6ft)—and beautiful, with many talents, she lacked judgement and was faced with a political and religious situation which might have baffled an older and wiser sovereign. She had been sent to France at the age of six, had briefly married the French King and was a childless widow not yet nineteen when she returned to Scotland in 1561.

Much had changed in Scotland during her absence. In particular the waves of a Protestant Reformation had broken over the land and the new religion had been accepted by Parliament in 1560; the Mass was abolished and the authority of the Pope rejected. True, there was still a large Catholic party but it was to a kingdom pledged to the new religion that Mary, herself a devout Catholic, returned. She can scarcely be blamed for her mistake in marrying her cousin Lord Darnley: he was tall and good-looking though also insolent and debauched. Furthermore, the union consolidated her claim on the throne of England (Table 14). Mary had already voiced this from France when Elizabeth ascended the throne, and had signified it by placing the arms of England on an escutcheon over the blazon of her husband and herself. Darnley was proclaimed as king (as had been Francis II of France). Unhappily Mary came to hate her husband, even before the birth of their only child, though it is far from certain that she was involved in his mysterious murder in January 1567. It is certain that her prompt marriage to Bothwell, who was implicated in the murder, outraged public opinion. Later in the year the hapless Queen was compelled to abdicate in favour of her infant son. A year later she fled over the border to take refuge with Elizabeth.

The English Queen was highly embarrassed. Mary was placed in captivity; but her name was involved in various plots, and in 1587 Elizabeth reluctantly consented to her execution. To the end her assumption of the English arms was a charge against her.

Not surprisingly the youthful James VI had a disturbed minority. As he grew older he feared domination by the Kirk, the reformed Church. As a measure of defence he fought long and successfully to keep some form of episcopal system. In external politics he moved closer to England; he married a Protestant princess from Denmark; he clearly had his eye firmly fixed on the English throne. His patience and powers of compromise were duly rewarded. In 1603, with 36 years of uneasy Scottish kingship behind him, he rode south to the richer land of England. He only once returned to Scotland.

James VI and I thus united the two Crowns on one head; but it was not until 1707 that the two realms were finally welded into the Kingdom of Great Britain.

Chapter 5

DENMARK

Of the three Scandinavian Kingdoms Denmark has always been the smallest and most fertile; in the Middle Ages it was also the most populous. In the eleventh century Canute the Great was briefly King of England and also ruler of Denmark, Norway and Sweden; he was the uncle of Sweyn Estridson who figures at the head of Tables 15 and 16.

The monarchy was elective, and no great attention was paid in the twelfth century to legitimacy of birth. It should also be remembered that almost throughout the Middle Ages the district of Scania, the southern tip of modern Sweden, was part of Denmark, which thus completely controlled the entrances to the Baltic. Waldemar I, the Great, brought some order after a period of violence and anarchy. He and both his sons carried on campaigns against the heathen Wends in Pomerania. Tradition relates that a red banner with a white cross descended from heaven (it was more plausibly a gift from the Pope) during an expedition of Waldemar II; this has become the national flag of Denmark and the insignia of the ancient Order of the Danebrog.

The attractive arms of Denmark first appear about 1190 in the reign of Canute VI. They consist of three running blue lions in a gold field dotted with red hearts. There were at first variations in the position of the lions' heads, which were at times crowned, and always in the number of hearts. Unluckily, the end of Waldemar II's reign was clouded by his capture and imprisonment and was followed by a period of instability.

Eric IV, nicknamed 'Ploughpenny' from putting a tax on ploughs, was murdered by his brother – a reversal of the biblical role of Abel. King Abel's wife was a daughter of the Count of Holstein. His curious and striking shield must have begun as an elaborate form of indented bordure; it came, however, to be regarded as a nettle leaf and even to be characteristic of the prickly nature of the folk of Holstein, an area whose fortunes were constantly involved with those of Denmark. Eric V inherited an uncertain Crown; surrounded by potentially hostile kinsmen, he was protected by his mother, a dark, able queen renowned as a horsewoman. In 1282 he was compelled to grant an extensive charter of liberties which established a parliamentary assembly (*hof*) as a check on royal power. Eric VI and Christopher II were unsuccessful kings who wasted their resources on futile wars. For eight years after the death of Christopher there was no king in Denmark and the country was overrun by the Counts of Holstein. In 1340 Waldemar IV, called Atterdag from his reiteration that 'Tomorrow would be a new day', began a long and painful task of reconstruction. Under his patronage Copenhagen became the capital of Denmark, and after long struggles a commercial relationship with the wealthy and powerful Hanseatic towns of north Germany was achieved, though parts of Denmark had to be mortgaged to them, and they were given a say in the choice of the Danish king.

Waldemar Atterdag left no son; his two daughters had married the rulers of Mecklenburg and Norway. The people of Denmark chose the youthful Olaf of Norway as their king, a decision with which the Hanseatic towns concurred. His mother, Margaret, was his guardian and mentor. She was an outstanding woman, shrewd, pious and above all tactful, who made it her goal to unite the three northern Kingdoms (Table 18). When her son Olaf, already King of Norway and Denmark, died in 1387, she was constituted regent of both countries; next year a body of Swedish nobility appealed to her for help, and Queen Margaret defeated Albrecht of Sweden and became regent of that Kingdom also. She had already chosen her great-nephew Eric, son of the Duke of Pomerania, as the heir of Norway and in 1397 at

TABLE 15

DENMARK
General survey

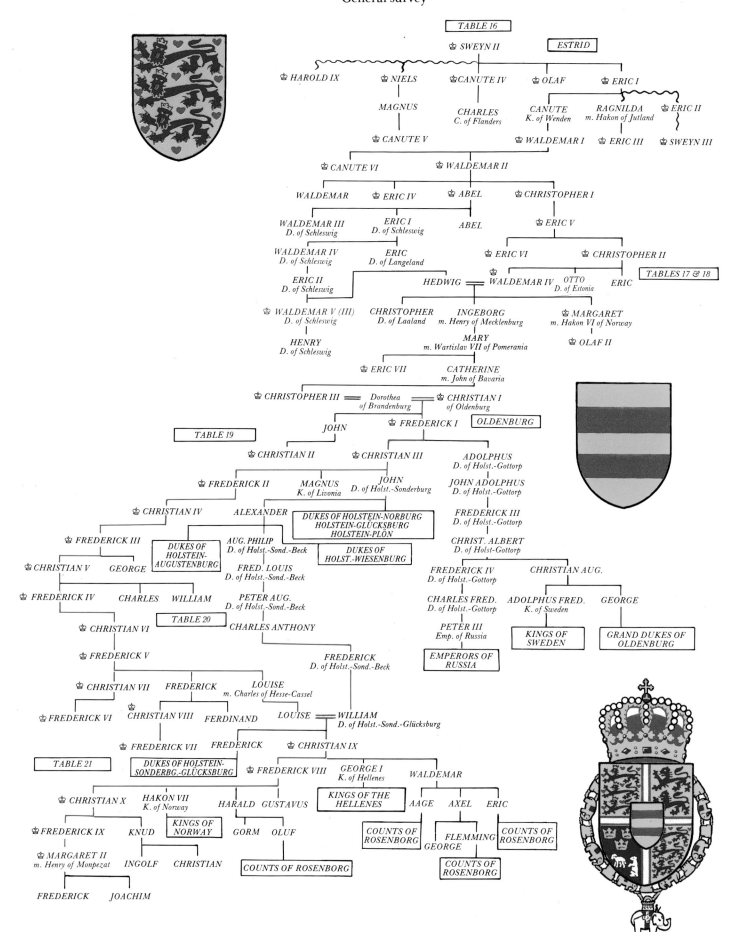

TABLE 16

SWEYN II   ESTRID

HAROLD IX   NIELS   CANUTE IV   OLAF   ERIC I

MAGNUS   CHARLES *C. of Flanders*   CANUTE *K. of Wenden*   RAGNILDA *m. Hakon of Jutland*   ERIC II

CANUTE V   WALDEMAR I   ERIC III   SWEYN III

CANUTE VI   WALDEMAR II

WALDEMAR   ERIC IV   ABEL   CHRISTOPHER I

WALDEMAR III *D. of Schleswig*   ERIC I *D. of Schleswig*   ABEL   ERIC V

WALDEMAR IV *D. of Schleswig*   ERIC *D. of Langeland*   ERIC VI   CHRISTOPHER II

ERIC II *D. of Schleswig*   HEDWIG ═ WALDEMAR IV   OTTO *D. of Estonia*   ERIC

TABLES 17 & 18

WALDEMAR V (III) *D. of Schleswig*   CHRISTOPHER *D. of Laaland*   INGEBORG *m. Henry of Mecklenburg*   MARGARET *m. Hakon VI of Norway*

HENRY *D. of Schleswig*   MARY *m. Wartislav VII of Pomerania*   OLAF II

ERIC VII   CATHERINE *m. John of Bavaria*

CHRISTOPHER III ═ *Dorothea of Brandenburg* ═ CHRISTIAN I *of Oldenburg*

OLDENBURG

TABLE 19

JOHN   FREDERICK I

CHRISTIAN II   CHRISTIAN III   ADOLPHUS *D. of Holst.-Gottorp*

FREDERICK II   MAGNUS *K. of Livonia*   JOHN *D. of Holst.-Sonderburg*   JOHN ADOLPHUS *D. of Holst.-Gottorp*

CHRISTIAN IV   ALEXANDER   DUKES OF HOLSTEIN-NORBURG HOLSTEIN-GLÜCKSBURG HOLSTEIN-PLÖN   FREDERICK III *D. of Holst.-Gottorp*

FREDERICK III   DUKES OF HOLSTEIN-AUGUSTENBURG   AUG. PHILIP *D. of Holst.-Sond.-Beck*   DUKES OF HOLST.-WIESENBURG   CHRIST. ALBERT *D. of Holst-Gottorp*

CHRISTIAN V   GEORGE   FRED. LOUIS *D. of Holst.-Sond.-Beck*   FREDERICK IV *D. of Holst.-Gottorp*   CHRISTIAN AUG.

FREDERICK IV   CHARLES   WILLIAM   PETER AUG. *D. of Holst.-Sond.-Beck*   CHARLES FRED. *D. of Holst.-Gottorp*   ADOLPHUS FRED. *K. of Sweden*   GEORGE

CHRISTIAN VI   TABLE 20   CHARLES ANTHONY   PETER III *Emp. of Russia*   KINGS OF SWEDEN   GRAND DUKES OF OLDENBURG

FREDERICK V   FREDERICK *D. of Holst.-Sond.-Beck*   EMPERORS OF RUSSIA

CHRISTIAN VII   FREDERICK   LOUISE *m. Charles of Hesse-Cassel*

FREDERICK VI   CHRISTIAN VIII   FERDINAND   LOUISE ═ WILLIAM *D. of Holst.-Sond.-Glücksburg*

FREDERICK VII   FREDERICK   CHRISTIAN IX

TABLE 21   DUKES OF HOLSTEIN-SONDERBG.-GLÜCKSBURG   FREDERICK VIII   GEORGE I *K. of Hellenes*   WALDEMAR

CHRISTIAN X   HAKON VII *K. of Norway*   HARALD   GUSTAVUS   KINGS OF THE HELLENES   AAGE   AXEL   ERIC

FREDERICK IX   KNUD   KINGS OF NORWAY   GORM   OLUF   COUNTS OF ROSENBORG   FLEMMING   COUNTS OF ROSENBORG

MARGARET II *m. Henry of Monpezat*   INGOLF   CHRISTIAN   COUNTS OF ROSENBORG   GEORGE   COUNTS OF ROSENBORG

FREDERICK   JOACHIM

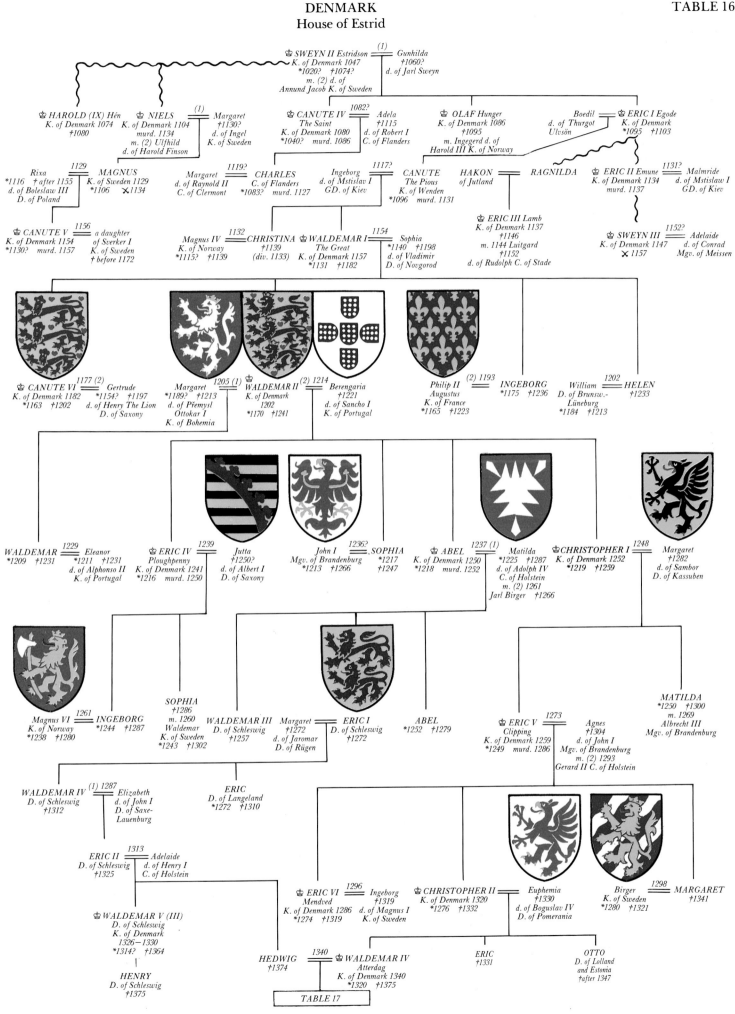

♔ SWEYN II Estridson (1) — Gunhilda
K. of Denmark 1047   †1060?
*1020? †1074?   d. of Jarl Sweyn
m. (2) d. of
Annund Jacob K. of Sweden

♔ HAROLD (IX) Hén
K. of Denmark 1074
†1080

♔ NIELS — (1) Margaret
K. of Denmark 1104   †1130?
murd. 1134   d. of Ingel
m. (2) Ulfhild   K. of Sweden
d. of Harold Finson

♔ CANUTE IV — Adela
The Saint   †1115
K. of Denmark 1080   d. of Robert I
*1040? murd. 1086   C. of Flanders

♔ OLAF Hunger
K. of Denmark 1086
†1095
m. Ingegerd d. of
Harold III K. of Norway

Boedil — ♔ ERIC I Egode
d. of Thurgot   K. of Denmark
Ulvsön   *1095 †1103

Rixa — 1129 MAGNUS
*1116 † after 1155   K. of Sweden 1129
d. of Boleslaw III   *1106 ✗1134
D. of Poland

Margaret — 1119? CHARLES
d. of Raynold II   C. of Flanders
C. of Clermont   *1083? murd. 1127

Ingeborg — 1117? CANUTE
d. of Mstislav I   The Pious
GD. of Kiev   K. of Wenden
*1096 murd. 1131

HAKON
of Jutland

RAGNILDA

♔ ERIC II Emune — 1131? Malmride
K. of Denmark 1134   d. of Mstislav I
murd. 1137   GD. of Kiev

♔ CANUTE V — 1156 a daughter
K. of Denmark 1154   of Sverker I
*1130? murd. 1157   K. of Sweden
† before 1172

Magnus IV — 1132 CHRISTINA
K. of Norway   †1139
*1115? †1139   (div. 1133)

♔ WALDEMAR I — 1154 Sophia
The Great   *1140 †1198
K. of Denmark 1157   d. of Vladimir
*1131 †1182   D. of Novgorod

♔ ERIC III Lamb
K. of Denmark 1137
†1146
m. 1144 Luitgard
†1152
d. of Rudolph C. of Stade

♔ SWEYN III — 1152? Adelaide
K. of Denmark 1147   d. of Conrad
✗1157   Mgv. of Meissen

♔ CANUTE VI — 1177 (2) Gertrude
K. of Denmark 1182   *1154? †1197
*1163 †1202   d. of Henry The Lion
D. of Saxony

Margaret — 1205 (1) ♔ WALDEMAR II — (2) 1214 Berengaria
*1189? †1213   K. of Denmark   †1221
d. of Přemysl   1202   d. of Sancho I
Ottokar I   *1170 †1241   K. of Portugal
K. of Bohemia

Philip II — (2) 1193 INGEBORG
Augustus   *1175 †1236
K. of France
*1165 †1223

William — 1202 HELEN
D. of Brunsw.-   †1233
Lüneburg
*1184 †1213

WALDEMAR — 1229 Eleanor
*1209 †1231   *1211 †1231
d. of Alphonso II
K. of Portugal

♔ ERIC IV — 1239 Jutta
Ploughpenny   †1250?
K. of Denmark 1241   d. of Albert I
*1216 murd. 1250   D. of Saxony

John I — 1236? SOPHIA
Mgv. of Brandenburg   †1247
*1213 †1266

♔ ABEL — 1237 (1) Matilda
K. of Denmark 1250   *1225 †1287
*1218 murd. 1252   d. of Adolph IV
C. of Holstein
m. (2) 1261
Jarl Birger †1266

♔ CHRISTOPHER I — 1248 Margaret
K. of Denmark 1252   †1282
*1219 †1259   d. of Sambor
D. of Kassuben

Magnus VI — 1261 INGEBORG
K. of Norway   *1244 †1287
*1238 †1280

SOPHIA
†1286
m. 1260
Waldemar
K. of Sweden
*1243 †1302

WALDEMAR III — Margaret — ERIC I
D. of Schleswig   †1272   D. of Schleswig
†1257   d. of Jaromar   †1272
D. of Rügen

ABEL
*1252 †1279

♔ ERIC V — 1273 Agnes
Clipping   †1304
K. of Denmark 1259   d. of John I
*1249 murd. 1286   Mgv. of Brandenburg
m. (2) 1293
Gerard II C. of Holstein

MATILDA
*1250 †1300
m. 1269
Albrecht III
Mgv. of Brandenburg

WALDEMAR IV — (1) 1287 Elizabeth
D. of Schleswig   d. of John I
†1312   D. of Saxe-
Lauenburg

ERIC
D. of Langeland
*1272 †1310

ERIC II — 1313 Adelaide
D. of Schleswig   d. of Henry I
†1325   C. of Holstein

♔ WALDEMAR V (III)
D. of Schleswig
K. of Denmark
1326–1330
*1314? †1364

HENRY
D. of Schleswig
†1375

♔ ERIC VI — 1296 Ingeborg
Mendved   †1319
K. of Denmark 1286   d. of Magnus I
*1274 †1319   K. of Sweden

♔ CHRISTOPHER II — Euphemia
K. of Denmark 1320   †1330
*1276 †1332   d. of Boguslav IV
D. of Pomerania

Birger — 1298 MARGARET
K. of Sweden   †1341
*1280 †1321

HEDWIG — 1340 ♔ WALDEMAR IV
†1374   Atterdag
K. of Denmark 1340
*1320 †1375

ERIC
†1331

OTTO
D. of Lolland
and Estonia
†after 1347

TABLE 17

TABLE 17

DENMARK
Accession of the House of Oldenburg

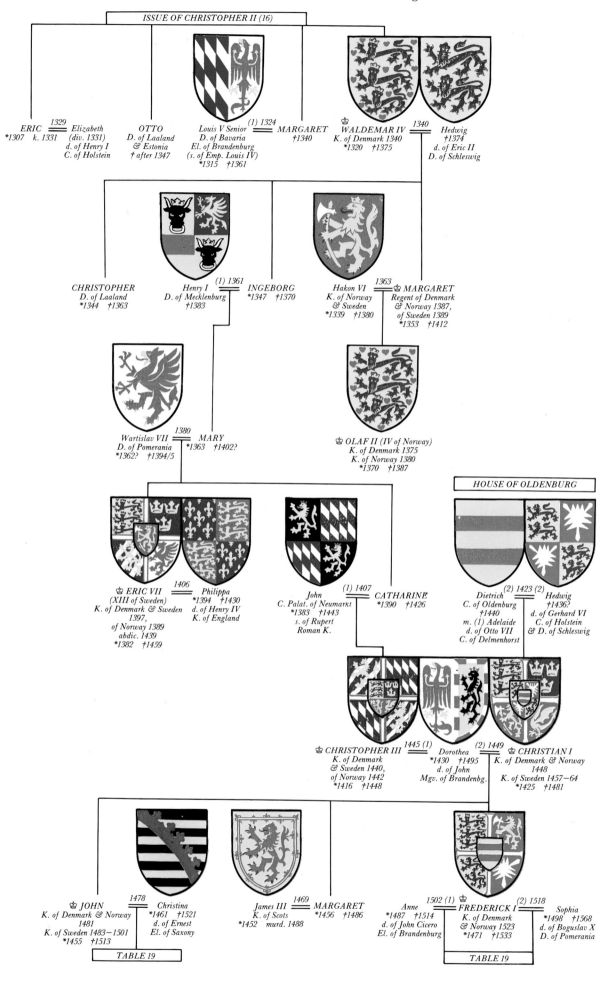

ISSUE OF CHRISTOPHER II (16)

ERIC — 1329 — Elizabeth
*1307 k. 1331 (div. 1331)
d. of Henry I
C. of Holstein

OTTO
D. of Laaland
& Estonia
† after 1347

Louis V Senior — (1) 1324 — MARGARET
D. of Bavaria †1340
El. of Brandenburg
(s. of Emp. Louis IV)
*1315 †1361

WALDEMAR IV — 1340 — Hedwig
K. of Denmark 1340 †1374
*1320 †1375 d. of Eric II
D. of Schleswig

CHRISTOPHER
D. of Laaland
*1344 †1363

Henry I — (1) 1361 — INGEBORG
D. of Mecklenburg *1347 †1370
†1383

Hakon VI — 1363 — MARGARET
K. of Norway Regent of Denmark
& Sweden & Norway 1387,
*1339 †1380 of Sweden 1389
*1353 †1412

Wartislav VII — 1380 — MARY
D. of Pomerania *1363 †1402?
*1362? †1394/5

OLAF II (IV of Norway)
K. of Denmark 1375
K. of Norway 1380
*1370 †1387

HOUSE OF OLDENBURG

ERIC VII — 1406 — Philippa
(XIII of Sweden) *1394 †1430
K. of Denmark & Sweden d. of Henry IV
1397, K. of England
of Norway 1389
abdic. 1439
*1382 †1459

John — (1) 1407 — CATHARINE
C. Palat. of Neumarkt *1390 †1426
*1383 †1443
s. of Rupert
Roman K.

Dietrich — (2) 1423 (2) — Hedwig
C. of Oldenburg †1436?
†1440 d. of Gerhard VI
m. (1) Adelaide C. of Holstein
d. of Otto VII & D. of Schleswig
C. of Delmenhorst

CHRISTOPHER III — 1445 (1) — Dorothea — (2) 1449 — CHRISTIAN I
K. of Denmark *1430 †1495 K. of Denmark & Norway
& Sweden 1440, d. of John 1448
of Norway 1442 Mgv. of Brandenbg. K. of Sweden 1457–64
*1416 †1448 *1425 †1481

JOHN — 1478 — Christina
K. of Denmark & Norway *1461 †1521
1481 d. of Ernest
K. of Sweden 1483–1501 El. of Saxony
*1455 †1513

James III — 1469 — MARGARET
K. of Scots *1456 †1486
*1452 murd. 1488

Anne — 1502 (1) — FREDERICK I — (2) 1518 — Sophia
*1487 †1514 K. of Denmark *1498 †1568
d. of John Cicero & Norway 1523 d. of Boguslav X
El. of Brandenburg *1471 †1533 D. of Pomerania

TABLE 19

TABLE 19

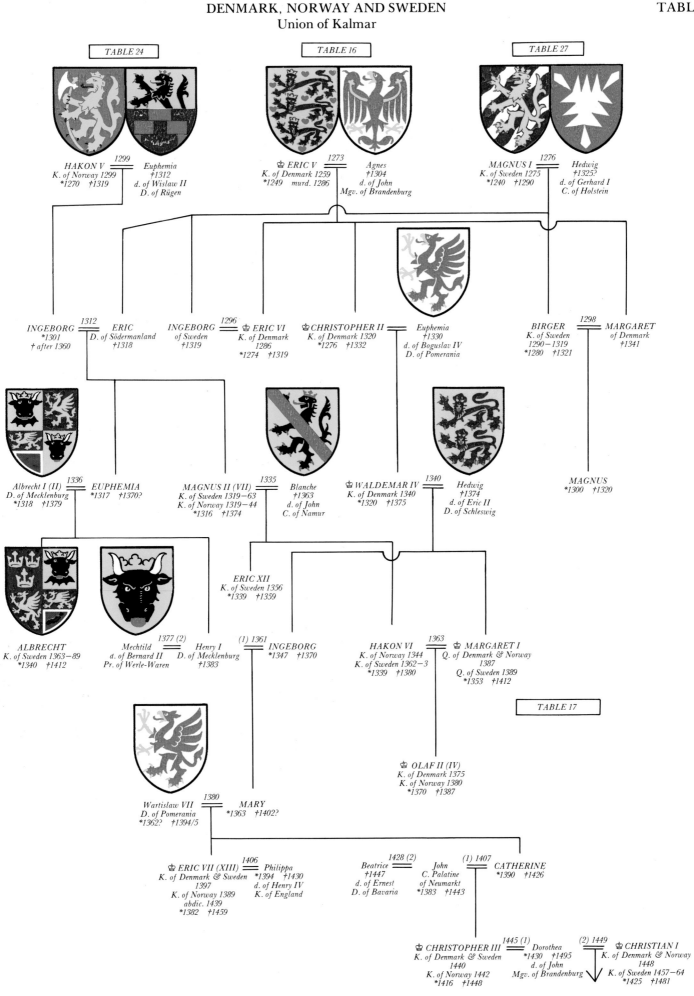

TABLE 24

TABLE 16

TABLE 27

HAKON V
K. of Norway 1299
*1270 †1319
— 1299 —
Euphemia
†1312
d. of Wislaw II
D. of Rügen

♔ **ERIC V**
K. of Denmark 1259
*1249 murd. 1286
— 1273 —
Agnes
†1304
d. of John
Mgv. of Brandenburg

MAGNUS I
K. of Sweden 1275
*1240 †1290
— 1276 —
Hedwig
†1325?
d. of Gerhard I
C. of Holstein

INGEBORG
*1301
† after 1360
— 1312 —
ERIC
D. of Södermanland
†1318

INGEBORG
of Sweden
†1319
— 1296 —
♔ **ERIC VI**
K. of Denmark
1286
*1274 †1319

♔ **CHRISTOPHER II**
K. of Denmark 1320
*1276 †1332
—
Euphemia
†1330
d. of Boguslav IV
D. of Pomerania

BIRGER
K. of Sweden
1290–1319
*1280 †1321
— 1298 —
MARGARET
of Denmark
†1341

Albrecht I (II)
D. of Mecklenburg
*1318 †1379
— 1336 —
EUPHEMIA
*1317 †1370?

MAGNUS II (VII)
K. of Sweden 1319–63
K. of Norway 1319–44
*1316 †1374
— 1335 —
Blanche
†1363
d. of John
C. of Namur

♔ **WALDEMAR IV**
K. of Denmark 1340
*1320 †1375
— 1340 —
Hedwig
†1374
d. of Eric II
D. of Schleswig

MAGNUS
*1300 †1320

ERIC XII
K. of Sweden 1356
*1339 †1359

ALBRECHT
K. of Sweden 1363–89
*1340 †1412
— 1377 (2) —
Mechtild
d. of Bernard II
Pr. of Werle-Waren
—
Henry I
D. of Mecklenburg
†1383

INGEBORG
*1347 †1370
— (1) 1361 —

HAKON VI
K. of Norway 1344
K. of Sweden 1362–3
*1339 †1380
— 1363 —
♔ **MARGARET I**
Q. of Denmark & Norway
1387
Q. of Sweden 1389
*1353 †1412

TABLE 17

♔ **OLAF II (IV)**
K. of Denmark 1375
K. of Norway 1380
*1370 †1387

Wartislaw VII
D. of Pomerania
*1362? †1394/5
— 1380 —
MARY
*1363 †1402?

♔ **ERIC VII (XIII)**
K. of Denmark & Sweden
1397
K. of Norway 1389
abdic. 1439
*1382 †1459
— 1406 —
Philippa
*1394 †1430
d. of Henry IV
K. of England

Beatrice
†1447
d. of Ernest
D. of Bavaria
— 1428 (2) —
John
C. Palatine
of Neumarkt
*1383 †1443
— (1) 1407 —
CATHERINE
*1390 †1426

♔ **CHRISTOPHER III**
K. of Denmark & Sweden
1440
K. of Norway 1442
*1416 †1448
— 1445 (1) —
Dorothea
*1430 †1495
d. of John
Mgv. of Brandenburg
— (2) 1449 —
♔ **CHRISTIAN I**
K. of Denmark & Norway
1448
K. of Sweden 1457–64
*1425 †1481

Kalmar she won recognition of Eric by Sweden and Denmark. The union which she so skilfully built up was one of Crowns rather than interests, but it survived uneasily until 1523.

Eric VII of Denmark (Eric XIII of Sweden) was less skilled in handling men than Queen Margaret; in 1439, after long and unrewarding conflict with Holstein and with the Hanseatic towns, he was compelled to abdicate in favour of his nephew, Duke Christopher of Bavaria (Table 17). Thereafter he became a pirate. By ill-fortune Christopher died childless at the age of 33. The Danish nobility promptly elected the young Count of Oldenburg (Table 112), who claimed descent from Eric V and consolidated his position by marrying Christopher's widow. Christian I was accepted with less alacrity by Norway and only after some years by Sweden; from him all subsequent rulers of Denmark are descended. Christian's mother came of the family ruling Schleswig and Holstein, and now his uncle, the Duke, died childless. Christian was successful in taking his place and in 1460 issued a famous declaration that Schleswig and Holstein should always be united. The risk implicit in this promise was that Schleswig was a Danish province while Holstein was technically part of the Holy Roman Empire. Nor did the money he had to spend on this southward expansion endear him to his Swedish subjects who spoke of him as 'an empty purse'. In 1462 he founded the Order of the Elephant.

John and Christian II continued the endeavour to rule over all three Kingdoms, but in the face of discontent, mainly in Sweden. Christian II was a striking figure, enlightened in his attitude to his humbler subjects but capable of barbaric revenges; he broke with the Pope and began the Reformation in Denmark. By 1523, when the wayward Christian fled his realms, Sweden had been lost for ever and the Union of Kalmar was over. But for two centuries Norway and Denmark continued under the same Crown (Table 19).

Christian II was followed by his uncle, Frederick I, who bestowed the Duchy of Holstein-Gottorp (which he himself held previously) on his younger son Adolphus, from whom descended the Emperors of Russia (from Peter III), some later Kings of Sweden and the Grand-Dukes of Oldenburg. Christian III was an avowed Lutheran and completed the process of Reformation in Denmark, but he was a man of moderation and dealt justly with all his subjects. In 1550 however he placed on his coat-of-arms the three crowns of Sweden as a reminder of the claims under the Union of Kalmar which he had not forgotten. Frederick II was a patron of learning, as his father had been before him, and was on good terms with the famous astronomer Tycho Brahe. An

King Christian IV of Denmark (1577–1648), by Karel van Mander, 1640.

aggravation of bad relations between Danes and Swedes was the establishment of Magnus, the King's brother, as King of Livonia.

Christian IV had the longest reign in Danish history. Handsome and robust, he was a great builder and the first part of his rule saw a long period of peace and many triumphs of architecture such as Frederiksborg and Rosenborg castles. From 1625 to 1629 he was involved without much advantage in the Thirty Years' War in Germany, and then in 1643 Denmark was attacked by the now formidable forces of Sweden. The King resisted valiantly and lost an eye in a sea-battle, but the Treaty of Brömsebro (1645) really made clear that Denmark was only the second power in the north. Sweden acquired the provinces of Scania and Halland and reached her natural frontier.

Hitherto the King of Denmark had always been elected by the nobility and had been compelled to recognize this fact by the 'Capitulations' which he then granted. Frederick III was coerced into signing a capitulation strongly in favour of the aristocracy, who exercised great power through a Council of State. In 1657 war broke out with Sweden. The ensuing winter (1657–8) was one of the coldest in history and the Swedes crossed from the mainland to the islands of Denmark on ice. The Treaty of Roskilde (1658) ratified the changes which were taking place: Sweden consolidated her control of her sea coast and even acquired part of Norway for a short spell. The general discontent manifested itself in favour of the King. In 1660 a popular delegation offered Frederick the throne of Denmark as an hereditary kingdom; the power of the nobility was broken, and it also proved to be the last meeting of the Estates for two centuries. A law was drawn up giving expression to royal absolutism; this declaration applied also to Norway, but unhappily it proved impossible to establish it because of the now fragmentary Duchies of Schleswig-Holstein which had been further sub-divided among the sons and grandsons of Duke John of Holstein-Sonderburg (d. 1622). The rulers of Holstein-Gottorp (Table 15) were already pursuing a policy of their own.

Christian V, whose brother was husband of the English Queen Anne, was in turn involved in wars with Sweden which brought triumphs to the growing Danish navy. In 1679 peace was achieved and the two realms began to lose some of their ancient antagonism. Trade was fostered both with Iceland and the Faroes, which belonged to Denmark of old, and also with more recent colonies in the East and West Indies and in Africa (the castle at Accra in Ghana is Danish by origin). Administration fell more into middle-class hands, and a new code of laws was promulgated. During the reign of Frederick IV the Swedes made an unsuccessful attempt to conquer Norway, but the consequent peace again brought the northern Powers closer. Frederick tired of his first wife and married Anne Sophia morganatically (and bigamously) in 1712; only nine years later could the union become official. In 1728 a great fire devastated Copenhagen. Christian VI (Table 20), a pious narrow man, whose wife was much disliked, enjoyed an unusually peaceful reign; indeed Denmark played small part in the affairs of Europe throughout the mid-eighteenth century. Christian was busy and pedantic; his son Frederick was more worldly and more indolent, allowing a series of able ministers, including the elder Bernstorff, a Hanoverian by birth, to govern for him and to keep the country clear of the Seven Years' War. In 1743 Frederick V had been a candidate for the vacant throne of Sweden, but Russian diplomacy installed Adolphus Frederick of Holstein-Gottorp. As Table 23 demonstrates, the successful incumbent of the Swedish throne was a kinsman of Frederick V. The ancestry of the latter was almost wholly confined to north German alliances, with the exception of his uterine descent which stemmed from Franconia (Table 22).

Dissipation may have ended the life of Frederick V prematurely; it crippled that of Christian VII, who is thought to have been a victim of *dementia praecox*. In 1768 the young King fell under the influence of his doctor who advanced to become first minister and lover of the Queen, a sister of George III of England.

Struensee was a liberal at heart and issued many reforming edicts, but his social background and methods stimulated a palace revolution and he was executed in 1772. The younger Bernstorff slowly rose to power and encouraged a policy of understanding with Russia. The Gottorp section of Holstein, belonging to the Czar, was exchanged for the detached German Counties of Oldenburg and Delmenhorst, which in due course became an independent grand-duchy (Chapter 29).

From 1784 the future Frederick VI was regent for his father, and with the aid of Bernstorff endeavoured to keep Denmark neutral in the convulsions which were overtaking Europe. Land reform was tackled and Denmark became the first nation to abolish and condemn the slave trade (1792). But neutrality has its perils; England in her desperate struggle against Napoleon felt compelled to eliminate the powerful Danish fleet. Nelson destroyed a part of it in 1801 and Canning mounted a more formidable attack in 1807 when Britain stood alone and the command of the sea was crucial. This arbitrary act drove Denmark into the arms of Bonaparte. By the peace treaty of 1814 she had to cede Norway to Sweden and Heligoland to Britain, and faced the future with a heavy debt and a capital in ruins.

Frederick VI, who had succeeded his mad father in 1808, was a liberal and popular ruler. Towards the end of his reign he introduced four diets, one for Jutland, one for the Islands, one each for Schleswig and Holstein; the last two also gained their own law courts. Unhappily, as the nineteenth century wore on, the sense of difference, the wide use of the German language and a long separatist tradition led to a movement for independence within the Duchies. Christian VIII, whose son was childless, announced that Schleswig was governed by the same rules of descent as Denmark, but voiced doubts about Holstein. Frederick VII on his accession in 1848, the year of revolutions, introduced a new constitution with a single assembly for all parts of the Kingdom. The Dukes of Holstein-Augustenburg proclaimed independence and called in the help of Prussia.

THE SCHLESWIG-HOLSTEIN QUESTION

After desultory campaigning, an international conference in London (1852) resolved that Duke Christian of Glücksburg should be recognized as Frederick's heir and should reign in Denmark and the Duchies. The nearest heir to Frederick VII was the Prince of Hesse-Cassel, but he obligingly resigned his claims in favour of his sister who was also Christian's wife. The last act of Frederick VII in 1863 was to promulgate a new constitution uniting Schleswig with Denmark and giving Holstein local government. On his death Christian IX succeeded

TABLE 19

DENMARK AND NORWAY
House of Oldenburg until the eighteenth century

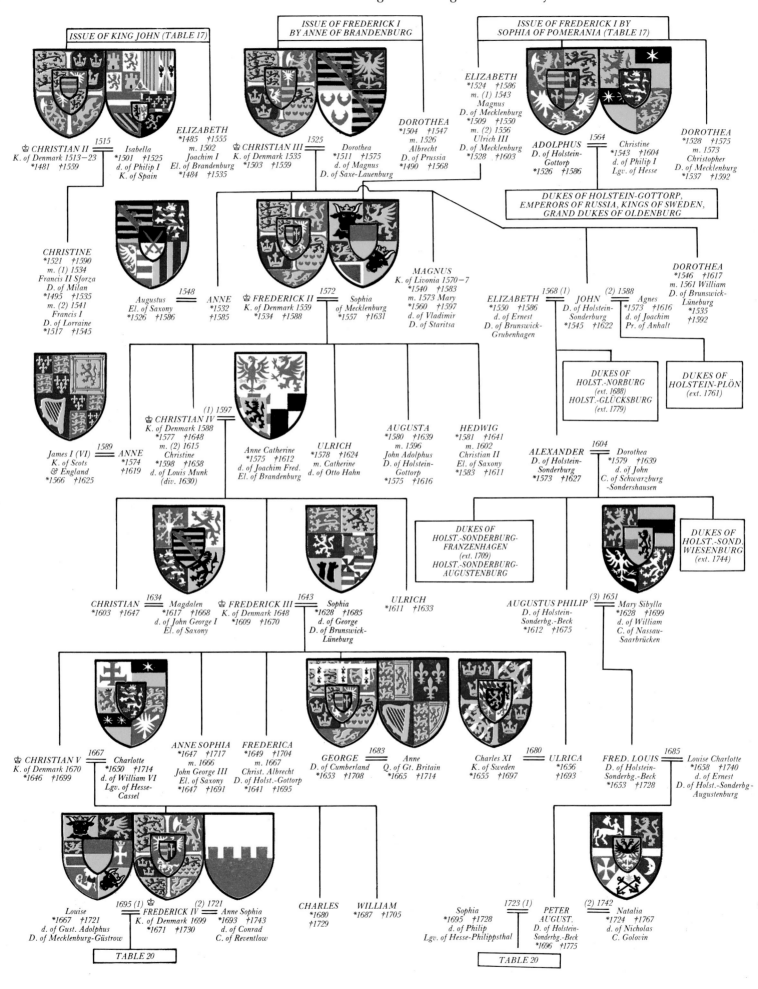

ISSUE OF KING JOHN (TABLE 17)

ISSUE OF FREDERICK I BY ANNE OF BRANDENBURG

ISSUE OF FREDERICK I BY SOPHIA OF POMERANIA (TABLE 17)

ELIZABETH
*1524 †1586
m. (1) 1543
Magnus
D. of Mecklenburg
*1509 †1550
m. (2) 1556
Ulrich III
D. of Mecklenburg
*1528 †1603

DOROTHEA
*1504 †1547
m. 1526
Albrecht
D. of Prussia
*1490 †1568

ADOLPHUS 1564
D. of Holstein-
Gottorp
*1526 †1586

Christine
*1543 †1604
d. of Philip I
Lgv. of Hesse

DOROTHEA
*1528 †1575
m. 1573
Christopher
D. of Mecklenburg
*1537 †1592

ELIZABETH
*1485 †1555
m. 1502
Joachim I
El. of Brandenburg
*1484 †1535

✠ **CHRISTIAN II** 1515
K. of Denmark 1513—23
*1481 †1559

Isabella
*1501 †1525
d. of Philip I
K. of Spain

✠ **CHRISTIAN III** 1525
K. of Denmark 1535
*1503 †1559

Dorothea
*1511 †1575
d. of Magnus
D. of Saxe-Lauenburg

DUKES OF HOLSTEIN-GOTTORP,
EMPERORS OF RUSSIA, KINGS OF SWEDEN,
GRAND DUKES OF OLDENBURG

CHRISTINE
*1521 †1590
m. (1) 1534
Francis II Sforza
D. of Milan
*1495 †1535
m. (2) 1541
Francis I
D. of Lorraine
*1517 †1545

Augustus 1548
El. of Saxony
*1526 †1586

ANNE
*1532
†1585

✠ **FREDERICK II** 1572
K. of Denmark 1559
*1534 †1588

Sophia
of Mecklenburg
*1557 †1631

MAGNUS
K. of Livonia 1570—7
*1540 †1583
m. 1573 Mary
*1560 †1597
d. of Vladimir
D. of Staritsa

ELIZABETH
*1550 †1586
d. of Ernest
D. of Brunswick-
Grubenhagen

JOHN 1568 (1)
D. of Holstein-
Sonderburg
*1545 †1622

(2) 1588
Agnes
*1573 †1616
d. of Joachim
Pr. of Anhalt

DOROTHEA
*1546 †1617
m. 1561 William
D. of Brunswick-
Lüneburg
*1535
†1592

DUKES OF
HOLST.-NORBURG
(ext. 1688)
HOLST.-GLÜCKSBURG
(ext. 1779)

DUKES OF
HOLSTEIN-PLÖN
(ext. 1761)

James I (VI) 1589
K. of Scots
& England
*1566 †1625

ANNE
*1574
†1619

✠ **CHRISTIAN IV** (1) 1597
K. of Denmark 1588
*1577 †1648
m. (2) 1615
Christine
*1598 †1658
d. of Louis Munk
(div. 1630)

Anne Catherine
*1575 †1612
d. of Joachim Fred.
El. of Brandenburg

ULRICH
*1578 †1624
m. Catherine
d. of Otto Hahn

AUGUSTA
*1580 †1639
m. 1596
John Adolphus
D. of Holstein-
Gottorp
*1575 †1616

HEDWIG
*1581 †1641
m. 1602
Christian II
El. of Saxony
*1583 †1611

ALEXANDER 1604
D. of Holstein-
Sonderburg
*1573 †1627

Dorothea
*1579 †1639
d. of John
C. of Schwarzburg
-Sondershausen

DUKES OF
HOLST.-SONDERBURG-
FRANZENHAGEN
(ext. 1709)
HOLST.-SONDERBURG-
AUGUSTENBURG

DUKES OF
HOLST.-SOND.
WIESENBURG
(ext. 1744)

CHRISTIAN 1634
*1603 †1647

Magdalen
*1617 †1668
d. of John George I
El. of Saxony

✠ **FREDERICK III** 1643
K. of Denmark 1648
*1609 †1670

Sophia
*1628 †1685
d. of George
D. of Brunswick-
Lüneburg

ULRICH
*1611 †1633

AUGUSTUS PHILIP
D. of Holstein-
Sonderbg.-Beck
*1612 †1675

(3) 1651
Mary Sibylla
*1628 †1699
d. of William
C. of Nassau-
Saarbrücken

✠ **CHRISTIAN V** 1667
K. of Denmark 1670
*1646 †1699

Charlotte
*1650 †1714
d. of William VI
Lgv. of Hesse-
Cassel

ANNE SOPHIA
*1647 †1717
m. 1666
John George III
El. of Saxony
*1647 †1691

FREDERICA
*1649 †1704
m. 1667
Christ. Albrecht
D. of Holst.-Gottorp
*1641 †1695

GEORGE 1683
D. of Cumberland
*1653 †1708

Anne
Q. of Gt. Britain
*1665 †1714

Charles XI 1680
K. of Sweden
*1655 †1697

ULRICA
*1656
†1693

FRED. LOUIS 1685
D. of Holstein-
Sonderbg.-Beck
*1653 †1728

Louise Charlotte
*1658 †1740
d. of Ernest
D. of Holst.-Sonderbg-
Augustenburg

Louise
*1667 †1721
d. of Gust. Adolphus
D. of Mecklenburg-Güstrow

1695 (1)
✠ **FREDERICK IV**
K. of Denmark 1699
*1671 †1730

(2) 1721
Anne Sophia
*1693 †1743
d. of Conrad
C. of Reventlow

CHARLES
*1680
†1729

WILLIAM
*1687 †1705

Sophia
*1695 †1728
d. of Philip
Lgv. of Hesse-Philippsthal

1723 (1)
**PETER
AUGUST.**
D. of Holstein-
Sonderbg.-Beck
*1696 †1775

(2) 1742
Natalia
*1724 †1767
d. of Nicholas
C. Golovin

TABLE 20

TABLE 20

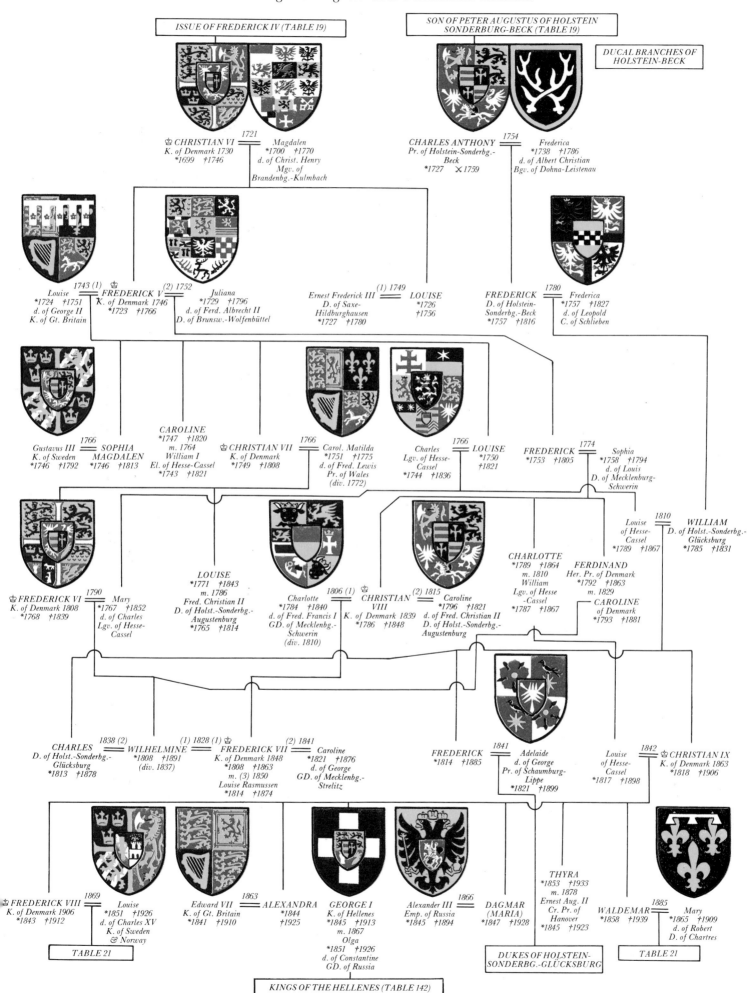

ISSUE OF FREDERICK IV (TABLE 19)

SON OF PETER AUGUSTUS OF HOLSTEIN SONDERBURG-BECK (TABLE 19)

DUCAL BRANCHES OF HOLSTEIN-BECK

♕ CHRISTIAN VI
K. of Denmark 1730
*1699 †1746

1721

Magdalen
*1700 †1770
d. of Christ. Henry
Mgv. of
Brandenbg.-Kulmbach

CHARLES ANTHONY
Pr. of Holstein-Sonderbg.-
Beck
*1727 ✕1759

1754

Frederica
*1738 †1786
d. of Albert Christian
Bgv. of Dohna-Leistenau

Louise
*1724 †1751
d. of George II
K. of Gt. Britain

1743 (1)

♕ FREDERICK V
K. of Denmark 1746
*1723 †1766

(2) 1752

Juliana
*1729 †1796
d. of Ferd. Albrecht II
D. of Brunsw.-Wolfenbüttel

Ernest Frederick III
D. of Saxe-
Hildburghausen
*1727 †1780

(1) 1749

LOUISE
*1726
†1756

FREDERICK
D. of Holstein-
Sonderbg.-Beck
*1757 †1816

1780

Frederica
*1757 †1827
d. of Leopold
C. of Schlieben

Gustavus III
K. of Sweden
*1746 †1792

1766

SOPHIA
MAGDALEN
*1746 †1813

CAROLINE
*1747 †1820
m. 1764
William I
El. of Hesse-Cassel
*1743 †1821

♕ CHRISTIAN VII
K. of Denmark
*1749 †1808

1766

Carol. Matilda
*1751 †1775
d. of Fred. Lewis
Pr. of Wales
(div. 1772)

Charles
Lgv. of Hesse-
Cassel
*1744 †1836

1766

LOUISE
*1750
†1821

FREDERICK
*1753 †1805

1774

Sophia
*1758 †1794
d. of Louis
D. of Mecklenburg-
Schwerin

Louise
of Holst.-Sonderbg.-
Cassel
*1789 †1867

1810

WILLIAM
D. of Holst.-Sonderbg.-
Glücksburg
*1785 †1831

♕ FREDERICK VI
K. of Denmark 1808
*1768 †1839

1790

Mary
*1767 †1852
d. of Charles
Lgv. of Hesse-
Cassel

LOUISE
*1771 †1843
m. 1786
Fred. Christian II
D. of Holst.-Sonderbg.-
Augustenburg
*1765 †1814

Charlotte
*1784 †1840
d. of Fred. Francis I
GD. of Mecklenbg.-
Schwerin
(div. 1810)

1806 (1)

♕ CHRISTIAN
VIII
K. of Denmark 1839
*1786 †1848

(2) 1815

Caroline
*1796 †1821
d. of Fred. Christian II
D. of Holst.-Sonderbg.-
Augustenburg

CHARLOTTE
*1789 †1864
m. 1810
William
Lgv. of Hesse
-Cassel
*1787 †1867

FERDINAND
Her. Pr. of Denmark
*1792 †1863
m. 1829

CAROLINE
of Denmark
*1793 †1881

CHARLES
D. of Holst.-Sonderbg.-
Glücksburg
*1813 †1878

1838 (2)

WILHELMINE
*1808 †1891
(div. 1837)

(1) 1828 (1)

♕ FREDERICK VII
K. of Denmark 1848
*1808 †1863
m. (3) 1850
Louise Rasmussen
*1814 †1874

(2) 1841

Caroline
*1821 †1876
d. of George
GD. of Mecklenbg.-
Strelitz

FREDERICK
*1814 †1885

1841

Adelaide
d. of George
Pr. of Schaumburg-
Lippe
*1821 †1899

Louise
of Hesse-Cassel
*1817 †1898

1842

♕ CHRISTIAN IX
K. of Denmark 1863
*1818 †1906

♕ FREDERICK VIII
K. of Denmark 1906
*1843 †1912

1869

Louise
*1851 †1926
d. of Charles XV
K. of Sweden
& Norway

Edward VII
K. of Gt. Britain
*1841 †1910

1863

ALEXANDRA
*1844
†1925

GEORGE I
K. of Hellenes
*1845 †1913
m. 1867
Olga
*1851 †1926
d. of Constantine
GD. of Russia

Alexander III
Emp. of Russia
*1845 †1894

1866

DAGMAR
(MARIA)
*1847 †1928

THYRA
*1853 †1933
m. 1878
Ernest Aug. II
Cr. Pr. of
Hanover
*1845 †1923

WALDEMAR
*1858 †1939

1885

Mary
*1865 †1909
d. of Robert
D. of Chartres

TABLE 21

KINGS OF THE HELLENES (TABLE 142)

DUKES OF HOLSTEIN-
SONDERBG.-GLÜCKSBURG

TABLE 21

TABLE 21

DENMARK
House of Holstein-Glücksburg

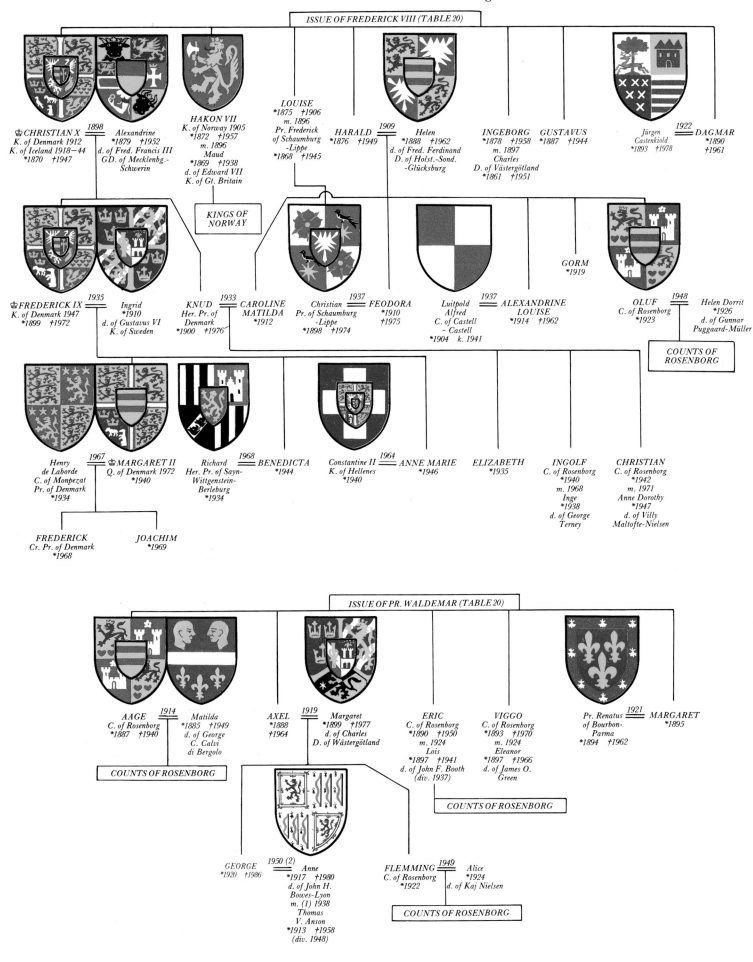

ISSUE OF FREDERICK VIII (TABLE 20)

♛ CHRISTIAN X
K. of Denmark 1912
K. of Iceland 1918–44
*1870 †1947

1898

Alexandrine
*1879 †1952
d. of Fred. Francis III
GD. of Mecklenbg.-
Schwerin

HAKON VII
K. of Norway 1905
*1872 †1957
m. 1896
Maud
*1869 †1938
d. of Edward VII
K. of Gt. Britain

LOUISE
*1875 †1906
m. 1896
Pr. Frederick
of Schaumburg
-Lippe
*1868 †1945

HARALD
*1876 †1949

1909

Helen
*1888 †1962
d. of Fred. Ferdinand
D. of Holst.-Sond.
-Glücksburg

INGEBORG
*1878 †1958
m. 1897
Charles
D. of Västergötland
*1861 †1951

GUSTAVUS
*1887 †1944

Jürgen
Castenkiold
*1893 †1978

1922

DAGMAR
*1890
†1961

KINGS OF
NORWAY

♛ FREDERICK IX
K. of Denmark 1947
*1899 †1972

1935

Ingrid
*1910
d. of Gustavus VI
K. of Sweden

KNUD
Her. Pr. of
Denmark
*1900 †1976

1933

CAROLINE
MATILDA
*1912

Christian
Pr. of Schaumburg
-Lippe
*1898 †1974

1937

FEODORA
*1910
†1975

Luitpold
Alfred
C. of Castell
- Castell
*1904 k. 1941

1937

ALEXANDRINE
LOUISE
*1914 †1962

GORM
*1919

OLUF
C. of Rosenborg
*1923

1948

Helen Dorrit
*1926
d. of Gunnar
Puggaard-Müller

COUNTS OF
ROSENBORG

Henry
de Laborde
C. of Monpezat
Pr. of Denmark
*1934

1967

♛ MARGARET II
Q. of Denmark 1972
*1940

Richard
Her. Pr. of Sayn-
Wittgenstein-
Berleburg
*1934

1968

BENEDICTA
*1944

Constantine II
K. of Hellenes
*1940

1964

ANNE MARIE
*1946

ELIZABETH
*1935

INGOLF
C. of Rosenborg
*1940
m. 1968
Inge
*1938
d. of George
Terney

CHRISTIAN
C. of Rosenborg
*1942
m. 1971
Anne Dorothy
*1947
d. of Villy
Maltofte-Nielsen

FREDERICK
Cr. Pr. of Denmark
*1968

JOACHIM
*1969

ISSUE OF PR. WALDEMAR (TABLE 20)

AAGE
C. of Rosenborg
*1887 †1940

1914

Matilda
*1885 †1949
d. of George
C. Calvi
di Bergolo

AXEL
*1888
†1964

1919

Margaret
*1899 †1977
d. of Charles
D. of Wästergötland

ERIC
C. of Rosenborg
*1890 †1950
m. 1924
Lois
*1897 †1941
d. of John F. Booth
(div. 1937)

VIGGO
C. of Rosenborg
*1893 †1970
m. 1924
Eleanor
*1897 †1966
d. of James O.
Green

Pr. Renatus
of Bourbon-
Parma
*1894 †1962

1921

MARGARET
*1895

COUNTS OF ROSENBORG

GEORGE
*1920 †1986

1950 (2)

Anne
*1917 †1980
d. of John H.
Bowes-Lyon
m. (1) 1938
Thomas
V. Anson
*1913 †1958
(div. 1948)

FLEMMING
C. of Rosenborg
*1922

1949

Alice
*1924
d. of Kaj Nielsen

COUNTS OF ROSENBORG

COUNTS OF ROSENBORG

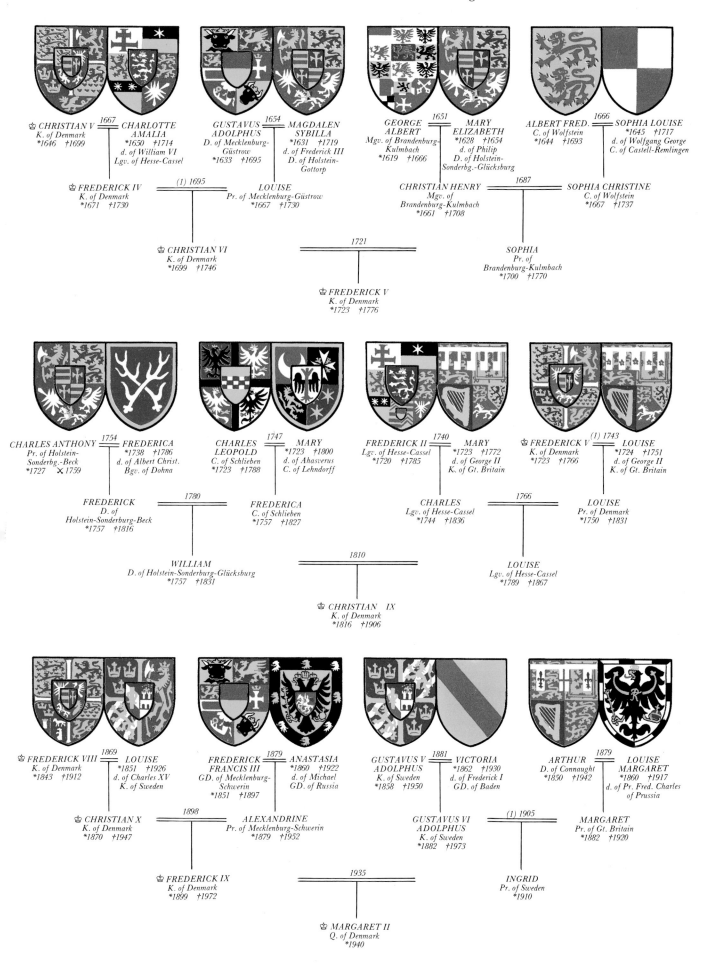

CHRISTIAN V ♔
K. of Denmark
*1646 †1699
— 1667 —
CHARLOTTE AMALIA
*1650 †1714
d. of William VI
Lgv. of Hesse-Cassel

GUSTAVUS ADOLPHUS
D. of Mecklenburg-Güstrow
*1633 †1695
— 1654 —
MAGDALEN SYBILLA
*1631 †1719
d. of Frederick III
D. of Holstein-Gottorp

GEORGE ALBERT
Mgv. of Brandenburg-Kulmbach
*1619 †1666
— 1651 —
MARY ELIZABETH
*1628 †1654
d. of Philip
D. of Holstein-Sonderbg.-Glücksburg

ALBERT FRED.
C. of Wolfstein
*1644 †1693
— 1666 —
SOPHIA LOUISE
*1645 †1717
d. of Wolfgang George
C. of Castell-Remlingen

FREDERICK IV ♔
K. of Denmark
*1671 †1730
— (1) 1695 —
LOUISE
Pr. of Mecklenburg-Güstrow
*1667 †1730

CHRISTIAN HENRY
Mgv. of Brandenburg-Kulmbach
*1661 †1708
— 1687 —
SOPHIA CHRISTINE
C. of Wolfstein
*1667 †1737

CHRISTIAN VI ♔
K. of Denmark
*1699 †1746

SOPHIA
Pr. of Brandenburg-Kulmbach
*1700 †1770

— 1721 —

FREDERICK V ♔
K. of Denmark
*1723 †1776

CHARLES ANTHONY
Pr. of Holstein-Sonderbg.-Beck
*1727 ✕1759
— 1754 —
FREDERICA
*1738 †1786
d. of Albert Christ.
Bgv. of Dohna

CHARLES LEOPOLD
C. of Schlieben
*1723 †1788
— 1747 —
MARY
*1723 †1800
d. of Ahasverus
C. of Lehndorff

FREDERICK II
Lgv. of Hesse-Cassel
*1720 †1785
— 1740 —
MARY
*1723 †1772
d. of George II
K. of Gt. Britain

FREDERICK V ♔
K. of Denmark
*1723 †1766
— (1) 1743 —
LOUISE
*1724 †1751
d. of George II
K. of Gt. Britain

FREDERICK
D. of Holstein-Sonderburg-Beck
*1757 †1816
— 1780 —
FREDERICA
C. of Schlieben
*1757 †1827

CHARLES
Lgv. of Hesse-Cassel
*1744 †1836
— 1766 —
LOUISE
Pr. of Denmark
*1750 †1831

WILLIAM
D. of Holstein-Sonderburg-Glücksburg
*1757 †1831

— 1810 —

LOUISE
Lgv. of Hesse-Cassel
*1789 †1867

CHRISTIAN IX ♔
K. of Denmark
*1816 †1906

FREDERICK VIII ♔
K. of Denmark
*1843 †1912
— 1869 —
LOUISE
*1851 †1926
d. of Charles XV
K. of Sweden

FREDERICK FRANCIS III
GD. of Mecklenburg-Schwerin
*1851 †1897
— 1879 —
ANASTASIA
*1860 †1922
d. of Michael
GD. of Russia

GUSTAVUS V ADOLPHUS
K. of Sweden
*1858 †1950
— 1881 —
VICTORIA
*1862 †1930
d. of Frederick I
GD. of Baden

ARTHUR
D. of Connaught
*1850 †1942
— 1879 —
LOUISE MARGARET
*1860 †1917
d. of Pr. Fred. Charles of Prussia

CHRISTIAN X ♔
K. of Denmark
*1870 †1947
— 1898 —
ALEXANDRINE
Pr. of Mecklenburg-Schwerin
*1879 †1952

GUSTAVUS VI ADOLPHUS
K. of Sweden
*1882 †1973
— (1) 1905 —
MARGARET
Pr. of Gt. Britain
*1882 †1920

FREDERICK IX ♔
K. of Denmark
*1899 †1972

— 1935 —

INGRID
Pr. of Sweden
*1910

MARGARET II ♔
Q. of Denmark
*1940

(Table 20) but one of the Augustenburgs declared himself Duke of Schleswig-Holstein. The background to the Schleswig-Holstein question, confused by a long litter of unresolved treaties running back from the London agreement of 1852 to the pronouncement of 1460, was a nightmare to diplomats (Chapter 29; Oldenburg). Adroitly Bismarck organized an invasion by Prussian and Austrian troops; Denmark was swiftly defeated and savage terms imposed. Not only German-speaking Holstein (and the smaller adjacent Duchy of Lauenburg) but Danish Schleswig were handed over to joint rule by Prussia and Austria, which meant within a few years incorporation in Prussian Germany.

Christian IX was mainly of German descent (Table 22) for his Hanoverian forebears were scarcely British. His kingdom had been brutally reduced by two-fifths of its land area. His long reign was devoted to reconstruction, the development of agriculture and dairy-farming, and the growth of a parliamentary democracy. His second son became King of Greece and his daughter a beloved Queen of England. His grandson became King of Norway.

Christian X had to face the impact of the First World War, but his country, acting in concert with Norway and Sweden, managed to maintain neutrality. None the less changes occurred: in 1916 Denmark sold her West Indian islands to the United States for $25 million; in 1918 the status of Iceland, long a subject of debate, was temporarily settled by pronouncing it an independent state under the Danish Crown. In 1944 the island went on to complete freedom and republican government. The onslaught of the Second World War was more ruthless. Without warning the Nazi hordes overran Denmark in April 1940 and subjected an innocent countryside to the barbarities of German occupation.

Frederick IX, who reigned from 1947 to 1972, was

King Christian IX of Denmark (1816–1906) with his wife, Queen Louise, and family, by Laurits Tuxen, 1883.

known for his interest in music and the sea. His arms can be seen on Table 21. The four main quarters, separated by the cross of the Danebrog Order, display *1* Denmark, *2* Schleswig, *3* the Union of Kalmar, with the ram of the Faroes and the polar bear of Greenland (the crowned fish-tail of Iceland can still be seen on Table 11), and *4* the kingdoms of the Goths and Wends; thereon is a shield with Holstein, Stormania, Ditmarschen and Lauenburg with over all Oldenburg impaling Delmenhorst – a rich pageant of the history of this ancient Kingdom and its neighbours.

The laws of Denmark require approval by the Rigsdag (assembly) for royal marriages; those princes who make unequal marriages are given the title of Count of Rosenborg. Prince Aage (Table 21) was, for example, an officer of the French Foreign Legion. In 1953 the law of succession was altered to permit the daughters of King Frederick IX to inherit; accordingly in 1972 he was succeeded by Queen Margaret, his eldest daughter who had married in 1967 Henry, Count Laborde of Monpezat, a French diplomat, who is now styled Henry, Prince of Denmark.

The arms of Queen Margaret, which can be seen at the foot of Table 15, are simpler than those of her father, as the basic quarterings only have an escutcheon of Oldenburg superimposed. They are surrounded with the collar of the Order of the Elephant. The shield of her husband, Prince Henry, can be seen on Table 21, where he quarters his own family blazon with the basic arms of Denmark, the lions and the hearts. The ancestors of the Queen (Table 22) show a representative selection of the Protestant powers of Northern Europe – Denmark, England, Prussia and Sweden, together with Orthodox Russia.

Chapter 6

NORWAY

In medieval times Norway was the largest of the Scandinavian countries, but its terrain was wild, indented by many fjords and thinly populated. In the ninth and tenth centuries Viking raiders from Norway and Denmark spread havoc up and down the western seaboard of Europe. Settlements were made in Ireland, in Scotland and its islands, in England and in France; in the last-named the wild Northmen created the Duchy of Normandy.

Harold III (Hardrada), who heads Tables 23 and 24, was a tough, romantic figure who had fought bravely in the Byzantine Army, campaigned in Sicily, reigned in Norway and perished in an effort to conquer England. The Crown passed, and often bloodily, from one of his descendants to another, with small regard for matrimony. Magnus III reasserted Norwegian rule over the islands round Scotland, but after his death came a period of confusion. In 1152 Nicholas Breakspear, later the only English Pope, reorganized the Church. At the end of the twelfth century King Sverker achieved a measure of unity and discipline. Hakon IV asserted his authority over the clergy at home and over Iceland and Greenland overseas. His son, Magnus VI, Lawmender, ceded the Hebrides to Scotland and gave Norway her first code of laws (Table 24).

The crowned lion holding an axe which forms the shield of Norway first appears at the end of the twelfth century; it may be a version of the Scottish lion, for the two countries were closely linked, and might have been united if Princess Margaret, the Fair Maid of Norway, had lived. Down the centuries the haft of the axe has grown shorter.

Eric II, who married two Scots wives, fell into conflict with the Hanseatic towns, which gained a stranglehold over the rich cod-fishing industry of Norwegian ports. His brother Hakon V left an only daughter whose son, Magnus, united the Crowns of Sweden and Norway (Table 18). However, Magnus was unable to maintain his position; the Norwegians elected his younger son, Hakon VI, while the Swedes turned to his nephew Albrecht of Mecklenburg. King Hakon VI of Norway married the ablest woman of the north, the wise and talented Margaret of Denmark. Their little son was briefly King of Denmark and Norway, presaging the long union of the two countries. After the death of young Olaf IV (1387), his mother Margaret engineered the union of all three northern Kingdoms at Kalmar in 1397.

When the Danes elected Christian I in 1448, the Norwegians after hesitation followed suit. They were ill repaid when in 1468 he yielded Orkney and Shetland to the King of Scotland. While Sweden stirred in rebellion, Norway sank into submission to Denmark and made less progress than the other two realms; but like both of them she accepted the Lutheran faith at the time of the Reformation. In 1536 King Christian III declared that Norway was no longer strong or wealthy enough to maintain a separate kingdom and must be subjected to Denmark. The Norwegian Council was suppressed and the country ruled by a governor, but in fact Norway still preserved considerable independence. During the frequent wars between Sweden and Denmark, Norway with its long inland frontier was repeatedly invaded. In 1658, by the Treaty of Roskilde, Charles X of Sweden was actually ceded a large slice of central Norway around Trondheim, but two years later he was compelled to return this area to Denmark. In 1665 the King of Denmark gained the right of hereditary succession; since this applied to Norway also, it gave the latter enhanced status. But throughout the eighteenth century Norwegian interests were continuously subordinated to those of Denmark.

TABLE 23

NORWAY
General survey

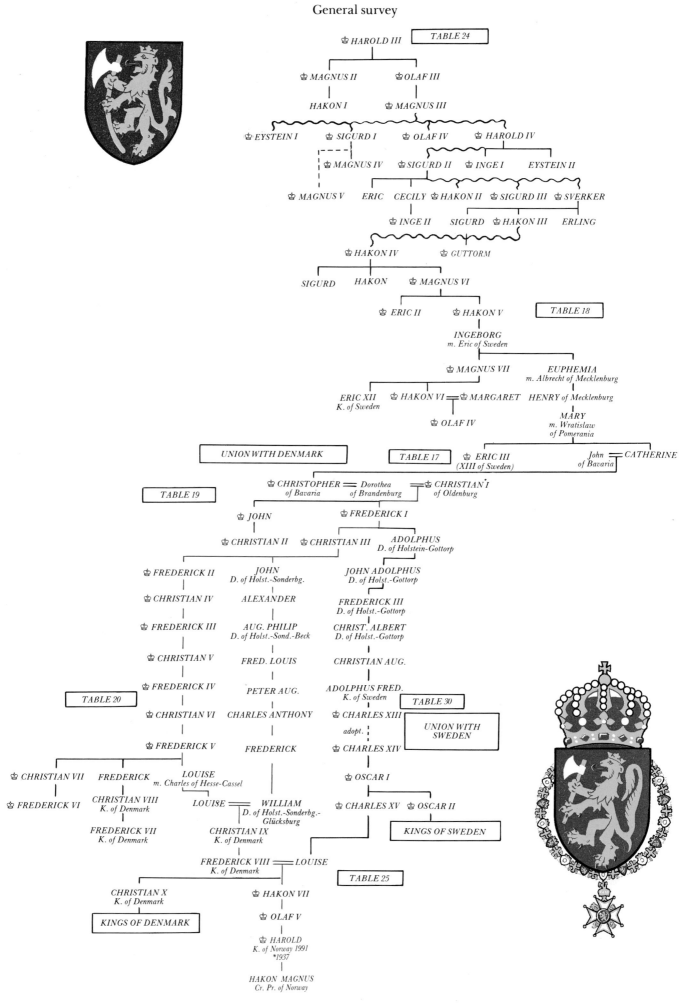

TABLE 24

♔ HAROLD III

♔ MAGNUS II   ♔ OLAF III

HAKON I   ♔ MAGNUS III

♔ EYSTEIN I   ♔ SIGURD I   ♔ OLAF IV   ♔ HAROLD IV

♔ MAGNUS IV   ♔ SIGURD II   ♔ INGE I   EYSTEIN II

♔ MAGNUS V   ERIC   CECILY   ♔ HAKON II   ♔ SIGURD III   ♔ SVERKER

♔ INGE II   SIGURD   ♔ HAKON III   ERLING

♔ HAKON IV   ♔ GUTTORM

SIGURD   HAKON   ♔ MAGNUS VI

♔ ERIC II   ♔ HAKON V   TABLE 18

INGEBORG
m. Eric of Sweden

♔ MAGNUS VII   EUPHEMIA
m. Albrecht of Mecklenburg

ERIC XII
K. of Sweden   ♔ HAKON VI ═ ♔ MARGARET   HENRY of Mecklenburg

♔ OLAF IV

MARY
m. Wratislaw
of Pomerania

UNION WITH DENMARK   TABLE 17   ♔ ERIC III
(XIII of Sweden)   John ═ CATHERINE
of Bavaria

TABLE 19

♔ CHRISTOPHER ═ Dorothea ═ ♔ CHRISTIAN I
of Bavaria   of Brandenburg   of Oldenburg

♔ JOHN   ♔ FREDERICK I

♔ CHRISTIAN II   ♔ CHRISTIAN III   ADOLPHUS
D. of Holstein-Gottorp

♔ FREDERICK II   JOHN
D. of Holst.-Sonderbg.   JOHN ADOLPHUS
D. of Holst.-Gottorp

♔ CHRISTIAN IV   ALEXANDER   FREDERICK III
D. of Holst.-Gottorp

♔ FREDERICK III   AUG. PHILIP
D. of Holst.-Sond.-Beck   CHRIST. ALBERT
D. of Holst.-Gottorp

♔ CHRISTIAN V   FRED. LOUIS   CHRISTIAN AUG.

♔ FREDERICK IV   PETER AUG.   ADOLPHUS FRED.
K. of Sweden   TABLE 30

TABLE 20

♔ CHRISTIAN VI   CHARLES ANTHONY   ♔ CHARLES XIII   UNION WITH
SWEDEN

adopt.

♔ FREDERICK V   FREDERICK   ♔ CHARLES XIV

♔ CHRISTIAN VII   FREDERICK   LOUISE
m. Charles of Hesse-Cassel   ♔ OSCAR I

♔ FREDERICK VI   CHRISTIAN VIII
K. of Denmark   LOUISE ═ WILLIAM
D. of Holst.-Sonderbg.-
Glücksburg   ♔ CHARLES XV   ♔ OSCAR II

FREDERICK VII
K. of Denmark   CHRISTIAN IX
K. of Denmark   KINGS OF SWEDEN

FREDERICK VIII ═ LOUISE
K. of Denmark   TABLE 25

CHRISTIAN X
K. of Denmark   ♔ HAKON VII

KINGS OF DENMARK   ♔ OLAF V

♔ HAROLD
K. of Norway 1991
*1937

HAKON MAGNUS
Cr. Pr. of Norway

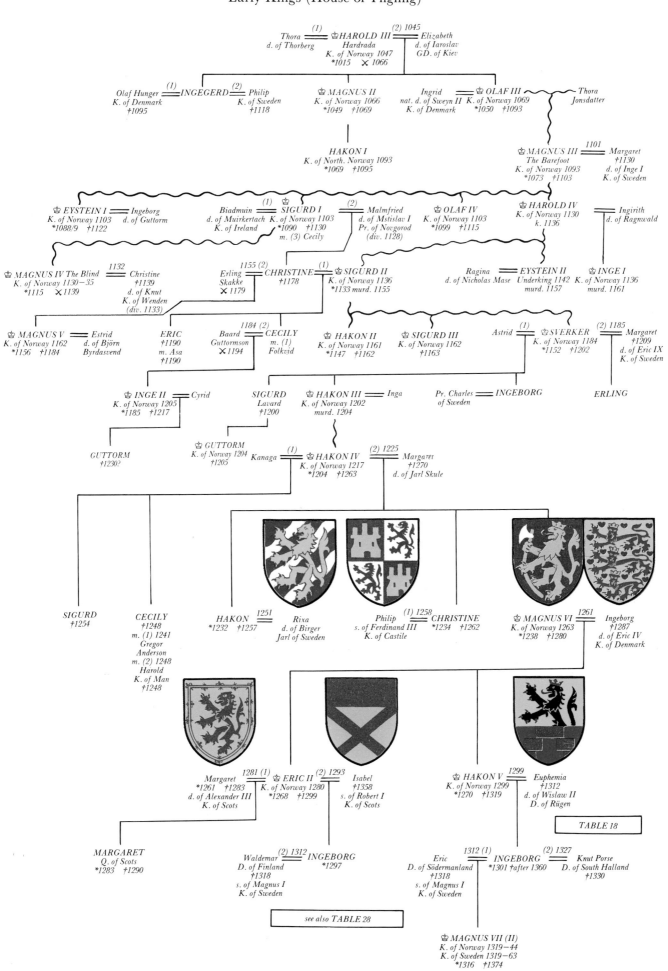

HAROLD III *(1)* Thora, d. of Thorberg — *(2)* 1045 Elizabeth, d. of Iaroslav, GD. of Kiev
Hardrada, K. of Norway 1047, *1015 ✗ 1066

Olaf Hunger, K. of Denmark †1095 *(1)* — **INGEGERD** — *(2)* Philip, K. of Sweden †1118

MAGNUS II, K. of Norway 1066, *1049 †1069

Ingrid, nat. d. of Sweyn II, K. of Denmark — **OLAF III**, K. of Norway 1069, *1050 †1093 — Thora Jonsdatter

HAKON I, K. of North. Norway 1093, *1069 †1095

MAGNUS III, The Barefoot, K. of Norway 1093, *1073 †1103 — 1101 Margaret †1130, d. of Inge I, K. of Sweden

EYSTEIN I, K. of Norway 1103, *1088/9 †1122 — Ingeborg, d. of Guttorm

Biadmuin, d. of Muirkertach, K. of Ireland *(1)* — **SIGURD I**, K. of Norway 1103, *1090 †1130, m. (3) Cecily — *(2)* Malmfried, d. of Mstislav I, Pr. of Novgorod (div. 1128)

OLAF IV, K. of Norway 1103, *1099 †1115

HAROLD IV, K. of Norway 1130, k. 1136 — Ingirith, d. of Ragnwald

MAGNUS IV The Blind, K. of Norway 1130—35, *1115 ✗1139 — 1132 Christine †1139, d. of Knut K. of Wenden (div. 1133)

Erling Skakke ✗1179 — 1155 *(2)* **CHRISTINE** †1178 *(1)* — **SIGURD II**, K. of Norway 1136, *1133 murd. 1155

Ragina, d. of Nicholas Mase — **EYSTEIN II**, Underking 1142, murd. 1157

INGE I, K. of Norway 1136, murd. 1161

MAGNUS V, K. of Norway 1162, *1156 †1184 — Estrid, d. of Björn Byrdasvend

ERIC †1190, m. Asa †1190

Baard Guttormson ✗1194 — 1184 *(2)* **CECILY**, m. (1) Folkvid

HAKON II, K. of Norway 1161, *1147 †1162

SIGURD III, K. of Norway 1162, †1163

Astrid *(1)* — **SVERKER**, K. of Norway 1184, *1152 †1202 — *(2)* 1185 Margaret †1209, d. of Eric IX, K. of Sweden

INGE II, K. of Norway 1205, *1185 †1217 — Cyrid

SIGURD Lavard †1200

HAKON III, K. of Norway 1202, murd. 1204 — Inga

Pr. Charles of Sweden — **INGEBORG**

ERLING

GUTTORM †1230?

GUTTORM, K. of Norway 1204 †1205

Kanaga *(1)* — **HAKON IV**, K. of Norway 1217, *1204 †1263 — *(2)* 1225 Margaret †1270, d. of Jarl Skule

SIGURD †1254

CECILY †1248, m. (1) 1241 Gregor Anderson, m. (2) 1248 Harold, K. of Man †1248

HAKON *1232 †1257 — 1251 Rixa, d. of Birger Jarl of Sweden

Philip, s. of Ferdinand III, K. of Castile *(1)* 1258 — **CHRISTINE** *1234 †1262

MAGNUS VI, K. of Norway 1263, *1238 †1280 — 1261 Ingeborg †1287, d. of Eric IV, K. of Denmark

Margaret *1261 †1283, d. of Alexander III, K. of Scots — 1281 *(1)* **ERIC II**, K. of Norway 1280, *1268 †1299 — *(2)* 1293 Isabel †1358, s. of Robert I, K. of Scots

HAKON V, K. of Norway 1299, *1270 †1319 — 1299 Euphemia †1312, d. of Wislaw II, D. of Rügen

TABLE 18

MARGARET, Q. of Scots *1283 †1290

Waldemar, D. of Finland †1318, s. of Magnus I, K. of Sweden — *(2)* 1312 **INGEBORG** *1297

Eric, D. of Södermanland †1318, s. of Magnus I, K. of Sweden — 1312 *(1)* **INGEBORG** *1301 †after 1360 — *(2)* 1327 Knut Porse, D. of South Halland †1330

see also TABLE 28

MAGNUS VII (II), K. of Norway 1319—44, K. of Sweden 1319—63, *1316 †1374

TABLE 25

NORWAY
Kings since separation from Sweden

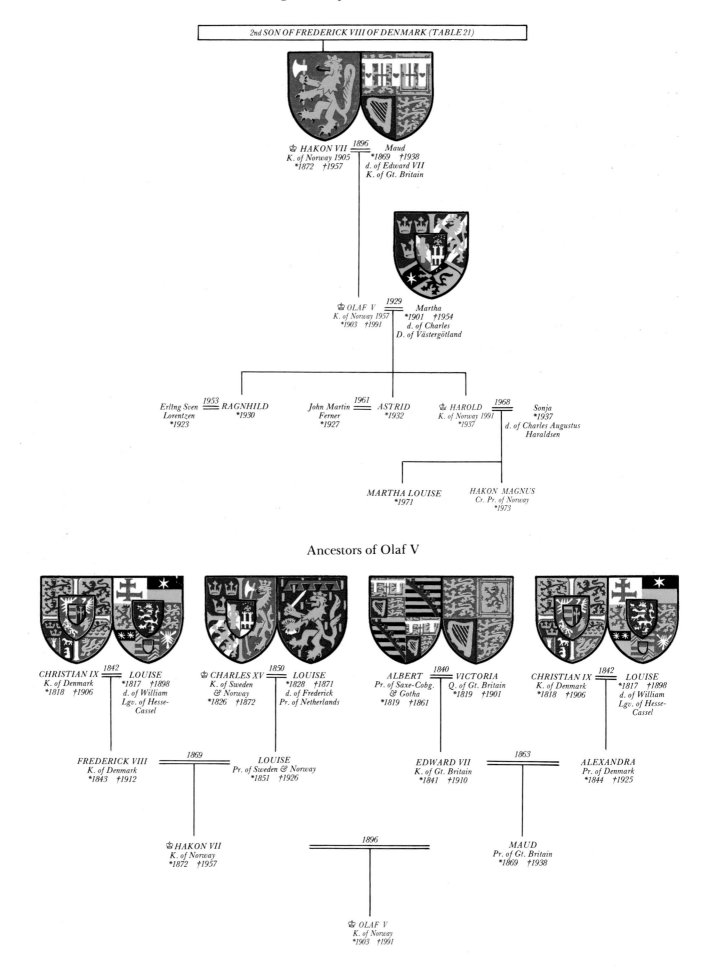

2nd SON OF FREDERICK VIII OF DENMARK (TABLE 21)

♔ HAKON VII ══1896══ Maud
K. of Norway 1905 *1869 †1938
*1872 †1957 d. of Edward VII
K. of Gt. Britain

♔ OLAF V ══1929══ Martha
K. of Norway 1957 *1901 †1954
*1903 †1991 d. of Charles
D. of Västergötland

Erling Sven ══1953══ RAGNHILD   John Martin ══1961══ ASTRID   ♔ HAROLD ══1968══ Sonja
Lorentzen *1930   Ferner *1932   K. of Norway 1991 *1937
*1923   *1927   *1937 d. of Charles Augustus
Haraldsen

MARTHA LOUISE   HAKON MAGNUS
*1971   Cr. Pr. of Norway
*1973

Ancestors of Olaf V

CHRISTIAN IX ══1842══ LOUISE   ♔ CHARLES XV ══1850══ LOUISE   ALBERT ══1840══ VICTORIA   CHRISTIAN IX ══1842══ LOUISE
K. of Denmark *1817 †1898   K. of Sweden *1828 †1871   Pr. of Saxe-Cobg. Q. of Gt. Britain   K. of Denmark *1817 †1898
*1818 †1906 d. of William   & Norway d. of Frederick   & Gotha *1819 †1901   *1818 †1906 d. of William
Lgv. of Hesse-   *1826 †1872 Pr. of Netherlands   *1819 †1861   Lgv. of Hesse-
Cassel   Cassel

FREDERICK VIII ══1869══ LOUISE   EDWARD VII ══1863══ ALEXANDRA
K. of Denmark Pr. of Sweden & Norway   K. of Gt. Britain Pr. of Denmark
*1843 †1912 *1851 †1926   *1841 †1910 *1844 †1925

♔ HAKON VII ══1896══ MAUD
K. of Norway   Pr. of Gt. Britain
*1872 †1957   *1869 †1938

♔ OLAF V
K. of Norway
*1903 †1991

CHRISTIAN DER ERSTE KO DORTHEA GEBORN ZV
NIG ZV DENNEMARCKEN BRANDEN BVRGK VND KONIG
SCHWEDEN VND NORWE CHRISTOFFERS VON BEYRE
GEN HERTZOG ZV SCHLE GELASSENE WIT FRAW
WIG HOLSTEIN · K · FRIDER · K · FRIDERICHS MOTTER
ICHS DES ERSTEN VATTER ·

*King Christian I of Denmark, Sweden and Norway
(1425–81) and his wife, Dorothea of Brandenburg, with
their shields. Copy of a painting commissioned on his death.*

COMPLETE INDEPENDENCE

In 1814 Denmark, which had supported Napoleon, was required to hand over Norway to Sweden. The Norwegians resented this transfer and elected their own king; in a lightning campaign they were overcome by the Crown Prince of Sweden (Marshal Bernadotte), who forthwith proffered generous terms. Norway became a separate kingdom. The union was one of Crowns only, but the people continued to long for complete freedom. Towards the end of the nineteenth century the Norwegian Parliament (Storting) chafed increasingly at Swedish dominance, demanded separate diplomatic representation and ultimately the dissolution of the union. A crisis developed in 1905; for a moment war threatened, but the Swedish King and his government were tactful and ready to yield; in June Norway became entirely independent.

The Crown of Norway was offered to Prince Charles of Denmark (a younger son of Frederick VIII) who took the name of Hakon VII; he was already married to a daughter of Edward VII of England (Table 25). During his long reign his country had to face the two world wars. In the first, like the other Scandinavian powers, Norway remained neutral; in the second she was given no choice. In April 1940 Norway was invaded by Germany; her stout resistance and an unprofitable intervention from Britain availed little against the weight of attack. King Hakon left the country, not to return until 1945.

His son King Olaf succeeded him in 1957 and his arms can be seen on Table 23 encircled by the Order of St Olaf, founded by Oscar I of Sweden and Norway in 1847. His ancestry (Table 25) shows a double descent from Christian IX of Denmark, linked with descent from the Kings of Sweden of the Bernadotte family and from Queen Victoria. Both his daughters have married commoners, for the Norwegian monarchy is rooted more in democracy than in pomp or protocol. In 1968 the Crown Prince followed their example and married another commoner, Miss Sonja Haraldsen.

Chapter 7

SWEDEN

Today Sweden is the most populous of the three Scandinavian Powers, but in the Middle Ages her situation was remote and backward. She had no access to the North Sea and till the seventeenth century the southernmost area of the peninsula (Scania) was part of Denmark. Sweden looked therefore towards the Baltic and the lands of Finland and Russia for commerce and expansion.

In the ninth century Swedish traders and warriors were already making their way across Russia to Constantinople and the rich routes of Asia; their main commodity was fur of various kinds. In Sweden itself the family of Stenkil (Tables 26 and 27) exercised an uneasy supremacy, but from 1134 onwards the descendants of Sverker and Eric IX occupied the throne in alternation. Later legend made a saint of Eric; in fact the first Swedish Archbishopric, at Uppsala, was founded in 1164. Eric X seems to have been the first ruler to have undergone a formal coronation. In the course of the twelfth century the position of 'Jarl', a single important nobleman, developed, and its holders were really more significant than the rival royal houses. Birger Jarl was leader of the army in campaigns against the eastern neighbours of Sweden – Finns and Estonians – which had a crusading character. The Jarl also encouraged the immigration of German merchants and the mining industry. After the death of Eric XI, the people elected Waldemar, son of Birger Jarl, and thus inaugurated a new dynasty which has been given the name of Folkunga.

The early heraldic history of the rulers of Sweden is complex. The seal of Eric X shows two crowned leopards, but not in the form of a coat-of-arms. His son Eric XI made use of the shield of his mother's family, the royal House of Denmark. Canute Johanson, the Tall, who deposed Eric in 1229, already had family arms which also served for the Kingdom (Table 27). Waldemar, who succeeded Eric XI, did not use the Folkunga arms, but continued to employ those of Denmark; on his private seal (*secretum*) he placed two crowns in pale. However, his successor Magnus I did adopt the blazon of his own family, a gold lion on a blue shield with three bends sinister of silver, but enriched the lion with a crown. Round the shield on his seal were three crowns, doubtless only an attribute of royalty.

Magnus I was a powerful ruler who consolidated his Kingdom and gave Sweden its first code of laws; to further his military ambitions he created a tax-free class of knights. But the reign of his son Birger was disfigured by bitter and confused struggles with his two brothers Eric and Waldemar; eventually Birger seized and murdered both after inviting them to dinner. In his turn Birger was driven into exile, and Magnus II, already heir to Norway, became ruler of both realms in 1319, while still a child (Table 28).

Magnus II was also a law-giver, and made an effort to extend Sweden's frontiers southwards by buying the province of Scania for 34,000 marks in 1333. Unhappily the sum was beyond his resources, and he lost the province again in 1360. He was castigated for his policies by Saint Bridget (Birgitta), when she could spare time from founding her order and correcting the Popes in Avignon. From 1356 to 1359 he was compelled to share his Kingdom with his son Eric XII; he had already been forced to give Norway to his younger son (1344). Finally, in 1363 the fractious but over-taxed nobility called in Magnus' nephew, Albrecht of Mecklenburg, who became King of Sweden. It was a sad end to the Folkunga dynasty.

The new ruler could scarcely continue to use the Folkunga blazon while Magnus still lived in exile. Accordingly he adopted a blue shield with three gold crowns which has since become the accepted coat-of-arms of Sweden. This is combined with the bull's head of Mecklenburg and quarterings for Rostock and Schwerin. Albrecht was a vigorous king but he favoured his German followers; in 1389 the nobles of Sweden appealed to the formidable figure of Queen Margaret, already Regent of Norway and Denmark. Her troops expelled Albrecht, and she became the effective ruler of all three Scandinavian realms. As has been seen in Chapter 5 she consolidated this union at Kalmar in 1397 in favour of her great-nephew the Duke of Pomerania, who thus became Eric XIII of Sweden and ruled in his own right from 1412, when the dynamic and dynastic Margaret died.

Revolts against the Danish dominance began as early as 1434. In the middle of the fifteenth century the leading figure was Charles Knutson who began as an official (Marshal) under the Danish Crown and then three times became King of Sweden. He was an ugly man and a tough politician with unusual powers of recovery; he placed his family arms of a boat in the centre of a shield with the arms of Sweden and Norway divided, on the Danish model, by a cross. This narrow cross has remained part of the Swedish royal arms.

After the death of Charles, Sweden was ruled by a series of regents. First came Sten Sture (1470–1503), then his namesake (but not kinsman) Svante Sture (1503–12) who was followed by his son Sten Sture the Younger (1512–20). None of them became king. Then, in 1520, Christian II of Denmark launched a successful attack on Sweden and was crowned. At the end of that year he executed 82 of the supporters of Sten Sture and even exhumed and burned the latter's corpse. Among the victims was Eric Vasa, a relation of Sten; his son Gustavus was a hostage in Denmark but escaped and began to raise a resistance movement. With some help from Lübeck and after many romantic escapes, he drove out the Danes and became regent and then king (1523).

Gustavus I, handsome with fair hair and long beard, was an outstanding ruler. He spoke brilliantly and with wit, he was not deterred by scruples and he combined industry and determination. In the course of his long reign he brought the Reformation to Sweden with the suppression of the monasteries in 1527. He established an hereditary monarchy in 1544, and instituted a national army. Above all he founded a dynasty of brilliant, if unstable, talent. Gustavus was a typical monarch of the sixteenth century, resolute in affairs of state, reformist in religion, the leader of a proud nation but autocratic in its management. In 1522 he was a hunted outlaw; he died in 1560 the father of princes and the hero of a free people, never again to know the Danish yoke. His family coat-of-arms was a canting one with a gold vase on the tripartite background; this he placed on an escutcheon over the three crowns and the traditional Folkunga arms, divided by a gold cross.

Eric XIV (Table 29), eldest son of Gustavus Vasa, was an able but unbalanced man. He extended Swedish rule on the east of the Baltic sea and used a new banner in naval warfare, a gold cross on a blue ground; in 1561 the people of Estonia invited him to be their king. But he fought a profitless war with Denmark, married the daughter of a lowborn soldier and began to put to death members of the nobility. In 1568 he was deposed in favour of his brother, John III. The new king was sympathetic to the Catholic faith and had married a Polish heiress; Sweden, however, remained loyal to the Reformation. John's son, Sigismund, a Catholic and already King of Poland, met sturdy resistance when he tried to reintroduce Romanism and was eventually deposed in favour of his uncle, Charles IX. This King was a firm Lutheran, and a reorganizer of the army; he was interested in extending the influence of Sweden in the Arctic and interfered successfully in the affairs of Russia. He founded the port of Gothenburg.

GUSTAVUS ADOLPHUS

The next King, Gustavus II Adolphus, was perhaps the greatest ruler in Swedish history. A brilliant leader and organizer of troops, an accomplished

King Gustavus I of Sweden (1496–1560), founder of the Vasa dynasty. A 17th-century painting by an unknown artist.

TABLE 26

SWEDEN
General survey

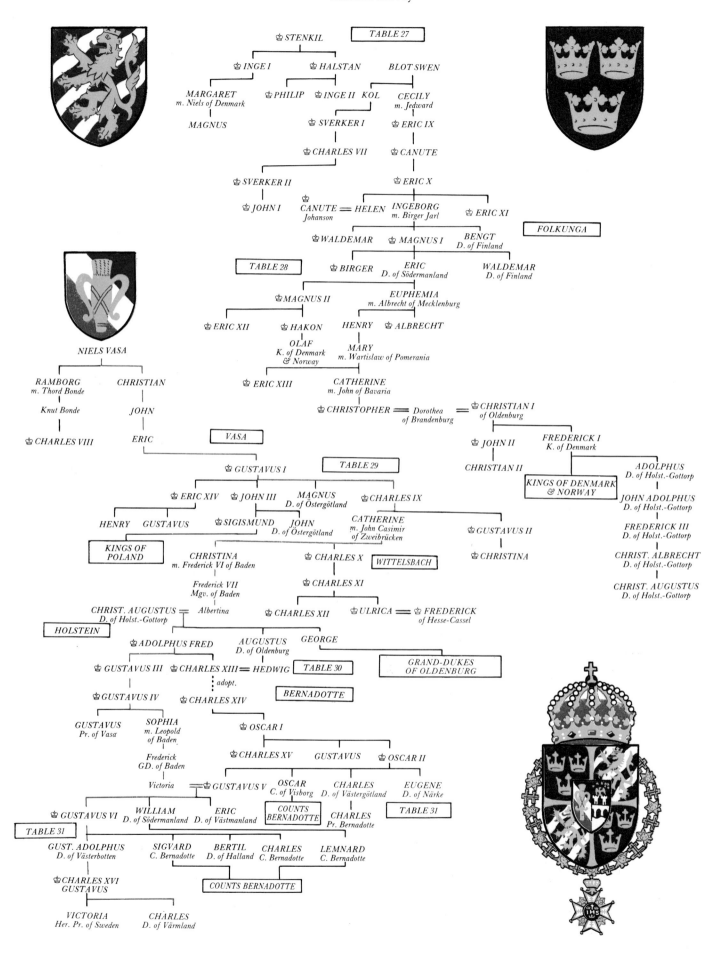

TABLE 27

✠ STENKIL

✠ INGE I   ✠ HALSTAN   BLOT SWEN

MARGARET
m. Niels of Denmark   ✠ PHILIP   ✠ INGE II KOL   CECILY
m. Jedward

MAGNUS   ✠ SVERKER I   ✠ ERIC IX

✠ CHARLES VII   ✠ CANUTE

✠ SVERKER II   ✠ ERIC X

✠ JOHN I   ✠ CANUTE = HELEN   INGEBORG   ✠ ERIC XI
      Johanson   *m. Birger Jarl*

FOLKUNGA

✠ WALDEMAR   ✠ MAGNUS I   BENGT
D. of Finland

TABLE 28   ✠ BIRGER   ERIC
D. of Södermanland   WALDEMAR
D. of Finland

✠ MAGNUS II   EUPHEMIA
m. Albrecht of Mecklenburg

✠ ERIC XII   ✠ HAKON   HENRY   ✠ ALBRECHT

OLAF
*K. of Denmark
& Norway*   MARY
m. Wartislaw of Pomerania

NIELS VASA

RAMBORG
m. Thord Bonde   CHRISTIAN   ✠ ERIC XIII   CATHERINE
m. John of Bavaria

Knut Bonde   JOHN   ✠ CHRISTOPHER == Dorothea == ✠ CHRISTIAN I
      of Brandenburg   *of Oldenburg*

✠ CHARLES VIII   ERIC   VASA   ✠ JOHN II   FREDERICK I
      K. of Denmark

ADOLPHUS
D. of Holst.-Gottorp

✠ GUSTAVUS I   TABLE 29   CHRISTIAN II

KINGS OF DENMARK
& NORWAY

JOHN ADOLPHUS
D. of Holst.-Gottorp

✠ ERIC XIV   ✠ JOHN III   MAGNUS
D. of Östergötland   ✠ CHARLES IX

FREDERICK III
D. of Holst.-Gottorp

HENRY   GUSTAVUS   ✠ SIGISMUND   JOHN
D. of Östergötland   CATHERINE
*m. John Casimir
of Zweibrücken*   ✠ GUSTAVUS II

CHRIST. ALBRECHT
D. of Holst.-Gottorp

KINGS OF
POLAND   CHRISTINA
m. Frederick VI of Baden   ✠ CHARLES X   WITTELSBACH   ✠ CHRISTINA

CHRIST. AUGUSTUS
D. of Holst.-Gottorp

Frederick VII
Mgv. of Baden   ✠ CHARLES XI

CHRIST. AUGUSTUS =   Albertina   ✠ CHARLES XII   ✠ ULRICA == ✠ FREDERICK
D. of Holst.-Gottorp   *of Hesse-Cassel*

HOLSTEIN

✠ ADOLPHUS FRED   AUGUSTUS
D. of Oldenburg   GEORGE

✠ GUSTAVUS III   ✠ CHARLES XIII == HEDWIG   TABLE 30

GRAND-DUKES
OF OLDENBURG

✠ GUSTAVUS IV   ⋯ *adopt.*   BERNADOTTE

✠ CHARLES XIV

GUSTAVUS
Pr. of Vasa   SOPHIA
*m. Leopold
of Baden*   ✠ OSCAR I

Frederick
GD. of Baden   ✠ CHARLES XV   GUSTAVUS   ✠ OSCAR II

Victoria == ✠ GUSTAVUS V   OSCAR
C. of Visborg   CHARLES
D. of Västergötland   EUGENE
D. of Närke

✠ GUSTAVUS VI   WILLIAM
D. of Södermanland   ERIC
D. of Västmanland   COUNTS
BERNADOTTE   CHARLES
Pr. Bernadotte   TABLE 31

TABLE 31

GUST. ADOLPHUS
D. of Västerbotten   SIGVARD
C. Bernadotte   BERTIL
D. of Halland   CHARLES
C. Bernadotte   LEMNARD
C. Bernadotte

✠ CHARLES XVI
GUSTAVUS   COUNTS BERNADOTTE

VICTORIA
Her. Pr. of Sweden   CHARLES
D. of Värmland

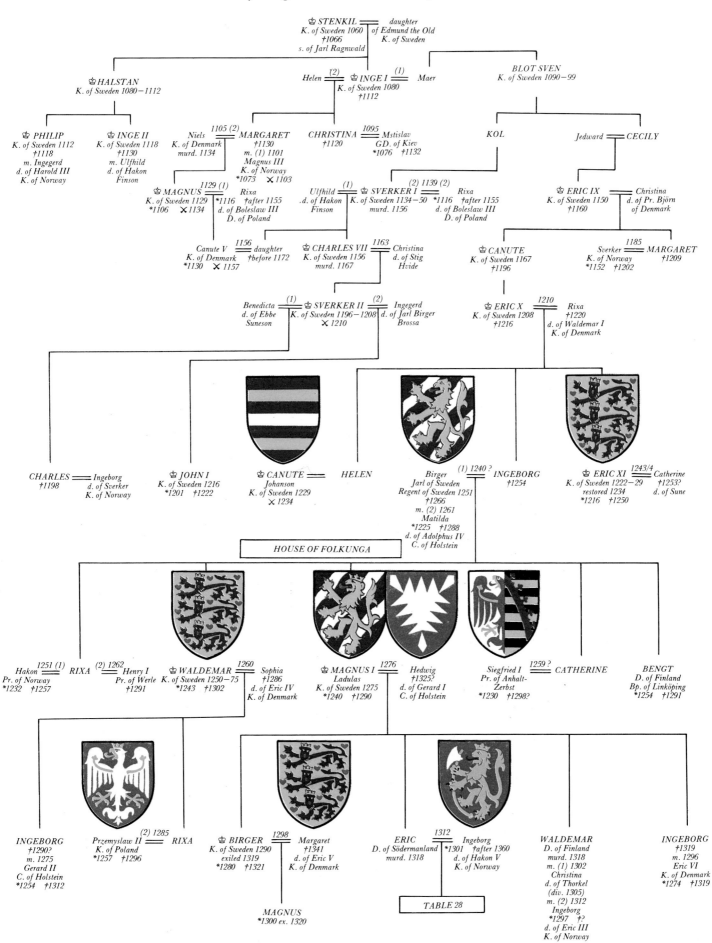

♔ *STENKIL* == *daughter*
K. of Sweden 1060 | *of Edmund the Old*
†1066 | *K. of Sweden*
s. of Jarl Ragnwald

♔ *HALSTAN*
K. of Sweden 1080–1112

Helen ==(2)== ♔ *INGE I* ==(1)== *Maer*
K. of Sweden 1080
†1112

BLOT SVEN
K. of Sweden 1090–99

♔ *PHILIP*
K. of Sweden 1112
†1118
m. Ingegerd
d. of Harold III
K. of Norway

♔ *INGE II*
K. of Sweden 1118
†1130
m. Ulfhild
d. of Hakon
Finson

Niels ==1105 (2)== *MARGARET*
K. of Denmark | *†1130*
murd. 1134 | *m. (1) 1101*
| *Magnus III*
| *K. of Norway*
| **1073* ✕*1103*

CHRISTINA ==1095== *Mstislav*
†1120 | *GD. of Kiev*
| **1076 †1132*

KOL

Jedward == *CECILY*

♔ *MAGNUS* ==1129 (1)==
K. of Sweden 1129
*1106 ✕*1134*

Rixa
*1116 †after 1155
d. of Boleslaw III
D. of Poland

Ulfhild ==(1)== ♔ *SVERKER I* ==(2) 1139 (2)== *Rixa*
.d. of Hakon | *K. of Sweden 1134–50* | **1116 †after 1155*
Finson | *murd. 1156* | *d. of Boleslaw III*
| | *D. of Poland*

♔ *ERIC IX* == *Christina*
K. of Sweden 1150 | *d. of Pr. Björn*
†1160 | *of Denmark*

Canute V ==1156== *daughter*
K. of Denmark | *†before 1172*
*1130 ✕*1157*

♔ *CHARLES VII* ==1163== *Christina*
K. of Sweden 1156 | *d. of Stig*
murd. 1167 | *Hvide*

♔ *CANUTE*
K. of Sweden 1167
†1196

Sverker ==1185== *MARGARET*
K. of Norway | *†1209*
*1152 †1202

Benedicta ==(1)== ♔ *SVERKER II* ==(2)== *Ingegerd*
d. of Ebbe | *K. of Sweden 1196–1208* | *d. of Jarl Birger*
Suneson | ✕*1210* | *Brossa*

♔ *ERIC X* ==1210== *Rixa*
K. of Sweden 1208 | *†1220*
†1216 | *d. of Waldemar I*
| *K. of Denmark*

CHARLES == *Ingeborg*
†1198 | *d. of Sverker*
| *K. of Norway*

♔ *JOHN I*
K. of Sweden 1216
*1201 †1222

♔ *CANUTE* == *HELEN*
Johanson
K. of Sweden 1229
✕*1234*

Birger ==(1) 1240 ?== *INGEBORG*
Jarl of Sweden | *†1254*
Regent of Sweden 1251
†1266
m. (2) 1261
Matilda
*1225 †1288
d. of Adolphus IV
C. of Holstein

♔ *ERIC XI* ==1243/4== *Catherine*
K. of Sweden 1222–29 | *†1253?*
restored 1234 | *d. of Sune*
*1216 †1250

HOUSE OF FOLKUNGA

Hakon ==1251 (1)== *RIXA* ==(2) 1262== *Henry I*
Pr. of Norway | | *Pr. of Werle*
*1232 †1257 | | *†1291*

♔ *WALDEMAR* ==1260== *Sophia*
K. of Sweden 1250–75 | *†1286*
*1243 †1302 | *d. of Eric IV*
| *K. of Denmark*

♔ *MAGNUS I* ==1276== *Hedwig*
Ladulas | *†1325?*
K. of Sweden 1275 | *d. of Gerard I*
*1240 †1290 | *C. of Holstein*

Siegfried I ==1259 ?== *CATHERINE*
Pr. of Anhalt-
Zerbst
*1230 †1298?

BENGT
D. of Finland
Bp. of Linköping
*1254 †1291

INGEBORG
†1290?
m. 1275
Gerard II
C. of Holstein
*1254 †1312

Przemyslaw II ==(2) 1285== *RIXA*
K. of Poland
*1257 †1296

♔ *BIRGER* ==1298== *Margaret*
K. of Sweden 1290 | *†1341*
exiled 1319 | *d. of Eric V*
*1280 †1321 | *K. of Denmark*

ERIC ==1312== *Ingeborg*
D. of Södermanland | **1301 †after 1360*
murd. 1318 | *d. of Hakon V*
| *K. of Norway*

WALDEMAR
D. of Finland
murd. 1318
m. (1) 1302
Christina
d. of Thorkel
(div. 1305)
m. (2) 1312
Ingeborg
*1297 †?
d. of Eric III
K. of Norway

INGEBORG
†1319
m. 1296
Eric VI
K. of Denmark
*1274 †1319

MAGNUS
*1300 ex. 1320

TABLE 28

TABLE 28

SWEDEN
House of Folkunga and accession of the House of Vasa

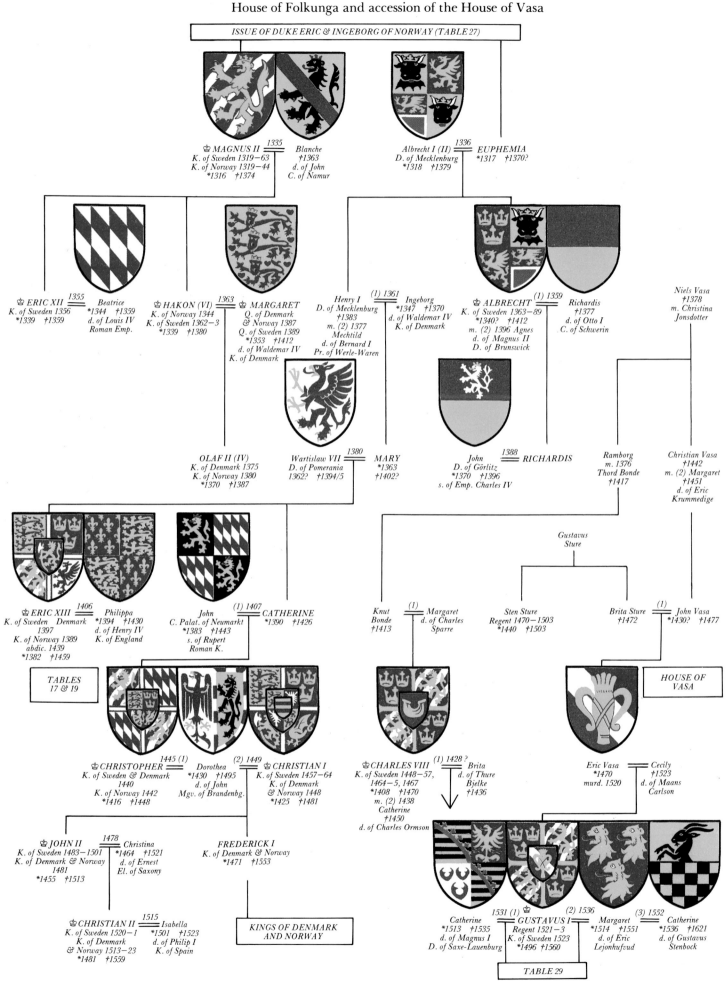

ISSUE OF DUKE ERIC & INGEBORG OF NORWAY (TABLE 27)

♚ MAGNUS II ══1335══ Blanche
K. of Sweden 1319–63 †1363
K. of Norway 1319–44 d. of John
*1316 †1374 C. of Namur

Albrecht I (II) ══1336══ EUPHEMIA
D. of Mecklenburg *1317 †1370?
*1318 †1379

♚ ERIC XII ══1355══ Beatrice
K. of Sweden 1356 *1344 †1359
*1339 †1359 d. of Louis IV
Roman Emp.

♚ HAKON (VI) ══1363══ MARGARET
K. of Norway 1344 Q. of Denmark
K. of Sweden 1362–3 & Norway 1387
*1339 †1380 Q. of Sweden 1389
*1353 †1412
d. of Waldemar IV
K. of Denmark

Henry I ══(1) 1361══ Ingeborg
D. of Mecklenburg *1347 †1370
†1383 d. of Waldemar IV
m. (2) 1377 K. of Denmark
Mechtild
d. of Bernard I
Pr. of Werle-Waren

♚ ALBRECHT ══(1) 1359══ Richardis
K. of Sweden 1363–89 †1377
*1340? †1412 d. of Otto I
m. (2) 1396 Agnes C. of Schwerin
d. of Magnus II
D. of Brunswick

Niels Vasa
†1378
m. Christina
Jonsdotter

OLAF II (IV) Wartislaw VII ══1380══ MARY
K. of Denmark 1375 D. of Pomerania *1363
K. of Norway 1380 1362? †1394/5 †1402?
*1370 †1387

John ══1388══ RICHARDIS
D. of Görlitz
*1370 †1396
s. of Emp. Charles IV

Ramborg
m. 1376
Thord Bonde
†1417

Christian Vasa
†1442
m. (2) Margaret
†1451
d. of Eric
Krummedige

Gustavus
Sture

♚ ERIC XIII ══1406══ Philippa
K. of Sweden Denmark *1394 †1430
1397 d. of Henry IV
K. of Norway 1389 K. of England
abdic. 1439
*1382 †1459

John ══(1) 1407══ CATHERINE
C. Palat. of Neumarkt *1390 †1426
*1383 †1443
s. of Rupert
Roman K.

Knut
Bonde
†1413

Margaret ══(1)══
d. of Charles
Sparre

Sten Sture
Regent 1470–1503
*1440 †1503

Brita Sture ══(1)══ John Vasa
†1472 *1430? †1477

TABLES
17 & 19

HOUSE OF
VASA

♚ CHRISTOPHER ══1445 (1)══ Dorothea ══(2) 1449══ ♚ CHRISTIAN I
K. of Sweden & Denmark *1430 †1495 K. of Sweden 1457–64
1440 d. of John K. of Denmark
K. of Norway 1442 Mgv. of Brandenbg. & Norway 1448
*1416 †1448 *1425 †1481

♚ CHARLES VIII ══(1) 1428 ?══ Brita
K. of Sweden 1448–57, d. of Thure
1464–5, 1467 Bjelke
*1408 †1470 †1436
m. (2) 1438
Catherine
†1450
d. of Charles Ormson

Eric Vasa ══ Cecily
*1470 †1523
murd. 1520 d. of Maans
Carlson

♚ JOHN II ══1478══ Christina
K. of Sweden 1483–1501 *1464 †1521
K. of Denmark & Norway d. of Ernest
1481 El. of Saxony
*1455 †1513

FREDERICK I
K. of Denmark & Norway
*1471 †1553

♚ CHRISTIAN II ══1515══ Isabella
K. of Sweden 1520–1 *1501 †1523
K. of Denmark d. of Philip I
& Norway 1513–23 K. of Spain
*1481 †1559

KINGS OF DENMARK
AND NORWAY

Catherine ══1531 (1)══ ♚ GUSTAVUS I ══(2) 1536══ Margaret ══(3) 1552══ Catherine
*1513 †1535 Regent 1521–3 *1514 †1551 *1536 †1621
d. of Magnus I K. of Sweden 1523 d. of Eric d. of Gustavus
D. of Saxe-Lauenburg *1496 †1560 Lejonhufvud Stenbock

TABLE 29

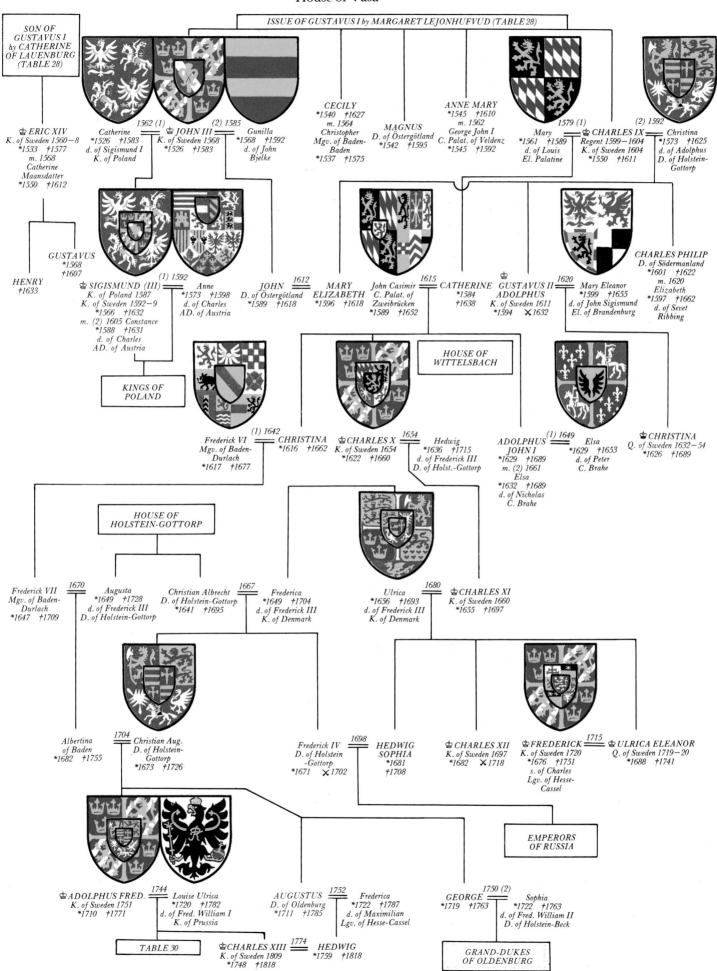

SON OF
GUSTAVUS I
by CATHERINE
OF LAUENBURG
(TABLE 28)

ISSUE OF GUSTAVUS I by MARGARET LEJONHUFVUD (TABLE 28)

♚ ERIC XIV
K. of Sweden 1560–8
*1533 †1577
m. 1568
Catherine
Maansdatter
*1550 †1612

Catherine
*1526 †1583
d. of Sigismund I
K. of Poland

1562 (1)

♚ JOHN III
K. of Sweden 1568
*1526 †1583

(2) 1585

Gunilla
*1568 †1592
d. of John
Bjelke

CECILY
*1540 †1627
m. 1564
Christopher
Mgv. of Baden-
Baden
*1537 †1575

MAGNUS
D. of Östergötland
*1542 †1595

ANNE MARY
*1545 †1610
m. 1562
George John I
C. Palat. of Veldenz
*1545 †1592

Mary
*1561 †1589
d. of Louis
El. Palatine

1579 (1)

♚ CHARLES IX
Regent 1599–1604
K. of Sweden 1604
*1550 †1611

(2) 1592

Christina
*1573 †1625
d. of Adolphus
D. of Holstein-
Gottorp

GUSTAVUS
*1568
†1607

HENRY
†1633

♚ SIGISMUND (III)
K. of Poland 1587
K. of Sweden 1592–9
*1566 †1632
m. (2) 1605 Constance
*1588 †1631
d. of Charles
AD. of Austria

(1) 1592

Anne
*1573 †1598
d. of Charles
AD. of Austria

JOHN
D. of Östergötland
*1589 †1618

1612

MARY
ELIZABETH
*1596 †1618

John Casimir
C. Palat. of
Zweibrücken
*1589 †1652

1615

CATHERINE
*1584
†1638

♚ GUSTAVUS II
ADOLPHUS
K. of Sweden 1611
*1594 ✕1632

1620

Mary Eleanor
*1599 †1655
d. of John Sigismund
El. of Brandenburg

CHARLES PHILIP
D. of Södermanland
*1601 †1622
m. 1620
Elizabeth
*1597 †1662
d. of Sevet
Ribbing

KINGS OF
POLAND

HOUSE OF
WITTELSBACH

Frederick VI
Mgv. of Baden-
Durlach
*1617 †1677

(1) 1642

CHRISTINA
*1616 †1662

♚ CHARLES X
K. of Sweden 1654
*1622 †1660

1654

Hedwig
*1636 †1715
d. of Frederick III
D. of Holst.-Gottorp

ADOLPHUS
JOHN I
*1629 †1689
m. (2) 1661
Elsa
*1632 †1689
d. of Nicholas
C. Brahe

(1) 1649

Elsa
*1629 †1653
d. of Peter
C. Brahe

♚ CHRISTINA
Q. of Sweden 1632–54
*1626 †1689

HOUSE OF
HOLSTEIN-GOTTORP

Frederick VII
Mgv. of Baden-
Durlach
*1647 †1709

1670

Augusta
*1649 †1728
d. of Frederick III
D. of Holstein-Gottorp

Christian Albrecht
D. of Holstein-Gottorp
*1641 †1695

1667

Frederica
*1649 †1704
d. of Frederick III
K. of Denmark

Ulrica
*1656 †1693
d. of Frederick III
K. of Denmark

1680

♚ CHARLES XI
K. of Sweden 1660
*1655 †1697

Albertina
of Baden
*1682 †1755

1704

Christian Aug.
D. of Holstein-
Gottorp
*1673 †1726

Frederick IV
D. of Holstein
-Gottorp
*1671 ✕1702

1698

HEDWIG
SOPHIA
*1681
†1708

♚ CHARLES XII
K. of Sweden 1697
*1682 ✕1718

♚ FREDERICK
K. of Sweden 1720
*1676 †1751
s. of Charles
Lgv. of Hesse-
Cassel

1715

♚ ULRICA ELEANOR
Q. of Sweden 1719–20
*1688 †1741

EMPERORS
OF RUSSIA

♚ ADOLPHUS FRED.
K. of Sweden 1751
*1710 †1771

1744

Louise Ulrica
*1720 †1782
d. of Fred. William I
K. of Prussia

AUGUSTUS
D. of Oldenburg
*1711 †1785

1752

Frederica
*1722 †1787
d. of Maximilian
Lgv. of Hesse-Cassel

GEORGE
*1719 †1763

1750 (2)

Sophia
*1722 †1763
d. of Fred. William II
D. of Holstein-Beck

TABLE 30

♚ CHARLES XIII
K. of Sweden 1809
*1748 †1818

1774

HEDWIG
*1759 †1818

GRAND-DUKES
OF OLDENBURG

Queen Christina of Sweden (1626–89), by Sebastian Bourdon, 1653. She often wore mannish clothes.

linguist, a skilled diplomat, he was kingly in appearance and lustrous in performance. With equal enthusiasm he fought for Sweden and for the Protestant religion. His early campaigns brought him triumphs against Denmark and Russia. The control which he thus won of the east coast of the Baltic embroiled him in turn with Poland; through four campaigns he perfected the training of his army, strengthened by Scottish exiles, and his own powers of leadership. His troops were among the earliest to wear uniform dress. In 1630 he landed on the German shore of the Baltic and prepared to take part in the Thirty Years' War and to become the ally of France against the empire. At Breitenfeld (1631) he destroyed the imperial forces under the veteran Tilly, but in the following year he fell at Lützen on the field of victory. With him idealism vanished from the Thirty Years' War.

The policies of Gustavus Adolphus, who left only a young daughter called Christina, were carried on by his able and loyal minister Oxenstjerna. A noble himself, he ruled with the support of his peers and favoured their interests. The seventeenth century saw the building of great mansions in the country and the splendid Riddarhuset in Stockholm itself. Abroad, the pupils of Gustavus continued to win battles; in 1648 the Peace of Westphalia gave Sweden part of Pomerania and the area round Bremen, two strategic footholds on the mainland of Europe.

Queen Christina lived up to the remarkable tradition of her dynasty. Not beautiful, but highly intelligent and well-educated, she favoured peace and moved gradually towards a sympathy with the old religion. Resenting her sex, she often dressed as a man, swore freely and was outspoken and forthright in speech. Her court was the most cultivated of its age. But in 1654 she abdicated, embraced the Catholic faith and retired (with many of her finest paintings) to Rome. As her successor she had already established her cousin, Charles X, a soldier who at once embarked upon campaigns against Poland and Denmark. In the bitter winter of 1657–8 he achieved an epic march over the ice from the Danish mainland, across the islands to Copenhagen where negotiations at last gave Sweden the southern provinces and a sea-frontier. Indeed for two years he also held the Trondheim district of Norway.

Charles XI was a man of peace and devoted himself to the reconstruction of his country's finances and to welding the new southern provinces into a united Sweden. He increased the royal estates until they represented a third of the realm and reduced both the lands of the nobility and their political influence. By contrast, Charles XII was a creature of war, who inherited a prosperous, stable and now autocratic kingdom from his father in 1697. As can be seen from Table 32, his ancestry was predominantly from the Protestant families of Germany, though his great-grandmother linked him to the House of Vasa; in the ascending male line he was a Wittelsbach (Table 96).

Russia, still deprived of access to the Baltic by Swedish possessions, and Poland both desired to humble their powerful neighbour. War broke out in 1700. Thin, tall, tough, seemingly inexperienced, Charles was like some northern meteor. At Narva he smashed the Russian army of Peter the Great; the prisoners taken outnumbered his own troops. He then devoted himself to a leisurely reduction of Poland and succeeded in dethroning King Augustus. Meanwhile Russia was rearming and reorganizing; Peter the Great had advanced to the Gulf of Finland and built St Petersburg (today known as Leningrad). In 1707 Charles XII moved into Russia; various disasters spoiled his plans to reach Moscow, and he suffered a severe defeat at Poltava in 1709 and had to retire into Turkey; he did not make his way back to Sweden until 1714. Undaunted, the taciturn genius, still popular with his troops, still believing that heaven was on his side, organized fresh armies and advanced into Norway (then united with Denmark). There he was killed, though it is still debated whether the bullet was fired by an enemy or a traitor. In 1721 Sweden was compelled to cede her most profitable Baltic provinces to Russia. It was the end of her period as a great power.

It was also the end of royal absolutism. Charles was succeeded by his sister Ulrica Eleanor who secured

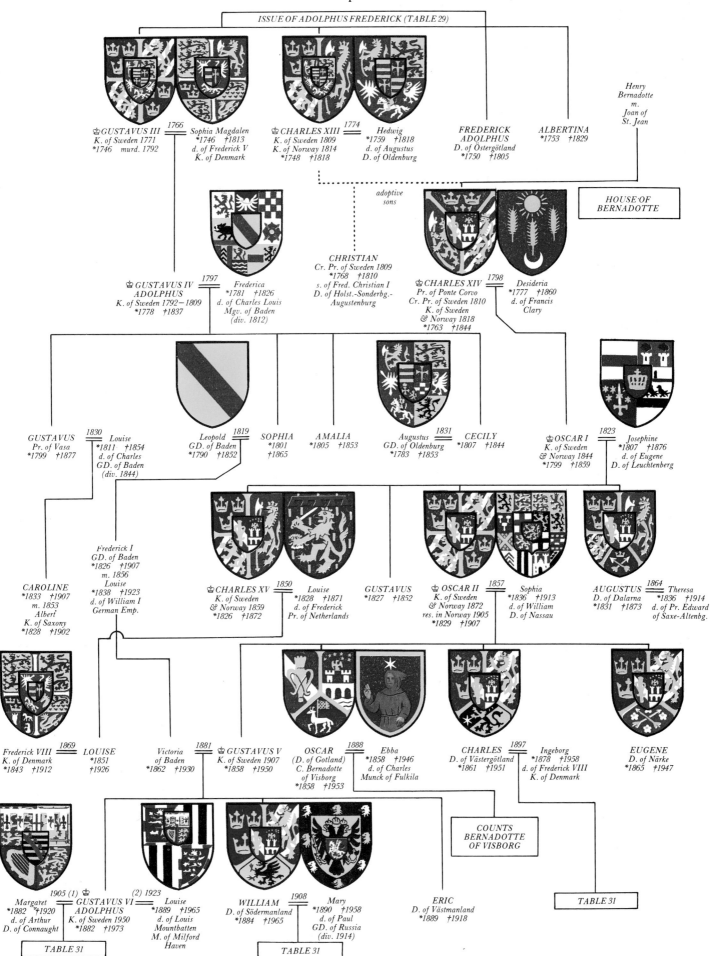

ISSUE OF ADOLPHUS FREDERICK (TABLE 29)

♔ GUSTAVUS III
K. of Sweden 1771
*1746   murd. 1792

1766

Sophia Magdalen
*1746   †1813
d. of Frederick V
K. of Denmark

♔ CHARLES XIII
K. of Sweden 1809
K. of Norway 1814
*1748   †1818

1774

Hedwig
*1759   †1818
d. of Augustus
D. of Oldenburg

FREDERICK
ADOLPHUS
D. of Östergötland
*1750   †1805

ALBERTINA
*1753   †1829

Henry
Bernadotte
m.
Joan of
St. Jean

adoptive
sons

HOUSE OF
BERNADOTTE

♔ GUSTAVUS IV
ADOLPHUS
K. of Sweden 1792–1809
*1778   †1837

1797

Frederica
*1781   †1826
d. of Charles Louis
Mgv. of Baden
(div. 1812)

CHRISTIAN
Cr. Pr. of Sweden 1809
*1768   †1810
s. of Fred. Christian I
D. of Holst.-Sonderbg.-
Augustenburg

♔ CHARLES XIV
Pr. of Ponte Corvo
Cr. Pr. of Sweden 1810
K. of Sweden
& Norway 1818
*1763   †1844

1798

Desideria
*1777   †1860
d. of Francis
Clary

GUSTAVUS
Pr. of Vasa
*1799   †1877

1830

Louise
*1811   †1854
d. of Charles
GD. of Baden
(div. 1844)

Leopold
GD. of Baden
*1790   †1852

1819

SOPHIA
*1801
†1865

AMALIA
*1805   †1853

Augustus
GD. of Oldenburg
*1783   †1853

1831

CECILY
*1807   †1844

♔ OSCAR I
K. of Sweden
& Norway 1844
*1799   †1859

1823

Josephine
*1807   †1876
d. of Eugene
D. of Leuchtenberg

CAROLINE
*1833   †1907
m. 1853
Albert
K. of Saxony
*1828   †1902

Frederick I
GD. of Baden
*1826   †1907
m. 1856
Louise
*1838   †1923
d. of William I
German Emp.

♔ CHARLES XV
K. of Sweden
& Norway 1859
*1826   †1872

1850

Louise
*1828   †1871
d. of Frederick
Pr. of Netherlands

GUSTAVUS
*1827   †1852

♔ OSCAR II
K. of Sweden
& Norway 1872
res. in Norway 1905
*1829   †1907

1857

Sophia
*1836   †1913
d. of William
D. of Nassau

AUGUSTUS
D. of Dalarna
*1831   †1873

1864

Theresa
*1836   †1914
d. of Pr. Edward
of Saxe-Altenbg.

Frederick VIII
K. of Denmark
*1843   †1912

1869

LOUISE
*1851
†1926

Victoria
of Baden
*1862   †1930

1881

♔ GUSTAVUS V
K. of Sweden 1907
*1858   †1950

OSCAR
(D. of Gotland)
C. Bernadotte
of Visborg
*1858   †1953

1888

Ebba
*1858   †1946
d. of Charles
Munck of Fulkila

CHARLES
D. of Västergötland
*1861   †1951

1897

Ingeborg
*1878   †1958
d. of Frederick VIII
K. of Denmark

EUGENE
D. of Närke
*1865   †1947

COUNTS
BERNADOTTE
OF VISBORG

Margaret
*1882   †1920
d. of Arthur
D. of Connaught

1905 (1)

♔ GUSTAVUS VI
ADOLPHUS
K. of Sweden 1950
*1882   †1973

(2) 1923

Louise
*1889   †1965
d. of Louis
Mountbatten
M. of Milford
Haven

WILLIAM
D. of Södermanland
*1884   †1965

1908

Mary
*1890   †1958
d. of Paul
GD. of Russia
(div. 1914)

ERIC
D. of Västmanland
*1889   †1918

TABLE 31

TABLE 31

TABLE 31

TABLE 31

TABLE 31

SWEDEN
House of Bernadotte

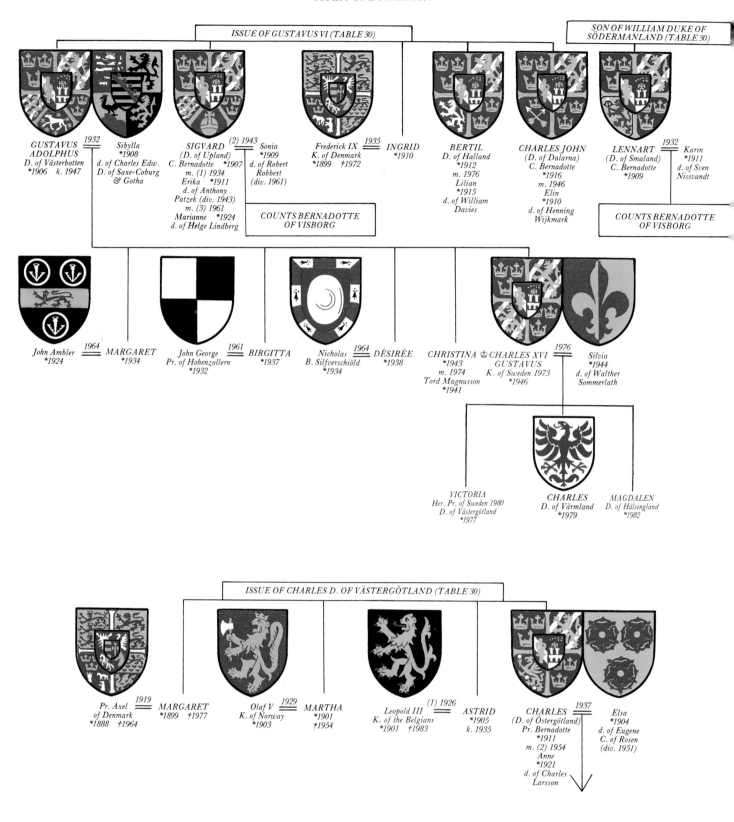

ISSUE OF GUSTAVUS VI (TABLE 30)

SON OF WILLIAM DUKE OF
SÖDERMANLAND (TABLE 30)

GUSTAVUS
ADOLPHUS
D. of Västerbotten
*1906 k. 1947

═══ 1932 ═══

Sibylla
*1908
d. of Charles Edw.
D. of Saxe-Coburg
& Gotha

SIGVARD
(D. of Upland)
C. Bernadotte *1907
m. (1) 1934
Erika *1911
d. of Anthony
Patzek (div. 1943)
m. (3) 1961
Marianne *1924
d. of Helge Lindberg

(2) 1943

Sonia
*1909
d. of Robert
Robbert
(div. 1961)

COUNTS BERNADOTTE
OF VISBORG

Frederick IX
K. of Denmark
*1899 †1972

═══ 1935 ═══

INGRID
*1910

BERTIL
D. of Halland
*1912
m. 1976
Lilian
*1915
d. of William
Davies

CHARLES JOHN
(D. of Dalarna)
C. Bernadotte
*1916
m. 1946
Elin
*1910
d. of Henning
Wijkmark

LENNART
(D. of Smaland)
C. Bernadotte
*1909

═══ 1932 ═══

Karin
*1911
d. of Sven
Nissvandt

COUNTS BERNADOTTE
OF VISBORG

John Ambler
*1924

═══ 1964 ═══

MARGARET
*1934

John George
Pr. of Hohenzollern
*1932

═══ 1961 ═══

BIRGITTA
*1937

Nicholas
B. Silfverschiöld
*1934

═══ 1964 ═══

DÉSIRÉE
*1938

CHRISTINA
*1943
m. 1974
Tord Magnusson
*1941

♔ CHARLES XVI
GUSTAVUS
K. of Sweden 1973
*1946

═══ 1976 ═══

Silvia
*1944
d. of Walther
Sommerlath

VICTORIA
Her. Pr. of Sweden 1980
D. of Västergötland
*1977

CHARLES
D. of Värmland
*1979

MAGDALEN
D. of Hälsingland
*1982

ISSUE OF CHARLES D. OF VÄSTERGÖTLAND (TABLE 30)

Pr. Axel
of Denmark
*1888 †1964

═══ 1919 ═══

MARGARET
*1899 †1977

Olaf V
K. of Norway
*1903

═══ 1929 ═══

MARTHA
*1901
†1954

Leopold III
K. of the Belgians
*1901 †1983

(1) 1926

ASTRID
*1905
k. 1935

CHARLES
(D. of Östergötland)
Pr. Bernadotte
*1911
m. (2) 1954
Anne
*1921
d. of Charles
Larsson

═══ 1937 ═══

Elsa
*1904
d. of Eugene
C. of Rosen
(div. 1951)

NOTE
The arms as given for Charles, D. of Värmland, are those of Värmland, not his personal arms.

SWEDEN
Ancestors of Charles XII, Gustavus VI and Charles XVI

TABLE 32

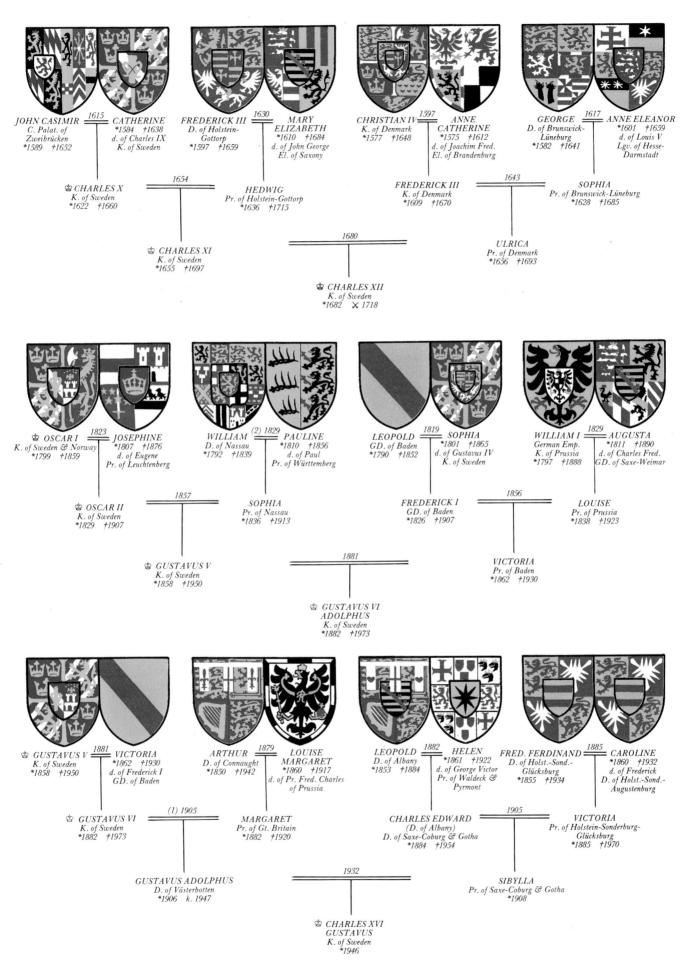

JOHN CASIMIR
C. Palat. of
Zweibrücken
*1589 †1652

1615

CATHERINE
*1584 †1638
d. of Charles IX
K. of Sweden

FREDERICK III
D. of Holstein-
Gottorp
*1597 †1659

1630

**MARY
ELIZABETH**
*1610 †1684
d. of John George
El. of Saxony

CHRISTIAN IV
K. of Denmark
*1577 †1648

1597

**ANNE
CATHERINE**
*1575 †1612
d. of Joachim Fred.
El. of Brandenburg

GEORGE
D. of Brunswick-
Lüneburg
*1582 †1641

1617

ANNE ELEANOR
*1601 †1659
d. of Louis V
Lgv. of Hesse-
Darmstadt

CHARLES X
K. of Sweden
*1622 †1660

1654

HEDWIG
Pr. of Holstein-Gottorp
*1636 †1715

FREDERICK III
K. of Denmark
*1609 †1670

1643

SOPHIA
Pr. of Brunswick-Lüneburg
*1628 †1685

CHARLES XI
K. of Sweden
*1655 †1697

1680

ULRICA
Pr. of Denmark
*1656 †1693

CHARLES XII
K. of Sweden
*1682 × 1718

OSCAR I
K. of Sweden & Norway
*1799 †1859

1823

JOSEPHINE
*1807 †1876
d. of Eugene
Pr. of Leuchtenberg

WILLIAM
D. of Nassau
*1792 †1839

(2) 1829

PAULINE
*1810 †1856
d. of Paul
Pr. of Württemberg

LEOPOLD
GD. of Baden
*1790 †1852

1819

SOPHIA
*1801 †1865
d. of Gustavus IV
K. of Sweden

WILLIAM I
German Emp.
K. of Prussia
*1797 †1888

1829

AUGUSTA
*1811 †1890
d. of Charles Fred.
GD. of Saxe-Weimar

OSCAR II
K. of Sweden
*1829 †1907

1857

SOPHIA
Pr. of Nassau
*1836 †1913

FREDERICK I
GD. of Baden
*1826 †1907

1856

LOUISE
Pr. of Prussia
*1838 †1923

GUSTAVUS V
K. of Sweden
*1858 †1950

1881

VICTORIA
Pr. of Baden
*1862 †1930

**GUSTAVUS VI
ADOLPHUS**
K. of Sweden
*1882 †1973

GUSTAVUS V
K. of Sweden
*1858 †1950

1881

VICTORIA
*1862 †1930
d. of Frederick I
GD. of Baden

ARTHUR
D. of Connaught
*1850 †1942

1879

**LOUISE
MARGARET**
*1860 †1917
d. of Pr. Fred. Charles
of Prussia

LEOPOLD
D. of Albany
*1853 †1884

1882

HELEN
*1861 †1922
d. of George Victor
Pr. of Waldeck &
Pyrmont

FRED. FERDINAND
D. of Holst.-Sond.-
Glücksburg
*1855 †1934

1885

CAROLINE
*1860 †1932
d. of Frederick
D. of Holst.-Sond.-
Augustenburg

GUSTAVUS VI
K. of Sweden
*1882 †1973

(1) 1905

MARGARET
Pr. of Gt. Britain
*1882 †1920

CHARLES EDWARD
(D. of Albany)
D. of Saxe-Coburg & Gotha
*1884 †1954

1905

VICTORIA
Pr. of Holstein-Sonderburg-
Glücksburg
*1885 †1970

GUSTAVUS ADOLPHUS
D. of Västerbotten
*1906 k. 1947

1932

SIBYLLA
Pr. of Saxe-Coburg & Gotha
*1908

**CHARLES XVI
GUSTAVUS**
K. of Sweden
*1946

the election of her husband, Frederick of Hesse-Cassel, as king. Charles X, XI and XII had borne the arms of the Palatinate on an escutcheon; Frederick replaced this with the blazon of Hesse-Cassel. Frederick also established in 1748 the Order of the Seraphim (Table 26) whose origin tradition placed without much warrant in the Middle Ages. A new constitution was imposed on the Crown which set up four Estates (Nobles, Priests, Burgesses and Peasants) but left power mainly in the hands of the first-named. Two parties grew up, distinguished as 'Caps' (originally 'Nightcaps') and 'Hats'. In 1741 the Hats lost Finland to the Russians, but regained most of the province by accepting Adolphus Frederick of Holstein-Gottorp, a kinsman of the Empress Elizabeth of Russia, as Crown Prince. He proved to be an ineffectual sovereign, dominated and browbeaten by the nobility until the close of his life.

Gustavus III (Table 30) was less pliant; by a *coup d'état* in 1772 he re-established royal authority. Clever, but lacking formal education, theatrical, at times indolent, he was none the less successful in bringing about a large measure of financial reform. In 1792 he was assassinated at the opera, a dramatic end to a dramatic life. Gustavus IV was a febrile and wayward king who saw himself as a rival to Napoleon. His futile campaigns lost Finland and Pomerania, and he was forcibly dethroned in 1809; the old constitution was restored and, after an interval, Charles XIII, uncle of Gustavus, became king with limited powers. He was childless and debates were held about a possible heir.

The first choice of a successor was a Danish prince, Christian, then Commander-in-chief in Norway, but he died in 1810. An astonishing selection was then made, and Jean Baptiste Bernadotte, one of Napoleon's ablest Marshals, was offered the reversion of the Swedish throne. A big, handsome Gascon, of proven military talent, he became a successful and popular king. Almost from his arrival he had to rule, for Charles XIII, who had adopted him, was now senile. He never learned Swedish but his good looks and good sense won the hearts of his new countrymen. In 1814 he conquered Norway in a lightning campaign and four years later succeeded his adoptive father as Charles XIV; his policy laid the foundation of the peace which Sweden has since enjoyed without a break.

His arms show the lions of Norway and the Folkunga combined with the three crowns of Sweden: on an escutcheon are the coats of Vasa and of Bernadotte – the latter a Napoleonic creation, since Charles XIV was the son of a small lawyer in Pau. His son, Oscar I, had been a liberal in youth but continued the main lines of his father's policy; domestic reforms, a campaign against drink, the advancement of agriculture and industry were the features of his reign. Charles XV was less vigorous, but put his confidence in good ministers who continued the pacific advance of the nation. True co-operation with Norway was still lacking, and many thousands of Swedes emigrated to the New World. During the reign of his brother, Oscar II, the separation of Norway from Sweden took place peacefully, partly thanks to the tact and moderation of the King. Gustavus V in his long reign led his country through two world wars without becoming involved in either. His son, Gustavus VI, was a distinguished archaeologist. It can be seen (Table 32) that his ancestry was mainly German; but through the Dukes of Baden he was descended from the former Swedish dynasty. Eugene, Prince of Leuchtenberg, was the son of the Empress Josephine by her first marriage.

The ancestry of his grandson King Charles XVI Gustavus (Table 32) shows a stronger infusion of British blood. In 1976 he married a commoner of German birth who has given birth to a daughter, born in 1977, and a son, Prince Charles Philip, born in 1979. At the time of his birth Prince Charles Philip was regarded as the heir to the throne, but the Swedish Parliament has since passed an Act of Succession which makes the eldest child of the monarch (irrespective of sex) heir to the throne. Accordingly on 1 January 1980, Princess Victoria replaced her younger brother as heir apparent. The various cadets of the royal family show versions of the arms of Sweden, Folkunga, Vasa and Bernadotte, usually with the arms of the province from which they take their title in base. Those who have made non-royal marriages are styled Counts of Visborg.

Chapter 8

NETHERLANDS AND LUXEMBURG

The early history of the Low Countries, which today in England are thought of as Holland, Belgium and Luxemburg, tells of a confusing welter of small states and varying allegiances. In the northern half of the Low Countries, men were already engaged in fishing and in the struggle against the sea, in maintenance of dykes and canals; in the southern section a powerful cloth trade developed with independent and wealthy cities such as Antwerp, Bruges and Ghent. At the end of the fourteenth century the invention of a better technique for salting herrings lent fresh impetus to the seaside towns. Town and country began to develop self-governing institutions and a tradition hostile to tyranny.

The first great unifying influence was the spread of the power of Burgundy (Chapter 18), which began with the wedding of Philip the Good to Margaret, heiress of Flanders. Then in 1477 Charles the Bold died leaving an only daughter, Mary. The cities and counties summoned a congress which extracted from Duchess Mary a charter of liberties, including a proviso that she should not marry without the leave of the Estates (assemblies) of her provinces. In the event Mary married Maximilian of Hapsburg, who became emperor (Table 79); his son Philip married Joanna, the heiress of Castile and Aragon, thus linking the fortunes of the Netherlands with Spain. Their son, Charles V, rounded off the Hapsburg dominions in the Low Countries by adding northern lands which included the Duchy of Guelders and the Bishopric of Utrecht. At his abdication in 1556 he allotted Spain, America and the Netherlands to his son Philip II; his brother Ferdinand succeeded him in the Empire and the Hapsburg territories.

Charles was the last natural prince of the Low Countries, in the sense that his upbringing and language naturally conformed to the Burgundian tradition. Philip II, paperbound and assiduous in

distant Spain, was never in touch with the problems of his northern lands, with their sturdy, burgher independence or with their sympathy with the reformed religion, of which Erasmus, the Dutch humanist, had been one of the prophets. It was at this juncture that the House of Nassau became embroiled with the fate of the Netherlands.

HOUSE OF NASSAU

The County of Nassau lies in Germany at the angle between the rivers Rhine and Main. In the second half of the thirteenth century the dynasty divided into two branches, the Walramian and the Ottonian (Table 33). To the former belonged Count Adolphus, who uneasily aspired from 1291 to 1298 to the position of emperor (Chapter 30): we are more concerned with the latter. The Counts of Nassau-Dillenburg showed the customary Teutonic tendency to subdivide and re-unite their estates, but Engelbert I made a fortunate marriage to Joanna, the heiress of Breda and other properties in Brabant. His grandson, Engelbert II, secured more estates in that region as a reward for his services to the Emperor Maximilian. In the next generation the family lands were again divided: Henry took Breda and the Flemish part, William, the less important German heritage (Table 34). Henry made a splendid alliance with the Princess of Orange, a tiny but independent sovereignty in the Rhône valley. His son René (Renatus) idly bequeathed the whole to his first cousin (although William had no Orange blood) and was then unexpectedly slain in battle.

Accordingly William the Silent resigned his German inheritance to a younger brother and prepared to take up his vast fortune in the Netherlands and elsewhere. He was good-looking, robust, charming and immensely accomplished: not taciturn, but a good listener and a skilful masker of his own

[71]

TABLE 33

NETHERLANDS AND LUXEMBURG
General survey of the House of Nassau

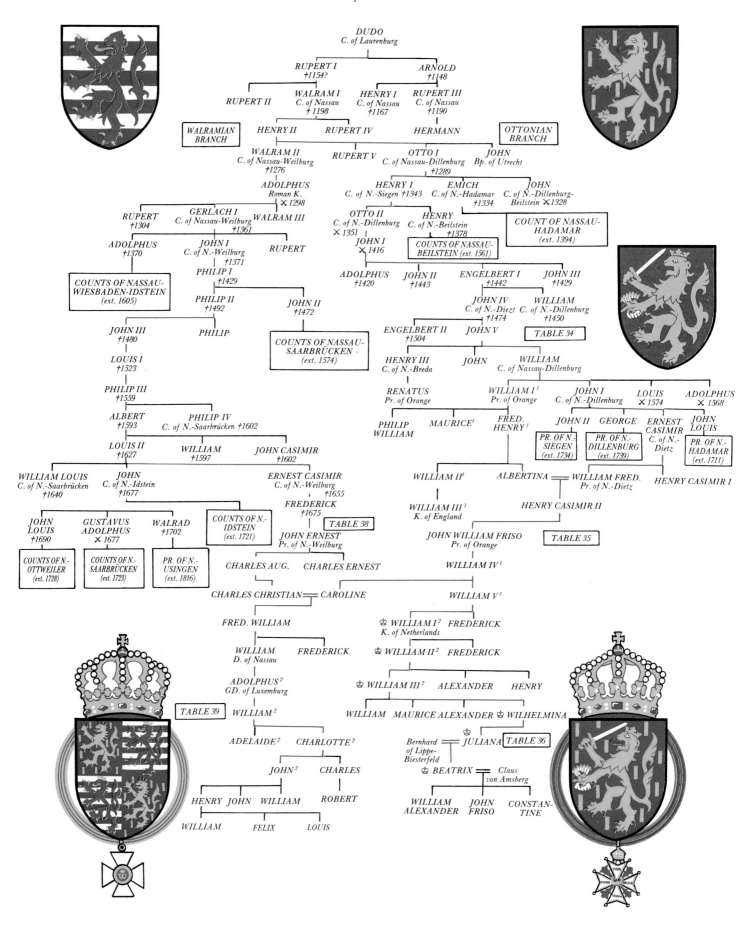

NOTE
[1] Stadholder
[2] Grand-Duke of Luxemburg

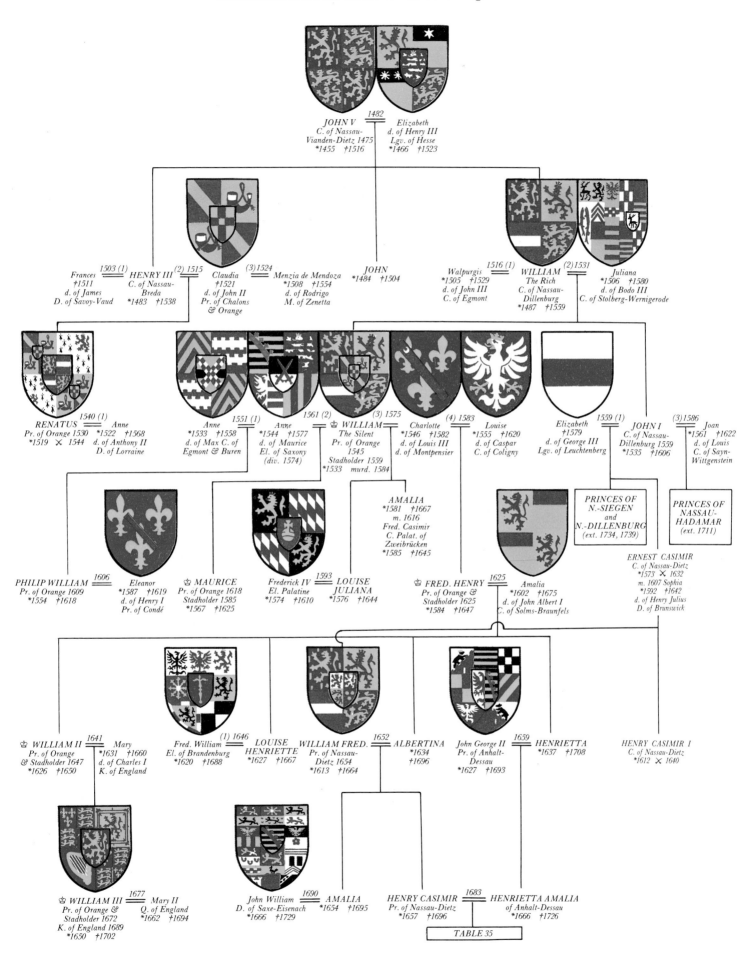

JOHN V ══ *1482* **Elizabeth**
C. of Nassau-
Vianden-Dietz 1475
*1455 †1516
d. of Henry III
Lgv. of Hesse
*1466 †1523

Frances ══ *1503 (1)* **HENRY III** ══ *(2) 1515* **Claudia** *(3)1524* ══ **Menzia de Mendoza**
†1511
d. of James
D. of Savoy-Vaud
C. of Nassau-
Breda
*1483 †1538
†1521
d. of John II
Pr. of Chalons
& Orange
*1508 †1554
d. of Rodrigo
M. of Zenetta

JOHN
*1484 †1504

Walpurgis ══ *1516 (1)* **WILLIAM** *(2)1531* ══ **Juliana**
*1505 †1529
d. of John III
C. of Egmont
The Rich
C. of Nassau-
Dillenburg
*1487 †1559
*1506 †1580
d. of Bodo III
C. of Stolberg-Wernigerode

RENATUS ══ *1540 (1)* **Anne**
Pr. of Orange 1530
*1519 ✕ 1544
*1522 †1568
d. of Anthony II
D. of Lorraine

Anne ══ *1551 (1)* **Anne** ══ *1561 (2)* 👑 **WILLIAM** *(3) 1575* ══ **Charlotte** *(4) 1583* ══ **Louise**
*1533 †1558
d. of Max C. of
Egmont & Buren
*1544 †1577
d. of Maurice
El. of Saxony
(div. 1574)
The Silent
Pr. of Orange
1545
Stadholder 1559
*1533 murd. 1584
*1546 †1582
d. of Louis III
d. of Montpensier
*1555 †1620
d. of Caspar
C. of Coligny

Elizabeth ══ *1559 (1)* **JOHN I** *(3)1586* ══ **Joan**
†1579
d. of George III
Lgv. of Leuchtenberg
C. of Nassau-
Dillenburg 1559
*1535 †1606
*1561 †1622
d. of Louis
C. of Sayn-
Wittgenstein

AMALIA
*1581 †1667
m. 1616
Fred. Casimir
C. Palat. of
Zweibrücken
*1585 †1645

**PRINCES OF
N.-SIEGEN**
and
N.-DILLENBURG
(ext. 1734, 1739)

**PRINCES OF
NASSAU-
HADAMAR**
(ext. 1711)

ERNEST CASIMIR
C. of Nassau-Dietz
*1573 ✕ 1632
m. 1607 Sophia
*1592 †1642
d. of Henry Julius
D. of Brunswick

PHILIP WILLIAM ══ *1606* **Eleanor**
Pr. of Orange 1609
*1554 †1618
*1587 †1619
d. of Henry I
Pr. of Condé

👑 **MAURICE**
Pr. of Orange 1618
Stadholder 1585
*1567 †1625

Frederick IV ══ *1593* **LOUISE**
El. Palatine
*1574 †1610
JULIANA
*1576 †1644

👑 **FRED. HENRY** ══ *1625* **Amalia**
Pr. of Orange &
Stadholder 1625
*1584 †1647
*1602 †1675
d. of John Albert I
C. of Solms-Braunfels

👑 **WILLIAM II** ══ *1641* **Mary**
Pr. of Orange
& Stadholder 1647
*1626 †1650
*1631 †1660
d. of Charles I
K. of England

Fred. William ══ *(1) 1646* **LOUISE
HENRIETTE**
El. of Brandenburg
*1620 †1688
*1627 †1667

WILLIAM FRED. ══ *1652* **ALBERTINA**
Pr. of Nassau-
Dietz 1654
*1613 †1664
*1634
†1696

John George II ══ *1659* **HENRIETTA**
Pr. of Anhalt-
Dessau
*1627 †1693
*1637 †1708

HENRY CASIMIR I
C. of Nassau-Dietz
*1612 ✕ 1640

👑 **WILLIAM III** ══ *1677* **Mary II**
Pr. of Orange &
Stadholder 1672
K. of England 1689
*1650 †1702
Q. of England
*1662 †1694

John William ══ *1690* **AMALIA**
D. of Saxe-Eisenach
*1666 †1729
*1654 †1695

HENRY CASIMIR ══ *1683* **HENRIETTA AMALIA**
Pr. of Nassau-Dietz
*1657 †1696
of Anhalt-Dessau
*1666 †1726

TABLE 35

TABLE 35

NETHERLANDS
Stadholders and Kings in the eighteenth and nineteenth centuries

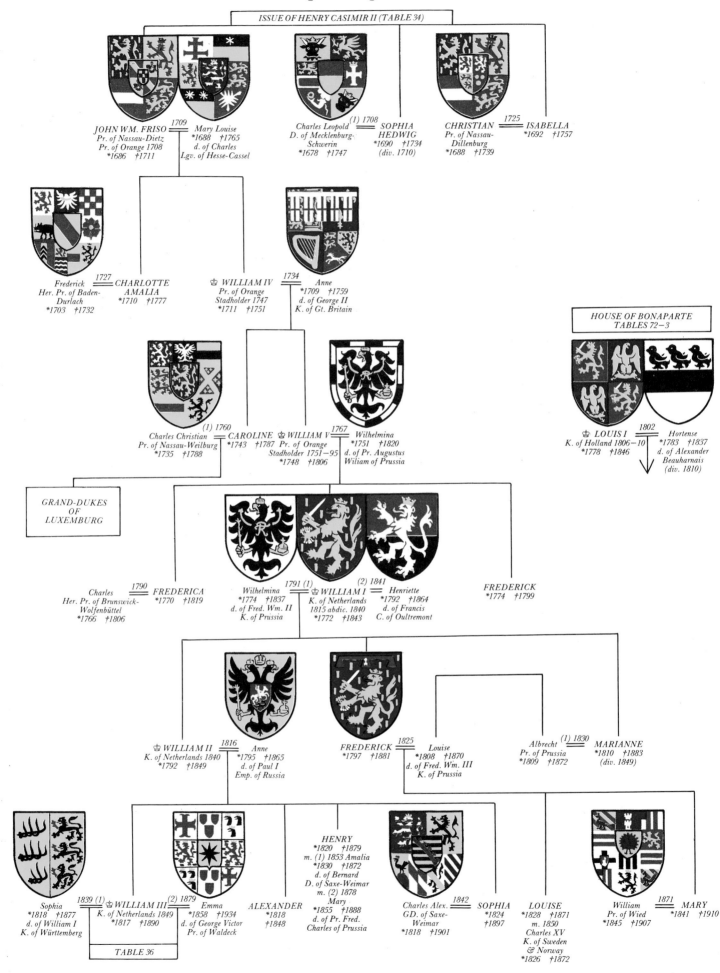

ISSUE OF HENRY CASIMIR II (TABLE 34)

JOHN WM. FRISO ══1709══ Mary Louise
Pr. of Nassau-Dietz *1688 †1765
Pr. of Orange 1708 d. of Charles
*1686 †1711 Lgv. of Hesse-Cassel

Charles Leopold ══(1) 1708══ SOPHIA HEDWIG
D. of Mecklenburg- *1690 †1734
Schwerin (div. 1710)
*1678 †1747

CHRISTIAN ══1725══ ISABELLA
Pr. of Nassau- *1692 †1757
Dillenburg
*1688 †1739

Frederick ══1727══ CHARLOTTE AMALIA
Her. Pr. of Baden- *1710 †1777
Durlach
*1703 †1732

♔ WILLIAM IV ══1734══ Anne
Pr. of Orange *1709 †1759
Stadholder 1747 d. of George II
*1711 †1751 K. of Gt. Britain

HOUSE OF BONAPARTE
TABLES 72–3

Charles Christian ══(1) 1760══ CAROLINE ══ ♔ WILLIAM V ══1767══ Wilhelmina
Pr. of Nassau-Weilburg *1743 †1787 Pr. of Orange *1751 †1820
*1735 †1788 Stadholder 1751–95 d. of Pr. Augustus
  *1748 †1806 Wiliam of Prussia

♔ LOUIS I ══1802══ Hortense
K. of Holland 1806–10 *1783 †1837
*1778 †1846 d. of Alexander
  Beauharnais
  (div. 1810)

GRAND-DUKES
OF
LUXEMBURG

Charles ══1790══ FREDERICA
Her. Pr. of Brunswick- *1770 †1819
Wolfenbüttel
*1766 †1806

Wilhelmina ══1791 (1)══ ♔ WILLIAM I ══(2) 1841══ Henriette
*1774 †1837 K. of Netherlands *1792 †1864
d. of Fred. Wm. II 1815 abdic. 1840 d. of Francis
K. of Prussia *1772 †1843 C. of Oultremont

FREDERICK
*1774 †1799

♔ WILLIAM II ══1816══ Anne
K. of Netherlands 1840 *1795 †1865
*1792 †1849 d. of Paul I
  Emp. of Russia

FREDERICK ══1825══ Louise
*1797 †1881 *1808 †1870
  d. of Fred. Wm. III
  K. of Prussia

Albrecht ══(1) 1830══ MARIANNE
Pr. of Prussia *1810 †1883
*1809 †1872 (div. 1849)

Sophia ══1839 (1)══ ♔ WILLIAM III ══(2) 1879══ Emma
*1818 †1877 K. of Netherlands 1849 *1858 †1934
d. of William I *1817 †1890 d. of George Victor
K. of Württemberg Pr. of Waldeck

ALEXANDER
*1818
†1848

HENRY
*1820 †1879
m. (1) 1853 Amalia
*1830 †1872
d. of Bernard
D. of Saxe-Weimar
m. (2) 1878
Mary
*1855 †1888
d. of Pr. Fred.
Charles of Prussia

Charles Alex. ══1842══ SOPHIA
GD. of Saxe- *1824
Weimar †1897
*1818 †1901

LOUISE
*1828 †1871
m. 1850
Charles XV
K. of Sweden
& Norway
*1826 †1872

William ══1871══ MARY
Pr. of Wied *1841 †1910
*1845 †1907

TABLE 36

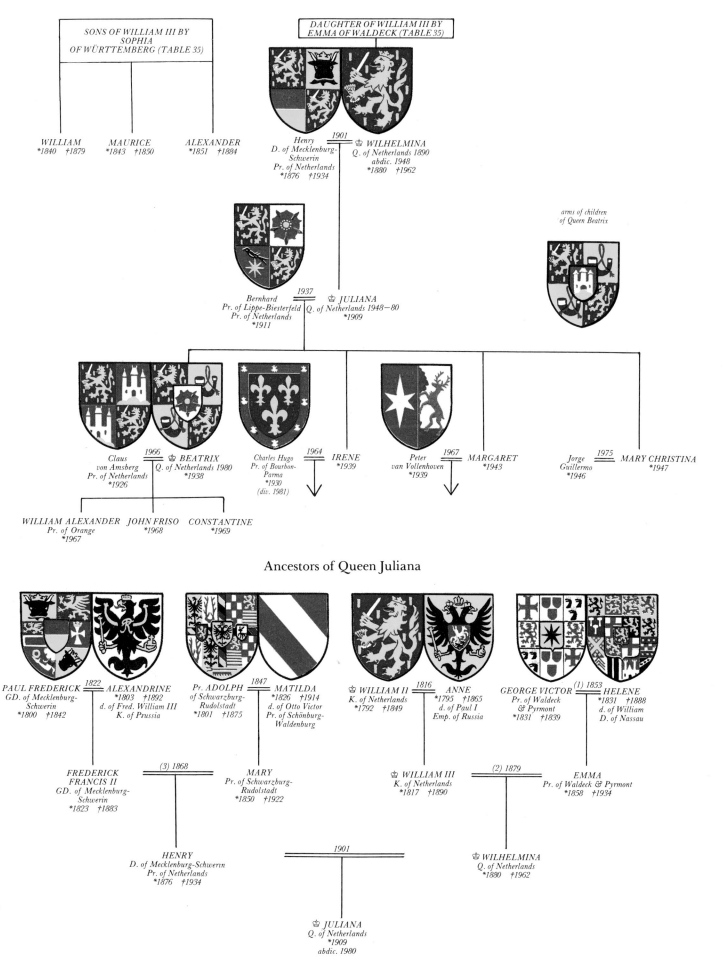

SONS OF WILLIAM III BY SOPHIA OF WÜRTTEMBERG (TABLE 35)

DAUGHTER OF WILLIAM III BY EMMA OF WALDECK (TABLE 35)

WILLIAM
*1840 †1879

MAURICE
*1843 †1850

ALEXANDER
*1851 †1884

Henry
D. of Mecklenburg-
Schwerin
Pr. of Netherlands
*1876 †1934

1901

♔ WILHELMINA
Q. of Netherlands 1890
abdic. 1948
*1880 †1962

arms of children
of Queen Beatrix

Bernhard
Pr. of Lippe-Biesterfeld
Pr. of Netherlands
*1911

1937

♔ JULIANA
Q. of Netherlands 1948—80
*1909

Claus
von Amsberg
Pr. of Netherlands
*1926

1966

♔ BEATRIX
Q. of Netherlands 1980
*1938

Charles Hugo
Pr. of Bourbon-
Parma
*1930
(div. 1981)

1964

IRENE
*1939

Peter
van Vollenhoven
*1939

1967

MARGARET
*1943

Jorge
Guillermo
*1946

1975

MARY CHRISTINA
*1947

WILLIAM ALEXANDER
Pr. of Orange
*1967

JOHN FRISO
*1968

CONSTANTINE
*1969

Ancestors of Queen Juliana

PAUL FREDERICK
GD. of Mecklenburg-
Schwerin
*1800 †1842

1822

ALEXANDRINE
*1803 †1892
d. of Fred. William III
K. of Prussia

Pr. ADOLPH
of Schwarzburg-
Rudolstadt
*1801 †1875

1847

MATILDA
*1826 †1914
d. of Otto Victor
Pr. of Schönburg-
Waldenburg

♔ WILLIAM II
K. of Netherlands
*1792 †1849

1816

ANNE
*1795 †1865
d. of Paul I
Emp. of Russia

GEORGE VICTOR
Pr. of Waldeck
& Pyrmont
*1831 †1839

(1) 1853

HELENE
*1831 †1888
d. of William
D. of Nassau

FREDERICK
FRANCIS II
GD. of Mecklenburg-
Schwerin
*1823 †1883

(3) 1868

MARY
Pr. of Schwarzburg-
Rudolstadt
*1850 †1922

♔ WILLIAM III
K. of Netherlands
*1817 †1890

(2) 1879

EMMA
Pr. of Waldeck & Pyrmont
*1858 †1934

♔ WILHELMINA
Q. of Netherlands
*1880 †1962

HENRY
D. of Mecklenburg-Schwerin
Pr. of Netherlands
*1876 †1934

1901

♔ JULIANA
Q. of Netherlands
*1909
abdic. 1980

NOTE
Arms shown for Queen Beatrix are those she used as a princess.

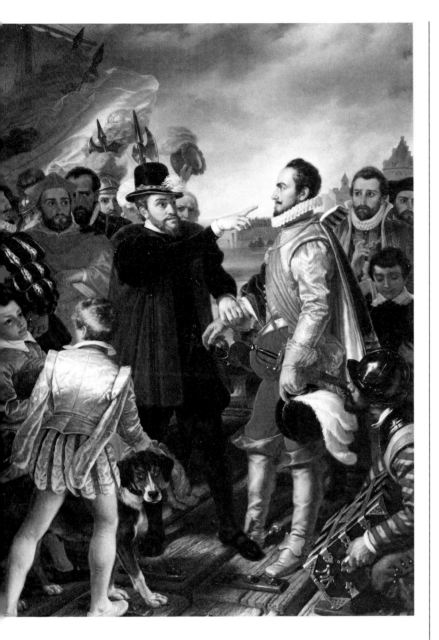

King Philip II of Spain (in hat) berating William the Silent in 1559, by Cornelis Kruseman, 1832.

emotions. At first he was a protégé and servant of Charles V, but as resistance to Philip II developed in the Low Countries he emerged as their natural and indomitable leader. He became a Calvinist, though he believed profoundly in tolerance, and lavished his enormous resources in the conflict against the repressive and bigoted government of Philip II. William's position was curious, for the power was vested in the Estates and he held only the office of stadholder, but his ability, diplomacy and resolution made him the founding father of the new republic. In 1579 the Union of Utrecht amalgamated the seven northern provinces, mainly those which had eschewed Catholicism, into a new European nation.

By the time of his assassination by a squalid and fanatic devotee of Rome, his work was achieved; 'when he died the little children cried in the streets' – so runs a contemporary report.

The territorial and religious division thus engendered proved to be a lasting one. Protestant Holland, under the guidance of the House of Orange, became the United Provinces; the Catholic southern provinces continued under alien rule until the time of Napoleon, and approximate to the modern Belgium.

The original arms of the Nassau family (Table 33) showed a gold lion rampant on a blue field strewn with gold billets (originally blocks of wood). John V quartered this (Table 34) with the arms of Dietz; his wife brought him the County of Katzenellenbogen. So his son William used four quarterings, for Nassau, Katzenellenbogen, Vianen and Dietz. On these William the Silent imposed a smaller escutcheon with Chalon quartering Orange, and Geneva over all. After his death the civil governance of the United Provinces was in the hands of the great statesman, John of Oldenbarnevelt, but Maurice of Nassau took over the military side, reconstituted the army and rapidly became celebrated as the finest commander of his age. In 1609 the Twelve Years' Truce amounted to Spanish recognition of Dutch independence. Maurice held the position of Stadholder of Holland, the most important of the seven provinces, from 1587 and came to hold the same office in three other provinces. Philip William, eldest son of William the Silent, had been taken to Spain as a hostage; he remained a Catholic and a stranger to his family. On his death in 1618, the Principality of Orange and Chalon passed to Maurice.

The early years of the seventeenth century witnessed an astonishing advance in Dutch prosperity. Amsterdam became one of the commercial centres of Europe; an East India company was founded; and the ships and seamanship, which had contributed so effectively to resistance against Spain, became controllers of the carrying trade in European waters. In 1619 Batavia was founded in the East Indies, in 1625 New Amsterdam (now known as New York) in America. At home the reclamation of land from the sea continued. In the Netherlands themselves there was also a powerful school of painting: such names as Rembrandt, Vermeer and Frans Hals could be followed by a long list of lesser masters.

When Spain renewed the war in 1621, the House of Orange provided another talented general to drive them back. Maurice died soon after, but his half-brother, Prince Frederick Henry, successfully invaded the Spanish Netherlands and captured Maastricht. At the time of his death (1647) he would have liked to continue the war, but the peace party prevailed. The merchants had won their

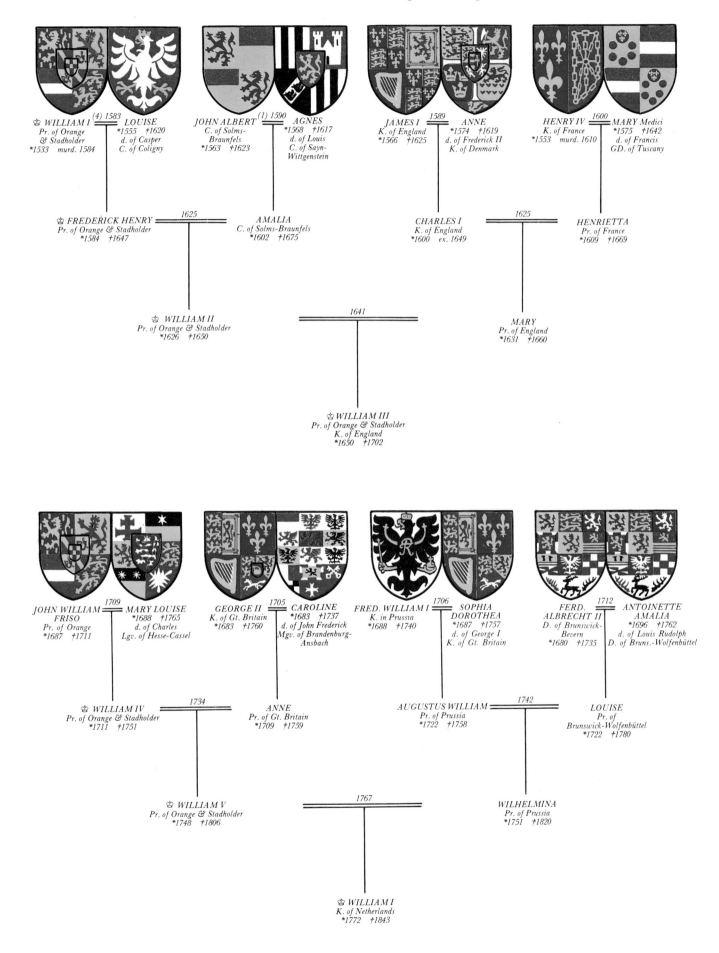

♔ WILLIAM I —(4) 1583— LOUISE
Pr. of Orange
& Stadholder
*1533 murd. 1584
*1555 †1620
d. of Casper
C. of Coligny

JOHN ALBERT —(1) 1590— AGNES
C. of Solms-
Braunfels
*1563 †1623
*1568 †1617
d. of Louis
C. of Sayn-
Wittgenstein

JAMES I —1589— ANNE
K. of England
*1566 †1625
*1574 †1619
d. of Frederick II
K. of Denmark

HENRY IV —1600— MARY Medici
K. of France
*1553 murd. 1610
*1575 †1642
d. of Francis
GD. of Tuscany

♔ FREDERICK HENRY —1625— AMALIA
Pr. of Orange & Stadholder
*1584 †1647
C. of Solms-Braunfels
*1602 †1675

CHARLES I —1625— HENRIETTA
K. of England
*1600 ex. 1649
Pr. of France
*1609 †1669

♔ WILLIAM II —1641—
Pr. of Orange & Stadholder
*1626 †1650

MARY
Pr. of England
*1631 †1660

♔ WILLIAM III
Pr. of Orange & Stadholder
K. of England
*1650 †1702

JOHN WILLIAM
FRISO —1709— MARY LOUISE
Pr. of Orange
*1687 †1711
*1688 †1765
d. of Charles
Lgv. of Hesse-Cassel

GEORGE II —1705— CAROLINE
K. of Gt. Britain
*1683 †1760
*1683 †1737
d. of John Frederick
Mgv. of Brandenburg-
Ansbach

FRED. WILLIAM I —1706— SOPHIA
DOROTHEA
K. in Prussia
*1688 †1740
*1687 †1757
d. of George I
K. of Gt. Britain

FERD.
ALBRECHT II —1712— ANTOINETTE
AMALIA
D. of Brunswick-
Bevern
*1680 †1735
*1696 †1762
d. of Louis Rudolph
D. of Bruns.-Wolfenbüttel

♔ WILLIAM IV —1734— ANNE
Pr. of Orange & Stadholder
*1711 †1751
Pr. of Gt. Britain
*1709 †1759

AUGUSTUS WILLIAM —1742— LOUISE
Pr. of Prussia
*1722 †1758
Pr. of
Brunswick-Wolfenbüttel
*1722 †1780

♔ WILLIAM V —1767—
Pr. of Orange & Stadholder
*1748 †1806

WILHELMINA
Pr. of Prussia
*1751 †1820

♔ WILLIAM I
K. of Netherlands
*1772 †1843

TABLE 38

LUXEMBURG
House of Nassau-Weilburg (eighteenth and nineteenth centuries)

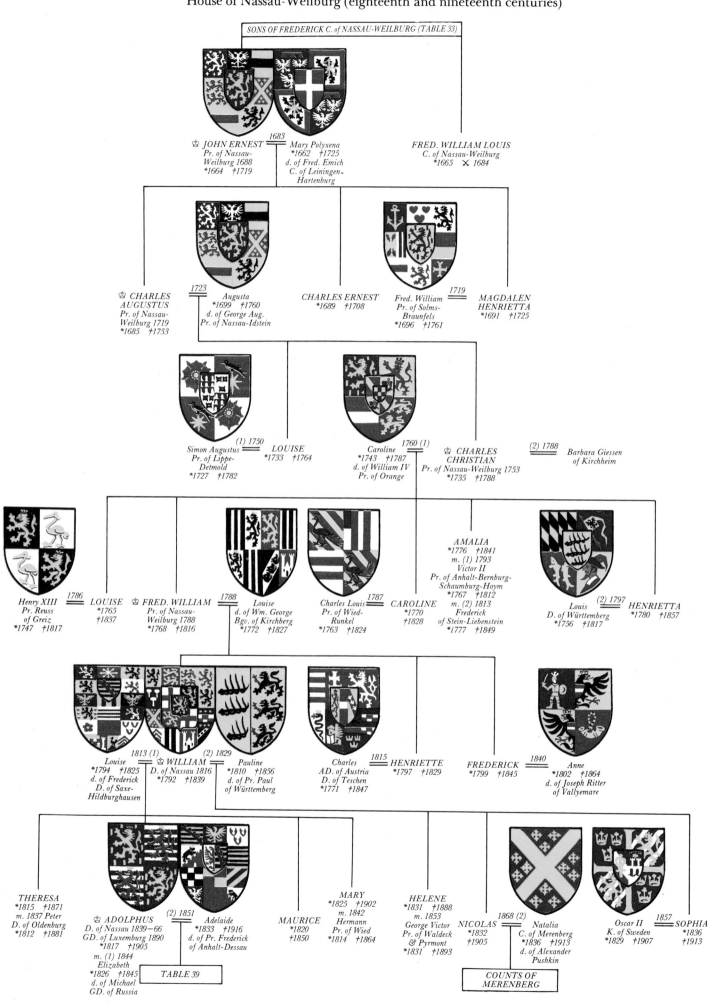

SONS OF FREDERICK C. of NASSAU-WEILBURG (TABLE 33)

♔ JOHN ERNEST
Pr. of Nassau-
Weilburg 1688
*1664 †1719
— 1683 —
Mary Polyxena
*1662 †1725
d. of Fred. Emich
C. of Leiningen-
Hartenburg

FRED. WILLIAM LOUIS
C. of Nassau-Weilburg
*1665 ✕ 1684

♔ CHARLES
AUGUSTUS
Pr. of Nassau-
Weilburg 1719
*1685 †1753
— 1723 —
Augusta
*1699 †1760
d. of George Aug.
Pr. of Nassau-Idstein

CHARLES ERNEST
*1689 †1708

Fred. William
Pr. of Solms-
Braunfels
*1696 †1761
— 1719 —
MAGDALEN
HENRIETTA
*1691 †1725

Simon Augustus
Pr. of Lippe-
Detmold
*1727 †1782
— (1) 1750 —
LOUISE
*1733 †1764

Caroline
*1743 †1787
d. of William IV
Pr. of Orange
— 1760 (1) —
♔ CHARLES
CHRISTIAN
Pr. of Nassau-Weilburg 1753
*1735 †1788
— (2) 1788 —
Barbara Giessen
of Kirchheim

Henry XIII
Pr. Reuss
of Greiz
*1747 †1817
— 1786 —
LOUISE
*1765 †1837

♔ FRED. WILLIAM
Pr. of Nassau-
Weilburg 1788
*1768 †1816
— 1788 —
Louise
d. of Wm. George
Bgv. of Kirchberg
*1772 †1827

Charles Louis
Pr. of Wied-
Runkel
*1763 †1824
— 1787 —
CAROLINE
*1770 †1828

AMALIA
*1776 †1841
m. (1) 1793
Victor II
Pr. of Anhalt-Bernburg-
Schaumburg-Hoym
*1767 †1812
m. (2) 1813
Frederick
of Stein-Liebenstein
*1777 †1849

Louis
D. of Württemberg
*1756 †1817
— (2) 1797 —
HENRIETTA
*1780 †1857

Louise
*1794 †1825
d. of Frederick
D. of Saxe-
Hildburghausen
— 1813 (1) —
☙ WILLIAM
D. of Nassau 1816
*1792 †1839
— (2) 1829 —
Pauline
*1810 †1856
d. of Pr. Paul
of Württemberg

Charles
AD. of Austria
D. of Teschen
*1771 †1847
— 1815 —
HENRIETTE
*1797 †1829

FREDERICK
*1799 †1845
— 1840 —
Anne
*1802 †1864
d. of Joseph Ritter
of Vallyemare

THERESA
*1815 †1871
m. 1837 Peter
D. of Oldenburg
*1812 †1881

♔ ADOLPHUS
D. of Nassau 1839—66
GD. of Luxemburg 1890
*1817 †1905
m. (1) 1844
Elizabeth
*1826 †1845
d. of Michael
GD. of Russia
— (2) 1851 —
Adelaide
*1833 †1916
d. of Pr. Frederick
of Anhalt-Dessau

MAURICE
*1820
†1850

MARY
*1825 †1902
m. 1842
Hermann
Pr. of Wied
*1814 †1864

HELENE
*1831 †1888
m. 1853
George Victor
Pr. of Waldeck
& Pyrmont
*1831 †1893

NICOLAS
*1832
†1905
— 1868 (2) —
Natalia
C. of Merenberg
*1836 †1913
d. of Alexander
Pushkin

Oscar II
K. of Sweden
*1829 †1907
— 1857 —
SOPHIA
*1836
†1913

TABLE 39

COUNTS OF
MERENBERG

TABLE 39

LUXEMBURG
Grand-Dukes in the twentieth century

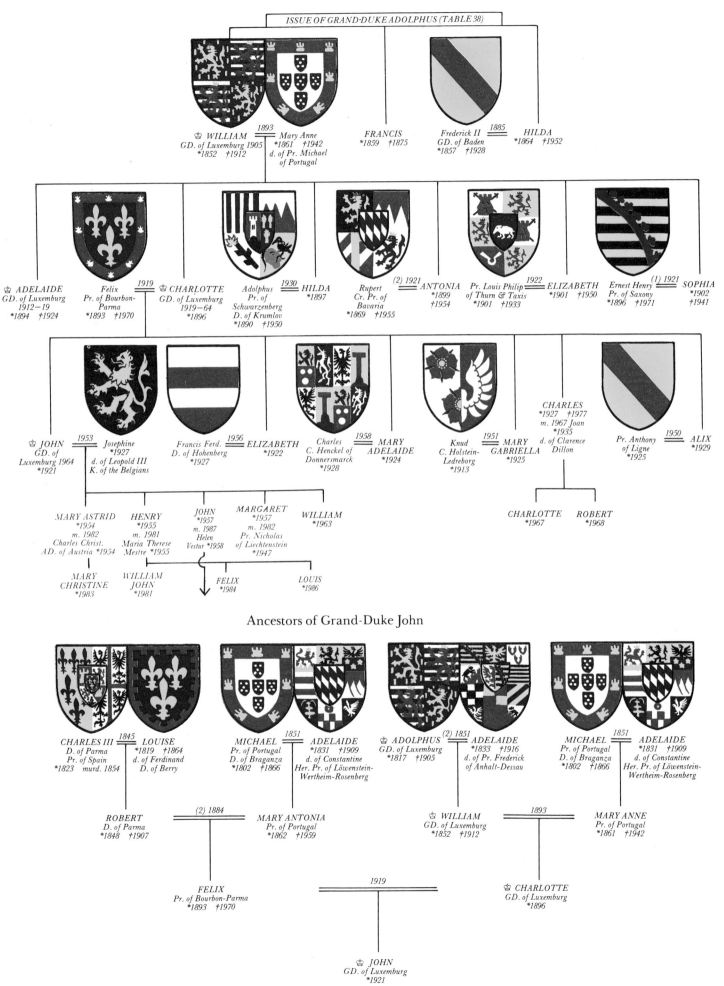

ISSUE OF GRAND-DUKE ADOLPHUS (TABLE 38)

♚ WILLIAM
GD. of Luxemburg 1905
*1852 †1912
— 1893 —
Mary Anne
*1861 †1942
d. of Pr. Michael
of Portugal

FRANCIS
*1859 †1875

Frederick II
GD. of Baden
*1857 †1928
— 1885 —
HILDA
*1864 †1952

♚ ADELAIDE
GD. of Luxemburg
1912—19
*1894 †1924

Felix
Pr. of Bourbon-
Parma
*1893 †1970
— 1919 —
♚ CHARLOTTE
GD. of Luxemburg
1919—64
*1896

Adolphus
Pr. of
Schwarzenberg
D. of Krumlov
*1890 †1950
— 1930 —
HILDA
*1897

Rupert
Cr. Pr. of
Bavaria
*1869 †1955
— (2) 1921 —
ANTONIA
*1899
†1954

Pr. Louis Philip
of Thurn & Taxis
*1901 †1933
— 1922 —
ELIZABETH
*1901 †1950

Ernest Henry
Pr. of Saxony
*1896 †1971
— (1) 1921 —
SOPHIA
*1902
†1941

♚ JOHN
GD. of
Luxemburg 1964
*1921
— 1953 —
Josephine
*1927
d. of Leopold III
K. of the Belgians

Francis Ferd.
D. of Hohenberg
*1927
— 1956 —
ELIZABETH
*1922

Charles
C. Henckel of
Donnersmarck
*1928
— 1958 —
MARY
ADELAIDE
*1924

Knud
C. Holstein-
Ledreborg
*1913
— 1951 —
MARY
GABRIELLA
*1925

CHARLES
*1927 †1977
m. 1967 Joan
*1935
d. of Clarence
Dillon

Pr. Anthony
of Ligne
*1925
— 1950 —
ALIX
*1929

MARY ASTRID
*1954
m. 1982
Charles Christ.
A.D. of Austria *1954

HENRY
*1955
m. 1981
Maria Therese
Mestre *1955

JOHN
*1957 †1987
Helen
Vestur *1958

MARGARET
*1957
m. 1982
Pr. Nicholas
of Liechtenstein
*1947

WILLIAM
*1963

CHARLOTTE
*1967

ROBERT
*1968

MARY
CHRISTINE
*1983

WILLIAM
JOHN
*1981

FELIX
*1984

LOUIS
*1986

Ancestors of Grand-Duke John

CHARLES III
D. of Parma
Pr. of Spain
*1823 murd. 1854
— 1845 —
LOUISE
*1819 †1864
d. of Ferdinand
D. of Berry

MICHAEL
Pr. of Portugal
D. of Braganza
*1802 †1866
— 1851 —
ADELAIDE
*1831 †1909
d. of Constantine
Her. Pr. of Löwenstein-
Wertheim-Rosenberg

ADOLPHUS
GD. of Luxemburg
*1817 †1905
— (2) 1851 —
ADELAIDE
*1833 †1916
d. of Pr. Frederick
of Anhalt-Dessau

MICHAEL
Pr. of Portugal
D. of Braganza
*1802 †1866
— 1851 —
ADELAIDE
*1831 †1909
d. of Constantine
Her. Pr. of Löwenstein-
Wertheim-Rosenberg

ROBERT
D. of Parma
*1848 †1907
— (2) 1884 —
MARY ANTONIA
Pr. of Portugal
*1862 †1959

♚ WILLIAM
GD. of Luxemburg
*1852 †1912
— 1893 —
MARY ANNE
Pr. of Portugal
*1861 †1942

FELIX
Pr. of Bourbon-Parma
*1893 †1970
— 1919 —
♚ CHARLOTTE
GD. of Luxemburg
*1896

♚ JOHN
GD. of Luxemburg
*1921

independence; they did not wish to intrude into the power politics of Europe. These ideas exacerbated the young and intelligent William II who saw himself as a future King of Holland. He carried out one coup against Amsterdam but died suddenly before the issue was truly joined. Alarmed by these events the State of Holland decided not to fill the office of stadholder; the principal power was exercised by the Grand Pensionary, John De Witt, for some twenty-two years. It was still an age of great prosperity and expansion at home and overseas; in 1652 Capetown was established and the foundations laid of Dutch South Africa. In Europe, however, France was replacing Spain as the main enemy by land, while England was emerging as a rival at sea. The arms used by the United Provinces in this period can be seen on Table 33. They comprised the lion of Nassau (but without the background of billets) crowned and holding a sword and a sheaf of seven arrows to symbolize the seven provinces.

In 1672 Louis XIV of France, buttressed by many allies, decided to invade the Netherlands, partly in order to facilitate his own ambitions on the Spanish Netherlands (Belgium of today). In the hour of crisis, the people turned once more to the House of Orange-Nassau. William III, young, inexperienced, and deliberately sheltered from public affairs, was appointed commander against the hosts of France with their distinguished Marshals, Turenne and Condé. His army was small and ill-trained. He resorted to the heroic remedy of breaching the dykes and flooding a defensive belt of country. At this difficult moment, the people rose against De Witt and demanded that William become stadholder like his forebears. By a narrow margin he succeeded in fending off the puissant French King, who – it must be admitted – had not employed his vast resources with energy, speed or strategy. The war continued till 1678 but the Republic had been saved, and William III was able to consolidate his position. Four of the seven provinces, including Holland, made the stadholdership hereditary in the family of Nassau; William was supreme and dominant in foreign policy and military affairs. In this capacity he was able to organize in 1688 the bold and dramatic stroke by which he replaced his father-in-law as King of England and stood forth as a European statesman inspiring the coalition against Louis XIV.

After he was acknowledged king in 1689, William placed a simple shield of Nassau over the royal arms of Britain (Table 34). His ancestry was varied; with his Germanic forebears mingled the blood of the Stuarts and of the illustrious French Protestant family of Coligny (Table 37). Before his death he recognized his cousin John William Friso as his heir in the Netherlands. The principality and title of Orange passed to Frederick of Prussia, child of William's aunt Louise Henriette, but were ceded to France at the Peace of Utrecht in 1713; the Dutch estates thereof stayed with the Nassau family who also used the style of Prince of Orange. John William Friso (Table 35) was descended from John, younger brother of William the Silent, but his grandmother was an aunt of William III; he was a brave soldier but was unluckily drowned on a tempestuous night in 1711. The heir, William IV, was born posthumously. His reign saw a reassertion of oligarchic control, but in 1747 he was appointed stadholder of the whole country; he died a few years later leaving an infant son.

The eighteenth century saw a great decline in Dutch prosperity and wealth, though her commerce continued to be considerable. The United Provinces remained neutral in the Seven Years' War, but most unprofitably came to the aid of the American Colonies in 1776; their shipping suffered severely and Britain became a rival in the East Indies. William V, a slow man with little capacity for government, was widely censured, but in fact he would have preferred to help his British kinsfolk. At one point (1787) he was barred from the province of Holland and only restored thither by the Prussian bayonets of his brother-in-law. Soon after, the French Revolution broke out, and in 1795 French republican troops entered Holland, meeting little resistance and setting up the Batavian Republic. From 1806 to 1810 Louis Bonaparte was King of Holland, but in the latter year his brother incorporated the Netherlands into France.

In 1815, as a result of the Treaty of Vienna, William VI became King of the united Low Countries, as William I, King of the Netherlands. In that year he founded the Military Order of William, which surrounds his shield on Table 33. The new King added to the arms of Nassau a crown on the head of the lion, a sword in his right hand and a bunch of seven arrows in his left; the lion with sword and arrows (representing the seven states) had been the arms of the United Provinces. None the less the union was unreal; Belgium, Catholic and French or Flemish speaking, had by now little in common with the Calvinistic Dutch. In 1830 there was a rebellion; the Great Powers took charge, with England and France in the lead, and in 1839 a separate Belgian kingdom was established (Chapter 9). In the next year William I abdicated. His ancestry (Table 37) shows a strong predominance of varying branches of the House of Brunswick, whether in Germany or England. His son, William II, during his brief reign embarked on a programme of reform and transformed the Netherlands into a constitutional monarchy, whose most striking feature was that ministers could be appointed from outside the two chambers.

Under William III Holland grew in industrial prosperity and aspired to neutrality in international politics; as a consequence The Hague became the seat of the International Court of Justice. When he died, Luxemburg passed to his distant cousin while Holland was ruled by Queen Wilhelmina, whose long reign spanned the first half of the twentieth century. The Netherlands were successful in avoiding any commitment in the First World War and gave refuge to the Kaiser at its end: but the country was invaded by Hitler in May 1940. The Dutch were forced to capitulate; Rotterdam was savagely and wantonly bombed; the royal family fled overseas. Soon after her return, the venerable Queen Wilhelmina abdicated in favour of her daughter, Juliana (Table 36), whose ancestry exhibits a cross-section of the Protestant families of northern Europe. Since the War the Netherlands have lost their valuable colonies in the East Indies, but have nevertheless retained a high level of prosperity.

In her turn Queen Juliana had only daughters. The eldest married a German nobleman, Claus von Amsberg, who bears the title of Prince of the Netherlands. They have three sons, the first male heirs in three generations. The marriage of Princess Irene to a Catholic provoked some reaction in the predominantly Protestant Netherlands. In 1980 Queen Juliana followed her mother's example and abdicated in favour of her eldest daughter, who thus became Queen Beatrix.

LUXEMBURG

In the Middle Ages Luxemburg was a district in the Low Countries, slightly isolated by the great Bishopric of Liège and the hills of the Ardennes. Its rulers rose in the fourteenth century to be Emperors of Germany and Kings of Bohemia (Table 87) but their last descendant sold the Duchy to Burgundy. Thereafter its fortunes lay with the Spanish Netherlands, which in the eighteenth century passed to Austria. In 1815 it was attached to the new Kingdom of Holland (which united the Holland and Belgium of today) as a compensation to the Nassau family for the lands they lost east of the Rhine, and was declared to be a grand-duchy. In 1839 when the independence of Belgium was established, Luxemburg, somewhat reduced in size, remained a separate domain of the King of Holland, who in 1841 founded the Order of the Oak Crown (Table 33).

William II (Table 35) gave the Grand-Duchy a liberal constitution. William III installed his brother Henry as his deputy with plenary powers. But in 1866, after the war between Prussia and Austria had dissolved the Germanic Confederation (of which Luxemburg was part), King William III conceived the idea of selling the province to France. Not surprisingly Prussia mistrusted this scheme, for the city of Luxemburg was deemed the strongest fortress in north Europe; and a conference of the major powers held in London (1867) guaranteed the sovereign independence of the Grand-Duchy.

When France and Prussia went to war in 1870 this freedom was precariously maintained. However, the death of William III in 1890 without male heirs posed a new problem since Luxemburg was under the Salic Law; accordingly the Grand-Duchy passed to Adolphus, Duke of Nassau, the senior male of the Walramian branch of the family, whose ancestors had been Princes of Nassau-Weilburg (Tables 33 and 38). His duchy had been annexed by Prussia in 1866.

Adolphus abandoned the complex quarterings of his former German fiefs and combined the lion of Nassau on its billety background with the ancient arms of Luxemburg, a red lion with two tails on a field of white and blue stripes. The Grand-Duke William (Table 39), who succeeded in 1905, strove to comply with the Salic Law, but finding himself the father of six daughters was constrained to modify the rules of succession. His eldest daughter Adelaide saw her territory invaded by the Germans in 1915, and abdicated in 1919 to enter a convent. Her sister Charlotte again saw Luxemburg's neutrality flouted by the German soldiery. Charlotte's son, Prince John, served in the British army during the war, in the course of which the Duchy saw heavy fighting when von Rundstedt counter-attacked in 1944–5, and re-entered his state in 1945 with the Allied Forces. In 1964 his mother abdicated and he became grand-duke in her stead; his ancestry (Table 39) shows a strong strain of Portuguese and Bourbon blood. An interesting morganatic marriage was made by Nicholas, younger brother of Grand-Duke Adolphus, with a daughter of the Russian poet Pushkin, himself half-negro. With the death of Grand-Duke William the numerous issue in tail male of the original twelfth-century Count of Nassau came to an end.

Chapter 9

BELGIUM

Something of the early history of Belgium has been described in the last chapter. There was little unity in the Low Countries between the break-up of the Carolingian Empire and the growth of the Burgundian dominions. In the division of his territories among the heirs of Charlemagne, Holland and Belgium (as known today) were part of the non-viable 'Middle Kingdom' set up for Lothair (Chapter 15: first section). The more stable powers of France and Germany both cast envious eyes on the lands between them, and have scarcely ceased to do so. The dramatic consolidation of territory, mainly south of the Scheldt, by the Dukes of Burgundy (Table 75) gave a new unity to the Belgic area, though the great Bishopric of Liège lay as a wedge between Luxemburg and the rest. The rich cultural evolution and commercial prosperity of the towns may be epitomized in the painting of van Eyck and his school and the towering churches and town halls of this epoch. The Burgundian territories passed to the Hapsburgs, and remained Catholic under their control while Protestant Holland battled to religious and political freedom. In 1713 the southern provinces were transferred from Spain to Austria.

The old map of Europe was in tatters at the end of the eighteenth century as a result of the French Revolution. Armies of fervent republicans invaded the Austrian Netherlands in 1792 and incorporated them in France. It was on Belgian soil that Napoleon was finally overthrown at Waterloo. In 1815 the two long-divided areas of the Netherlands were united into a single kingdom under William I of Orange-Nassau. The amalgamation did not work. William was a fussy and stubborn monarch; geography and politics might dictate the alliance, but tradition, religion, language and sentiment were hostile to it. In 1830 an uprising in Belgium enforced separation; the Great Powers met in London to regularize what had

taken place. At first the Crown was offered to the Duc de Nemours, son of Louis Philippe of France (Table 70), who refused. Ultimately the congress agreed to nominate Prince Leopold of Saxe-Coburg-Saalfeld. He had already been married to the only child of George IV, but the death in childbirth of Princess Charlotte robbed him of the throne of Britain; he now

Leopold I (1790–1865), King of the Belgians. He is wearing the insignia of the Golden Fleece.

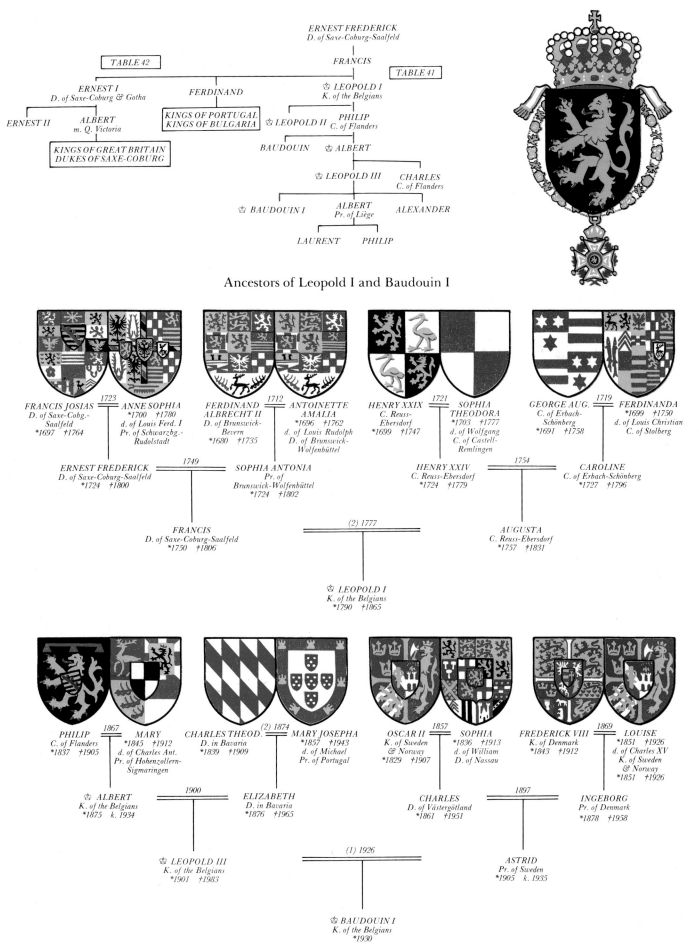

ERNEST FREDERICK
D. of Saxe-Coburg-Saalfeld

FRANCIS

TABLE 42

TABLE 41

ERNEST I
D. of Saxe-Coburg & Gotha

FERDINAND

♚ LEOPOLD I
K. of the Belgians

ERNEST II

ALBERT
m. Q. Victoria

KINGS OF PORTUGAL
KINGS OF BULGARIA

♚ LEOPOLD II

PHILIP
C. of Flanders

KINGS OF GREAT BRITAIN
DUKES OF SAXE-COBURG

BAUDOUIN

♚ ALBERT

♚ LEOPOLD III

CHARLES
C. of Flanders

♚ BAUDOUIN I

ALBERT
Pr. of Liège

ALEXANDER

LAURENT   PHILIP

Ancestors of Leopold I and Baudouin I

FRANCIS JOSIAS
D. of Saxe-Cobg.-
Saalfeld
*1697 †1764

1723

ANNE SOPHIA
*1700   †1780
d. of Louis Ferd. I
Pr. of Schwarzbg.-
Rudolstadt

FERDINAND
ALBRECHT II
D. of Brunswick-
Bevern
*1680 †1735

1712

ANTOINETTE
AMALIA
*1696 †1762
d. of Louis Rudolph
D. of Brunswick-
Wolfenbüttel

HENRY XXIX
C. Reuss-
Ebersdorf
*1699 †1747

1721

SOPHIA
THEODORA
*1703 †1777
d. of Wolfgang
C. of Castell-
Remlingen

GEORGE AUG.
C. of Erbach-
Schönberg
*1691 †1758

1719

FERDINANDA
*1699 †1750
d. of Louis Christian
C. of Stolberg

ERNEST FREDERICK
D. of Saxe-Coburg-Saalfeld
*1724 †1800

1749

SOPHIA ANTONIA
Pr. of
Brunswick-Wolfenbüttel
*1724 †1802

HENRY XXIV
C. Reuss-Ebersdorf
*1724 †1779

1754

CAROLINE
C. of Erbach-Schönberg
*1727 †1796

FRANCIS
D. of Saxe-Coburg-Saalfeld
*1750 †1806

(2) 1777

AUGUSTA
C. Reuss-Ebersdorf
*1757 †1831

♚ LEOPOLD I
K. of the Belgians
*1790 †1865

PHILIP
C. of Flanders
*1837 †1905

1867

MARY
*1845 †1912
d. of Charles Ant.
Pr. of Hohenzollern-
Sigmaringen

CHARLES THEOD.
D. in Bavaria
*1839 †1909

(2) 1874

MARY JOSEPHA
*1857 †1943
d. of Michael
Pr. of Portugal

OSCAR II
K. of Sweden
& Norway
*1829 †1907

1857

SOPHIA
*1836 †1913
d. of William
D. of Nassau

FREDERICK VIII
K. of Denmark
*1843 †1912

1869

LOUISE
*1851 †1926
d. of Charles XV
K. of Sweden
& Norway
*1851 †1926

♚ ALBERT
K. of the Belgians
*1875 k. 1934

1900

ELIZABETH
D. in Bavaria
*1876 †1965

CHARLES
D. of Västergötland
*1861 †1951

1897

INGEBORG
Pr. of Denmark
*1878 †1958

♚ LEOPOLD III
K. of the Belgians
*1901 †1983

(1) 1926

ASTRID
Pr. of Sweden
*1905 k. 1935

♚ BAUDOUIN I
K. of the Belgians
*1930

TABLE 41

BELGIUM
House of Saxe-Coburg

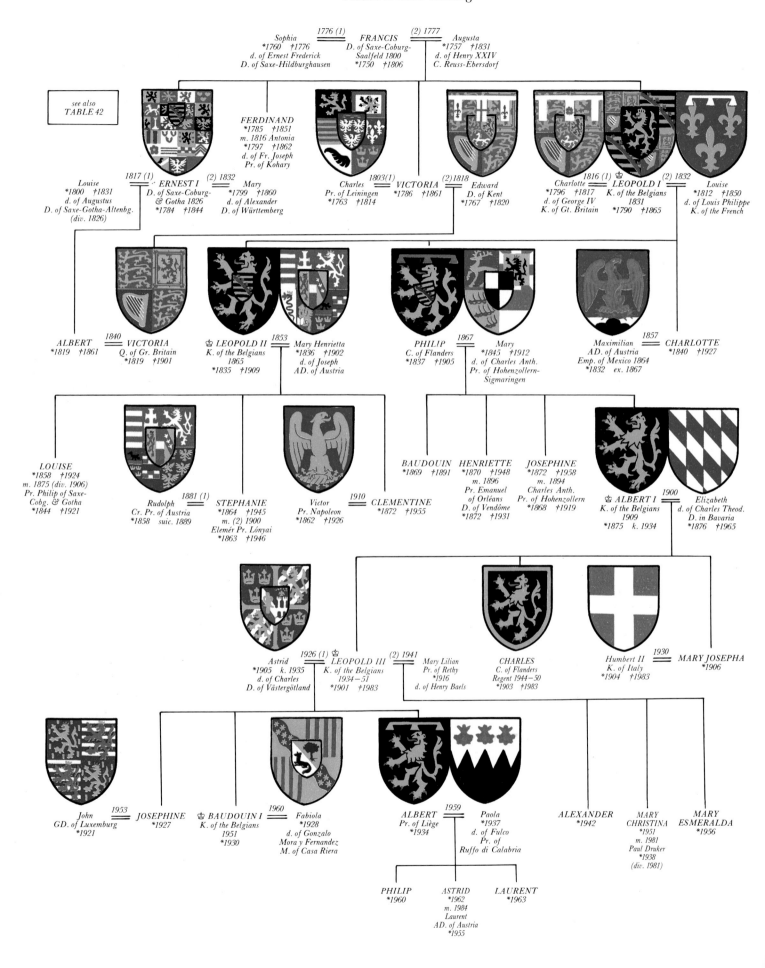

FRANCIS *1776 (1)* Sophia *1760 †1776 d. of Ernest Frederick D. of Saxe-Hildburghausen — FRANCIS D. of Saxe-Coburg-Saalfeld 1800 *1750 †1806 — *(2) 1777* Augusta *1757 †1831 d. of Henry XXIV C. Reuss-Ebersdorf

see also TABLE 42

FERDINAND *1785 †1851 m. 1816 Antonia *1797 †1862 d. of Fr. Joseph Pr. of Kohary

1817 (1) Louise *1800 †1831 d. of Augustus D. of Saxe-Gotha-Altenbg. (div. 1826) — **ERNEST I** D. of Saxe-Coburg-& Gotha 1826 *1784 †1844 — *(2) 1832* Mary *1799 †1860 d. of Alexander D. of Württemberg

1803(1) Charles Pr. of Leiningen *1763 †1814 — **VICTORIA** *1786 †1861 — *(2)1818* Edward D. of Kent *1767 †1820

1816 (1) Charlotte *1796 †1817 d. of George IV K. of Gt. Britain — **LEOPOLD I** K. of the Belgians 1831 *1790 †1865 — *(2) 1832* Louise *1812 †1850 d. of Louis Philippe K. of the French

ALBERT *1819 †1861 — *1840* **VICTORIA** Q. of Gr. Britain *1819 †1901

LEOPOLD II K. of the Belgians 1865 *1835 †1909 — *1853* Mary Henrietta *1836 †1902 d. of Joseph AD. of Austria

PHILIP C. of Flanders *1837 †1905 — *1867* Mary *1845 †1912 d. of Charles Anth. Pr. of Hohenzollern-Sigmaringen

Maximilian AD. of Austria Emp. of Mexico 1864 *1832 ex. 1867 — *1857* **CHARLOTTE** *1840 †1927

LOUISE *1858 †1924 m. 1875 (div. 1906) Pr. Philip of Saxe-Cobg. & Gotha *1844 †1921

Rudolph Cr. Pr. of Austria *1858 suic. 1889 — *1881 (1)* **STEPHANIE** *1864 †1945 m. (2) 1900 Elemér Pr. Lónyai *1863 †1946

Victor Pr. Napoleon *1862 †1926 — *1910* **CLEMENTINE** *1872 †1955

BAUDOUIN *1869 †1891

HENRIETTE *1870 †1948 m. 1896 Pr. Emanuel of Orléans D. of Vendôme *1872 †1931

JOSEPHINE *1872 †1958 m. 1894 Charles Anth. Pr. of Hohenzollern *1868 †1919

ALBERT I K. of the Belgians 1909 *1875 k. 1934 — *1900* Elizabeth d. of Charles Theod. D. in Bavaria *1876 †1965

Astrid *1905 k. 1935 d. of Charles D. of Västergötland — *1926 (1)* **LEOPOLD III** K. of the Belgians 1934−51 *1901 †1983 — *(2) 1941* Mary Lilian Pr. of Rethy *1916 d. of Henry Baels

CHARLES C. of Flanders Regent 1944−50 *1903 †1983

Humbert II K. of Italy *1904 †1983 — *1930* **MARY JOSEPHA** *1906

John GD. of Luxemburg *1921 — *1953* **JOSEPHINE** *1927

BAUDOUIN I K. of the Belgians 1951 *1930 — *1960* Fabiola *1928 d. of Gonzalo Mora y Fernandez M. of Casa Riera

ALBERT Pr. of Liège *1934 — *1959* Paola *1937 d. of Fulco Pr. of Ruffo di Calabria

ALEXANDER *1942

MARY CHRISTINA *1951 m. 1981 Paul Druker *1938 (div. 1981)

MARY ESMERALDA *1956

PHILIP *1960

ASTRID *1962 m. 1984 Laurent AD. of Austria *1955

LAURENT *1963

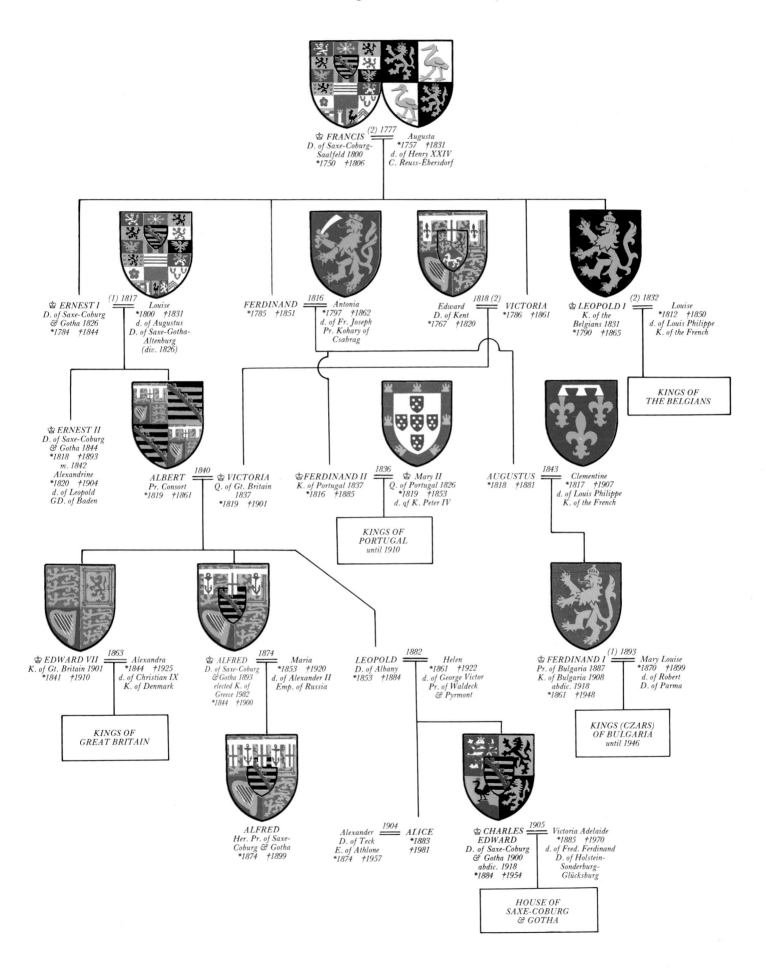

♔ **FRANCIS**
D. of Saxe-Coburg-
Saalfeld 1800
*1750 †1806
— (2) 1777 —
Augusta
*1757 †1831
d. of Henry XXIV
C. Reuss-Ebersdorf

♔ **ERNEST I**
D. of Saxe-Coburg
& Gotha 1826
*1784 †1844
— (1) 1817 —
Louise
*1800 †1831
d. of Augustus
D. of Saxe-Gotha-
Altenburg
(div. 1826)

FERDINAND
*1785 †1851
— 1816 —
Antonia
*1797 †1862
d. of Fr. Joseph
Pr. Kohary of
Csabrag

Edward
D. of Kent
*1767 †1820
— 1818 (2) —
♔ **VICTORIA**
*1786 †1861

♔ **LEOPOLD I**
K. of the
Belgians 1831
*1790 †1865
— (2) 1832 —
Louise
*1812 †1850
d. of Louis Philippe
K. of the French

**KINGS OF
THE BELGIANS**

♔ **ERNEST II**
D. of Saxe-Coburg
& Gotha 1844
*1818 †1893
m. 1842
Alexandrine
*1820 †1904
d. of Leopold
GD. of Baden

ALBERT
Pr. Consort
*1819 †1861
— 1840 —
♔ **VICTORIA**
Q. of Gt. Britain
1837
*1819 †1901

♔ **FERDINAND II**
K. of Portugal 1837
*1816 †1885
— 1836 —
♔ **Mary II**
Q. of Portugal 1826
*1819 †1853
d. of K. Peter IV

AUGUSTUS
*1818 †1881
— 1843 —
Clementine
*1817 †1907
d. of Louis Philippe
K. of the French

**KINGS OF
PORTUGAL
until 1910**

♔ **EDWARD VII**
K. of Gt. Britain 1901
*1841 †1910
— 1863 —
Alexandra
*1844 †1925
d. of Christian IX
K. of Denmark

♔ **ALFRED**
D. of Saxe-Coburg
& Gotha 1893
elected K. of
Greece 1982
*1844 †1900
— 1874 —
Maria
*1853 †1920
d. of Alexander II
Emp. of Russia

LEOPOLD
D. of Albany
*1853 †1884
— 1882 —
Helen
*1861 †1922
d. of George Victor
Pr. of Waldeck
& Pyrmont

♔ **FERDINAND I**
Pr. of Bulgaria 1887
K. of Bulgaria 1908
abdic. 1918
*1861 †1948
— (1) 1893 —
Mary Louise
*1870 †1899
d. of Robert
D. of Parma

**KINGS OF
GREAT BRITAIN**

**KINGS (CZARS)
OF BULGARIA
until 1946**

ALFRED
Her. Pr. of Saxe-
Coburg & Gotha
*1874 †1899

Alexander
D. of Teck
E. of Athlone
*1874 †1957
— 1904 —
ALICE
*1883
†1981

♔ **CHARLES
EDWARD**
D. of Saxe-Coburg
& Gotha 1900
abdic. 1918
*1884 †1954
— 1905 —
Victoria Adelaide
*1885 †1970
d. of Fred. Ferdinand
D. of Holstein-
Sonderburg-
Glücksburg

**HOUSE OF
SAXE-COBURG
& GOTHA**

acquired that of Belgium and married a daughter of Louis Philippe (Table 41). Leopold I was of exclusively German ancestry, mainly from minor princely families (Table 40), but he proved an able, popular and resourceful ruler, combining tact with shrewd political sense. He was uncle to both Queen Victoria and the Prince Consort (Table 42) and lavished good advice upon them. The last difficulties with Holland were not resolved until 1839, when the neutrality of Belgium was guaranteed by treaty (the famous 'scrap of paper' of 1914), but, before he died, Leopold had firmly established Belgian freedom and nationality. He adopted as the arms of his realm the gold lion on black which was the ancient insignia of Brabant; this he combined with his personal arms (still including those of Princess Charlotte). In 1832 he founded the Order of Leopold (Table 40).

Leopold II is best known for his interest in colonial expansion. His initiative found a notorious opening in the Congo, where he became the ruler of an area 80 times that of Belgium, rich in rubber and ivory. But he was also concerned with the threat to his frontiers occasioned by the German occupation of Alsace and Lorraine in 1870. It fell to his nephew, Albert, to offer an heroic resistance to the Teutonic hordes which in 1914 ignored the treaty signed in 1839. King Albert's bravery and resolution won the admiration of his subjects; he and his wife were deeply loved. Not surprisingly, he ceased to use the German blazon of Saxony; as can be seen, his younger son and grandson have differenced the simple lion of Belgium with a bordure and label of gold respectively.

Leopold III married a charming Swedish princess who was killed in a car accident the year after his father died from a fall while climbing. Battered by these losses, he had to face the second aggression of the German nation. He chose to stay in his conquered country until deported to Germany in 1944, but his second, morganatic, marriage to a commoner and the bitter circumstances of the occupation reduced his prestige. When Belgium was liberated, his brother Charles, Count of Flanders, acted as regent until 1950 when a plebiscite invited Leopold to return; the latter, however, deemed it prudent to abdicate in 1951 in favour of his son, Baudouin. The young King had to face contentious problems, including linguistic discords between French and Flemish speakers and the loss into anarchy of the Congo (which had been annexed to Belgium in 1908). He and his brother have both sought their wives from the Mediterranean nobility, Baudouin from Spain and Albert from southern Italy. The ancestry of the King, who is so far childless, shows a wide spread from Catholic Portugal to the northern forebears of his mother, who was brought up a Lutheran.

THE HOUSE OF SAXE-COBURG

The ability and success of Leopold I and the illustrious marriage of his nephew Albert, the Prince Consort, constituted a good advertisement for the little dynasty of Saxe-Coburg (Table 42). Another nephew of Leopold of Belgium had made a distinguished alliance when he married Mary II, already Queen Regent of Portugal. Their descendants ruled in Portugal until the country became a republic in 1910 (Table 119). Meanwhile in 1878 an independent Bulgaria (Chapter 38) was set up by the Treaty of Berlin.

The first prince allotted to the new state was Alexander of Battenberg, a scion of the other great expanding family of this era. Alexander was deposed and exiled by a revolt in 1886; in his place the Bulgars chose Ferdinand of Saxe-Coburg, who reigned until 1918, promoting himself to King in 1908 but backing the wrong side in 1914. His grandson Simeon II was dethroned by the Communists in 1946 (Table 150). Thus at the accession of Edward VII of Great Britain in 1901, no less than four European realms were ruled by direct male descendants of Duke Francis of Saxe-Coburg-Saalfeld, a circumstance which would most certainly have astonished that rather obscure Saxon princeling.

Chapter 10

SPAIN: MEDIEVAL

The Iberian peninsula is one of the best defined geographical entities in Europe. The land mass, roughly rectangular, is bounded by sea on three sides: the fourth faces the Bay of Biscay and the formidable barrier of the Pyrenees. Yet the whole area has but seldom been united; nor have the Pyrenees always furnished the frontier which they seem so clearly to offer. Many races have occupied the peninsula and mixed their blood with the Celtic inhabitants who were conquered by Rome: Visigoths and Vandals have entered from the north, Arabs and Berbers from the south. In the seventh century AD almost the whole was occupied by a great wave of Islamic invaders, some of whom passed on to attack Gaul. Only in the bleak northwest and among the foothills of the Pyrenees did Christian societies survive. Charlemagne extended his dominions over the mountains to include Navarre at their western end and the Spanish March, down to Barcelona, at the east.

Meanwhile the whole of central and southern Spain constituted the prosperous and cultured Emirate of Cordova, ruled by the powerful Ommayad dynasty with every manifestation of civilized life. Christians were tolerated, the arts flourished and technical advances (such as the use of paper instead of animal skins) were fostered. At the beginning of the eleventh century, after the death in 1002 of the famous Almanzor, there was a sudden change. The political potency of Cordova collapsed and a period of civil war resulted. A great opportunity developed for the Christian kinglets who only a generation before were penned against the harsh Pyrenees and the chill Atlantic. At this epoch, the principal Christian states were, from west to east, Leon occupying the northwest corner and including the national shrine of St James at Santiago de Compostela, Castile centred round Burgos, Navarre

bestriding the Biscay end of the Pyrenees, Aragon, still small and crouched under the south flank of the mountains, and Barcelona, controlling the Mediterranean seaboard from that city north to Perpignan.

The epic of the reconquest, which dominates medieval Spain, may begin with Sancho III (1000–35), King of Navarre (Tables 43, 44 and 45), who conquered both Leon and Castile. A chance of Christian unity was forfeited when his realm was divided at his death. Garcias, his eldest son, took Navarre, Ferdinand received Castile, to which he soon added Leon on the death of his brother-in-law; Ramiro, an illegitimate brother, became the first King of Aragon. It was Ferdinand (Table 45) who launched the attack on the Moors; although he did defeat and kill his elder brother in 1054, his gaze was fixed to the south. The frontier of Castile was carried further inland, and most of the warring Moorish emirs paid tribute to him. Less sensational progress was made by Aragon and by the Count of Barcelona. It was, however, already becoming apparent that Navarre, dynastically the parent kingdom, was likely to lose in wealth and prestige by having almost no frontier with Islam and therefore less possibility of expansion.

Unhappily Ferdinand divided his kingdom between three sons; there was internecine warfare between them and their cousin Sancho IV of Navarre. In these futile struggles El Cid (Ruy Diaz de Bivar), the great Spanish hero of legend, made his name. In more sober history he seems also to have fought for the Moors or anyone who would pay him, ending up as an independent princeling in Valencia. In 1085 Alphonso VI of Castile captured the important city of Toledo, almost 300km (200 miles) south of Burgos, an indication of the scale of Castilian advance. His death was followed by a period of lamentable wars between the Christian states, including the

TABLE 43

SPAIN
General survey

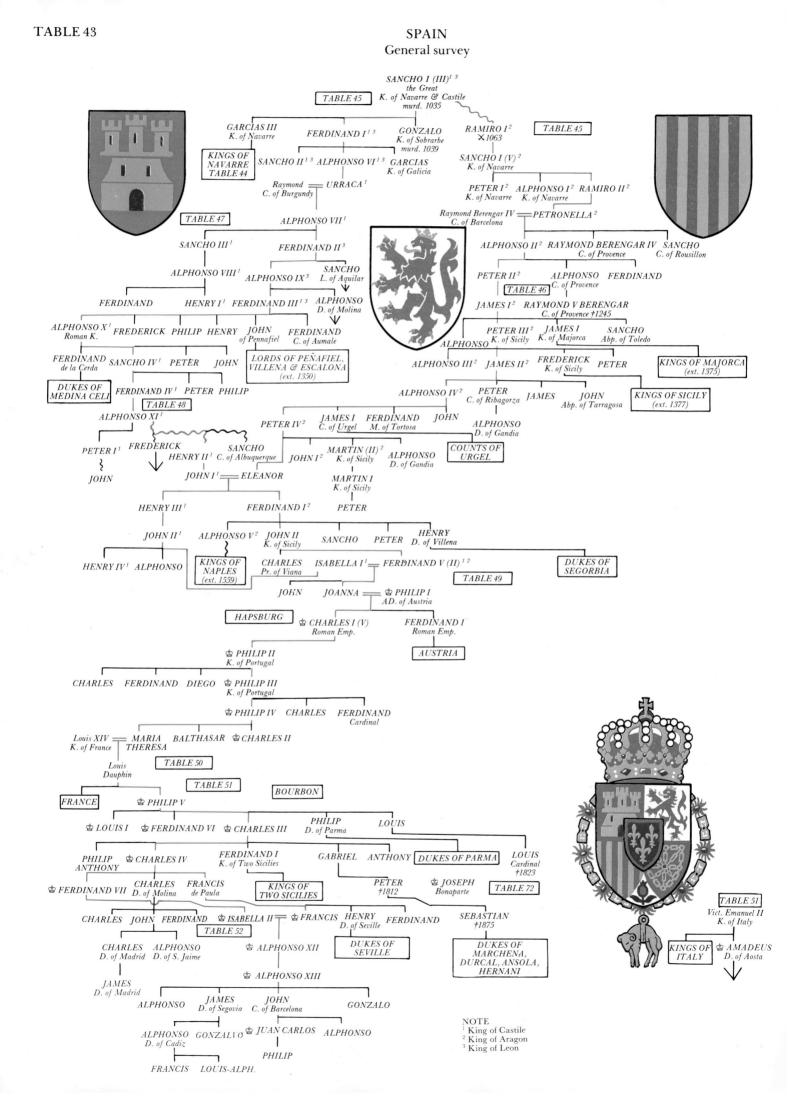

TABLE 45

SANCHO I (III)[1][3]
the Great
K. of Navarre & Castile
murd. 1035

TABLE 45

GARCIAS III
K. of Navarre

FERDINAND I[1][3]

GONZALO
K. of Sobrarbe
murd. 1039

RAMIRO I[2]
× 1063

KINGS OF
NAVARRE
TABLE 44

SANCHO II[1][3]   ALPHONSO VI[1][3]   GARCIAS
K. of Galicia

SANCHO I (V)[2]
K. of Navarre

Raymond
C. of Burgundy — URRACA[1]

PETER I[2]   ALPHONSO I[2]   RAMIRO II[2]
K. of Navarre   K. of Navarre

TABLE 47

ALPHONSO VII[1]

Raymond Berengar IV
C. of Barcelona — PETRONELLA[2]

SANCHO III[1]

FERDINAND II[3]

ALPHONSO II[2]   RAYMOND BERENGAR IV   SANCHO
C. of Provence   C. of Rousillon

ALPHONSO VIII[1]   ALPHONSO IX[3]   SANCHO
L. of Aquilar

PETER II[2]   ALPHONSO   FERDINAND
C. of Provence

FERDINAND   HENRY I[1]   FERDINAND III[1][3]   ALPHONSO
D. of Molina

JAMES I[2]   RAYMOND V BERENGAR
C. of Provence †1245

ALPHONSO X[1]   FREDERICK   PHILIP   HENRY   JOHN   FERDINAND
Roman K.   of Pennafiel   C. of Aumale

PETER III[2]   JAMES I   SANCHO
K. of Sicily   K. of Majorca   Abp. of Toledo

ALPHONSO

FERDINAND   SANCHO IV[1]   PETER   JOHN
de la Cerda

ALPHONSO III[2]   JAMES II[2]   FREDERICK   PETER
K. of Sicily

KINGS OF MAJORCA
(ext. 1375)

DUKES OF
MEDINA CELI

FERDINAND IV[1]   PETER   PHILIP

LORDS OF PEÑAFIEL,
VILLENA & ESCALONA
(ext. 1350)

ALPHONSO IV[2]   PETER   JAMES   JOHN
C. of Ribagorza   Abp. of Tarragosa

KINGS OF SICILY
(ext. 1377)

TABLE 48

ALPHONSO XI[1]

PETER IV[2]   JAMES I   FERDINAND   JOHN
C. of Urgel   M. of Tortosa

ALPHONSO
D. of Gandia

PETER I[1]   FREDERICK   HENRY II[1]   SANCHO
C. of Albuquerque

JOHN I[2]   MARTIN (II)[2]   ALPHONSO
K. of Sicily   D. of Gandia

COUNTS OF
URGEL

JOHN   JOHN I[1] — ELEANOR   MARTIN I
K. of Sicily

HENRY III[1]   FERDINAND I[2]   PETER

JOHN II[1]   ALPHONSO V[2]   JOHN II   SANCHO   PETER   HENRY
K. of Sicily   D. of Villena

HENRY IV[1]   ALPHONSO   KINGS OF
NAPLES
(ext. 1559)

CHARLES   ISABELLA I[1] — FERDINAND V (II)[1][2]
Pr. of Viana

DUKES OF
SEGORBIA

TABLE 49

JOHN   JOANNA — PHILIP I
AD. of Austria

HAPSBURG   CHARLES I (V)
Roman Emp.

FERDINAND I
Roman Emp.

AUSTRIA

PHILIP II
K. of Portugal

CHARLES   FERDINAND   DIEGO   PHILIP III
K. of Portugal

PHILIP IV   CHARLES   FERDINAND
Cardinal

Louis XIV — MARIA   BALTHASAR   CHARLES II
K. of France   THERESA

Louis
Dauphin   TABLE 50

TABLE 51

FRANCE   PHILIP V   BOURBON

LOUIS I   FERDINAND VI   CHARLES III   PHILIP   LOUIS
D. of Parma

PHILIP   CHARLES IV   FERDINAND I   GABRIEL   ANTHONY   DUKES OF PARMA   LOUIS
ANTHONY   K. of Two Sicilies   Cardinal
†1823

FERDINAND VII   CHARLES   FRANCIS   KINGS OF   PETER   JOSEPH   TABLE 72
D. of Molina   de Paula   TWO SICILIES   †1812   Bonaparte

CHARLES   JOHN   FERDINAND   ISABELLA II — FRANCIS   HENRY   FERDINAND   SEBASTIAN
D. of Seville   †1875

TABLE 52   DUKES OF   DUKES OF
SEVILLE   MARCHENA,
DURCAL, ANSOLA,
HERNANI

CHARLES   ALPHONSO   ALPHONSO XII
D. of Madrid   D. of S. Jaime

JAMES   ALPHONSO XIII
D. of Madrid

ALPHONSO   JAMES   JOHN   GONZALO
D. of Segovia   C. of Barcelona

ALPHONSO   GONZALVO   JUAN CARLOS   ALPHONSO
D. of Cadiz

PHILIP

FRANCIS   LOUIS-ALPH.

TABLE 51
Vict. Emanuel II
K. of Italy

KINGS OF   AMADEUS
ITALY   D. of Aosta

NOTE
[1] King of Castile
[2] King of Aragon
[3] King of Leon

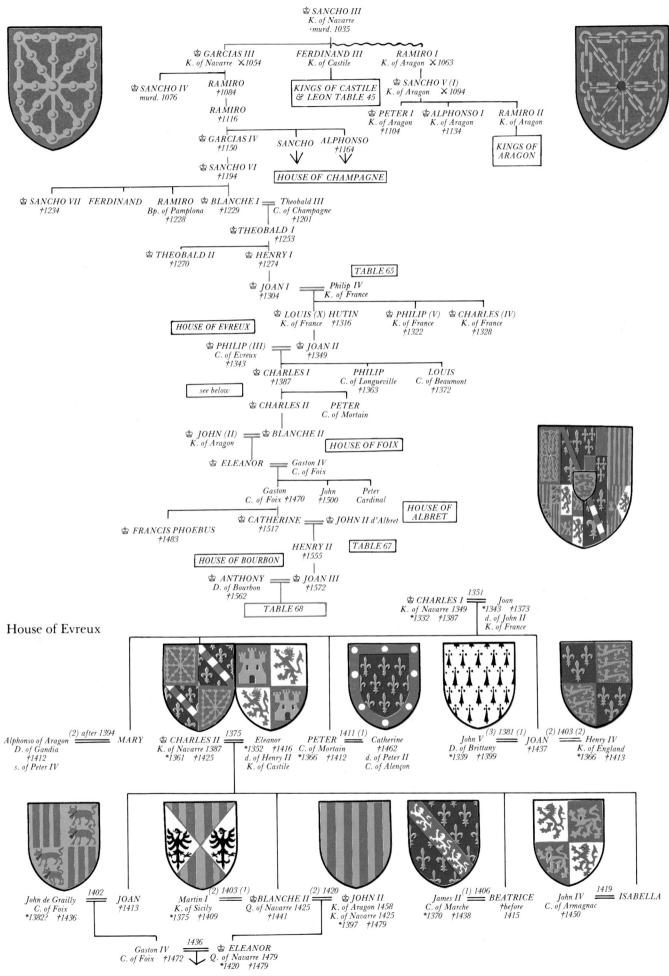

☖ SANCHO III
K. of Navarre
·murd. 1035

☖ GARCIAS III
K. of Navarre ✕1054

FERDINAND III
K. of Castile

RAMIRO I
K. of Aragon ✕1063

☖ SANCHO IV
murd. 1076

RAMIRO
†1084

KINGS OF CASTILE
& LEON TABLE 45

☖ SANCHO V (I)
K. of Aragon ✕1094

RAMIRO
†1116

PETER I
K. of Aragon
†1104

ALPHONSO I
K. of Aragon
†1134

RAMIRO II
K. of Aragon

☖ GARCIAS IV
†1150

SANCHO

ALPHONSO
†1164

KINGS OF
ARAGON

☖ SANCHO VI
†1194

HOUSE OF CHAMPAGNE

☖ SANCHO VII
†1234

FERDINAND

RAMIRO
Bp. of Pamplona
†1228

☖ BLANCHE I
†1229

Theobald III
C. of Champagne
†1201

☖ THEOBALD I
†1253

☖ THEOBALD II
†1270

☖ HENRY I
†1274

TABLE 65

☖ JOAN I
†1304

Philip IV
K. of France

☖ LOUIS (X) HUTIN
K. of France †1316

☖ PHILIP (V)
K. of France
†1322

☖ CHARLES (IV)
K. of France
†1328

HOUSE OF EVREUX

☖ PHILIP (III)
C. of Evreux
†1343

☖ JOAN II
†1349

☖ CHARLES I
†1387

PHILIP
C. of Longueville
†1363

LOUIS
C. of Beaumont
†1372

see below

☖ CHARLES II

PETER
C. of Mortain

☖ JOHN (II)
K. of Aragon

☖ BLANCHE II

HOUSE OF FOIX

☖ ELEANOR

Gaston IV
C. of Foix

Gaston
C. of Foix †1470

John
†1500

Peter
Cardinal

HOUSE OF
ALBRET

☖ FRANCIS PHOEBUS
†1483

☖ CATHERINE
†1517

☖ JOHN II d'Albret

HENRY II
†1555

TABLE 67

HOUSE OF BOURBON

☖ ANTHONY
D. of Bourbon
†1562

☖ JOAN III
†1572

TABLE 68

☖ CHARLES I
K. of Navarre 1349
*1332 †1387

1351
Joan
*1343 †1373
d. of John II
K. of France

House of Evreux

Alphonso of Aragon
D. of Gandia
†1412
s. of Peter IV

(2) after 1394
MARY

☖ CHARLES II
K. of Navarre 1387
*1361 †1425

1375
Eleanor
*1352 †1416
d. of Henry II
K. of Castile

PETER
C. of Mortain
*1366 †1412

1411 (1)
Catherine
†1462
d. of Peter II
C. of Alençon

John V
D. of Brittany
*1339 †1399

(3) 1381 (1)
JOAN
†1437

(2) 1403 (2)
Henry IV
K. of England
*1366 †1413

John de Grailly
C. of Foix
*1382? †1436

1402
JOAN
†1413

Martin I
K. of Sicily
*1375 †1409

(2) 1403 (1)
☖ BLANCHE II
Q. of Navarre 1425
†1441

(2) 1420
☖ JOHN II
K. of Aragon 1458
K. of Navarre 1425
*1397 †1479

James II
C. of Marche
*1370 †1438

(1) 1406
BEATRICE
†before
1415

John IV
C. of Armagnac
†1450

1419
ISABELLA

Gaston IV
C. of Foix †1472

1436
☖ ELEANOR
Q. of Navarre 1479
*1420 †1479

new country of Portugal (Chapter 31) established by the husband of his illegitimate daughter, Theresa. Matters could have gone worse for Christendom if the revival of Moorish military might under the Berber dynasty of the Almoravides had not turned out to be so short-lived.

The attempt to unite northern Spain by the marriage of Urraca of Castile with Alphonso I of Aragon foundered on their incompatibility and the union was annulled on grounds of consanguinity. However, Alphonso enlarged Aragon by capturing Saragossa, which became his capital, and by severely defeating the Moors in 1120. He was abetted by the Count of Barcelona, who had also acquired by marriage the distant county of Provence.

Alphonso I of Aragon was childless and toyed with

King Alphonso VII of Castile and Leon (1105–57) rides to his coronation (1126) with shield and banner of those arms. 14th-century MS.

the idea of bequeathing his realm to the Orders of the Temple and of St John. This concept did not commend itself to the nobility and they prevailed upon his younger brother, Ramiro II, to leave the monastery to which he had retired and to take a wife. This he dutifully did and, having engendered a daughter, Petronella, returned to his celibate cell. Her marriage to Raymond Berengar IV of Barcelona created an imposing power on the east coast of Spain. It was at this point that Navarre (which had been united with Aragon since 1076) broke away and chose Garcias IV (Table 44) as king.

Alphonso VII of Castile was a dominant king, who called himself emperor and led his forces far into the south, actually capturing Cordova but leaving the Muslim ruler as his vassal. At his death Castile and Leon were divided again between his two sons, and remained separate for three generations. In the second half of the twelfth century there was another Moorish revival under a second Berber dynasty from Africa, the Almohades. Alphonso VIII of Castile (Table 47), after a turbulent minority, had to face this attack and was beaten at Alarcos (1198); Toledo was besieged and with sorry particularism Leon and Navarre both invaded Castile in her hour of trouble. Before the end of his long reign the King had re-established his authority and married his talented daughter Berengaria to the unattractive King of Leon, Alphonso the Slobberer. In 1212 he led southwards a great host and inflicted a decisive defeat on the Almohades at Las Navas de Tolosa, a campaign which was proclaimed a crusade by Pope Innocent III. Considerable assistance was given by the three military Orders which combined the profession of arms (generally as cavalry) with the vows of a monk. That of Calatrava was founded in 1164, and quickly followed by those of Alcantara and Santiago (St James).

The coinage and seals of the Spanish kings give evidence of the development of their heraldry. The lion of Leon appears on the money of Alphonso VII, and the castle of Castile – both are obviously a play on words – on the money and seal of Alphonso VIII (Table 47). Ferdinand III finally united the two Kingdoms in 1230 and his great seal shows the arms of Castile and Leon quartered on his shield and separately on the trappings of his horse. This is probably the first example of 'quartering' known to heraldry. In Aragon the distinctive coat of four vertical red stripes on gold is to be seen on the seal of Alphonso II (Table 45). The earliest shields of the rulers of Navarre (Table 44) show an eagle, but one seal of Sancho VII exhibits an escarbuncle, that is a series of rays outwards from a central boss. Not till the seal of Theobald (1234–53) does the full pattern of escarbuncle and bordure of chains seem to appear.

The suggestion that the final coat-of-arms (Table 44: top right) is a play upon the words *una vara* (a chain) seems strained.

CASTILE

After the great victory of Las Navas, the Christian Powers were poised for further advance. The amalgamation of Castile and Leon under Ferdinand III (1230) created a power in the west to match that of Aragon in the east. At the same moment the throne of Navarre (Table 44) was inherited by the Counts of Champagne, whose interests lay more in France than in Spain. Alphonso II of Aragon (Table 45) had defined his complete independence from Castile; indeed he and Alphonso VIII had agreed in 1179 on their respective spheres of expansion. To Aragon fell Valencia and the Balearic Islands, but their conquest lay in the future. Alphonso II had seized Provence from his kinswoman there and bestowed it upon his second son. Peter II of Aragon was embroiled in the Albigensian crusade and perished at Muret in 1213; not until James I did expansion begin again. Through the mid-thirteenth century St Ferdinand III of Castile (Table 47: he was canonized in 1671) and James I of Aragon (Table 46) directed a series of campaigns against the now disorganized Islamic kingdoms. Ferdinand took Cordova in 1236 and Seville in 1248; James acquired the Balearics (1229-35) and Valencia in 1238, and assisted in the conquest of Murcia (1266), which the agreement of 1179 had allotted to Castile. Only the Kingdom of Granada remained to the Moors, defended by a ring of mountains and cultivating the delicacies of architecture exemplified in the Alhambra.

Alphonso X of Castile is called the Learned; he was indeed a poet and a lawgiver, but he wasted his resources competing for the Crown of Germany (Chapter 30) and failed to control his restless nobility. Ferdinand de la Cerda, the eldest son, died in Alphonso's lifetime; his splendid vesture and armorial sword-belt have been recovered from his grave at Burgos. Medieval opinion on succession was still apt to prefer a living son to a grandson; and Sancho IV successfully claimed the throne, thus disinheriting his nephews, the younger of whom was progenitor of the Dukes of Medina Celi. Their attractive shield (Table 47) combines their French ancestry with their paternal arms. No mistake could be greater than to think of Castile as a united kingdom. Particularism was still strong among the component provinces along the Biscayan coast, where men thought of themselves as belonging to Galicia or Leon or old Castile rather than the larger state. Equally, in the newly conquered lands was a welter of mixed populations, many Jews, Mozarabic Christians, converted Moors and adherents of Islam. The rich civilization of the south had already made notable contributions to European learning. Initially, the Kings of Castile exercised wide tolerance towards their subjects, but by the end of the fourteenth century a harsher attitude was arising.

The death of Alphonso the Learned introduced a period of disturbance. Sancho IV gained the throne at the expense of his nephews: his early demise left Ferdinand IV exposed to the rivalry of the Infante John and of the de la Cerda family, from which he was saved by the skill of his mother. But Ferdinand IV, a weak ruler, in turn died young, leaving a one-year-old son (Table 48). Once he came of age Alphonso XI devoted himself with some effect to restoring order. The rebellious nobility were brought to heel, privileges granted to the towns and the royal income augmented. The threat from Granada had been increased by the Sultan of Morocco, who seized Tarifa, near Gibraltar. Alphonso XI shattered the Moors at the battle of Salado (1340), and was besieging Gibraltar itself when he died of the Black Death. By the Ordinance of Alcala (1348) he did much to put into effect the laws made by Alphonso the Learned.

His private life did not match his political success, for he neglected his Portuguese Queen in favour of Leonora (Eleanor) Guzman. The cooking vessels (*calderas*) on her shield are an essentially Spanish charge and were once a mark of nobility (*rica hombría*). His death unleashed a frantic family struggle. Peter I, the Cruel, not lightly so named, was his only lawful son; Henry of Trastamara and his twin, Frederick, Grand-Master of the Order of Santiago, were supported by many of the nobility. The dead King's mistress was swiftly despatched, probably by the dead King's widow. Other acts of savagery followed: with his own hand Peter struck down a suppliant and exiled King of Granada, and two of his half-brothers were slain at his command. French aid placed Henry II on the throne, but he was evicted by Edward, the Black Prince, of England in alliance with Peter (1367); finally Peter was killed by Henry in a personal brawl.

Peter's private life was no more rewarding than that of his father. The spread of Islamic thought, which accepted polygamy, had encouraged in Spain a form of secondary marriage called *baragania*. Peter, wed to Blanche of Bourbon for political reasons, treated her abominably, was infatuated with Mary de Padilla and espoused her in this left-handed fashion; it was the marriage of her daughter to John of Gaunt which gave him, at least in his own eyes, a claim to Castile. The arms of Padilla show the unusual feature of three frying pans. The shield of Peter's bastard, John de Castella, shows a very Spanish feature, a bend *engolada*: that is, issuing from

two animal heads. Equally Hispanic is the dice-like arrangement of the six roundels of Castro.

Heraldic insignia were of course required for the brothers of Henry II. The House of Albuquerque used the lion of Leon (which began to be crowned again under Sancho IV) in a pointed base between two castles of Castile: this can be seen (Table 48) for the wife of Ferdinand I. The cognate family of Henriques, descended from Henry II's twin, surrounded the same blazon with a bordure charged with anchors (after his grandson became Admiral of Castile), such charged borders being another Spanish usage: this can be seen for the second wife of John II of Aragon. Henry II himself had a difficult reign: invasions from Portugal, Navarre and England had to be rebuffed. His contentious nobility were partially placated with his new titles, such as duke and marquess, but the epithet of 'Generous' was a poor return for the wastage of Crown lands.

ARAGON

The fortunes of Aragon had been more engaged in the Mediterranean than within Spain. The splendid harbours of her east coast bred generations of sailors who travelled to the related ports of Provence and also overseas to Sicily. Like Castile, this kingdom lacked basic unity; Aragon was an inland and Catalonia (or Barcelona) a maritime society, while Valencia shared the ambitions of both. It might be added that the speech of Catalonia (then as now) differed considerably from that of Aragon, and that an instinct for separatism was already well-established here. James I (Table 46), in his long reign, had extended the borders of Aragon southwards; he had also married his son, Peter III, to the daughter of Manfred, King of Sicily; less wisely perhaps he had bestowed upon his younger son, James, the Balearic Islands and his French fiefs of Rousillon and Montpellier. This imprudent disposition was not liquidated until 1344, by which date the ruthless Peter IV of Aragon had dispossessed his island cousins.

After the death of the Emperor Frederick II, his bastard Manfred had established himself as ruler of Sicily. Against him was embodied the implacable hostility of the Papacy, which conferred the Crown of Sicily on Charles of Anjou, the younger brother of St Louis IX of France and also the husband of the heiress of Provence. Charles' government was harsh, and at Eastertide 1282 the revolt broke out known as the Sicilian Vespers. Peter III of Aragon accepted the challenge and became King of Sicily; the south Italian mainland remained in the grasp of Charles of Anjou and his heirs. One decisive battle, at sea off Naples, was won in 1284 by the Catalan fleet under a Sicilian admiral. At his death, Peter bequeathed Aragon to his eldest son and Sicily to his second; the early death of Alphonso III necessitated some re-arrangement. James gave up Sicily, after reaching an agreement with the Papacy, and reigned in Aragon. The third brother became Frederick II of Sicily. In 1299 Frederick II won a great victory over the forces of Naples, and secured the title of King of Trinacria; he then married the daughter of Charles II of Anjou, King of Naples. These struggles had very greatly reduced the prosperity of his island kingdom. The settlement left unemployed the highly competent Catalan mercenaries who had fought for Frederick: moving eastwards by a bizarre set of circumstances, they seized and controlled the Duchy of Athens.

The branch of Aragon in Majorca differenced the family coat with a blue bend (Table 46). Frederick II of Sicily divided his coat saltire-wise with the black eagle of Sicily; a similar arrangement was adopted by James, Count of Urgel, with the black and gold chequers of that lordship. On the whole the administration of Aragon was more orderly than that of Castile. In both states an assembly grew up which was known as the 'Cortes'. In Aragon this body was composed of nobles, clerics and townsmen; they normally met separately for Aragon, Catalonia and Valencia, thus emphasizing the intense localism of Spain.

Peter IV was a tough monarch who added Majorca to his Kingdom and worked powerfully to assert his authority in his fourfold realm. His vigorous revenge won him the nickname of 'Peter of the Poniard', though he was more generally known as Peter the Ceremonious. He even secured the homage of the distant Catalan Duchy in Athens (1381). His two sons (John and Martin) reigned in turn after him; but at the end of his life Martin I succeeded his own son, another Martin, as King of Sicily. The death of Martin I, now childless, in 1410 raised a formidable succession problem, for the male line of Aragon had become extinct. It is to the credit of the Aragonese Cortes that the issue was peaceably solved in favour of Ferdinand (younger son of John I of Castile and his wife, Eleanor of Aragon) who inherited both Aragon and Sicily.

CASTILE AND ARAGON

When the illegitimate Henry II of Castile, who had attained the throne by stabbing his half-brother, Peter the Cruel, died in 1379, he had made his position secure. Castilian fleets had scoured the English Channel; her rivals at home had been disciplined. Unluckily both the next two kings, John I and Henry III (Table 48), died young after relatively brief reigns. John I attempted to claim the Crown of Portugal but sustained a crushing defeat in 1385. Under Henry III hostility to the Jews, accompanied by wanton massacres, began to appear. John II proved to be a feeble creature, dominated by his friend, Alphonso de Lara, Grand-Master of the Order of Santiago. His son, Henry IV, the Impotent, was if anything worse: it was widely rumoured that his daughter Joanna was not his child. In 1465 his half-brother Alphonso was briefly put forward as king; Castile had reached a low ebb in her fortunes when Henry IV died in 1474, leaving his sister Isabella as one possible recognized heiress and his daughter as another.

As has been seen, Ferdinand of Castile became King of Aragon and Sicily in 1412; he was scarcely established when he died. Alphonso V, his eldest son, was a highly successful king. It is true that he spent little time in his native land, but he married his younger brother, John, to the heiress of Navarre. Alphonso had been adopted as her heir by the lecherous (though childless) Joanna, Queen of Naples, and from 1435 he devoted his energies to establishing himself on the Italian mainland and reuniting the Two Sicilies. He was well-placed, for his tastes and patronage inclined him to the Renaissance and he was admirably suited to an Italian court. At his death (1458), he left Naples to his illegitimate son Ferdinand (Ferrante).

John II, brother of Alphonso V, had ruled Navarre in right of his wife since 1425 and had acted as regent in Aragon while Alphonso was busy in Naples; he had effectually disinherited his own son, the Prince of Viana, after the death of Blanche of Navarre. The mysterious death of Prince Charles brought forth a formidable Catalan revolt. John II's fortunes wavered a while but ultimately triumphed, for in 1469 he engineered the all-important marriage between Ferdinand, son of his second marriage and heir of Aragon, and Isabella, half-sister and heiress presumptive of Henry IV of Castile. The nobles of Castile, fearful of the enhanced strength of the monarchy, opposed the match, which actually took place in sordid and furtive circumstances in a private house in Valladolid. When Henry IV died in 1474, civil strife broke out forthwith in the best Castilian tradition. Portugal supported the claim of 'La Beltraneja' – as Joanna was nicknamed from her putative father – and might, under firmer leadership, have obtained part or all of Castile just as the New World was opened up; in 1479, however, Ferdinand and Isabella were accepted as the rulers of Aragon and Castile. Spain was united at last (Table 48).

NAVARRE

To write thus may seem to ignore the fate of Navarre. The death of Sancho VII in 1234 allowed the Kingdom to pass to Theobald of Champagne (Table 44). His two sons were more concerned with their French county than with the little Spanish Kingdom which straddled the Pyrenees. His granddaughter, Joan, married Philip IV of France. Although her eldest son, Louis X, had only a daughter who should have succeeded to Navarre, that province was retained by Philip V and Charles IV. On the death of the last-named, Navarre was relinquished to Joan II and her husband, the Count of Evreux, although Champagne was held by the French Crown. It may be noted that Joan and her issue had, by accepted standards, a better claim to the French Crown than Edward III of England. Such a claim was understood by Charles I, the Bad, one of the more intransigent subjects of John II of France. Able, eloquent and unscrupulous, Charles even began to negotiate with Edward III for a partition of France, However his misdeeds and his treachery belong more to the history of France than of Spain. By contrast, his son Charles II had a long and peaceful reign lacking alike in pretensions and incident.

At his death Navarre passed to his daughter Blanche, the wife of John II of Aragon; at her death it passed to her son, Charles of Viana (Table 48), but that slightly ineffectual Prince was dispossessed by his more vigorous father. John II arranged with the King of France that he should be followed in Navarre by his daughter Eleanor and Gaston IV of Foix (Table 44). In the event, Eleanor was succeeded by her grandson, Francis Phoebus, Count of Foix. His sister Catherine married John d'Albret, from whom Ferdinand of Aragon easily seized Spanish Navarre in 1512. Their granddaughter Joan III married Anthony of Bourbon and was mother of Henry IV who united French Navarre with the Crown of France. The arms of Anthony, King of Navarre (Table 44), show eight quarterings, namely: *1* Navarre, *2* Bourbon, *3* Albret, *4* Aragon, *5* Foix and Bearn, *6* Armagnac and Rodez, *7* Evreux and *8* Bigorre.

THE CATHOLIC KINGS

The long reigns of Ferdinand II of Aragon and his wife, Isabella the Catholic of Castile (Table 48), mark more than the union of the two great, crusading, Spanish Kingdoms. Indeed, for all that union, strong local feeling and patriotism, and separate languages like Catalan and Gallegan (the speech of Galicia) continued to flourish, and do so today. But the reigns of the two sovereigns mark a turning point in the history of Spain and her emergence as a world power. By 1479 both were secure upon their thrones. Three years later they embarked upon the capture of Granada, the last Moorish Kingdom. The campaign was deliberate, and Granada itself did not fall until 1492. Thus ended the long sojourn of Islam in Iberia; it is permissible to regret the extinction of this civilized little society with its tolerance, learning and airy architecture. At first the inhabitants were

TABLE 47

CASTILE
Union with Leon until the beginning of the fourteenth century

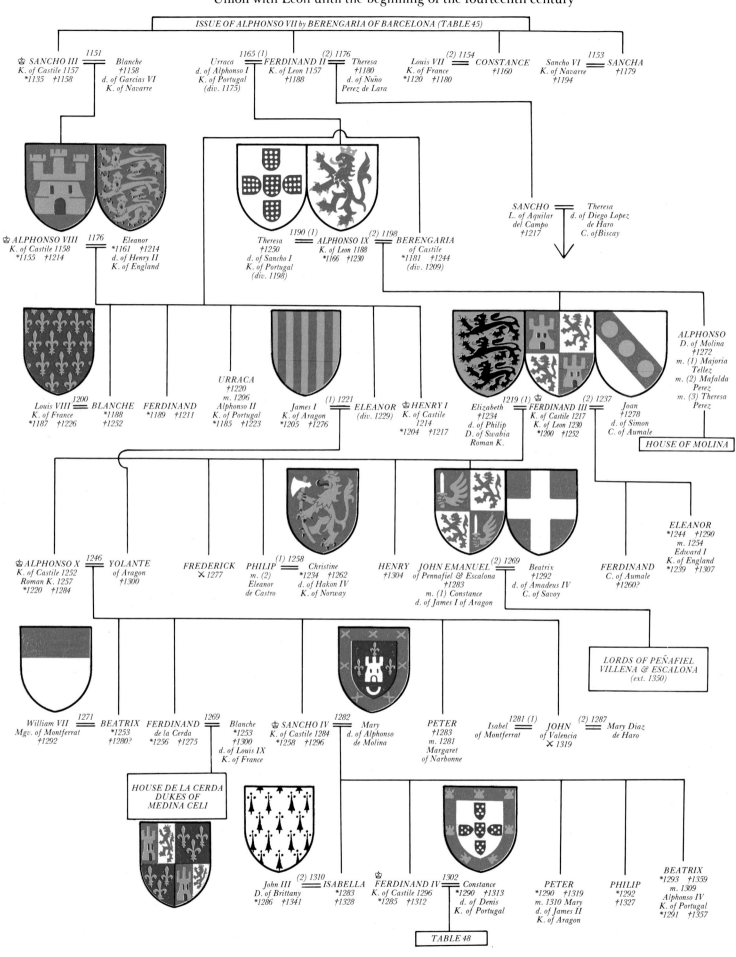

ISSUE OF ALPHONSO VII by BERENGARIA OF BARCELONA (TABLE 45)

♔ SANCHO III
K. of Castile 1157
*1135 †1158
— 1151 —
Blanche
†1158
d. of Garcias VI
K. of Navarre

Urraca
d. of Alphonso I
K. of Portugal
(div. 1175)
— 1165 (1) —
FERDINAND II
K. of Leon 1157
†1188
— (2) 1176 —
Theresa
†1180
d. of Nuño
Perez de Lara

Louis VII
K. of France
*1120 †1180
— (2) 1154 —
CONSTANCE
†1160

Sancho VI
K. of Navarre
†1194
— 1153 —
SANCHA
†1179

♔ ALPHONSO VIII
K. of Castile 1158
*1155 †1214
— 1176 —
Eleanor
*1161 †1214
d. of Henry II
K. of England

Theresa
†1250
d. of Sancho I
K. of Portugal
(div. 1198)
— 1190 (1) —
ALPHONSO IX
K. of Leon 1188
*1166 †1230
— (2) 1198 —
BERENGARIA
of Castile
*1181 †1244
(div. 1209)

SANCHO
L. of Aquilar
del Campo
†1217
═══
Theresa
d. of Diego Lopez
de Haro
C. of Biscay

ALPHONSO
D. of Molina
†1272
m. (1) Majoria
Tellez
m. (2) Mafalda
Perez
m. (3) Theresa
Perez

Louis VIII
K. of France
*1187 †1226
— 1200 —
BLANCHE
*1188
†1252

FERDINAND
*1189 †1211

URRACA
†1220
m. 1206
Alphonso II
K. of Portugal
*1185 †1223

James I
K. of Aragon
*1205 †1276
— (1) 1221 —
ELEANOR
(div. 1229)

♔ HENRY I
K. of Castile
1214
*1204 †1217

Elizabeth
†1234
d. of Philip
D. of Swabia
Roman K.
— 1219 (1) —
FERDINAND III
K. of Castile 1217
K. of Leon 1230
*1200 †1252
— (2) 1237 —
Joan
†1278
d. of Simon
C. of Aumale

HOUSE OF MOLINA

ELEANOR
*1244 †1290
m. 1254
Edward I
K. of England
*1239 †1307

♔ ALPHONSO X
K. of Castile 1252
Roman K. 1257
*1220 †1284
— 1246 —
YOLANTE
of Aragon
†1300

FREDERICK
✕ 1277

PHILIP
m. (2)
Eleanor
de Castro
— (1) 1258 —
Christine
*1234 †1262
d. of Hakon IV
K. of Norway

HENRY
†1304

JOHN EMANUEL
of Pennafiel & Escalona
†1283
m. (1) Constance
d. of James I of Aragon
— (2) 1269 —
Beatrix
†1292
d. of Amadeus IV
C. of Savoy

FERDINAND
C. of Aumale
†1260?

LORDS OF PEÑAFIEL
VILLENA & ESCALONA
(ext. 1350)

William VII
Mgv. of Montferrat
†1292
— 1271 —
BEATRIX
*1253
†1280?

FERDINAND
de la Cerda
*1256 †1275
— 1269 —
Blanche
*1253
†1300
d. of Louis IX
K. of France

♔ SANCHO IV
K. of Castile 1284
*1258 †1296
— 1282 —
Mary
d. of Alphonso
de Molina

PETER
†1283
m. 1281
Margaret
of Narbonne

Isabel
of Montferrat
— 1281 (1) —
JOHN
of Valencia
✕ 1319
— (2) 1287 —
Mary Diaz
de Haro

HOUSE DE LA CERDA
DUKES OF
MEDINA CELI

John III
D. of Brittany
*1286 †1341
— (2) 1310 —
ISABELLA
*1283
†1328

♔ FERDINAND IV
K. of Castile 1296
*1285 †1312
— 1302 —
Constance
*1290 †1313
d. of Denis
K. of Portugal

PETER
*1290 †1319
m. 1310 Mary
d. of James II
K. of Aragon

PHILIP
*1292
†1327

BEATRIX
*1293 †1359
m. 1309
Alphonso IV
K. of Portugal
*1291 †1357

TABLE 48

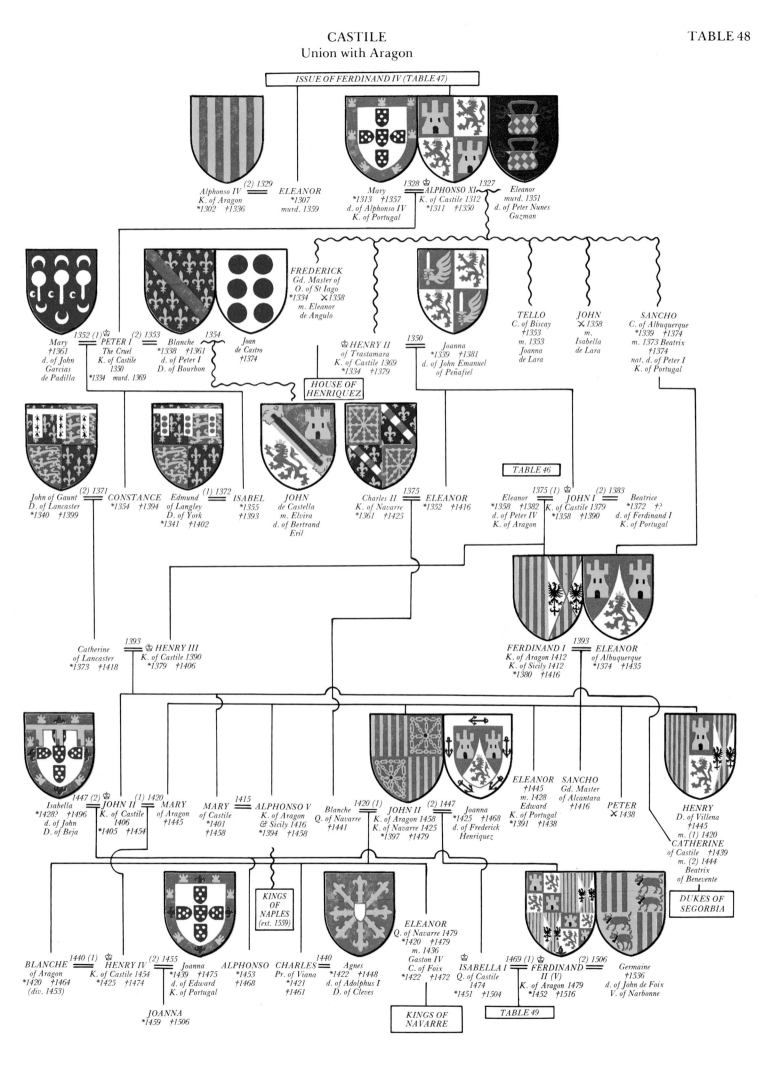

ISSUE OF FERDINAND IV (TABLE 47)

Alphonso IV (2) 1329 *ELEANOR*
K. of Aragon *1307
*1302 †1336 murd. 1359

Mary 1328 ⚜ *ALPHONSO XI* 1327 *Eleanor*
*1313 †1357 K. of Castile 1312 murd. 1351
d. of Alphonso IV *1311 †1350 d. of Peter Nunes
K. of Portugal Guzman

Mary 1352 (1) ⚜ *PETER I* (2) 1353 *Blanche* 1354 *Joan* *FREDERICK* *HENRY II* 1350 *Joanna* *TELLO* *JOHN* *SANCHO*
†1361 *PETER I* *Blanche* *de Castro* Gd. Master of of Trastamara *1339 †1381 C. of Biscay ✕ 1358 C. of Albuquerque
d. of John The Cruel *1338 †1361 †1374 O. of St Iago K. of Castile 1369 d. of John Emanuel †1353 m. *1339 †1374
Garcias K. of Castile d. of Peter I *1334 ✕ 1358 *1334 †1379 of Peñafiel m. 1353 Isabella m. 1373 Beatrix
de Padilla 1350 D. of Bourbon m. Eleanor Joanna de Lara nat. d. of Peter I
*1334 murd. 1369 de Angulo de Lara K. of Portugal

HOUSE OF
HENRIQUEZ

John of Gaunt (2) 1371 *CONSTANCE* *Edmund* (1) 1372 *ISABEL* *JOHN* *Charles II* 1375 *ELEANOR* TABLE 46 *Eleanor* 1375 (1) ⚜ *JOHN I* (2) 1383 *Beatrice*
D. of Lancaster *1354 †1394 of Langley *1355 de Castella K. of Navarre *1352 †1416 *1358 †1382 K. of Castile 1379 *1372 †?
*1340 †1399 D. of York †1393 m. Elvira *1361 †1425 d. of Peter IV *1358 †1390 d. of Ferdinand I
*1341 †1402 d. of Bertrand K. of Aragon K. of Portugal
Eril

Catherine 1393 ⚜ *HENRY III* *FERDINAND I* 1393 *ELEANOR*
of Lancaster K. of Castile 1390 K. of Aragon 1412 of Albuquerque
*1373 †1418 *1379 †1406 K. of Sicily 1412 *1374 †1435
*1380 †1416

Isabella 1447 (2) ⚜ *JOHN II* (1) 1420 *MARY* *MARY* 1415 *ALPHONSO V* *Blanche* 1420 (1) *JOHN II* (2) 1447 *Joanna* *ELEANOR* *SANCHO* *PETER* *HENRY*
*1428? †1496 K. of Castile of Aragon of Castile K. of Aragon Q. of Navarre K. of Aragon 1458 *1425 †1468 †1445 Gd. Master ✕ 1438 D. of Villena
d. of John 1406 †1445 *1401 & Sicily 1416 †1441 K. of Navarre 1425 d. of Frederick m. 1428 of Alcantara †1445
D. of Beja *1405 †1454 †1458 *1394 †1458 *1397 †1479 Henriquez Edward †1416 m. (1) 1420
K. of Portugal CATHERINE
KINGS *1391 †1438 of Castile †1439
OF m. (2) 1444
NAPLES Beatrix
(ext. 1559) of Benevente

DUKES OF
SEGORBIA

BLANCHE 1440 (1) *HENRY IV* (2) 1455 *Joanna* *ALPHONSO* *CHARLES* 1440 *Agnes* *ELEANOR* *ISABELLA I* 1469 (1) ⚜ *FERDINAND* (2) 1506 *Germaine*
of Aragon K. of Castile 1454 *1439 †1475 *1453 Pr. of Viana *1422 †1448 Q. of Navarre 1479 Q. of Castile II (V) †1536
*1420 †1464 *1425 †1474 d. of Edward †1468 *1421 d. of Adolphus I *1420 †1479 1474 K. of Aragon 1479 d. of John de Foix
(div. 1453) K. of Portugal †1461 D. of Cleves m. 1436 *1451 †1504 *1452 †1516 V. of Narbonne
Gaston IV
JOANNA C. of Foix KINGS OF TABLE 49
*1459 †1506 *1422 †1472 NAVARRE

KINGS OF
NAVARRE

treated in a liberal manner, but soon a harsher climate prevailed.

Later in that year came an event of shattering importance. After much hesitation Isabella had conferred her patronage on the Genoese mariner, Christopher Columbus: on 12 October 1492, he landed in the Bahamas. Whether or not Irish monks and Viking adventurers had already made perilous voyages to America is immaterial, the discovery – and exploitation – of the New World dates from this moment. With a renowned and dramatic gesture the Spanish Pope, Alexander VI, drew a line of demarcation down the Atlantic dividing the spheres of interest of Spain and Portugal. Columbus was able to make a valuable staging point at the Canaries, which were then being added to the Spanish dominions. The adventures of the Spanish conquerors in Mexico and Peru cannot concern us here.

There was, however, a more sombre side to the rule of the Catholic sovereigns. In 1478 the Spanish Inquisition was established. In 1492 all Jews were abruptly expelled from Spain and a decade later the same fate overtook the resident Muslims. Any gain to fanaticism was savagely offset by the loss to commerce occasioned by the persecution of these diligent and skilful communities. To the credit of Ferdinand and Isabella is the restoration of order, especially in Castile, which was the leading partner in the union. Brigandage was suppressed; the military orders, now obsolete in aim, were taken over by the Crown; alienated royal lands were resumed. Of more doubtful long term value was the encouragement of sheepfarming at the expense of agriculture.

In 1496 a marriage was finally arranged between their daughter Joanna and the young, handsome and wealthy Philip the Fair, Duke of Burgundy. At the same time her eldest sister married the King of Portugal, and a little later her ill-fated younger sister Catherine married the son of the King of England (Table 49). The death in 1497 of John, the only son of Ferdinand and Isabella, altered the picture and Charles, the eldest son of Joanna, emerged as the heir of Spain, Burgundy and the Empire. The ancestry of the Emperor Charles V (Table 53) – Charles I in Spanish history – shows that five of his great-grandparents came from the peninsula: he was more Hispanic than anything else. His coat-of-arms (Table 49) shows in the upper half Castile and Leon, Aragon and Sicily with the pomegranate of Granada: in the lower, Austria, Burgundy ancient and modern and Brabant, with Flanders and Tyrol over all.

Joanna herself, lacking the love of her husband, drifted into insanity, and the inconstant Philip died before his father in 1506. Accordingly Ferdinand II of Aragon acted as regent for his mad daughter and infant grandson. His second marriage to Germaine de Foix (Table 48) even raised the possibility that he might beget a son to inherit Aragon and undo the union. His main preoccupation, an emphatic continuation of Aragonese interests in the western Mediterranean, was with war in Italy and the ejection of the French from Naples. In these sterile campaigns the Spanish infantry began to win its great reputation under the *Gran Capitan* Gonzalvo de Cordova. In addition, Ferdinand II, as has been seen, annexed Spanish Navarre and regained Rousillon from France. He even invaded North Africa; and it has been argued that the true overseas interests of Spain lay here rather than in Italy. The multiple inheritance of Charles V ensured however that Spain would be drawn fully into the complicated politics of central Europe and the Reformation. The comparative isolation of the Iberian peninsula was now at an end.

Chapter 11

SPAIN: HAPSBURG AND BOURBON

Two reigns spanned almost all of the sixteenth century for Spain, those of Charles I and Philip II. The two were very different men. Charles V (he is better known by his notation as Emperor than as King of Spain) was resolute in the hideous toil and travel required to maintain his scattered dominions, though in consequence each realm supposed it was being neglected for others. He was the inheritor of perhaps the largest European burden since Charlemagne. A competent captain with a dislike for bloodshed, an accomplished negotiator, too much perhaps of a centralizer, crippled latterly with gout, he laboured to overcome his twin enemies of heresy and debt. In 1506 he became heir to Burgundy and the Low Countries; in 1516 King of Spain; and in 1519, after profuse expenditure on the Electors, he was chosen King of the Romans, and called himself Emperor-Elect. His actual coronation took place at Bologna in 1530; he was the last Emperor to be crowned by a pope. He was in Spain from 1522 to 1529, but was not a popular sovereign. Not without reason his Spanish subjects suspected him of disbursing their own wealth (and also the untold sums which began to come in from the New World) on greedy German princelings and a seemingly endless war with France.

The great victory of his forces at Pavia (1525) secured his hold on Naples and Milan, but did not finish the conflict. In 1527 Spanish troops brutally sacked Rome. In Germany he was involved in heavy fighting against the Protestants and won an important battle at Mühlberg in 1547. In weariness, he joined the select company of Diocletian and a few others by voluntarily resigning great power (1556). His brother Ferdinand (Chapter 19) succeeded him in Austria and the Empire; his son Philip II followed him in Spain, Italy and the Netherlands (Table 49).

Philip II was intensely industrious, but he was also suspicious, sinister and secretive. Like a mole, he wor-ried away, beset by detail, in the great palace-monastery of the Escorial, which he built north of Madrid. Disaster outweighed triumph in his reign. It is true that in 1580 he added Portugal, to which he had a claim through his mother and his first wife, to his dominions, and for sixty years one ruler was to govern the whole peninsula. But Philip II's second marriage to Mary Tudor of England was childless and frustrated: nor did it bring alliance with England. His efforts to stamp out heresy in the Low Countries led, after the bitterest strife and persecution, to the independence of the Netherlands. Later, his gigantic invasion plan for England, the Armada, came to nothing thanks to the brilliance of Drake and his colleagues, abetted by foul weather. He did, however, achieve peace with France in 1559, which he sealed by marrying a French wife, his third. Worst of all, the extravagance of the court and the misunderstanding of the economic consequences of the vast imports of gold and silver from the New World began a steady deterioration in the financial position of Spain. Rumour also accused Philip of having encompassed the deaths of his own eldest son (Charles) and his more glamorous (illegitimate) half-brother, Don John of Austria, the victor of Lepanto. The arms of Philip II show a small escutcheon of Portugal added to the blazon of his father (Table 49).

SIGLO DE ORO

The history of Spain in the next two reigns presents a curious contrast. Her political power, her influence abroad, her military repute, her general finance were all on the decline, but in the world of arts this was her golden century (*Siglo de Oro*). The names of Lope de Vega, Cervantes, creator of Don Quixote, and Calderon in Literature, or El Greco and Velazquez in painting, and the splendid achievements in architecture, lend a rare glory to the hundred years or so

TABLE 49

SPAIN
House of Hapsburg

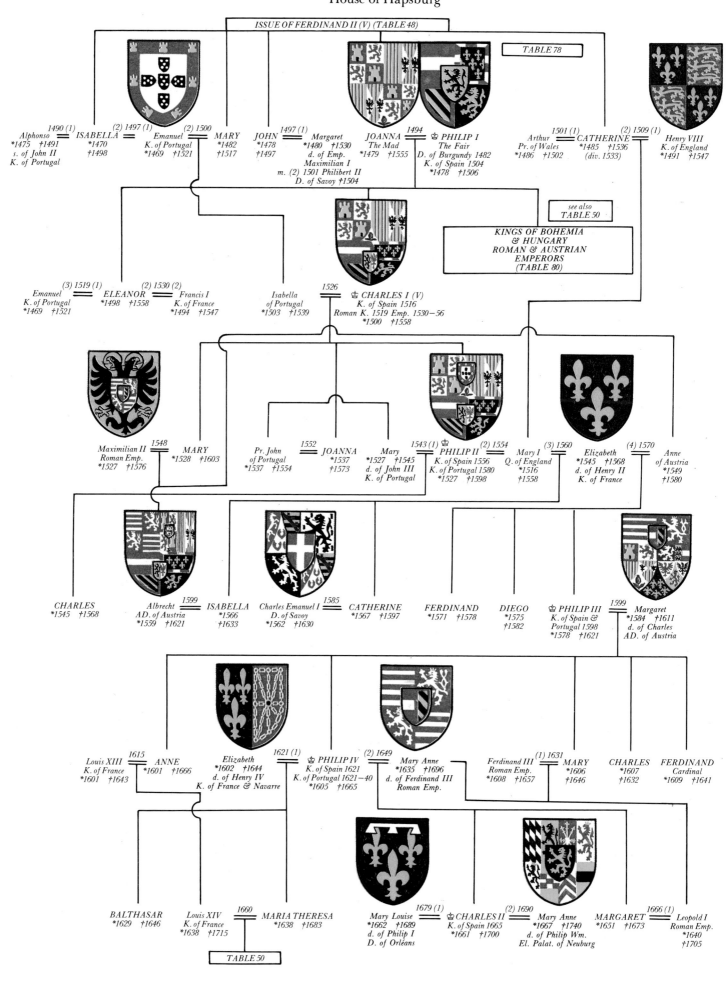

ISSUE OF FERDINAND II (V) (TABLE 48)

TABLE 78

Alphonso
*1475 †1491
s. of John II
K. of Portugal

1490 (1)

ISABELLA
*1470
†1498

(2) 1497 (1)

Emanuel
K. of Portugal
*1469 †1521

(2) 1500

MARY
*1482
†1517

JOHN
*1478
†1497

1497 (1)

Margaret
*1480 †1530
d. of Emp.
Maximilian I
m. (2) 1501 Philibert II
D. of Savoy †1504

JOANNA
The Mad
*1479 †1555

1494

♔ **PHILIP I**
The Fair
D. of Burgundy 1482
K. of Spain 1504
*1478 †1506

Arthur
Pr. of Wales
*1486 †1502

1501 (1)

CATHERINE
*1485 †1536
(div. 1533)

(2) 1509 (1)

Henry VIII
K. of England
*1491 †1547

see also TABLE 50

KINGS OF BOHEMIA
& HUNGARY
ROMAN & AUSTRIAN
EMPERORS
(TABLE 80)

Emanuel
K. of Portugal
*1469 †1521

(3) 1519 (1)

ELEANOR
*1498 †1558

(2) 1530 (2)

Francis I
K. of France
*1494 †1547

Isabella
of Portugal
*1503 †1539

1526

♔ **CHARLES I (V)**
K. of Spain 1516
Roman K. 1519 Emp. 1530−56
*1500 †1558

Maximilian II
Roman Emp.
*1527 †1576

1548

MARY
*1528 †1603

Pr. John
of Portugal
*1537 †1554

1552

JOANNA
*1537
†1573

Mary
*1527 †1545
d. of John III
K. of Portugal

1543 (1)

♔ **PHILIP II**
K. of Spain 1556
K. of Portugal 1580
*1527 †1598

(2) 1554

Mary I
Q. of England
*1516
†1558

(3) 1560

Elizabeth
*1545 †1568
d. of Henry II
K. of France

(4) 1570

Anne
of Austria
*1549
†1580

CHARLES
*1545 †1568

Albrecht
AD. of Austria
*1559 †1621

1599

ISABELLA
*1566
†1633

Charles Emanuel I
D. of Savoy
*1562 †1630

1585

CATHERINE
*1567 †1597

FERDINAND
*1571 †1578

DIEGO
*1575
†1582

♔ **PHILIP III**
K. of Spain &
Portugal 1598
*1578 †1621

1599

Margaret
*1584 †1611
d. of Charles
AD. of Austria

Louis XIII
K. of France
*1601 †1643

1615

ANNE
*1601 †1666

Elizabeth
*1602 †1644
d. of Henry IV
K. of France & Navarre

1621 (1)

♔ **PHILIP IV**
K. of Spain 1621
K. of Portugal 1621−40
*1605 †1665

(2) 1649

Mary Anne
*1635 †1696
d. of Ferdinand III
Roman Emp.

Ferdinand III
Roman Emp.
*1608 †1657

(1) 1631

MARY
*1606
†1646

CHARLES
*1607
†1632

FERDINAND
Cardinal
*1609 †1641

BALTHASAR
*1629 †1646

Louis XIV
K. of France
*1638 †1715

1660

MARIA THERESA
*1638 †1683

Mary Louise
*1662 †1689
d. of Philip I
D. of Orléans

1679 (1)

♔ **CHARLES II**
K. of Spain 1665
*1661 †1700

(2) 1690

Mary Anne
*1667 †1740
d. of Philip Wm.
El. Palat. of Neuburg

MARGARET
*1651 †1673

1666 (1)

Leopold I
Roman Emp.
*1640
†1705

TABLE 50

TABLE 50

SPAIN
War of Succession (Houses of Hapsburg and Bourbon)

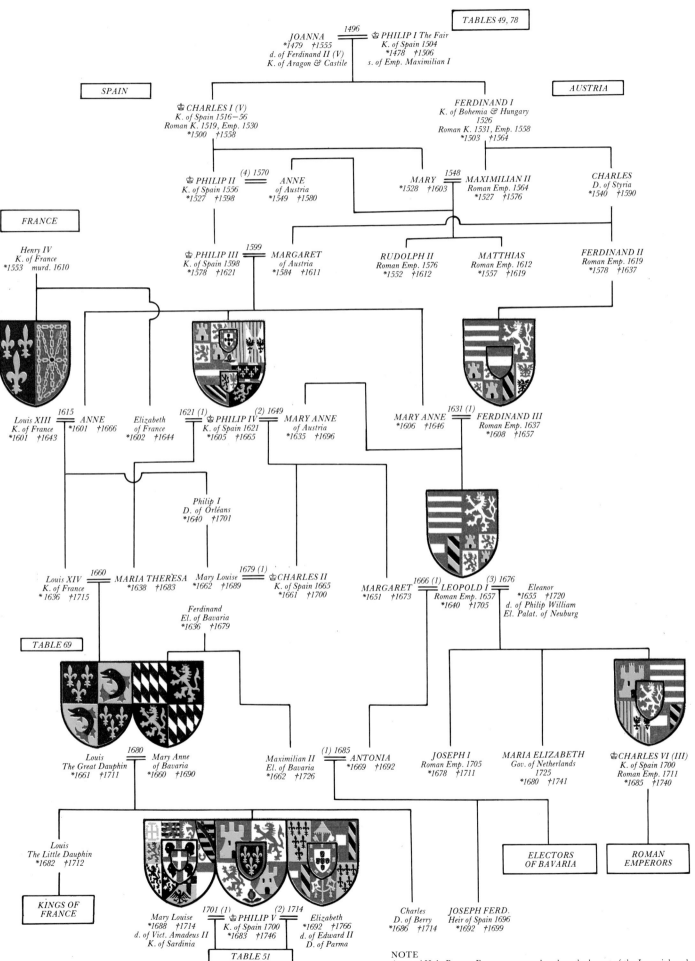

TABLES 49, 78

JOANNA
*1479 †1555
d. of Ferdinand II (V)
K. of Aragon & Castile

1496

PHILIP I The Fair
K. of Spain 1504
*1478 †1506
s. of Emp. Maximilian I

SPAIN

AUSTRIA

CHARLES I (V)
K. of Spain 1516−56
Roman K. 1519, Emp. 1530
*1500 †1558

FERDINAND I
K. of Bohemia & Hungary
1526
Roman K. 1531, Emp. 1558
*1503 †1564

PHILIP II
K. of Spain 1556
*1527 †1598

(4) 1570

ANNE
of Austria
*1549 †1580

MARY
*1528 †1603

1548

MAXIMILIAN II
Roman Emp. 1564
*1527 †1576

CHARLES
D. of Styria
*1540 †1590

FRANCE

Henry IV
K. of France
*1553 murd. 1610

PHILIP III
K. of Spain 1598
*1578 †1621

1599

MARGARET
of Austria
*1584 †1611

RUDOLPH II
Roman Emp. 1576
*1552 †1612

MATTHIAS
Roman Emp. 1612
*1557 †1619

FERDINAND II
Roman Emp. 1619
*1578 †1637

Louis XIII
K. of France
*1601 †1643

1615

ANNE
*1601 †1666

Elizabeth
of France
*1602 †1644

1621 (1)

PHILIP IV
K. of Spain 1621
*1605 †1665

(2) 1649

MARY ANNE
of Austria
*1635 †1696

MARY ANNE
*1606 †1646

1631 (1)

FERDINAND III
Roman Emp. 1637
*1608 †1657

Philip I
D. of Orléans
*1640 †1701

Louis XIV
K. of France
*1636 †1715

1660

MARIA THERESA
*1638 †1683

Mary Louise
*1662 †1689

1679 (1)

CHARLES II
K. of Spain 1665
*1661 †1700

MARGARET
*1651 †1673

1666 (1)

LEOPOLD I
Roman Emp. 1657
*1640 †1705

(3) 1676

Eleanor
*1655 †1720
d. of Philip William
El. Palat. of Neuburg

Ferdinand
El. of Bavaria
*1636 †1679

TABLE 69

Louis
The Great Dauphin
*1661 †1711

1680

Mary Anne
of Bavaria
*1660 †1690

Maximilian II
El. of Bavaria
*1662 †1726

(1) 1685

ANTONIA
*1669 †1692

JOSEPH I
Roman Emp. 1705
*1678 †1711

MARIA ELIZABETH
Gov. of Netherlands
1725
*1680 †1741

CHARLES VI (III)
K. of Spain 1700
Roman Emp. 1711
*1685 †1740

Louis
The Little Dauphin
*1682 †1712

ELECTORS
OF BAVARIA

ROMAN
EMPERORS

KINGS OF
FRANCE

Mary Louise
*1688 †1714
d. of Vict. Amadeus II
K. of Sardinia

1701 (1)

PHILIP V
K. of Spain 1700
*1683 †1746

(2) 1714

Elizabeth
*1692 †1766
d. of Edward II
D. of Parma

Charles
D. of Berry
*1686 †1714

JOSEPH FERD.
Heir of Spain 1696
*1692 †1699

TABLE 51

NOTE
Arms of Holy Roman Emperors were placed on the breast of the Imperial eagle.

before 1680. The reign of Philip III witnessed the expulsion of the Moriscos (Christianized Moors); power at this time was in the hands of the King's favourites. Philip IV allowed a free hand to his minister, the Count-Duke of Olivares. Portugal broke away in 1640, and the last years of his reign were disfigured by a series of provincial revolts. In 1659 he ceded Cerdagne and Rousillon to France.

Charles II, the last Hapsburg King of Spain, was an even more pathetic figure. Flimsy and epileptic, he was sadly inbred. Philip IV had married his Austrian niece; Philip III had wed another Austrian princess; so the now debilitated Hapsburg blood ran too profusely in the veins of Charles. He married twice but it was widely believed that fatherhood was beyond him; like vultures, the great European Powers brooded over the disposition of the corpse. For while the internal condition of Spain was distressing, her possessions still commanded envy. The wealth of the New World, the Belgian half of the Low Countries, Milan, Naples, Sicily and Sardinia were a strong lure to the contenders.

By the closing years of the seventeenth century three candidates were in the field (Table 50). Two great sovereigns were closely related to the sickly King (who was not weaned until he was four and had the use of fourteen wet-nurses). His half-sister had married her first cousin Louis XIV of France; his sister had been the wife of the Emperor Leopold I of Austria, whose mother was also a sister of Philip IV. Neither monarch dared claim the inheritance for himself; Louis XIV sponsored his grandson, Philip, Duke of Anjou, while Leopold put forward Charles, the younger son of his second marriage. In 1698 the diplomacy of William III of England engineered the First Partition Treaty, which gave the lion's share to a third candidate, Joseph Ferdinand of Bavaria, son of the Elector Maximilian and Antonia, daughter of the first marriage of the Emperor Leopold. Unluckily the Electoral Prince died in 1699 at the age of six. The ailing Charles II bequeathed all his dominions to Philip of Anjou and died in 1700: he stipulated that if the French prince did not accept the entire bequest, it should pass *en bloc* to the Archduke Charles.

THE BOURBON KINGS

Philip V became King of Spain in 1700 at the age of 17. As his ascending pedigree shows (Table 53), he had a strong strain of Hapsburg blood and a strong strain of Bourbon: the remaining quarter was divided between Savoy and Bavaria. The first 13 years of his reign were occupied with the War of the Spanish Succession. Spain did not play an active part, but at the peace she had to forfeit Gibraltar and Minorca to England and her possessions in Italy and the Low Countries to Austria. In the meantime the Archduke

Charles, who had claimed the Spanish throne in 1700, had become emperor. It may be noted in passing that Gibraltar was only in Spanish hands from 1462 to 1704 (242 years) and has already been in British possession for 277 years. The Catalans, who had supported Charles, were ruthlessly suppressed and their language banned from official use. Philip also renounced any claim to the throne of France: during the childless and delicate youth of Louis XV, this was an important proviso.

Philip V himself wearied of his throne, and in 1724 abdicated in favour of his son, Louis I (Table 51). The young King died later in the same year, and Philip resumed the throne until his own death in 1746, to be succeeded by his colourless second son, Ferdinand VI. In 1759 Charles III became king: he was born of the second marriage of Philip V to the vigorous and able Elizabeth Farnese, who became the heiress of Parma on the death of her uncle. She secured the province for Charles (Table 130) and indeed orientated the policy of Spain towards Italy with the aim of providing for her family. Charles went on to become King of Naples in 1734 and transmitted that throne to his younger son Ferdinand on inheriting Spain; Philip, younger brother of Charles III, became Duke of Parma in 1748. During the intervening years (1735–48) Parma was governed by the Hapsburgs from Vienna. The youngest brother, Louis, rose to be an archbishop and a cardinal before abandoning the church for matrimony.

Charles III was the most experienced and competent of the Bourbons; Spain became more prosperous under his rule, absolute as it was. Authority was asserted over the Church and the Jesuits were expelled (1767). Towards the end of his reign he joined France in assisting the American colonies in their successful revolt from Britain. At the peace of 1783 he recovered Minorca and Florida, though the long siege of Gibraltar was unsuccessful. His arms, in their simpler form, show Castile and Leon, with Granada in base, and over all France within a red border for Anjou (Table 51); his son and brother combined these with the blazons of their Italian dominions. The famous chivalric Order of the Golden Fleece had, of course, been founded in Burgundy, and had been maintained by the Hapsburg Kings of Spain. In 1700, at the death of Charles II, it was claimed by the Austrian Hapsburgs; in 1713 the archives were transferred to Vienna. But the Bourbon Kings of Spain also asserted their right to appoint; in 1748 agreement was reached that there should be two branches of the Order, one Austrian (Table 76) and one Spanish (Table 43).

The long, melancholy, prognathous faces of the Hapsburgs have been immortalized by Velazquez. The sorry countenances of the next two rulers and

their court were immortalized by Goya. Charles IV was of limited intelligence and dominated by his wife: complaisantly he accepted as his first minister her lover, Manuel Godoy, who was even permitted to marry an unimportant princess (herself the child of an Archbishop of Toledo). Outraged by the execution of Louis XVI, this gimcrack regime attacked France, which invaded and occupied Catalonia. Godoy negotiated a treaty with the French Republic and was rewarded with the slightly absurd title of 'Prince of the Peace'. Spain was now allied to France, in maintenance of the Bourbon tradition, and was to pay dearly for this when Napoleon came to power.

The events of 1808 read almost like the plot of a light opera. Charles IV abdicated in favour of his son Ferdinand VII at the behest of a mob, who found him wrapped up in a carpet; later in the year, Ferdinand was lured to Bayonne by Napoleon and there witnessed his father first resume the throne and then assign it to Joseph, the brother of Napoleon. Ferdinand was detained in France, but his supporters in Spain were not slow to rise against King Joseph Bonaparte; thus began the long struggle known in England as the Peninsular War but in Spain as the War of Independence; to Napoleon it was the Spanish ulcer. In 1808 Wellington first landed in Portugal; in 1813 he crossed the Bidassoa into France.

In 1814 Ferdinand VII returned to Spain. His reign was tyrannical and disastrous. The lessons of recent years had not been lost on the Spanish colonies in America: one by one they revolted, until only Cuba and Puerto Rico remained to Spain. For a brief period Ferdinand flirted with liberalism, but then turned to French bayonets to restore autocracy. Finally, he failed to provide a male heir; although he was four times married, twice to his own nieces, he engen-

King Charles IV of Spain (1747–1819) with wife and family, painted with unflattering realism by Francisco Goya in 1800.

dered only two daughters. It was not certain whether a queen could succeed, though of course the Bourbons had inherited through a woman; conservative opinion favoured the King's brother, Charles (Don Carlos). It may be observed that most Spanish titles of nobility can pass through a female.

Ferdinand had only taken his fourth wife Mary Christina in 1829: Isabella was born in 1830. The King died in 1833. The baby Queen was proclaimed, with her mother as regent, but the followers of Charles, Count of Molina, proclaimed him as king. A bitter civil war ensued, fought mainly in the northern provinces, and lasted for seven years. Mary Christina made a secret morganatic marriage with an ex-sergeant: a dukedom of Riansares might conceal his vulgar origins, but it was less easy to keep dark the Queen Mother's frequent pregnancies. Isabella was a wayward and ill-educated princess with whose morals rumour made free. The choice of her husband perplexed the chanceries of Europe for five years (1841–6) but Mary Christina finally married the Queen to Francis, Duke of Cadiz, who was Isabella's first cousin and her own nephew. He was a hypochondriacal and effeminate bigot. Few royal families have been so closely inbred as the Spanish Bourbons in the nineteenth century.

Meanwhile political power was seized in turn by a series of generals of whom Espartero, Narvaez and O'Donnell were the most noteworthy. The passing of years did nothing to improve Isabella's reputation, and in 1868 General Prim, who had made his name in Morocco, organized a revolution which drove the Queen into exile: she finally abdicated in 1870. For

TABLE 51

SPAIN
House of Bourbon and the Carlist branch

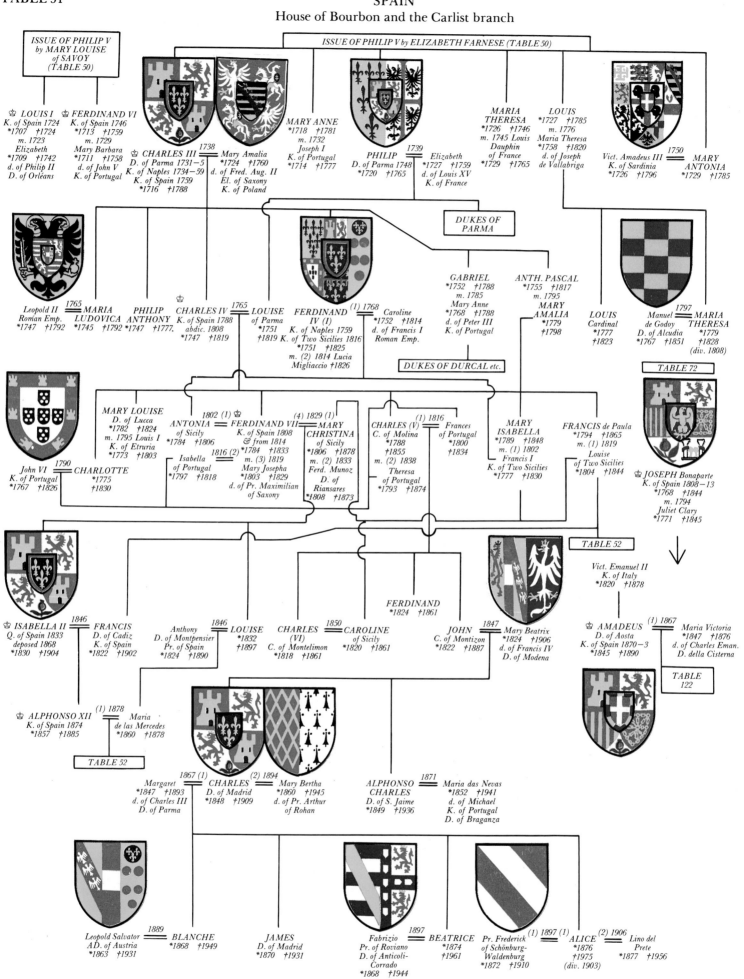

ISSUE OF PHILIP V by MARY LOUISE of SAVOY (TABLE 50)

ISSUE OF PHILIP V by ELIZABETH FARNESE (TABLE 50)

♔ LOUIS I
K. of Spain 1724
*1707 †1724
m. 1723
Elizabeth
*1709 †1742
d. of Philip II
D. of Orléans

♔ FERDINAND VI
K. of Spain 1746
*1713 †1759
m. 1729
Mary Barbara
*1711 †1758
d. of John V
K. of Portugal

CHARLES III 1738
D. of Parma 1731–5
K. of Naples 1734–59
K. of Spain 1759
*1716 †1788

Mary Amalia
*1724 †1760
d. of Fred. Aug. II
El. of Saxony
K. of Poland

MARY ANNE
*1718 †1781
m. 1732
Joseph I
K. of Portugal
*1714 †1777

PHILIP 1739
D. of Parma 1748
*1720 †1765

Elizabeth
*1727 †1759
d. of Louis XV
K. of France

MARIA THERESA
*1726 †1746
m. 1745 Louis
Dauphin
of France
*1729 †1765

LOUIS
*1727 †1785
m. 1776
Maria Theresa
*1758 †1820
d. of Joseph
de Vallabriga

Vict. Amadeus III
K. of Sardinia
*1726 †1796 1750

MARY ANTONIA
*1729 †1785

DUKES OF PARMA

Leopold II
Roman Emp.
*1747 †1792 1765

MARIA LUDOVICA
*1745 †1792

PHILIP ANTHONY
*1747 †1777.

CHARLES IV
K. of Spain 1788
abdic. 1808
*1747 †1819 1765

LOUISE
of Parma
*1751
†1819

FERDINAND IV (I) (1) 1768
K. of Naples 1759
K. of Two Sicilies 1816
*1751 †1825
m. (2) 1814 Lucia
Migliaccio †1826

Caroline
*1752 †1814
d. of Francis I
Roman Emp.

GABRIEL
*1752 †1788
m. 1785
Mary Anne
*1768 †1788
d. of Peter III
K. of Portugal

ANTH. PASCAL
*1755 †1817
m. 1795
MARY AMALIA
*1779
†1798

LOUIS
Cardinal
*1777
†1823

Manuel
de Godoy
D. of Alcudia
*1767 †1851 1797

MARIA THERESA
*1779
†1828
(div. 1808)

DUKES OF DURCAL etc.

TABLE 72

MARY LOUISE
D. of Lucca
*1782 †1824
m. 1795 Louis I
K. of Etruria
*1773 †1803

ANTONIA 1802 (1)
of Sicily
*1784 †1806

FERDINAND VII
K. of Spain 1808
& from 1814
*1784 †1833
m. (3) 1819
Mary Josepha
*1803 †1829
d. of Pr. Maximilian
of Saxony

MARY CHRISTINA
of Sicily
*1806 †1878
m. (2) 1833
Ferd. Munoz
D. of
Riansares
*1808 †1873

(4) 1829 (1)

Isabella
of Portugal
*1797 †1818 1816 (2)

CHARLES (V) (1) 1816
C. of Molina
*1788
†1855
m. (2) 1838
Theresa
of Portugal
*1793 †1874

Frances
of Portugal
*1800
†1834

MARY ISABELLA
*1789 †1848
m. (1) 1802
Francis I
K. of Two Sicilies
*1777 †1830

FRANCIS de Paula
*1794 †1865
m. (1) 1819
Louise
of Two Sicilies
*1804 †1844

JOSEPH Bonaparte
K. of Spain 1808–13
*1768 †1844
m. 1794
Juliet Clary
*1771 †1845

John VI 1790
K. of Portugal
*1767 †1826

CHARLOTTE
*1775
†1830

FERDINAND
*1824 †1861

TABLE 52

Vict. Emanuel II
K. of Italy
*1820 †1878

♔ ISABELLA II 1846
Q. of Spain 1833
deposed 1868
*1830 †1904

FRANCIS
D. of Cadiz
K. of Spain
*1822 †1902

Anthony
D. of Montpensier
Pr. of Spain
*1824 †1890

LOUISE 1846
*1832
†1897

CHARLES (VI)
C. of Montelimon
*1818 †1861

CAROLINE 1850
of Sicily
*1820 †1861

JOHN 1847
C. of Montizon
*1822 †1887

Mary Beatrix
*1824 †1906
d. of Francis IV
D. of Modena

♔ AMADEUS
D. of Aosta
K. of Spain 1870–3
*1845 †1890

Maria Victoria (1) 1867
*1847 †1876
d. of Charles Eman.
D. della Cisterna

TABLE 122

♔ ALPHONSO XII (1) 1878
K. of Spain 1874
*1857 †1885

Maria
de las Mercedes
*1860 †1878

TABLE 52

Margaret 1867 (1)
*1847 †1893
d. of Charles III
D. of Parma

CHARLES
D. of Madrid
*1848 †1909

(2) 1894 Mary Bertha
*1860 †1945
d. of Pr. Arthur
of Rohan

ALPHONSO CHARLES 1871
D. of S. Jaime
*1849 †1936

Maria das Nevas
*1852 †1941
d. of Michael
K. of Portugal
D. of Braganza

Leopold Salvator 1889
AD. of Austria
*1863 †1931

BLANCHE
*1868 †1949

JAMES
D. of Madrid
*1870 †1931

Fabrizio 1897
Pr. of Roviano
D. of Anticoli-
Corrado
*1868 †1944

BEATRICE
*1874
†1961

Pr. Frederick (1) 1897 (1)
of Schönburg-
Waldenburg
*1872 †1910

ALICE
*1876
†1975
(div. 1903)

(2) 1906 Lino del
Prete
*1877 †1956

TABLE 52

SPAIN
House of Bourbon since the Restoration in 1874

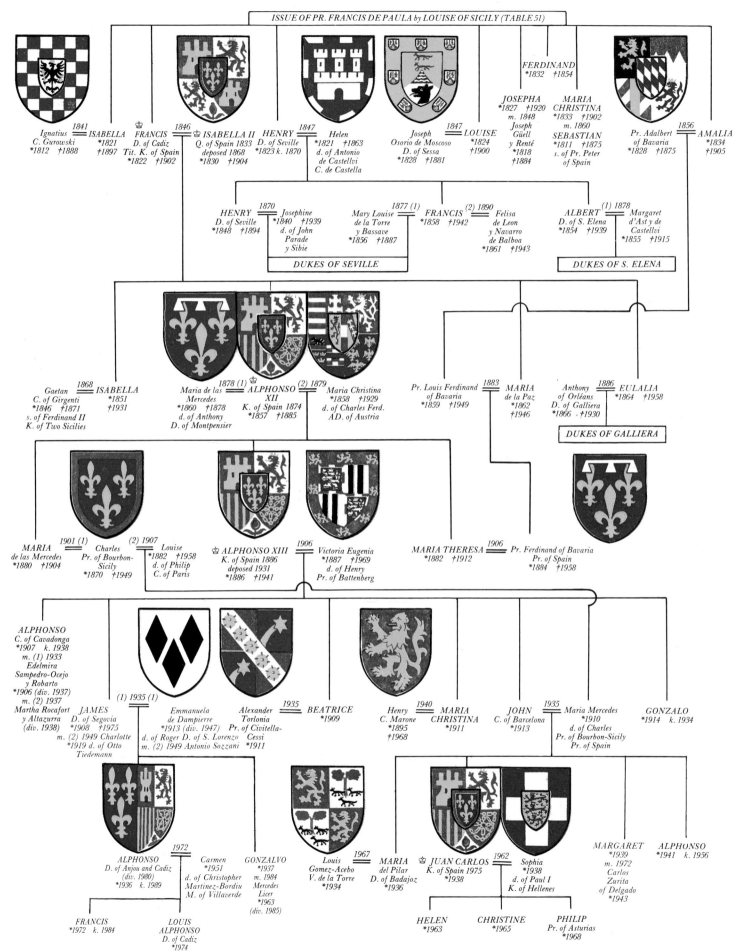

ISSUE OF PR. FRANCIS DE PAULA by LOUISE OF SICILY (TABLE 51)

Ignatius
C. Gurowski
*1812 †1888

1841

ISABELLA
*1821
†1897

FRANCIS
D. of Cadiz
Tit. K. of Spain
*1822 †1902

1846

ISABELLA II
Q. of Spain 1833
deposed 1868
*1830 †1904

HENRY
D. of Seville
*1823 k. 1870

1847

Helen
*1821 †1863
d. of Antonio
de Castellvi
C. de Castella

Joseph
Osorio de Moscoso
D. of Sessa
*1828 †1881

1847

LOUISE
*1824
†1900

JOSEPHA
*1827 †1920
m. 1848
Joseph
Güell
y Renté
*1818
†1884

MARIA
CHRISTINA
*1833 †1902
m. 1860
SEBASTIAN
*1811 †1875
s. of Pr. Peter
of Spain

FERDINAND
*1832 †1854

Pr. Adalbert
of Bavaria
*1828 †1875

1856

AMALIA
*1834
†1905

HENRY
D. of Seville
*1848 †1894

1870

Josephine
*1840 †1939
d. of John
Parade
y Sibie

Mary Louise
de la Torre
y Bassavo
*1856 †1887

1877 (1)

FRANCIS
*1858 †1942

(2) 1890

Felisa
de Leon
y Navarro
de Balboa
*1861 †1943

ALBERT
D. of S. Elena
*1854 †1939

(1) 1878

Margaret
d'Ast y de
Castellvi
*1855 †1915

DUKES OF SEVILLE

DUKES OF S. ELENA

Gaetan
C. of Girgenti
*1846 †1871
s. of Ferdinand II
K. of Two Sicilies

1868

ISABELLA
*1851
†1931

Maria de las
Mercedes
*1860 †1878
d. of Anthony
D. of Montpensier

1878 (1)

ALPHONSO
XII
K. of Spain 1874
*1857 †1885

(2) 1879

Maria Christina
*1858 †1929
d. of Charles Ferd.
AD. of Austria

Pr. Louis Ferdinand
of Bavaria
*1859 †1949

1883

MARIA
de la Paz
*1862
†1946

Anthony
of Orléans
D. of Galliera
*1866 †1930

1886

EULALIA
*1864 †1958

DUKES OF GALLIERA

MARIA
de las Mercedes
*1880 †1904

1901 (1)

Charles
Pr. of Bourbon-
Sicily
*1870 †1949

(2) 1907

Louise
*1882 †1958
d. of Philip
C. of Paris

ALPHONSO XIII
K. of Spain 1886
deposed 1931
*1886 †1941

1906

Victoria Eugenia
*1887 †1969
d. of Henry
Pr. of Battenberg

MARIA THERESA
*1882 †1912

1906

Pr. Ferdinand of Bavaria
Pr. of Spain
*1884 †1958

ALPHONSO
C. of Cavadonga
*1907 k. 1938
m. (1) 1933
Edelmira
Sampedro-Ocejo
y Robarto
*1906 (div. 1937)
m. (2) 1937
Martha Rocafort
y Altazurra
(div. 1938)

JAMES
D. of Segovia
*1908 †1975
m. (2) 1949 Charlotte
*1919 d. of Otto
Tiedemann

(1) 1935 (1)

Emmanuela
de Dampierre
*1913 (div. 1947)
d. of Roger D. of S. Lorenzo
m. (2) 1949 Antonio Sozzani

Alexander
Torlonia
Pr. of Civitella-
Cessi *1911

1935

BEATRICE
*1909

Henry
C. Marone
*1895
†1968

1940

MARIA
CHRISTINA
*1911

JOHN
C. of Barcelona
*1913

1935

Maria Mercedes
*1910
d. of Charles
Pr. of Bourbon-Sicily
Pr. of Spain

GONZALO
*1914 k. 1934

ALPHONSO
D. of Anjou and Cadiz
(div. 1980)
*1936 k. 1989

1972

Carmen
*1951
d. of Christopher
Martinez-Bordiu
M. of Villaverde

GONZALVO
*1937
m. 1984
Mercedes
Licer
*1963
(div. 1985)

Louis
Gomez-Acebo
V. de la Torre
*1934

1967

MARIA
del Pilar
D. of Badajoz
*1936

JUAN CARLOS
K. of Spain 1975
*1938

1962

Sophia
*1938
d. of Paul I
K. of Hellenes

MARGARET
*1939
m. 1972
Carlos
Zurita
of Delgado
*1943

ALPHONSO
*1941 k. 1956

FRANCIS
*1972 k. 1984

LOUIS
ALPHONSO
D. of Cadiz
*1974

HELEN
*1963

CHRISTINE
*1965

PHILIP
Pr. of Asturias
*1968

TABLE 53

SPAIN
Ancestors of Charles I, Philip V and Juan Carlos

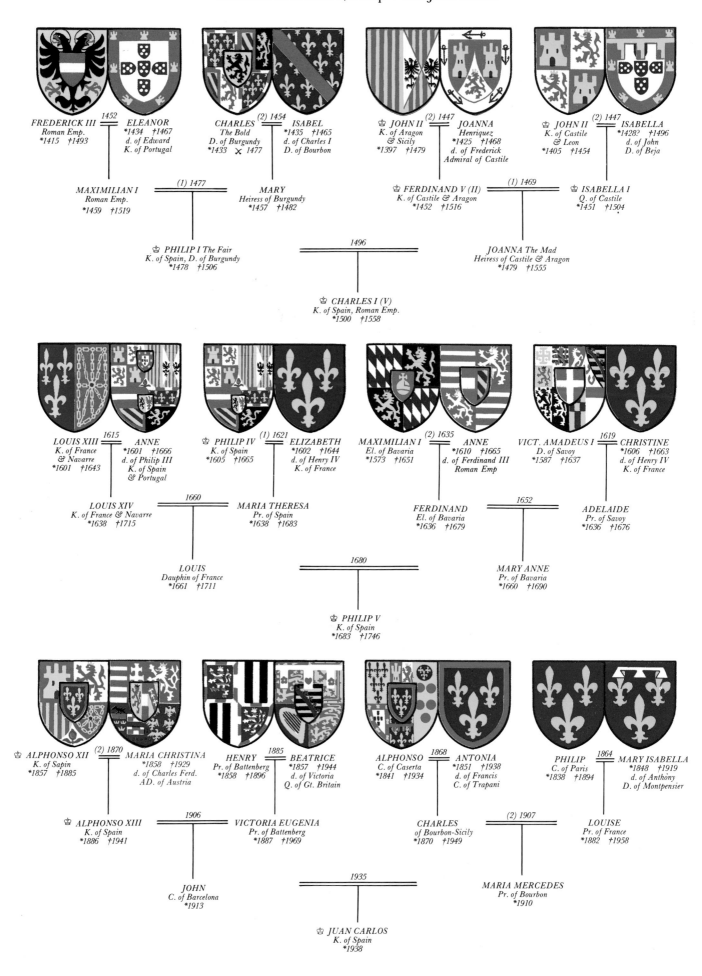

FREDERICK III Roman Emp. *1415 †1493 ══1452══ **ELEANOR** *1434 †1467 d. of Edward K. of Portugal

CHARLES The Bold D. of Burgundy *1433 ✕ 1477 ══(2) 1454══ **ISABEL** *1435 †1465 d. of Charles I D. of Bourbon

♔ **JOHN II** K. of Aragon & Sicily *1397 †1479 ══(2) 1447══ **JOANNA** Henriquez *1425 †1468 d. of Frederick Admiral of Castile

♔ **JOHN II** K. of Castile & Leon *1405 †1454 ══(2) 1447══ **ISABELLA** *1428? †1496 d. of John D. of Beja

MAXIMILIAN I Roman Emp. *1459 †1519 ══(1) 1477══ **MARY** Heiress of Burgundy *1457 †1482

♔ **FERDINAND V (II)** K. of Castile & Aragon *1452 †1516 ══(1) 1469══ ♔ **ISABELLA I** Q. of Castile *1451 †1504

♔ **PHILIP I** The Fair K. of Spain, D. of Burgundy *1478 †1506 ══1496══ **JOANNA** The Mad Heiress of Castile & Aragon *1479 †1555

♔ **CHARLES I (V)** K. of Spain, Roman Emp. *1500 †1558

LOUIS XIII K. of France & Navarre *1601 †1643 ══1615══ **ANNE** *1601 †1666 d. of Philip III K. of Spain & Portugal

♔ **PHILIP IV** K. of Spain *1605 †1665 ══(1) 1621══ **ELIZABETH** *1602 †1644 d. of Henry IV K. of France

MAXIMILIAN I El. of Bavaria *1573 †1651 ══(2) 1635══ **ANNE** *1610 †1665 d. of Ferdinand III Roman Emp

VICT. AMADEUS I D. of Savoy *1587 †1637 ══1619══ **CHRISTINE** *1606 †1663 d. of Henry IV K. of France

LOUIS XIV K. of France & Navarre *1638 †1715 ══1660══ **MARIA THERESA** Pr. of Spain *1638 †1683

FERDINAND El. of Bavaria *1636 †1679 ══1652══ **ADELAIDE** Pr. of Savoy *1636 †1676

LOUIS Dauphin of France *1661 †1711 ══1680══ **MARY ANNE** Pr. of Bavaria *1660 †1690

♔ **PHILIP V** K. of Spain *1683 †1746

♔ **ALPHONSO XII** K. of Sapin *1857 †1885 ══(2) 1870══ **MARIA CHRISTINA** *1858 †1929 d. of Charles Ferd. AD. of Austria

HENRY Pr. of Battenberg *1858 †1896 ══1885══ **BEATRICE** *1857 †1944 d. of Victoria Q. of Gt. Britain

ALPHONSO C. of Caserta *1841 †1934 ══1868══ **ANTONIA** *1851 †1938 d. of Francis C. of Trapani

PHILIP C. of Paris *1838 †1894 ══1864══ **MARY ISABELLA** *1848 †1919 d. of Anthony D. of Montpensier

♔ **ALPHONSO XIII** K. of Spain *1886 †1941 ══1906══ **VICTORIA EUGENIA** Pr. of Battenberg *1887 †1969

CHARLES of Bourbon-Sicily *1870 †1949 ══(2) 1907══ **LOUISE** Pr. of France *1882 †1958

JOHN C. of Barcelona *1913 ══1935══ **MARIA MERCEDES** Pr. of Bourbon *1910

♔ **JUAN CARLOS** K. of Spain *1938

the best part of two years the Crown of Spain was hawked round Europe. The Duke of Montpensier was considered; then overtures were made to Prince Leopold of Hohenzollern-Sigmaringen, which helped to start the Franco-Prussian War; the King of Portugal and his Saxe-Coburg father were both discussed; at last the throne was accepted, late in 1870, by Amadeus of Savoy, Duke of Aosta and younger son of the first King of United Italy (Tables 51 and 122). His arms show the normal smaller shield of Spain, with his own differenced coat of Savoy over all. His reign was short and unhappy; opposition mounted, some in favour of Isabella's son, some advocating Charles, Duke of Madrid, grandson of the original Carlist claimant. In 1873 Amadeus abdicated and returned to Italy.

For a year there was an uneasy republic under four fleeting presidents. In the north the Carlists set up an independent state, centred on the Basque area of Navarre. At the very end of 1874 part of the army declared for Alphonso XII; the young King, then a cadet at Sandhurst, entered upon his short reign. He insisted on marrying his first cousin, a daughter of the Duke of Montpensier, but she died five months later. His second marriage was to an Austrian princess who provided him with two daughters. The King's rule was constitutional: a Conservative Government was followed by a Liberal one, and a more promising era for Spain seemed about to materialize. Unhappily the King developed consumption and died, genuinely mourned by his subjects, at the end of 1885. The Queen was pregnant and six months later had a son, Alphonso XIII, who was thus a king from the moment of his birth. In 1883 there had died the exiled Count of Chambord, the last male descendant of Louis XV. Alphonso XII thus became head of the House of Bourbon and the senior heir of Hugh Capet. Accordingly he adopted the undifferenced arms of France, which can be seen over the traditional shield of Spain on Table 52.

Under the regency of the Queen Mother the minority of Alphonso XIII was passed in parliamentary government. The end of the century saw a crisis in Cuba, where a revolution, which broke out in 1895, led finally to war with the United States and the loss of the island. In 1906 the King made a marriage of affection with Princess Victoria of Battenberg, who had been brought up in England as a Protestant. Though she became a Catholic, the King's choice was criticized on the score of religion and non-royal birth. The neutrality of Spain in the First World War brought considerable prosperity to the country. At the same time socialist movements were spreading and there was a resurgence of Catalan separatism. From 1923 to 1930 there was a dictatorship under General Primo de Rivera; it was followed

by massive manifestations of republicanism. In 1931 the King left Spain, partly with the aim of avoiding civil war, but he never abdicated. He died in 1941. The eldest son of Alphonso XIII resigned all his rights in 1933 on marrying a commoner; the second, who was born deaf and dumb, did the same although he has sometimes advanced claims to the thrones of both France and Spain.

The Second Republic had a brief and violent career. In 1936 a military rising in Morocco spread to Spain and the civil war began. Like the internal conflicts between the supporters of Queen Isabella and the Carlists in the nineteenth century, it was waged with extreme bitterness and brutality. But in this savage conflict alien powers were all too ready to interfere, whether from Fascist right or Communist left; the war ended in 1939 with victory for the right. From that date until his death in 1975 the ruler of Spain was a Gallegan soldier, General Francisco Franco, styled the *Caudillo*. This is no place to judge his regime. Against the indubitable woes of internal dictatorship may be set his success in not involving Spain in the Second World War, despite his obligations to the Axis.

General Franco declared that Spain was a monarchy and in 1969 chose as his successor the son of Juan, Count of Barcelona, the Bourbon claimant (Table 52). The Prince, Juan Carlos, was partly brought up in Spain, while his father maintained his exile in Portugal. After Franco's death, he was duly proclaimed and crowned as King of Spain in November 1975, but it was not until 1977 that the Count of Barcelona actually resigned his rights in his son's favour. King Juan Carlos is married to a Greek princess and their son bears the traditional title of Prince of the Asturias. He has courageously embarked upon a policy of transforming Spain into a parliamentary monarchy.

Many traditional problems such as the separatist ambitions of some areas survive all changes of constitution. The true Carlist branch came to an end with the death of Alphonso, Duke of San Jaime, in 1936 (Table 51). However, he designated as head of the Carlist movement Prince Xavier of Bourbon-Parma (Table 130) who was banned from Spain in 1968 (though his genealogical claims were remote) and died in 1977. His eldest son, Charles Hugo, is married to a Dutch princess (Table 36) and lives in Paris.

The King's formal arms can be seen at the foot of Table 43; they show the ancient Spanish quarterings of Castile, Leon, Aragon and Navarre, with Granada in base, ensigned with an escutcheon of France and surrounded by the Golden Fleece. For King Juan Carlos is the heir male of Hugh Capet, who ascended the French throne in 987, a line of direct descent not easily equalled.

Chapter 12

LIECHTENSTEIN

Scattered around Europe are five tiny states whose survival stems from a series of historical accidents and from their ability to evade the grasp of larger neighbours. In central Italy is the minute republic (61 square kilometres) of San Marino; in the heart of the Pyrenees, between France and Spain, is the little state of Andorra (452 square kilometres) which boasts as joint princes the Bishop of Urgel and the President of the French Republic – the latter representing the former Counts of Foix. Smallest of all these entities is the Vatican City (less than half a square kilometre) ruled over by the Pope. The other two are the Principalities of Liechtenstein and Monaco.

Liechtenstein today comprises an area of 157 square kilometres between Switzerland and Austria. In the Middle Ages there were two separate feudal fiefs, the Lordship of Schellenberg and the County of Vaduz, both parts of the Duchy of Swabia. In about 1200 the County of Vaduz passed by descent to the family of Montfort, which in 1396 succeeded in making it a direct fief of the Holy Roman Empire. The Montforts, whose principal title was Count of Werdenberg, also secured the neighbouring Lordship of Schellenberg; but in the fifteenth century both properties passed to their kinsmen the Brandis family, and from them to the Counts of Sulz, who eventually sold the two estates in 1613 to the Count of Hohenems.

It must be remembered that all this time the cantons of Switzerland to the west had been growing in strength and independence. During the Thirty Years' War (1618–48) the various lands of the Hohenems were repeatedly devastated; by the end of the century they were in serious financial difficulties. In 1699 they were compelled to sell Schellenberg for 115,000 guilders; in 1712 they parted with Vaduz for a further 290,000. In both cases the purchaser was Prince John Adam of Liechtenstein.

The earliest ancestor of this dynasty (Table 54) is a certain Hugo, who belonged to the official class of *ministeriales*. His grandson became Lord of Nikolsburg (now Mikulov in Moravia): Liechtenstein itself was a castle no great distance from Vienna. No members of the family attained great distinction until the beginning of the seventeenth century. Then Charles, eldest son of Hartmann II, was made Governor of Bohemia by the Emperor, with orders to bring the country to heel and to suppress Protestantism. It was easy to combine this task with making a fortune. Charles became in succession a Prince of the Empire (1608), Duke of Troppau (1613) and Duke of Jägerndorf (1623); in this last year the princely title was conferred on his younger brothers, Maximilian and Gundakar. Prince John Adam, who bought Vaduz and Schellenberg from the bankrupt James Hannibal III of Hohenems, was the last male descendant of Prince Charles, and died later in 1712.

All his possessions were inherited by his cousin, Anthony Florian (Table 55), the heir of Prince Gundakar. In 1719 the Emperor Charles VI erected the two Lordships of Vaduz and Schellenberg into an hereditary and independent principality under the Holy Roman Empire to which he transferred the name of Liechtenstein. The new Princes continued to live mainly in Vienna and to play their part in the affairs of the Empire: none of them bothered to visit Liechtenstein until 1842. Many of them married Czech wives. Prince Wenceslas (d. 1772) was a distinguished diplomat, soldier, and field-marshal in the Seven Years' War; he was also interested in painting. His great-nephew Aloys I was also a celebrated connoisseur and patron of the arts; the next Prince, John I, was another distinguished general, fighting against Napoleon at Aspern-Essling and Wagram and commanding the whole Austrian army from 1809.

In 1806 Napoleon's conquests in Europe put an

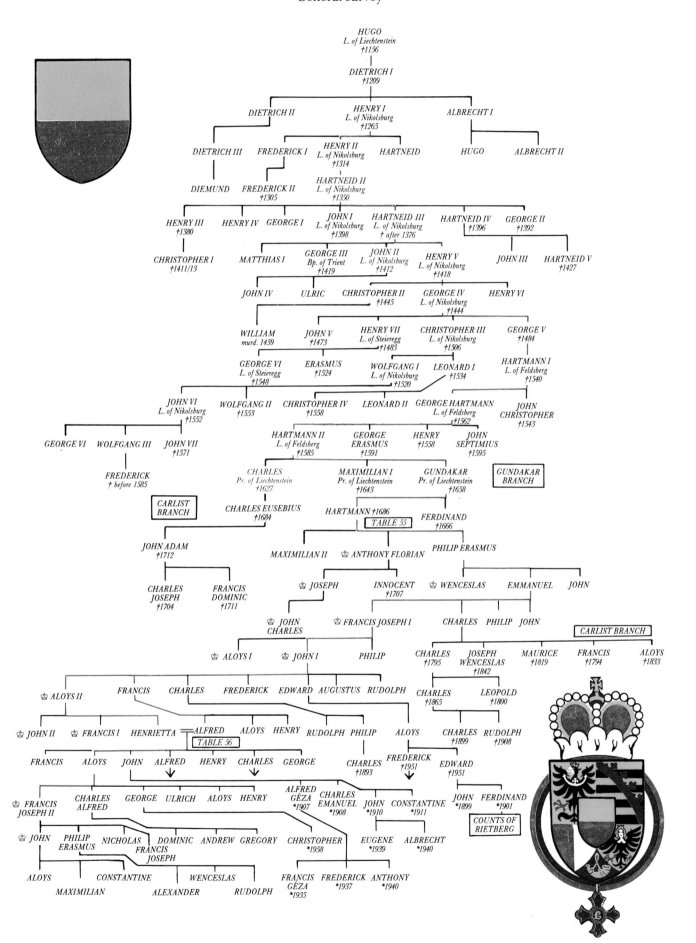

HUGO L. of Liechtenstein †1156

DIETRICH I †1209

DIETRICH II — **HENRY I** L. of Nikolsburg †1265 — **ALBRECHT I**

DIETRICH III — **FREDERICK I** — **HENRY II** L. of Nikolsburg †1314 — **HARTNEID** — **HUGO** — **ALBRECHT II**

DIEMUND — **FREDERICK II** †1305 — **HARTNEID II** L. of Nikolsburg †1350

HENRY III †1380 — **HENRY IV** — **GEORGE I** — **JOHN I** L. of Nikolsburg †1398 — **HARTNEID III** L. of Nikolsburg † after 1376 — **HARTNEID IV** †1396 — **GEORGE II** †1392

CHRISTOPHER I †1411/13 — **MATTHIAS I** — **GEORGE III** Bp. of Trient †1419 — **JOHN II** L. of Nikolsburg †1412 — **HENRY V** L. of Nikolsburg †1418 — **JOHN III** — **HARTNEID V** †1427

JOHN IV — **ULRIC** — **CHRISTOPHER II** †1445 — **GEORGE IV** L. of Nikolsburg †1444 — **HENRY VI**

WILLIAM murd. 1459 — **JOHN V** †1473 — **HENRY VII** L. of Steieregg †1483 — **CHRISTOPHER III** L. of Nikolsburg †1506 — **GEORGE V** †1484

GEORGE VI L. of Steieregg †1548 — **ERASMUS** †1524 — **WOLFGANG I** L. of Nikolsburg †1520 — **LEONARD I** †1534 — **HARTMANN I** L. of Feldsberg †1540

JOHN VI L. of Nikolsburg †1552 — **WOLFGANG II** †1553 — **CHRISTOPHER IV** †1558 — **LEONARD II** — **GEORGE HARTMANN** L. of Feldsberg †1562 — **JOHN CHRISTOPHER** †1543

GEORGE VI — **WOLFGANG III** — **JOHN VII** †1571 — **HARTMANN II** L. of Feldsberg †1585 — **GEORGE ERASMUS** †1591 — **HENRY** †1558 — **JOHN SEPTIMIUS** †1595

FREDERICK † before 1585 — **CHARLES** Pr. of Liechtenstein †1627 — **MAXIMILIAN I** Pr. of Liechtenstein †1643 — **GUNDAKAR** Pr. of Liechtenstein †1658

[GUNDAKAR BRANCH]

[CARLIST BRANCH]

CHARLES EUSEBIUS †1684 — **HARTMANN †1686** [TABLE 55] — **FERDINAND** †1666

JOHN ADAM †1712 — **MAXIMILIAN II** — ☘ **ANTHONY FLORIAN** — **PHILIP ERASMUS**

CHARLES JOSEPH †1704 — **FRANCIS DOMINIC** †1711 — ☘ **JOSEPH** — **INNOCENT** †1707 — ☘ **WENCESLAS** — **EMMANUEL** — **JOHN**

☘ **JOHN CHARLES** — ☘ **FRANCIS JOSEPH I** — **CHARLES** — **PHILIP** — **JOHN**

[CARLIST BRANCH]

☘ **ALOYS I** — ☘ **JOHN I** — **PHILIP** — **CHARLES** †1795 — **JOSEPH WENCESLAS** †1842 — **MAURICE** †1819 — **FRANCIS** †1794 — **ALOYS** †1833

☘ **ALOYS II** — **FRANCIS** — **CHARLES** — **FREDERICK** — **EDWARD** — **AUGUSTUS** — **RUDOLPH** — **CHARLES** †1865 — **LEOPOLD** †1800

☘ **JOHN II** — ☘ **FRANCIS I** — **HENRIETTA** — **ALFRED** — **ALOYS** — **HENRY** — **RUDOLPH** — **PHILIP** — **ALOYS** — **CHARLES** †1899 — **RUDOLPH** †1908

[TABLE 56]

FRANCIS — **ALOYS** — **JOHN** — **ALFRED** — **HENRY** — **CHARLES** — **GEORGE** — **CHARLES** †1893 — **FREDERICK** †1951 — **EDWARD** †1951

☘ **FRANCIS JOSEPH II** — **CHARLES ALFRED** — **GEORGE** — **ULRICH** — **ALOYS** — **HENRY** — **ALFRED GÉZA** *1907 — **CHARLES EMANUEL** *1908 — **JOHN** *1910 — **CONSTANTINE** *1911 — **JOHN** *1899 — **FERDINAND** *1901

[COUNTS OF RIETBERG]

☘ **JOHN** — **PHILIP ERASMUS** — **NICHOLAS** — **DOMINIC** — **ANDREW** — **GREGORY** — **CHRISTOPHER** *1958 — **EUGENE** *1939 — **ALBRECHT** *1940

FRANCIS JOSEPH

ALOYS — **CONSTANTINE** — **WENCESLAS** — **FRANCIS GÉZA** *1935 — **FREDERICK** *1937 — **ANTHONY** *1940

MAXIMILIAN — **ALEXANDER** — **RUDOLPH**

TABLE 55

LIECHTENSTEIN
First sovereign Princes

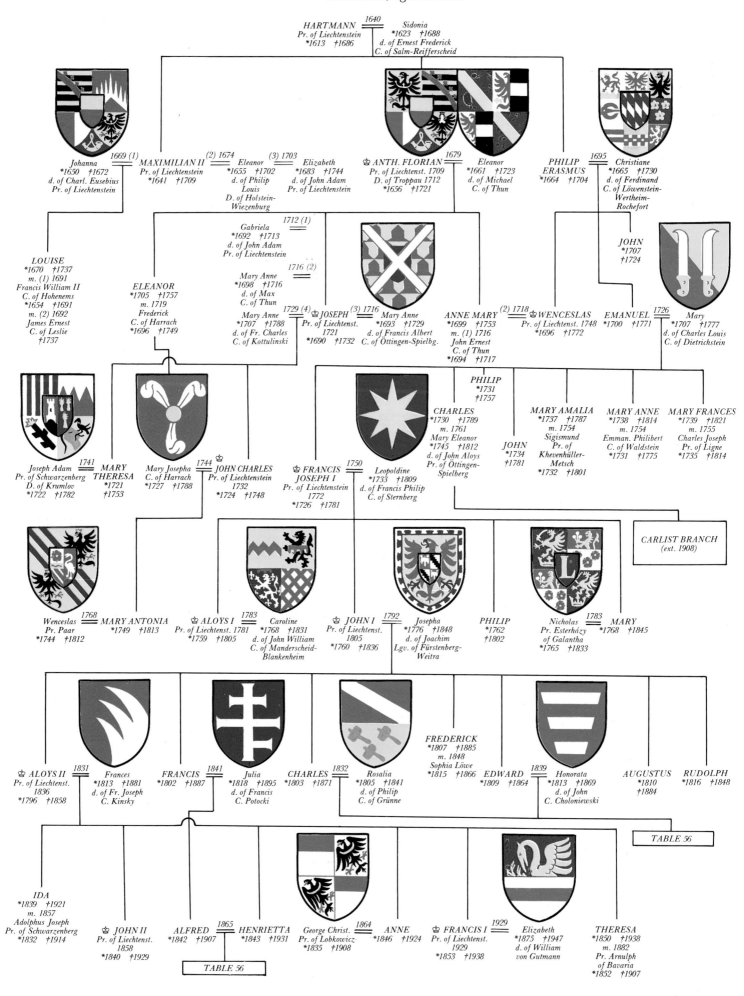

HARTMANN 1640 — Sidonia
Pr. of Liechtenstein *1623 †1688
*1613 †1686 d. of Ernest Frederick
C. of Salm-Reifferscheid

Johanna 1669 (1) **MAXIMILIAN II** (2) 1674 Eleanor (3) 1703 Elizabeth | **ANTH. FLORIAN** 1679 Eleanor | **PHILIP** 1695 Christiane
*1650 †1672 Pr. of Liechtenstein *1655 †1702 *1683 †1744 | Pr. of Liechtenst. 1709 *1661 †1723 | **ERASMUS** *1665 †1730
d. of Charl. Eusebius *1641 †1709 d. of Philip d. of John Adam | D. of Troppau 1712 d. of Michael | *1664 †1704 d. of Ferdinand
Pr. of Liechtenstein Louis Pr. of Liechtenstein | *1656 †1721 C. of Thun | C. of Löwenstein-
D. of Holstein- | | Wertheim-
Wiezenburg | | Rochefort

Gabriela 1712 (1)
*1692 †1713
d. of John Adam **JOHN**
Pr. of Liechtenstein *1707
†1724

1716 (2)
Mary Anne
*1698 †1716
d. of Max
C. of Thun **EMANUEL** 1726 Mary

LOUISE **ELEANOR** Mary Anne 1729 (4) **JOSEPH** (3) 1716 Mary Anne | **ANNE MARY** (2) 1718 **WENCESLAS** *1700 †1771 *1707 †1777
*1670 †1737 *1705 †1757 *1707 †1788 Pr. of Liechtenst. *1693 †1729 | *1699 †1753 Pr. of Liechtenst. 1748 d. of Charles Louis
m. (1) 1691 m. 1719 d. of Fr. Charles 1721 d. of Francis Albert | m. (1) 1716 *1696 †1772 C. of Dietrichstein
Francis William II Frederick C. of Kottulinski *1690 †1732 C. of Öttingen-Spielbg. | John Ernest
C. of Hohenems C. of Harrach | C. of Thun
*1654 †1691 *1696 †1749 | *1694 †1717
m. (2) 1692
James Ernest
C. of Leslie
†1737

PHILIP
*1731
†1757

CHARLES MARY AMALIA MARY ANNE MARY FRANCES
*1730 †1789 *1737 †1787 *1738 †1814 *1739 †1821
m. 1761 m. 1754 m. 1754 m. 1755
Mary Eleanor Sigismund Emman. Philibert Charles Joseph
*1745 †1812 Pr. of C. of Waldstein Pr. of Ligne
d. of John Aloys Khevenhüller- *1731 †1775 *1735 †1814
Pr. of Öttingen- Metsch
JOHN Spielberg *1732 †1801
*1734
†1781

Joseph Adam 1741 **MARY** Mary Josepha 1744 **JOHN CHARLES** **FRANCIS** 1750 Leopoldine
Pr. of Schwarzenberg **THERESA** C. of Harrach Pr. of Liechtenstein **JOSEPH I** *1733 †1809
D. of Krumlov *1721 *1727 †1788 1732 Pr. of Liechtenstein d. of Francis Philip
*1722 †1782 †1753 *1724 †1748 1772 C. of Sternberg
*1726 †1781

CARLIST BRANCH
(ext. 1908)

Wenceslas 1768 **MARY ANTONIA** **ALOYS I** 1783 Caroline | **JOHN I** 1792 Josepha | PHILIP Nicholas 1783 **MARY**
Pr. Paar *1749 †1813 Pr. of Liechtenst. 1781 *1768 †1831 | Pr. of Liechtenst. *1776 †1848 | *1762 Pr. Esterházy *1768 †1845
*1744 †1812 *1759 †1805 d. of John William | 1805 d. of Joachim | *1802 of Galantha
C. of Manderscheid- | *1760 †1836 Lgv. of Fürstenberg- | *1765 †1833
Blankenheim | Weitra |

FREDERICK
*1807 †1885
m. 1848
Sophia Löwe
*1815 †1866

ALOYS II 1831 Frances **FRANCIS** 1841 Julia CHARLES 1832 Rosalia **EDWARD** 1839 Honorata AUGUSTUS RUDOLPH
Pr. of Liechtenst. *1813 †1881 *1802 †1887 *1818 †1895 *1803 †1871 *1805 †1841 *1809 †1864 *1813 †1869 *1810 *1816 †1848
1836 d. of Fr. Joseph d. of Francis d. of Philip d. of John †1884
*1796 †1858 C. Kinsky C. Potocki C. of Grünne C. Choloniewski

TABLE 56

IDA **JOHN II** ALFRED 1865 HENRIETTA George Christ. 1864 ANNE **FRANCIS I** 1929 Elizabeth THERESA
*1839 †1921 Pr. of Liechtenst. *1842 †1907 *1843 †1931 Pr. of Lobkowicz *1846 †1924 Pr. of Liechtenst. *1875 †1947 *1850 †1938
m. 1857 1858 *1835 †1908 1929 d. of William m. 1882
Adolphus Joseph *1840 †1929 *1853 †1938 von Gutmann Pr. Arnulph
Pr. of Schwarzenberg of Bavaria
*1832 †1914 TABLE 56 *1852 †1907

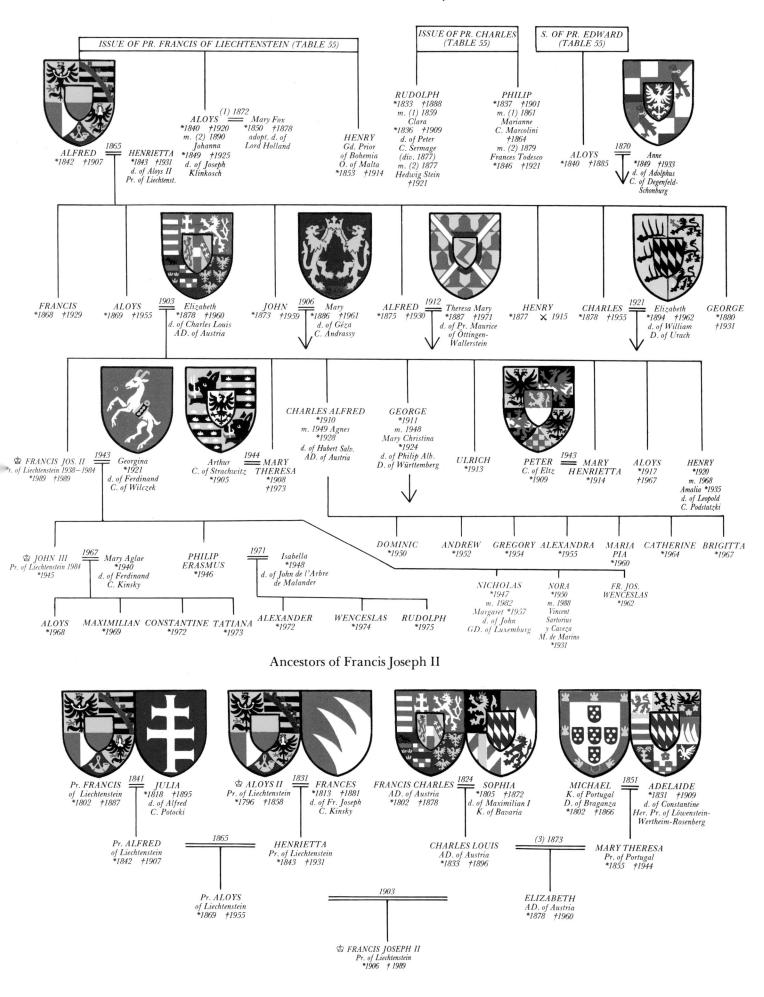

Ancestors of Francis Joseph II

Wenceslas (1696–1772), Prince of Liechtenstein, with the insignia of the Golden Fleece, by H. Rigaud, c. 1740.

stein to mediatized status, like so many petty German fiefs of the former Empire, but included it in the new Confederation of the Rhine. After Waterloo Prince John was able to regain independence. His son, Aloys II, took a more positive interest in the Principality, which formed part of the Germanic Confederation, and engineered in 1852 a Customs Union with Austria. He was succeeded in 1858 by his 18-year-old son, John II, who ruled until 1929, a reign of 71 years without minority, which is believed to be a European record. Prince John saw many changes; at first he minted Germanic thalers, then Austrian crowns, and finally Swiss francs. He witnessed the rise and fall of the German Empire, the collapse of the Austrian and Russian Empires, but he continued to care for his people, often out of his private fortune. In 1924 he arranged a Customs Union with Switzerland; when he died he was honoured and esteemed by all his subjects.

His brother Francis I founded the Order of Merit which encircles the coat-of-arms on Table 54. The five divisions of the shield represent five of the family estates – Silesia, Künring, Troppau, Ostfriesland-Rietberg, and (in base) Jägerndorf. The arms of Künring are easily confused with those of Saxony, but have only eight bars – with gold at the top. Ostfriesland, acquired by the marriage of Prince Gundakar in 1604, has the unusual charge of a crowned harpy with human head and breasts. Over all is the gold and red escutcheon of Liechtenstein.

When Francis I died in 1938, he was followed by his cousin (and also great-nephew) Francis Joseph II (Table 56), whose father, Prince Aloys, had renounced his rights of succession in 1923. The young ruler was successful in preserving the neutrality of Liechtenstein during the Second World War. His ancestry shows an international flavour, ranging from Poland to Portugal, with a double strain of his own long-lived family. Post-war years have brought financial prosperity to his miniature state, with its low taxation attractive to foreign companies. All lovers of history will hope that it long retains its freedom.

end to the Holy Roman Empire. Despite the fact that Prince John was leading troops against him, Napoleon did not reduce the principality of Liechten-

Chapter 13

MONACO

The Principality of Monaco, a mere one and a half square kilometres in area, is a narrow strip along the shore of the Mediterranean. Today the Côte d'Azur is renowned as an international holiday resort; its early history was more violent and chequered. Fraxinetum, a famous nest of Saracen pirates who preyed on the shipping of those waters, was not extirpated until the end of the tenth century; the various steep promontories were a temptation to the castle-building and restless nobility. In the twelfth century the Emperor Frederick I (Barbarossa) gave the Republic of Genoa certain rights over the coastline near Nice. Among the leading families of Genoa was that of Grimaldi, and its scions began to interest themselves in the excellent harbour of Monaco and the rocky headland beside it.

In 1297 Francis Grimaldi (Table 57) seized Monaco and established himself there. By tradition he and his companions got into the castle by disguising themselves as friars; and two Franciscans with swords are still the supporters of the princely arms, which consist of a bold pattern of fifteen red diamonds on a white background. Charles I of Monaco (d. 1363) was an admiral in the service of France, and raided Southampton in 1339; he also fought at Crécy. He was, however, ejected from Monaco by the Genoese ruler Simone de Boccanegra, commemorated in the opera by Verdi. Rainier II recaptured the town; of his sons Ambrose was drowned and John became an Admiral of France. He laid down in his will that any heiress must marry another Grimaldi; this duly occurred when his granddaughter, Claudine, was won by her cousin Lambert, Lord of Antibes, after a certain amount of competition. Gradually Monaco began to assert its independence. In 1489 the Dukes of Savoy recognized that the Lordship was free of other suzerains; in 1512 the King of France admitted that Lucien (k. 1523)

was entirely independent, in consequence of which Lucien began to mint his own coins.

In 1525 the Emperor Charles V in turn conceded independence and protection to Monaco, in favour of Augustine (who was also Bishop of Grasse), and paid a state visit a few years later. Honoré I fought during the siege of Malta and at the Battle of Lepanto against the Turks. Honoré II abandoned the protection of Spain for that of France; he was the first of the Grimaldi to give up the use of the surname in official documents and to style himself prince; in 1642 he was created Duke of Valentinois and a peer of France.

His descendants made a series of marriages which added to their wealth and their titles, if not to their happiness. Louis I (Table 58), who was finally recognized as sovereign prince by Louis XIV (his godfather) in 1688, married Charlotte de Gramont, who furnished Dumas with material for one of his novels. Their son Anthony espoused a member of the House of Lorraine, but she bore him only daughters. In 1715 James de Goyon de Matignon, the head of an ancient Breton family (the Goyon-Matignon alliance took place in about 1200) was prepared to give up his name and arms (which are shown on Table 57) to assume those of Grimaldi and marry the heiress Louise-Hyppolite. Archbishop Honoré ceded his rights to James, who at first incurred the wrath of Prince Anthony by combining the blazons of Matignon and Monaco. Louise died shortly after her father, and, after ruling for two years, James withdrew to the comforts of Paris. Their son Honoré III also acquired a wealthy wife, but she left him to live for half a lifetime with the Prince of Condé whom she eventually married after a liaison of 48 years. In 1793 the French Revolutionaries incorporated the little state in the *département* of Alpes Maritimes and for a while the Principality vanished.

Honoré IV was too ill to rule in person after the

Rainier III (b.1923), Prince of Monaco, broke with precedent by marrying the film star, Grace Kelly.

restoration of 1814, but he did make a profitable alliance; his wife brought him the Duchy of Mazarin – though she divorced him during the Revolution and re-married several times. Honoré V entered the service of Napoleon, was Grand Equerry to the Empress Josephine, and was created a Baron of the Empire. Returning to his father's domain in 1815, he met Napoleon just returned from Elba, but declined to exchange the reality of Monaco for the hazards of the Hundred Days. In 1816 he was compelled to do homage to the King of Sardinia for the outlying lands of Menton and Roquebrune.

In the early nineteenth century the tiny Principality was barren and impoverished. It was Charles III who took the sensational step of giving Louis Blanc in 1863 a concession to establish sea-bathing and a casino. Complaints from the French Government were met by a threat to abdicate in favour of his German nephew the Duke of Urach. He thus established the modern prosperity of his state and began the now traditional lure of Monte Carlo, though his dominions were diminished by the cession of Menton and Roquebrune to France in 1861. In 1858 he founded the Order of St Charles (Table 57).

Albert I, who followed Charles III, was a distinguished scholar in marine biology who built up an important aquarium in Monaco. His marriage with a daughter of the British Duke of Hamilton was unhappy; and his wife left him having borne one son. This son, Prince Louis, showed no inclination to marry at all, which became a source of disquiet to the French Government; the next heir was still the Duke of Urach, a subject of the German Emperor. Accordingly, in 1911 an illegitimate daughter, whom Louis had casually begotten in North Africa, was brought to Monaco and by stages declared legitimate, and made heiress to the Principality. She was created Duchess of Valentinois and married to a Frenchman, Count Peter of Polignac in 1920. The union was scarcely successful, but a son and a daughter were born and the dynasty ensured. Count Peter assumed the name and arms of Grimaldi.

Prince Louis II, though his appearance was Teutonic, joined the French Army in the First World War. His grandson, Prince Rainier, fought in the Second under General de Lattre de Tassigny. Towards the end of his life Prince Louis married an actress; meanwhile his daughter had already (1944) resigned her rights in favour of her son. Accordingly, on the death of Prince Louis, his grandson succeeded as Prince Rainier III. In 1956 he married the American actress, Grace Kelly, a romantic alliance of princely lineage and rare beauty, designed to perpetuate this small, enduring state into the uncertain future.

Chapter 14

DYNASTIC RELATIONS

Such alliances as that between the Prince of Monaco and a glamorous actress of the international screen would have been quite impossible, for more reasons than one, only a short time ago. A long tradition has prevailed that the members of royal or reigning families marry only among their own class. When a new family, such as the Tudors in England or the Bonapartes in France, secured a throne, one of its first impulses was to marry into an established princely dynasty. In consequence the ruling Houses of Europe have always been closely related one to another. Marriages were arranged to cement old and enduring friendships, such as those between France and Scotland or between England and Portugal; but more often they were designed to ratify treaties or to end a period of hostility. The pages of history are spattered with sad examples of the illusion that a wedding between two rival kingdoms must bring peace in its wake. A parallel error was the belief that the loyalty of cadets of the royal House could be secured by the bestowal of large domains. York and Lancaster in England or Burgundy in France are illustrations of the failure of such plans.

The passage of time strengthened the convention that royalty only allied with royalty, and from the sixteenth century onwards marriages between crown and commoner became rarer and rarer. At the same time the impact of the Reformation and the subsequent wars of religion tended to divide the ruling princes of Europe into two groups, Catholic and Protestant, between which intermarriage was infrequent. Thus in the eighteenth and nineteenth centuries the sovereigns of England, Holland and the Scandinavian Powers normally sought their wives among themselves or among the Reformed dynasties of Germany. On the other hand the Bourbons, Hapsburgs and Savoyards of France, Spain, Austria and Italy wedded among their own numerous branches or with the Catholic Houses in Germany. The bar was in no sense complete, because one partner in the alliance (more usually the wife) could change religion to conform to the spouse's faith. Orthodox Russia in general sought marriages in Protestant Germany or Sweden.

Nowhere was the principle of dynastic purity taken more seriously than in Germany, where various reigning families laid down codes regulating possible marriages. To lend some status to weddings between non-equal persons, the morganatic marriage was evolved, whereby the issue were given a title, and a status below that of truly royal alliances. These refinements never prevailed in England; two German families, the Dukes of Teck and the Princes of Battenberg (later Mountbatten), morganatically descended from the Houses of Württemberg and Hesse respectively, married into the British dynasty in the reign of Queen Victoria.

Tables 59–60 show the close connection which existed between the kings of Europe in 1914. The important rulers were all intimately related to each other, and even the remoter Balkan rulers were linked to the historic dynasties. Thus, King George V of England was first cousin of his ally the Emperor of Russia, to whom he bore a striking resemblance. But he was also first cousin of Emperor William II of Germany, whom he was to defeat after four catastrophic years of war. Similarly, in southern, Catholic Europe, Victor Emanuel III of Italy was the second cousin of his enemy the Emperor Francis Joseph of Austria. Mere kinship was no protection against rising economic and national hostility.

COMMON ANCESTRY

Tables 61–2 illustrate how all the reigning sovereigns of the present day are descended from William the Conqueror. It may be added that the same descent

Relationship of European monarchs before and at the time of the First World War

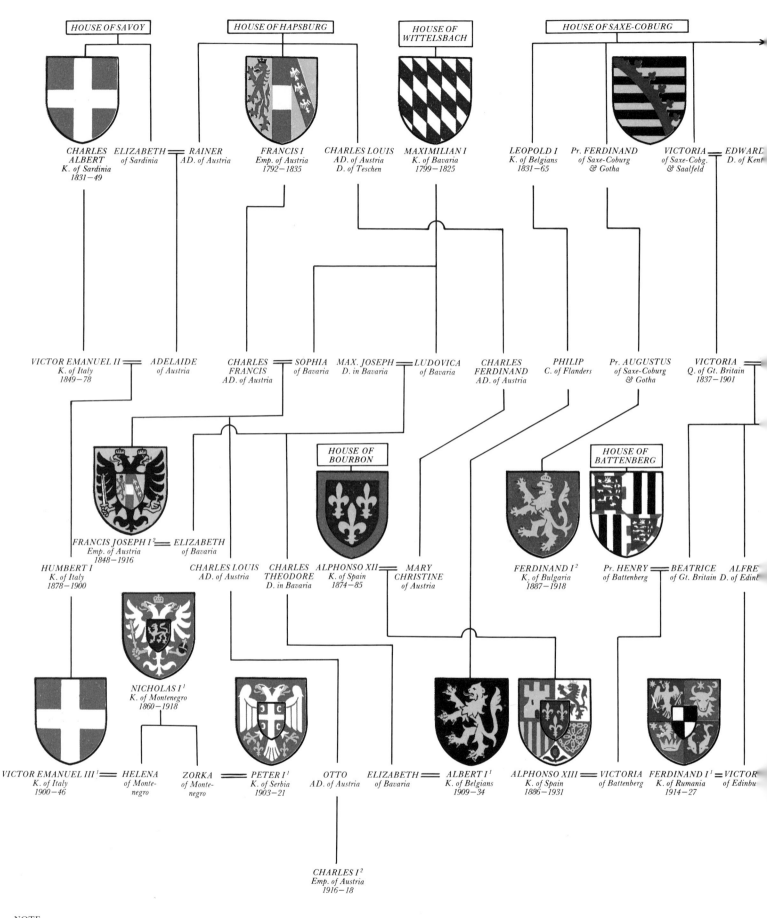

NOTE
[1] Allied sovereign
[2] Sovereign of the Central Powers
All dates are those of regnal years.
The dynastic arms of a House are shown beneath its name.

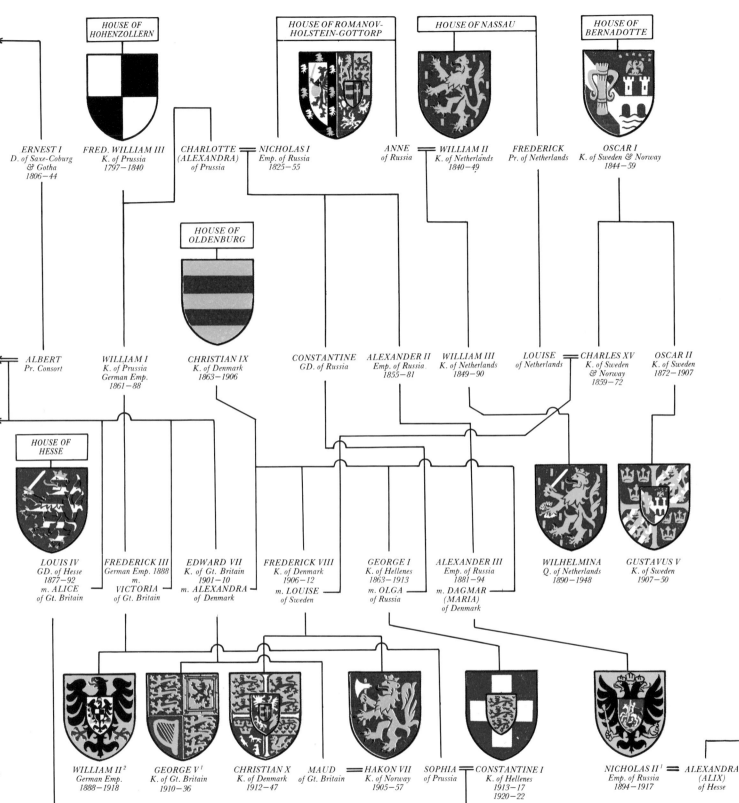

HOUSE OF HOHENZOLLERN

HOUSE OF ROMANOV-HOLSTEIN-GOTTORP

HOUSE OF NASSAU

HOUSE OF BERNADOTTE

ERNEST I
D. of Saxe-Coburg
& Gotha
1806—44

FRED. WILLIAM III
K. of Prussia
1797—1840

CHARLOTTE
(ALEXANDRA)
of Prussia

NICHOLAS I
Emp. of Russia
1825—55

ANNE
of Russia

WILLIAM II
K. of Netherlands
1840—49

FREDERICK
Pr. of Netherlands

OSCAR I
K. of Sweden & Norway
1844—59

HOUSE OF OLDENBURG

ALBERT
Pr. Consort

WILLIAM I
K. of Prussia
German Emp.
1861—88

CHRISTIAN IX
K. of Denmark
1863—1906

CONSTANTINE
GD. of Russia

ALEXANDER II
Emp. of Russia
1855—81

WILLIAM III
K. of Netherlands
1849—90

LOUISE
of Netherlands

CHARLES XV
K. of Sweden
& Norway
1859—72

OSCAR II
K. of Sweden
1872—1907

HOUSE OF HESSE

LOUIS IV
GD. of Hesse
1877—92
m. ALICE
of Gt. Britain

FREDERICK III
German Emp. 1888
m.
VICTORIA
of Gt. Britain

EDWARD VII
K. of Gt. Britain
1901—10
m. ALEXANDRA
of Denmark

FREDERICK VIII
K. of Denmark
1906—12
m. LOUISE
of Sweden

GEORGE I
K. of Hellenes
1863—1913
m. OLGA
of Russia

ALEXANDER III
Emp. of Russia
1881—94
m. DAGMAR
(MARIA)
of Denmark

WILHELMINA
Q. of Netherlands
1890—1948

GUSTAVUS V
K. of Sweden
1907—50

WILLIAM II[2]
German Emp.
1888—1918

GEORGE V[1]
K. of Gt. Britain
1910—36

CHRISTIAN X
K. of Denmark
1912—47

MAUD
of Gt. Britain

HAKON VII
K. of Norway
1905—57

SOPHIA
of Prussia

CONSTANTINE I
K. of Hellenes
1913—17
1920—22

NICHOLAS II[1]
Emp. of Russia
1894—1917

ALEXANDRA
(ALIX)
of Hesse

ALEXANDER[1]
K. of Hellenes
1917—20

Common descent of the present European sovereigns since William the Conqueror

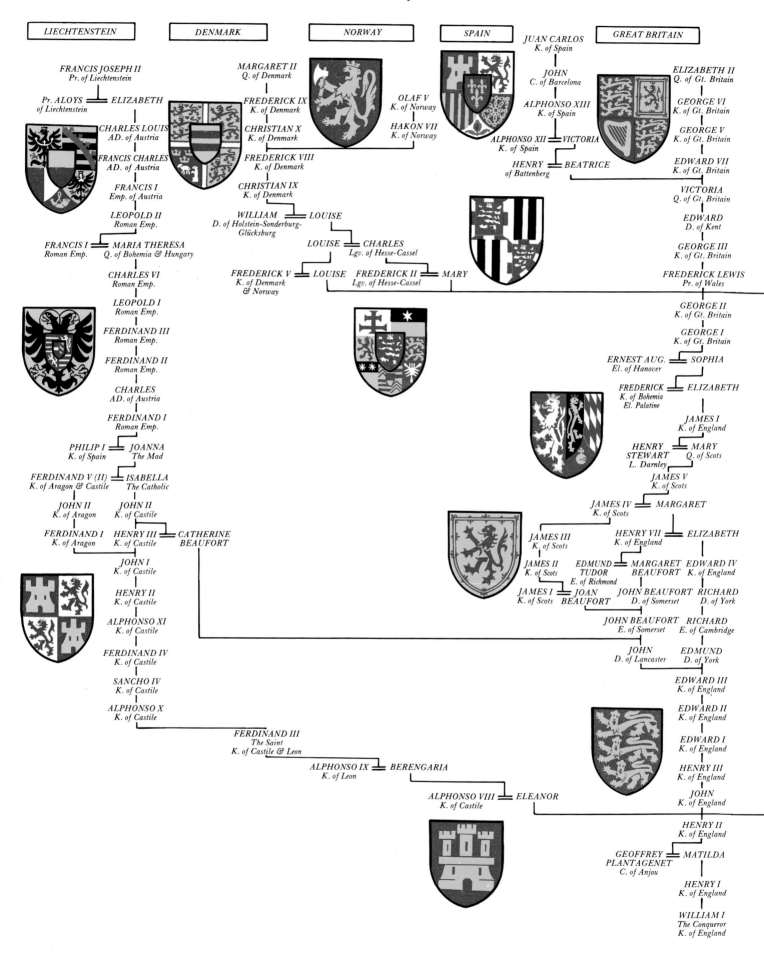

LIECHTENSTEIN	DENMARK	NORWAY	SPAIN	GREAT BRITAIN

FRANCIS JOSEPH II
Pr. of Liechtenstein

Pr. ALOYS ══ **ELIZABETH**
of Liechtenstein

CHARLES LOUIS
AD. of Austria

FRANCIS CHARLES
AD. of Austria

FRANCIS I
Emp. of Austria

LEOPOLD II
Roman Emp.

FRANCIS I ══ **MARIA THERESA**
Roman Emp. · *Q. of Bohemia & Hungary*

CHARLES VI
Roman Emp.

LEOPOLD I
Roman Emp.

FERDINAND III
Roman Emp.

FERDINAND II
Roman Emp.

CHARLES
AD. of Austria

FERDINAND I
Roman Emp.

PHILIP I ══ **JOANNA**
K. of Spain · *The Mad*

FERDINAND V (II) ══ **ISABELLA**
K. of Aragon & Castile · *The Catholic*

JOHN II   **JOHN II**
K. of Aragon · *K. of Castile*

FERDINAND I   **HENRY III** ══ **CATHERINE BEAUFORT**
K. of Aragon · *K. of Castile*

JOHN I
K. of Castile

HENRY II
K. of Castile

ALPHONSO XI
K. of Castile

FERDINAND IV
K. of Castile

SANCHO IV
K. of Castile

ALPHONSO X
K. of Castile

FERDINAND III
The Saint
K. of Castile & Leon

ALPHONSO IX ══ **BERENGARIA**
K. of Leon

ALPHONSO VIII ══ **ELEANOR**
K. of Castile

MARGARET II
Q. of Denmark

FREDERICK IX
K. of Denmark

CHRISTIAN X
K. of Denmark

FREDERICK VIII
K. of Denmark

CHRISTIAN IX
K. of Denmark

WILLIAM ══ **LOUISE**
D. of Holstein-Sonderburg-Glücksburg

LOUISE ══ **CHARLES**
Lgv. of Hesse-Cassel

FREDERICK V ══ **LOUISE**   **FREDERICK II** ══ **MARY**
K. of Denmark & Norway · *Lgv. of Hesse-Cassel*

OLAF V
K. of Norway

HAKON VII
K. of Norway

JUAN CARLOS
K. of Spain

JOHN
C. of Barcelona

ALPHONSO XIII
K. of Spain

ALPHONSO XII ══ **VICTORIA**
K. of Spain

HENRY ══ **BEATRICE**
of Battenberg

ELIZABETH II
Q. of Gt. Britain

GEORGE VI
K. of Gt. Britain

GEORGE V
K. of Gt. Britain

EDWARD VII
K. of Gt. Britain

VICTORIA
Q. of Gt. Britain

EDWARD
D. of Kent

GEORGE III
K. of Gt. Britain

FREDERICK LEWIS
Pr. of Wales

GEORGE II
K. of Gt. Britain

GEORGE I
K. of Gt. Britain

ERNEST AUG. ══ **SOPHIA**
El. of Hanover

FREDERICK ══ **ELIZABETH**
K. of Bohemia
El. Palatine

JAMES I
K. of England

HENRY STEWART ══ **MARY**
L. Darnley · *Q. of Scots*

JAMES V
K. of Scots

JAMES IV ══ **MARGARET**
K. of Scots

JAMES III   **HENRY VII** ══ **ELIZABETH**
K. of Scots · *K. of England*

JAMES II   **EDMUND TUDOR** ══ **MARGARET BEAUFORT**   **EDWARD IV**
K. of Scots · *E. of Richmond* · *K. of England*

JAMES I ══ **JOAN BEAUFORT**   **JOHN BEAUFORT**   **RICHARD**
K. of Scots · *D. of Somerset* · *D. of York*

JOHN BEAUFORT   **RICHARD**
E. of Somerset · *E. of Cambridge*

JOHN   **EDMUND**
D. of Lancaster · *D. of York*

EDWARD III
K. of England

EDWARD II
K. of England

EDWARD I
K. of England

HENRY III
K. of England

JOHN
K. of England

HENRY II
K. of England

GEOFFREY PLANTAGENET ══ **MATILDA**
C. of Anjou

HENRY I
K. of England

WILLIAM I
The Conqueror
K. of England

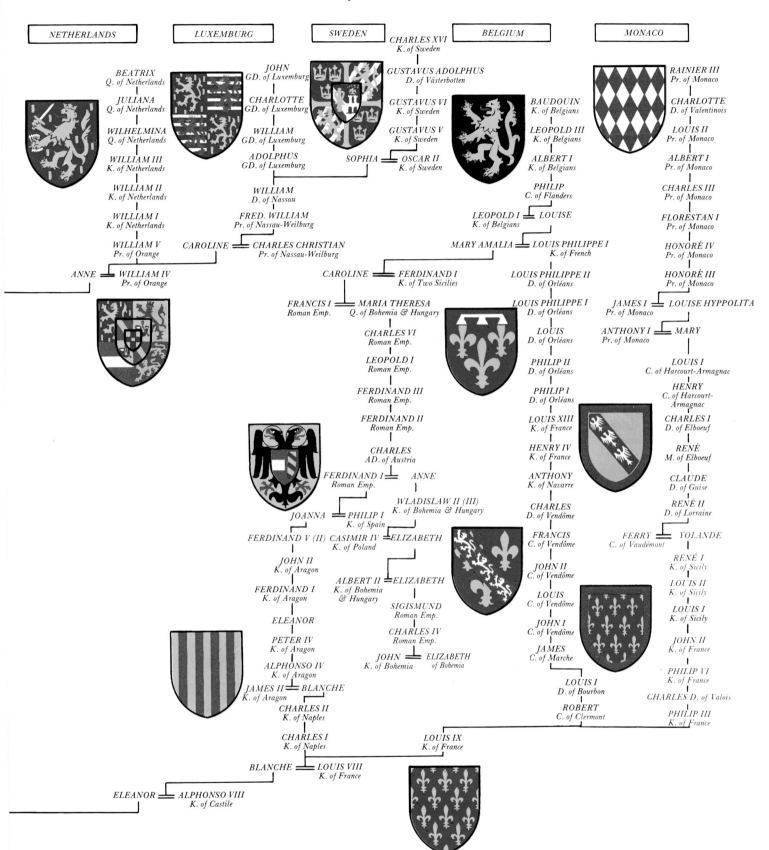

NETHERLANDS

BEATRIX
Q. of Netherlands

JULIANA
Q. of Netherlands

WILHELMINA
Q. of Netherlands

WILLIAM III
K. of Netherlands

WILLIAM II
K. of Netherlands

WILLIAM I
K. of Netherlands

WILLIAM V
Pr. of Orange

ANNE ⚯ WILLIAM IV
Pr. of Orange

LUXEMBURG

JOHN
GD. of Luxemburg

CHARLOTTE
GD. of Luxemburg

WILLIAM
GD. of Luxemburg

ADOLPHUS
GD. of Luxemburg

WILLIAM
D. of Nassau

FRED. WILLIAM
Pr. of Nassau-Weilburg

CAROLINE ⚯ CHARLES CHRISTIAN
Pr. of Nassau-Weilburg

SWEDEN

CHARLES XVI
K. of Sweden

GUSTAVUS ADOLPHUS
D. of Västerbotten

GUSTAVUS VI
K. of Sweden

GUSTAVUS V
K. of Sweden

SOPHIA ⚯ OSCAR II
K. of Sweden

CAROLINE ⚯ FERDINAND I
K. of Two Sicilies

FRANCIS I ⚯ MARIA THERESA
Roman Emp.   Q. of Bohemia & Hungary

CHARLES VI
Roman Emp.

LEOPOLD I
Roman Emp.

FERDINAND III
Roman Emp.

FERDINAND II
Roman Emp.

CHARLES
AD. of Austria

FERDINAND I ⚯ ANNE
Roman Emp.

JOANNA ⚯ PHILIP I   WLADISLAW II (III)
K. of Spain   K. of Bohemia & Hungary

FERDINAND V (II) CASIMIR IV ⚯ ELIZABETH
K. of Poland

JOHN II
K. of Aragon

FERDINAND I   ALBERT II ⚯ ELIZABETH
K. of Aragon   K. of Bohemia
& Hungary

ELEANOR   SIGISMUND
Roman Emp.

PETER IV   CHARLES IV
K. of Aragon   Roman Emp.

ALPHONSO IV   JOHN ⚯ ELIZABETH
K. of Aragon   K. of Bohemia of Bohemia

JAMES II ⚯ BLANCHE
K. of Aragon

CHARLES II
K. of Naples

CHARLES I   LOUIS IX
K. of Naples   K. of France

BLANCHE ⚯ LOUIS VIII
K. of France

ELEANOR ⚯ ALPHONSO VIII
K. of Castile

BELGIUM

BAUDOUIN
K. of Belgians

LEOPOLD III
K. of Belgians

ALBERT I
K. of Belgians

PHILIP
C. of Flanders

LEOPOLD I ⚯ LOUISE
K. of Belgians

MARY AMALIA ⚯ LOUIS PHILIPPE I
K. of French

LOUIS PHILIPPE II
D. of Orléans

LOUIS PHILIPPE I
D. of Orléans

LOUIS
D. of Orléans

PHILIP II
D. of Orléans

PHILIP I
D. of Orléans

LOUIS XIII
K. of France

HENRY IV
K. of France

ANTHONY
K. of Navarre

CHARLES
D. of Vendôme

FRANCIS
C. of Vendôme

JOHN II
C. of Vendôme

LOUIS
C. of Vendôme

JOHN I
C. of Vendôme

JAMES
C. of Marche

LOUIS I
D. of Bourbon

ROBERT
C. of Clermont

MONACO

RAINIER III
Pr. of Monaco

CHARLOTTE
D. of Valentinois

LOUIS II
Pr. of Monaco

ALBERT I
Pr. of Monaco

CHARLES III
Pr. of Monaco

FLORESTAN I
Pr. of Monaco

HONORÉ IV
Pr. of Monaco

HONORÉ III
Pr. of Monaco

JAMES I ⚯ LOUISE HYPPOLITA
Pr. of Monaco

ANTHONY I ⚯ MARY
Pr. of Monaco

LOUIS I
C. of Harcourt-Armagnac

HENRY
C. of Harcourt-
Armagnac

CHARLES I
D. of Elboeuf

RENÉ
M. of Elboeuf

CLAUDE
D. of Guise

RENÉ II
D. of Lorraine

FERRY ⚯ YOLANDE
C. of Vaudémont

RENÉ I
K. of Sicily

LOUIS II
K. of Sicily

LOUIS I
K. of Sicily

JOHN II
K. of France

PHILIP VI
K. of France

CHARLES D. of Valois

PHILIP III
K. of France

TABLE 63

FRANCE
General survey

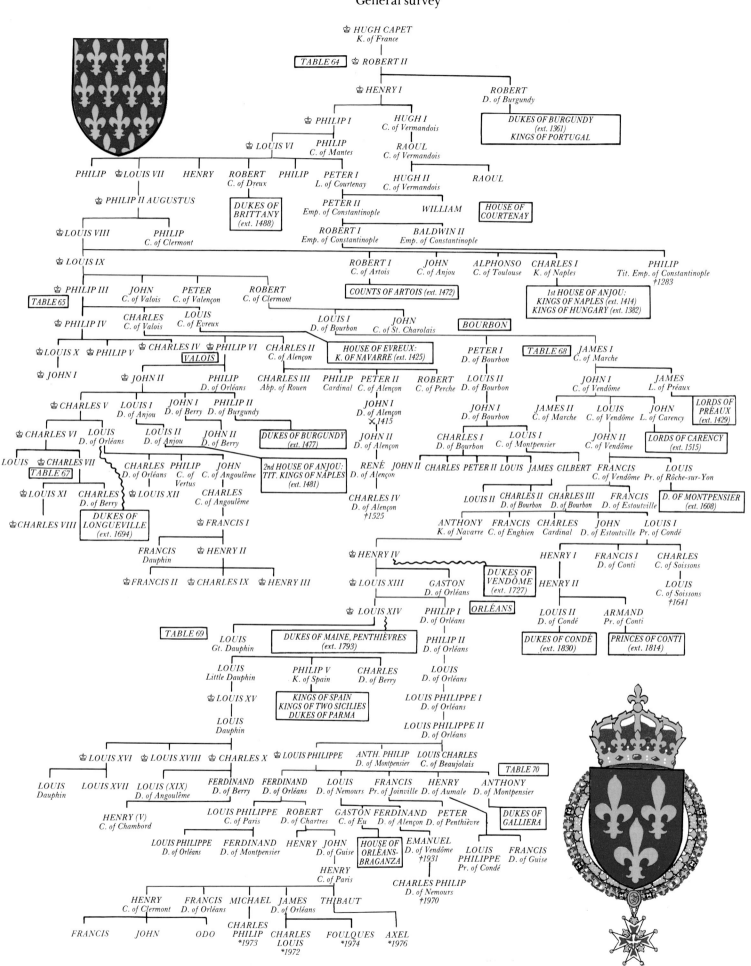

HUGH CAPET
K. of France

TABLE 64 · ROBERT II

HENRY I · ROBERT D. of Burgundy

PHILIP I · HUGH I C. of Vermandois · DUKES OF BURGUNDY (ext. 1361) KINGS OF PORTUGAL

LOUIS VI · PHILIP C. of Mantes · RAOUL C. of Vermandois

PHILIP · LOUIS VII · HENRY · ROBERT C. of Dreux · PHILIP · PETER I L. of Courtenay · HUGH II C. of Vermandois · RAOUL

PHILIP II AUGUSTUS · DUKES OF BRITTANY (ext. 1488) · PETER II Emp. of Constantinople · WILLIAM · HOUSE OF COURTENAY

LOUIS VIII · PHILIP C. of Clermont · ROBERT I Emp. of Constantinople · BALDWIN II Emp. of Constantinople

LOUIS IX · ROBERT I C. of Artois · JOHN C. of Anjou · ALPHONSO C. of Toulouse · CHARLES I K. of Naples · PHILIP Tit. Emp. of Constantinople †1283

PHILIP III · JOHN C. of Valois · PETER C. of Valençon · ROBERT C. of Clermont · COUNTS OF ARTOIS (ext. 1472) · 1st HOUSE OF ANJOU: KINGS OF NAPLES (ext. 1414) KINGS OF HUNGARY (ext. 1382)

TABLE 65

PHILIP IV · CHARLES C. of Valois · LOUIS C. of Evreux · LOUIS I D. of Bourbon · JOHN C. of St. Charolais · BOURBON

HOUSE OF EVREUX: K. OF NAVARRE (ext. 1425) · PETER I D. of Bourbon · TABLE 68 · JAMES I C. of Marche

LOUIS X · PHILIP V · CHARLES IV · PHILIP VI · CHARLES II C. of Alençon · LOUIS II D. of Bourbon · JOHN I C. of Vendôme · JAMES L. of Préaux

VALOIS

JOHN I · JOHN II · PHILIP D. of Orléans · CHARLES III Abp. of Rouen · PHILIP Cardinal · PETER II C. of Alençon · ROBERT C. of Perche · JOHN I D. of Bourbon · JAMES II C. of Marche · LOUIS C. of Vendôme · JOHN L. of Carency · LORDS OF PRÉAUX (ext. 1429)

CHARLES V · LOUIS I D. of Anjou · JOHN I D. of Berry · PHILIP II D. of Burgundy · JOHN I D. of Alençon ×1415 · CHARLES I D. of Bourbon · LOUIS I C. of Montpensier · JOHN II C. of Vendôme · LORDS OF CARENCY (ext. 1515)

CHARLES VI · LOUIS D. of Orléans · LOUIS II D. of Anjou · JOHN II D. of Berry · DUKES OF BURGUNDY (ext. 1477) · JOHN II D. of Alençon · CHARLES PETER II LOUIS JAMES GILBERT · FRANCIS C. of Vendôme · LOUIS Pr. of Rôche-sur-Yon

LOUIS · CHARLES VII · CHARLES D. of Orléans · PHILIP C. of Vertus · JOHN C. of Angoulême · 2nd HOUSE OF ANJOU: TIT. KINGS OF NAPLES (ext. 1481) · RENÉ D. of Alençon · JOHN II · LOUIS II · CHARLES II D. of Bourbon · CHARLES III D. of Bourbon · FRANCIS D. of Estoutville · D. OF MONTPENSIER (ext. 1608)

TABLE 67

LOUIS XI · CHARLES D. of Berry · LOUIS XII · CHARLES C. of Angoulême · CHARLES IV D. of Alençon †1525 · ANTHONY K. of Navarre · FRANCIS C. of Enghien · CHARLES Cardinal · JOHN D. of Estoutville · LOUIS I Pr. of Condé

CHARLES VIII · DUKES OF LONGUEVILLE (ext. 1694) · FRANCIS I · HENRY I · FRANCIS I D. of Conti · CHARLES C. of Soissons

FRANCIS Dauphin · HENRY II · HENRY IV · LOUIS XIII · GASTON D. of Orléans · DUKES OF VENDÔME (ext. 1727) · HENRY II · LOUIS C. of Soissons †1641

FRANCIS II · CHARLES IX · HENRY III · LOUIS XIV · PHILIP I D. of Orléans · ORLÉANS · LOUIS II D. of Condé · ARMAND Pr. of Conti

TABLE 69 · LOUIS Gt. Dauphin · DUKES OF MAINE, PENTHIÈVRES (ext. 1793) · PHILIP II D. of Orléans · DUKES OF CONDÉ (ext. 1830) · PRINCES OF CONTI (ext. 1814)

LOUIS Little Dauphin · PHILIP V K. of Spain · CHARLES D. of Berry · LOUIS D. of Orléans

LOUIS XV · KINGS OF SPAIN KINGS OF TWO SICILIES DUKES OF PARMA · LOUIS PHILIPPE I D. of Orléans

LOUIS Dauphin · LOUIS PHILIPPE II D. of Orléans

LOUIS XVI · LOUIS XVIII · CHARLES X · LOUIS PHILIPPE · ANTH. PHILIP D. of Montpensier · LOUIS CHARLES C. of Beaujolais · TABLE 70

LOUIS Dauphin · LOUIS XVII · LOUIS (XIX) D. of Angoulême · FERDINAND D. of Berry · FERDINAND D. of Orléans · LOUIS D. of Nemours · FRANCIS Pr. of Joinville · HENRY D. of Aumale · ANTHONY D. of Montpensier

HENRY (V) C. of Chambord · LOUIS PHILIPPE C. of Paris · ROBERT D. of Chartres · GASTON C. of Eu · FERDINAND D. of Alençon · PETER D. of Penthièvre · DUKES OF GALLIERA

LOUIS PHILIPPE D. of Orléans · FERDINAND D. of Montpensier · HENRY D. of Guise · JOHN D. of Guise · HOUSE OF ORLÉANS-BRAGANZA · EMANUEL D. of Vendôme †1931 · LOUIS PHILIPPE Pr. of Condé · FRANCIS D. of Guise

HENRY C. of Paris · CHARLES PHILIP D. of Nemours †1970

HENRY C. of Clermont · FRANCIS D. of Orléans · MICHAEL · JAMES D. of Orléans · THIBAUT

FRANCIS · JOHN · ODO · CHARLES PHILIP *1973 · CHARLES LOUIS *1972 · FOULQUES *1974 · AXEL *1976

TABLE 64

FRANCE
Early Capetian Kings

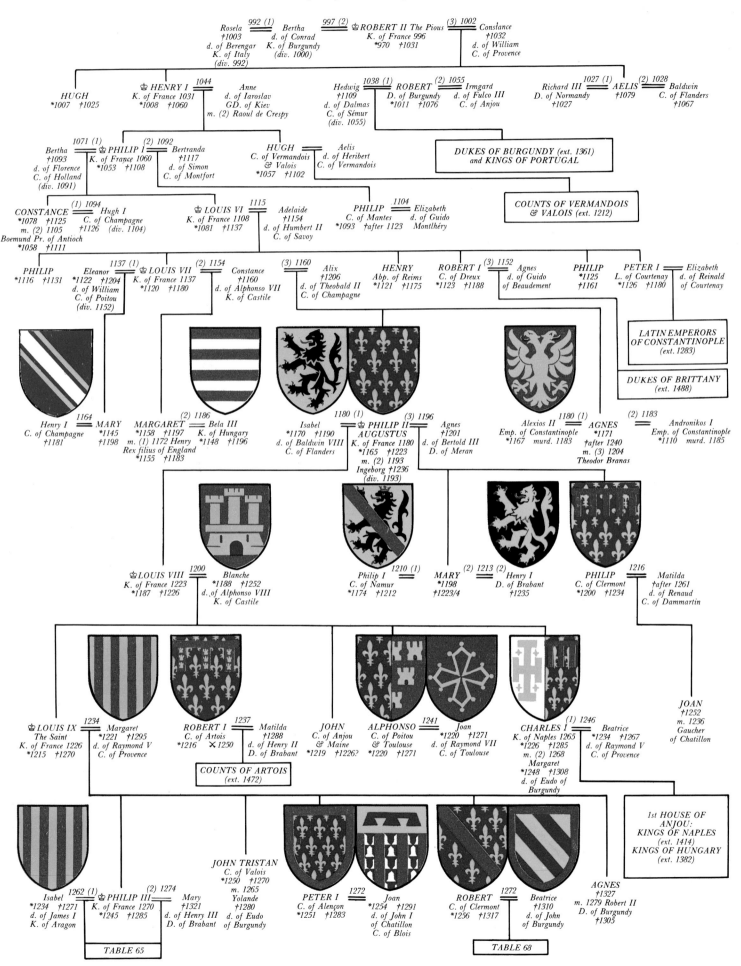

Rosela †1003 d. of Berengar K. of Italy (div. 992) ═══ 992 (1) ═══ *Bertha* d. of Conrad K. of Burgundy (div. 1000) ═══ 997 (2) ═══ ♛ *ROBERT II The Pious* K. of France 996 *970 †1031 ═══ (3) 1002 ═══ *Constance* †1032 d. of William C. of Provence

HUGH *1007 †1025

♛ **HENRY I** K. of France 1031 *1008 †1060 ═══ 1044 ═══ *Anne* d. of Iaroslav GD. of Kiev m. (2) Raoul de Crespy

Hedwig †1109 d. of Dalmas C. of Sémur (div. 1055) ═══ 1038 (1) ═══ **ROBERT** D. of Burgundy *1011 †1076 ═══ (2) 1055 ═══ *Irmgard* d. of Fulco III C. of Anjou

Richard III D. of Normandy †1027 ═══ 1027 (1) ═══ **AELIS** *1079 ═══ (2) 1028 ═══ *Baldwin* C. of Flanders †1067

Bertha †1093 d. of Florence C. of Holland (div. 1091) ═══ 1071 (1) ═══ ♛ **PHILIP I** K. of France 1060 *1053 †1108 ═══ (2) 1092 ═══ *Bertranda* †1117 d. of Simon C. of Montfort

HUGH C. of Vermandois & Valois *1057 †1102 ═══ *Aelis* d. of Heribert C. of Vermandois

DUKES OF BURGUNDY (ext. 1361) **and KINGS OF PORTUGAL**

COUNTS OF VERMANDOIS & VALOIS (ext. 1212)

CONSTANCE *1078 †1125 m. (2) 1105 Boemund Pr. of Antioch *1058 †1111 ═══ (1) 1094 ═══ *Hugh I* C. of Champagne †1126 (div. 1104)

♛ **LOUIS VI** K. of France 1108 *1081 †1137 ═══ 1115 ═══ *Adelaide* †1154 d. of Humbert II C. of Savoy

PHILIP C. of Mantes *1093 †after 1123 ═══ 1104 ═══ *Elizabeth* d. of Guido Montlhéry

PHILIP *1116 †1131

Eleanor *1122 †1204 d. of William C. of Poitou (div. 1152) ═══ 1137 (1) ═══ ♛ **LOUIS VII** K. of France 1137 *1120 †1180 ═══ (2) 1154 ═══ *Constance* †1160 d. of Alphonso VII K. of Castile ═══ (3) 1160 ═══ *Alix* †1206 d. of Theobald II C. of Champagne

HENRY Abp. of Reims *1121 †1175

ROBERT I C. of Dreux *1123 †1188 ═══ (3) 1152 ═══ *Agnes* d. of Guido of Beaudement

PHILIP *1125 †1161

PETER I L. of Courtenay *1126 †1180 ═══ *Elizabeth* d. of Reinald of Courtenay

LATIN EMPERORS OF CONSTANTINOPLE (ext. 1283)

DUKES OF BRITTANY (ext. 1488)

Henry I C. of Champagne †1181 ═══ 1164 ═══ **MARY** *1145 †1198

MARGARET *1158 †1197 m. (1) 1172 Henry Rex filius of England *1155 †1183 ═══ (2) 1186 ═══ *Bela III* K. of Hungary *1148 †1196

Isabel *1170 †1190 d. of Baldwin VIII C. of Flanders ═══ 1180 (1) ═══ ♛ **PHILIP II AUGUSTUS** K. of France 1180 *1165 †1223 m. (2) 1193 Ingeborg †1236 (div. 1193) ═══ (3) 1196 ═══ *Agnes* †1201 d. of Bertold III D. of Meran

Alexios II Emp. of Constantinople *1167 murd. 1183 ═══ 1180 (1) ═══ **AGNES** *1171 †after 1240 m. (3) 1204 Theodor Branas ═══ (2) 1183 ═══ *Andronikos I* Emp. of Constantinople *1110 murd. 1185

♛ **LOUIS VIII** K. of France 1223 *1187 †1226 ═══ 1200 ═══ *Blanche* *1188 †1252 d. of Alphonso VIII K. of Castile

Philip I C. of Namur *1174 †1212 ═══ 1210 (1) ═══ **MARY** *1198 †1223/4 ═══ (2) 1213 (2) ═══ *Henry I* D. of Brabant †1235

PHILIP C. of Clermont *1200 †1234 ═══ 1216 ═══ *Matilda* †after 1261 d. of Renaud C. of Dammartin

♛ **LOUIS IX The Saint** K. of France 1226 *1215 †1270 ═══ 1234 ═══ *Margaret* *1221 †1295 d. of Raymond V C. of Provence

ROBERT I C. of Artois *1216 ✕1250 ═══ 1237 ═══ *Matilda* †1288 d. of Henry II D. of Brabant

JOHN C. of Anjou & Maine *1219 †1226? ═══ **ALPHONSO** C. of Poitou & Toulouse *1220 †1271 ═══ 1241 ═══ *Joan* *1220 †1271 d. of Raymond VII C. of Toulouse

CHARLES I K. of Naples 1265 *1226 †1285 m. (2) 1268 Margaret *1248 †1308 d. of Eudo of Burgundy ═══ (1) 1246 ═══ *Beatrice* *1234 †1267 d. of Raymond V C. of Provence

JOAN †1252 m. 1236 Gaucher of Chatillon

COUNTS OF ARTOIS (ext. 1472)

1st HOUSE OF ANJOU: KINGS OF NAPLES (ext. 1414) **KINGS OF HUNGARY** (ext. 1382)

Isabel *1234 †1271 d. of James I K. of Aragon ═══ 1262 (1) ═══ ♛ **PHILIP III** K. of France 1270 *1245 †1285 ═══ (2) 1274 ═══ *Mary* †1321 d. of Henry III D. of Brabant

JOHN TRISTAN C. of Valois *1250 †1270 m. 1265 Yolande d. of Eudo of Burgundy

PETER I C. of Alençon *1251 †1283 ═══ 1272 ═══ *Joan* *1254 †1291 d. of John I of Chatillon C. of Blois

ROBERT C. of Clermont *1256 †1317 ═══ 1272 ═══ *Beatrice* †1310 d. of John of Burgundy

AGNES †1327 m. 1279 Robert II D. of Burgundy †1305

TABLE 65

TABLE 68

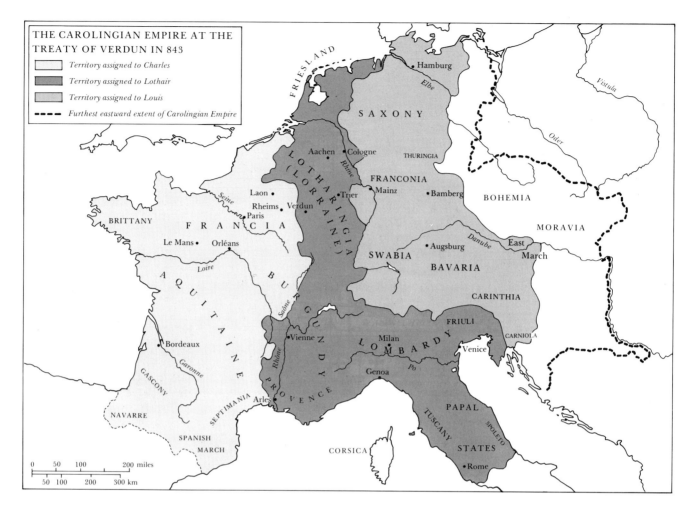

and lilies had been placed on the coinage of Louis VI and VII. Later generations liked to think of the flower as an emblem of the Virgin and of blue as her colour; but it is doubtful if these sentiments prevailed in the twelfth century. As in England the problem arose of distinguishing cadet branches of the family; Tables 64 and 65 reveal that the French made use of the label and the bordure but also frequently employed the bend, or diagonal stripe. Examples of each can be seen in the two lowest rows of Table 64; Robert, Count of Artois (whose label reflects the blazon of his mother), Peter, Count of Alençon, and Robert, Count of Clermont. It will be seen that Agnes, sister of Philip II, married the Emperor Alexios II; the arms displayed for him are what western authorities thought he ought to use, for heraldry in its western usage was not known in the Byzantine Empire.

RISE OF CAPETIAN POWER

Philip Augustus was a great and successful King of France. Talented, agile and unscrupulous, he was able to detach large portions of the Angevin inheritance and to extend his domain in other directions: Normandy, Maine and Anjou were wrested from John of England and he also acquired Artois and Berry. These provinces were to provide titles for generations of French princes. His son even invaded England unsuccessfully at the end of the reign of John, and during his short reign, as Louis VIII, conquered Poitou and lands in the south. Louis IX (Saint Louis) survived the perils of minority, partly thanks to his determined mother. He proved the pattern of medieval kingship. Austere but not weakly, brave and just, he ruled France devotedly and also spent much money and energy on crusades which were less successful. We know a lot about him because one of his admiring followers (Joinville) wrote a full life of the holy monarch. His father had bestowed large apanages on all his children and St Louis did the same. One of his brothers, Charles, Duke of Anjou, fared better still: first he married the heiress of Raymond IV of Provence, which was not then part of France, and secondly, at the request of the Pope, he undertook the conquest of the Kingdom of Naples and founded a dynasty there, which later briefly acquired Hungary also (Tables 125 and 90). These royal princes could at first be controlled by the head of the family, but later became a cause of trouble. Robert, Count of Clermont, a son of St Louis, was the ancestor of all the Kings of France from Henry IV onwards. It will be noticed that the arms of the wife of Louis IX (and that of Charles of Anjou), coming from Provence, and those of Isabel of Aragon, wife of Philip III, are the same, because they both belonged to branches of the same family.

One of the statesmanlike acts of St Louis was to renounce any claims south of the Pyrenees in favour of Aragon which equally gave up any claims on Languedoc. During the thirteenth century the potency of the German monarchy declined, and at the death of St Louis the Kingdom of France was the outstanding power in western Europe. This power was maintained by Philip III and Philip IV, who ruled with a series of professional advisers, well-read in law and devoted to the interests of the French monarchy. Their fortunes were linked with those of the Papacy. In 1271 Philip III inherited the wide estates of his childless uncle, Alphonse, Count of Poitou, whose arms include the blazon of his county; as an act of piety this rather colourless King bestowed upon the Pope the little County of Venaissin on the Rhône with Avignon as its chief town. His son Philip IV was a more sinister ruler, whose character is difficult to discern behind the acts of his ruthless and legalistic ministers. He became embroiled with Pope Boniface VIII, principally over the right of the lay rulers to tax the clergy of their own realms, and eventually sent agents to Italy who briefly seized the person of the Pontiff. The next Pope was a Frenchman and abandoned the turmoil of Rome for residence in Avignon.

King Philip IV made an important marriage with the heiress of Henry I, King of Navarre and also Count of Champagne (Table 65). Navarre was to pass, as has been seen, into other hands, but the Kings of France kept the rich and prosperous lands of Champagne; its chief city, Troyes, has given its name to troy weight. Philip also called, in 1302, the first meeting of the Three Estates – nobles, clergy and burgesses. In 1314 he completed his unscrupulous suppression of the Order of the Temple; the last Grand-Master was burned and is rumoured to have called upon the King to meet him hereafter. Within the year Philip was dead. He had enhanced the power of France, even if by doubtful means, and had gained some important towns on his eastern frontier, including Lyons. He also began in 1295 the long alliance with Scotland against England.

Philip IV left three sons who all succeeded to the throne, and who confronted France with the first succession problem since 987. Louis X died after a brief reign leaving a daughter and a pregnant wife; the latter gave birth to a son, John I, who lived only a few days. Promptly, Philip V, the next brother of Louis X, seized the throne. Some voices were raised in favour of his niece, Joanna, but an assembly in Paris declared that no female could inherit the throne of France. Accordingly, when Philip V died in 1322, leaving four daughters, he was naturally succeeded by his brother Charles IV, but the death of Charles IV six years later, also without sons, posed a more difficult problem.

His widow was pregnant, and Philip of Valois, the King's first cousin, was declared regent. When the Queen gave birth to a daughter, one thing was clear; Navarre would have to pass to Joanna, the senior heiress of Philip IV and his wife. But who should succeed to France? Edward III of England was male and a nephew of the late King; Philip of Valois was the nearest agnatic relation, that is by male descent. Not surprisingly the nobles who met in the capital decided in favour of their compatriot who became Philip VI, and inaugurated the House of Valois. Meanwhile Joanna married her cousin Philip, Count of Evreux, who reigned as Philip III of Navarre and whose descendants ruled there until 1425.

THE HUNDRED YEARS' WAR

Like many of his predecessors, Philip VI sought to extend his influence in Flanders. The towns of Flanders were already exceedingly prosperous centres of weaving and had a natural alliance with England which was a supplier of raw wool. Two parties in the area bore quasi-heraldic names; the mercantile upper classes, who had been linked with Philip IV against their Count, were called *leliaerts* from the lilies of France, while the lower ranks called themselves *clauwerts* (claw-men) in allusion to the lion in the arms of Flanders (Table 64, top row). By 1328 the reigning Count had allied himself to the *leliaerts* and called in the help of his overlord, Philip VI, against the workers. At the battle of Mount Cassel, the latter were massacred by the French cavalry, an event which may have given the French knights an inflated opinion of their military value. The Flemings, undaunted, turned again to England and besought Edward III to renew his claim to the Crown of France (Table 66).

As has been seen (Chapter 2) Edward responded to this challenge in 1340 by quartering the arms of France with his own as a symbol of his pretensions, and the long struggle of the Hundred Years' War began. On the one side Philip VI and his son John II, and on the other Edward III, were all very much children of their age and saw life and war in terms of chivalry. Not much strategy entered into their campaigns. In both Kingdoms the war meant increased taxation; at first it was more popular in England than in France, not least because it was fought on the soil of France with intermittent but destructive raids. The early pitched battles went in favour of England, and at Poitiers (1356), John II was captured. The

TABLE 65

FRANCE
Succession of the House of Valois

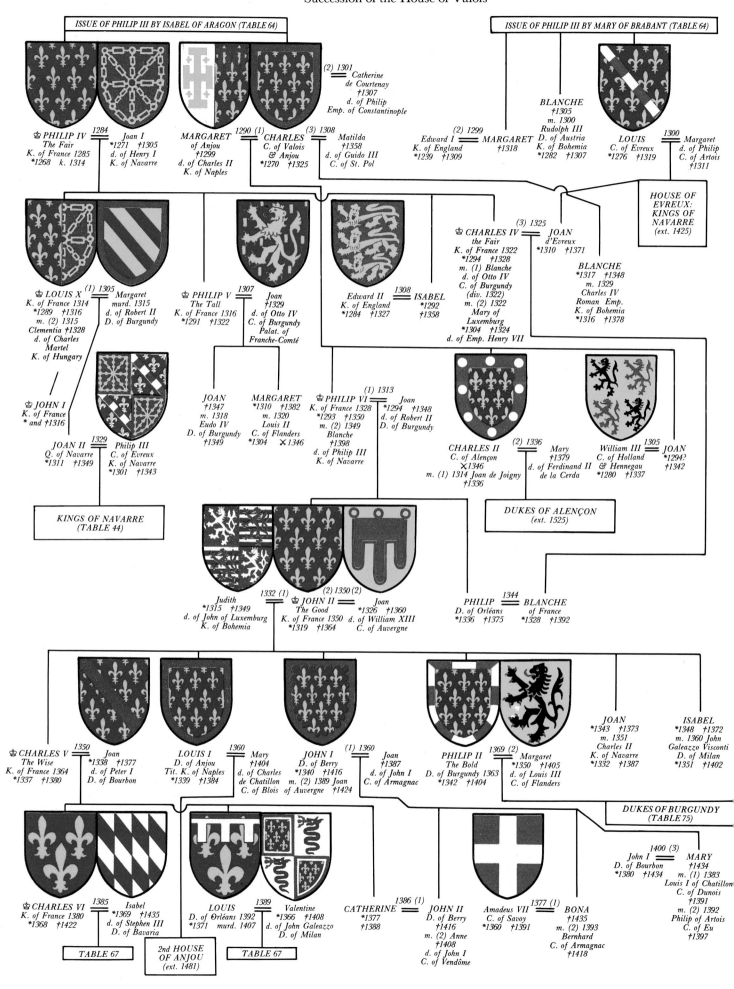

ISSUE OF PHILIP III BY ISABEL OF ARAGON (TABLE 64)

ISSUE OF PHILIP III BY MARY OF BRABANT (TABLE 64)

♛ PHILIP IV | 1284 | Joan I
The Fair | | *1271 †1305
K. of France 1285 | | d. of Henry I
*1268 k. 1314 | | K. of Navarre

MARGARET | 1290 (1) | CHARLES | (3) 1308 | Matilda
of Anjou | | C. of Valois | | †1358
†1299 | | & Anjou | | d. of Guido III
d. of Charles II | | *1270 †1325 | | C. of St. Pol
K. of Naples

(2) 1301
Catherine
de Courtenay
†1307
d. of Philip
Emp. of Constantinople

(2) 1299
Edward I | MARGARET
K. of England | †1318
*1239 †1309

BLANCHE
†1305
m. 1300
Rudolph III
D. of Austria
K. of Bohemia
*1282 †1307

LOUIS | 1300 | Margaret
C. of Evreux | | d. of Philip
*1276 †1319 | | C. of Artois
| | †1311

HOUSE OF
EVREUX:
KINGS OF
NAVARRE
(ext. 1425)

♛ LOUIS X | (1) 1305 | Margaret
K. of France 1314 | | murd. 1315
*1289 †1316 | | d. of Robert II
m. (2) 1315 | | D. of Burgundy
Clementia †1328
d. of Charles
Martel
K. of Hungary

♛ PHILIP V | 1307 | Joan
The Tall | | †1329
K. of France 1316 | | d. of Otto IV
*1291 †1322 | | C. of Burgundy
| | Palat. of
| | Franche-Comté

Edward II | 1308 | ISABEL
K. of England | | *1292
*1284 †1327 | | †1358

♛ CHARLES IV | (3) 1325 | JOAN
the Fair | | d'Evreux
K. of France 1322 | | *1310 †1371
*1294 †1328
m. (1) Blanche
d. of Otto IV
C. of Burgundy
(div. 1322)
m. (2) 1322
Mary of
Luxemburg
*1304 †1324
d. of Emp. Henry VII

BLANCHE
*1317 †1348
m. 1329
Charles IV
Roman Emp.
K. of Bohemia
*1316 †1378

♛ JOHN I
K. of France
* and †1316

JOAN II | 1329 | Philip III
Q. of Navarre | | C. of Evreux
*1311 †1349 | | K. of Navarre
| | *1301 †1343

KINGS OF NAVARRE
(TABLE 44)

JOAN
†1347
m. 1318
Eudo IV
D. of Burgundy
†1349

MARGARET
*1310 †1382
m. 1320
Louis II
C. of Flanders
*1304 ✕1346

♛ PHILIP VI | (1) 1313 | Joan
K. of France 1328 | | *1294 †1348
*1293 †1350 | | d. of Robert II
m. (2) 1349 | | D. of Burgundy
Blanche
†1398
d. of Philip III
K. of Navarre

CHARLES II
C. of Alençon
✕1346
m. (1) 1314 Joan de Joigny
†1336

(2) 1336
Mary
†1379
d. of Ferdinand II
de la Cerda

William III | 1305 | JOAN
C. of Holland | | *1294?
& Hennegau | | †1342
*1280 †1337

DUKES OF ALENÇON
(ext. 1525)

Judith | 1332 (1) | ♛ JOHN II | (2) 1350 (2) | Joan
*1315 †1349 | | The Good | | *1326 †1360
d. of John of Luxemburg | | K. of France 1350 | | d. of William XIII
K. of Bohemia | | *1319 †1364 | | C. of Auvergne

PHILIP | 1344 | BLANCHE
D. of Orléans | | of France
*1336 †1375 | | *1328 †1392

♛ CHARLES V | 1350 | Joan
The Wise | | *1338 †1377
K. of France 1364 | | d. of Peter I
*1337 †1380 | | D. of Bourbon

LOUIS I | 1360 | Mary
D. of Anjou | | †1404
Tit. K. of Naples | | d. of Charles
*1339 †1384 | | de Chatillon
| | C. of Blois

JOHN I | (1) 1360 | Joan
D. of Berry | | †1387
*1340 †1416 | | d. of John I
m. (2) 1389 Joan | | C. of Armagnac
of Auvergne †1424

PHILIP II | 1369 (2) | Margaret
The Bold | | *1350 †1405
D. of Burgundy 1363 | | d. of Louis III
*1342 †1404 | | C. of Flanders

JOAN
*1343 †1373
m. 1351
Charles II
K. of Navarre
*1332 †1387

ISABEL
*1348 †1372
m. 1360 John
Galeazzo Visconti
D. of Milan
*1351 †1402

DUKES OF BURGUNDY
(TABLE 75)

♛ CHARLES VI | 1385 | Isabel
K. of France 1380 | | *1369 †1435
*1368 †1422 | | d. of Stephen III
| | D. of Bavaria

LOUIS | 1389 | Valentine
D. of Orléans 1392 | | *1366 †1408
*1371 murd. 1407 | | d. of John Galeazzo
| | D. of Milan

CATHERINE | 1386 (1)
*1377
†1388

JOHN II
D. of Berry
†1416
m. (2) Anne
†1408
d. of John I
C. of Vendôme

Amadeus VII | 1377 (1) | BONA
C. of Savoy | | †1435
*1360 †1391 | | m. (2) 1393
| | Bernhard
| | C. of Armagnac
| | †1418

John I | 1400 (3) | MARY
D. of Bourbon | | †1434
*1380 †1434 | | m. (1) 1383
| | Louis I of Chatillon
| | C. of Dunois
| | †1391
| | m. (2) 1392
| | Philip of Artois
| | C. of Eu
| | †1397

TABLE 67

2nd HOUSE
OF ANJOU
(ext. 1481)

TABLE 67

chivalry of France was quite unable to cope with the archers of England and suffered hideous losses in these battles. The condition of France was now sombre; her King was in prison and needing ransom, her treasury empty, her coinage debased and her fields devastated. There were risings of the miserable peasants known as *Jacquerie*. In 1360 peace was concluded between Edward III and the Dauphin of France; a large area of Aquitaine and also Calais was ceded to the English King absolutely while John II was to be ransomed for 3,000,000 gold crowns.

The future Charles V was the first French heir apparent to use the title of Dauphin. It was derived from the province of Dauphiné, between Savoy and Provence, whose ruler had sold it to Philip VI with the condition that the eldest son of the King of France should be so styled. One great chance fell in favour of John II. The first line of Dukes of Burgundy, descended from Robert II (Tables 63 and 74), died out in the male line in 1361, and the Duchy of Burgundy, lying within France, therefore escheated to the French Crown. John II then bestowed it on his fourth son. The County of Burgundy (the later Franche-Comté), lying within the Empire of Germany, passed to the descendants of Philip V of France, but was reunited with the French province by the marriage of Philip the Bold. France was unable to raise the ransom required for John II; one of his hostages fled and with typical, if futile, chivalric spirit the King returned to London and died there.

Charles V was a very different man from his father. He was scholarly, he was not interested in battles but in law, he had a sense of order. Good fortune brought him a distinguished and successful Breton soldier, Bertrand du Guesclin, who was rewarded with the Constableship of France. Artillery was introduced into the reformed French army, pitched battles were avoided and the English conquests were gradually whittled away. With some art, the so-called Free Companies, which had been ravaging the soil of France, were lured into Spain, then, as often, the scene of civil war. Gradually the French gained command of the Channel and began to plunder the south coast harbours of England. When Charles V died in 1380, France was again in the ascendant; but triumph had not been achieved without heavy taxation. The salt-tax (*Gabelle*), first raised in 1341, had become permanent, and a crippling hearth tax had been introduced to pay the ransom (never in fact fully delivered) of King John II. If there were signs of revival, France had still not won back the position which she had held at the death of Philip IV. For this the long, savage war was a prime cause.

THE THREAT OF BURGUNDY

It will be seen that the coat-of-arms of Charles VI displays only three fleurs-de-lys (Table 65). The general view is that Charles V altered the blazon of France to this form in about 1365 and in honour of the Holy Trinity. In fact there had been a period of indecision and a pattern of only three fleurs-de-lys can be found as early as 1228 (on a seal of the town of Lens). Equally, Charles VI has the old arrangement, known briefly as 'France ancient', on his counter-seal, though he uses 'France modern' everywhere else. Some earlier writers associate the Trinity with the three petals of the fleur-de-lys. In any case the change must be associated with the reign of Charles V, and was echoed in the arms of his descendants. It is possible that the alteration was not unwelcome since it distinguished the current blazon of France from that usurped by England in 1340; but Henry IV of England adopted 'France modern' in his turn (Table 66).

Unhappily for France, the revival of her fortunes under Charles V was not maintained. Like his contemporary, Richard of England, Charles VI was a minor surrounded by powerful uncles with large estates. The Dukes of Anjou, Berry and Burgundy had no common purpose and little sense of what was needed for France. Nor had Louis, Duke of Bourbon,

King Charles VI of France (1368–1422) on an expedition, with shield and banner of France modern. 15th- century MS.

TABLE 66

FRANCE
The Hundred Years' War

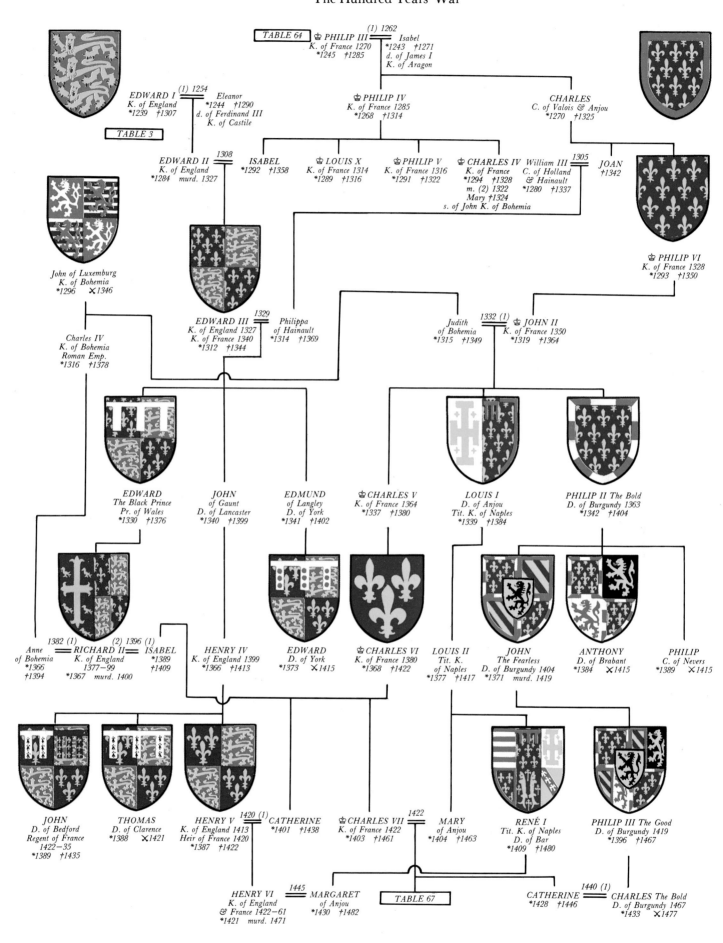

TABLE 64 ♛ *PHILIP III* (1) 1262 *Isabel*
K. of France 1270 *1243 †1271
*1245 †1285 d. of James I
K. of Aragon

EDWARD I (1) 1254 *Eleanor*
K. of England *1244 †1290
*1239 †1307 d. of Ferdinand III
K. of Castile

TABLE 3

♛ *PHILIP IV*
K. of France 1285
*1268 †1314

CHARLES
C. of Valois & Anjou
*1270 †1325

EDWARD II 1308 *ISABEL* ♛ *LOUIS X* ♛ *PHILIP V* ♛ *CHARLES IV* William III 1305 *JOAN*
K. of England *1292 †1358 K. of France 1314 K. of France 1316 K. of France C. of Holland †1342
*1284 murd. 1327 *1289 †1316 *1291 †1322 *1294 †1328 & Hainault
m. (2) 1322 *1280 †1337
Mary †1324
s. of John K. of Bohemia

John of Luxemburg
K. of Bohemia
*1296 ✕1346

♛ *PHILIP VI*
K. of France 1328
*1293 †1350

EDWARD III 1329 *Philippa* Judith 1332 (1) ♛ *JOHN II*
K. of England 1327 of Hainault of Bohemia K. of France 1350
K. of France 1340 *1314 †1369 *1315 †1349 *1319 †1364
*1312 †1344

Charles IV
K. of Bohemia
Roman Emp.
*1316 †1378

EDWARD JOHN EDMUND ♛ *CHARLES V* LOUIS I PHILIP II The Bold
The Black Prince of Gaunt of Langley K. of France 1364 D. of Anjou D. of Burgundy 1363
Pr. of Wales D. of Lancaster D. of York *1337 †1380 Tit. K. of Naples *1342 †1404
*1330 †1376 *1340 †1399 *1341 †1402 *1339 †1384

Anne 1382 (1) RICHARD II 1396 (1) *ISABEL* HENRY IV EDWARD ♛ *CHARLES VI* LOUIS II JOHN ANTHONY PHILIP
of Bohemia K. of England *1389 K. of England 1399 D. of York K. of France 1380 Tit. K. The Fearless D. of Brabant C. of Nevers
*1366 1377–99 †1409 *1366 †1413 *1373 ✕1415 *1368 †1422 of Naples D. of Burgundy 1404 *1384 ✕1415 *1389 ✕1415
†1394 *1367 murd. 1400 *1377 †1417 *1371 murd. 1419

JOHN THOMAS HENRY V 1420 (1) *CATHERINE* ♛ *CHARLES VII* 1422 *MARY* RENÉ I PHILIP III The Good
D. of Bedford D. of Clarence K. of England 1413 *1401 †1438 K. of France 1422 of Anjou Tit. K. of Naples D. of Burgundy 1419
Regent of France *1388 ✕1421 Heir of France 1420 *1403 †1461 *1404 †1463 D. of Bar *1396 †1467
1422–35 *1387 †1422 *1409 †1480
*1389 †1435

HENRY VI 1445 *MARGARET* **TABLE 67** CATHERINE 1440 (1) CHARLES The Bold
K. of England of Anjou *1428 †1446 D. of Burgundy 1467
& France 1422–61 *1430 †1482 *1433 ✕1477
*1421 murd. 1471

Houses of Valois-Orléans and Angoulême

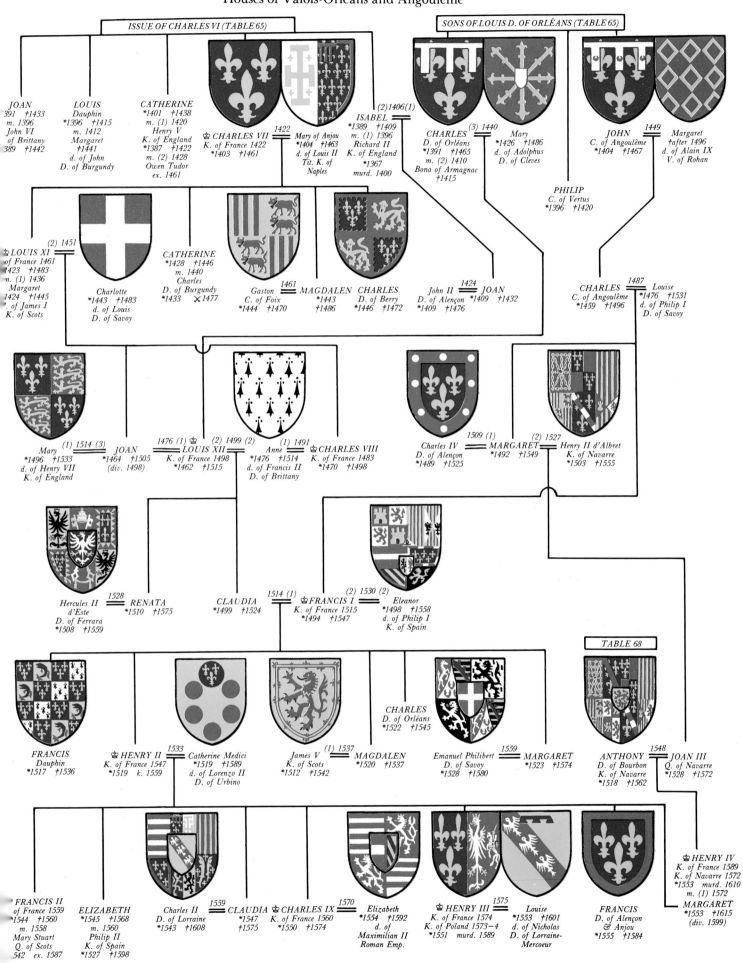

ISSUE OF CHARLES VI (TABLE 65)

SONS OF LOUIS D. OF ORLÉANS (TABLE 65)

JOAN
*391 †1433
m. 1396
John VI
of Brittany
389 †1442

LOUIS
Dauphin
*1396 †1415
m. 1412
Margaret
†1441
d. of John
D. of Burgundy

CATHERINE
*1401 †1438
m. (1) 1420
Henry V
K. of England
*1387 †1422
m. (2) 1428
Owen Tudor
ex. 1461

♚ CHARLES VII   1422
K. of France 1422
*1403 †1461

Mary of Anjou
*1404 †1463
d. of Louis II
Tit. K. of
Naples

(2)1406(1)   ISABEL
*1389 †1409
m. (1) 1396
Richard II
K. of England
*1367
murd. 1400

CHARLES   (3) 1440
D. of Orléans
*1391 †1465
m. (2) 1410
Bona of Armagnac
†1415

Mary
*1426 †1486
d. of Adolphus
D. of Cleves

JOHN   1449
C. of Angoulême
*1404 †1467

Margaret
†after 1496
d. of Alain IX
V. of Rohan

PHILIP
C. of Vertus
*1396 †1420

♚ LOUIS XI   (2) 1451
of France 1461
*1423 †1483
m. (1) 1436
Margaret
1424 †1445
d. of James I
K. of Scots

Charlotte
*1443 †1483
d. of Louis
D. of Savoy

CATHERINE
*1428 †1446
m. 1440
Charles
D. of Burgundy
*1433 ✕ 1477

Gaston   1461
C. of Foix
*1444 †1470

MAGDALEN
*1443
†1486

CHARLES
D. of Berry
*1446 †1472

John II   1424   JOAN
D. of Alençon   *1409 †1432
*1409 †1476

CHARLES   1487   Louise
C. of Angoulême   *1476 †1531
*1459 †1496   d. of Philip I
D. of Savoy

Mary   (1) 1514 (3)
*1496 †1533
d. of Henry VII
K. of England

JOAN
*1464 †1505
(div. 1498)

LOUIS XII   1476 (1) ♚
K. of France 1498
*1462 †1515

Anne   (2) 1499 (2)   (1) 1491
*1476 †1514
d. of Francis II
D. of Brittany

♚ CHARLES VIII
K. of France 1483
*1470 †1498

Charles IV   1509 (1)   MARGARET   (2) 1527   Henry II d'Albret
D. of Alençon   *1492 †1549   K. of Navarre
*1489 †1525   *1503 †1555

Hercules II   1528   RENATA
d'Este   *1510 †1575
D. of Ferrara
*1508 †1559

CLAUDIA
*1499 †1524

♚ FRANCIS I   1514 (1)   (2) 1530 (2)   Eleanor
K. of France 1515   *1498 †1558
*1494 †1547   d. of Philip I
K. of Spain

TABLE 68

FRANCIS
Dauphin
*1517 †1536

♚ HENRY II   1533   Catherine Medici
K. of France 1547   *1519 †1589
*1519 k. 1559   d. of Lorenzo II
D. of Urbino

James V   (1) 1537   MAGDALEN
K. of Scots   *1520 †1537
*1512 †1542

CHARLES
D. of Orléans
*1522 †1545

Emanuel Philibert   1559   MARGARET
D. of Savoy   *1523 †1574
*1528 †1580

ANTHONY   1548   JOAN III
D. of Bourbon   Q. of Navarre
K. of Navarre   *1528 †1572
*1518 †1562

FRANCIS II
of France 1559
*1544 †1560
m. 1558
Mary Stuart
Q. of Scots
542 ex. 1587

ELIZABETH
*1545 †1568
m. 1560
Philip II
K. of Spain
*1527 †1598

Charles II   1559   CLAUDIA
D. of Lorraine   *1547
*1543 †1608   †1575

♚ CHARLES IX   1570
K. of France 1560
*1550 †1574

Elizabeth
*1554 †1592
d. of
Maximilian II
Roman Emp.

♚ HENRY III   1575   Louise
K. of France 1574   *1553 †1601
K. of Poland 1573–4   d. of Nicholas
*1551 murd. 1589   D. of Lorraine-
Mercoeur

FRANCIS
D. of Alençon
& Anjou
*1555 †1584

♚ HENRY IV
K. of France 1589
K. of Navarre 1572
*1553 murd. 1610
m. (1) 1572

MARGARET
*1553 †1615
(div. 1599)

the King's maternal uncle, who shared the guardianship with Burgundy, any greater capacity for statesmanship (Table 65). The reimposition of the hearth tax brought widespread uprisings in 1382, possibly influenced by the Peasants' Revolt in England a year before. In 1388 the King, now 20, declared himself of age, but unfortunately in 1392 he had a mental collapse and was never again capable of a vigorous interest in affairs. Two of his uncles were in their way men of talent. Philip II, Duke of Burgundy, married the heiress of Flanders whose inheritance also included Franche-Comté, and was the founder of the remarkable fifteenth-century state of Burgundy. John, Duke of Berry, with his seat at Bourges, was a magnificent patron of the arts for whom splendid books were illuminated.

During the King's madness, his brother Louis, Duke of Orléans, became a rival of Burgundy. Orléans also married an heiress, the daughter of the Visconti Duke of Milan; he was a lover of literature and a profligate. The famous soldier, Dunois, was one of his bastards. Embittered relations between Orléans and John the Fearless, Duke of Burgundy (Table 66), led to the murder of Orléans in Paris by supporters of Burgundy. The stage was set for civil war. The new Duke of Orléans, Charles (Table 67), was an attractive, youthful figure, a poet of merit but doomed to spend his best years in an English prison. He had married Bona, the daughter of a tough southern French nobleman, Bernard, Count of Armagnac, who gave his name to the anti-Burgundian party and became Constable of France.

While France was sinking into internecine strife and disorder, a new and vigorous King had ascended the English throne. In 1415 Henry V invaded France; the French commanders forgot all that du Guesclin had taught them and were savagely defeated with heavy mortality at Agincourt. Among the captives were the Dukes of Orléans and Bourbon. Henry V set about the systematic reduction of northern France. In 1419 John the Fearless, Duke of Burgundy, was wantonly slain during an interview with the Dauphin, and in 1420 Henry V was able to negotiate the Treaty of Troyes whereby he married Catherine of France and was accepted as heir to the French throne.

Resistance to Henry V was still organized by the Dauphin and the Armagnacs south of the Loire; England was now linked to Burgundy. But speculation as to whether the great talents of Henry V could have enforced the Treaty of Troyes are otiose because of his unexpected and early death in 1422, a year which also saw the death of the hapless Charles VI, his father-in-law. The tide was partly turned in favour of France by the appearance in 1429 of the singular figure of Joan of Arc whose simple faith in the beastliness of the English led her to attempt their expulsion.

Later that year she successfully engineered the coronation of Charles VII at Rheims. In 1430 she was captured, and in 1431 burned for heresy; her treatment by the authorities of the Catholic Church (which canonized her 500 years later) was probably no better or worse than that of many other religious suspects. Charles VII, a weak and inconstant man, may be censured for making no effort to save her.

Nor did the tide of battle turn at once, but in 1435 a treaty was achieved between France and Burgundy; and England, now isolated, began to be preoccupied with domestic discord. The French forces were still ill-organized and often ill-led, but they paid some attention to the developing weapon of artillery. By 1453 the English had been driven out of Normandy and Gascony and only retained Calais. They did not, however, abate their claims; fresh invasion was a possibility and the rulers of England styled themselves Kings of France until 1801.

The end of his reign saw Charles VII a successful, though scarcely an estimable king. His servants were loyal, industrious, and drawn from the middle classes; the power of the nobility was tamed, though the threat of Burgundy remained. Charles never returned to Paris, which had been in English hands for much of his reign, and the Loire valley with its great châteaux set in a lovely landscape became the centre of the reunited Kingdom. His reign witnessed also an advantageous settlement with the Papacy and the beginnings of provincial *Parlements*; the *Parlement* of Paris had long been the chief law-court of the land.

WARS WITH ITALY

Louis XI, shabby, miserly, suspicious and unpompous, was none the less an important King of France. In 1465 he successfully broke a powerful aristocratic conspiracy, which included his younger brother, the Duke of Berry, and had some backing from the quasi-independent Dukes of Brittany and Burgundy, by giving the rebels good terms, which he gradually undermined in the years that followed. In 1469 he founded the Order of St Michael, whose collar surrounds his shield at the head of this chapter. His intelligence made clear to him that Burgundy was the real enemy of French development; it was lucky for him that Charles the Bold (Table 75) died without male heirs which made it easy for Louis to seize his French estates. An equally fortunate event was the extinction of the family of René of Anjou which gave the Crown the county of Maine, and the valuable fief of Provence across the Rhône. René of Anjou was an attractive figure. His proud blazon (Table 66) vaunts claims to the Kingdoms of Naples, Hungary and Jerusalem, but in truth he lived off his French estates in Provence and Lorraine. He was a writer in prose and verse, even a painter of a sort, and a patron of the arts interested in the work of both Italians and Flemings (Chapter 28).

Charles VIII, delicate and romantic, was brought up by his sister Anne. By marrying the heiress of Brittany, he finally united that maritime and separatist province to the Crown. But he also began the sad series of profitless incursions into Italy which are a feature of the sixteenth century and which only added to the political distress of that turbulent peninsula. Reasserting the claim to Naples, which had been but feebly voiced by the second House of Anjou (Table 63), he invaded and swiftly conquered south Italy. His licentious army provoked a rapid reaction and he was as swiftly flung back into France, though with considerable booty. Dying childless, he was succeeded by his cousin Louis XII, the head of the House of Orléans, who had ambitions on Milan as the descendant of the Visconti (Table 65), and occasionally quartered their alarming, serpentine arms (sometimes alleged to refer to a monster slain by the founder of the family). For 12 years he held Milan (1500–12), Naples was won and lost, but he gained nothing permanent.

His cousin and heir, Francis I, was young, handsome and high-spirited, a generous lover of the arts. Again the lure of Italy was too much for him, but four successive wars against the Emperor Charles V, in one of which Francis himself was captured at Pavia (1525), brought little in the way of enduring success. He used a famous badge of a salamander amid flames which is widely displayed on his castles in the Loire valley, or at Fontainebleau. Francis I also began the palace of the Louvre in Paris, today one of the great museums of the world. The shield of his eldest son, Francis, who predeceased his father, has the arms of the Dauphin quartered with those of the heir of Brittany. His son Henry II carried on the struggle against Charles V. Calais was captured from the English, but in 1559 a moment of realism prevailed and he finally abandoned the Italian claims of France at the Treaty of Cateau-Cambrésis. Later in the same year he was accidentally killed in one of the tournaments which were so popular and lavish an entertainment. Henry married the Florentine, Catherine dei Medici. Her family originally bore six red roundels, but Louis XII had granted them the right of turning the uppermost into a roundel of France.

WARS OF RELIGION

The preoccupation of France with Italy was replaced by the equally disastrous wars of religion. Protestantism had grown in France in the reigns of Francis I and his son, and had been persecuted fairly savagely: none the less it spread over much of the country. By ill fortune none of the children of Henry II were strong rulers. Francis II was sickly and reigned but a year; Charles IX was unbalanced and died young; Henry III, though valiant in youth, proved an effeminate king under the influence of men friends. All died childless. Much influence devolved upon Catherine the Queen Mother and also on the House of Lorraine (Table 110) and its junior branch the Dukes of Guise, to which the mother of Queen Mary Stuart belonged. Catherine dei Medici strove for peace and toleration, but often by paths so serpentine as to arouse suspicion.

The Guise faction led the Catholics; the reformers looked to the Kings of Navarre, heads of the House of Bourbon and (if the Valois died out, as became increasingly probable) heirs male of France. It would be tedious to trace the long and savage conflict in detail: both sides enlisted foreign aid. The future Henry III, while still Duke of Anjou, was suggested as a husband for Elizabeth of England; indeed on the strength of battles gained against the Huguenots (as the Protestants were termed) he was actually chosen King of Poland (1573–4) (Chapter 35). At one point (1561) the Third Estate even contemplated the complete nationalization of the Church. In 1570 an agreement was reached, of which one clause arranged for the marriage of the King's sister to Henry of Navarre. This wedding took place in Paris in August 1572. A week later, on the feast of St Bartholomew, a ghastly massacre of the Huguenots, who had flocked to Paris, was organized: several thousand were butchered by the Paris mob and the hirelings of the Guise faction. The Pope celebrated with a Mass, and Philip II of Spain smiled; happily Henry escaped.

The war broke out again; by now many moderate men, the *Politiques*, were moving towards the Protestant side. Power at the court was increasingly usurped by the Guises and the fanatical Catholic League, particularly strong in Paris. Eventually the unmanly Henry III was goaded into murdering the Duke of Guise and his brother the Cardinal. When the degenerate monarch was himself assassinated by a crackpot friar, opinion rallied on all sides to Henry of Navarre: his military talents were already clear, his shrewdness was evident and a long list of gallantries attested his virility. Henry IV was a realist and after fighting for some years to establish order, he announced his conversion to the Catholic faith. Only then was he able to enter Paris.

The middle years of this sombre century in French history were ennobled by a group of poets – the *Pléiade* – who, headed by Pierre de Ronsard, strove to improve the lyric verse of their language and who introduced the sonnet to France. Henry III also established the Order of the Holy Ghost, which replaced that of St Michael as the principal order of France; its insignia can be seen on Table 63 and at the head of the next chapter.

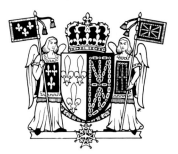

Chapter 16

FRANCE: MODERN

The accession of the Protestant Henry IV, already King of Navarre, to the throne of France in 1589 did not bring immediate peace. The bitter dissensions and the harsh doctrinal persecutions of the long religious wars were not to be dispelled overnight. Although Henry adopted the Catholic faith in 1593, he was not able to enter Paris until the following year. His conversion was one of policy rather than belief: 'Paris is well worth a Mass', he is reputed to have exclaimed. In 1598 by the Edict of Nantes he gave liberty of worship to the Protestants of France; and as the seventeenth century dawned France was gathering her powers and resources for the great role which lay ahead of her. The basic difference between Henry IV and the effete and shadowy Valois kings whom he followed, was Henry's concern for the ordinary folk of France. He worked, with his great minister and friend, the Duke of Sully, for prosperity as well as peace: agriculture was encouraged, roads built, commerce fostered, and above all the national debt was redeemed and taxation meanwhile actually reduced. When the knife of a deranged Catholic assassin ended Henry's life, the Kingdom was almost miraculously different from its condition 21 years earlier.

It can be seen that Henry IV was only a remote relation of Henry III, but both were descended from St Louis IX, and they became brothers-in-law. The throne of Navarre had passed, as has been explained, to the daughter of Louis X who married her cousin, the Count of Evreux (Table 65). Their male descendants gave out in 1425, and marriages were made with two local families, the Counts of Foix and the Lords of Albret. In 1512 Ferdinand of Aragon wrested from John d'Albret (see also Chapter 10) that part of Navarre which lay south of the Pyrenees, leaving him only lower Navarre. None the less Henry IV of France added the ancient arms of Navarre to those of France (Table 68); although it

has been suggested, the elaborate pattern of chains is probably not a pun on the Spanish words *una vara* – a chain. This shield was used occasionally by Louis XIII but abandoned by Louis XIV.

The first wife of Henry IV was barren, and he divorced her accordingly. For his second he chose Mary, daughter of the Grand-Duke of Tuscany and a cousin of Catherine dei Medici, wife of Henry II. It was part of an Italian policy aimed against Spain, in pursuit of which Henry IV also won from Savoy the two Duchies of Bresse and Bugey. His sudden death altered the situation. His widow became regent for the youthful Louis XIII, and arranged a Spanish wife for him. The moment of his majority (1614) saw the last summons of the Estates General (the Three Estates) until 1789. Once in power, Louis set himself to reduce the might of the nobility and to curb the separatism of the Huguenot communities in the southern half of the Kingdom, The latter was achieved by the Treaty of Montpellier (1622), a year which also saw the entry into the King's council of Cardinal Richelieu whose statesmanship dominated the remainder of the reign.

Richelieu was not concerned, as were Henry IV and Sully, with internal reforms and prosperity: his dominant concern was for the expansion and prestige of France. The branches of the Hapsburg family controlled the Low Countries (approximately the Belgium of today), the Empire of Germany, Spain and Portugal. The Cardinal endeavoured to extend the frontiers of France and thus react against the threat of encirclement. To do this he was prepared to ally himself with Catholics or non-Catholics as circumstances suggested; it was a naked display of power politics. By intervening in the Thirty Years' War in Germany (1635) he changed the character of that struggle from a religious to a dynastic contest. In 1648 France gained Alsace and some lands in

TABLE 68

FRANCE
House of Bourbon

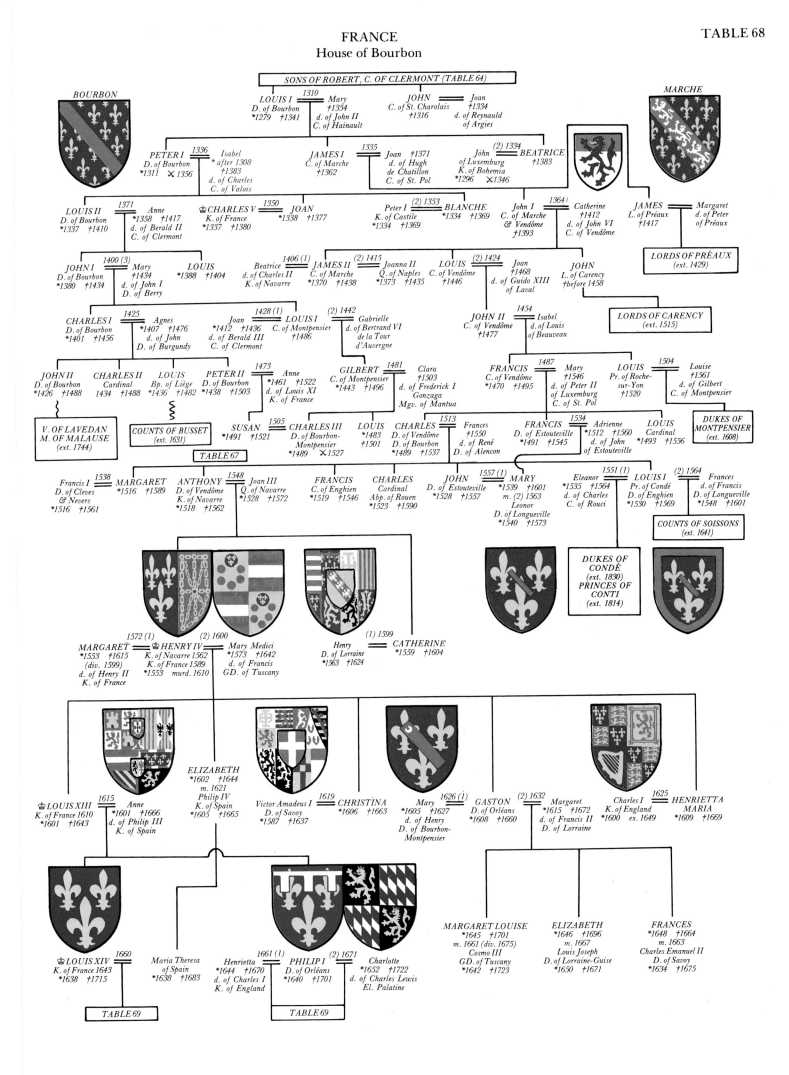

SONS OF ROBERT, C. OF CLERMONT (TABLE 64)

BOURBON

MARCHE

LOUIS I — 1310 — Mary
D. of Bourbon — †1354
*1279 †1341 — d. of John II
C. of Hainault

JOHN — Joan
C. of St. Charolais — †1334
†1316 — d. of Reynauld
of Argies

PETER I — 1336 — Isabel
D. of Bourbon — * after 1308
*1311 ✕1356 — †1383
d. of Charles
C. of Valois

JAMES I — 1335 — Joan †1371
C. of Marche — d. of Hugh
†1362 — de Chatillon
C. of St. Pol

(2) 1334 — BEATRICE
John — †1383
of Luxemburg
K. of Bohemia
*1296 ✕1346

JAMES — Margaret
L. of Préaux — d. of Peter
†1417 — of Préaux

LOUIS II — 1371 — Anne
D. of Bourbon — *1358 †1417
*1337 †1410 — d. of Berald II
C. of Clermont

♛ CHARLES V — 1350 — JOAN
K. of France — *1338 †1377
*1337 †1380

Peter I — (2) 1353 — BLANCHE
K. of Castile — *1334 †1369
*1334 †1369

John I — 1364 — Catherine
C. of Marche — †1412
& Vendôme — d. of John VI
†1393 — C. of Vendôme

LORDS OF PRÉAUX
(ext. 1429)

JOHN I — 1400 (3) — Mary
D. of Bourbon — †1434
*1380 †1434 — d. of John I
D. of Berry

LOUIS
*1388 †1404

Beatrice — 1406 (1)
d. of Charles II
K. of Navarre

JAMES II — (2) 1415 — Joanna II
C. of Marche — Q. of Naples
*1370 †1438 — †1373 †1435

LOUIS — (2) 1424 — Joan
C. of Vendôme — †1468
†1446 — d. of Guido XIII
of Laval

JOHN
L. of Carency
†before 1458

LORDS OF CARENCY
(ext. 1515)

CHARLES I — 1425 — Agnes
D. of Bourbon — *1407 †1476
*1401 †1456 — d. of John
D. of Burgundy

Joan — 1428 (1) — LOUIS I
*1412 †1436 — C. of Montpensier
d. of Berald III — †1486
C. of Clermont

(2) 1442 — Gabrielle
d. of Bertrand VI
de la Tour
d'Auvergne

JOHN II — 1454 — Isabel
C. of Vendôme — d. of Louis
†1477 — of Beauveau

JOHN II
D. of Bourbon
*1426 †1488

CHARLES II
Cardinal
1434 †1488

LOUIS
Bp. of Liège
*1436 †1482

PETER II — 1473 — Anne
D. of Bourbon — *1461 †1522
*1438 †1503 — d. of Louis XI
K. of France

GILBERT — 1481 — Clara
C. of Montpensier — †1503
*1443 †1496 — d. of Frederick I
Gonzaga
Mgv. of Mantua

FRANCIS — 1487 — Mary
C. of Vendôme — †1546
*1470 †1495 — d. of Peter II
of Luxemburg
C. of St. Pol

LOUIS — 1504 — Louise
Pr. of Roche- — †1561
sur-Yon — d. of Gilbert
†1520 — C. of Montpensier

**V. OF LAVEDAN
M. OF MALAUSE**
(ext. 1744)

COUNTS OF BUSSET
(ext. 1631)

SUSAN — 1505 — CHARLES III
*1491 †1521 — D. of Bourbon-
Montpensier
*1489 ✕1527

LOUIS
*1483 †1501

CHARLES — 1513 — Frances
D. of Vendôme — †1550
D. of Bourbon — d. of René
*1489 †1537 — D. of Alencon

FRANCIS — 1534 — Adrienne
D. of Estouteville — *1512 †1560
*1491 †1545 — d. of John
of Estouteville

LOUIS
Cardinal
*1493 †1556

**DUKES OF
MONTPENSIER**
(ext. 1608)

TABLE 67

Francis I — 1538 — MARGARET
D. of Cleves — *1516 †1589
& Nevers
*1516 †1561

ANTHONY — 1548 — Joan III
D. of Vendôme — Q. of Navarre
K. of Navarre — *1528 †1572
*1518 †1562

FRANCIS
C. of Enghien
*1519 †1546

CHARLES
Cardinal
Abp. of Rouen
*1523 †1590

JOHN
D. of Estouteville
*1528 †1557

1557 (1) — MARY
*1539 †1601
m. (2) 1563
Leonor
D. of Longueville
*1540 †1573

Eleanor — 1551 (1) — LOUIS I
*1535 †1564 — Pr. of Condé
d. of Charles — D. of Enghien
C. of Rouci — *1530 †1569

(2) 1564 — Frances
d. of Francis
D. of Longueville
*1548 †1601

COUNTS OF SOISSONS
(ext. 1641)

**DUKES OF
CONDÉ**
(ext. 1830)
**PRINCES OF
CONTI**
(ext. 1814)

MARGARET — 1572 (1) — ♛ HENRY IV — (2) 1600 — Mary Medici
*1553 †1615 — K. of Navarre 1562 — *1573 †1642
(div. 1599) — K. of France 1589 — d. of Francis
d. of Henry II — *1553 murd. 1610 — GD. of Tuscany
K. of France

Henry — (1) 1599 — CATHERINE
D. of Lorraine — *1559 †1604
*1563 †1624

♛ LOUIS XIII — 1615 — Anne
K. of France 1610 — *1601 †1666
*1601 †1643 — d. of Philip III
K. of Spain

ELIZABETH
*1602 †1644
m. 1621
Philip IV
K. of Spain

Victor Amadeus I — 1619 — CHRISTINA
D. of Savoy — *1606 †1663
*1587 †1637

Mary — 1626 (1) — GASTON — (2) 1632 — Margaret
*1605 †1627 — D. of Orléans — *1615 †1672
d. of Henry — *1608 †1660 — d. of Francis II
D. of Bourbon- — D. of Lorraine
Montpensier

Charles I — 1625 — HENRIETTA
K. of England — MARIA
*1600 ex. 1649 — *1609 †1669

♛ LOUIS XIV — 1660 — Maria Theresa
K. of France 1643 — of Spain
*1638 †1715 — *1638 †1683

Henrietta — 1661 (1) — PHILIP I — (2) 1671 — Charlotte
*1644 †1670 — D. of Orléans — *1652 †1722
d. of Charles I — *1640 †1701 — d. of Charles Lewis
K. of England — El. Palatine

MARGARET LOUISE
*1645 †1701
m. 1661 (div. 1675)
Cosmo III
GD. of Tuscany
*1642 †1723

ELIZABETH
*1646 †1696
m. 1667
Louis Joseph
D. of Lorraine-Guise
*1650 †1671

FRANCES
*1648 †1664
m. 1663
Charles Emanuel II
D. of Savoy
*1634 †1675

TABLE 69

TABLE 69

TABLE 69

FRANCE
End of the monarchy

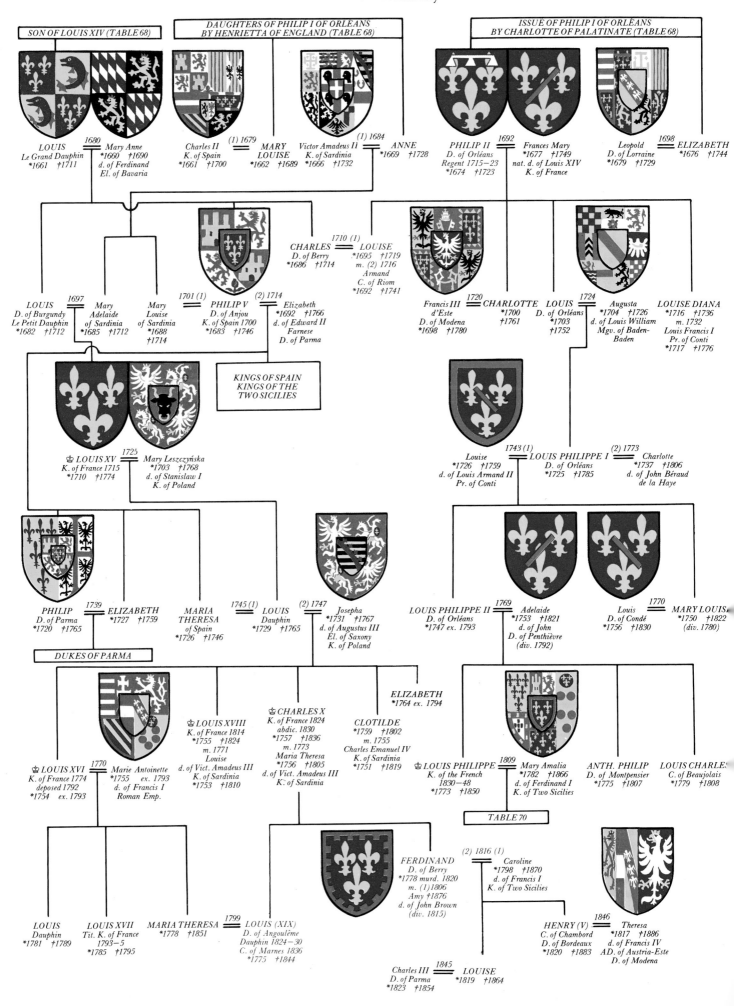

SON OF LOUIS XIV (TABLE 68)

DAUGHTERS OF PHILIP I OF ORLEANS
BY HENRIETTA OF ENGLAND (TABLE 68)

ISSUE OF PHILIP I OF ORLEANS
BY CHARLOTTE OF PALATINATE (TABLE 68)

LOUIS Le Grand Dauphin *1661 †1711 — 1680 — Mary Anne *1660 †1690 d. of Ferdinand El. of Bavaria

Charles II K. of Spain *1661 †1700 — (1) 1679 — MARY LOUISE *1662 †1689

Victor Amadeus II K. of Sardinia *1666 †1732 — (1) 1684 — ANNE *1669 †1728

PHILIP II D. of Orléans Regent 1715—23 *1674 †1723 — 1692 — Frances Mary *1677 †1749 nat. d. of Louis XIV K. of France

Leopold D. of Lorraine *1679 †1729 — 1698 — ELIZABETH *1676 †1744

CHARLES D. of Berry *1686 †1714 — 1710 (1) — LOUISE *1695 †1719 m. (2) 1716 Armand C. of Riom *1692 †1741

Francis III d'Este D. of Modena *1698 †1780 — 1720 — CHARLOTTE *1700 †1761

LOUIS D. of Orléans *1703 †1752 — 1724 — Augusta *1704 †1726 d. of Louis William Mgv. of Baden-Baden

LOUISE DIANA *1716 †1736 m. 1732 Louis Francis I Pr. of Conti *1717 †1776

LOUIS D. of Burgundy Le Petit Dauphin *1682 †1712 — 1697 — Mary Adelaide of Sardinia *1685 †1712

Mary Louise of Sardinia *1688 †1714 — 1701 (1) — PHILIP V D. of Anjou K. of Spain 1700 *1683 †1746 — (2) 1714 — Elizabeth *1692 †1766 d. of Edward II Farnese D. of Parma

KINGS OF SPAIN
KINGS OF THE
TWO SICILIES

♔ LOUIS XV K. of France 1715 *1710 †1774 — 1725 — Mary Leszczyńska *1703 †1768 d. of Stanislaw I K. of Poland

Louise *1726 †1759 d. of Louis Armand II Pr. of Conti — 1743 (1) — LOUIS PHILIPPE I D. of Orléans *1725 †1785 — (2) 1773 — Charlotte *1737 †1806 d. of John Béraud de la Haye

PHILIP D. of Parma *1720 †1765 — 1739 — ELIZABETH *1727 †1759

MARIA THERESA of Spain *1726 †1746 — 1745 (1) — LOUIS Dauphin *1729 †1765 — (2) 1747 — Josepha *1731 †1767 d. of Augustus III El. of Saxony K. of Poland

LOUIS PHILIPPE II D. of Orléans *1747 ex. 1793 — 1769 — Adelaide *1753 †1821 d. of John D. of Penthièvre (div. 1792)

Louis D. of Condé *1756 †1830 — 1770 — MARY LOUISA *1750 †1822 (div. 1780)

DUKES OF PARMA

ELIZABETH *1764 ex. 1794

♔ LOUIS XVIII K. of France 1814 *1755 †1824 m. 1771 Louise d. of Vict. Amadeus III K. of Sardinia *1753 †1810

♔ CHARLES X K. of France 1824 abdic. 1830 *1757 †1836 m. 1773 Maria Theresa *1756 †1805 d. of Vict. Amadeus III K. of Sardinia

CLOTILDE *1759 †1802 m. 1755 Charles Emanuel IV K. of Sardinia *1751 †1819

♔ LOUIS PHILIPPE K. of the French 1830—48 *1773 †1850 — 1809 — Mary Amalia *1782 †1866 d. of Ferdinand I K. of Two Sicilies

ANTH. PHILIP D. of Montpensier *1775 †1807

LOUIS CHARLES C. of Beaujolais *1779 †1808

TABLE 70

♔ LOUIS XVI K. of France 1774 deposed 1792 *1754 ex. 1793 — 1770 — Marie Antoinette *1755 ex. 1793 d. of Francis I Roman Emp.

FERDINAND D. of Berry *1778 murd. 1820 m. (1)1806 Amy †1876 d. of John Brown (div. 1815) — (2) 1816 (1) — Caroline *1798 †1870 d. of Francis I K. of Two Sicilies

LOUIS Dauphin *1781 †1789

LOUIS XVII Tit. K. of France 1793—5 *1785 †1795

MARIA THERESA *1778 †1851 — 1799 — LOUIS (XIX) D. of Angoulême Dauphin 1824—30 C. of Marnes 1836 *1775 †1844

HENRY (V) C. of Chambord D. of Bordeaux *1820 †1883 — 1846 — Theresa *1817 †1886 d. of Francis IV AD. of Austria-Este D. of Modena

Charles III D. of Parma *1823 †1854 — 1845 — LOUISE *1819 †1864

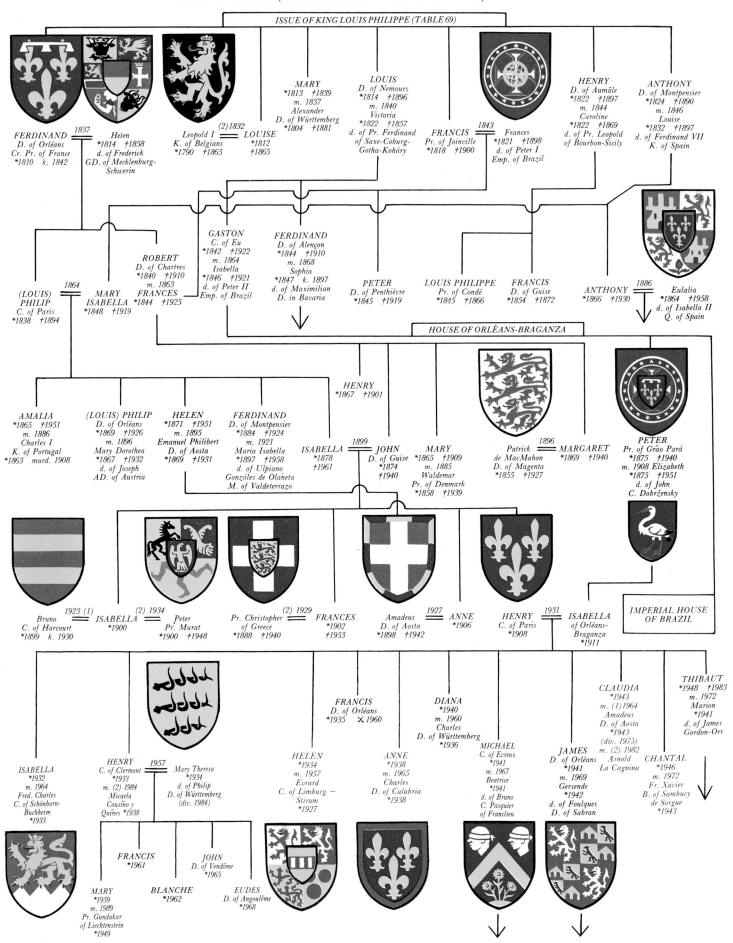

ISSUE OF KING LOUIS PHILIPPE (TABLE 69)

MARY
*1813 †1839
m. 1837
Alexander
D. of Württemberg
*1804 †1881

LOUIS
D. of Nemours
*1814 †1896
m. 1840
Victoria
*1822 †1857
d. of Pr. Ferdinand
of Saxe-Coburg-
Gotha-Koháry

HENRY
D. of Aumâle
*1822 †1897
m. 1844
Caroline
*1822 †1869
d. of Pr. Leopold
of Bourbon-Sicily

ANTHONY
D. of Montpensier
*1824 †1890
m. 1846
Louise
*1832 †1897
d. of Ferdinand VII
K. of Spain

FERDINAND
D. of Orléans
Cr. Pr. of France
*1810 k. 1842

1837

Helen
*1814 †1858
d. of Frederick
GD. of Mecklenburg-
Schwerin

Leopold I
K. of Belgians
*1790 †1865

(2)1832 **LOUISE**
*1812 †1865

FRANCIS
Pr. of Joinville
*1818 †1900

1843

Frances
*1821 †1898
d. of Peter I
Emp. of Brazil

GASTON
C. of Eu
*1842 †1922
m. 1864
Isabella
*1846 †1921
m. 1863
d. of Peter II
Emp. of Brazil

FERDINAND
D. of Alençon
*1844 †1910
m. 1868
Sophia
*1847 k. 1897
d. of Maximilian
D. in Bavaria

ROBERT
D. of Chartres
*1840 †1910
m. 1863
FRANCES
*1844 †1925

(LOUIS) PHILIP
C. of Paris
*1838 †1894

1864

MARY ISABELLA
*1848 †1919

PETER
D. of Penthièvre
*1845 †1919

LOUIS PHILIPPE
Pr. of Condé
*1845 †1866

FRANCIS
D. of Guise
*1854 †1872

ANTHONY
*1866 †1930

1886

Eulalia
*1864 †1958
d. of Isabella II
Q. of Spain

HOUSE OF ORLÉANS-BRAGANZA

HENRY
*1867 †1901

AMALIA
*1865 †1951
m. 1886
Charles I
K. of Portugal
*1863 murd. 1908

(LOUIS) PHILIP
D. of Orléans
*1869 †1926
m. 1896
Mary Dorothea
*1867 †1932
d. of Joseph
AD. of Austria

HELEN
*1871 †1951
m. 1895
Emanuel Philibert
D. of Aosta
*1869 †1931

FERDINAND
D. of Montpensier
*1884 †1924
m. 1921
Maria Isabella
*1897 †1958
d. of Ulpiano
Gonzáles de Olañeta
M. of Valdeterrazo

ISABELLA
*1878 †1961

1899 **JOHN**
D. of Guise
*1874 †1940

MARY
*1865 †1909
m. 1885
Waldemar
Pr. of Denmark
*1858 †1939

Patrick
de MacMahon
D. of Magenta
*1855 †1927

1896 **MARGARET**
*1869 †1940

PETER
Pr. of Grão Pará
*1875 †1940
m. 1908 Elizabeth
*1875 †1951
d. of John
C. Dobrzensky

Bruno
C. of Harcourt
*1899 k. 1930

1923 (1) **ISABELLA**
*1900

(2) 1934 **Peter**
Pr. Murat
*1900 †1948

Pr. Christopher
of Greece
*1888 †1940

(2) 1929 **FRANCES**
*1902 †1953

Amadeus
D. of Aosta
*1898 †1942

1927 **ANNE**
*1906

HENRY
C. of Paris
*1908

1931 **ISABELLA**
of Orléans-
Braganza
*1911

IMPERIAL HOUSE OF BRAZIL

ISABELLA
*1932
m. 1964
Fred. Charles
C. of Schönborn-
Buchheim
*1933

HENRY
C. of Clermont
*1933
m. (2) 1984
Micaela
Cousiño y
Quiñes *1938

1957 **Mary Theresa**
*1934
d. of Philip
D. of Württemberg
(div. 1984)

HELEN
*1934
m. 1957
Evrard
C. of Limburg-
Stirum
*1927

FRANCIS
D. of Orléans
*1935 ✕ 1960

ANNE
*1938
m. 1965
Charles
D. of Calabria
*1938

DIANA
*1940
m. 1960
Charles
D. of Württemberg
*1936

MICHAEL
C. of Evreux
*1941
m. 1967
Beatrice
*1941
d. of Bruno
C. Pasquier
of Franclieu

JAMES
D. of Orléans
*1941
m. 1969
Gersende
*1942
d. of Foulques
D. of Sabran

CLAUDIA
*1943
m. (1)1964
Amadeus
D. of Aosta
*1943
(div. 1975)
m. (2) 1982
Arnold
La Cagnina

THIBAUT
*1948 †1983
m. 1972
Marion
*1941
d. of James
Gordon-Orr

CHANTAL
*1946
m. 1972
Fr. Xavier
B. of Sambucy
de Sorgue
*1943

ISABELLA
*1932
m. 1964
Fred. Charles
C. of Schönborn-
Buchheim
*1933

FRANCIS
*1961

JOHN
D. of Vendôme
*1965

MARY
*1959
m. 1989
Pr. Gundakar
of Liechtenstein
*1949

BLANCHE
*1962

EUDES
D. of Angoulême
*1968

TABLE 71

FRANCE
Ancestors of Louis XIV, Louis XVI and Louis Philippe

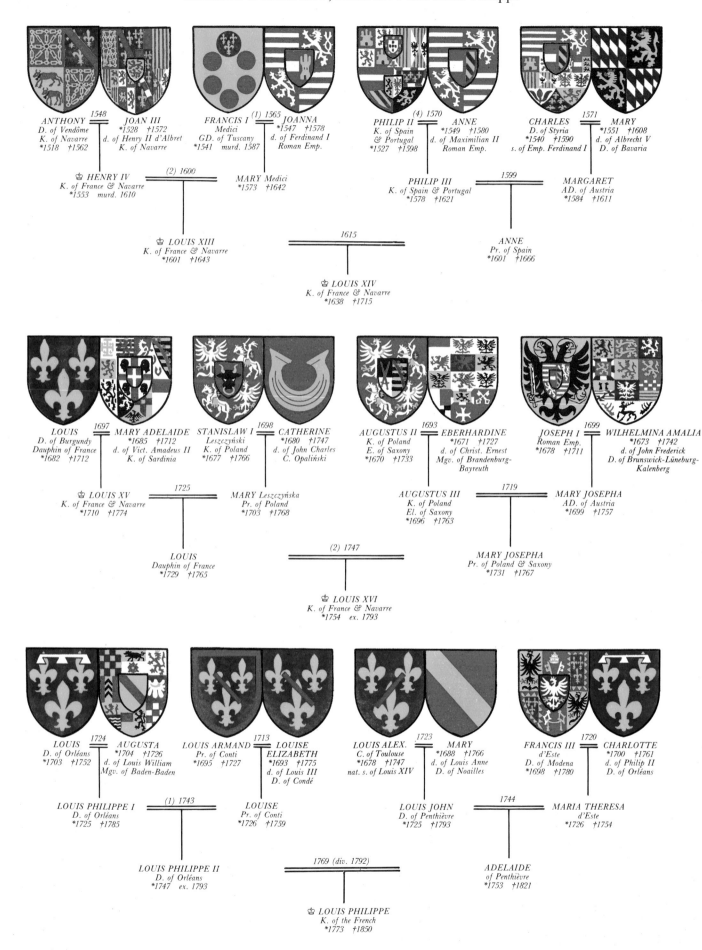

ANTHONY
D. of Vendôme
K. of Navarre
*1518 †1562

— 1548 —

JOAN III
*1528 †1572
d. of Henry II d'Albret
K. of Navarre

FRANCIS I
Medici
GD. of Tuscany
*1541 murd. 1587

— (1) 1565 —

JOANNA
*1547 †1578
d. of Ferdinand I
Roman Emp.

PHILIP II
K. of Spain
& Portugal
*1527 †1598

— (4) 1570 —

ANNE
*1549 †1580
d. of Maximilian II
Roman Emp.

CHARLES
D. of Styria
*1540 †1590
s. of Emp. Ferdinand I

— 1571 —

MARY
*1551 †1608
d. of Albrecht V
D. of Bavaria

♔ **HENRY IV**
K. of France & Navarre
*1553 murd. 1610

— (2) 1600 —

MARY Medici
*1573 †1642

PHILIP III
K. of Spain & Portugal
*1578 †1621

— 1599 —

MARGARET
AD. of Austria
*1584 †1611

♔ **LOUIS XIII**
K. of France & Navarre
*1601 †1643

— 1615 —

ANNE
Pr. of Spain
*1601 †1666

♔ **LOUIS XIV**
K. of France & Navarre
*1638 †1715

LOUIS
D. of Burgundy
Dauphin of France
*1682 †1712

— 1697 —

MARY ADELAIDE
*1685 †1712
d. of Vict. Amadeus II
K. of Sardinia

STANISLAW I
Leszczyński
K. of Poland
*1677 †1766

— 1698 —

CATHERINE
*1680 †1747
d. of John Charles
C. Opaliński

AUGUSTUS II
K. of Poland
E. of Saxony
*1670 †1733

— 1693 —

EBERHARDINE
*1671 †1727
d. of Christ. Ernest
Mgv. of Brandenburg-
Bayreuth

JOSEPH I
Roman Emp.
*1678 †1711

— 1699 —

WILHELMINA AMALIA
*1673 †1742
d. of John Frederick
D. of Brunswick-Lüneburg-
Kalenberg

♔ **LOUIS XV**
K. of France & Navarre
*1710 †1774

— 1725 —

MARY Leszczyńska
Pr. of Poland
*1703 †1768

AUGUSTUS III
K. of Poland
El. of Saxony
*1696 †1763

— 1719 —

MARY JOSEPHA
AD. of Austria
*1699 †1757

LOUIS
Dauphin of France
*1729 †1765

— (2) 1747 —

MARY JOSEPHA
Pr. of Poland & Saxony
*1731 †1767

♔ **LOUIS XVI**
K. of France & Navarre
*1754 ex. 1793

LOUIS
D. of Orléans
*1703 †1752

— 1724 —

AUGUSTA
*1704 †1726
d. of Louis William
Mgv. of Baden-Baden

LOUIS ARMAND
Pr. of Conti
*1695 †1727

— 1713 —

**LOUISE
ELIZABETH**
*1693 †1775
d. of Louis III
D. of Condé

LOUIS ALEX.
C. of Toulouse
*1678 †1747
nat. s. of Louis XIV

— 1723 —

MARY
*1688 †1766
d. of Louis Anne
D. of Noailles

FRANCIS III
d'Este
D. of Modena
*1698 †1780

— 1720 —

CHARLOTTE
*1700 †1761
d. of Philip II
D. of Orléans

LOUIS PHILIPPE I
D. of Orléans
*1725 †1785

— (1) 1743 —

LOUISE
Pr. of Conti
*1726 †1759

LOUIS JOHN
D. of Penthièvre
*1725 †1793

— 1744 —

MARIA THERESA
d'Este
*1726 †1754

LOUIS PHILIPPE II
D. of Orléans
*1747 ex. 1793

— 1769 (div. 1792) —

ADELAIDE
of Penthièvre
*1753 †1821

♔ **LOUIS PHILIPPE**
K. of the French
*1773 †1850

the less a modicum of good sense. True, he had to bolt from his capital for the Hundred Days which ended with Waterloo, but he contrived to avoid the grosser right-wing antics of some of the returned nobility while preserving a natural fear of radicalism. The murder of the Duke of Berry in 1820 compelled the old King to move towards the right; the process was accelerated by his brother Charles X, who was deliberately crowned at Rheims with all the old ceremony, and even 'touched' sufferers for the King's Evil (scrofula) which no English monarch had done since Anne. His finest action was the capture of Algiers and the foundation of the French dominion in North Africa. In 1830 a revolution in Paris easily dismissed the obstinate and obsolete monarch to exile, first in Scotland and then in Bohemia.

Many Frenchmen were still Republican, and others Bonapartist; others supported Louis Philippe, Duke of Orléans, who narrowly won the day. His father had attacked the court of Louis XVI, embraced the Revolution and adopted the name of Philippe Egalité, voted for the execution of the King, but was himself guillotined a few months later. The son, pear-shaped but well-educated, had a reputation for liberalism. He became King of the French, adopted the Napoleonic tricolor and modelled his constitutional monarchy on that of England. To fervent royalists the true king was the Count of Chambord (Henry V), grandson of Charles X. The July monarchy saw a sober, worthy but slightly dull pursuit of the middle path; in the wave of revolutions which swept Europe in 1848, the Orléans family quietly disappeared into bourgeois exile. France returned (Chapter 17) to her Bonapartist loyalty. It can be seen from Table 71 that Louis Philippe was in fact of mainly French (if royal French) ancestry.

When the Second Empire fell in 1870, the future constitution of France was once more in debate. France, defeated by Germany, had to endure the shattering loss of Alsace and Lorraine. The Count of Chambord, senior heir of Henry IV and Louis XVI, was a middle-aged and childless exile; his nearest heir was the Count of Paris who belonged to the Orléans line (Tables 69 and 70). The supporters of Orléans were prepared to accept 'Henry V' in confident expectation of the eventual succession. But the royalist claimant was unbending. Ready enough to resume the throne of his ancestors, he would not abandon the white banner of the Bourbons for the tricolor. To almost all Frenchmen the tricolor was the symbol not only of great glory won but also of the heritage of the Revolution. Chambord would not move and France has been a republic, whether the republic of Clemenceau, Laval or de Gaulle, ever since.

The death of 'Henry V' in 1883 meant that the senior heir of Hugh Capet was a Spanish Bourbon,

Louis Philippe (1773–1850), King of the French, with his five sons, by H. Vernet, 1846.

the Carlist claimant (see Table 51); with the death of his son in 1936, the representation passed to King Alphonso XIII. Both were descended from the second grandson of Louis XIV, but both were inhibited from claiming the throne of France by the Treaty of Utrecht (1713). Accordingly the Orleanist line, the heirs of Louis Philippe, have continued to make their stand as pretenders to the throne of France. Any claims to the French Crown by the heirs of Alphonso XIII must have been reduced by the accession of King Juan Carlos to the Crown of Spain in 1975.

A younger branch has inherited claims to the short-lived Empire of Brazil (Table 70) but Henry, Count of Paris, is the only serious, present-day competitor for the throne which Hugh Capet, his direct male progenitor, acquired almost a thousand years ago (987). His immediate ancestry is unusual, and complicated; like every human being, he has eight great-great-grandfathers and as many great-great-grandmothers, but among them Louis Philippe and his Queen each occur four times. The Count of Paris continued family tradition by marrying a cousin, but his consort's mother brought in an unaccustomed strain from the Slav domains of the old Austro-Hungarian Empire. His eldest son, another Henry, carries the title of Count of Clermont, originally held by that son of St Louis who founded the Bourbons. But of his later twin sons, the elder, Prince Michael, has made a marriage of non-dynastic character, with Beatrice Pasquier de Franclieu, while the union of the younger with Gersende de Sabran conforms to Capetian tradition and standards.

An alliance which cuts across the lines of history is that of the sister of the Count of Paris with Prince Peter Murat, who was both the descendant of Napoleon's brother-in-law and an officer in the British army in the Second World War.

[141]

Chapter 17

NAPOLEON

The family of Bonaparte appears to have originated in Florence, and passed over to Corsica in 1529 where they mainly devoted themselves to the law. The family could count itself as noble, and the original coat-of-arms is shown at the bottom of Table 72.

The French Revolution made possible a career for anybody of talent. The reign of terror was followed by the Directory, which had to seek artillery to maintain itself. General Bonaparte, when he rose to his first independent command, promptly quelled a Parisian riot. In 1796–7 he made his own revolution in the art of war by the brilliance and speed of his north Italian victories. In 1799 he became First Consul (the names of his two colleagues are not remembered) and in 1804 the Senate begged him to become emperor. The Pope was brought from Italy to consecrate Napoleon in Paris; visits to Aachen, the one-time capital of Charlemagne, and to Milan, where he assumed the Iron Crown of Lombardy, made it clear that the shadow of European dominion fell over the new monarch.

Military genius raised Napoleon to his throne but he had already given evidence of his omnivorous interest in government of all kinds. The Code Napoleon of 1804 is a masterpiece of legal clarity and sense, which is perhaps the most widespread legacy of the Napoleonic regime, though its conquests were also instrumental in extending the area which used the metric system (fully adopted in 1801). Nelson at Trafalgar (1805) denied the Emperor command of the sea, but his armies swept across Europe and he was able to redraw the political map on entirely new lines, often to the benefit of his own family. His elder brother Joseph was made King of Naples and then of Spain; the vacant throne of Naples went to his brother-in-law Marshal Murat, one of the most dazzling cavalry leaders of all time but politically incompetent. Louis Bonaparte became King of Holland and Jerome King of an artificial German province of Westphalia.

The desire for a dynasty was dominant in Napoleon's mind. He had quarrelled with his ablest brother, Lucien, over the latter's second marriage (to a former mistress of no birth); Joseph had only daughters; Jerome had been coerced into divorcing his American wife. The Emperor's own wife, the beautiful Josephine Tascher de la Pagerie, was childless by him, though her daughter was married to Louis of Holland. In 1809 Napoleon divorced Josephine and extorted from the Emperor of Austria his daughter. The proud blood of Hapsburg-Lorraine was joined with that of the Corsican genius. Only one son graced the union, and his delighted father bestowed upon him the traditional style of King of Rome.

For his own arms Napoleon adopted a Roman eagle clutching a thunderbolt. After becoming emperor he instituted a new system of heraldry to match the new honours which he bestowed upon his marshals and his civil servants. His brothers combined the imperial eagle with the ancient blazon of the provinces over which they ruled. To his brother-in-law Joachim Murat of Naples he allowed a chief of the Empire. Each rank in the peerage also had a particular heraldic distinction. Thus every duke had a red chief sown with silver stars. In 1802 he founded the Legion of Honour, an order which was maintained by Louis XVIII and is still the principal decoration of France: the collar and badge surround his shield on Table 73.

Like so many conquerors Napoleon found it difficult to halt or withdraw. More than once he was offered terms which allowed France her so-called 'natural frontiers' – the Rhine, the Alps and the Pyrenees – but he refused them. His invasion of Russia in 1812, followed by the bitter retreat from

Moscow, marked a definite stage in his downfall. His new armies were shattered at Leipzig in 1813, and in 1814 he was compelled to abdicate. Exiled to Elba, he made a sensational but futile excursion which ended at Waterloo. From St Helena there was no physical return, but he cultivated a spiritual legend which served his nephew well. His son was borne off to Austria and given an Austrian title and Austrian arms. The Empress, allotted the Duchy of Parma, slid into adultery with a one-eyed general.

Napoleon ruled as an autocrat. Yet on three separate occasions, in 1800, 1802 and 1804, he sought the endorsement of the French people. He reigned as an Emperor, and yet he was the heir of the French Revolution. For example, in 1802 he made a Concordat with the Vatican, but the church as restored in France lacked all the privileges and splendour of the *ancien régime* and was almost an adjunct of the civil power. After royalist risings had taken place in France, he committed an arbitrary but effective act of violence against the old dynasty by kidnapping and executing the Duc d'Enghien, last of the Condé line of Bourbons. His personal interest in law reform and the aspects of civil government was detailed and indubitable; and both Goethe and Heine admired him. The creation of his own Empire caused the extinction of the centuries-old Holy Roman Empire (Chapter 30). One thing was certain: after his career Europe could never be the same again.

In France, the memory of Napoleon's greatness and glory outlived the recollection of his blunders and the carnage of his ceaseless campaigns. After the early death in Vienna of his son, King of Rome or Duke of Reichstadt, the leadership of the family was asserted by Louis Napoleon, son of the King of Holland (and grandson of Josephine). After the downfall of the July monarchy in 1848, he came forward as a candidate for the Presidency of the Second Republic. Such was now the repute of Bonapartism that this awkward, unimpressive little man, with no success to his name, was elected president by a vast majority. In 1852 he became emperor and, as a recognition of the Duke of Reichstadt, took the title of Napoleon III. The princesses of Europe fought shy of this new Prince, and he married for love a ravishingly beautiful Spanish countess.

Napoleon promised France peace, but he became involved in the Crimean War (allied with England against Russia), in campaigns against Austria in northern Italy (where the slaughter at Solferino in 1864 prompted the inauguration of the Red Cross), in an unprofitable expedition to Mexico and finally in conflict with Prussia. The Emperor lacked all trace of his uncle's grasp of warfare; Paris, which Napoleon III had done much to develop and beautify, was besieged and the Second Empire collapsed. His only

The Emperor Napoleon (1769–1821) wearing his coronation robes and the Legion of Honour, by Ingres, 1806.

child was killed with the British army in Zululand. Any legacy which remains to Bonapartism is now vested in the descendants of Jerome, King of Westphalia. Ironically, the heir, Prince Charles, has married a Bourbon princess, thus linking Bonapartism with the traditional rulers of France.

FRANCE
House of Bonaparte

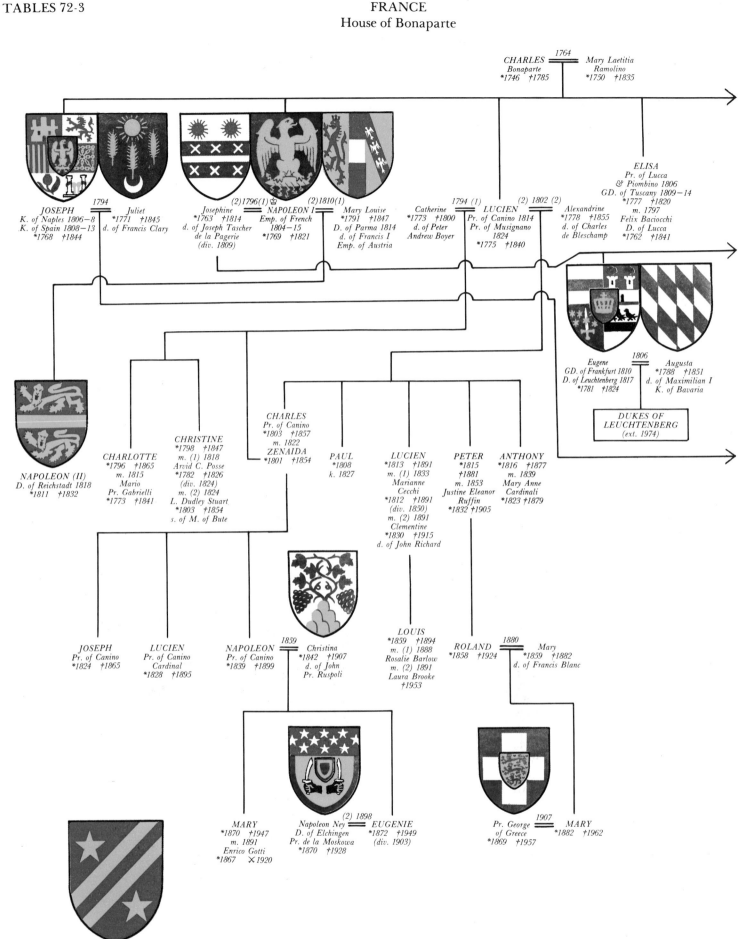

CHARLES 1764 Mary Laetitia
Bonaparte Ramolino
*1746 †1785 *1750 †1835

JOSEPH 1794 Juliet
K. of Naples 1806–8 *1771 †1845
K. of Spain 1808–13 d. of Francis Clary
*1768 †1844

Josephine (2)1796(1) **NAPOLEON I** (2)1810(1) Mary Louise
*1763 †1814 Emp. of French *1791 †1847
d. of Joseph Tascher 1804–15 D. of Parma 1814
de la Pagerie *1769 †1821 d. of Francis I
(div. 1809) Emp. of Austria

Catherine 1794 (1) **LUCIEN** (2) 1802 (2) Alexandrine
*1773 †1800 Pr. of Canino 1814 *1778 †1855
d. of Peter Pr. of Musignano d. of Charles
Andrew Boyer 1824 de Bleschamp
*1775 †1840

ELISA
Pr. of Lucca
& Piombino 1806
GD. of Tuscany 1809–14
*1777 †1820
m. 1797
Felix Baciocchi
D. of Lucca
*1762 †1841

Eugene 1806 Augusta
GD. of Frankfurt 1810 *1788 †1851
D. of Leuchtenberg 1817 d. of Maximilian I
*1781 †1824 K. of Bavaria

**DUKES OF
LEUCHTENBERG**
(ext. 1974)

NAPOLEON (II)
D. of Reichstadt 1818
*1811 †1832

CHARLOTTE
*1796 †1865
m. 1815
Mario
Pr. Gabrielli
*1773 †1841

CHRISTINE
*1798 †1847
m. (1) 1818
Arvid C. Posse
*1782 †1826
(div. 1824)
m. (2) 1824
L. Dudley Stuart
*1803 †1854
s. of M. of Bute

CHARLES
Pr. of Canino
*1803 †1857
m. 1822
ZENAIDA
*1801 †1854

PAUL
*1808
k. 1827

LUCIEN
*1813 †1891
m. (1) 1833
Marianne
Cecchi
*1812 †1891
(div. 1850)
m. (2) 1891
Clementine
*1830 †1915
d. of John Richard

PETER
*1815
†1881
m. 1853
Justine Eleanor
Ruffin
*1832 †1905

ANTHONY
*1816 †1877
m. 1839
Mary Anne
Cardinali
*1823 †1879

JOSEPH
Pr. of Canino
*1824 †1865

LUCIEN
Pr. of Canino
Cardinal
*1828 †1895

NAPOLEON 1859 Christina
Pr. of Canino *1842 †1907
*1839 †1899 d. of John
Pr. Ruspoli

LOUIS
*1859 †1894
m. (1) 1888
Rosalie Barlow
m. (2) 1891
Laura Brooke
†1953

ROLAND 1880 Mary
*1858 †1924 *1859 †1882
d. of Francis Blanc

MARY
*1870 †1947
m. 1891
Enrico Gotti
*1867 ✕1920

Napoleon Ney (2) 1898 **EUGENIE**
D. of Elchingen *1872 †1949
Pr. de la Moskowa (div. 1903)
*1870 †1928

Pr. George 1907 **MARY**
of Greece *1882 †1962
*1869 †1957

FRANCE
House of Bonaparte

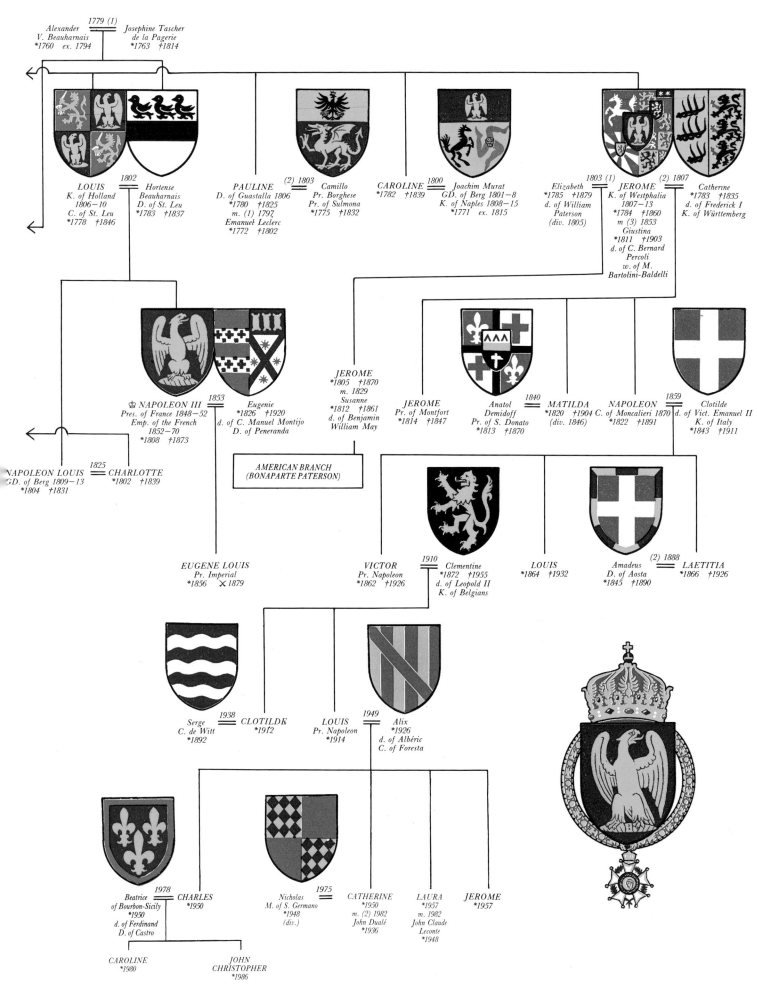

1779 (1)

Alexander
V. Beauharnais
*1760 ex. 1794

Josephine Tascher
de la Pagerie
*1763 †1814

LOUIS
K. of Holland
1806−10
C. of St. Leu
*1778 †1846

1802

Hortense
Beauharnais
D. of St. Leu
*1783 †1837

PAULINE
D. of Guastalla 1806
*1780 †1825
m. (1) 1797
Emanuel Leclerc
*1772 †1802

(2) 1803

Camillo
Pr. Borghese
Pr. of Sulmona
*1775 †1832

CAROLINE
*1782 †1839

1800

Joachim Murat
GD. of Berg 1801−8
K. of Naples 1808−15
*1771 ex. 1815

Elizabeth
*1785 †1879
d. of William
Paterson
(div. 1805)

1803 (1)

JEROME
K. of Westphalia
1807−13
*1784 †1860
m (3) 1853
Giustina
*1811 †1903
d. of C. Bernard
Percoli
w. of M.
Bartolini-Baldelli

(2) 1807

Catherine
*1783 †1835
d. of Frederick I
K. of Württemberg

NAPOLEON III
Pres. of France 1848−52
Emp. of the French
1852−70
*1808 †1873

1853

Eugenie
*1826 †1920
d. of C. Manuel Montijo
D. of Peneranda

JEROME
*1805 †1870
m. 1829
Susanne
*1812 †1861
d. of Benjamin
William May

JEROME
Pr. of Montfort
*1814 †1847

Anatol
Demidoff
Pr. of S. Donato
*1813 †1870

1840

MATILDA
*1820 †1904
(div. 1846)

NAPOLEON
C. of Moncalieri 1870
*1822 †1891

1859

Clotilde
d. of Vict. Emanuel II
K. of Italy
*1843 †1911

NAPOLEON LOUIS
GD. of Berg 1809−13
*1804 †1831

1825

CHARLOTTE
*1802 †1839

AMERICAN BRANCH
(BONAPARTE PATERSON)

EUGENE LOUIS
Pr. Imperial
*1856 × 1879

VICTOR
Pr. Napoleon
*1862 †1926

1910

Clementine
*1872 †1955
d. of Leopold II
K. of Belgians

LOUIS
*1864 †1932

Amadeus
D. of Aosta
*1845 †1890

(2) 1888

LAETITIA
*1866 †1926

Serge
C. de Witt
*1892

1938

CLOTILDE
*1912

LOUIS
Pr. Napoleon
*1914

1949

Alix
*1926
d. of Albéric
C. of Foresta

Beatrice
of Bourbon-Sicily
*1950
d. of Ferdinand
D. of Castro

1978

CHARLES
*1950

Nicholas
M. of S. Germano
*1948
(div.)

1975

CATHERINE
*1950
m. (2) 1982
John Dualé
*1936

LAURA
*1957
m. 1982
John Claude
Leconte
*1948

JEROME
*1957

CAROLINE
*1980

JOHN
CHRISTOPHER
*1986

Chapter 18

BURGUNDY

As a geographical expression Burgundy has had a complicated history. The Burgundians were a relatively minor Teutonic people who broke into Gaul in the early fifth century and settled in the valleys of the Rhône and Saône. In the early Middle Ages all this area constituted a Kingdom of Burgundy whose capital was at Arles. Gradually the name came to be applied only to the northern part. Even here there were two different regions which bore the name. The Duchy of Burgundy was part of France, and its dukes, whose pedigree is drawn out on Table 74, were subjects of the French Crown: their capital was at Dijon and their territory included the famous wine-producing hills round Beaune. But there was also a County of Burgundy (later known as Franche-Comté) with its centre at Besançon, which was part of the Holy Roman Empire. At times the two were united.

Robert II of France gave the French Duchy, which had lapsed into his hands, to his son Robert who founded the first House of Burgundy. This donation took place before the age of heraldry. In the thirteenth century the dukes devised their own coat-of-arms of six diagonal stripes of gold and blue within a red bordure. This appears on the seal of Hugh IV in 1234. The family flourished in its rich provinces, but its younger sons needed to make their own way. Henry, younger brother of Hugh I, made his way south and became Count of Portugal and ancestor of the kings of that country (Table 114). Hugh III married twice; his second wife was heiress of Vienne and their child Guido (or Guiges) inherited that fief and the unusual title of Dauphin which ultimately passed to the eldest sons of the Kings of France (Chapter 15: The Hundred Years' War). The last Count of imperial Burgundy left a sister who married Philip V of France. Their elder daughter married Eudo IV, Duke of French Burgundy, and the two parts were thus united in 1330. However Philip I, grandson of this alliance, died childless in 1361 and the Duchy reverted to the French Crown while the county passed to Margaret of Flanders.

In 1363 John II of France granted French Burgundy to his youngest son, Philip the Bold, and inaugurated the second and more glorious line of Capetian dukes (Table 75). Philip II proceeded to make a splendid marriage with the widow of the last

Charles the Bold (1433–77), Duke of Burgundy, in the midst of his court. MS of 1473.

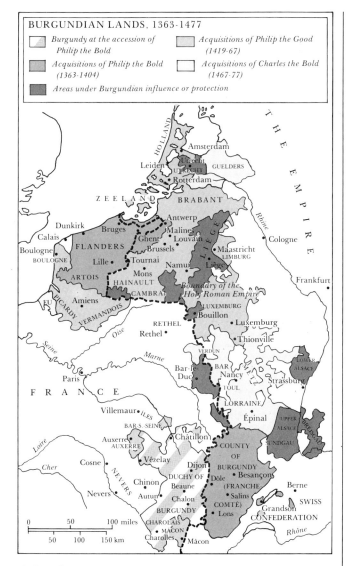

Belgium and more; their capital was at Brussels, their riches were the envy of most kings. Philip the Good founded in 1430 the Knights of the Golden Fleece, which became the most lustrous order of chivalry on the Continent. Its collar and badge surround his shield at the head of this chapter and on Table 74. The first and fourth quarterings show the differenced arms of France used by Philip the Bold; in the second, Burgundy ancient is united with the lion of Brabant, and in the third, with that of Limburg; over all is the black lion on gold of Flanders. The dukes were buried at Dijon, but the heart of their power was in the Low Countries; in both they made profuse use of heraldic display. They also fostered the notable port of Antwerp. It was in the Low Countries that the great artistic movement, headed by Jan van Eyck, developed and that the technique of painting in oils was worked out. In this medium northern Europe for the first time contributed something to the galaxy of Italian art.

The long reign of Philip the Good (1419–67) marked the high tide of Burgundian power. His epithet is flattering, for he was a tough and demanding ruler and the father of many bastards. His court was splendid, he encouraged literature and the arts, but his rule was ruthless and his taxation severe. A principal handicap was that his various lordships in the Netherlands were cut off from his ancestral lands in Burgundy. Nor was he king. Ancient memories of the Middle Kingdom fabricated for the eldest grandson of Charlemagne (Chapter 15: first section) stirred in his fancy, but this could not be achieved; he spurned the lesser title of King of Brabant.

His son, Charles the Bold, was of a different type. Chaste and basically stupid, he failed to engender an heir and became involved in the complicated politics of Switzerland and the Hapsburgs. His efforts to bridge the gap between Burgundy and Brabant by acquisitions in Alsace and Lorraine were unrewarded; his battles with the Swiss were disastrous. At Grandson (1476) he was heavily defeated, and at Nancy he was killed in January 1477. Three marriages had only produced one daughter, Mary, the most sensational heiress in Europe. Louis XI of France coveted her hand for the Dauphin, but the County of Flanders was against the alliance. In August Mary espoused Maximilian, son and heir to the Hapsburg Emperor of Germany. The consequences of this wedding were to lour over the map of Europe for 500 years. It is true that French Burgundy, Artois and other minor fiefs escheated to Louis XI, but the County of Burgundy and the more important and more affluent provinces of the Low Countries were added to the Hapsburg dominions, and there remained until the French Revolution. The brief, brilliant ballad of Burgundy was at an end.

duke of the old line. Margaret was daughter of Louis III de Mâle, Count of Flanders: she was heiress not only to Flanders but to the Counties of Nevers, Rethel, Artois and non-French Burgundy. In addition Philip devoted long diplomatic and military endeavour to securing the reversion of the Duchies of Brabant and Limburg which belonged to the sister of his mother-in-law. He succeeded in the year of his death in gaining them for his second son Anthony, but in due course they passed to his eldest grandson, Philip the Good. The two marriages made with the Bavarian rulers of Holland (and Hainault) also yielded a golden dividend when those Counties in turn passed to Philip the Good, who in addition purchased the County of Namur and the Duchy of Luxemburg.

The fifteenth-century Dukes of Burgundy were an extraordinary phenomenon. Technically they were not independent sovereigns, for all their lands were held of the King of France or the Emperor. But they had succeeded in consolidating most of what is now

TABLE 74

BURGUNDY
General survey

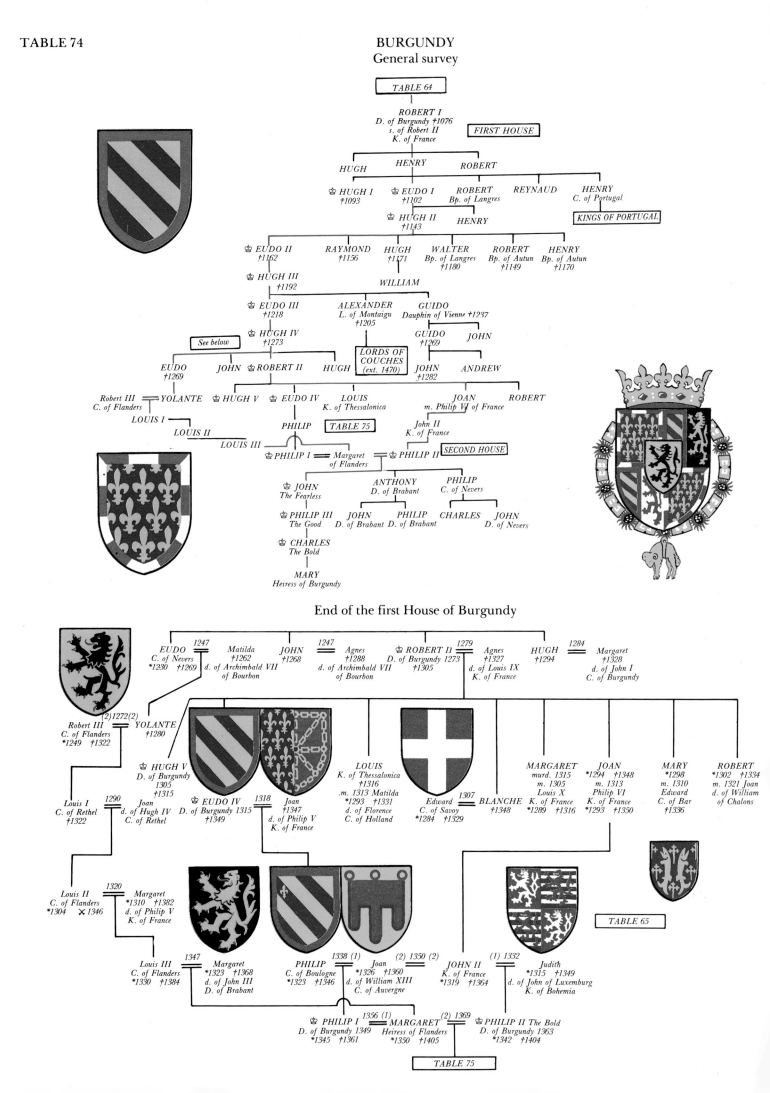

TABLE 64

ROBERT I
D. of Burgundy †1076
s. of Robert II
K. of France

FIRST HOUSE

HUGH   HENRY   ROBERT

♔ HUGH I †1093   ♔ EUDO I †1102   ROBERT Bp. of Langres   REYNAUD   HENRY C. of Portugal

♔ HUGH II †1143   HENRY

KINGS OF PORTUGAL

♔ EUDO II †1162   RAYMOND †1156   HUGH †1171   WALTER Bp. of Langres †1180   ROBERT Bp. of Autun †1149   HENRY Bp. of Autun †1170

♔ HUGH III †1192   WILLIAM

♔ EUDO III †1218   ALEXANDER L. of Montaigu †1205   GUIDO Dauphin of Vienne †1237

♔ HUGH IV †1273   GUIDO †1269   JOHN

See below   LORDS OF COUCHES (ext. 1470)

EUDO †1269   JOHN   ♔ ROBERT II   HUGH   JOHN †1282   ANDREW

Robert III C. of Flanders ══ YOLANTE   ♔ HUGH V   ♔ EUDO IV   LOUIS K. of Thessalonica   JOAN m. Philip VI of France   ROBERT

LOUIS I   PHILIP   TABLE 75   John II K. of France

LOUIS II   LOUIS III   ♔ PHILIP I ══ Margaret of Flanders ══ ♔ PHILIP II   SECOND HOUSE

♔ JOHN The Fearless   ANTHONY D. of Brabant   PHILIP C. of Nevers

♔ PHILIP III The Good   JOHN D. of Brabant   PHILIP D. of Brabant   CHARLES   JOHN D. of Nevers

♔ CHARLES The Bold

MARY Heiress of Burgundy

End of the first House of Burgundy

EUDO C. of Nevers *1230 †1269   1247 ══ Matilda †1262 d. of Archimbald VII of Bourbon   JOHN †1268   1247 ══ Agnes †1288 d. of Archimbald VII of Bourbon   ♔ ROBERT II D. of Burgundy 1273 †1305   1279 ══ Agnes †1327 d. of Louis IX K. of France   HUGH †1294   1284 ══ Margaret †1328 d. of John I C. of Burgundy

Robert III C. of Flanders *1249 †1322   (2) 1272 (2) ══ YOLANTE †1280   ♔ HUGH V D. of Burgundy 1305 †1315   ♔ EUDO IV D. of Burgundy 1315 †1349   1318 ══ Joan †1347 d. of Philip V K. of France   LOUIS K. of Thessalonica †1316 .m. 1313 Matilda *1293 †1331 d. of Florence C. of Holland   Edward C. of Savoy *1284 †1329   1307 ══ BLANCHE †1348   MARGARET murd. 1315 m. 1305 Louis X K. of France *1289 †1316   JOAN *1294 †1348 m. 1313 Philip VI K. of France *1293 †1350   MARY *1298 m. 1310 Edward C. of Bar †1336   ROBERT *1302 †1334 m. 1321 Joan d. of William of Chalons

Louis I C. of Rethel †1322   1290 ══ Joan d. of Hugh IV C. of Rethel

Louis II C. of Flanders *1304 ✕ 1346   1320 ══ Margaret *1310 †1382 d. of Philip V K. of France

TABLE 65

Louis III C. of Flanders *1330 †1384   1347 ══ Margaret *1323 †1368 d. of John III D. of Brabant   PHILIP C. of Boulogne *1323 †1346   1338 (1) ══ Joan *1326 †1360 d. of William XIII C. of Auvergne ══ (2) 1350 (2)   JOHN II K. of France *1319 †1364   (1) 1332 ══ Judith *1315 †1349 d. of John of Luxemburg K. of Bohemia

♔ PHILIP I ══ 1356 (1) ══ MARGARET ══ (2) 1369 ══ ♔ PHILIP II The Bold
D. of Burgundy 1349   Heiress of Flanders   D. of Burgundy 1363
*1345 †1361   *1350 †1405   *1342 †1404

TABLE 75

TABLE 75

BURGUNDY
Second House

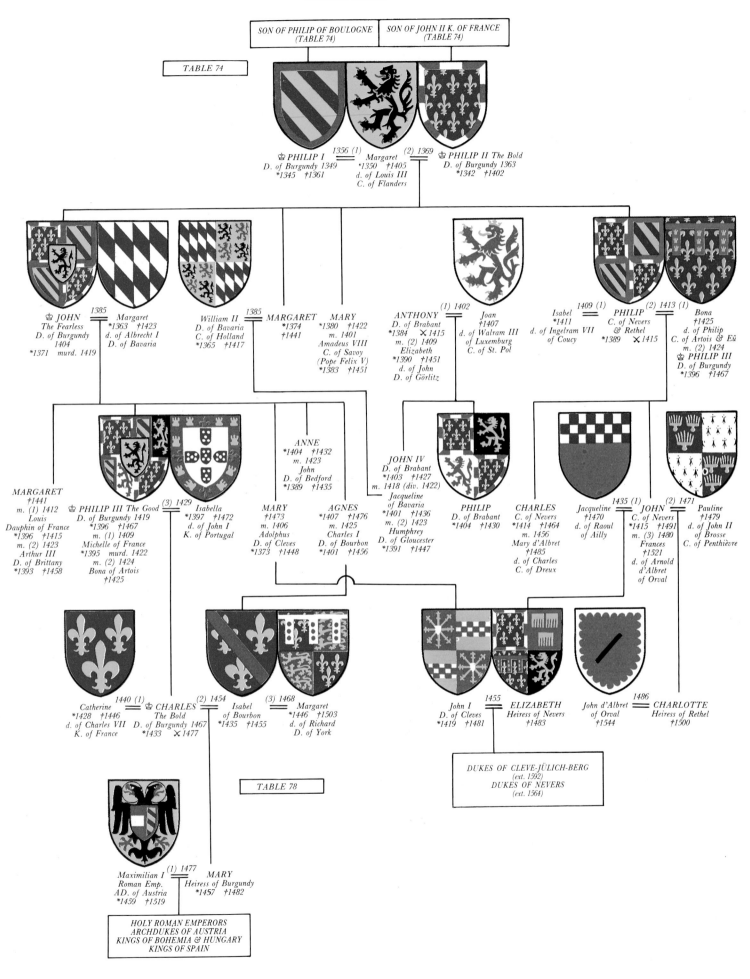

SON OF PHILIP OF BOULOGNE
(TABLE 74)

SON OF JOHN II K. OF FRANCE
(TABLE 74)

TABLE 74

♚ PHILIP I
D. of Burgundy 1349
*1345 †1361

1356 (1)
Margaret
*1350 †1405
d. of Louis III
C. of Flanders

(2) 1369

♚ PHILIP II The Bold
D. of Burgundy 1363
*1342 †1402

♚ JOHN
The Fearless
D. of Burgundy
1404
*1371 murd. 1419

1385
Margaret
*1363 †1423
d. of Albrecht I
D. of Bavaria

William II
D. of Bavaria
C. of Holland
*1365 †1417

1385
MARGARET
*1374
†1441

MARY
*1380 †1422
m. 1401
Amadeus VIII
C. of Savoy
(Pope Felix V)
*1383 †1451

ANTHONY
D. of Brabant
*1384 ✕1415
m. (2) 1409
Elizabeth
*1390 †1451
d. of John
D. of Görlitz

(1) 1402
Joan
†1407
d. of Walram III
of Luxemburg
C. of St. Pol

Isabel
*1411
d. of Ingelram VII
of Coucy

1409 (1)
PHILIP
C. of Nevers
& Rethel
*1389 ✕1415

(2) 1413 (1)
Bona
†1425
d. of Philip
C. of Artois & Eû
m. (2) 1424

♚ PHILIP III
D. of Burgundy
*1396 †1467

MARGARET
†1441
m. (1) 1412
Louis
Dauphin of France
*1396 †1415
m. (2) 1423
Arthur III
D. of Brittany
*1393 †1458

♚ PHILIP III The Good
D. of Burgundy 1419
*1396 †1467
m. (1) 1409
Michelle of France
*1395 murd. 1422
m. (2) 1424
Bona of Artois
†1425

(3) 1429
Isabella
*1397 †1472
d. of John I
K. of Portugal

ANNE
*1404 †1432
m. 1423
John
D. of Bedford
*1389 †1435

MARY
†1473
m. 1406
Adolphus
D. of Cleves
*1373 †1448

AGNES
*1407 †1476
m. 1425
Charles I
D. of Bourbon
*1401 †1456

JOHN IV
D. of Brabant
*1403 †1427
m. 1418 (div. 1422)
Jacqueline
of Bavaria
*1401 †1436
m. (2) 1423
Humphrey
D. of Gloucester
*1391 †1447

PHILIP
D. of Brabant
*1404 †1430

CHARLES
C. of Nevers
*1414 †1464
m. 1456
Mary d'Albret
†1485
d. of Charles
C. of Dreux

Jacqueline
†1470
d. of Raoul
of Ailly

1435 (1)
JOHN
C. of Nevers
*1415 †1491
m. (3) 1480
Frances
†1521
d. of Arnold
d'Albret
of Orval

(2) 1471
Pauline
†1479
d. of John II
of Brosse
C. of Penthièvre

1440 (1)
Catherine
*1428 †1446
d. of Charles VII
K. of France

♚ CHARLES
The Bold
D. of Burgundy 1467
*1433 ✕1477

(2) 1454
Isabel
of Bourbon
*1435 †1455

(3) 1468
Margaret
*1446 †1503
d. of Richard
D. of York

John I
D. of Cleves
*1419 †1481

1455
ELIZABETH
Heiress of Nevers
†1483

John d'Albret
of Orval

1486
CHARLOTTE
Heiress of Rethel
†1500

TABLE 78

DUKES OF CLEVE-JÜLICH-BERG
(ext. 1592)
DUKES OF NEVERS
(ext. 1564)

Maximilian I
Roman Emp.
AD. of Austria
*1459 †1519

(1) 1477
MARY
Heiress of Burgundy
*1457 †1482

HOLY ROMAN EMPERORS
ARCHDUKES OF AUSTRIA
KINGS OF BOHEMIA & HUNGARY
KINGS OF SPAIN

Chapter 19

AUSTRIA: HAPSBURG

Bella gerant alii, tu felix Austria nube
(Let others make wars, you, fortunate Austria, marry)

The great historic name of Austria began as a frontier province of Germany. In the time of Charlemagne Bavaria had been a border state resisting the hosts of the Avars. Gradually German arms and the Christian religion spread eastwards and a group of marcher lordships developed beyond Bavaria; noteworthy among them (from north to south) were Austria, Styria, Carinthia and Carniola. In the tenth century a fresh and terrible menace assaulted Christian Europe, the Hungarians or Magyars, who swept across the Continent leaving a track of destruction. Otto I of Germany defeated them decisively at the battle of the Lechfeld near Augsburg in 955. The Magyars were driven back to the area which they have since occupied as Hungary, while Otto named a certain Burchard as ruler of Ostmark or eastern march. By the end of the century the holder of this position was known as a margrave, that is 'graf' or count of a border area or 'mark'.

In 976 Leopold I of Babenberg (the modern Bamberg) appears as Margrave of the Ostmark and his descendants continued to govern Austria under the Emperor until 1246. His great-grandson, Leopold III (Table 76), was a warm patron of the Church and benefactor of monasteries; he was proclaimed a saint in 1485, but had enjoyed a local reputation for sanctity long before formal canonization. His wife, Agnes, was the widow of Frederick of Hohenstaufen. This made his numerous sons half-brothers of the first Swabian Emperor, Conrad III. One of them, Leopold, became briefly Duke of Bavaria; his successor Henry 'Jasomirgott' (so-called from his favourite oath, 'So help me God') became the first Duke of Austria in 1156 by gift of the Emperor Frederick Barbarossa. In the course of the Second Crusade

Henry married a Byzantine princess. A third son, Otto, Bishop of Freising, was one of the most important German historians of the twelfth century; yet another was Archbishop of Salzburg.

Leopold V took part in the Third Crusade and was present at the capture of Acre (July 1190). Here he had a furious quarrel with Richard I of England, when the latter tore down the Austrian banner from a conquered tower. Duke Leopold had his revenge when he seized the English King who was seeking to travel home through Austria in disguise, handed him over to the Emperor and shared in the vast ransom extorted from Richard's domains. He extended his own importance by acquiring the Duchy of Styria (1192) as a legacy from its last duke.

Leopold VI was a prosperous ruler and acted as mediator between Empire and Papacy; by this time Vienna was one of the wealthiest cities of Germany. However, his son Frederick was involved in conflict with the Emperor Frederick II, was briefly deprived of his duchies and perished childless in battle against the Hungarians in 1246. It was the Babenberg family which had laid the solid basis of the Austrian state, had encouraged colonization of the land and established great monasteries in their dominions. The Duchy itself was a union of the two districts of Upper and Lower Austria: the arms of the latter can be seen on Table 76 with five eagles, and are sometimes styled Austria ancient. They have been overshadowed by the white bar on red of Austria modern, one of the historic blazons of European heraldry, and long linked with the Hapsburg dynasty, who virtually abandoned for it the use of their ancestral arms, a red lion on gold with a blue crown (Tables 76 and 77).

The extinction of the Babenberg dynasty almost coincided with the collapse of central authority in Germany following the death of Frederick II (1250). That Emperor had declared Austria and Styria to be

[150]

escheated to the Crown, despite efforts by Hermann V of Baden, a nephew of the last Babenberg duke, to establish a claim to them. In 1251 Ottokar II, King of Bohemia, seized the duchies and proceeded to marry Margaret of Babenberg. He was a powerful and ambitious prince who aimed at dominating the German scene. In 1269 he extended his influence south of Austria by acquiring the Duchies of Carinthia and Carniola. It was a serious blow to his lofty aims when the Electors in 1273 chose Rudolph of Hapsburg to be King of the Romans (Chapter 30). In two campaigns (1276 and 1278) Ottokar was stripped of his conquests and finally slain.

THE HAPSBURGS

The family of the Counts of Hapsburg came originally from Alsace and had considerable property there and in what today is Switzerland: the actual castle of Hapsburg is in the Aargau. Rudolph was no longer young when chosen, but he was solid, respected, not too powerful, and had been a loyal adherent of the vanished Hohenstaufen dynasty. In 1282 he persuaded the Electors to sanction the grant of Austria and Styria to his sons Albrecht and Rudolph: here began the long connection between his descendants and Vienna.

Rudolph had hoped to obtain the succession of his younger son and namesake to Germany, but the boy died young: when Rudolph eventually died in 1291, the Electors regarded Albrecht of Austria as too powerful and chose Adolphus of Nassau, the 'Priests' King'. Seven years later they deposed him and did elect Albrecht of Austria, a tough and successful soldier but a less kindly and generous prince than his father. For a short time he secured Bohemia for his eldest son, presaging its future union with Austria, but in 1308 Albrecht was barbarously murdered by his nephew John the Parricide. For all Albrecht's power he had difficulty in maintaining control over some of the Alpine valleys; later legend has placed the story of William Tell in his reign. One of his sons, Leopold I (Table 78), was decisively defeated at Morgarten in 1315 by the Swiss peasantry, a blunt reminder to the feudal classes that their superiority in war could be challenged, and challenged effectively.

In 1314 there was a double election to the Empire, though more princes supported Louis of Bavaria than Frederick the Fair of Austria. Frederick and his brothers were beaten at the Battle of Mühldorf in 1322 and Frederick was made prisoner; his more capable brother Leopold directed Austria in his absence. Bit by bit the successive Hapsburg dukes built up their power, In 1363 they secured the Tyrol on the death of Count Meinhard V (Table 78). Rudolph IV gained the title of archduke in the same year. His shield shows the quarterings for Styria, Carinthia,

Hapsburg and Carniola with Austria over all. The arms of Styria were unusual and originally showed a mad bull, breathing flames, on a green field: this was a canting coat on the name 'Stier' or ox; later generations of heralds concluded that these fire-throwing exercises were more suited to a panther and sometimes altered the main charge to that monster. At this time an arrangement was made with the House of Luxemburg that if one family died out, the other would succeed to its possessions. Rudolph IV had high ambitions and even fabricated documents allegedly bestowing privileges on Austria by Julius Caesar: among the expert witnesses who condemned them was the poet Petrarch.

One of the basic factors in medieval German history was the slow adoption of the hereditary system and the passage of undiminished domains to the eldest son. In the fourteenth and fifteenth centuries the Hapsburgs were affected by the old Teutonic practice of subdivision of lands, which will be encountered in many other principalities. Thus Leopold III, youngest brother of Rudolph IV, became Duke of Styria, and his youngest son, Frederick, was Count of Tyrol. The full Hapsburg territories were not reunited until the time of Frederick V. But by that date a wider destiny was opening up before the Hapsburgs. The Electors to the Holy Roman Empire (Chapter 30) increasingly manifested a preference for emperors whose main power lay outside Germany. Sigismund of Hungary and Bohemia reigned from 1410 to 1437. His only child Elizabeth was married to Albrecht V, Duke of Austria, who in 1438 was elected to the vacant throne, as Albrecht II. His immediate demise makes his own reign unimportant save that it begins the long connection from 1438 to 1918 between the Hapsburgs and the Empire, a connection severed only for one short spell. On Albrecht's death the Electors turned to his cousin Frederick V who (with his brother Albrecht) was Duke of Styria, Carinthia and Carniola; his youth and good looks seemed to promise a vigorous reign.

Appearances were deceptive. Frederick III, as he became, was perhaps the most ineffectual of all the heirs of Charlemagne; his long reign saw scant political achievement though it offers certain landmarks. He was the last Emperor to be crowned in Rome; he was the first to show the famous Hapsburg jutting lower lip. An early difficulty arose when the widow of his predecessor gave birth to a posthumous son: Ladislas V was nominal King of Bohemia and Hungary and Duke of Austria for his brief life. By 1463 Frederick had reunited the family lands, except Tyrol, in his person and assumed the title of Archduke of Austria. If he was a bad monarch of Germany, he was a good Hapsburg. Ambitious schemes flitted across his mind, indulged by his hobbies of

TABLE 76

AUSTRIA
General survey

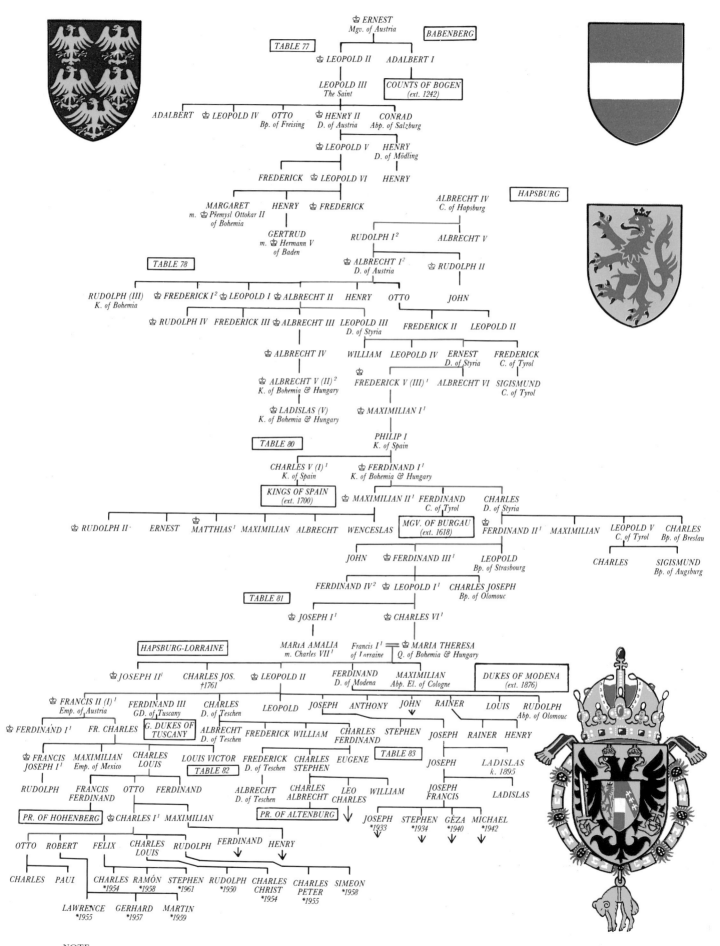

ERNEST
Mgv. of Austria — BABENBERG

TABLE 77

LEOPOLD II   ADALBERT I

LEOPOLD III
The Saint   COUNTS OF BOGEN
(ext. 1242)

ADALBERT   LEOPOLD IV   OTTO
Bp. of Freising   HENRY II
D. of Austria   CONRAD
Abp. of Salzburg

LEOPOLD V   HENRY
D. of Mödling

FREDERICK   LEOPOLD VI   HENRY

MARGARET
m. Přemysl Ottokar II
of Bohemia   HENRY   FREDERICK   ALBRECHT IV
C. of Hapsburg   HAPSBURG

GERTRUD
m. Hermann V
of Baden   RUDOLPH I²   ALBRECHT V

ALBRECHT I²
D. of Austria   RUDOLPH II

TABLE 78

RUDOLPH (III)   FREDERICK I²   LEOPOLD I   ALBRECHT II   HENRY   OTTO   JOHN
K. of Bohemia

RUDOLPH IV   FREDERICK III   ALBRECHT III   LEOPOLD III   FREDERICK II   LEOPOLD II
D. of Styria

ALBRECHT IV   WILLIAM   LEOPOLD IV   ERNEST   FREDERICK
D. of Styria   C. of Tyrol

ALBRECHT V (II)²   FREDERICK V (III)¹   ALBRECHT VI   SIGISMUND
K. of Bohemia & Hungary   C. of Tyrol

LADISLAS (V)   MAXIMILIAN I¹
K. of Bohemia & Hungary

PHILIP I
K. of Spain

TABLE 80

CHARLES V (I)¹   FERDINAND I¹
K. of Spain   K. of Bohemia & Hungary

KINGS OF SPAIN
(ext. 1700)   MAXIMILIAN II¹   FERDINAND
C. of Tyrol   CHARLES
D. of Styria

RUDOLPH II   ERNEST   MATTHIAS¹   MAXIMILIAN   ALBRECHT   WENCESLAS   MGV. OF BURGAU
(ext. 1618)   FERDINAND II¹   MAXIMILIAN   LEOPOLD V   CHARLES
C. of Tyrol   Bp. of Breslau

JOHN   FERDINAND III¹   LEOPOLD   CHARLES   SIGISMUND
Bp. of Strasbourg   Bp. of Augsburg

FERDINAND IV²   LEOPOLD I¹   CHARLES JOSEPH
Bp. of Olomouc

TABLE 81

JOSEPH I¹   CHARLES VI¹

HAPSBURG-LORRAINE   MARIA AMALIA
m. Charles VII¹   Francis I¹
of Lorraine   MARIA THERESA
Q. of Bohemia & Hungary

JOSEPH II¹   CHARLES JOS.
†1761   LEOPOLD II   FERDINAND
D. of Modena   MAXIMILIAN
Abp. El. of Cologne   DUKES OF MODENA
(ext. 1876)

FRANCIS II (I)¹
Emp. of Austria   FERDINAND III
GD. of Tuscany   CHARLES
D. of Teschen   LEOPOLD   JOSEPH   ANTHONY   JOHN   RAINER   LOUIS   RUDOLPH
Abp. of Olomouc

FERDINAND I¹   FR. CHARLES   G. DUKES OF
TUSCANY   ALBRECHT
D. of Teschen   FREDERICK   WILLIAM   CHARLES
FERDINAND   STEPHEN   JOSEPH   RAINER   HENRY

FRANCIS
JOSEPH I¹   MAXIMILIAN
Emp. of Mexico   CHARLES
LOUIS   LOUIS VICTOR   FREDERICK
D. of Teschen   CHARLES
STEPHEN   EUGENE   TABLE 83   JOSEPH   LADISLAS
k. 1895

RUDOLPH   FRANCIS
FERDINAND   OTTO   FERDINAND   TABLE 82   ALBRECHT
D. of Teschen   CHARLES
ALBRECHT   LEO
CHARLES   WILLIAM   JOSEPH
FRANCIS   LADISLAS

PR. OF HOHENBERG   CHARLES I¹   MAXIMILIAN   PR. OF ALTENBURG   JOSEPH
*1933   STEPHEN
*1934   GÉZA
*1940   MICHAEL
*1942

OTTO   ROBERT   FELIX   CHARLES
LOUIS   RUDOLPH   FERDINAND   HENRY

CHARLES   PAUL   CHARLES
*1954   RAMÓN
*1958   STEPHEN
*1961   RUDOLPH
*1950   CHARLES
CHRIST
*1954   CHARLES
PETER
*1955   SIMEON
*1958

LAWRENCE
*1955   GERHARD
*1957   MARTIN
*1959

NOTE
¹ Holy Roman Emperor or, later, Emperor of Austria
² King of the Romans

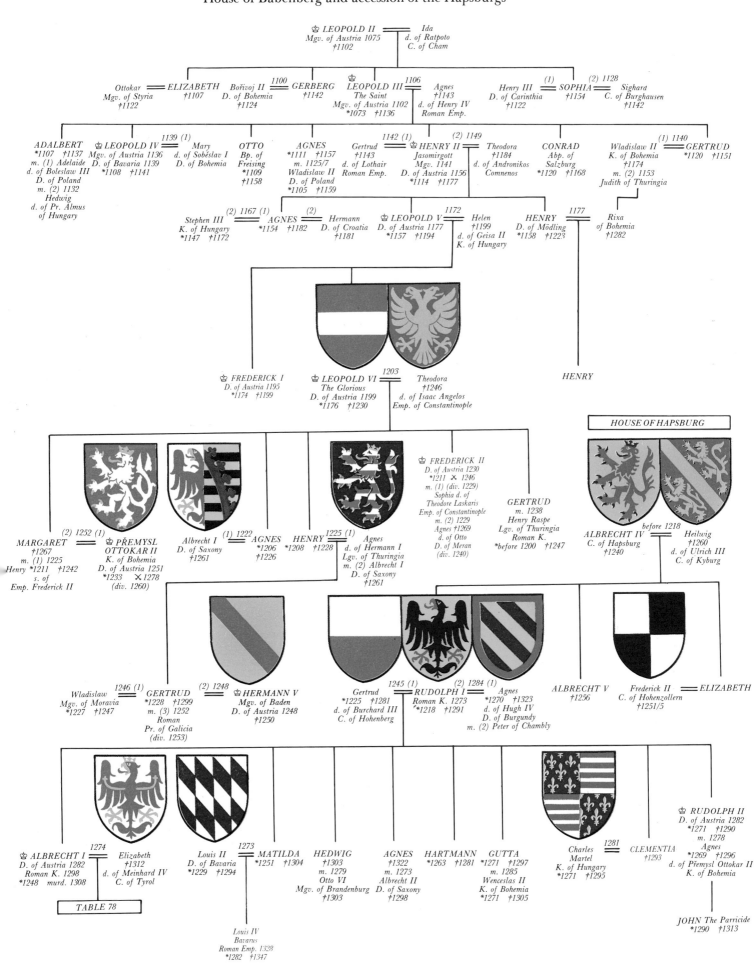

♔ LEOPOLD II
Mgv. of Austria 1075
†1102

Ida
d. of Ratpoto
C. of Cham

Ottokar
Mgv. of Styria
†1122

ELIZABETH
†1107

Bořivoj II
D. of Bohemia
†1124

1100

GERBERG
†1142

♔ LEOPOLD III
The Saint
Mgv. of Austria 1102
*1073 †1136

1106

Agnes
†1143
d. of Henry IV
Roman Emp.

Henry III
D. of Carinthia
†1122

(1)

SOPHIA
†1154

(2) 1128

Sighard
C. of Burghausen
†1142

ADALBERT
*1107 †1137
m. (1) Adelaide
d. of Boleslaw III
D. of Poland
m. (2) 1132
Hedwig
d. of Pr. Almus
of Hungary

♔ LEOPOLD IV
Mgv. of Austria 1136
D. of Bavaria 1139
*1108 †1141

1139 (1)

Mary
d. of Soběslav I
D. of Bohemia

OTTO
Bp. of
Freising
*1109
†1158

AGNES
*1111 †1157
m. 1125/7
Wladislaw II
D. of Poland
*1105 †1159

1142 (1)

Gertrud
†1143
d. of Lothair
Roman Emp.

♔ HENRY II
Jasomirgott
Mgv. 1141
D. of Austria 1156
*1114 †1177

(2) 1149

Theodora
†1184
d. of Andronikos
Comnenos

CONRAD
Abp. of
Salzburg
*1120 †1168

Wladislaw II
K. of Bohemia
†1174
m. (2) 1153
Judith of Thuringia

(1) 1140

GERTRUD
*1120 †1151

Stephen III
K. of Hungary
*1147 †1172

(2) 1167 (1)

AGNES
*1154 †1182

(2)

Hermann
D. of Croatia
†1181

♔ LEOPOLD V
D. of Austria 1177
*1157 †1194

1172

Helen
†1199
d. of Geisa II
K. of Hungary

HENRY
D. of Mödling
*1158 †1223

1177

Rixa
of Bohemia
†1282

♔ FREDERICK I
D. of Austria 1195
*1174 †1199

♔ LEOPOLD VI
The Glorious
D. of Austria 1199
*1176 †1230

1203

Theodora
†1246
d. of Isaac Angelos
Emp. of Constantinople

HENRY

HOUSE OF HAPSBURG

MARGARET
†1267
m. (1) 1225
Henry *1211 †1242
s. of
Emp. Frederick II

(2) 1252 (1)

♔ PŘEMYSL
OTTOKAR II
K. of Bohemia
D. of Austria 1251
*1233 ✕1278
(div. 1260)

Albrecht I
D. of Saxony
†1261

(1) 1222

AGNES
*1206 †1226

HENRY
*1208 †1228

1225 (1)

Agnes
d. of Hermann I
Lgv. of Thuringia
m. (2) Albrecht I
D. of Saxony
†1261

♔ FREDERICK II
D. of Austria 1230
*1211 ✕ 1246
m. (1) (div. 1229)
Sophia d. of
Theodore Laskaris
Emp. of Constantinople
m. (2) 1229
Agnes †1269
d. of Otto
D. of Meran
(div. 1240)

GERTRUD
m. 1238
Henry Raspe
Lgv. of Thuringia
Roman K.
*before 1200 †1247

ALBRECHT IV
C. of Hapsburg
†1240

before 1218

Heilwig
†1260
d. of Ulrich III
C. of Kyburg

Wladislaw
Mgv. of Moravia
*1227 †1247

1246 (1)

GERTRUD
*1228 †1299
m. (3) 1252
Roman
Pr. of Galicia
(div. 1253)

(2) 1248

♔ HERMANN V
Mgv. of Baden
D. of Austria 1248
†1250

Gertrud
*1225 †1281
d. of Burchard III
C. of Hohenberg

1245 (1)

♔ RUDOLPH I
Roman K. 1273
*1218 †1291

(2) 1284 (1)

Agnes
*1270 †1323
d. of Hugh IV
D. of Burgundy
m. (2) Peter of Chambly

ALBRECHT V
†1256

Frederick II
C. of Hohenzollern
†1251/5

ELIZABETH

♔ ALBRECHT I
D. of Austria 1282
Roman K. 1298
*1248 murd. 1308

1274

Elizabeth
†1312
d. of Meinhard IV
C. of Tyrol

Louis II
D. of Bavaria
*1229 †1294

1273

MATILDA
*1251 †1304

HEDWIG
†1303
m. 1279
Otto VI
Mgv. of Brandenburg
†1303

AGNES
†1322
m. 1273
Albrecht II
D. of Saxony
†1298

HARTMANN
*1263 †1281

GUTTA
*1271 †1297
m. 1285
Wenceslas II
K. of Bohemia
*1271 †1305

Charles
Martel
K. of Hungary
*1271 †1295

1281

CLEMENTIA
†1293

♔ RUDOLPH II
D. of Austria 1282
*1271 †1290
m. 1278
Agnes
*1269 †1296
d. of Přemysl Ottokar II
K. of Bohemia

TABLE 78

Louis IV
Bavarus
Roman Emp. 1328
*1282 †1347

JOHN The Parricide
*1290 †1313

The Holy Roman Emperor Maximilian I (1459–1519) with his family, by B. Strigel, c. 1515. The characteristic Hapsburg jaw is very evident.

alchemy and the acquisition of gems. He invented, to adorn his possessions, the monogram AEIOU announcing with fortunate prophecy the sentiment *Austriae est imperare orbi universo* (it is for Austria to rule over all the world). Above all, in 1477 he arranged the marriage of his son to the heiress of Burgundy and much of the Netherlands (Chapter 18). The election of that son, the vigorous and warlike Maximilian, as King of the Romans in 1486 may have been some consolation to Frederick III who had been evicted from his own capital by the King of Hungary. Finally, in 1490, Tyrol was secured by pensioning off the last Count (Table 78). At the least this sad, craven, dreaming Emperor bequeathed to a vigorous heir an inheritance of high potential.

MAXIMILIAN I AND CHARLES V

Maximilian I succeeded to the Empire without difficulty. He had been in real control of the family dominions for the last years of his father's long reign, and had been consolidating his power there. New influences were making themselves felt. To the southeast pressure from the Ottoman Turks was increasing; to the north and west the control of Germany was becoming more shadowy and elusive, while the invention of printing and the spread of the new learning over the Alps stimulated the intellectual ferment of the times. Two alliances arranged by

Maximilian were to have great consequences, though in neither case were these predictable at the time. First, he married his son and daughter (Table 79) to the daughter and the son of Ferdinand of Aragon; secondly he betrothed his grandson and granddaughter to the two children of Wladislaw, King of Bohemia and Hungary. He himself was often short of money, which he had to seek from the Estates, or assemblies of his provinces, and was embroiled in war with France to establish his Burgundian inheritance.

Maximilian knew in his lifetime that the young Prince of Aragon, his son-in-law, was dead and without issue, and that his son Philip (also destined to an early death) was heir to Castile and Aragon in right of his wife, the mad Joanna. He was not to know that Louis of Bohemia would perish at Mohács in 1526, leaving his sister as heiress of Bohemia and Hungary. The great inheritance of the Hapsburgs was building up. Albrecht II had placed Austria alone on the breast of a one-headed eagle. Maximilian I impaled Austria with old Burgundy on a two-headed eagle after he became emperor (Table 78). His great-grandson Maximilian II (Table 79) has two superimposed escutcheons, the lower for Bohemia and Hungary and the upper for Austria and Burgundy.

Charles I of Austria is better known as the Emperor Charles V and on him descended the formidable burden of the Hapsburg territories. He followed one grandfather as King of Spain in 1516 and the other as Holy Roman Emperor in 1519. He was thus ruler of Spain, of Burgundy and the Netherlands, overlord of Germany and Archduke of Austria. The fortunate series of alliances by which this great dominion was achieved can be seen on Table 79. There also can be seen the heraldic display of his honours. Four quarters stand in turn for Castile and Leon, Aragon and Sicily, Austria and old Burgundy, Burgundy modern and Brabant; in the centre of the upper shield is the pomegranate of Granada and, on the escutcheon below it, Flanders and Tyrol. The load was too great. In 1521 Charles assigned the Austrian duchies to his brother Ferdinand with the title of Imperial Lieutenant.

The new Prince had been educated entirely in Spain, but he proceeded to celebrate the marriage with Anne of Bohemia, planned by his grandfather. After the death in battle of his brother-in-law, he became King of Bohemia and part of Hungary as well as ruler of Austria. Other Hapsburgs had reigned in these lands, but from now on the Danubian character of the Hapsburg monarchy is firmly established. So is its role as a protector of Europe from the Turks, for most of Hungary remained in Turkish hands after Mohács. Ferdinand had to contend also with the impact of the Reformation, which had serious repercussions in Bohemia and in Austria. He was a pious Catholic; he protected the Council of Trent and encouraged the brisk successes of the Jesuits in rescuing Austria from Protestant beliefs. In 1558, after his brother Charles had abdicated, Ferdinand finally became emperor, while Spain and the Low Countries passed to his nephew, Philip II. The latter inherited Portugal through his mother and married Mary of England. However Mary had no children: the march of the Hapsburgs was not destined to cross the channel.

Ferdinand I reverted to the practice of division. His eldest son Maximilian II became emperor and received Austria, Bohemia and Hungary; Ferdinand became Count of Tyrol and Charles, Duke of Styria. The younger sons (Table 80) bore elaborate shields reflecting their proud ancestry and also a large number of relatively unimportant lordships, such as the fief of Windeschenmark with its distinctive black hat. In all the provinces religious questions were paramount. Maximilian II was a kindly and tolerant man, but ineffectual in public life. His son Rudolph II, that rarity an unmarried emperor, was a shy and superstitious eccentric. Devoted to astrology and hating crowds, he lived mainly in Prague, which he greatly beautified, and whither be brought Kepler and Tycho Brahe. So remote and disastrous was his government that his brothers united against him, and in 1608 Matthias, who ultimately succeeded him, was named as his deputy. Another brother, Maximilian, was Grand-Master of the Teutonic Order, the black cross of which is superimposed on his quarterings.

Matthias was childless and took great care to pass on his dominions to his cousin Ferdinand. Ferdinand II was a zealous and passionate Catholic educated by Jesuits. Already he had persecuted the reformed religions in his Duchy of Styria. His second son, Leopold, was placed in the Church and at the age of eleven was in charge of two bishoprics and four abbeys to vindicate paternal piety. Unhappily Ferdinand's intransigent and arid virtue was of small service to his Empire. The celebrated 'Defenestration of Prague' had begun the Thirty Years' War, the worst disaster (before Hitler) in German history.

This conflict, which began as a religious uprising in Bohemia, was gradually enlarged until almost all the nations of western Europe played some part, not least France and Sweden. But the main theatre of war was always on German soil or in Bohemia itself; and it was the peasantry of these lands which bore the grimmest burden. The effects in devastation and suffering were fearful; furthermore the decline in imperial authority left Germany disunited and ineffective for two centuries. Ferdinand II himself had reunited the Austrian lands, but in 1625 he conferred the Tyrol upon his brother: final reunion did not take place until 1665. At his death in 1637, his good intentions had brought his domains to a sorry pass. His ancestry (Table 84) was strongly Hapsburg, for Ferdinand I was his grandfather on one side, his great-grandfather on the other; the least likely elements were provided by the blood of Spain and Foix. His industry was attested by the savage persecution of the Bohemian Protestants after the battle of the White Mountain.

To his son, Ferdinand III, fell the conduct of the later part of the Thirty Years' War, and the negotiation of peace. The greatest general on the Imperial side, Wallenstein (more properly Waldstein), was suspected of leniency and bluntly assassinated by some Irish hirelings. By 1635 the war had ceased to be mainly concerned with religion and was centred upon the political ambitions of Sweden and France; the possible profits for Austria were negligible. When the Peace of Westphalia was finally negotiated in 1648, the main gain to Ferdinand III was that the Crown of Bohemia was recognized as hereditary in the Hapsburg dynasty; on the other hand the ancient Alsatian estates of the Hapsburgs were ceded to France, and any hope of establishing a unified or central form of government in Germany was dead. The future of that country lay in the hands of a collection of princes, divided in religion and disparate in power. The future for the Hapsburg dynasty lay outside the traditional boundaries of the Empire. Ferdinand III, in his later years, was successful in securing the acceptance of his eldest son as King of Bohemia and King of the Romans, but Ferdinand IV predeceased his father, and the inheritance came in 1657 to Leopold I.

TABLE 78

AUSTRIA
House of Hapsburg in the fourteenth and fifteenth centuries

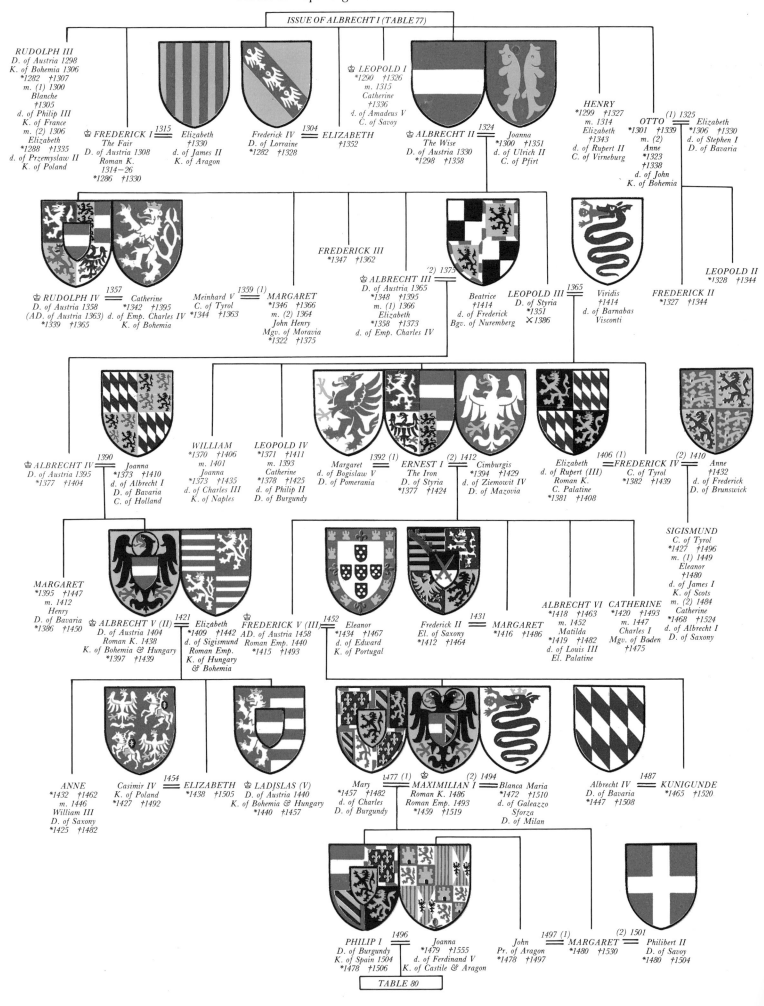

ISSUE OF ALBRECHT I (TABLE 77)

RUDOLPH III
D. of Austria 1298
K. of Bohemia 1306
*1282 †1307
m. (1) 1300
Blanche
†1305
d. of Philip III
K. of France
m. (2) 1306
Elizabeth
*1288 †1335
d. of Przemyslaw II
K. of Poland

♔ **FREDERICK I** ══1315══ Elizabeth
The Fair   †1330
D. of Austria 1308   d. of James II
Roman K.   K. of Aragon
1314—26
*1286 †1330

Frederick IV ══1304══ **ELIZABETH**
D. of Lorraine   †1352
*1282 †1328

♔ **LEOPOLD I**
*1290 †1326
m. 1315
Catherine
†1336
d. of Amadeus V
C. of Savoy

♔ **ALBRECHT II** ══1324══ Joanna
The Wise   *1300 †1351
D. of Austria 1330   d. of Ulrich II
*1298 †1358   C. of Pfirt

HENRY
*1299 †1327
m. 1314
Elizabeth
†1343
d. of Rupert II
C. of Virneburg

OTTO (1) 1325
*1301 †1339
m. (2)
Anne
*1323
†1338
d. of John
K. of Bohemia

Elizabeth
*1306 †1330
d. of Stephen I
D. of Bavaria

LEOPOLD II
*1328 †1344

FREDERICK II
*1327 †1344

FREDERICK III
*1347 †1362

♔ **ALBRECHT III** '2) 1375
D. of Austria 1365
*1348 †1395
m. (1) 1366
Elizabeth
*1358 †1373
d. of Emp. Charles IV

Beatrice
†1414
d. of Frederick
Bgv. of Nuremberg

LEOPOLD III 1365
D. of Styria
*1351
✕1386

Viridis
†1414
d. of Barnabas
Visconti

♔ **RUDOLPH IV** 1357 Catherine
D. of Austria 1358   *1342 †1395
(AD. of Austria 1363) d. of Emp. Charles IV
*1339 †1365   K. of Bohemia

Meinhard V ══1359 (1)══ **MARGARET**
C. of Tyrol   *1346 †1366
*1344 †1363   m. (2) 1364
                    John Henry
                    Mgv. of Moravia
                    *1322 †1375

♔ **ALBRECHT IV** 1390 Joanna
D. of Austria 1395   *1373 †1410
*1377 †1404   d. of Albrecht I
                D. of Bavaria
                C. of Holland

WILLIAM
*1370 †1406
m. 1401
Joanna
*1373 †1435
d. of Charles III
K. of Naples

LEOPOLD IV
*1371 †1411
m. 1393
Catherine
*1378 †1425
d. of Philip II
D. of Burgundy

Margaret ══1392 (1)══ **ERNEST I** (2) 1412 Cimburgis
d. of Bogislaw V   The Iron   *1394 †1429
D. of Pomerania   D. of Styria   d. of Ziemowit IV
                   *1377 †1424   D. of Mazovia

Elizabeth ══1406 (1)══ **FREDERICK IV** (2) 1410 Anne
d. of Rupert (III)   C. of Tyrol   †1432
Roman K.   *1382 †1439   d. of Frederick
C. Palatine   D. of Brunswick
*1381 †1408

SIGISMUND
C. of Tyrol
*1427 †1496
m. (1) 1449
Eleanor
†1480
d. of James I
K. of Scots
m. (2) 1484
Catherine
*1468 †1524
d. of Albrecht I
D. of Saxony

MARGARET
*1395 †1447
m. 1412
Henry
D. of Bavaria
*1386 †1450

♔ **ALBRECHT V (II)** 1421 Elizabeth
D. of Austria 1404   *1409 †1442
Roman K. 1438   d. of Sigismund
K. of Bohemia & Hungary Roman Emp.
*1397 †1439   K. of Hungary
                & Bohemia

♔ **FREDERICK V (III)** 1452 Eleanor
AD. of Austria 1458   *1434 †1467
Roman Emp. 1440   d. of Edward
*1415 †1493   K. of Portugal

Frederick II ══1431══ **MARGARET**
El. of Saxony   *1416 †1486
*1412 †1464

ALBRECHT VI
*1418 †1463
m. 1452
Matilda
*1419 †1482
d. of Louis III
El. Palatine

CATHERINE
*1420 †1493
m. 1447
Charles I
Mgv. of Baden
†1475

ANNE
*1432 †1462
m. 1446
William III
D. of Saxony
*1425 †1482

Casimir IV ══1454══ **ELIZABETH**
K. of Poland   *1438 †1505
*1427 †1492

♔ **LADISLAS (V)**
D. of Austria 1440
K. of Bohemia & Hungary
*1440 †1457

Mary ══1477 (1)══ ♔ **MAXIMILIAN I** (2) 1494 Blanca Maria
*1457 †1482   Roman K. 1486   *1472 †1510
d. of Charles   Roman Emp. 1493   d. of Galeazzo
D. of Burgundy   *1459 †1519   Sforza
                                    D. of Milan

Albrecht IV ══1487══ **KUNIGUNDE**
D. of Bavaria   *1465 †1520
*1447 †1508

PHILIP I 1496 Joanna
D. of Burgundy   *1479 †1555
K. of Spain 1504   d. of Ferdinand V
*1478 †1506   K. of Castile & Aragon

John ══1497 (1)══ **MARGARET** (2) 1501 Philibert II
Pr. of Aragon   *1480 †1530   D. of Savoy
*1478 †1497   *1480 †1504

TABLE 80

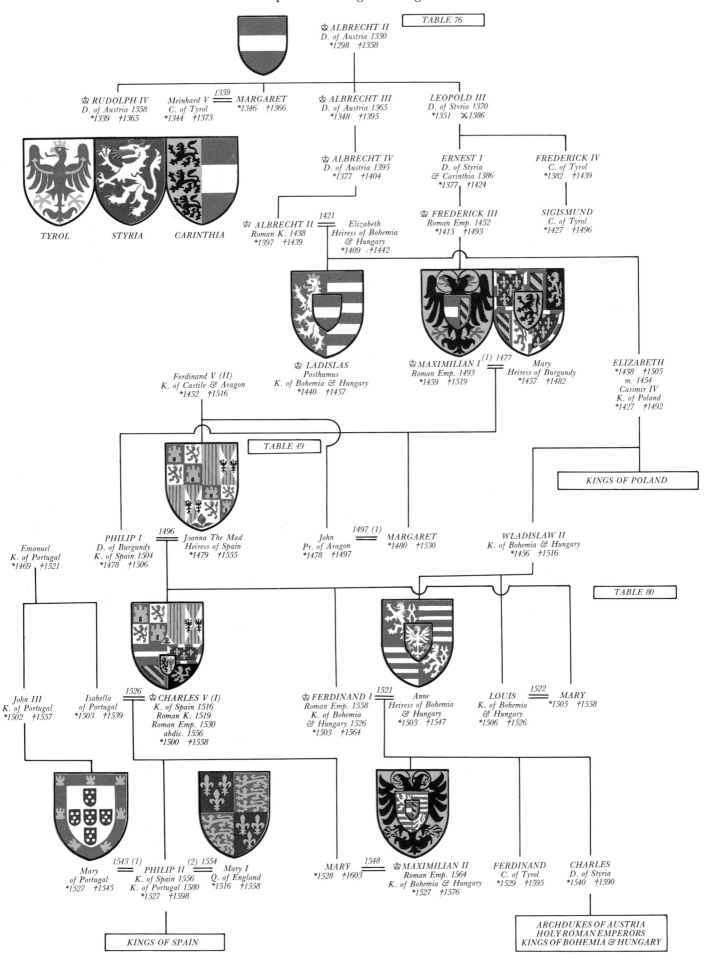

AUSTRIA
Expansion through marriages

TABLE 76

♔ ALBRECHT II
D. of Austria 1330
*1298 †1358

♔ RUDOLPH IV
D. of Austria 1358
*1339 †1365

Meinhard V
C. of Tyrol
*1344 †1373

— 1359 — MARGARET
*1346 †1366

♔ ALBRECHT III
D. of Austria 1365
*1348 †1395

LEOPOLD III
D. of Styria 1370
*1351 ✕1386

TYROL   STYRIA   CARINTHIA

♔ ALBRECHT IV
D. of Austria 1395
*1377 †1404

ERNEST I
D. of Styria
& Carinthia 1386
*1377 †1424

FREDERICK IV
C. of Tyrol
*1382 †1439

♔ ALBRECHT II
Roman K. 1438
*1397 †1439

— 1421 — Elizabeth
Heiress of Bohemia
& Hungary
*1409 †1442

♔ FREDERICK III
Roman Emp. 1452
*1415 †1493

SIGISMUND
C. of Tyrol
*1427 †1496

♔ LADISLAS
Posthumus
K. of Bohemia & Hungary
*1440 †1457

♔ MAXIMILIAN I (1) 1477
Roman Emp. 1493
*1459 †1519

Mary
Heiress of Burgundy
*1457 †1482

ELIZABETH
*1438 †1505
m. 1454
Casimir IV
K. of Poland
*1427 †1492

Ferdinand V (II)
K. of Castile & Aragon
*1452 †1516

TABLE 49

KINGS OF POLAND

Emanuel
K. of Portugal
*1469 †1521

PHILIP I
D. of Burgundy
K. of Spain 1504
*1478 †1506

— 1496 — Joanna The Mad
Heiress of Spain
*1479 †1555

John
Pr. of Aragon
*1478 †1497

— 1497 (1) — MARGARET
*1480 †1530

WLADISLAW II
K. of Bohemia & Hungary
*1456 †1516

TABLE 80

John III
K. of Portugal
*1502 †1557

Isabella
of Portugal
*1503 †1539

— 1526 — ♔ CHARLES V (I)
K. of Spain 1516
Roman K. 1519
Roman Emp. 1530
abdic. 1556
*1500 †1558

♔ FERDINAND I
Roman Emp. 1558
K. of Bohemia
& Hungary 1526
*1503 †1564

Anne
Heiress of Bohemia
& Hungary
*1503 †1547

LOUIS
K. of Bohemia
& Hungary
*1506 †1526

— 1522 — MARY
*1505 †1558

Mary
of Portugal
*1527 †1545

— 1543 (1) — PHILIP II
K. of Spain 1556
K. of Portugal 1580
*1527 †1598

— (2) 1554 — Mary I
Q. of England
*1516 †1558

MARY
*1528 †1603

— 1548 — ♔ MAXIMILIAN II
Roman Emp. 1564
K. of Bohemia & Hungary
*1527 †1576

FERDINAND
C. of Tyrol
*1529 †1595

CHARLES
D. of Styria
*1540 †1590

KINGS OF SPAIN

ARCHDUKES OF AUSTRIA
HOLY ROMAN EMPERORS
KINGS OF BOHEMIA & HUNGARY

Chapter 20

AUSTRIA: MODERN

The long agony of the Thirty Years' War (1618–48) made clear the immediate destiny of the Hapsburgs. German unity had for the nonce become an impossibility, not to be achieved until the nineteenth century, and then under the banner of the Hohenzollerns. By the Treaty of Westphalia the Crown of Bohemia was acknowledged as the hereditary possession of the Hapsburgs. Over three hundred different states were recognized in Germany, many of them minute in land and resources; in general the worship of the inhabitants was dictated by the faith of the prince–*cujus regio ejus religio* was an oft-quoted maxim. Meanwhile the threat of the Turks continued to lour over Austria's eastern flank. It was perhaps fortunate for Europe that the Ottoman dynasty went through a period of weakness and instability just at this time.

Ferdinand, eldest son of Ferdinand III, had been elected King of Bohemia, but died in his father's lifetime. In 1657 Leopold I, the next brother, began his long reign. He was to add extensively to the Hapsburg domains, increasing their area by almost a half. The Emperor was an ugly, lonely man with a reserved and unwarlike disposition; in his features the family lip was almost a deformity. He was pious and a patron of learning, much under the influence of the Catholic Church. His second marriage brought him the Tyrol with the extinction of that branch of the Hapsburgs (Table 80); his first had been to his own niece, the Spanish Infanta. In 1664 his armies, with some help from France, defeated the Turks at St Gotthard and proved that Islam was vulnerable. But in 1683 the Sultan, now allied to France, set in motion a formidable attack on Austria, and reached the gates of Vienna. Leopold fled, but his brother-in-law, Charles of Lorraine, improvised a defence and the King of Poland, John Sobieski, came to his aid. In a desperate battle the Turks were routed and the city

saved; never again was the Ottoman Empire to be a threat to central Europe. The returned Emperor was ungrateful: 'How does one receive an elected king?' he sneered. 'With open arms,' replied the Duke of Lorraine, 'if he has saved one's capital'.

In 1686 Lorraine captured Buda and in the following year savagely defeated the Turks on the historic field of Mohács. The Hungarian Diet now resolved that their Crown should descend with the male line of the Hapsburg dynasty. By the Treaty of Karlowitz (1699) the Sultan ceded almost all Hungary and Croatia to the Emperor. One consequence of these triumphant campaigns, all led by foreign generals, was the establishment in 1680 of a regular, standing Austrian army.

But the Turkish problem was not Leopold's only anxiety. French aggression in western Germany threatened imperial interests, and in 1689 Austria joined an alliance with England and the Netherlands. Over international affairs at the end of the seventeenth century loomed the question of the childless, mad King of Spain (Charles II: Table 50). There was general agreement that the vast Spanish dominions must be broken up, but there were various claimants. By unanimity among the Great Powers Joseph Ferdinand of Bavaria, Leopold's grandson by his first marriage, was accepted as the main heir, but unluckily died in 1699. A second solution was elaborated which divided the Spanish inheritance between Philip of Anjou and Charles, younger son of Leopold, but in vain. The Austrian Hapsburgs aspired to the entire spoil and Leopold rejected the compromise, an act of ambition and folly. When Charles II of Spain died in 1700, he bequeathed all his lands to the French Duke of Anjou.

Most of the reign of Joseph I (Table 81) was taken up with the consequent War of the Spanish Succession; under Prince Eugene of Savoy the Emperor's

forces campaigned beside their English allies, led by
Marlborough, at Blenheim and in the Low Countries.
Joseph's death without sons brought his brother
Charles VI to the imperial throne and, as a substantial
ruler in his own right, he was clearly unacceptable to
the Powers as an heir to Spain; by the Treaty of Ras-
tatt (1714) Austria acquired the Spanish Netherlands
(which Britain was resolved to withhold from
France), Naples, Milan and Sardinia. The Austrian
Empire thus became a considerable Italian power; its
own future was, however, in serious hazard.

Joseph I begat only two girls; Charles VI devoted
much of his reign and vast efforts to securing the
succession of his own elder daughter, Maria Theresa,
and to reversing the natural order of inheritance
which would have favoured his nieces. The settlement designed to this end was known as the Pragmatic Sanction; one by one the constituent parts of
the Empire acceded to it, and after them the various
Great Powers of Europe. Not till 1735 did France and
Spain agree to it at the Treaty of Vienna (which
settled a brief and futile contest over the succession to
Poland). This triumph of French diplomacy arranged also that Naples and Sicily should pass to Spain,
and that Maria Theresa should marry Francis, Duke
of Lorraine, who would give up his own duchy and
receive that of Florence in its place.

MARIA THERESA

When Charles VI died in 1740, it might have been
thought that his daughter's position was secure. But
the presence of an inexperienced and youthful queen
weighed more with some powers than the sanctity of
treaties. Led by Prussia, Saxony, Spain and Bavaria
all claimed portions of Maria Theresa's heritage.
Charles of Bavaria was elected King of the Romans
and then Emperor (1742) – the only non-Hapsburg
to hold the imperial Crown since 1437; however, he
died in 1745 and was replaced by Maria Theresa's
husband, Francis. In 1741 a French statesman could
declare that the House of Hapsburg was finished.
Cardinal Fleury was wrong, and the Queen of Hungary (as Maria Theresa was styled at this time) made
a marked recovery. Britain continued to be her
ally and to subsidize her efforts; her Magyar subjects
rallied with valour to her cause. The perfidious
Frederick of Prussia, bribed with Silesia, turned, if
only briefly, to her support. In 1748 she emerged
from the War of the Austrian Succession, recognized,
and with only minor losses in Italy. But the permanent Prussian seizure of Silesia, a wealthy
province, left Austria with an antipathy to the
Hohenzollerns; in the Seven Years' War (1756–63)
the Empress was allied, though without much profit,

[159]

TABLE 80

AUSTRIA, BOHEMIA AND HUNGARY
Hapsburgs in the sixteenth and seventeenth centuries

ISSUE OF PHILIP I K. OF SPAIN (TABLE 78)

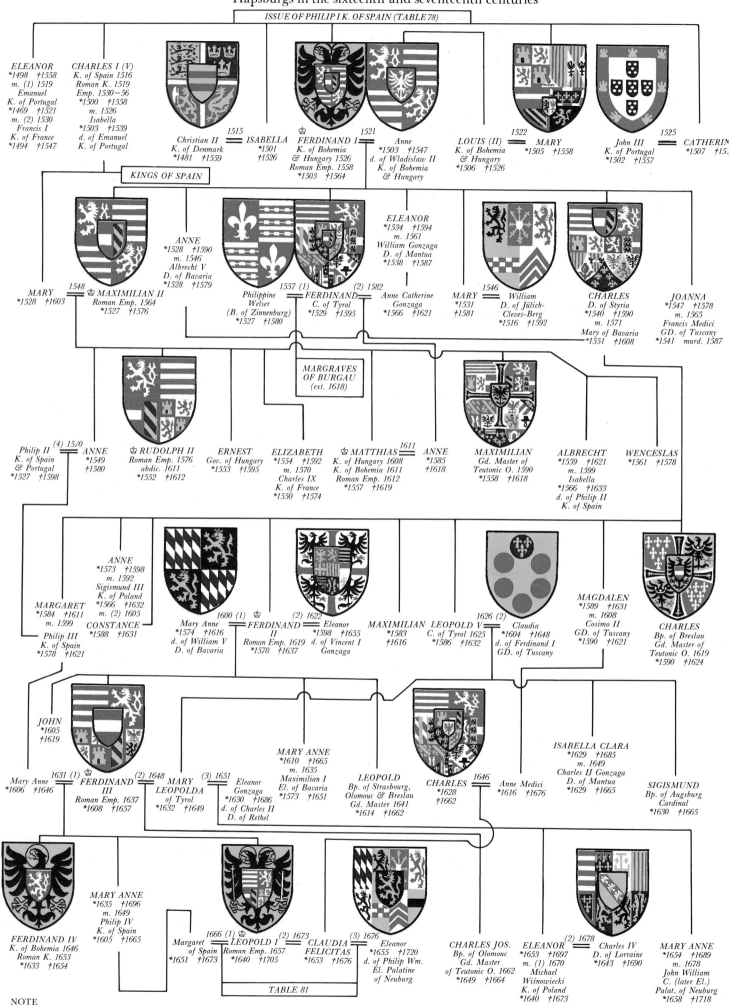

ELEANOR
*1498 †1558
m. (1) 1519
Emanuel
K. of Portugal
*1469 †1521
m. (2) 1530
Francis I
K. of France
*1494 †1547

CHARLES I (V)
K. of Spain 1516
Roman K. 1519
Emp. 1530—56
*1500 †1558
m. 1526
Isabella
d. of Emanuel
K. of Portugal

Christian II
K. of Denmark
*1481 †1559
— ISABELLA
*1501
†1526

1515

FERDINAND I
K. of Bohemia
& Hungary 1526
Roman Emp. 1558
*1503 †1564

1521

Anne
*1503 †1547
d. of Wladislaw II
K. of Bohemia
& Hungary

LOUIS (II)
K. of Bohemia
& Hungary
*1506 †1526

1522

MARY
*1505 †1558

John III
K. of Portugal
*1502 †1557

1525

CATHERIN
*1507 †15..

KINGS OF SPAIN

MARY
*1528 †1603

1548

MAXIMILIAN II
Roman Emp. 1564
*1527 †1576

ANNE
*1528 †1590
m. 1546
Albrecht V
D. of Bavaria
*1528 †1579

Philippine
Welser
(B. of Zinnenburg)
*1527 †1580

1557 (1)

FERDINAND
C. of Tyrol
*1529 †1595

(2) 1582

Anne Catherine
Gonzaga
*1566 †1621

ELEANOR
*1534 †1594
m. 1561
William Gonzaga
D. of Mantua
*1538 †1587

MARY
*1531
†1581

William
D. of Jülich-
Cleves-Berg
*1516 †1592

1546

CHARLES
D. of Styria
*1540 †1590
m. 1571
Mary of Bavaria
*1551 †1608

JOANNA
*1547 †1578
m. 1565
Francis Medici
GD. of Tuscany
*1541 murd. 1587

MARGRAVES
OF BURGAU
(ext. 1618)

Philip II
K. of Spain
& Portugal
*1527 †1598

(4) 15/0

ANNE
*1549
†1580

RUDOLPH II
Roman Emp. 1576
abdic. 1611
*1552 †1612

ERNEST
Gov. of Hungary
*1553 †1595

ELIZABETH
*1554 †1592
m. 1570
Charles IX
K. of France
*1550 †1574

MATTHIAS
K. of Hungary 1608
K. of Bohemia 1611
Roman Emp. 1612
*1557 †1619

1611

ANNE
*1585
†1618

MAXIMILIAN
Gd. Master of
Teutonic O. 1590
*1558 †1618

ALBRECHT
*1559 †1621
m. 1599
Isabella
*1566 †1633
d. of Philip II
K. of Spain

WENCESLAS
*1561 †1578

ANNE
*1573 †1598
m. 1592
Sigismund III
K. of Poland
*1566 †1632
m. (2) 1605
CONSTANCE
*1588 †1631

MARGARET
*1584 †1611
m. 1599
Philip III
K. of Spain
*1578 †1621

Mary Anne
*1574 †1616
d. of William V
D. of Bavaria

1600 (1)

FERDINAND
II
Roman Emp. 1619
*1578 †1637

(2) 1622

Eleanor
*1598 †1655
d. of Vincent I
Gonzaga

MAXIMILIAN
*1583
†1616

LEOPOLD V
C. of Tyrol 1625
*1586 †1632

1626 (2)

Claudia
*1604 †1648
d. of Ferdinand I
GD. of Tuscany

MAGDALEN
*1589 †1631
m. 1608
Cosimo II
GD. of Tuscany
*1590 †1621

CHARLES
Bp. of Breslau
Gd. Master of
Teutonic O. 1619
*1590 †1624

JOHN
*1605
†1619

Mary Anne
*1606 †1646

1631 (1)

FERDINAND
III
Roman Emp. 1637
*1608 †1657

(2) 1648

MARY
LEOPOLDA
of Tyrol
*1632 †1649

(3) 1651

Eleanor
Gonzaga
*1630 †1686
d. of Charles II
D. of Rethel

MARY ANNE
*1610 †1665
m. 1635
Maximilian I
El. of Bavaria
*1573 †1651

LEOPOLD
Bp. of Strasbourg,
Olomouc & Breslau
Gd. Master 1641
*1614 †1662

CHARLES
*1628
†1662

1646

Anne Medici
*1616 †1676

ISABELLA CLARA
*1629 †1685
m. 1649
Charles II Gonzaga
D. of Mantua
*1629 †1665

SIGISMUND
Bp. of Augsburg
Cardinal
*1630 †1665

FERDINAND IV
K. of Bohemia 1646
Roman K. 1653
*1633 †1654

MARY ANNE
*1635 †1696
m. 1649
Philip IV
K. of Spain
*1605 †1665

Margaret
of Spain
*1651 †1673

1666 (1)

LEOPOLD I
Roman Emp. 1657
*1640 †1705

(2) 1673

CLAUDIA
FELICITAS
*1653 †1676

(3) 1676

Eleanor
*1655 †1720
d. of Philip Wm.
El. Palatine
of Neuburg

CHARLES JOS.
Bp. of Olomouc
Gd. Master
of Teutonic O. 1662
*1649 †1664

ELEANOR
*1653 †1697
m. (1) 1670
Michael
Wiśnowiecki
K. of Poland
*1640 †1673

(2) 1678

Charles IV
D. of Lorraine
*1643 †1690

MARY ANNE
*1654 †1689
m. 1678
John William
C. (later El.)
Palat. of Neuburg
*1658 †1718

TABLE 81

NOTE
Holy Roman Emperors placed their arms on the breast of the double-headed Imperial eagle,
while Kings of the Romans (Roman K.) used the single-headed eagle.

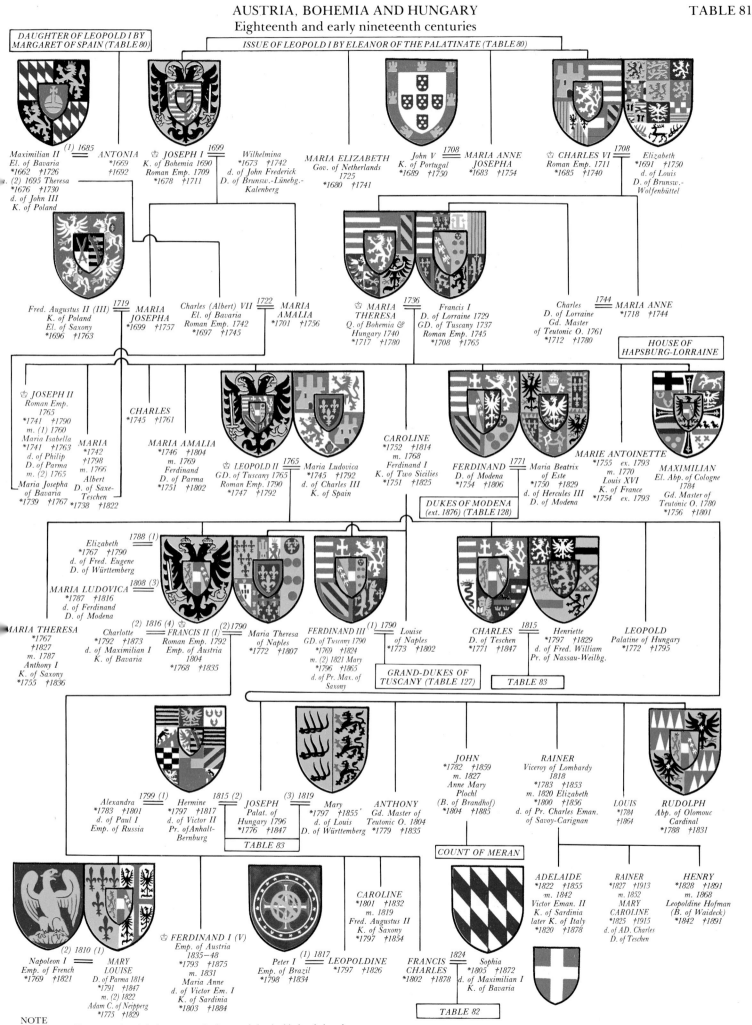

DAUGHTER OF LEOPOLD I BY MARGARET OF SPAIN (TABLE 80)

ISSUE OF LEOPOLD I BY ELEANOR OF THE PALATINATE (TABLE 80)

Maximilian II
El. of Bavaria
*1662 †1726
a. (2) 1695 Theresa
*1676 †1730
d. of John III
K. of Poland
— (1) 1685 — ANTONIA
*1669
†1692

☼ JOSEPH I — 1699 — Wilhelmina
K. of Bohemia 1690
Roman Emp. 1709
*1678 †1711
*1673 †1742
d. of John Frederick
D. of Brunsw.-Lünebg.-Kalenberg

MARIA ELIZABETH
Gov. of Netherlands
1725
*1680 †1741

John V — 1708 — MARIA ANNE
K. of Portugal
*1689 †1750
JOSEPHA
*1683 †1754

☼ CHARLES VI — 1708 — Elizabeth
Roman Emp. 1711
*1685 †1740
*1691 †1750
d. of Louis
D. of Brunsw.-Wolfenbüttel

Fred. Augustus II (III)
K. of Poland
El. of Saxony
*1696 †1763
— 1719 — MARIA JOSEPHA
*1699 †1757

Charles (Albert) VII — 1722 — MARIA AMALIA
El. of Bavaria
Roman Emp. 1742
*1697 †1745
*1701 †1756

☼ MARIA THERESA — 1736 — Francis I
Q. of Bohemia &
Hungary 1740
*1717 †1780
D. of Lorraine 1729
GD. of Tuscany 1737
Roman Emp. 1745
*1708 †1765

Charles — 1744 — MARIA ANNE
D. of Lorraine
Gd. Master
of Teutonic O. 1761
*1712 †1780
*1718 †1744

HOUSE OF HAPSBURG-LORRAINE

☼ JOSEPH II
Roman Emp.
1765
*1741 †1790
m. (1) 1760
Maria Isabella
*1741 †1763
d. of Philip
D. of Parma
m. (2) 1765
Maria Josepha
of Bavaria
*1739 †1767

MARIA
*1742
†1798
m. 1766
Albert
D. of Saxe-Teschen
*1738 †1822

CHARLES
*1745 †1761

MARIA AMALIA
*1746 †1804
m. 1769
Ferdinand
D. of Parma
*1751 †1802

☼ LEOPOLD II — 1765 — Maria Ludovica
GD. of Tuscany 1765
Roman Emp. 1790
*1747 †1792
*1745 †1792
d. of Charles III
K. of Spain

CAROLINE
*1752 †1814
m. 1768
Ferdinand I
K. of Two Sicilies
*1751 †1825

FERDINAND — 1771 — Maria Beatrix
D. of Modena
*1754 †1806
of Este
*1750 †1829
d. of Hercules III
D. of Modena

MARIE ANTOINETTE
*1755 ex. 1793
m. 1770
Louis XVI
K. of France
*1754 ex. 1793

MAXIMILIAN
El. Abp. of Cologne
1784
Gd. Master of
Teutonic O. 1780
*1756 †1801

DUKES OF MODENA
(ext. 1876) (TABLE 128)

Elizabeth
*1767 †1790
d. of Fred. Eugene
D. of Württemberg
— 1788 (1)

MARIA LUDOVICA
*1787 †1816
d. of Ferdinand
D. of Modena
— 1808 (3)

MARIA THERESA
*1767
†1827
m. 1787
Anthony I
K. of Saxony
*1755 †1836

Charlotte
*1792 †1873
d. of Maximilian I
K. of Bavaria
— (2) 1816 (4) ☼ FRANCIS II (1) — (2) 1790 — Maria Theresa
Roman Emp. 1792
Emp. of Austria
1804
*1768 †1835
of Naples
*1772 †1807

FERDINAND III — (1) 1790 — Louise
GD. of Tuscany 1790
*1769 †1824
m. (2) 1821 Mary
*1796 †1865
d. of Pr. Max. of Saxony
of Naples
*1773 †1802

CHARLES — 1815 — Henriette
D. of Teschen
*1771 †1847
*1797 †1829
d. of Fred. William
Pr. of Nassau-Weilbg.

LEOPOLD
Palatine of Hungary
*1772 †1795

GRAND-DUKES OF TUSCANY (TABLE 127)

TABLE 83

Alexandra
*1783 †1801
d. of Paul I
Emp. of Russia
— 1799 (1)

Hermine
*1797 †1817
d. of Victor II
Pr. of Anhalt-Bernburg
— 1815 (2)

JOSEPH — (3) 1819
Palat. of
Hungary 1796
*1776 †1847

Mary
*1797 †1855
d. of Louis
D. of Württemberg

ANTHONY
Gd. Master of
Teutonic O. 1804
*1779 †1835

JOHN
*1782 †1859
m. 1827
Anne Mary
Plochl
(B. of Brandhof)
*1804 †1885

RAINER
Viceroy of Lombardy
1818
*1783 †1853
m. 1820 Elizabeth
*1800 †1856
d. of Pr. Charles Eman.
of Savoy-Carignan

LOUIS
*1784
†1864

RUDOLPH
Abp. of Olomouc
Cardinal
*1788 †1831

TABLE 83

COUNT OF MERAN

Napoleon I — (2) 1810 (1)
Emp. of French
*1769 †1821

MARY LOUISE
D. of Parma 1814
*1791 †1847
m. (2) 1822
Adam C. of Neipperg
*1775 †1829

☼ FERDINAND I (V)
Emp. of Austria
1835–48
*1793 †1875
m. 1831
Maria Anne
d. of Victor Em. I
K. of Sardinia
*1803 †1884

Peter I — (1) 1817 — LEOPOLDINE
Emp. of Brazil
*1798 †1834
*1797 †1826

CAROLINE
*1801 †1832
m. 1819
Fred. Augustus II
K. of Saxony
*1797 †1854

FRANCIS CHARLES — 1824 — Sophia
*1802 †1878
*1805 †1872
d. of Maximilian I
K. of Bavaria

ADELAIDE
*1822 †1855
m. 1842
Victor Eman. II
K. of Sardinia
later K. of Italy
*1820 †1878

RAINER
*1827 †1913
m. 1852
MARY CAROLINE
*1825 †1915
d. of AD. Charles
D. of Teschen

HENRY
*1828 †1891
m. 1868
Leopoldine Hofman
(B. of Waideck)
*1842 †1891

TABLE 82

NOTE
Holy Roman Emperors placed their arms on the breast of the double-headed eagle, which in the 17th century usually held in its claws a sword and a sceptre, and in the 18th century an orb instead of the sceptre.

TABLE 82

AUSTRIA, BOHEMIA AND HUNGARY
End of the monarchy

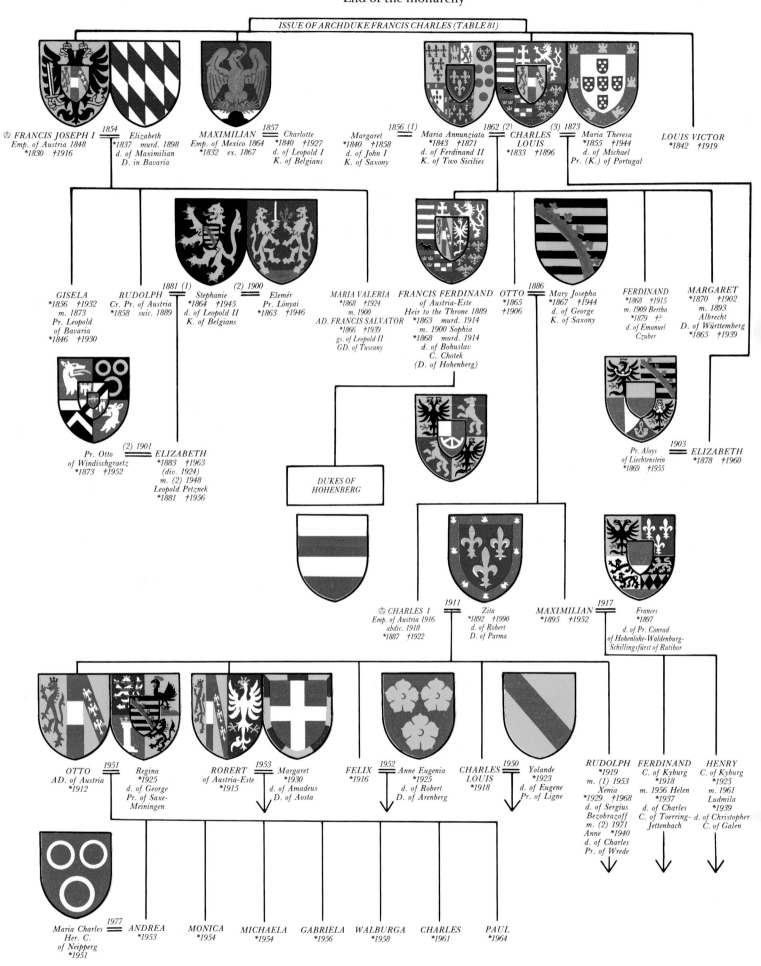

ISSUE OF ARCHDUKE FRANCIS CHARLES (TABLE 81)

♔ FRANCIS JOSEPH I
Emp. of Austria 1848
*1830 †1916

1854
Elizabeth
*1837 murd. 1898
d. of Maximilian
D. in Bavaria

MAXIMILIAN
Emp. of Mexico 1864
*1832 ex. 1867

1857
Charlotte
*1840 †1927
d. of Leopold I
K. of Belgians

Margaret
*1840 †1858
d. of John I
K. of Saxony

1856 (1)
Maria Annunziata
*1843 †1871
d. of Ferdinand II
K. of Two Sicilies

1862 (2)
CHARLES
LOUIS
*1833 †1896

(3) 1873
Maria Theresa
*1855 †1944
d. of Michael
Pr. (K.) of Portugal

LOUIS VICTOR
*1842 †1919

GISELA
*1856 †1932
m. 1873
Pr. Leopold
of Bavaria
*1846 †1930

RUDOLPH
Cr. Pr. of Austria
*1858 suic. 1889

1881 (1)
Stephanie
*1864 †1945
d. of Leopold II
K. of Belgians

(2) 1900
Elemér
Pr. Lónyai
*1863 †1946

MARIA VALERIA
*1868 †1924
m. 1900
AD. FRANCIS SALVATOR
*1866 †1939
gs. of Leopold II
GD. of Tuscany

FRANCIS FERDINAND
of Austria-Este
Heir to the Throne 1889
*1863 murd. 1914
m. 1900 Sophia
*1868 murd. 1914
d. of Bohuslav
C. Chotek
(D. of Hohenberg)

OTTO
*1865
†1906

1886
Mary Josepha
*1867 †1944
d. of George
K. of Saxony

FERDINAND
*1868 †1915
m. 1909 Bertha
*1879 †?
d. of Emanuel
Czuber

MARGARET
*1870 †1902
m. 1893
Albrecht
D. of Württemberg
*1865 †1939

Pr. Otto
of Windischgraetz
*1873 †1952

(2) 1901
ELIZABETH
*1883 †1963
(div. 1924)
m. (2) 1948
Leopold Petznek
*1881 †1956

DUKES OF
HOHENBERG

Pr. Aloys
of Liechtenstein
*1869 †1955

1903
ELIZABETH
*1878 †1960

♔ CHARLES I
Emp. of Austria 1916
abdic. 1918
*1887 †1922

1911
Zita
*1892 †1990
d. of Robert
D. of Parma

MAXIMILIAN
*1895 †1952

1917
Frances
*1897
d. of Pr. Conrad
of Hohenlohe-Waldenburg-
Schillingsfürst of Ratibor

OTTO
AD. of Austria
*1912

1951
Regina
*1925
d. of George
Pr. of Saxe-
Meiningen

ROBERT
of Austria-Este
*1915

1953
Margaret
*1930
d. of Amadeus
D. of Aosta

FELIX
*1916

1952
Anne Eugenia
*1925
d. of Robert
D. of Arenberg

CHARLES
LOUIS
*1918

1950
Yolande
*1923
d. of Eugene
Pr. of Ligne

RUDOLPH
*1919
m. (1) 1953
Xenia
*1929 †1968
d. of Sergius
Bezobrazoff
m. (2) 1971
Anne *1940
d. of Charles
Pr. of Wrede

FERDINAND
C. of Kyburg
*1918
m. 1956 Helen
*1937
d. of Charles
C. of Toerring-
Jettenbach

HENRY
C. of Kyburg
*1925
m. 1961
Ludmila
*1939
d. of Christopher
C. of Galen

Maria Charles
Her. C.
of Neipperg
*1951

1977
ANDREA
*1953

MONICA
*1954

MICHAELA
*1954

GABRIELA
*1956

WALBURGA
*1958

CHARLES
*1961

PAUL
*1964

with France against England and Prussia.

In 1765 Joseph II followed his father as Holy Roman Emperor, and shared the government with his mother. The decay of Poland prompted her powerful neighbours to plunder: in 1772 Austria shared in the first partition of Poland and acquired Galicia, a gain which could scarcely be justified on either historical or geographical grounds. But Maria Theresa, whose comely if unexciting features gaze down from so many state portraits in her dominions, was a great ruler in the domestic sphere also. Central organs of government were developed; noble and ecclesiastical privileges were reduced; she ended her reign with a larger revenue and a better established army than her mixed domains had known before. By her death in 1780 she had by courage and endurance transformed her challenged inheritance into an enlarged monarchy with a tincture of reform.

The ancestry of Maria Theresa (Table 84) shows a wide mixture of German blood; considering the degree of intermarriage among the Hapsburgs, the variety is noteworthy. She used several different arrangements of her arms; that shown on Table 81 displays four quarterings for Hungary, Austria and Burgundy, Moravia and Silesia, with the lion of Bohemia over all. The blazon of her husband, the Emperor Francis, shows the many pretensions of his House (Chapter 28) with the shield of his two Duchies of Lorraine and Tuscany in pretence.

Joseph II belonged to the group of late eighteenth-century sovereigns who are known as the enlightened despots. His ambitions and endeavours were shared by his younger brother Leopold, to whom the Grand-Duchy of Tuscany had been assigned as an apanage, and who strove with more flexibility and intelligence to modernize the antique system of the Medici grand-dukes. Joseph believed that a beneficent emperor could best achieve the happiness of his peoples. On the one hand he attacked and diminished the position of the Church; on the other his tendency to centralize provoked disquiet in his polyglot lands. Before the end of his reign he was compelled to modify many of his reforms, but education was widely encouraged and the sublime talent of Mozart adorned the Austria of his day.

The brief imperial reign of Leopold II served to tidy up some of the confusion left by Joseph. His shield (Table 81) shows the imperial two-headed eagle, to which in the eighteenth century a sword and orb were added in either claw, with a superimposed shield of Hungary, Bohemia, Burgundy and Bar, and over all Lorraine, Austria and Tuscany. His younger brother Ferdinand married the heiress of the Este Dukes of Modena (Chapter 34), in north Italy, and founded a cadet branch which died out in 1876. Their coat-of-arms showed quarterings of the Empire

and Ferrara (a version of France), with a central pale of the papal insignia surmounted by the family arms of Este, a white eagle, gold crowned, on a blue field.

NAPOLEONIC WARS

The Emperor Francis II had to face the wind of change engendered by the French Revolution, and the more positive gale of Napoleon thereafter. The first impact of the new climate was the execution of his aunt, Marie Antoinette, Queen of France, and the occupation of the Austrian Netherlands (Belgium) by the revolutionary armies. Poor compensation was achieved in 1795 when Austria annexed western Galicia from the third partition of Poland. During the campaigns of Bonaparte in Italy, boundaries were drawn and redrawn on many occasions; in Germany Francis lost the last vestiges of control or power. Accordingly, in August, 1804, he solemnly assumed the title of Emperor of Austria, thus matching the style of Emperor of the French asserted by Napoleon a few months earlier. His honorific availed him little when it came to war: at Austerlitz (1805) the parvenu French ruler overwhelmed the traditional Hapsburg dynast. Napoleon proceeded to redesign the map of Europe; in 1806 Francis II proclaimed the dissolution of the Holy Roman Empire. The long line of emperors, stemming (with some interruptions) from the coronation of Charles the Great in 800, thus sadly terminated a thousand years later in the limp hands of Francis. Four years later he was compelled to give his daughter in marriage to the Corsican upstart (Tables 72–3). The alliance was one of the earliest achievements of Metternich, the able minister who was to dominate Austrian politics for the next generation. In 1813 Napoleon was at last defeated at Leipzig by a coalition including imperial troops; the resulting peace congress met at Vienna in 1814, and – though rudely interrupted by the Hundred Days and Waterloo – set about reconstituting Europe.

From the furnace of this period a new Austria was forged. Belgium and western Galicia were lost, but virtually the whole of north Italy, including Venice, came under Hapsburg control. Modena was restored to the younger branch; Ferdinand, the Emperor's next brother, was reinstated in Tuscany; the Archduke Charles, who had commanded the Austrian armies with more skill than success, was Duke of Teschen (Těšín to the Czechs or Cieszyn to the Poles); two other brothers successively held rank as Palatine of Hungary and another as Viceroy of Lombardy: Anthony was Grand-Master of the Teutonic Order and Rudolph held the historic See of Olomouc (Olmütz). These Princes add the serpent of Milan and the winged lion of Venice together with the arms of Galicia to the older quarterings of Hungary and Bohemia: Rudolph places this blazon over the arms

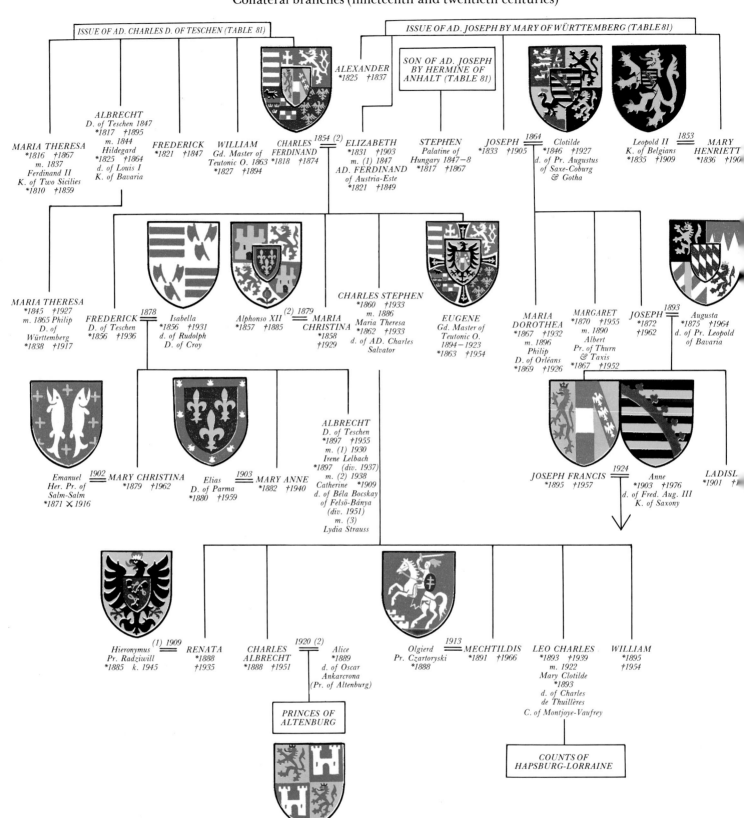

ISSUE OF AD. CHARLES D. OF TESCHEN (TABLE 81)

ISSUE OF AD. JOSEPH BY MARY OF WÜRTTEMBERG (TABLE 81)

ALEXANDER
*1825 †1837

SON OF AD. JOSEPH
BY HERMINE OF
ANHALT (TABLE 81)

ALBRECHT
D. of Teschen 1847
*1817 †1895
m. 1844
Hildegard
*1825 †1864
d. of Louis I
K. of Bavaria

MARIA THERESA
*1816 †1867
m. 1837
Ferdinand II
K. of Two Sicilies
*1810 †1859

FREDERICK
*1821 †1847

WILLIAM
Gd. Master of
Teutonic O. 1863
*1827 †1894

CHARLES ——1854 (2)—— ELIZABETH
FERDINAND   *1831 †1903
*1818 †1874   m. (1) 1847
                AD. FERDINAND
                of Austria-Este
                *1821 †1849

STEPHEN
Palatine of
Hungary 1847–8
*1817 †1867

JOSEPH ——1864—— Clotilde
*1833 †1905   *1846 †1927
                  d. of Pr. Augustus
                  of Saxe-Coburg
                  & Gotha

Leopold II ——1853—— MARY
K. of Belgians   HENRIETT
*1835 †1909   *1836 †190

MARIA THERESA
*1845 †1927
m. 1865 Philip
D. of
Württemberg
*1838 †1917

FREDERICK ——1878—— Isabella
D. of Teschen   *1856 †1931
*1856 †1936   d. of Rudolph
                     D. of Croy

Alphonso XII ——(2) 1879—— MARIA
*1857 †1885   CHRISTINA
                         *1858
                         †1929

CHARLES STEPHEN
*1860 †1933
m. 1886
Maria Theresa
*1862 †1933
d. of AD. Charles
Salvator

EUGENE
Gd. Master of
Teutonic O.
1894–1923
*1863 †1954

MARIA
DOROTHEA
*1867 †1932
m. 1896
Philip
D. of Orléans
*1869 †1926

MARGARET
*1870 †1955
m. 1890
Albert
Pr. of Thurn
& Taxis
*1867 †1952

JOSEPH ——1893—— Augusta
*1872   *1875 †1964
†1962   d. of Pr. Leopold
                 of Bavaria

Emanuel ——1902—— MARY CHRISTINA
Her. Pr. of   *1879 †1962
Salm-Salm
*1871 ✕ 1916

Elias ——1903—— MARY ANNE
D. of Parma   *1882 †1940
*1880 †1959

ALBRECHT
D. of Teschen
*1897 †1955
m. (1) 1930
Irene Lelbach
*1897 (div. 1937)
m. (2) 1938
Catherine *1909
d. of Béla Bocskay
of Felsö-Bánya
(div. 1951)
m. (3)
Lydia Strauss

JOSEPH FRANCIS ——1924—— Anne
*1895 †1957   *1903 †1976
                         d. of Fred. Aug. III
                         K. of Saxony

LADISL
*1901 †

Hieronymus ——(1) 1909—— RENATA
Pr. Radziwill   *1888
*1885 k. 1945   †1935

CHARLES ——1920 (2)—— Alice
ALBRECHT   *1889
*1888 †1951   d. of Oscar
                      Ankarcrona
                      (Pr. of Altenburg)

Olgierd ——1913—— MECHTILDIS
Pr. Czartoryski   *1891 †1966
*1888

LEO CHARLES
*1893 †1939
m. 1922
Mary Clotilde
*1893
d. of Charles
de Thuillères
C. of Montjoye-Vaufrey

WILLIAM
*1895
†1954

PRINCES OF
ALTENBURG

COUNTS OF
HAPSBURG-LORRAINE

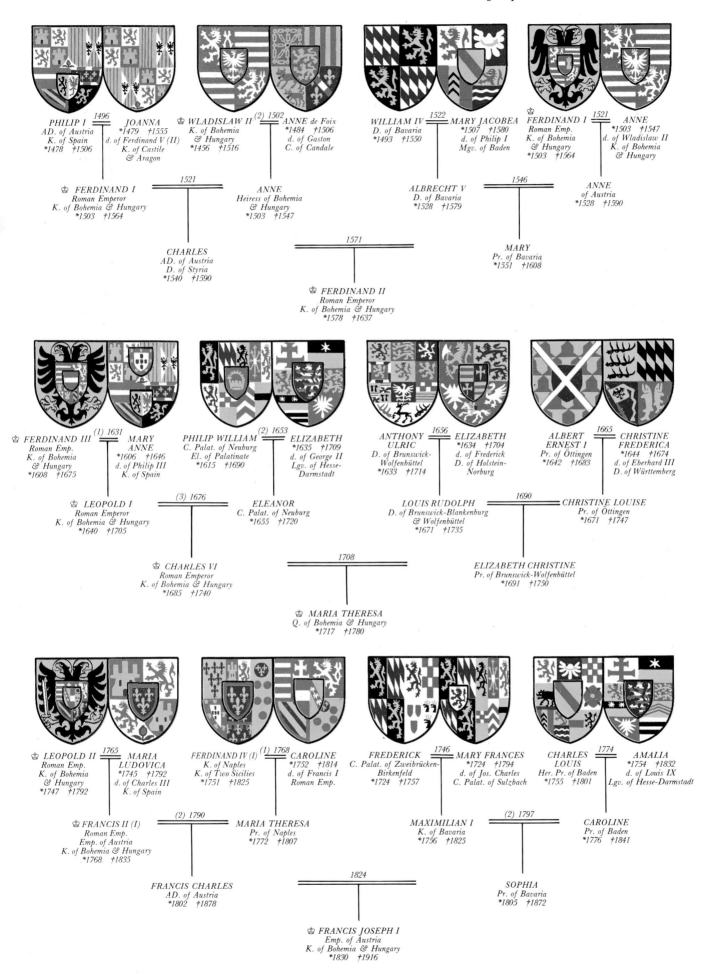

PHILIP I
AD. of Austria
K. of Spain
*1478 †1506

1496

JOANNA
*1479 †1555
d. of Ferdinand V (II)
K. of Castile
& Aragon

WLADISLAW II
K. of Bohemia
& Hungary
*1456 †1516

(2) *1502*

ANNE de Foix
*1484 †1506
d. of Gaston
C. of Candale

WILLIAM IV
D. of Bavaria
*1493 †1550

1522

MARY JACOBEA
*1507 †1580
d. of Philip I
Mgv. of Baden

FERDINAND I
Roman Emp.
K. of Bohemia
& Hungary
*1503 †1564

1521

ANNE
*1503 †1547
d. of Wladislaw II
K. of Bohemia
& Hungary

FERDINAND I
Roman Emperor
K. of Bohemia & Hungary
*1503 †1564

1521

ANNE
Heiress of Bohemia
& Hungary
*1503 †1547

ALBRECHT V
D. of Bavaria
*1528 †1579

1546

ANNE
of Austria
*1528 †1590

CHARLES
AD. of Austria
D. of Styria
*1540 †1590

MARY
Pr. of Bavaria
*1551 †1608

1571

FERDINAND II
Roman Emperor
K. of Bohemia & Hungary
*1578 †1637

FERDINAND III
Roman Emp.
K. of Bohemia
& Hungary
*1608 †1675

(1) *1631*

MARY ANNE
*1606 †1646
d. of Philip III
K. of Spain

PHILIP WILLIAM
C. Palat. of Neuburg
El. of Palatinate
*1615 †1690

(2) *1653*

ELIZABETH
*1635 †1709
d. of George II
Lgv. of Hesse-Darmstadt

ANTHONY ULRIC
D. of Brunswick-Wolfenbüttel
*1633 †1714

1656

ELIZABETH
*1634 †1704
d. of Frederick
D. of Holstein-Norburg

ALBERT ERNEST I
Pr. of Öttingen
*1642 †1683

1665

CHRISTINE FREDERICA
*1644 †1674
d. of Eberhard III
D. of Württemberg

LEOPOLD I
Roman Emperor
K. of Bohemia & Hungary
*1640 †1705

(3) *1676*

ELEANOR
C. Palat. of Neuburg
*1655 †1720

LOUIS RUDOLPH
D. of Brunswick-Blankenburg
& Wolfenbüttel
*1671 †1735

1690

CHRISTINE LOUISE
Pr. of Öttingen
*1671 †1747

CHARLES VI
Roman Emperor
K. of Bohemia & Hungary
*1685 †1740

ELIZABETH CHRISTINE
Pr. of Brunswick-Wolfenbüttel
*1691 †1750

1708

MARIA THERESA
Q. of Bohemia & Hungary
*1717 †1780

LEOPOLD II
Roman Emp.
K. of Bohemia
& Hungary
*1747 †1792

1765

MARIA LUDOVICA
*1745 †1792
d. of Charles III
K. of Spain

FERDINAND IV (I)
K. of Naples
K. of Two Sicilies
*1751 †1825

(1) *1768*

CAROLINE
*1752 †1814
d. of Francis I
Roman Emp.

FREDERICK
C. Palat. of Zweibrücken-Birkenfeld
*1724 †1757

1746

MARY FRANCES
*1724 †1794
d. of Jos. Charles
C. Palat. of Sulzbach

CHARLES LOUIS
Her. Pr. of Baden
*1755 †1801

1774

AMALIA
*1754 †1832
d. of Louis IX
Lgv. of Hesse-Darmstadt

FRANCIS II (I)
Roman Emp.
Emp. of Austria
K. of Bohemia & Hungary
*1768 †1835

(2) *1790*

MARIA THERESA
Pr. of Naples
*1772 †1807

MAXIMILIAN I
K. of Bavaria
*1756 †1825

(2) *1797*

CAROLINE
Pr. of Baden
*1776 †1841

FRANCIS CHARLES
AD. of Austria
*1802 †1878

1824

SOPHIA
Pr. of Bavaria
*1805 †1872

FRANCIS JOSEPH I
Emp. of Austria
K. of Bohemia & Hungary
*1830 †1916

of Olomouc. From Lombardy to Lemberg the Hapsburgs ruled over a solid block of prosperous territories. Good ports on the Adriatic were in fact worth more than distant harbours in the Low Countries.

The Holy Roman Empire was not restored; instead a German Confederation of 39 states was established, in which Austria strove to play the leading part. When Francis II reached the end of his long reign, he gave his son the advice, 'Rule, and change nothing.' His Empire had settled into a course of conservative stagnation. Ferdinand I was feeble-minded; it is rumoured that, having shot an eagle, he enquired why it had only one head. Discontent spread and reached a climax in 1848, the year of revolutions. Ferdinand abdicated; Metternich fled; the Archduke Francis Charles renounced the succession; his son, Francis Joseph (Table 82) began his long and often tragic reign. The pedigree of the young Emperor (Table 84) shows that his maternal ancestry derived from several German families, with a strong Wittelsbach infusion, while his paternal forebears were exclusively Hapsburg and Bourbon.

FRANCIS JOSEPH

The first years of Francis Joseph were devoted to the restoration of authority and the suppression of rebellion in Hungary. Thereafter the Emperor ruled in an increasingly autocratic manner; his absolutism was tinged with reform, and the general tenor of government was both more vigorous and more enlightened than under his uncle. He had, however, to contend with rising tides of nationalism in Italy, in Germany, in the Balkans and in his own dominions. His first losses were in Italy, where an alliance of the Savoyard Kings of Sardinia and Napoleon III transferred Lombardy to the former (1859); the Hapsburg Duke of Modena and Grand-Duke of Tuscany lost their territories a year later; the unification of Italy was under way. Within the Empire the various races, particularly the Magyars, were seeking a measure of independence. The Emperor oscillated between simple constitutionalism and some form of federalism. These manoeuvres were overshadowed by the involvement of Francis Joseph in a remote dispute over the Duchies of Schleswig and Holstein (Chapter 5), which culminated in a lightning attack by Prussia on Austria in 1866, and the Prussian victory at Sadowa. In consequence, Venetia had to be ceded to Italy and Austria was excluded from Germany, in whose affairs she had had a voice for over four hundred years.

The Emperor now settled for federalism. Through the *Ausgleich* (1867) the former Empire of Austria was transformed into the Dual Monarchy of Austria-Hungary. Broadly, the areas of Galicia, Bohemia and Austria constituted the first; Hungary, Transylvania and Croatia the second. The settlement, while flattering to the Magyars, left the Slav races unsatisfied; nevertheless it lasted 50 years.

Francis Joseph endured a series of personal disasters. His brother had been lured by Napoleon III into accepting the throne of Mexico. Adequate military support and sufficient local enthusiasm alike were lacking and Maximilian was ignominiously shot in 1867. In 1889 the Crown Prince Rudolph committed suicide in company with a girl not his wife; in 1898 the Empress Elizabeth, a wild and lovely horsewoman, was wantonly assassinated in Switzerland. In 1900 the Archduke Francis Ferdinand, the next heir to the throne, made a morganatic marriage with Countess Chotek which debarred his children from succession. In the Balkans the surge of Slavic nationalism was thrown back on itself by the Austrian annexation of Bosnia and Hercegovina in 1908. In the summer of 1914 the Archduke and his wife were assassinated at Sarajevo (Chapter 38). Still the ageing Emperor toiled on until death relieved him in 1916. When he ascended the throne Metternich had just left office: when he quitted it, Woodrow Wilson was already President of the United States.

Francis Joseph was followed by his great-nephew Charles who abdicated in 1918. The peace terms of the Allies fragmented the Austrian Empire irretrievably and the long story of the Hapsburg and Hapsburg-Lorraine dynasties was ended. After the loss of the north Italian duchies, the Austrian archdukes used a shield which can be seen for Charles Louis (top of Table 82) or Charles Ferdinand (Table 83); it comprised quarterings for Hungary, Bohemia, Galicia and Austria ancient, with over all Hapsburg, Austria modern and Lorraine. Francis Ferdinand had been given the name of Este (after the extinction of the Dukes of Modena) and added their eagle to his escutcheon. This can be seen on Table 82. The Emperors themselves sometimes employed a highly elaborate device with the shields of their provinces spread over a two-headed eagle; more normally they used the simple pattern on Table 76 where the imperial eagle bears on its breast Hapsburg, Austria and Lorraine, and is surrounded by the ancient Burgundian Order of the Golden Fleece. Charles I died in Madeira in 1922, a remote grave for the last Hapsburg Emperor. His claims were inherited by his eldest son, the Archduke Otto, whose interests have been mainly academic. The younger brother, Robert, has been granted the name and arms of Este. Otto, however, has renounced all dynastic ambition and taken on West German citizenship; he is now a member of the European Parliament for Bavaria. Thus, by the ironies of history, the potential successor to the throne of Charlemagne sits as Herr von Hapsburg in a democratic assembly whose frontiers are not so very different from those of the ninth-century Emperor.

Chapter 21

BOHEMIA

Slav settlements took place all over eastern and central Europe in the Dark Ages. They may have appeared in what is now Czechoslovakia early in the Christian era; there was certainly a considerable infiltration into the Balkan peninsula in the sixth century. The Byzantine Empire was above all a Christian state: it sought not only to preserve its own boundaries but to extend those of Christendom. In about 867 two Greek missionaries, St Cyril and St Methodius, were sent to convert the inhabitants of Moravia. Methodius baptized a leading noble called Bořivoj, who was the founder of the first Bohemian dynasty, the Přemyslids. Cyril's achievement was even greater, for he invented the first Slavonic alphabet, whose successors still bear his name. A grandson of Bořivoj was St Wenceslas, murdered in 929, the hero of the famous carol and the patron saint of his people.

As can now be seen from Table 85, the idea of an hereditary succession was slow to establish itself among the rulers of Bohemia and Moravia, who at that time came under the general suzerainty of the Roman emperors. In 1086 Henry IV conferred the personal title of King on Wratislaw II. In 1158 Frederick Barbarossa not only ceded Upper Lusatia to that ruler's grandson, Wladislaw II (Table 86), but gave him the hereditary rank of king. However, a period of confusion ensued and it was not until the reign of Wenceslas I that the Bohemian monarchy was well established. Wladislaw II used as arms a crowned silver lion on a red field; his nephew Děpolt II dimidiated this coat with an eagle, which was associated with St Wenceslas. The Kingdom was also becoming increasingly independent of the Empire, and inclined to interfere in the affairs of Austria. Přemysl Ottokar II took possession of Austria and Styria and married the heiress of the Babenberg line; later he added Carinthia and Carniola so that his power reached the Adriatic. His dominions thus briefly possessed the coastline with which Shakespeare credited Bohemia in *The Winter's Tale*. His northern adventures led this great King into Lithuania, and Königsberg was so named in his honour. But his ambitions for the Empire were frustrated by the election of Rudolph of Hapsburg. In 1278 he was slain in battle and Austria passed to the Hapsburgs. In this reign we find the Bohemian lion assuming its familiar double tail; the two tails are always drawn crossed. His brother, Wladislaw, displays the checky eagle of Moravia, of which he was Margrave.

Ottokar's son, Wenceslas II, looked east rather than south. After a long minority, he was recognized as King of Poland in 1300 and a year later saw his son accepted as King of Hungary. A golden future for Bohemia seemed assured, but the hope was shattered when the childless Wenceslas III was murdered after a reign of only one year. The thirteenth century had been a period of great prosperity for Bohemia; commerce and the arts had flourished, new towns and abbeys had been founded. It was a sad ending to the native dynasty.

THE LUXEMBURGS

After a brief Hapsburg rule, a new dynasty emerged. In 1310 the Emperor Henry VII bestowed Bohemia on his son John, and married him to the sister of the last Přemyslid, Elizabeth.

John of Luxemburg was an active and chivalrous king who enlarged the boundaries of Bohemia to the north. But he was often absent and allowed the nobility to dominate his country; during his last absence he died, sightless, fighting for the French against the English at Crécy. His son, Charles I (Table 87), was a far abler ruler. He became emperor (as Charles IV) in 1355 and promulgated the famous Golden Bull of 1356, which gave Bohemia first place among the lay

TABLE 85

BOHEMIA
General survey and the 'Winter King'

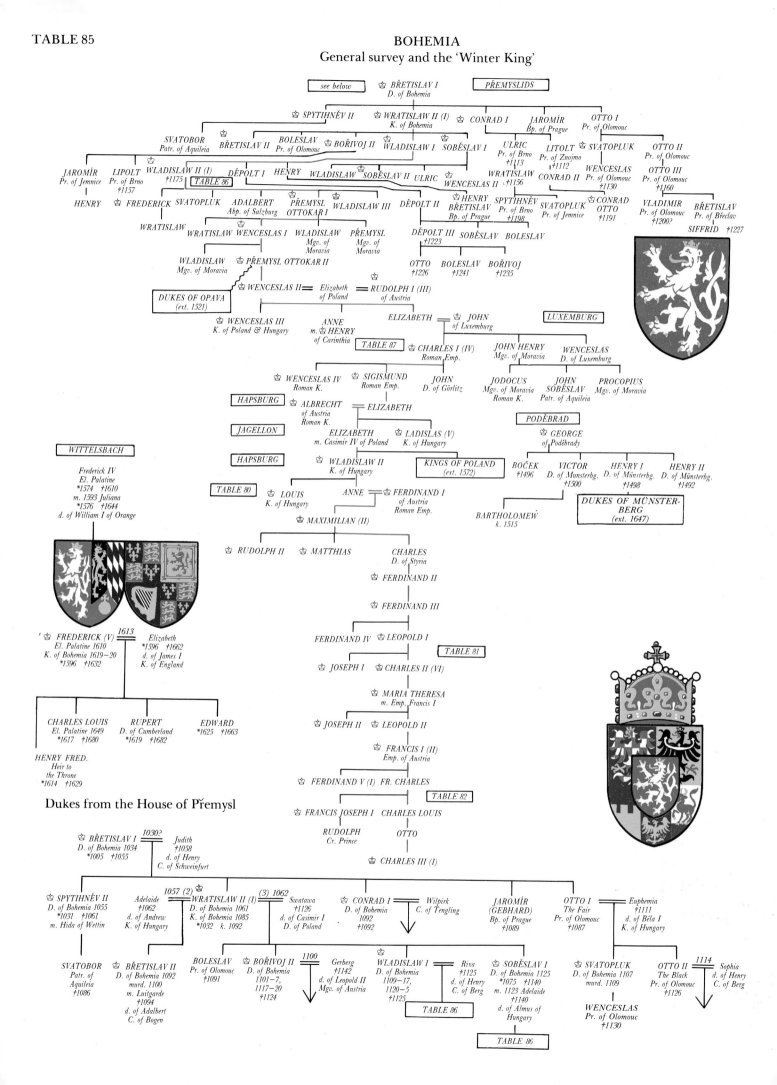

see below

♔ BŘETISLAV I
D. of Bohemia

PŘEMYSLIDS

♔ SPYTIHNĚV II   ♔ WRATISLAW II (I)   CONRAD I   JAROMÍR   OTTO I
K. of Bohemia   Bp. of Prague   Pr. of Olomouc

SVATOBOR   ♔ BŘETISLAV II   BOLESLAV   ♔ BOŘIVOJ II   ♔ WLADISLAW I   SOBĚSLAV I   ULRIC   LITOLT   ♔ SVATOPLUK   OTTO II
Patr. of Aquileia   Pr. of Olomouc   Pr. of Brno   Pr. of Znojmo   Pr. of Olomouc
†1113   †1112

JAROMÍR   LIPOLT   WLADISLAW II (I)   DĚPOLT I   HENRY   WLADISLAW   SOBĚSLAV II   ULRIC   WRATISLAW   CONRAD II   WENCESLAS   OTTO III
Pr. of Jemnice   Pr. of Brno   †1175   †1156   Pr. of Olomouc   Pr. of Olomouc
†1157   TABLE 86   †1130   †1160

HENRY   ♔ FREDERICK   SVATOPLUK   ADALBERT   ♔ PŘEMYSL   WLADISLAW III   DĚPOLT II   ♔ HENRY   SPYTIHNĚV   SVATOPLUK   CONRAD   VLADIMIR   BŘETISLAV
Abp. of Salzburg   OTTOKAR I   BŘETISLAV   Pr. of Brno   Pr. of Jemnice   OTTO   Pr. of Olomouc   Pr. of Břeclav
Bp. of Prague   †1198   †1191   †1200?
WRATISLAW   †1223   SIFFRID   †1227

WRATISLAW   WENCESLAS I   WLADISLAW   PŘEMYSL   DĚPOLT III   SOBĚSLAV   BOLESLAV
Mgv. of   Mgv. of
Moravia   Moravia

WLADISLAW   ♔ PŘEMYSL OTTOKAR II   OTTO   BOLESLAV   BOŘIVOJ
Mgv. of Moravia   †1226   †1241   †1235

DUKES OF OPAVA   ♔ WENCESLAS II ══ Elizabeth ══ RUDOLPH I (III)
(ext. 1521)   of Poland   of Austria

♔ WENCESLAS III   ANNE   ELIZABETH ═══ ♔ JOHN   LUXEMBURG
K. of Poland & Hungary   m. ♔ HENRY   of Luxemburg
of Carinthia
TABLE 87   ♔ CHARLES I (IV)   JOHN HENRY   WENCESLAS
Roman Emp.   Mgv. of Moravia   D. of Luxemburg

♔ WENCESLAS IV   ♔ SIGISMUND   JOHN   JODOCUS   JOHN   PROCOPIUS
Roman K.   Roman Emp.   D. of Görlitz   Mgv. of Moravia   SOBĚSLAV   Mgv. of Moravia
Roman K.   Patr. of Aquileia

HAPSBURG   ♔ ALBRECHT ═══ ELIZABETH   PODĚBRAD
of Austria
Roman K.   ♔ GEORGE
of Poděbrady

JAGELLON   ELIZABETH   ♔ LADISLAS (V)   BOČEK   VICTOR   HENRY I   HENRY II
m. Casimir IV of Poland   K. of Hungary   †1496   D. of Munsterbg.   D. of Münsterbg.   D. of Münsterbg.
†1500   †1498   †1492

HAPSBURG   ♔ WLADISLAW II   KINGS OF POLAND
K. of Hungary   (ext. 1572)   DUKES OF MÜNSTER-
BERG
TABLE 80   ♔ LOUIS   ANNE ═══ ♔ FERDINAND I   (ext. 1647)
K. of Hungary   of Austria   BARTHOLOMEW
Roman Emp.   k. 1515

♔ MAXIMILIAN (II)

♔ RUDOLPH II   ♔ MATTHIAS   CHARLES
D. of Styria

WITTELSBACH   ♔ FERDINAND II

Frederick IV   ♔ FERDINAND III
El. Palatine
*1574 †1610
m. 1593 Juliana   FERDINAND IV   ♔ LEOPOLD I   TABLE 81
*1576 †1644
d. of William I of Orange   ♔ JOSEPH I   ♔ CHARLES II (VI)

♔ MARIA THERESA
m. Emp. Francis I

♔ JOSEPH II   ♔ LEOPOLD II

♔ FRANCIS I (II)
Emp. of Austria

♔ FREDERICK (V) ══1613══ Elizabeth   ♔ FERDINAND V (I)   FR. CHARLES
El. Palatine 1610   *1596 †1662
K. of Bohemia 1619–20   d. of James I   TABLE 82
*1596 †1632   K. of England

Dukes from the House of Přemysl   ♔ FRANCIS JOSEPH I   CHARLES LOUIS

CHARLES LOUIS   RUPERT   EDWARD   RUDOLPH   OTTO
El. Palatine 1649   D. of Cumberland   *1625 †1663   Cr. Prince
*1617 †1680   *1619 †1682

HENRY FRED.
Heir to   ♔ CHARLES III (I)
the Throne
*1614 †1629

♔ BŘETISLAV I ══1030?══ Judith
D. of Bohemia 1034   †1058
*1005 †1055   d. of Henry
C. of Schweinfurt

♔ SPYTIHNĚV II   Adelaide ══1057 (2)══ ♔ WRATISLAW II (I) ══(3) 1062══ Swatawa   ♔ CONRAD I ═══ Wilpirk   JAROMÍR   OTTO I ═══ Euphemia
D. of Bohemia 1055   †1062   D. of Bohemia 1061   †1126   D. of Bohemia   C. of Tengling   (GEBHARD)   The Fair   †1111
*1031 †1061   d. of Andrew   K. of Bohemia 1085   d. of Casimir I   1092   Bp. of Prague   Pr. of Olomouc   d. of Béla I
m. Hida of Wettin   K. of Hungary   *1032 k. 1092   D. of Poland   †1092   †1089   †1087   K. of Hungary

SVATOBOR   ♔ BŘETISLAV II   BOLESLAV   ♔ BOŘIVOJ II ══1100══ Gerberg   ♔ WLADISLAW I ═══ Rixa   ♔ SOBĚSLAV I   ♔ SVATOPLUK   OTTO II ══1114══ Sophia
Patr. of   D. of Bohemia 1092   Pr. of Olomouc   D. of Bohemia   †1142   D. of Bohemia   †1125   D. of Bohemia 1125   D. of Bohemia 1107   The Black   d. of Henry
Aquileia   murd. 1100   †1091   1101–7,   d. of Leopold II   1109–17,   d. of Henry   *1075 †1140   murd. 1109   †1126   C. of Berg
†1086   m. Luitgarde   1117–20   Mgv. of Austria   1120–5   C. of Berg   m. 1123 Adelaide
†1094   †1124   †1125   †1140   WENCESLAS
d. of Adalbert   d. of Almus of   Pr. of Olomouc
C. of Bogen   TABLE 86   Hungary   †1130

TABLE 86

TABLE 86

BOHEMIA
Kings from the House of Přemysl

ISSUE OF WLADISLAW I (TABLE 85)

ISSUE OF SOBĚSLAV I (TABLE 85)

WLADISLAW
Pr. of Olomouc
†1165
m. a daughter of
Albrecht I
The Bear
Mgv. of
Brandenburg

SOBĚSLAV II
D. of Bohemia
1173–8
*1128 †1180
m. 1173?
Elizabeth
†1209
d. of Mieszko III
D. of Poland

MARY
m. (1) 1139
Leopold IV
Mgv. of Austria
*1108 †1141
m. (2)
Hermann II
D. of Carinthia
†1181

ULRIC
Pr. of Olomouc
*1134 †1177
m. (1) Cecily
d. of Louis I
Lgv. of Thuringia
m. (2) Sophia
d. of Otto
Mgv. of Meissen

WENCESLAS II
D. of Bohemia 1191
*1137 †1192

DĚPOLT I
†1167
m. Sibyl
d. of Albrecht I
The Bear

HENRY
† after 1169
m. Margaret
† before 1186

Gertrud
*1129 †1150
d. of Leopold III
Mgv. of Austria
1140 (1)

WLADISLAW II (I)
D. of Bohemia 1140
K. of Bohemia 1158
abdic. 1172
†1174

(2) 1153
Judith
† after 1174
d. of Louis I
Lgv. of Thuringia

FREDERICK
D. of Bohemia
1172–3, 1178
†1189
m. 1147
Elizabeth
† after 1190
d. of Geisa II
K. of Hungary

SVATOPLUK
† after 1169

ADALBERT
Abp. of Salzburg
†1200

Adelaide
†1211
d. of Otto
Mgv. of Meissen
(div. 1198)
1187 (1)

**PŘEMYSL
OTTOKAR I**
D. of Bohemia
1192–3
K. of Bohemia 1198
*1155? †1230

(2) 1198
Constance
†1240
d. of Béla III
K. of Hungary

WLADISLAW III
D. of Bohemia 1197
abdic. 1197
Mgv. of Moravia
*1160? †1222
m. Hedwig

RIXA
†1182
m. 1177
Henry
of Austria
D. of Mödling
†1223

DĚPOLT II
†1190

HENRY BŘETISLAV
Bp. of Prague 1182
D. of Bohemia 1193
†1197

DĚPOLT BRANCH
(ext. 1241)

WRATISLAW
† before 1180

SOPHIA
†1195
m. 1186
Albrecht
Mgv. of Meissen
*1158 †1195

LUDMILA
*1170 †1240
m. (1) Albrecht
C. of Bogen
†1198
m. (2) 1204
Louis I
D. of Bavaria
*1174 murd. 1231

WRATISLAW
enfeoffed
by Otto IV 1212
† after 1225

Waldemar II
K. of Denmark
*1170 †1241
(2) 1205
**MARGARET
(DAGMAR)**
*1189? †1213

Henry II
D. of Wroclaw
✗ 1241
1216
ANNE
*1204
†1265

WENCESLAS I
K. of Bohemia 1230
*1205 †1253
1224
Kunigunde
*1200 †1248
d. of Philip
Roman K.

WLADISLAW
Mgv. of Moravia
1224
*1207 †1227

PŘEMYSL
Mgv. of Moravia 1227
*1209 †1239
m. 1233
Margaret
d. of Otto
D. of Meran

AGNES
The Saint
*1211 †1282

WLADISLAW
Mgv. of Moravia
1246
*1227 †1247
1246 (1)
Gertrud
*1228 †1299
d. of Henry
D. of Austria

Margaret
†1267
d. of Leopold VI
Mgv. of Austria
(div. 1260)
(2) 1252 (1)
**PŘEMYSL
OTTOKAR II**
K. of Bohemia 1253
*1233 ✗ 1278

(2) 1261 (1)
Kunigunde
*1245 †1285
d. of Rostislaw
Pr. of Galicia

(2) 1285 (1)
Záviš
L. of Falkenstein
ex. 1290

Otto III
Mgv. of Brandenburg
†1268
1243
BEATRICE
†1286

Henry
The Serene
Mgv. of Meissen
*1216 †1288
(2) 1245
AGNES
†1268

Boleslaw II
D. of Mazovia
†1313
1291
KUNIGUNDE
*1265 †1321
(div. 1302)

Rudolph II
D. of Austria
*1271 †1290
1278
AGNES
*1268 †1296

Guta
*1271 †1297
d. of Rudolph I
Roman K.
1287 (1)
WENCESLAS II
K. of Bohemia 1283
K. of Poland 1300
*1271 †1305

(2) 1300 (1)
Elizabeth
*1286 †1335
d. of Przemyslaw II
K. of Poland

RUDOLPH I (III)
D. of Austria
K. of Bohemia
1306
*1282 †1307
(2) 1306 (2)

Otto V
Mgv. of Brandenbg
Regent 1278–83
†1299
1268
Judith
†1317?
d. of Hermann II
C. of Henneberg

WENCESLAS III
K. of Hungary 1301–5
K. of Bohemia
& Poland 1305
*1289 murd. 1306
1306 (1)
Viola
†1317
d. of Mieszko I
D. of Těšin
m. (2) 1316
Peter
L. of Rožmberk
†1347

HENRY
D. of Carinthia
K. of Bohemia 1307–10
*1270 †1335
(2)
Adelaide
*1285 †1320
d. of Henry I
D. of Brunswick-
Grubenhagen
m. (3) 1328 Beatrix
of Savoy †1331

(1) 1306
ANNE
*1290 †1313

ELIZABETH
*1292 †1330
1310 (1)
JOHN
of Luxemburg
*1296 ✗ 1346
s. of Emp. Henry VII
K. of Bohemia 1310

(2) 1334
Beatrix
†1383
d. of Louis I
D. of Bourbon

Boleslaw III
D. of Wroclaw
& Legnica
*1291 †1352
(1) 1303
MARGARET
*1296 †1322

AGNES
*1305 †1336?
m. 1316
Henry
D. of Jawor
†1346

TABLE 87

TABLE 87

TABLE 87

BOHEMIA
Houses of Luxemburg & Jagellon

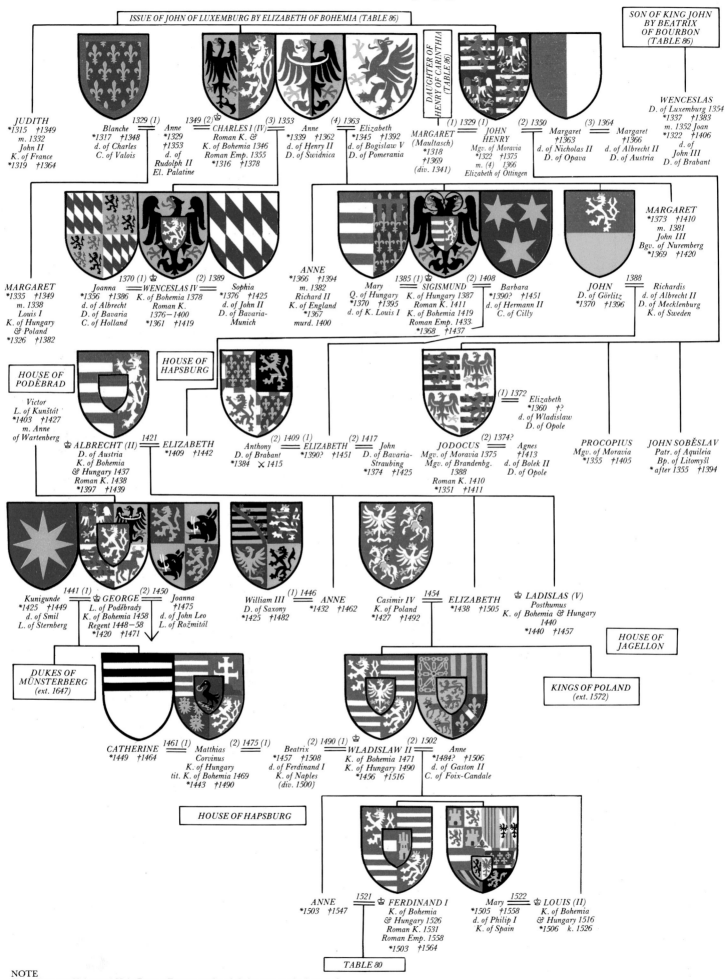

ISSUE OF JOHN OF LUXEMBURG BY ELIZABETH OF BOHEMIA (TABLE 86)

DAUGHTER OF HENRY OF CARINTHIA (TABLE 86)

SON OF KING JOHN BY BEATRIX OF BOURBON (TABLE 86)

JUDITH
*1315 †1349
m. 1332
John II
K. of France
*1319 †1364

1329 (1)
Blanche
*1317 †1348
d. of Charles
C. of Valois

1349 (2)
CHARLES I (IV)
Roman K. &
K. of Bohemia 1346
Roman Emp. 1355
*1316 †1378

Anne
*1329
†1353
d. of
Rudolph II
El. Palatine

(3) 1353
Anne
*1339 †1362
d. of Henry II
D. of Swidnica

(4) 1363
Elizabeth
*1345 †1392
d. of Bogislaw V
D. of Pomerania

(1) 1329
MARGARET
(Maultasch)
*1318
†1369
(div. 1341)

JOHN HENRY
Mgv. of Moravia
*1322 †1375
m. (4) 1366
Elizabeth of Öttingen

(2) 1350
Margaret
†1363
d. of Nicholas II
D. of Opava

(3) 1364
Margaret
†1366
d. of Albrecht II
D. of Austria

WENCESLAS
D. of Luxemburg 1354
*1337 †1383
m. 1352 Joan
*1322 †1406
d. of
John III
D. of Brabant

MARGARET
*1373 †1410
m. 1381
John III
Bgv. of Nuremberg
*1369 †1420

MARGARET
*1335 †1349
m. 1338
Louis I
K. of Hungary
& Poland
*1326 †1382

1370 (1)
Joanna
*1356 †1386
d. of Albrecht
D. of Bavaria
C. of Holland

WENCESLAS IV
K. of Bohemia 1378
Roman K.
1376–1400
*1361 †1419

(2) 1389
Sophia
*1376 †1425
d. of John II
D. of Bavaria-
Munich

ANNE
*1366 †1394
m. 1382
Richard II
K. of England
*1367
murd. 1400

Mary
Q. of Hungary
*1370 †1395
d. of K. Louis I

1385 (1)
SIGISMUND
K. of Hungary 1387
Roman K. 1411
K. of Bohemia 1419
Roman Emp. 1433
*1368 †1437

(2) 1408
Barbara
*1390? †1451
d. of Hermann II
C. of Cilly

JOHN
D. of Görlitz
*1370 †1396

1388
Richardis
d. of Albrecht II
D. of Mecklenburg
K. of Sweden

HOUSE OF PODĚBRAD

Victor
L. of Kunštát
*1403 †1427
m. Anne
of Wartenberg

HOUSE OF HAPSBURG

ALBRECHT (II)
D. of Austria
K. of Bohemia
& Hungary 1437
Roman K. 1438
*1397 †1439

1421
ELIZABETH
*1409 †1442

(2) 1409 (1)
Anthony
D. of Brabant
*1384 ✕ 1415

ELIZABETH
*1390? †1451

(2) 1417
John
D. of Bavaria-
Straubing
*1374 †1425

JODOCUS
Mgv. of Moravia 1375
Mgv. of Brandenbg.
1388
Roman K. 1410
*1351 †1411

(1) 1372
Elizabeth
*1360 †?
d. of Wladislaw
D. of Opole

(2) 1374?
Agnes
†1413
d. of Bolek II
D. of Opole

PROCOPIUS
Mgv. of Moravia
*1355 †1405

JOHN SOBĚSLAV
Patr. of Aquileia
Bp. of Litomyšl
*after 1355 †1394

Kunigunde
*1425 †1449
d. of Smil
L. of Sternberg

1441 (1)
GEORGE
L. of Poděbrady
K. of Bohemia 1458
Regent 1448–58
*1420 †1471

(2) 1450
Joanna
†1475
d. of John Leo
L. of Rožmitál

William III
D. of Saxony
*1425 †1482

(1) 1446
ANNE
*1432 †1462

Casimir IV
K. of Poland
*1427 †1492

1454
ELIZABETH
*1438 †1505

LADISLAS (V)
Posthumus
K. of Bohemia & Hungary
1440
*1440 †1457

DUKES OF MÜNSTERBERG
(ext. 1647)

HOUSE OF JAGELLON

KINGS OF POLAND
(ext. 1572)

CATHERINE
*1449 †1464

1461 (1)
Matthias
Corvinus
K. of Hungary
tit. K. of Bohemia 1469
*1443 †1490

(2) 1475 (1)
Beatrix
*1457 †1508
d. of Ferdinand I
K. of Naples
(div. 1500)

(2) 1490 (1)
WLADISLAW II
K. of Bohemia 1471
K. of Hungary 1490
*1456 †1516

(2) 1502
Anne
*1484? †1506
d. of Gaston II
C. of Foix-Candale

HOUSE OF HAPSBURG

ANNE
*1503 †1547

1521
FERDINAND I
K. of Bohemia
& Hungary 1526
Roman K. 1531
Roman Emp. 1558
*1503 †1564

Mary
*1505 †1558
d. of Philip I
K. of Spain

1522
LOUIS (II)
K. of Bohemia
& Hungary 1516
*1506 k. 1526

TABLE 80

NOTE
Since Emperor Sigismund Holy Roman Emperors placed their arms on the breast of
the double-headed eagle, and Kings of the Romans on that of a single-headed one.

electors to the imperial dignity. Charles IV perceived that a strong Bohemia was essential as a firm base for the government of the Holy Roman Empire, so he added Lusatia and the Margravate of Brandenburg to the family lands: for a brief moment Berlin was in Bohemia. He founded the University of Prague which still bears his name, as does the magnificent bridge across the Vltava below his cathedral of St Vitus. In the arts and learning Prague was the outstanding imperial city. Charles himself impaled Bohemia with the Empire; other members of his family quartered the red lion of Luxemburg on its striped background with another province (Table 87: John of Moravia).

Wenceslas IV was a less effective ruler. He lost Brandenburg, but more serious was the growth of religious heterodoxy. The marriage of Anne of Bohemia to Richard II of England had no doubt facilitated the transmission of the opinions of John Wycliffe to Europe; the preaching in Bohemia of John Hus (c. 1369–1415) marked the onset of the Reformation. Wenceslas himself had ceased to be King of the Romans in 1400; it was his brother, Sigismund, who incinerated Hus in 1415. But the Czech people would not accept this verdict, and bitterly resented the succession of Sigismund to Bohemia in 1419. Under John Žižka they flung back the German armies of invasion. Sigismund was not finally accepted till 1436, and even then had to make concessions to his subjects, such as Communion in both kinds.

Sigismund died in 1437: his son-in-law Albrecht of Austria died in 1439. The throne passed to the latter's posthumous son, Ladislas. In Bohemia, the real ruler was a powerful noble, George Poděbrady, who ultimately became king himself in 1458 by election. A tolerant follower of Hus, he strove to reduce religious tension and to increase commerce. The family arms of Poděbrady can be seen beside those of his son-in-law, Matthias Corvinus on Table 87. Although George chose as his heir Wladislaw, son of the King of Poland, Matthias Corvinus for a time occupied Moravia. But on the death of Matthias, Wladislaw acceded in turn to the thrones of Bohemia and Hungary, while Poland went to a brother. On his death in 1516 he bequeathed these Crowns to his son Louis. By now the Turkish threat from the Balkans was omnipresent: at the fatal battle of Mohács, the King, just over twenty years of age,

perished without issue before the hosts of Süleyman the Lawgiver.

His only sister was married to Ferdinand of Hapsburg (Table 80), later the Emperor Ferdinand I. From this point onward the fortunes of Bohemia were mainly linked with those of Austria and Hungary. There was, however, a decisive break early in the seventeenth century. It followed a considerable period of religious dissension between the Protestant elements of Bohemia and their Catholic rulers. In May of 1618 two councillors of the Emperor Matthias were flung from a window of the royal palace – the 'Defenestration of Prague'. The councillors survived, but the issue had been ventilated. The Protestant German princes gave no clear lead, and when Matthias was succeeded in the next year by a more intransigent Catholic (Ferdinand II), the Lutherans of Bohemia proceeded to offer their throne to Frederick V, the Elector Palatine and a well-known Protestant prince (Table 96). The manoeuvre was not a success. Frederick and his wife, a daughter of James I of England (Table 7), came to Prague and were duly crowned, but defeat at the battle of the White Mountain in 1620 put an end to their hopes. There ensued for Bohemia a period of rigid, Catholic repression led by Jesuit priests and German civilians.

Unhappily for Europe, the conflict did not cease at this point. Reeling under the successes of the Catholic Emperor, the Protestant princes of Germany reorganized and eventually were aided by the forces of Denmark, France and Sweden. For 30 years the war raged, with the Defenestration long forgotten. But, except as a battlefield, these events did not much concern Bohemia. Her interests remained subjected to Hapsburg rule from Vienna. It is true that Prague was occupied briefly by the Bavarian Emperor Charles VII in 1741, but this had scant effect. Mild concessions were made to Czech autonomy, but German continued to be the dominant language. Only in 1918 was the Hapsburg Empire dismembered and a Czechoslovak republic proclaimed.

The arms of Bohemia at the foot of Table 85 show the two-tailed lion over five quarterings. These are for Moravia and Silesia above, with Upper Lusatia (a masoned wall), Teschen and the ox of Lower Lusatia below.

TABLE 88

HUNGARY
General survey

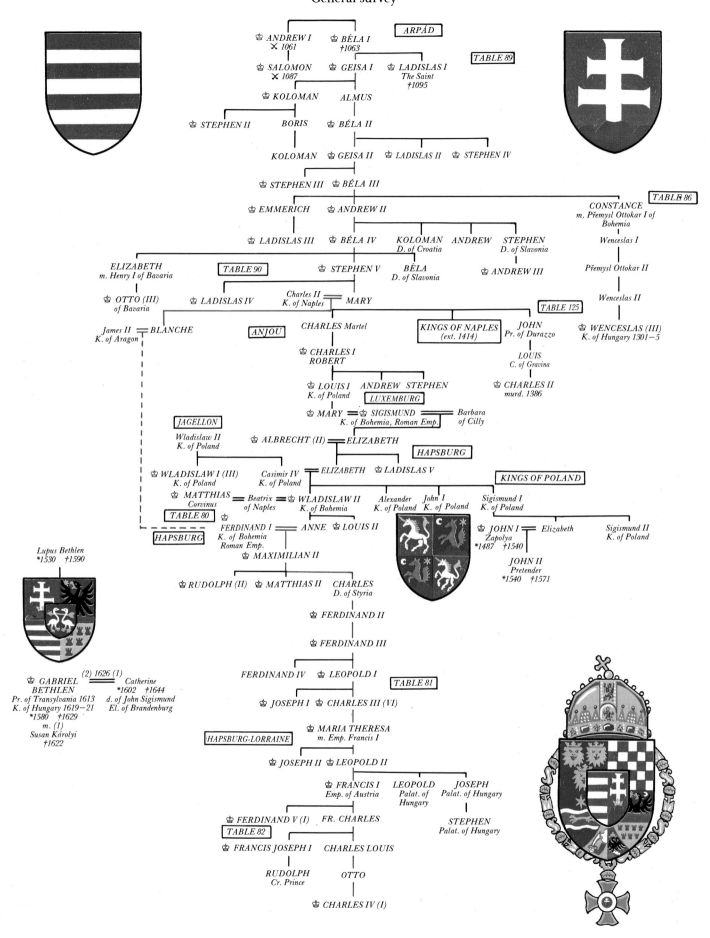

TABLE 89

ARPÁD

♔ ANDREW I
✕ 1061

♔ BÉLA I
†1063

♔ SALOMON
✕ 1087

♔ GEISA I

♔ LADISLAS I
The Saint
†1095

♔ KOLOMAN   ALMUS

♔ STEPHEN II   BORIS   ♔ BÉLA II

KOLOMAN   ♔ GEISA II   ♔ LADISLAS II   ♔ STEPHEN IV

♔ STEPHEN III   ♔ BÉLA III

TABLE 86

♔ EMMERICH   ♔ ANDREW II   CONSTANCE
m. Přemysl Ottokar I of
Bohemia

♔ LADISLAS III   ♔ BÉLA IV   KOLOMAN
D. of Croatia   ANDREW   STEPHEN
D. of Slavonia   Wenceslas I

ELIZABETH
m. Henry I of Bavaria   TABLE 90   ♔ STEPHEN V   BÉLA
D. of Slavonia   ♔ ANDREW III   Přemysl Ottokar II

♔ OTTO (III)
of Bavaria   ♔ LADISLAS IV   Charles II
K. of Naples   MARY   TABLE 125   Wenceslas II

James II
K. of Aragon   BLANCHE   ANJOU   CHARLES Martel   KINGS OF NAPLES
(ext. 1414)   JOHN
Pr. of Durazzo   ♔ WENCESLAS (III)
K. of Hungary 1301–5

♔ CHARLES I
ROBERT   LOUIS
C. of Gravina

♔ LOUIS I
K. of Poland   ANDREW   STEPHEN
LUXEMBURG   ♔ CHARLES II
murd. 1386

JAGELLON   ♔ MARY ══ ♔ SIGISMUND ══ Barbara
K. of Bohemia, Roman Emp.   of Cilly

Wladislaw II
K. of Poland   ♔ ALBRECHT (II) ══ ELIZABETH   HAPSBURG

♔ WLADISLAW I (III)
K. of Poland   Casimir IV ══ ELIZABETH
K. of Poland   ♔ LADISLAS V   KINGS OF POLAND

♔ MATTHIAS
Corvinus ══ Beatrix ══ ♔ WLADISLAW II
of Naples   K. of Bohemia   Alexander
K. of Poland   John I
K. of Poland   Sigismund I
K. of Poland

TABLE 80

♔ FERDINAND I
K. of Bohemia
Roman Emp. ══ ANNE   ♔ LOUIS II   ♔ JOHN I ══ Elizabeth
Zápolya
*1487 †1540   Sigismund II
K. of Poland

HAPSBURG

♔ MAXIMILIAN II   JOHN II
Pretender
*1540 †1571

Lupus Bethlen
*1530 †1590

♔ RUDOLPH (II)   ♔ MATTHIAS II   CHARLES
D. of Styria

♔ FERDINAND II

♔ FERDINAND III

(2) 1626 (1)
♔ GABRIEL ══ Catherine
BETHLEN   *1602 †1644
Pr. of Transylvania 1613   d. of John Sigismund
K. of Hungary 1619–21   El. of Brandenburg
*1580 †1629
m. (1)
Susan Károlyi
†1622   FERDINAND IV   ♔ LEOPOLD I   TABLE 81

♔ JOSEPH I   ♔ CHARLES III (VI)

♔ MARIA THERESA
m. Emp. Francis I

HAPSBURG-LORRAINE

♔ JOSEPH II   ♔ LEOPOLD II

♔ FRANCIS I
Emp. of Austria   LEOPOLD
Palat. of
Hungary   JOSEPH
Palat. of Hungary

♔ FERDINAND V (I)   FR. CHARLES   STEPHEN
Palat. of Hungary

TABLE 82

♔ FRANCIS JOSEPH I   CHARLES LOUIS

RUDOLPH
Cr. Prince   OTTO

♔ CHARLES IV (I)

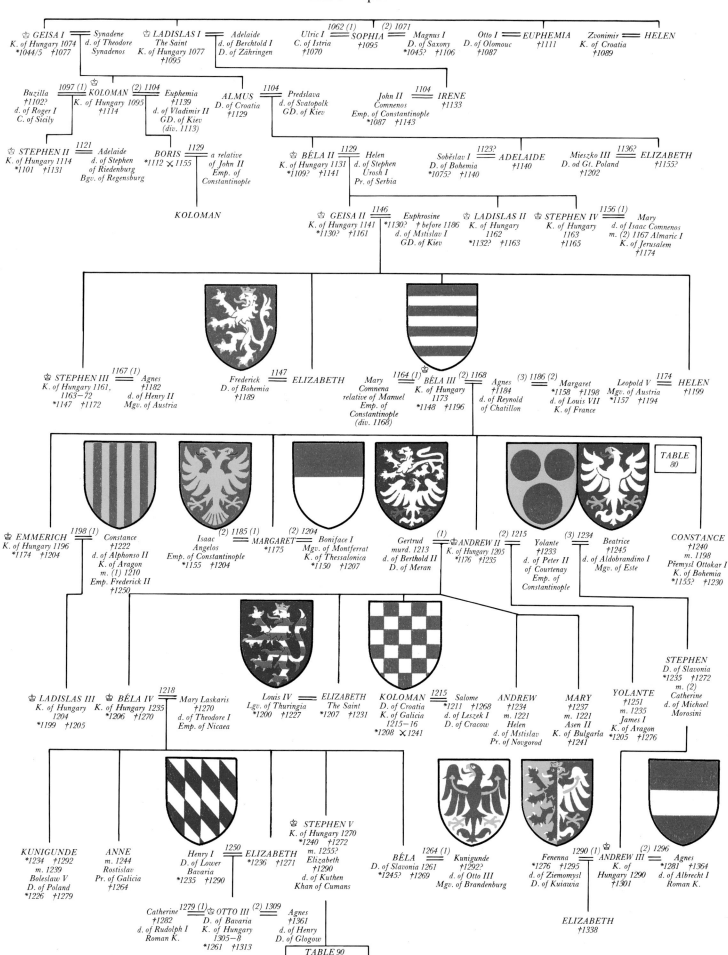

GEISA I
K. of Hungary 1074
*1044/5 †1077
— Synadene
d. of Theodore
Synadenos

LADISLAS I
The Saint
K. of Hungary 1077
†1095
— Adelaide
d. of Berchtold I
D. of Zähringen

Ulric I
C. of Istria
†1070
— 1062 (1) SOPHIA †1095 (2) 1071 — Magnus I
D. of Saxony
*1045? †1106

Otto I
D. of Olomouc
†1087
— EUPHEMIA
†1111

Zvonimir
K. of Croatia
†1089
— HELEN

Buzilla
†1102?
d. of Roger I
C. of Sicily
— 1097 (1) KOLOMAN
K. of Hungary 1095
†1114
(2) 1104 — Euphemia
†1139
d. of Vladimir II
GD. of Kiev
(div. 1113)

ALMUS
D. of Croatia
†1129
— 1104 — Predslava
d. of Svatopolk
GD. of Kiev

John II
Comnenos
Emp. of Constantinople
*1087 †1143
— 1104 — IRENE
†1133

STEPHEN II
K. of Hungary 1114
*1101 †1131
— 1121 — Adelaide
d. of Stephen
of Riedenburg
Bgv. of Regensburg

BORIS
*1112 ✕1155
— 1129 — a relative
of John II
Emp. of
Constantinople

BÉLA II
K. of Hungary 1131
*1109? †1141
— 1129 — Helen
d. of Stephen
Urosh I
Pr. of Serbia

Soběslav I
D. of Bohemia
*1075? †1140
— 1123? — ADELAIDE
†1140

Mieszko III
D. od Gt. Poland
†1202
— 1136? — ELIZABETH
†1155?

KOLOMAN

GEISA II
K. of Hungary 1141
*1130? †1161
— 1146 — Euphrosine
*1130? † before 1186
d. of Mstislav I
GD. of Kiev

LADISLAS II
K. of Hungary
1162
*1132? †1163

STEPHEN IV
K. of Hungary
1163
†1165
— 1156 (1) Mary
d. of Isaac Comnenos
m. (2) 1167 Almaric I
K. of Jerusalem
†1174

STEPHEN III
K. of Hungary 1161,
1163—72
*1147 †1172
— 1167 (1) Agnes
†1182
d. of Henry II
Mgv. of Austria

Frederick
D. of Bohemia
†1189
— 1147 — ELIZABETH

Mary
Comnena
relative of Manuel
Emp. of
Constantinople
(div. 1168)
— 1164 (1) BÉLA III
K. of Hungary 1173
*1148 †1196
(2) 1168 — Agnes
†1184
d. of Reynold
of Chatillon
(3) 1186 (2) — Margaret
*1158 †1198
d. of Louis VII
K. of France

Leopold V
Mgv. of Austria
*1157 †1194
— 1174 — HELEN
†1199

TABLE 80

EMMERICH
K. of Hungary 1196
*1174 †1204
— 1198 (1) Constance
†1222
d. of Alphonso II
K. of Aragon
m. (1) 1210
Emp. Frederick II
†1250

Isaac
Angelos
Emp. of Constantinople
*1155 †1204
— (2) 1185 (1) MARGARET
*1175
(2) 1204 — Boniface I
Mgv. of Montferrat
K. of Thessalonica
*1150 †1207

Gertrud
murd. 1213
d. of Berthold II
D. of Meran
— (1) ANDREW II
K. of Hungary 1205
*1176 †1235
(2) 1215 — Yolante
†1233
d. of Peter II
of Courtenay
Emp. of
Constantinople
(3) 1234 — Beatrice
†1245
d. of Aldobrandino I
Mgv. of Este

CONSTANCE
†1240
m. 1198
Přemysl Ottokar I
K. of Bohemia
*1155? †1230

LADISLAS III
K. of Hungary
1204
*1199 †1205

BÉLA IV
K. of Hungary 1235
*1206 †1270
— 1218 — Mary Laskaris
†1270
d. of Theodore I
Emp. of Nicaea

Louis IV
Lgv. of Thuringia
*1200 †1227
— ELIZABETH
The Saint
*1207 †1231

KOLOMAN
D. of Croatia
K. of Galicia
1215—16
*1208 ✕1241
— 1215 — Salome
*1211 †1268
d. of Leszek I
D. of Cracow

ANDREW
†1234
m. 1221
Helen
d. of Mstislav
Pr. of Novgorod

MARY
†1237
m. 1221
Asen II
K. of Bulgaria
†1241

YOLANTE
†1251
m. 1235
James I
K. of Aragon
*1205 †1276

STEPHEN
D. of Slavonia
*1235 †1272
m. (2)
Catherine
d. of Michael
Morosini

KUNIGUNDE
*1234 †1292
m. 1239
Boleslaw V
D. of Poland
*1226 †1279

ANNE
m. 1244
Rostislav
Pr. of Galicia
†1264

Henry I
D. of Lower
Bavaria
*1235 †1290
— 1250 — ELIZABETH
*1236 †1271

STEPHEN V
K. of Hungary 1270
*1240 †1272
m. 1255?
Elizabeth
†1290
d. of Kuthen
Khan of Cumans

BÉLA
D. of Slavonia 1261
*1245? †1269
— 1264 (1) Kunigunde
†1292?
d. of Otto III
Mgv. of Brandenburg

Fenenna
*1276 †1295
d. of Ziemomysl
D. of Kuiawia
— 1290 (1) ANDREW III
K. of
Hungary 1290
†1301
(2) 1296 — Agnes
*1281 †1364
d. of Albrecht I
Roman K.

Catherine
†1282
d. of Rudolph I
Roman K.
— 1279 (1) OTTO III
D. of Bavaria
K. of Hungary
1305—8
*1261 †1313
(2) 1309 — Agnes
†1361
d. of Henry
D. of Glogow

TABLE 90

ELIZABETH
†1338

TABLE 90

HUNGARY
Houses of Anjou, Luxemburg and Jagellon

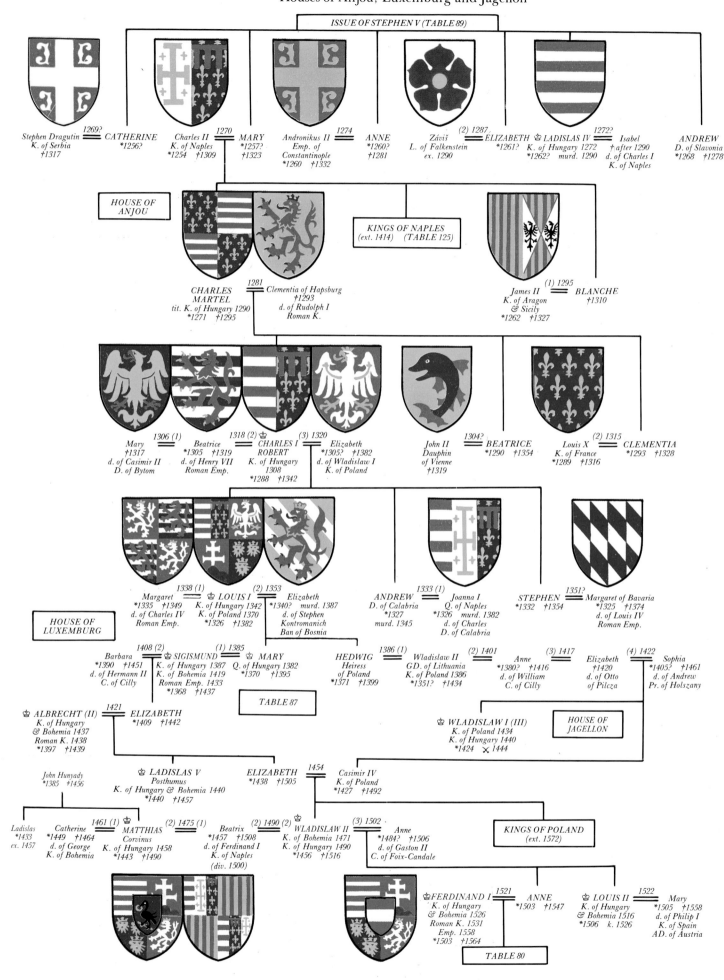

ISSUE OF STEPHEN V (TABLE 89)

Stephen Dragutin ═══ CATHERINE
K. of Serbia   *1256?*
†1317   *1269?*

Charles II ═══ MARY
K. of Naples   *1257?*
*1254 †1309   †1323
1270

Andronikus II ═══ ANNE
Emp. of   *1260?*
Constantinople †1281
*1260 †1332
1274

Záviš
L. of Falkenstein
ex. 1290
(2) 1287

ELIZABETH ⚜ LADISLAS IV ═══ Isabel
1261?   K. of Hungary 1272   †after 1290
          *1262? murd. 1290   d. of Charles I
          1272?   K. of Naples

ANDREW
D. of Slavonia
*1268 †1278

HOUSE OF ANJOU

KINGS OF NAPLES
(ext. 1414)   (TABLE 125)

CHARLES MARTEL ═══ Clementia of Hapsburg
tit. K. of Hungary 1290   †1293
*1271 †1295   d. of Rudolph I
1281   Roman K.

James II ═══ BLANCHE
K. of Aragon   †1310
& Sicily
*1262 †1327
(1) 1295

Mary ═══ Beatrice ═══ CHARLES I ═══ Elizabeth
†1317   *1305 †1319   ROBERT   *1305? †1382
d. of   d. of Henry VII K. of Hungary   d. of Wladislaw I
Casimir II Roman Emp.   1308   K. of Poland
D. of Bytom   *1288 †1342
1306 (1) *1318 (2)* ⚜   *(3) 1320*

John II
Dauphin
of Vienne
†1319

BEATRICE ═══ Louis X ═══ CLEMENTIA
*1290 †1354   K. of France   *1293 †1328
              *1289 †1316
1304?   *(2) 1315*

Margaret ═══ ⚜ LOUIS I ═══ Elizabeth
*1335 †1349   K. of Hungary 1342   *1340? murd. 1387
d. of Charles IV K. of Poland 1370   d. of Stephen
Roman Emp.   *1326 †1382   Kontromanich
1338 (1)   *(2) 1353*   Ban of Bosnia

ANDREW ═══ Joanna I
D. of Calabria   Q. of Naples
*1327   *1326 murd. 1382
murd. 1345   d. of Charles
1333 (1)   D. of Calabria

STEPHEN ═══ Margaret of Bavaria
*1332 †1354   *1325 †1374
1351?   d. of Louis IV
               Roman Emp.

HOUSE OF LUXEMBURG

Barbara ═══ ⚜ SIGISMUND ═══ ⚜ MARY
*1390 †1451   K. of Hungary 1387   Q. of Hungary 1382
d. of Hermann II K. of Bohemia 1419   *1370 †1395
C. of Cilly   Roman Emp. 1433
1408 (2)   *1368 †1437
               (1) 1385

HEDWIG
Heiress
of Poland
*1371 †1399

Wladislaw II ═══ Anne ═══ Elizabeth ═══ Sophia
GD. of Lithuania *1380? †1416   †1420   *1405? †1461
K. of Poland 1386 d. of William   d. of Otto   d. of Andrew
*1351? †1434   C. of Cilly   of Pilcza   Pr. of Holszany
1386 (1)   *(2) 1401*   *(3) 1417*   *(4) 1422*

TABLE 87

⚜ ALBRECHT (II) ═══ ELIZABETH
K. of Hungary   *1409 †1442
& Bohemia 1437
Roman K. 1438
*1397 †1439
1421

⚜ WLADISLAW I (III)
K. of Poland 1434
K. of Hungary 1440
*1424 ✕ 1444

HOUSE OF JAGELLON

John Hunyady
*1385 †1456

⚜ LADISLAS V
Posthumus
K. of Hungary & Bohemia 1440
*1440 †1457

ELIZABETH ═══ Casimir IV
*1438 †1505   K. of Poland
               *1427 †1492
1454

KINGS OF POLAND
(ext. 1572)

Ladislas
*1433
ex. 1457

Catherine ═══ ⚜ MATTHIAS ═══ Beatrix
*1449 †1464   Corvinus   *1457 †1508
d. of George   K. of Hungary 1458   d. of Ferdinand I
K. of Bohemia *1443 †1490   K. of Naples
1461 (1) ⚜   *(2) 1475 (1)*   (div. 1500)

⚜ WLADISLAW II ═══ Anne
K. of Bohemia 1471   *1484? †1506
K. of Hungary 1490   d. of Gaston II
*1456 †1516   C. of Foix-Candale
(2) 1490 (2) ⚜   *(3) 1502*

⚜ FERDINAND I ═══ ANNE
K. of Hungary   *1503 †1547
& Bohemia 1526
Roman K. 1531
Emp. 1558
*1503 †1564
1521

⚜ LOUIS II ═══ Mary
K. of Hungary   *1505 †1558
& Bohemia 1516   d. of Philip I
*1506 k. 1526   K. of Spain
                AD. of Austria
1522

TABLE 80

descent from his mother. This long reign and his generous, chivalric qualities have won him the epithet 'Great'.

At the moment of his death, his elder daughter was engaged to Sigismund of Luxemburg-Bohemia. The people of Poland repudiated this union and preferred his younger daughter, Hedwig, as queen (Table 133). Sigismund was also Emperor and King of Bohemia; it cannot be contended that he did a great deal for Hungary, though he became fonder of that country as his reign wore on. By now it was clear that the principal consideration in Magyar policy was defence against the Turkish menace to the southeast; Sigismund perceived this and among other successes established the strong-point of Belgrade.

Sigismund's son-in-law, Albrecht of Austria, only survived two years; he died in 1439. Four months later his son was born, Ladislas V Posthumus, heir to Hungary and Bohemia. His position was briefly disputed by Wladislaw III, King of Poland. The true leader of Magyar resistance was the able soldier, John Hunyadi. Although he lost battles at Varna (1444), where Wladislaw III fell, and at Kossovo (1448), he won a great victory at Belgrade in 1456, and died of the plague shortly after. Next year (1457) Ladislas himself died, aged seventeen. The lesser nobles, to whom Hunyadi had belonged, contrived to ensure the election of his son, Matthias Corvinus, aged fifteen. Matthias ruled with considerable ability; he conquered part of Bohemia, he built up an efficient army, he reformed the system of taxation, he was a conspicuous patron of the new learning. But although he perceived the need for building up a potent Christian land power against the Turkish menace, he failed to achieve the required power base. His arms (on Table 90) show Hungary, old and new, Dalmatia and Bohemia, with his own raven coat over all.

Matthias had groomed his natural son, János, to follow him, but the Hungarian nobles sought a more pliable master and chose Wladislaw II, King of Bohemia. He was called 'King All Right' because he agreed to everything. When he died in 1516 he left behind him a son of ten, as King of Hungary and of Bohemia. At twenty years old Louis II had to face the massive invasion of Sultan Süleyman; he was overwhelmed and killed at the battle of Mohács in 1526. The event was disastrous for Hungary. Süleyman advanced and captured Buda. The Hungarian nobility chose John Zapolya (Table 88) as king, but his claim was contested by the Archduke Ferdinand (Table 90), brother-in-law of the slain King. In 1538 a compromise was reached: Ferdinand kept Croatia and Slavonia and western Hungary, while John retained eastern Hungary and the title of king until his death in 1540. He was the last native-born and independent ruler of Hungary.

At the death of John Zapolya, it had been agreed that Ferdinand should succeed. An attempt by the Estates of Hungary to choose John's baby son, John II (Table 88), merely led to a fresh Turkish invasion and a continued fragmentation of Hungary. But over the fragmentation lay the shadow of Hapsburg domination, at first from Prague and later from Vienna. Resistance continued in various provinces, notably in Transylvania, but the Magyar lands were in general regarded as an unremunerative part of the Empire. The exclusion of the Austrian Empire from any share in Germany in 1866 made some form of compromise with Hungary essential: in 1867 the Dual Monarchy was established (the *Ausgleich*). Francis Joseph was solemnly crowned as King of Hungary: henceforward all government was to be called Imperial *and* Royal (Kaiserlich und König-lich).

After the First World War, Hungary remained a monarchy, but without a king. Admiral Horthy was regent from 1920 till 1945. The full arms of Hungary, surrounded by the collar of the Order of St Stephen, founded by Maria Theresa in 1764 (Table 88), show a shield of Hungary, old and new, set over quarterings for Dalmatia, Croatia, Slavonia and Transylvania, with in base Bosnia and Fiume.

Chapter 23

BRANDENBURG, PRUSSIA AND GERMANY

The two Powers which have exercised the greatest influence on German history both grew out of frontier provinces. The growth of the Ostmark into Austria has been discussed in Chapter 19: the Mark of Brandenburg is the ancient core of Prussia and hence of the German Empire. Early medieval Germany was divided into five duchies, Lorraine, Franconia, Swabia, Bavaria and Saxony. On the eastern boundary of Saxony, which then covered the north German plain, developed the Mark of Brandenburg. In 1133 the title of Margrave of Brandenburg was conferred on Albrecht the Bear (Table 91) who was also briefly Duke of Saxony. His family is named Ascanian from the Latin name of their castle of Aschersleben; the elder branch ruled Brandenburg until their extinction in 1320, while the younger is still represented by the Princes of Anhalt. The successors of Albrecht the Bear steadily pushed eastwards, first across the Elbe and then across the Oder. New towns like Berlin and Frankfurt marked their progress. Otto II was invested with Pomerania; though not taken up, the claim remained.

After the death of Henry II in 1320, control of the Mark passed to the Wittelsbachs of Bavaria, who exercised it loosely, and from them to the Kings of Bohemia of the Luxemburg House. In 1351 the Emperor Charles IV finally attached the rank of Elector to the Margravate. In 1411 the Emperor Sigismund pawned the province to Frederick of Hohenzollern; he was unable to redeem it and in 1417 Frederick was solemnly installed as Elector and Margrave of Brandenburg. The province was impoverished; the peasants were mainly of Wendish stock, but the squires, or 'Junkers', were predominantly German.

BRANDENBURG

The castle of Zollern, later (1170) Hohenzollern, is in Swabia, not in fact far distant from the castle of Haps-burg. Counts of Zollern are known from the early twelfth century and one of them married the heiress of the Burgraves of Nuremberg. Their son, Frederick, who became Burgrave in 1192, founded the two branches of the Hohenzollern family: both used the dramatically simple shield of four white and black quarters (Table 91). Since the cadet branch became the more important, it may be simpler to deal with the elder first. The descendants of Frederick II acquired the Lordship of Sigmaringen in 1534, and became Princes of the Holy Roman Empire in 1576. There were two main branches, Hohenzollern-Sigmaringen and Hohenzollern-Hechingen, but the latter became extinct in 1869; both had already renounced their territories to Prussia in 1849. In 1866 Prince Charles of Hohenzollern-Sigmaringen became Prince (and later King) of Rumania (Table 147); in 1870 the candidature of his elder brother Leopold for the throne of Spain was a proximate cause of the Franco-Prussian War which ended in 1871.

Conrad, the younger son, maintained the title over Nuremberg. Other Lordships were acquired, including Bayreuth (by marriage, 1234) and Ansbach (by purchase, 1331). Frederick V was a friend and supporter of the Emperor Charles IV, who made him a prince of the Empire in 1363; he divided his lands between his two sons. The younger Frederick, who received Nuremberg (which he later sold to the citizens thereof), was able to purchase the Margravate of Brandenburg and, after his elder brother's death, to reunite the Hohenzollern fiefs. The second great step up the ladder of power had been taken; and Frederick perceived with acumen that the future lay in the north rather than in Nuremberg and Swabia. His province was in disorder, but his resolve was firm: using the new weapon of artillery, he battered his nobility into submission. But for all his realism he was

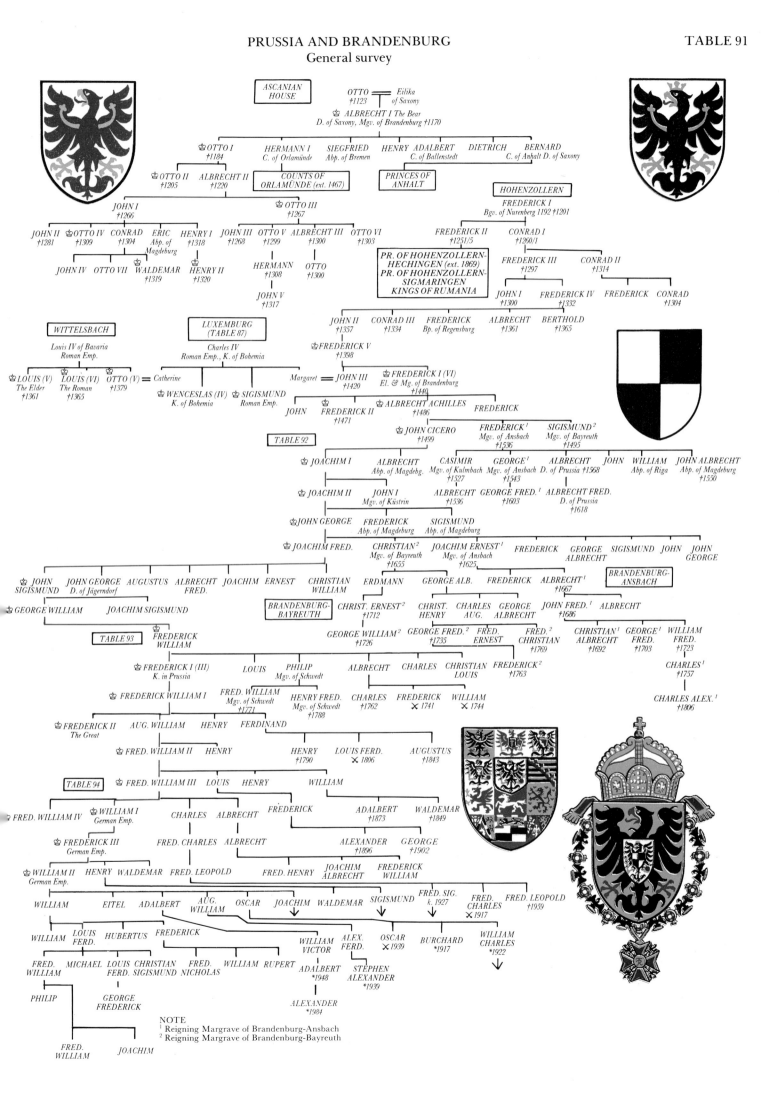

ASCANIAN HOUSE

OTTO †1123 — Eilika of Saxony

☙ ALBRECHT I The Bear D. of Saxony, Mgv. of Brandenburg †1170

OTTO I †1184   HERMANN I C. of Orlamünde   SIEGFRIED Abp. of Bremen   HENRY   ADALBERT C. of Ballenstedt   DIETRICH   BERNARD C. of Anhalt D. of Saxony

OTTO II †1205   ALBRECHT II †1220   COUNTS OF ORLAMÜNDE (ext. 1467)   PRINCES OF ANHALT

HOHENZOLLERN
FREDERICK I Bgv. of Nurenberg 1192 †1201

JOHN I †1266   OTTO III †1267

JOHN II †1281   OTTO IV †1309   CONRAD †1304   ERIC Abp. of Magdeburg   HENRY I †1318   JOHN III †1268   OTTO V †1299   ALBRECHT III †1300   OTTO VI †1303

FREDERICK II †1251/5   CONRAD I †1260/1

JOHN IV   OTTO VII   WALDEMAR †1319   HENRY II †1320   HERMANN †1308   OTTO †1300

FREDERICK III †1297   CONRAD II †1314

PR. OF HOHENZOLLERN-HECHINGEN (ext. 1869)
PR. OF HOHENZOLLERN-SIGMARINGEN
KINGS OF RUMANIA

JOHN V †1317

JOHN I †1300   FREDERICK IV †1332   FREDERICK   CONRAD †1304

WITTELSBACH
Louis IV of Bavaria Roman Emp.

LUXEMBURG (TABLE 87)
Charles IV Roman Emp., K. of Bohemia

JOHN II †1357   CONRAD III †1334   FREDERICK Bp. of Regensburg   ALBRECHT †1361   BERTHOLD †1365

LOUIS (V) The Elder †1361   LOUIS (VI) The Roman †1365   OTTO (V) †1379 = Catherine

FREDERICK V †1398

WENCESLAS (IV) K. of Bohemia   SIGISMUND Roman Emp.

Margaret = JOHN III †1420   FREDERICK I (VI) El. & Mg. of Brandenburg †1440

JOHN   FREDERICK II †1471   ALBRECHT ACHILLES †1486   FREDERICK

TABLE 92

JOHN CICERO †1499   FREDERICK¹ Mgv. of Ansbach †1536   SIGISMUND² Mgv. of Bayreuth †1495

JOACHIM I   ALBRECHT Abp. of Magdebg.   CASIMIR Mgv. of Kulmbach †1527   GEORGE¹ Mgv. of Ansbach †1543   ALBRECHT D. of Prussia †1568   JOHN   WILLIAM Abp. of Riga   JOHN ALBRECHT Abp. of Magdeburg †1550

JOACHIM II   JOHN I Mgv. of Küstrin   ALBRECHT †1536   GEORGE FRED.¹ †1603   ALBRECHT FRED. D. of Prussia †1618

JOHN GEORGE   FREDERICK Abp. of Magdeburg   SIGISMUND Abp. of Magdeburg

JOACHIM FRED.   CHRISTIAN² Mgv. of Bayreuth †1655   JOACHIM ERNEST¹ Mgv. of Ansbach †1625   FREDERICK   GEORGE ALBRECHT   SIGISMUND   JOHN   JOHN GEORGE

JOHN SIGISMUND   JOHN GEORGE D. of Jägerndorf   AUGUSTUS   ALBRECHT FRED.   JOACHIM ERNEST   CHRISTIAN WILLIAM   ERDMANN   GEORGE ALB.   FREDERICK   ALBRECHT¹ †1667   BRANDENBURG-ANSBACH

GEORGE WILLIAM   JOACHIM SIGISMUND   BRANDENBURG-BAYREUTH   CHRIST. ERNEST² †1712   CHRIST. HENRY   CHARLES AUG.   GEORGE ALBRECHT   JOHN FRED.¹ †1686   ALBRECHT

TABLE 93   FREDERICK WILLIAM   GEORGE WILLIAM² †1726   GEORGE FRED.² †1735   FRED. ERNEST   FRED.² CHRISTIAN †1769   CHRISTIAN¹ ALBRECHT †1692   GEORGE¹ FRED. †1703   WILLIAM FRED. †1723

FREDERICK I (III) K. in Prussia   LOUIS   PHILIP Mgv. of Schwedt   ALBRECHT   CHARLES   CHRISTIAN LOUIS   FREDERICK² †1763   CHARLES¹ †1757

FREDERICK WILLIAM I   FRED. WILLIAM Mgv. of Schwedt †1771   HENRY FRED. Mgv. of Schwedt †1788   CHARLES †1762   FREDERICK ✕ 1741   WILLIAM ✕ 1744   CHARLES ALEX.¹ †1806

FREDERICK II The Great   AUG. WILLIAM   HENRY   FERDINAND

FRED. WILLIAM II   HENRY   HENRY †1790   LOUIS FERD. ✕ 1806   AUGUSTUS †1843

TABLE 94   FRED. WILLIAM III   LOUIS   HENRY   WILLIAM

FRED. WILLIAM IV   WILLIAM I German Emp.   CHARLES   ALBRECHT   FREDERICK   ADALBERT †1873   WALDEMAR †1849

FREDERICK III German Emp.   FRED. CHARLES   ALBRECHT   ALEXANDER †1896   GEORGE †1902

WILLIAM II German Emp.   HENRY   WALDEMAR   FRED. LEOPOLD   FRED. HENRY   JOACHIM ALBRECHT   FREDERICK WILLIAM

WILLIAM   EITEL   ADALBERT   AUG. WILLIAM   OSCAR   JOACHIM ↓   WALDEMAR   SIGISMUND ↘   FRED. SIG. k. 1927 ↓   FRED. CHARLES ✕ 1917   FRED. LEOPOLD †1959

WILLIAM   LOUIS FERD.   HUBERTUS   FREDERICK   WILLIAM VICTOR   ALEX. FERD.   OSCAR ✕ 1939   BURCHARD *1917   WILLIAM CHARLES *1922

FRED. WILLIAM   MICHAEL   LOUIS FERD.   CHRISTIAN SIGISMUND   FRED. NICHOLAS   WILLIAM   RUPERT   ADALBERT *1948   STEPHEN ALEXANDER *1939 ↓

PHILIP   GEORGE FREDERICK   ALEXANDER *1984

FRED. WILLIAM   JOACHIM

NOTE
¹ Reigning Margrave of Brandenburg-Ansbach
² Reigning Margrave of Brandenburg-Bayreuth

not proof against the German weakness: at his demise he shared his domains among his offspring. The death without issue of his two eldest sons brought the whole inheritance to Albrecht Achilles. In 1473 he ordained the *Dispositio Achillea* by which the Margravate of Brandenburg was to descend undivided in the male line, while Ansbach and Bayreuth could be allotted to younger sons, but not further divided. It was a momentous decision for the family's future greatness.

Accordingly his eldest son became Margrave while the Franconian fiefs went to the two younger sons. Successive Electors showed themselves men of ability and sense, and bit by bit built up their territories by diplomacy and purchase rather than by war. The shield of Joachim I (Table 92) shows quarterings for Brandenburg, Pomerania, Nuremberg and Hohenzollern, with the sceptre of the Grand-Chamberlain of the Empire over all. His brother Albrecht bears a wider range of quarterings and over all the shields of his three Sees, Halberstadt, Magdeburg and Mainz. The red eagle of Brandenburg can also be seen at the head of Table 91; the gold outline on the wings was originally a suggestion of anatomical structure, but developed into an addition, the *kleestengel* (clover-stalk), susceptible to variations and very typical of German heraldry. The Electors embraced the Lutheran faith, and Joachim II added three secularized bishoprics to his lands. But a greater prize was already in sight.

PRUSSIA

The Teutonic Order of Knights had been established at the end of the twelfth century to combat the infidel in the Holy Land. In 1229 a contingent was sent to fight the pagans in Prussia, and this became their only theatre of activity. The lands they conquered were controlled by great castles and towns like Königsberg. In 1511 the Order, after a period of decline, chose Albrecht of Hohenzollern-Ansbach (Table 91) as Grand-Master. Fourteen years later, the soldier-priest secularized the Order, married, and became Duke of Prussia under the King of Poland. His kinsmen were quick to see their chance. Duke Albrecht's son, Albrecht Frederick, proved to be an imbecile; and he sired only daughters. The Elector Joachim Frederick married one as his second wife, and his son, John Sigismund (Table 92) espoused the eldest. In 1618 the Duchy of Prussia passed to the latter. Nor was this all. The wife of the unhappy Duke Albrecht Frederick was a sister of the Duke of Cleves and Jülich, who died childless in 1609. His inheritance in the Rhineland was wealthy, and the claimants turned to the sword. The local struggle became part of the Thirty Years' War, and it was not until 1666 that Cleves, Mark and Ravenstein were finally allotted to Brandenburg as its share. Mean-

while Bayreuth and Ansbach, which had reverted to Elector Joachim Frederick, had been regranted to his younger brothers, Christian and Joachim Ernest. The shield of Elector George William, at the base of Table 92, now shows, beneath the imperial sceptre, quarterings for Prussia (a black eagle), Brandenburg (a red one), Berg, Cleves, Jülich, Nuremberg and Hohenzollern. George William himself was more interested in hunting than statecraft; he had great difficulty in making up his mind, and achieved only a policy of unrewarded neutrality until in 1631 he allied with his brother-in-law, Gustavus Adolphus of Sweden. In 1637 the last Duke of Pomerania died and the Elector claimed the Duchy as his right. Brandenburg was ravaged by war when he died in 1640.

His son was of different mettle. Not for nothing is Frederick William (Table 93) called the Great Elector. His long reign transformed his state and laid the foundations of future Prussian greatness. His resources were meagre, his realm devastated, but his supple diplomacy and dynamic powers of organization triumphed over these handicaps. At the Treaty of Westphalia he secured the eastern half of Pomerania (Sweden kept the west), the bishoprics of Halberstadt and Minden and the reversion of the larger diocese of Magdeburg. Already Brandenburg looked more powerful. In the wars between Sweden and Poland he adroitly changed sides and freed the Duchy of Prussia from any Polish suzerainty: the Elector was now its independent prince, though Prussia was still cut off by part of Poland from Brandenburg. The prestige of his forces was greatly enhanced by a victory over the hitherto invincible Swedes at Fehrbellin in 1679. Behind the complicated and unscrupulous foreign policy of the Elector lay a thorough reorganization of his realm. Berlin was mainly his creation and he was interested in science. But above all he welded Prussia and Brandenburg into an efficient and militarist instrument of absolute monarchy. The Prussian army was henceforward a factor in European politics.

In 1701, with the consent of the Emperor, Frederick III, son of the Great Elector, took the title of King *in* Prussia. This was permissible because that province lay outside the boundaries of the Holy Roman Empire, but it had also to be recognized that much of West Prussia was still in Polish hands. He crowned himself, with no priestly aid, at Königsberg; and on the same day founded the Order of the Black Eagle, whose collar can be seen on Table 91. Furthermore, he placed his initials FR on the breast of the Prussian eagle on his shield (Table 93). Despite his participation in the War of the Spanish Succession against Louis XIV his gains were negligible save for the general recognition of his kingship. The arms of his half-brother Philip show the black eagle of Prussia and the red of Brandenburg in a black and white border.

Frederick William I was a boorish and beery figure. For 27 years he ruled his Kingdom with routine military efficiency, lavishing attention on an army which was seldom launched into battle, and for which he collected outsize men with the zeal of a circus-proprietor. This army was increased from under 40,000 to over 80,000 men, but was only maintained at this figure by the use of mercenaries, merciless conscription and iron discipline. On his deathbed, hearing the words 'Naked I came into this world, and naked I shall leave it,' the King muttered, 'No, no, I shall have my uniform'. He had added Stettin and most of western Pomerania to his territory, but Sweden clung to Stralsund and the isle of Rügen.

FREDERICK THE GREAT

Frederick II, the Great, is one of the dazzling figures of history. His talents and success are indisputable; his behaviour at times was odious. Much may be attributed to his bitter youth under a drill-sergeant father, when he had to learn French or the flute by subterfuge. The German tongue he grew to loathe. Cynic, atheist, follower of Voltaire, he was without scruple and without a real friend. His first action was shamelessly to attack Maria Theresa of Austria and to seize the rich province of Silesia; in his first battle he fled, though his troops triumphed. With brutal self-interest he then switched sides: by the Treaty of Berlin (1742) he legitimized his conquest and augmented Brandenburg with Silesia. At this juncture his title was altered to King *of* Prussia. Many of his later campaigns were waged to defend this conquest, particularly the Seven Years' War (1756–63) in which he was allied with Britain against France and Austria; Britain laid the foundation of her overseas Empire at the expense of France. On the Continent Frederick II was hard pushed to preserve Prussia, and his victories against odds at Rosbach and Leuthen (1757) are clear evidence of his military brilliance. In 1759 he was again almost defeated; the highly trained army of his father was no more, and his country was ravaged by the Russians. With poison ready for suicide, the King fought on and his reputation hindered his adversaries from pressing home their attacks. A change of sovereign in Russia removed one foe; and when peace came in 1763, Frederick had just contrived to preserve Silesia and the prestige of Prussia. He was ably assisted by his brother Henry, a highly competent commander.

The ensuing years were devoted to refashioning the material resources of Prussia. Agriculture and trade were fostered: a new army constituted. The next coup came in 1772, when, in alliance with Russia, he coerced Austria into the first partition of Poland. West Prussia fell to Frederick's share, and his two principal provinces were no longer separated. Prussia was now beyond all question a major European Power: Frederick II had more than doubled her area and far more than doubled the size of her army. A master of war and movement, a diplomat devoid of any principle save the aggrandizement of Prussia, the little King in the faded blue coat had triumphed from the very edge of ruin. His ancestry (Table 95) shows a predominance of Hanover-Brunswick blood, and a quarter descent from Bavaria. It is tempting to connect Frederick II's affection for the French language with his French forebear, Eleanor d'Olbreuse.

PRUSSIA AND NAPOLEON

The marriage of Frederick II was childless as it was loveless; his successor was his nephew Frederick William II. Faced with the impact of the French Revolution, he made peace with the Republicans and turned his attention to further subdivision of the hapless Polish Kingdom. In 1793 Russia and Prussia cold-bloodedly helped themselves to vast areas of northern Poland; two years later Prussia acquired a further sizeable block of territory including Warsaw. Poland had been obliterated. Frederick William II added to the arms of Prussia the sceptre and orb of royalty. Frederick William III saw no point in attacking Napoleon; when Napoleon attacked him, he was without friends. At Jena in 1806 the French Emperor annihilated the old Prussian army and its reputation, a few weeks after Francis of Austria had jettisoned the ghostly title of Holy Roman Emperor. Bonaparte entered Berlin and desecrated the tomb of Frederick the Great, dead a mere twenty years. It was the nadir of the Prussian fortunes.

The Treaty of Tilsit (1807) deprived Prussia of all provinces west of the river Elbe and of all she had gained from the partitions of Poland; in the circumstances the terms were not ungenerous. Frederick William III, though more virtuous than his father, was a sovereign of limited imagination and powers; fortunately for his dynasty he was able to recruit an able group of ministers, mainly from outside his own realms. Scharnhorst and Gneisenau set about military reform of the army; Humboldt tackled education; over and above all Stein began the general reorganization of the administration. Serfdom was abolished (1807); centralization was diminished; teaching was modernized. Meanwhile a new army was being created with Blücher as its commander, and proved its worth at the battles of Leipzig (1813) and Waterloo (1815).

The Treaty of Vienna constitutes another milestone in the growth of Prussia. It is true she did not recover all the lands she had filched from Poland, but the compensation elsewhere was more than adequate. Most important was the acquisition of a

TABLE 92

BRANDENBURG
House of Hohenzollern in the sixteenth and early seventeenth centuries

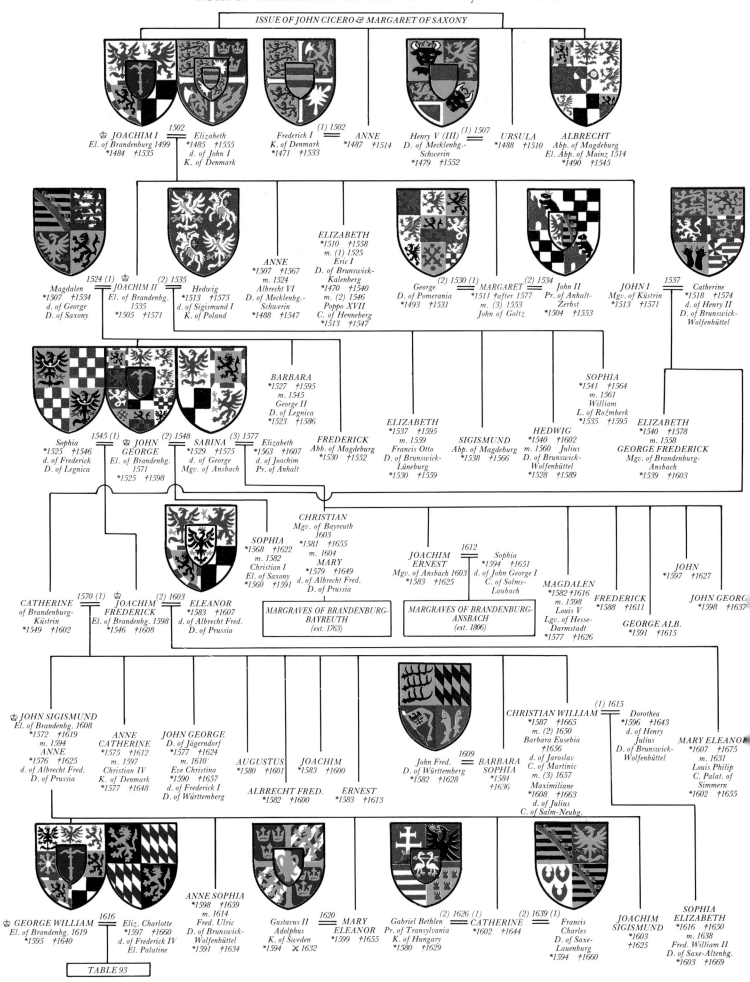

ISSUE OF JOHN CICERO & MARGARET OF SAXONY

♔ JOACHIM I
El. of Brandenburg 1499
*1484 †1535

1502

Elizabeth
*1485 †1555
d. of John I
K. of Denmark

Frederick I
K. of Denmark
*1471 †1533

(1) 1502

ANNE
*1487 †1514

Henry V (III)
D. of Mecklenbg.-
Schwerin
*1479 †1552

(1) 1507

URSULA
*1488 †1510

ALBRECHT
Abp. of Magdeburg
El. Abp. of Mainz 1514
*1490 †1545

Magdalen
*1507 †1534
d. of George
D. of Saxony

1524 (1)

♔ JOACHIM II
El. of Brandenbg.
1535
*1505 †1571

(2) 1535

Hedwig
*1513 †1573
d. of Sigismund I
K. of Poland

ANNE
*1507 †1567
m. 1524
Albrecht VI
D. of Mecklenbg.-
Schwerin
*1488 †1547

ELIZABETH
*1510 †1558
m. (1) 1525
Eric I
D. of Brunswick-
Kalenberg
*1470 †1540
m. (2) 1546
Poppo XVII
C. of Henneberg
*1513 †1547

George
D. of Pomerania
*1493 †1531

(2) 1530 (1)

MARGARET
*1511 †after 1577
m. (3) 1553
John of Goltz

(2) 1534

John II
Pr. of Anhalt-
Zerbst
*1504 †1553

JOHN I
Mgv. of Küstrin
*1513 †1571

1537

Catherine
*1518 †1574
d. of Henry II
D. of Brunswick-
Wolfenbüttel

Sophia
*1525 †1546
d. of Frederick
D. of Legnica

1545 (1)

♔ JOHN
GEORGE
El. of Brandenbg.
1571
*1525 †1598

(2) 1548

SABINA
*1529 †1575
d. of George
Mgv. of Ansbach

(3) 1577

Elizabeth
*1563 †1607
d. of Joachim
Pr. of Anhalt

BARBARA
*1527 †1595
m. 1545
George II
D. of Legnica
*1523 †1586

FREDERICK
Abb. of Magdeburg
*1530 †1552

ELIZABETH
*1537 †1595
m. 1559
Francis Otto
D. of Brunswick-
Lüneburg
*1530 †1559

SIGISMUND
Abp. of Magdeburg
*1538 †1566

SOPHIA
*1541 †1564
m. 1561
William
L. of Rožmberk
*1535 †1595

HEDWIG
*1540 †1602
m. 1560 Julius
D. of Brunswick-
Wolfenbüttel
*1528 †1589

ELIZABETH
*1540 †1578
m. 1558
GEORGE FREDERICK
Mgv. of Brandenburg-
Ansbach
*1539 †1603

SOPHIA
*1568 †1622
m. 1582
Christian I
El. of Saxony
*1560 †1591

CHRISTIAN
Mgv. of Bayreuth
1603
*1581 †1655
m. 1604
MARY
*1579 †1649
d. of Albrecht Fred.
D. of Prussia

JOACHIM
ERNEST
Mgv. of Ansbach 1603
*1583 †1625

1612

Sophia
*1594 †1651
d. of John George I
C. of Solms-
Laubach

MAGDALEN
*1582 †1616
m. 1598
Louis V
Lgv. of Hesse-
Darmstadt
*1577 †1626

FREDERICK
*1588 †1611

JOHN
*1597 †1627

JOHN GEORG
*1598 †1637

GEORGE ALB.
*1591 †1615

MARGRAVES OF BRANDENBURG-
BAYREUTH
(ext. 1763)

MARGRAVES OF BRANDENBURG-
ANSBACH
(ext. 1806)

CATHERINE
of Brandenburg-
Küstrin
*1549 †1602

1570 (1)

♔ JOACHIM
FREDERICK
El. of Brandenbg. 1598
*1546 †1608

(2) 1603

ELEANOR
*1583 †1607
d. of Albrecht Fred.
D. of Prussia

♔ JOHN SIGISMUND
El. of Brandenbg. 1608
*1572 †1619
m. 1594
ANNE
*1576 †1625
d. of Albrecht Fred.
D. of Prussia

ANNE
CATHERINE
*1575 †1612
m. 1597
Christian IV
K. of Denmark
*1577 †1648

JOHN GEORGE
D. of Jägerndorf
*1577 †1624
m. 1610
Eve Christina
*1590 †1657
d. of Frederick I
D. of Württemberg

AUGUSTUS
*1580 †1601

JOACHIM
*1583 †1600

ALBRECHT FRED.
*1582 †1600

ERNEST
*1583 †1613

John Fred.
D. of Württemberg
*1582 †1628

1609

BARBARA
SOPHIA
*1584
†1636

CHRISTIAN WILLIAM
*1587 †1665
m. (2) 1650
Barbara Eusebia
†1656
d. of Jaroslav
C. of Martinic
m. (3) 1657
Maximiliane
*1608 †1663
d. of Julius
C. of Salm-Neubg.

(1) 1615

Dorothea
*1596 †1643
d. of Henry
Julius
D. of Brunswick-
Wolfenbüttel

MARY ELEANOR
*1607 †1675
m. 1631
Louis Philip
C. Palat. of
Simmern
*1602 †1655

♔ GEORGE WILLIAM
El. of Brandenbg. 1619
*1595 †1640

1616

Eliz. Charlotte
*1597 †1660
d. of Frederick IV
El. Palatine

ANNE SOPHIA
*1598 †1659
m. 1614
Fred. Ulric
D. of Brunswick-
Wolfenbüttel
*1591 †1634

Gustavus II
Adolphus
K. of Sweden
*1594 ✕ 1632

1620

MARY
ELEANOR
*1599 †1655

Gabriel Bethlen
Pr. of Transylvania
K. of Hungary
*1580 †1629

(2) 1626 (1)

CATHERINE
*1602 †1644

(2) 1639 (1)

Francis
Charles
D. of Saxe-
Lauenburg
*1594 †1660

JOACHIM
SIGISMUND
*1603
†1625

SOPHIA
ELIZABETH
*1616 †1650
m. 1638
Fred. William II
D. of Saxe-Altenbg.
*1603 †1669

TABLE 93

TABLE 93

PRUSSIA
First Kings

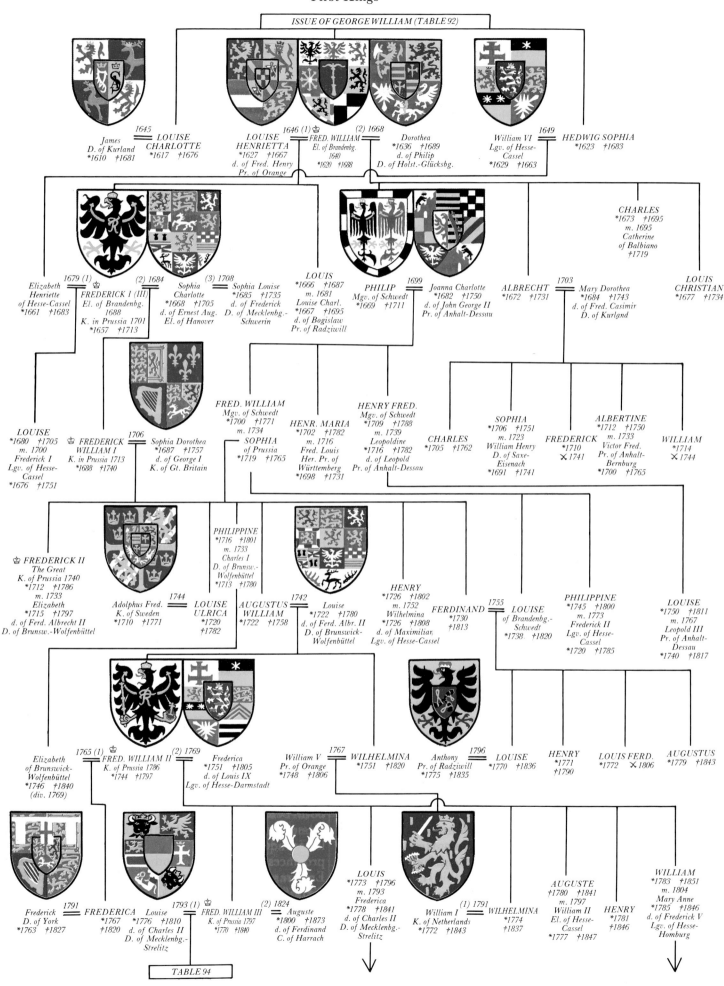

ISSUE OF GEORGE WILLIAM (TABLE 92)

1645 — *James D. of Kurland* *1610 †1681 = **LOUISE CHARLOTTE** *1617 †1676

LOUISE HENRIETTA *1627 †1667 d. of Fred. Henry Pr. of Orange = **1646 (1)** **FRED. WILLIAM** El. of Brandenbg. 1640 *1620 †1688 **(2) 1668** = *Dorothea* *1636 †1689 d. of Philip D. of Holst.-Glücksbg.

William VI Lgv. of Hesse-Cassel *1629 †1663 = **1649** **HEDWIG SOPHIA** *1623 †1683

CHARLES *1673 †1695 m. 1695 Catherine of Balbiano †1719

Elizabeth Henriette of Hesse-Cassel *1661 †1683 = **1679 (1)** **FREDERICK I (III)** El. of Brandenbg. 1688 K. in Prussia 1701 *1657 †1713 **(2) 1684** = *Sophia Charlotte* *1668 †1705 d. of Ernest Aug. El. of Hanover **(3) 1708** = *Sophia Louise* *1685 †1735 D. of Mecklenbg.-Schwerin

LOUIS *1666 †1687 m. 1681 Louise Charl. *1667 †1695 d. of Bogislaw Pr. of Radziwill

PHILIP Mgv. of Schwedt *1669 †1711 = **1699** *Joanna Charlotte* *1682 †1750 d. of John George II Pr. of Anhalt-Dessau

ALBRECHT *1672 †1731 = **1703** *Mary Dorothea* *1684 †1743 d. of Fred. Casimir D. of Kurland

LOUIS CHRISTIAN *1677 †1734

LOUISE *1680 †1705 m. 1700 Frederick Lgv. of Hesse-Cassel *1676 †1751

FREDERICK WILLIAM I K. in Prussia 1713 *1688 †1740 = **1706** *Sophia Dorothea* *1687 †1757 d. of George I K. of Gt. Britain

FRED. WILLIAM Mgv. of Schwedt *1700 †1771 m. 1734 **SOPHIA** of Prussia *1719 †1765

HENR. MARIA *1702 †1782 m. 1716 Fred. Louis Her. Pr. of Württemberg *1698 †1731

HENRY FRED. Mgv. of Schwedt *1709 †1788 m. 1739 Leopoldine *1716 †1782 d. of Leopold Pr. of Anhalt-Dessau

CHARLES *1705 †1762

SOPHIA *1706 †1751 m. 1723 William Henry D. of Saxe-Eisenach *1691 †1741

FREDERICK *1710 ✕1741

ALBERTINE *1712 †1750 m. 1733 Victor Fred. Pr. of Anhalt-Bernburg *1700 †1765

WILLIAM *1714 ✕1744

*Elizabeth *1715 †1797 d. of Ferd. Albrecht II D. of Brunsw.-Wolfenbüttel* = **FREDERICK II** The Great K. of Prussia 1740 *1712 †1786 m. 1733

Adolphus Fred. K. of Sweden *1710 †1771 = **1744** **LOUISE ULRICA** *1720 †1782

AUGUSTUS WILLIAM *1722 †1758 = **1742** *Louise *1722 †1780 d. of Ferd. Albr. II D. of Brunswick-Wolfenbüttel*

HENRY *1726 †1802 m. 1752 Wilhelmina *1726 †1808 d. of Maximilian Lgv. of Hesse-Cassel

FERDINAND *1730 †1813 = **1755** **LOUISE** of Brandenbg.-Schwedt *1738 †1820

PHILIPPINE *1716 †1801 m. 1733 Charles I D. of Brunsw.-Wolfenbüttel *1713 †1780

PHILIPPINE *1745 †1800 m. 1773 Frederick II Lgv. of Hesse-Cassel *1720 †1785

LOUISE *1750 †1811 m. 1767 Leopold III Pr. of Anhalt-Dessau *1740 †1817

Elizabeth of Brunswick-Wolfenbüttel *1746 †1840 (div. 1769) = **1765 (1)** **FRED. WILLIAM II** K. of Prussia 1786 *1744 †1797 **(2) 1769** = *Frederica* *1751 †1805 d. of Louis IX Lgv. of Hesse-Darmstadt

William V Pr. of Orange *1748 †1806 = **1767** **WILHELMINA** *1751 †1820

Anthony Pr. of Radziwill *1775 †1835 = **1796** **LOUISE** *1770 †1836

HENRY *1771 †1790

LOUIS FERD. *1772 ✕1806

AUGUSTUS *1779 †1843

Frederick D. of York *1763 †1827 = **1791** **FREDERICA** *1767 †1820

*Louise *1776 †1810 d. of Charles II D. of Mecklenbg.-Strelitz* = **1793 (1)** **FRED. WILLIAM III** K. of Prussia 1797 *1770 †1840 **(2) 1824** = *Auguste *1800 †1873 d. of Ferdinand C. of Harrach*

LOUIS *1773 †1796 m. 1793 Frederica *1778 †1841 d. of Charles II D. of Mecklenbg.-Strelitz

William I K. of Netherlands *1772 †1843 = **(1) 1791** **WILHELMINA** *1774 †1837

AUGUSTE *1780 †1841 m. 1797 William II El. of Hesse-Cassel *1777 †1847

HENRY *1781 †1846

WILLIAM *1783 †1851 m. 1804 Mary Anne *1785 †1846 d. of Frederick V Lgv. of Hesse-Homburg

TABLE 94

TABLE 94

PRUSSIA AND THE GERMAN EMPIRE
End of the monarchy

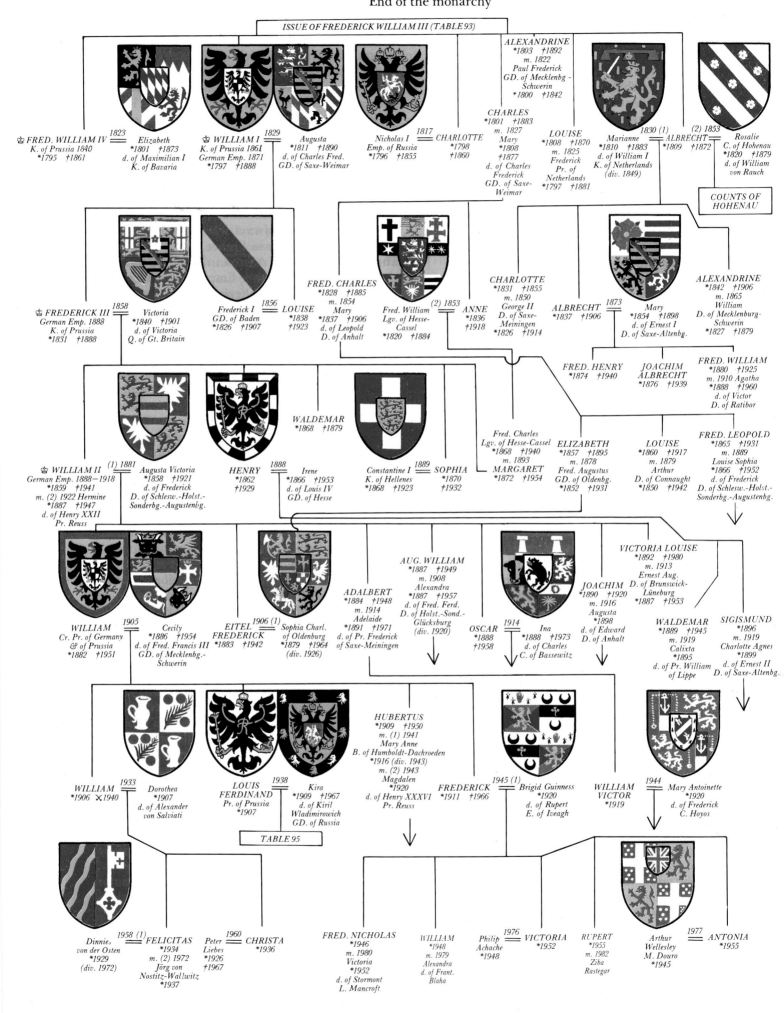

ISSUE OF FREDERICK WILLIAM III (TABLE 93)

♚ FRED. WILLIAM IV
K. of Prussia 1840
*1795 †1861
— 1823 —
Elizabeth
*1801 †1873
d. of Maximilian I
K. of Bavaria

♚ WILLIAM I
K. of Prussia 1861
German Emp. 1871
*1797 †1888
— 1829 —
Augusta
*1811 †1890
d. of Charles Fred.
GD. of Saxe-Weimar

Nicholas I
Emp. of Russia
*1796 †1855
— 1817 —
CHARLOTTE
*1798
†1860

CHARLES
*1801 †1883
m. 1827
Mary
*1808
†1877
d. of Charles
Frederick
GD. of Saxe-
Weimar

ALEXANDRINE
*1803 †1892
m. 1822
Paul Frederick
GD. of Mecklenbg.-
Schwerin
*1800 †1842

LOUISE
*1808 †1870
m. 1825
Frederick
Pr. of
Netherlands
*1797 †1881

Marianne
*1810 †1883
d. of William I
K. of Netherlands
(div. 1849)
— 1830 (1) —
ALBRECHT
*1809 †1872
— (2) 1853 —
Rosalie
C. of Hohenau
*1820 †1879
d. of William
von Rauch

COUNTS OF
HOHENAU

♚ FREDERICK III
German Emp. 1888
K. of Prussia
*1831 †1888
— 1858 —
Victoria
*1840 †1901
d. of Victoria
Q. of Gt. Britain

Frederick I
GD. of Baden
*1826 †1907
— 1856 —
LOUISE
*1838
†1923

FRED. CHARLES
*1828 †1885
m. 1854
Mary
*1837 †1906
d. of Leopold
D. of Anhalt

Fred. William
Lgv. of Hesse-
Cassel
*1820 †1884
— (2) 1853 —
ANNE
*1836
†1918

CHARLOTTE
*1831 †1855
m. 1850
George II
D. of Saxe-
Meiningen
*1826 †1914

ALBRECHT
*1837 †1906
— 1873 —
Mary
*1854 †1898
d. of Ernest I
D. of Saxe-Altenbg.

ALEXANDRINE
*1842 †1906
m. 1865
William
D. of Mecklenburg-
Schwerin
*1827 †1879

FRED. HENRY
*1874 †1940

JOACHIM
ALBRECHT
*1876 †1939

FRED. WILLIAM
*1880 †1925
m. 1910 Agatha
*1888 †1960
d. of Victor
D. of Ratibor

♚ WILLIAM II
German Emp. 1888–1918
*1859 †1941
m. (2) 1922 Hermine
*1887 †1947
d. of Henry XXII
Pr. Reuss
— (1) 1881 —
Augusta Victoria
*1858 †1921
d. of Frederick
D. of Schlesw.-Holst.-
Sonderbg.-Augustenbg.

HENRY
*1862
†1929
— 1888 —
Irene
*1866 †1953
d. of Louis IV
GD. of Hesse

WALDEMAR
*1868 †1879

Constantine I
K. of Hellenes
*1868 †1923
— 1889 —
SOPHIA
*1870
†1932

Fred. Charles
Lgv. of Hesse-Cassel
*1868 †1940
m. 1893
MARGARET
*1872 †1954

ELIZABETH
*1857 †1895
m. 1878
Fred. Augustus
GD. of Oldenbg.
*1852 †1931

LOUISE
*1860 †1917
m. 1879
Arthur
D. of Connaught
*1850 †1942

FRED. LEOPOLD
*1865 †1931
Louise Sophia
*1866 †1952
d. of Frederick
D. of Schlesw.-Holst.-
Sonderbg.-Augustenbg.

WILLIAM
Cr. Pr. of Germany
& of Prussia
*1882 †1951
— 1905 —
Cecily
*1886 †1954
d. of Fred. Francis III
GD. of Mecklenburg.-
Schwerin

EITEL
FREDERICK
*1883 †1942
— 1906 (1) —
Sophia Charl.
of Oldenburg
*1879 †1964
(div. 1926)

ADALBERT
*1884 †1948
m. 1914
Adelaide
*1891 †1971
d. of Pr. Frederick
of Saxe-Meiningen

AUG. WILLIAM
*1887 †1949
m. 1908
Alexandra
*1887 †1957
d. of Fred. Ferd.
D. of Holst.-Sond.-
Glücksburg
(div. 1920)

OSCAR
*1888
†1958
— 1914 —
Ina
*1888 †1973
d. of Charles
C. of Bassewitz

JOACHIM
*1890 †1920
m. 1916
Augusta
*1898
d. of Edward
D. of Anhalt

VICTORIA LOUISE
*1892 †1980
m. 1913
Ernest Aug.
D. of Brunswick-
Lüneburg
*1887 †1953

WALDEMAR
*1889 †1945
m. 1919
Calixta
*1895
d. of Pr. William
of Lippe

SIGISMUND
*1896
m. 1919
Charlotte Agnes
*1899
d. of Ernest II
D. of Saxe-Altenbg.

WILLIAM
*1906 ×1940
— 1933 —
Dorothea
*1907
d. of Alexander
von Salviati

LOUIS
FERDINAND
Pr. of Prussia
*1907
— 1938 —
Kira
*1909 †1967
d. of Kiril
Wladimirowich
GD. of Russia

TABLE 95

HUBERTUS
*1909 †1950
m. (1) 1941
Mary Anne
B. of Humboldt-Dachroeden
*1916 (div. 1943)
m. (2) 1943
Magdalen
*1920
d. of Henry XXXVI
Pr. Reuss

FREDERICK
*1911 †1966
— 1945 (1) —
Brigid Guinness
*1920
d. of Rupert
E. of Iveagh

WILLIAM
VICTOR
*1919

Mary Antoinette
*1920
d. of Frederick
C. Hoyos
— 1944 —

Dinnies
von der Osten
*1929
(div. 1972)
— 1958 (1) —
FELICITAS
*1934
m. (2) 1972
Jörg von
Nostitz-Wallwitz
*1937

Peter
Liebes
*1926
†1967
— 1960 —
CHRISTA
*1936

FRED. NICHOLAS
*1946
m. 1980
Victoria
*1952
d. of Stormont
L. Mancroft

WILLIAM
*1948
m. 1979
Alexandra
d. of Frant.
Blaha

Philip
Achache
*1948
— 1976 —
VICTORIA
*1952

RUPERT
*1955
m. 1982
Ziba
Rastegar

Arthur
Wellesley
M. Douro
*1945
— 1977 —
ANTONIA
*1955

TABLE 95

PRUSSIA
Main line in the twentieth century

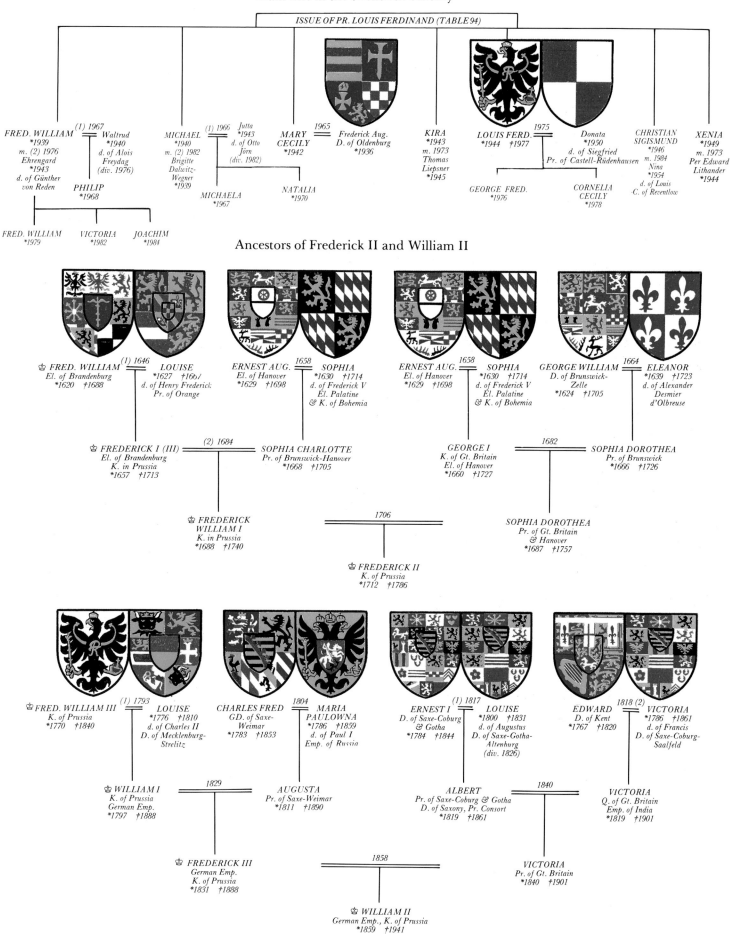

ISSUE OF PR. LOUIS FERDINAND (TABLE 94)

FRED. WILLIAM — (1) 1967 — Waltrud
*1939   *1940
m. (2) 1976   d. of Alois
Ehrengard   Freydag
*1943   (div. 1976)
d. of Günther
von Reden
      PHILIP
      *1968

MICHAEL — (1) 1966 — Jutta
*1940   *1943
m. (2) 1982   d. of Otto
Brigitte   Jörn
Dalwitz-   (div. 1982)
Wegner
*1939
   MICHAELA
   *1967

MARY
CECILY   1965   Frederick Aug.
*1942   D. of Oldenburg
         *1936

NATALIA
*1970

KIRA
*1943
m. 1973
Thomas
Liepsner
*1945

LOUIS FERD. — 1975 — Donata
*1944 †1977   *1950
          d. of Siegfried
         Pr. of Castell-Rüdenhausen

GEORGE FRED.   CORNELIA
*1976   CECILY
             *1978

CHRISTIAN
SIGISMUND
*1946
m. 1984
Nina
*1954
d. of Louis
C. of Reventlow

XENIA
*1949
m. 1973
Per Edward
Lithander
*1944

FRED. WILLIAM   VICTORIA   JOACHIM
*1979   *1982   *1984

Ancestors of Frederick II and William II

♛ FRED. WILLIAM — (1) 1646 — LOUISE
El. of Brandenburg   *1627 †166/
*1620 †1688   d. of Henry Frederick
            Pr. of Orange

ERNEST AUG. — 1658 — SOPHIA
El. of Hanover   *1630 †1714
*1629 †1698   d. of Frederick V
          Él. Palatine
          & K. of Bohemia

ERNEST AUG. — 1658 — SOPHIA
El. of Hanover   *1630 †1714
*1629 †1698   d. of Frederick V
          Él. Palatine
          & K. of Bohemia

GEORGE WILLIAM — 1664 — ELEANOR
D. of Brunswick-   *1639 †1723
Zelle   d. of Alexander
*1624 †1705   Desmier
            d'Olbreuse

♛ FREDERICK I (III) — (2) 1684 — SOPHIA CHARLOTTE
El. of Brandenburg   Pr. of Brunswick-Hanover
K. in Prussia   *1668 †1705
*1657 †1713

GEORGE I — 1682 — SOPHIA DOROTHEA
K. of Gt. Britain   Pr. of Brunswick
El. of Hanover   *1666 †1726
*1660 †1727

♛ FREDERICK
WILLIAM I
K. in Prussia
*1688 †1740

— 1706 —

SOPHIA DOROTHEA
Pr. of Gt. Britain
& Hanover
*1687 †1757

♛ FREDERICK II
K. of Prussia
*1712 †1786

♛ FRED. WILLIAM III — (1) 1793 — LOUISE
K. of Prussia   *1776 †1810
*1770 †1840   d. of Charles II
           D. of Mecklenburg-
           Strelitz

CHARLES FRED — 1804 — MARIA
GD. of Saxe-   PAULOWNA
Weimar   *1786 †1859
*1783 †1853   d. of Paul I
           Emp. of Russia

ERNEST I — (1) 1817 — LOUISE
D. of Saxe-Coburg   *1800 †1831
& Gotha   d. of Augustus
*1784 †1844   D. of Saxe-Gotha-
          Altenburg
          (div. 1826)

EDWARD — 1818 (2) — VICTORIA
D. of Kent   *1786 †1861
*1767 †1820   d. of Francis
          D. of Saxe-Coburg-
          Saalfeld

♛ WILLIAM I — 1829 — AUGUSTA
K. of Prussia   Pr. of Saxe-Weimar
German Emp.   *1811 †1890
*1797 †1888

ALBERT — 1840 — VICTORIA
Pr. of Saxe-Coburg & Gotha   Q. of Gt. Britain
D. of Saxony, Pr. Consort   Emp. of India
*1819 †1861   *1819 †1901

♛ FREDERICK III — 1858 — VICTORIA
German Emp.   Pr. of Gt. Britain
K. of Prussia   *1840 †1901
*1831 †1888

♛ WILLIAM II
German Emp., K. of Prussia
*1859 †1941

Chapter 24

BAVARIA AND THE PALATINATE

Bavaria was conquered by Charlemagne at the end of the eighth century and added to his empire. It was the most independent of the great German duchies and in the twelfth century was temporarily united with Saxony (Chapter 26). After the fall of Henry the Lion (1180) the Duchy was given to Otto of Wittelsbach. In the meantime the growth of Austria and Carinthia to the east and of the county of Tyrol to the south had somewhat diminished the importance of Bavaria and had curtailed the possibility of any expansion.

The family of Wittelsbach was already of some antiquity; one Count of Scheyern had been Duke of Bavaria and fell in battle against the Hungarians in 907. It is probable that they shared a common ancestor with the Babenbergs who became Dukes of Austria (Table 77). In 1124 they moved from Scheyern to the castle of Wittelsbach, which has furnished their name. Their coat-of-arms (Table 96) – 'paly bendy argent and azure' – is of striking simplicity and beauty. Louis I was a considerable figure in the troubled Germany of the early thirteenth century: his first cousin, another Otto, was the assassin of Philip of Swabia just when the latter seemed about to vindicate his claim to the German throne (1208). Otto was put under the ban of the Empire and slain the next year. During the lifetime of Duke Louis his infant son Otto was created Count Palatine of the Rhine and betrothed to the heiress of that fief by the Emperor Frederick II as a reward for the loyalty of his father. Since that date (1214) both the Palatinate – the lands extending to the left and right of the middle Rhine – and Bavaria have belonged to the Wittelsbachs.

Originally the title of count palatine designated an official detached from the imperial palace, and often given special powers over various districts; hence the word came to mean a noble with extended or unusual functions. There were counts palatine at early dates in many parts of Germany; but the term Palatinate (or *Pfalz*) has come to be applied particularly to a part of the Duchy of Franconia lying mainly to the west of the Rhine, with Heidelberg as its chief city. The rank of palatine was not, however, confined to Germany; it had great importance in Hungary and was conferred in the nineteenth century on archdukes of the Hapsburg family (Tables 81 and 83). In Poland it signified a provincial governor; and in England the term was applied to counties whose lord had powers normally reserved for the Crown (Durham was a county palatine under its bishop).

Otto II grew up to marry Agnes, daughter of the Palatine Henry. He was a successful ruler and augmented the size of his Duchy; sometimes he is styled 'the illustrious'. Unfortunately, his sons began that process of subdivision which has been debilitating to so many of the German states. Such sharing within the family did, however, represent good Teutonic custom. After two years of joint rule, Louis II, the Severe, kept Upper Bavaria and the Palatinate while his brother Henry became Duke of Lower Bavaria (the eastern part of the Duchy, towards the Austrian frontier). Louis derived his nickname from inflexibly executing his first wife. His third wife was a Hapsburg and he supported the claims of Rudolph I (Table 77).

But on the death of Louis II further subdivision took place. For a brief season his two sons ruled their domains in harmony, but quarrels erupted and they partitioned Upper Bavaria and then fought over the partition. Louis, the younger disputant, was victorious, and succeeded in putting himself forward in 1314 as a candidate for the Holy Roman Empire in opposition to Frederick of Austria. Victory at Mühldorf (1322) after a dreary and desultory war gave Louis IV the advantage. In 1329 the Emperor bestowed upon his nephews, Rudolph and Rupert, the Palatinate of the Rhine (or Lower Palatinate) and also a segment of northern Bavaria, adjacent to Nuremberg, which came to be known as the Upper Palatinate. From this date the Palatinate and

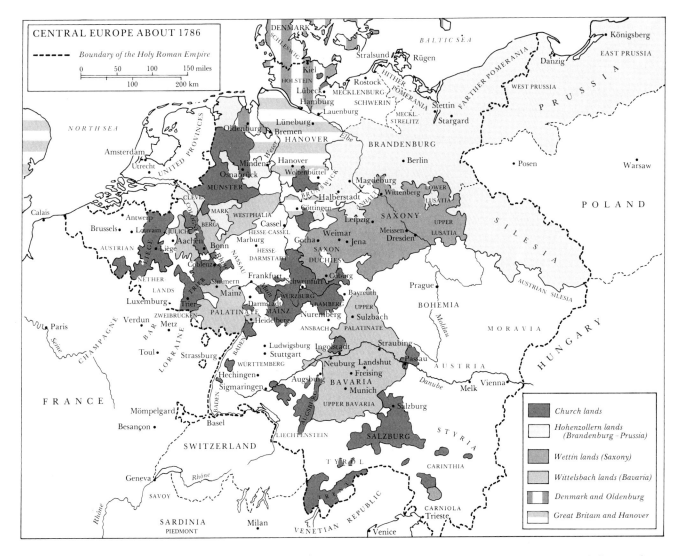

Church lands

Hohenzollern lands
(Brandenburg – Prussia)

Wettin lands (Saxony)

Wittelsbach lands (Bavaria)

Denmark and Oldenburg

Great Britain and Hanover

Bavaria were separated until 1777. The arms of the Palatinate were a gold lion, with red crown, tongue and claws on a black field (Table 96).

BAVARIA

The Emperor Louis IV had high ambitions for Germany and his family but normally lacked resources and the support of the other princes in putting them into effect. His first achievement was to invest his eldest son with the Electorate of Brandenburg on the extinction of the Ascanian dynasty (Chapter 23). His next was to ensure the succession of the sons of his second marriage to the County of Holland, of which their mother was heiress. His efforts to win part of the Tyrol were less successful and he became embroiled in a bitter contest with the Papacy at Avignon, where successive popes disputed his right to the Empire. In his defence he enlisted brilliant foreign philosophers, the Englishman, William of Ockham, and the Italian, Marsiglio of Padua – for the schools of war-torn Germany were unproductive. The death of his cousin, John I of Lower Bavaria, without children,

enabled him to reunite Bavaria in 1340. When at last he died in 1347, excommunicated, he was struggling bravely to retain his grasp of empire against the assaults of Charles IV of Bohemia (Chapter 21). Germany at this time lay devastated not only by the prolonged and uninteresting campaigns but also by the onset of the Black Death.

Louis bequeathed Bavaria to his six sons, of whom some also had interests in Holland and Brandenburg. Three of them died without male issue and it was, in the event, upon the children of Stephen that the future of Bavaria depended. The Golden Bull of Charles IV (1356) had laid down firmly that the electorship belonged to the Palatinate branch, for this also had been in dispute. Stephen and Albrecht of Holland had begun by dividing Bavaria into Bavaria-Landshut and Bavaria-Straubing. In 1392 the sons of Stephen divided their portion into the Duchies of Ingolstadt, Landshut and Munich. On the death of William II, Count of Holland, his brother John, Bishop of Liège, abandoned his mitre to reign over Bavaria-Straubing, but his tardy

TABLE 96

BAVARIA AND THE PALATINATE
General survey (House of Wittelsbach)

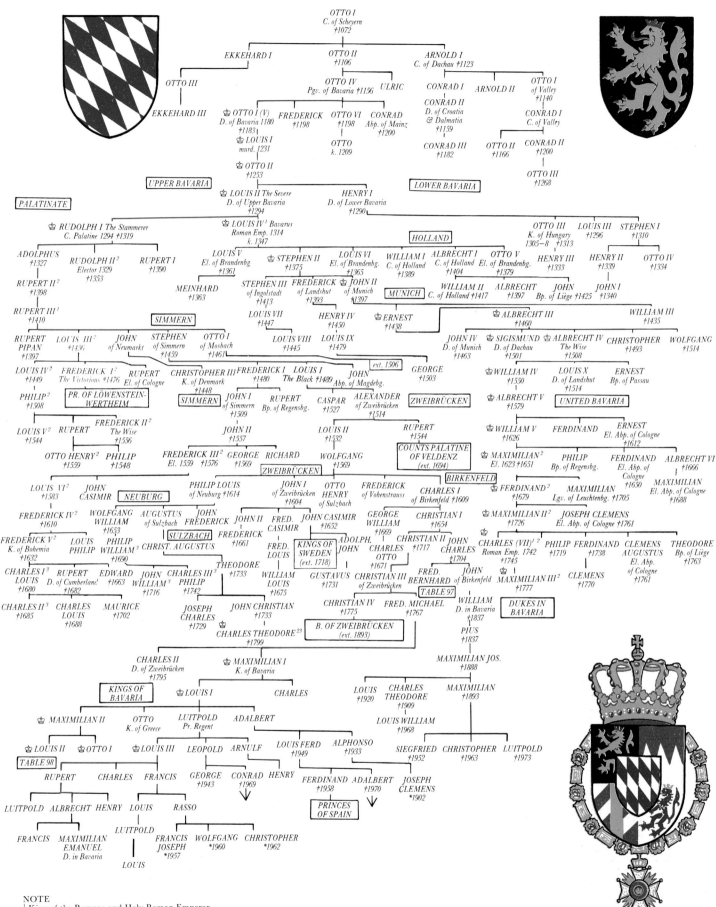

NOTE
[1] King of the Romans and Holy Roman Emperor
[2] Elector of the Palatinate (the original Electorship which was transferred in 1623 to Bavaria)
[3] Elector of the Palatinate (the new Electorship created in 1649)
Both Electorships were united in 1777 in the person of Charles Theodore of Sulzbach.

TABLE 97

BAVARIA
Kings until the end of the monarchy

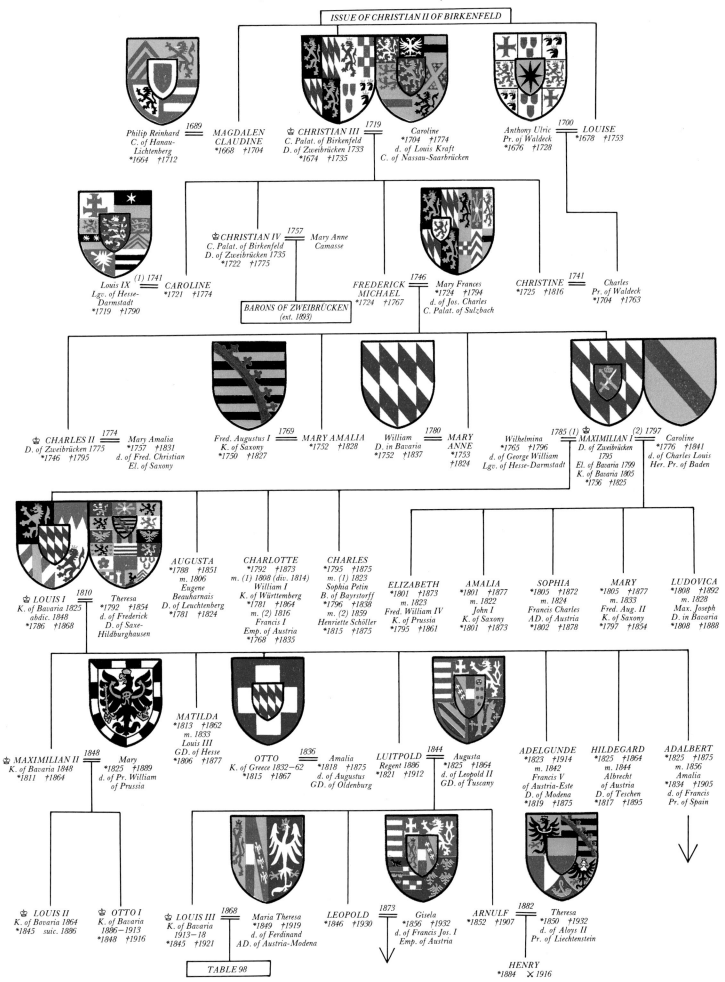

ISSUE OF CHRISTIAN II OF BIRKENFELD

Philip Reinhard
C. of Hanau-
Lichtenberg
*1664 †1712
— 1689 —
MAGDALEN
CLAUDINE
*1668 †1704

CHRISTIAN III
C. Palat. of Birkenfeld
D. of Zweibrücken 1733
*1674 †1735
— 1719 —
Caroline
*1704 †1774
d. of Louis Kraft
C. of Nassau-Saarbrücken

Anthony Ulric
Pr. of Waldeck
*1676 †1728
— 1700 —
LOUISE
*1678 †1753

CHRISTIAN IV
C. Palat. of Birkenfeld
D. of Zweibrücken 1735
*1722 †1775
— 1757 —
Mary Anne
Camasse

Louis IX
Lgv. of Hesse-
Darmstadt
*1719 †1790
— (1) 1741 —
CAROLINE
*1721 †1774

BARONS OF ZWEIBRÜCKEN
(ext. 1893)

FREDERICK
MICHAEL
*1724 †1767
— 1746 —
Mary Frances
*1724 †1794
d. of Jos. Charles
C. Palat. of Sulzbach

CHRISTINE
*1725 †1816
— 1741 —
Charles
Pr. of Waldeck
*1704 †1763

CHARLES II
D. of Zweibrücken 1775
*1746 †1795
— 1774 —
Mary Amalia
*1757 †1831
d. of Fred. Christian
El. of Saxony

Fred. Augustus I
K. of Saxony
*1750 †1827
— 1769 —
MARY AMALIA
*1752 †1828

William
D. in Bavaria
*1752 †1837
— 1780 —
MARY
ANNE
*1753 †1824

Wilhelmina
*1765 †1796
d. of George William
Lgv. of Hesse-Darmstadt
— 1785 (1) —
MAXIMILIAN I
D. of Zweibrücken
1795
El. of Bavaria 1799
K. of Bavaria 1805
*1756 †1825
— (2) 1797 —
Caroline
*1776 †1841
d. of Charles Louis
Her. Pr. of Baden

LOUIS I
K. of Bavaria 1825
abdic. 1848
*1786 †1868
— 1810 —
Theresa
*1792 †1854
d. of Frederick
D. of Saxe-
Hildburghausen

AUGUSTA
*1788 †1851
m. 1806
Eugene
Beauharnais
D. of Leuchtenberg
*1781 †1824

CHARLOTTE
*1792 †1873
m. (1) 1808 (div. 1814)
William I
K. of Württemberg
*1781 †1864
m. (2) 1816
Francis I
Emp. of Austria
*1768 †1835

CHARLES
*1795 †1875
m. (1) 1823
Sophia Petin
B. of Bayrstorff
*1796 †1838
m. (2) 1859
Henriette Schöller
*1815 †1875

ELIZABETH
*1801 †1873
m. 1823
Fred. William IV
K. of Prussia
*1795 †1861

AMALIA
*1801 †1877
m. 1822
John I
K. of Saxony
*1801 †1873

SOPHIA
*1805 †1872
m. 1824
Francis Charles
AD. of Austria
*1802 †1878

MARY
*1805 †1877
m. 1833
Fred. Aug. II
K. of Saxony
*1797 †1854

LUDOVICA
*1808 †1892
m. 1828
Max. Joseph
D. in Bavaria
*1808 †1888

MAXIMILIAN II
K. of Bavaria 1848
*1811 †1864
— 1848 —
Mary
*1825 †1889
d. of Pr. William
of Prussia

MATILDA
*1813 †1862
m. 1833
Louis III
GD. of Hesse
*1806 †1877

OTTO
K. of Greece 1832–62
*1815 †1867
— 1836 —
Amalia
*1818 †1875
d. of Augustus
GD. of Oldenburg

LUITPOLD
Regent 1886
*1821 †1912
— 1844 —
Augusta
*1825 †1864
d. of Leopold II
GD. of Tuscany

ADELGUNDE
*1823 †1914
m. 1842
Francis V
of Austria-Este
D. of Modena
*1819 †1875

HILDEGARD
*1825 †1864
m. 1844
Albrecht
of Austria
D. of Teschen
*1817 †1895

ADALBERT
*1825 †1875
m. 1856
Amalia
*1834 †1905
d. of Francis
Pr. of Spain

LOUIS II
K. of Bavaria 1864
*1845 suic. 1886

OTTO I
K. of Bavaria
1886–1913
*1848 †1916

LOUIS III
K. of Bavaria
1913–18
*1845 †1921
— 1868 —
Maria Theresa
*1849 †1919
d. of Ferdinand
AD. of Austria-Modena

LEOPOLD
*1846 †1930

Gisela
*1856 †1932
d. of Francis Jos. I
Emp. of Austria
— 1873 —

ARNULF
*1852 †1907
— 1882 —
Theresa
*1850 †1932
d. of Aloys II
Pr. of Liechtenstein

HENRY
*1884 ✕ 1916

TABLE 98

marriage was unproductive; at his death in 1425 his Duchy was shared among his cousins, Louis VII, Henry IV and Ernest, not without some acrimony.

It would be tedious to rehearse the bickering between the various princelings which rendered Bavaria ineffective as a German state and uncomfortable as a domicile. It is perhaps enough to say that the reign of Albrecht IV, the Wise, saw a reunion of the fragmented Bavarian territory. It was not achieved without effort: Albrecht's main rival was his distant kinsman, Rupert of the Palatinate (son of the Elector Philip, and sometime Bishop of Freising), who had wed the daughter of George of Landshut. By 1504 Albrecht had consolidated the greater part of Bavaria proper under his rule. More important was his action in 1506 in laying down that henceforward the Duchy of Bavaria should descend without division to the eldest son. Old tradition yet prevailed; William IV was coerced to share his Duchy with his brother, Louis X, but mercifully the latter died without issue. Thereafter the Duchy of Bavaria remained in one piece. Moreover, its dukes secured a dominant influence over the Prince-Archbishopric of Cologne. From 1583 to 1761 this important ecclesiastical Electorate was monopolized by five successive cadets of the House of Wittelsbach.

THE REFORMATION

Duke William IV and Duke Albrecht V were both on the side of the Catholic faith; as a result of their endeavours any tendency towards Protestantism in the Duchy was effectually checked. William V, the Pious, actually abdicated in favour of his son and retired to a monastery (1597). The reign of that son, Maximilian I, coincided with the outbreak of the Thirty Years' War. In 1618 the throne of Bohemia was offered to Maximilian's distant kinsman, that ardent Protestant, the Elector Palatine Frederick V. Maximilian had already carried out thoroughgoing reforms of his Duchy; in 1623 he was given the Electorate which Frederick V was deemed to have forfeited. In the course of the war Maximilian regained the Upper Palatinate, and though Bavaria was afflicted severely by the operations of the various militants, a more united and cohesive state emerged from the struggle.

This local consolidation was to some extent offset by an increased dynastic involvement in European politics. Maximilian (Emanuel) II married the daughter of Leopold of Austria, through whose wife his son Joseph Ferdinand (not shown on Table 96: see Table 50) inherited a claim to the extensive dominions of the Spanish Hapsburgs. Louis XIV of France and Leopold I of Austria both also coveted the inheritance for junior members of their dynasties. The relatively inconspicuous Joseph Ferdinand was

accepted by the major Powers as a neutral solution; but, sadly, he died in 1699 before the ailing King of Spain. None the less his father, Maximilian II, flung himself unfruitfully into the War of the Spanish Succession. Bavaria was on the losing side at Blenheim, and was briefly divided between the victors, with scant advantage to the inhabitants. Maximilian recovered his lands, somewhat the worse for wear, at the Treaty of Utrecht (1713), but his son Charles rashly engaged in further political adventure. Seeking to draw profit from the equivocal position of Maria Theresa (Chapter 20), he advanced his claims to the Empire. On the day he was crowned as Charles VII at Frankfurt, his enemies occupied his own capital of Munich. His son, Maximilian III, was happy to accept the Pragmatic Sanction and to devote his energies to the rehabilitation of the fields of Bavaria across which remorseless hosts had been marching and countermarching for two generations. Unhappily, this enlightened and able ruler was the last of his line; at his death (1777) the Electorate of Bavaria passed to his distant cousin, Charles Theodore of Sulzbach, the Elector Palatine, himself middle-aged and childless.

THE PALATINATE

The division between Bavaria and the Palatinate, as has been seen, dated back to 1329. Rupert II of the Palatinate reigned alone from 1390 until 1398 and added to his domains by prudent purchase, so much so that his son, Rupert III, was able to act as an honest, if totally ineffectual, King of the Romans (1400–10). At his death the Palatinate was divided among his four sons. Louis inherited the Palatinate of the Rhine; John the Upper Palatinate (i.e. northern Bavaria) which returned to the eldest line on the death of his son, Christopher of Denmark (Table 17); Stephen acquired Zweibrücken and Simmern, and Otto got Mosbach. Otto's line expired in 1506.

The senior line of Electors Palatine lasted till 1559. Frederick I made an unconventional marriage with a lady called Klara Tott from Augsburg and founded thereby the family of Princes of Löwenstein, still extant. As has been seen (above: Bavaria) his great-nephew Rupert tried hard to claim the Duchy of Bavaria-Landshut, but only won the detached districts of Neuburg and Sulzbach: Rupert's son, Otto Henry, was the last of this branch. The Electorate then passed (Table 96) to Frederick III of Simmern. Frederick was a Calvinist and his successors all adhered to some branch of the reformed faith. It was his descendant, Frederick V (married to a daughter of James I of England: Table 85), who imprudently accepted the throne of Bohemia, and thus launched the Thirty Years' War. In 1623 he gave up the title of elector, which was awarded to his

TABLE 98

BAVARIA
Royal House since the end of the monarchy

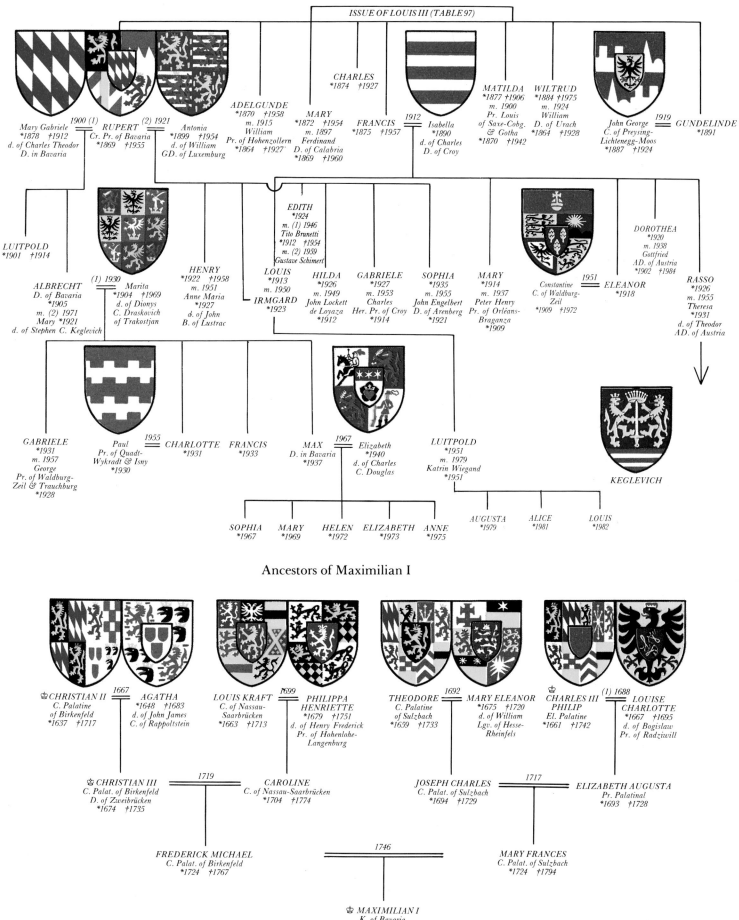

ISSUE OF LOUIS III (TABLE 97)

Mary Gabriele
*1878 †1912
d. of Charles Theodor
D. in Bavaria

1900 (1)

RUPERT
Cr. Pr. of Bavaria
*1869 †1955

(2) 1921

Antonia
*1899 †1954
d. of William
GD. of Luxemburg

ADELGUNDE
*1870 †1958
m. 1915
William
Pr. of Hohenzollern
*1864 †1927

MARY
*1872 †1954
m. 1897
Ferdinand
D. of Calabria
*1869 †1960

CHARLES
*1874 †1927

FRANCIS
*1875 †1957

1912

Isabella
*1890
d. of Charles
D. of Croy

MATILDA
*1877 †1906
m. 1900
Pr. Louis
of Saxe-Cobg.
& Gotha
*1870 †1942

WILTRUD
*1884 †1975
m. 1924
William
D. of Urach
*1864 †1928

John George
C. of Preysing-
Lichtenegg-Moos
*1887 †1924

1919

GUNDELINDE
*1891

LUITPOLD
*1901 †1914

ALBRECHT
D. of Bavaria
*1905
m. (2) 1971
Mary *1921
d. of Stephen C. Keglevich

(1) 1930

Marita
*1904 †1969
d. of Dionys
C. Draskovich
of Trakostjan

HENRY
*1922 †1958
m. 1951
Anne Maria
*1927
d. of John
B. of Lustrac

EDITH
*1924
m. (1) 1946
Tito Brunetti
*1912 †1954
m. (2) 1959
Gustave Schimert

LOUIS
*1913
m. 1950
IRMGARD
*1923

HILDA
*1926
m. 1949
John Lockett
de Loyaza
*1912

GABRIELE
*1927
m. 1953
Charles
Her. Pr. of Croy
*1914

SOPHIA
*1935
m. 1955
John Engelbert
D. of Arenberg
*1921

MARY
*1914
m. 1937
Peter Henry
Pr. of Orléans-
Braganza
*1909

Constantine
C. of Waldburg-
Zeil
*1909 †1972

1951

ELEANOR
*1918

DOROTHEA
*1920
m. 1938
Gottfried
AD. of Austria
*1902 †1984

RASSO
*1926
m. 1955
Theresa
*1931
d. of Theodor
AD. of Austria

GABRIELE
*1931
m. 1957
George
Pr. of Waldburg-
Zeil & Trauchburg
*1928

Paul
Pr. of Quadt-
Wykradt & Isny
*1930

1955

CHARLOTTE
*1931

FRANCIS
*1933

MAX
D. in Bavaria
*1937

1967

Elizabeth
*1940
d. of Charles
C. Douglas

LUITPOLD
*1951
m. 1979
Katrin Wiegand
*1951

KEGLEVICH

SOPHIA
*1967

MARY
*1969

HELEN
*1972

ELIZABETH
*1973

ANNE
*1975

AUGUSTA
*1979

ALICE
*1981

LOUIS
*1982

Ancestors of Maximilian I

♔ CHRISTIAN II
C. Palatine
of Birkenfeld
*1637 †1717

1667

AGATHA
*1648 †1683
d. of John James
C. of Rappoltstein

LOUIS KRAFT
C. of Nassau-
Saarbrücken
*1663 †1713

1699

PHILIPPA
HENRIETTE
*1679 †1751
d. of Henry Frederick
Pr. of Hohenlohe-
Langenburg

THEODORE
C. Palatine
of Sulzbach
*1659 †1733

1692

MARY ELEANOR
*1675 †1720
d. of William
Lgv. of Hesse-
Rheinfels

♔ CHARLES III
PHILIP
El. Palatine
*1661 †1742

(1) 1688

LOUISE
CHARLOTTE
*1667 †1695
d. of Bogislaw
Pr. of Radziwill

♔ CHRISTIAN III
C. Palat. of Birkenfeld
D. of Zweibrücken
*1674 †1735

1719

CAROLINE
C. of Nassau-Saarbrücken
*1704 †1774

JOSEPH CHARLES
C. Palat. of Sulzbach
*1694 †1729

1717

ELIZABETH AUGUSTA
Pr. Palatinal
*1693 †1728

FREDERICK MICHAEL
C. Palat. of Birkenfeld
*1724 †1767

1746

MARY FRANCES
C. Palat. of Sulzbach
*1724 †1794

♔ MAXIMILIAN I
K. of Bavaria
*1756 †1825

cousin of Bavaria. By the Treaty of Westphalia (1648), the next Count Palatine, Charles I (Louis), was accorded an extra electorate, but had to forfeit the Upper Palatinate. His younger brother, Rupert, made a remarkable career in England, first as a cavalry leader under his uncle Charles I and later as an admiral and patron of science under Charles II.

The death of Charles II in 1685 brought an end to the line of Simmern, for his two younger half-brothers came of a morganatic marriage and only bore the title of Raugraf. The next Elector Palatine was Philip William of Neuburg (the senior representative of Alexander of Zweibrücken, d. 1514). His father Wolfgang William had been a competitor in the contest over the Duchies of Cleves, Jülich and Berg (Chapter 23: Prussia) and had gained the two latter, and with them the distinguished Order of St Hubert, founded in 1444. In 1742 the Neuburg line died out, and the succession passed to Charles Theodore of Sulzbach, who later inherited the Duchy of Bavaria as well.

The new ruler lacked legitimate children and wasted much effort endeavouring to improve the status of his irregular progeny; he even aspired to barter Bavaria for the Austrian Netherlands. Bavaria itself profited little from his rule, and was abandoned by him to the conflicting forces of Austria and the French Revolution.

KINGDOM OF BAVARIA

The unlamented death of Charles Theodore entailed another genealogical jump. Maximilian I (Table 97), Duke of Zweibrücken, was now heir male of Stephen, Count of Simmern (d. 1459), and inheritor both of the Palatinate and of Bavaria. His ancestry (Table 98) shows three strains of Bavarian blood, a dash of Polish and the rest German. The arms of the Elector Palatine, Charles III Philip, show quarterings for the Palatinate, Bavaria, Jülich, Cleves, Berg, Veldenz, Mark, Ravensberg and Meurs. The small red shield is blank because of uncertainty as to which line should display the gold orb of the Stewardship of the Empire (claimed at that date by the Elector-Dukes of Bavaria). Unlike many Germanic princes, Maximilian committed himself to a positive policy of alliance with Napoleon. His reward was a substantial accretion of territory to the north, and, in 1805, the title of king. At the treaties after Waterloo, he preserved this rank and most of his acquisitions. His arms (Table 97) show simply Bavaria with the attributes of kingship on a red escutcheon. Those of his grandfather, Christian III of Birkenfeld, display the blazons of the Palatinate and Wittelsbach (twice each), and the Lordships of Veldenz, Spanheim, Rappoltstein and Hohenach. The younger branch of the Birkenfeld line, descending from Christian III's uncle, were given in 1799 the title of Dukes *in*

Bavaria. Two of the most striking queens of Europe in recent years came from this family, both called Elizabeth – the wives of Francis Joseph of Austria and Albert I of Belgium.

Louis I of Bavaria was an artistic ruler who added greatly to the distinction of Munich as his capital: his appreciation of beauty led him too far in his attachment to an Irish girl who passed under the name of Lola Montez. In 1848, the year of revolutions, he was driven to abdicate. His second son, Otto, was King of Greece (Chapter 37). Maximilian II, his eldest son, was mainly concerned in resisting, without success, the growing tide of Prussian aggrandizement and in aiming at a consolidation of the Catholic Powers of southern Germany. Neither of Maximilian's sons was stable mentally. Louis II witnessed the triumphs of Prussia over Austria and France: compelled to abandon any dream of Bavarian separatism, he formally proposed at Versailles in 1871 that the Imperial Crown be offered to William I. Bavaria, it is true, retained more independence than any other German state.

The King's conduct became increasingly eccentric. Patronage of Wagner was not acceptable to contemporaries; still less was the financial burden of fantastic castles, such as Neuschwanstein, which he erected on the less accessible Bavarian peaks. In 1886 his uncle Luitpold was proclaimed regent; a week later Louis drowned himself (and his hapless keeper). His brother Otto had been more definitively mad for some time, and was removed from the throne in 1913. Louis III, the son of the Regent, found himself involved in the First World War, at the end of which, after the defeat of Germany, he was compelled to abdicate. His marriage to Maria of Austria-Este made the Crown Prince Rupert (Table 98) heir to the Jacobite claim to the throne of Great Britain. His son Albrecht married an Austrian (actually Croatian) countess. At first the union was ruled (1930) to be morganatic, but before his death Crown Prince Rupert accepted it as valid for succession to the throne of Bavaria. After his first wife's death, Duke Albrecht married Mary, Countess Keglevich, whose arms can be seen in the right hand margin (Table 98). In 1965 the last of the Dukes *in* Bavaria, who was without heirs, adopted as his son Prince Max, the second son of Duke Albrecht; Max is thus styled Duke *in* Bavaria and has married a Swedish countess who, like so many of that nobility, has a Scottish name.

The arms of the Kingdom of Bavaria (Table 96) show quarterings for the Palatinate, Franconia, Burgau and Veldenz, surmounted by the family arms of Wittelsbach, which have come to stand for Bavaria. They are surrounded by the collar of St Hubert, founded by Gerhard V, Duke of Jülich and Berg, which passed to the Counts Palatine in 1609.

Chapter 25

BRUNSWICK AND HANOVER

Sometimes a family falls from prominence and after many centuries rises again. Such was the case with the Dukes of Brunswick. A series of fortunate marriages brought Henry the Proud and Henry the Lion to a dominant position among the German princes. The former (Table 99) espoused Gertrude, daughter of the Emperor Lothair and granddaughter of Gertrude, heiress of the original Lords of Brunswick, who were called Bruno and gave the place its name. But although alliances within Germany brought importance to one line of the family, it was in fact of Italian origin, stemming from the little town of Este, near Padua. A younger branch remaining in the south eventually became Dukes of Modena (Table 128).

In 1180 Henry the Lion fell from power and was stripped of his Duchies of Bavaria and Saxony. However, he was allowed to keep his family lands of Brunswick and Lüneburg. Henry was married to Matilda, the eldest daughter of Henry II of England. It has been suggested that the two gold lions, or leopards, on the red shield of Brunswick might be connected with the arms of England which were then evolving; the blue lion rampant surrounded by hearts for Lüneburg was related to the arms of Denmark, its northern neighbour. Otto IV was brought up in England and according to one chronicler enjoyed the earldom of York; on returning to Germany he became emperor in 1208, but his alliance with his uncle John of England brought him to complete disaster in 1214, at Bouvines, one of the truly decisive battles of the Middle Ages.

By its frequency the baptismal name Welf, or in its Italian form Guelph, was transferred to the dynasty as a whole and even to its political cause. Thus followers of later emperors or would-be emperors, who like Otto IV were opposed to the Hohenstaufen tradition or who enjoyed the support of the Papacy, styled themselves Guelphs. Their opponents were known as Ghibellines from an Italian version of the Staufen fortress of Waiblingen, near Stuttgart (Chapter 30).

The Emperor Frederick II, anxious to win the Guelphs to his side, created Otto I, the Child, Duke of Brunswick and Lüneburg in 1235. Before his death Otto added Hanover to his territories; all subsequent members of the dynasty are descended from him. The Teutonic principle of subdivision began to operate here also. Albrecht I divided his possessions with his younger brother in 1267, and his three sons later partitioned their father's Duchy of Brunswick. The first line of Dukes of Lüneburg died out in 1369, and after a considerable contest the sons of Magnus II, Duke of Brunswick, vindicated their right to succeed. Any reunion was short-lived. In 1428 Bernhard I made a fresh redistribution. His own descendants became Dukes of Brunswick-Lüneburg; those of his brother were Dukes of Brunswick-Wolfenbüttel, to which in 1463 they added Göttingen, on the death of Otto the One-Eyed.

Another significant division occurred in 1569 among the children of Duke Ernest I after a period of discord among them. Henry, Duke of Dannenburg, and William, Duke of Lüneburg, established two lines which existed separately until 1884. In 1635 these two families divided the estates of the Wolfenbüttel branch. The elder line was now known as Brunswick-Wolfenbüttel; its first duke, Augustus (d. 1666), was a celebrated bibliophile, but most of his race were renowned as soldiers. Charles I hired his troops to Britain to fight in the War of American Independence. His brother Ferdinand served under both Frederick the Great and George II of England, but devoted his later years to the study of freemasonry. Charles II also served in the Prussian army and later commanded against the French Republic at Valmy; he was mortally wounded at

TABLE 99

BRUNSWICK AND HANOVER
General survey (House of Guelph)

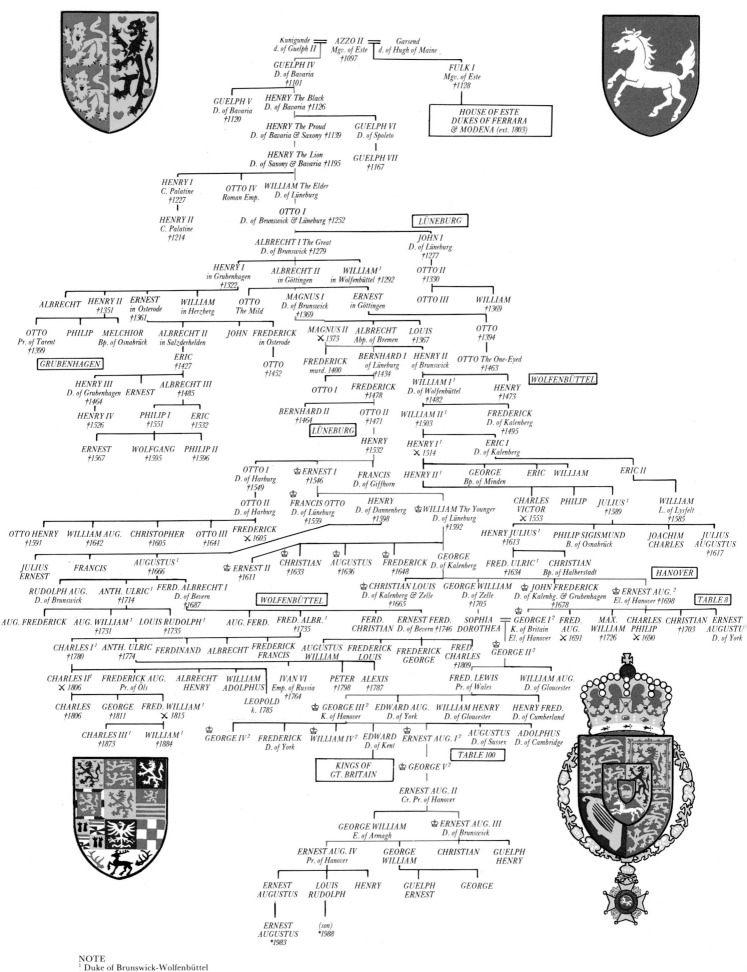

Kunigunde d. of Guelph II ══ AZZO II Mgv. of Este †1097 ══ Garsend d. of Hugh of Maine

GUELPH IV D. of Bavaria †1101

FULK I Mgv. of Este †1128

GUELPH V D. of Bavaria †1120

HENRY The Black D. of Bavaria †1126

HOUSE OF ESTE DUKES OF FERRARA & MODENA (ext. 1803)

HENRY The Proud D. of Bavaria & Saxony †1139

GUELPH VI D. of Spoleto

HENRY The Lion D. of Saxony & Bavaria †1195

GUELPH VII †1167

HENRY I C. Palatine †1227

OTTO IV Roman Emp.

WILLIAM The Elder D. of Lüneburg

HENRY II C. Palatine †1214

OTTO I D. of Brunswick & Lüneburg †1252

LÜNEBURG

ALBRECHT I The Great D. of Brunswick †1279

JOHN I D. of Lüneburg †1277

HENRY I in Grubenhagen †1322

ALBRECHT II in Göttingen

WILLIAM[1] in Wolfenbüttel †1292

OTTO II †1330

ALBRECHT · HENRY II †1351 · ERNEST in Osterode †1361 · WILLIAM in Herzberg · OTTO The Mild · MAGNUS I D. of Brunswick †1369 · ERNEST in Göttingen · OTTO III · WILLIAM †1369

OTTO Pr. of Tarent †1399 · PHILIP · MELCHIOR Bp. of Osnabrück · ALBRECHT II in Salzderhelden · JOHN · FREDERICK in Osterode · MAGNUS II ✕1373 · ALBRECHT Abp. of Bremen · LOUIS †1367 · OTTO †1394

GRUBENHAGEN

ERIC †1427

OTTO †1452

FREDERICK murd. 1400 · BERNHARD I of Lüneburg †1434 · HENRY II of Brunswick · OTTO The One-Eyed †1463

WOLFENBÜTTEL

HENRY III D. of Grubenhagen †1464 · ERNEST · ALBRECHT III †1485

OTTO I · FREDERICK †1478 · WILLIAM I[1] D. of Wolfenbüttel †1482 · HENRY †1473

HENRY IV †1526 · PHILIP I †1551 · ERIC †1532

BERNHARD II †1464 · OTTO II †1471 · WILLIAM II[1] †1503 · FREDERICK D. of Kalenberg †1495

LÜNEBURG

ERNEST †1567 · WOLFGANG †1595 · PHILIP II †1596

HENRY †1532

HENRY I[1] ✕1514 · ERIC I D. of Kalenberg

OTTO I D. of Harburg †1549 · ⚜ERNEST I †1546 · FRANCIS D. of Giffhorn · HENRY II[1] · GEORGE Bp. of Minden · ERIC · WILLIAM · ERIC II

OTTO II D. of Harburg · ⚜FRANCIS OTTO D. of Lüneburg †1559 · HENRY D. of Dannenberg · ⚜WILLIAM The Younger D. of Lüneburg †1592 · CHARLES VICTOR ✕1553 · PHILIP · JULIUS[1] †1589 · WILLIAM L. of Lysfelt †1585

OTTO HENRY †1591 · WILLIAM AUG. †1642 · CHRISTOPHER †1605 · OTTO III †1641 · FREDERICK ✕1605 · HENRY JULIUS[1] †1613 · PHILIP SIGISMUND B. of Osnabrück · JOACHIM CHARLES · JULIUS AUGUSTUS †1617

JULIUS ERNEST · FRANCIS · AUGUSTUS[1] †1666 · ⚜ERNEST II †1611 · CHRISTIAN †1633 · AUGUSTUS †1636 · FREDERICK †1648 · GEORGE D. of Kalenberg · FRED. ULRIC[1] †1634 · CHRISTIAN Bp. of Halberstadt

HANOVER

RUDOLPH AUG. D. of Brunswick · ANTH. ULRIC[1] †1714 · FERD. ALBRECHT I D. of Bevern †1687 · ⚜CHRISTIAN LOUIS D. of Kalenberg & Zelle †1665 · GEORGE WILLIAM D. of Zelle †1705 · ⚜JOHN FREDERICK D. of Kalenbg. & Grubenhagen †1678 · ⚜ERNEST AUG.[2] El. of Hanover †1698

WOLFENBÜTTEL

TABLE 8

AUG. FREDERICK · AUG. WILLIAM[1] †1731 · LOUIS RUDOLPH[1] †1735 · AUG. FERD. · FRED. ALBR.[1] †1735 · FERD. CHRISTIAN D. of Bevern †1746 · ERNEST FERD. · SOPHIA DOROTHEA ══ ⚜GEORGE I[2] K. of Britain El. of Hanover · FRED. AUG. ✕1691 · MAX. WILLIAM †1726 · CHARLES PHILIP ✕1690 · CHRISTIAN †1703 · ERNEST AUGUSTUS D. of York

CHARLES I[1] †1780 · ANTH. ULRIC †1774 · FERDINAND · ALBRECHT · FREDERICK FRANCIS · AUGUSTUS WILLIAM · FREDERICK LOUIS · FREDERICK GEORGE · FRED. CHARLES †1809 · ⚜GEORGE II[2]

CHARLES II[1] ✕1806 · FREDERICK AUG. Pr. of Öls · ALBRECHT HENRY · WILLIAM ADOLPHUS · IVAN VI Emp. of Russia †1764 · PETER †1798 · ALEXIS †1787 · FRED. LEWIS Pr. of Wales · WILLIAM AUG. D. of Gloucester

CHARLES †1806 · GEORGE †1811 · FRED. WILLIAM[1] ✕1815 · LEOPOLD k. 1785 · ⚜GEORGE III[2] K. of Hanover · EDWARD AUG. D. of York · WILLIAM HENRY D. of Gloucester · HENRY FRED. D. of Cumberland

CHARLES III[1] †1873 · WILLIAM[1] †1884 · GEORGE IV[2] · FREDERICK D. of York · WILLIAM IV[2] · EDWARD D. of Kent · ERNEST AUG. I[2] · AUGUSTUS D. of Sussex · ADOLPHUS D. of Cambridge

KINGS OF GT. BRITAIN

TABLE 100

⚜GEORGE V[2]

ERNEST AUG. II Cr. Pr. of Hanover

GEORGE WILLIAM E. of Armagh · ⚜ERNEST AUG. III D. of Brunswick

ERNEST AUG. IV Pr. of Hanover · GEORGE WILLIAM · CHRISTIAN · GUELPH HENRY

ERNEST AUGUSTUS · LOUIS RUDOLPH · HENRY · GUELPH ERNEST · GEORGE

ERNEST AUGUSTUS *1983 · (son) *1988

NOTE
[1] Duke of Brunswick-Wolfenbüttel
[2] Elector and King of Hanover

TABLE 100

HANOVER
Kings since the separation from Great Britain

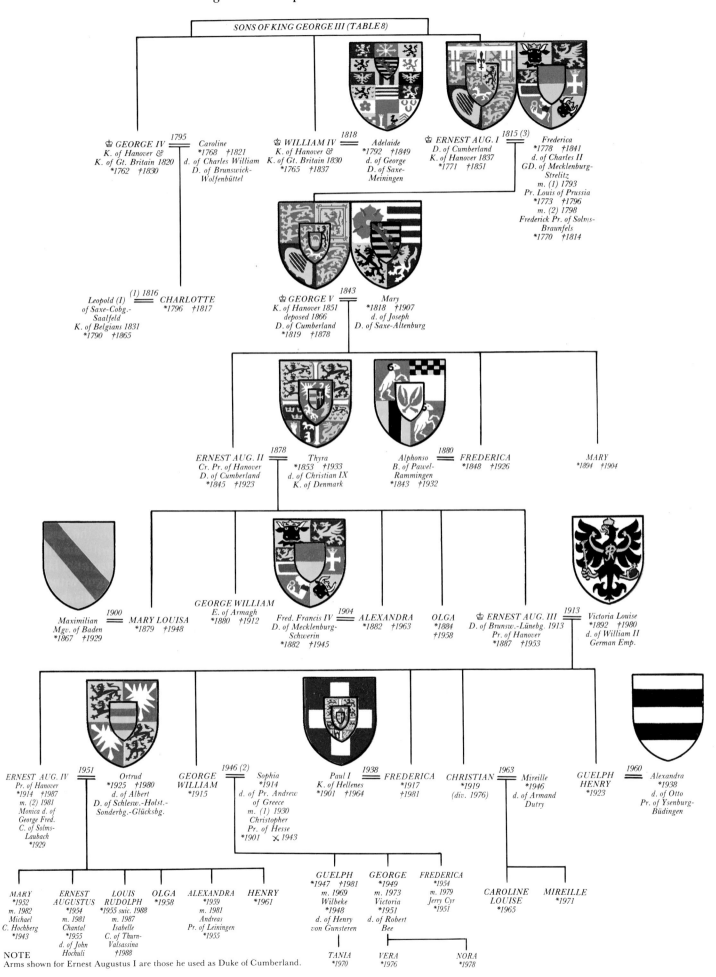

SONS OF KING GEORGE III (TABLE 8)

♛ GEORGE IV 1795
K. of Hanover &
K. of Gt. Britain 1820
*1762 †1830

Caroline
*1768 †1821
d. of Charles William
D. of Brunswick-
Wolfenbüttel

♛ WILLIAM IV 1818
K. of Hanover &
K. of Gt. Britain 1830
*1765 †1837

Adelaide
*1792 †1849
d. of George
D. of Saxe-
Meiningen

♛ ERNEST AUG. I 1815 (3)
D. of Cumberland
K. of Hanover 1837
*1771 †1851

Frederica
*1778 †1841
d. of Charles II
GD. of Mecklenburg-
Strelitz
m. (1) 1793
Pr. Louis of Prussia
*1773 †1796
m. (2) 1798
Frederick Pr. of Solms-
Braunfels
*1770 †1814

Leopold (I) (1) 1816
of Saxe-Cobg.-
Saalfeld
K. of Belgians 1831
*1790 †1865

CHARLOTTE
*1796 †1817

♛ GEORGE V 1843
K. of Hanover 1851
deposed 1866
D. of Cumberland
*1819 †1878

Mary
*1818 †1907
d. of Joseph
D. of Saxe-Altenburg

ERNEST AUG. II 1878
Cr. Pr. of Hanover
D. of Cumberland
*1845 †1923

Thyra
*1853 †1933
d. of Christian IX
K. of Denmark

Alphonso
B. of Pawel-
Rammingen
*1843 †1932

FREDERICA 1880
*1848 †1926

MARY
*1894 †1904

Maximilian 1900
Mgv. of Baden
*1867 †1929

MARY LOUISA
*1879 †1948

GEORGE WILLIAM
E. of Armagh
*1880 †1912

Fred. Francis IV 1904
D. of Mecklenburg-
Schwerin
*1882 †1945

ALEXANDRA
*1882 †1963

OLGA
*1884
†1958

♛ ERNEST AUG. III 1913
D. of Brunsw.-Lünebg. 1913
Pr. of Hanover
*1887 †1953

Victoria Louise
*1892 †1980
d. of William II
German Emp.

ERNEST AUG. IV 1951
Pr. of Hanover
*1914 †1987
m. (2) 1981
Monica d. of
George Fred.
C. of Solms-
Laubach
*1929

Ortrud
*1925 †1980
d. of Albert
D. of Schlesw.-Holst.-
Sonderbg.-Glücksbg.

GEORGE 1946 (2)
WILLIAM
*1915

Sophia
*1914
d. of Pr. Andrew
of Greece
m. (1) 1930
Christopher
Pr. of Hesse
*1901 ✕ 1943

Paul I 1938
K. of Hellenes
*1901 †1964

FREDERICA
*1917
†1981

CHRISTIAN 1963
*1919
(div. 1976)

Mireille
*1946
d. of Armand
Dutry

GUELPH
HENRY
*1923

Alexandra 1960
*1938
d. of Otto
Pr. of Ysenburg-
Büdingen

MARY
*1952
m. 1982
Michael
C. Hochberg
*1943

ERNEST
AUGUSTUS
*1954
m. 1981
Chantal
*1955
d. of John
Hochuli

LOUIS
RUDOLPH
*1955 suic. 1988
m. 1987
Isabelle
C. of Thurn-
Valsassina
†1988

OLGA
*1958

ALEXANDRA
*1959
m. 1981
Andreas
Pr. of Leiningen
*1955

HENRY
*1961

GUELPH
*1947 †1981
m. 1969
Wilbeke
*1948
d. of Henry
von Gunsteren

GEORGE
*1949
m. 1973
Victoria
*1951
d. of Robert
Bee

FREDERICA
*1954
m. 1979
Jerry Cyr
*1951

CAROLINE
LOUISE
*1965

MIREILLE
*1971

TANIA
*1970

VERA
*1976

NORA
*1978

NOTE
Arms shown for Ernest Augustus I are those he used as Duke of Cumberland.

TABLE 101

SAXONY
General survey

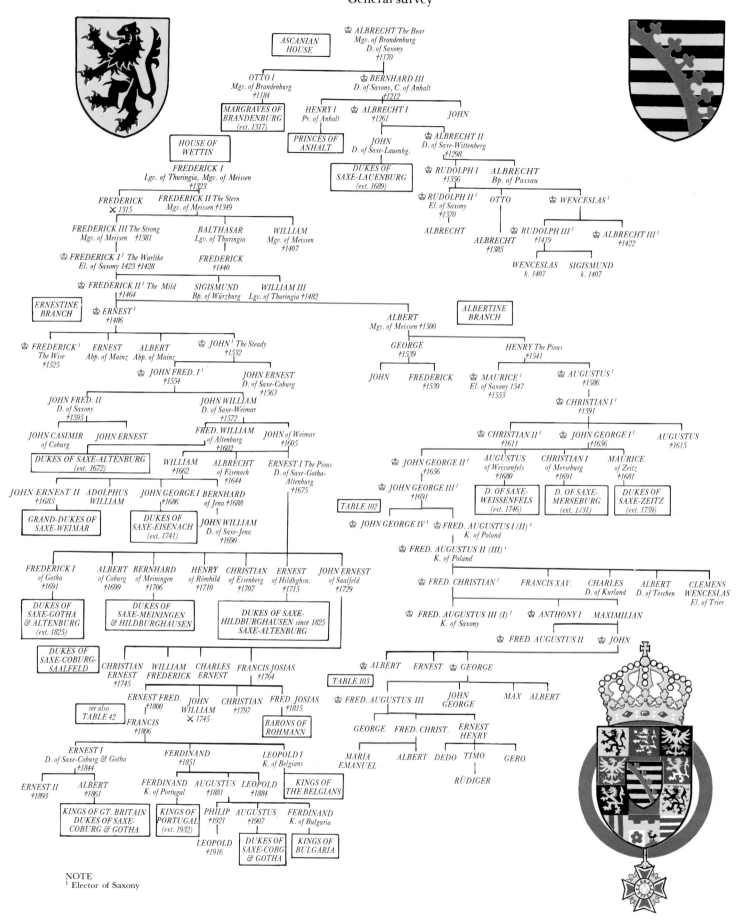

ASCANIAN HOUSE

👑 ALBRECHT The Bear
Mgv. of Brandenburg
D. of Saxony
†1170

OTTO I
Mgv. of Brandenburg
†1184

👑 BERNHARD III
D. of Saxony, C. of Anhalt
†1212

MARGRAVES OF BRANDENBURG (ext. 1317)

HENRY I
Pr. of Anhalt

👑 ALBRECHT I
†1261

JOHN

PRINCES OF ANHALT

JOHN
D. of Saxe-Lauenbg.

👑 ALBRECHT II
D. of Saxe-Wittenberg
†1298

DUKES OF SAXE-LAUENBURG (ext. 1689)

HOUSE OF WETTIN

FREDERICK I
Lgv. of Thuringia, Mgv. of Meissen
†1323

👑 RUDOLPH I
†1356

ALBRECHT
Bp. of Passau

FREDERICK
✕ 1315

FREDERICK II The Stern
Mgv. of Meissen †1349

👑 RUDOLPH II
El. of Saxony
†1370

OTTO

👑 WENCESLAS I

FREDERICK III The Strong
Mgv. of Meissen †1381

BALTHASAR
Lgv. of Thuringia

WILLIAM
Mgv. of Meissen
†1407

ALBRECHT

ALBRECHT
†1385

👑 RUDOLPH III I
†1419

👑 ALBRECHT III I
†1422

👑 FREDERICK I I The Warlike
El. of Saxony 1423 †1428

FREDERICK
†1440

WENCESLAS
k. 1407

SIGISMUND
k. 1407

👑 FREDERICK II I The Mild
†1464

SIGISMUND
Bp. of Würzburg

WILLIAM III
Lgv. of Thuringia †1482

ALBERT
Mgv. of Meissen †1500

ERNESTINE BRANCH

👑 ERNEST I
†1486

ALBERTINE BRANCH

👑 FREDERICK I
The Wise
†1525

ERNEST
Abp. of Mainz

ALBERT
Abp. of Mainz

👑 JOHN I The Steady
†1532

GEORGE
†1539

HENRY The Pious
†1541

👑 JOHN FRED. I I
†1554

JOHN ERNEST
D. of Saxe-Coburg
†1563

JOHN

FREDERICK
†1539

👑 MAURICE I
El. of Saxony 1547
†1553

👑 AUGUSTUS I
†1586

JOHN FRED. II
D. of Saxony
†1595

JOHN WILLIAM
D. of Saxe-Weimar
†1572

👑 CHRISTIAN I I
†1591

JOHN CASIMIR
of Coburg

JOHN ERNEST

FRED. WILLIAM
of Altenburg
†1602

JOHN of Weimar
†1605

👑 CHRISTIAN II I
†1611

👑 JOHN GEORGE I I
†1656

AUGUSTUS
†1615

DUKES OF SAXE-ALTENBURG (ext. 1672)

WILLIAM
†1662

ALBRECHT
of Eisenach
†1644

ERNEST I The Pious
D. of Saxe-Gotha-Altenburg
†1675

👑 JOHN GEORGE II I
†1656

AUGUSTUS
of Weissenfels
†1680

CHRISTIAN I
of Merseburg
†1691

MAURICE
of Zeitz
†1681

JOHN ERNEST II
†1683

ADOLPHUS
WILLIAM

JOHN GEORGE I
†1686

BERNHARD
of Jena †1688

👑 JOHN GEORGE III I
†1691

D. OF SAXE-WEISSENFELS (ext. 1746)

D. OF SAXE-MERSEBURG (ext. 1731)

DUKES OF SAXE-ZEITZ (ext. 1759)

GRAND-DUKES OF SAXE-WEIMAR

DUKES OF SAXE-EISENACH (ext. 1741)

JOHN WILLIAM
D. of Saxe-Jena
†1690

TABLE 102

👑 JOHN GEORGE IV I
†

👑 FRED. AUGUSTUS I (II) I
K. of Poland

FREDERICK I
of Gotha
†1691

ALBERT
of Coburg
†1699

BERNHARD
of Meiningen
†1706

HENRY
of Römhild
†1710

CHRISTIAN
of Eisenberg
†1707

ERNEST
of Hildbghsn.
†1715

JOHN ERNEST
of Saalfeld
†1729

👑 FRED. AUGUSTUS II (III) I
K. of Poland

DUKES OF SAXE-GOTHA & ALTENBURG (ext. 1825)

DUKES OF SAXE-MEININGEN & HILDBURGHAUSEN

DUKES OF SAXE-HILDBURGHAUSEN since 1825 SAXE-ALTENBURG

👑 FRED. CHRISTIAN I

FRANCIS XAV.

CHARLES
D. of Kurland

ALBERT
D. of Teschen

CLEMENS
WENCESLAS
El. of Trier

DUKES OF SAXE-COBURG-SAALFELD

CHRISTIAN
ERNEST
†1745

WILLIAM
FREDERICK

CHARLES
ERNEST

FRANCIS JOSIAS
†1764

👑 FRED. AUGUSTUS III (I) I
K. of Saxony

👑 ANTHONY I

MAXIMILIAN

TABLE 103

ERNEST FRED.
†1800

JOHN
WILLIAM
✕ 1745

CHRISTIAN
†1797

FRED. JOSIAS
†1815

👑 FRED. AUGUSTUS II

👑 JOHN

see also **TABLE 42**

FRANCIS
†1806

BARONS OF ROHMANN

👑 ALBERT

ERNEST

👑 GEORGE

ERNEST I
D. of Saxe-Coburg & Gotha
†1844

FERDINAND
†1851

LEOPOLD I
K. of Belgians

👑 FRED. AUGUSTUS III

JOHN
GEORGE

MAX

ALBERT

ERNEST II
†1893

ALBERT
†1861

FERDINAND
K. of Portugal

AUGUSTUS
†1881

LEOPOLD
†1884

KINGS OF THE BELGIANS

GEORGE

FRED. CHRIST.

ERNEST
HENRY

KINGS OF GT. BRITAIN DUKES OF SAXE-COBURG & GOTHA

KINGS OF PORTUGAL (ext. 1932)

PHILIP
†1921

AUGUSTUS
†1907

FERDINAND
K. of Bulgaria

MARIA
EMANUEL

ALBERT

DEDO

TIMO

GERO

LEOPOLD
†1916

DUKES OF SAXE-COBG. & GOTHA

KINGS OF BULGARIA

RÜDIGER

NOTE
[1] Elector of Saxony

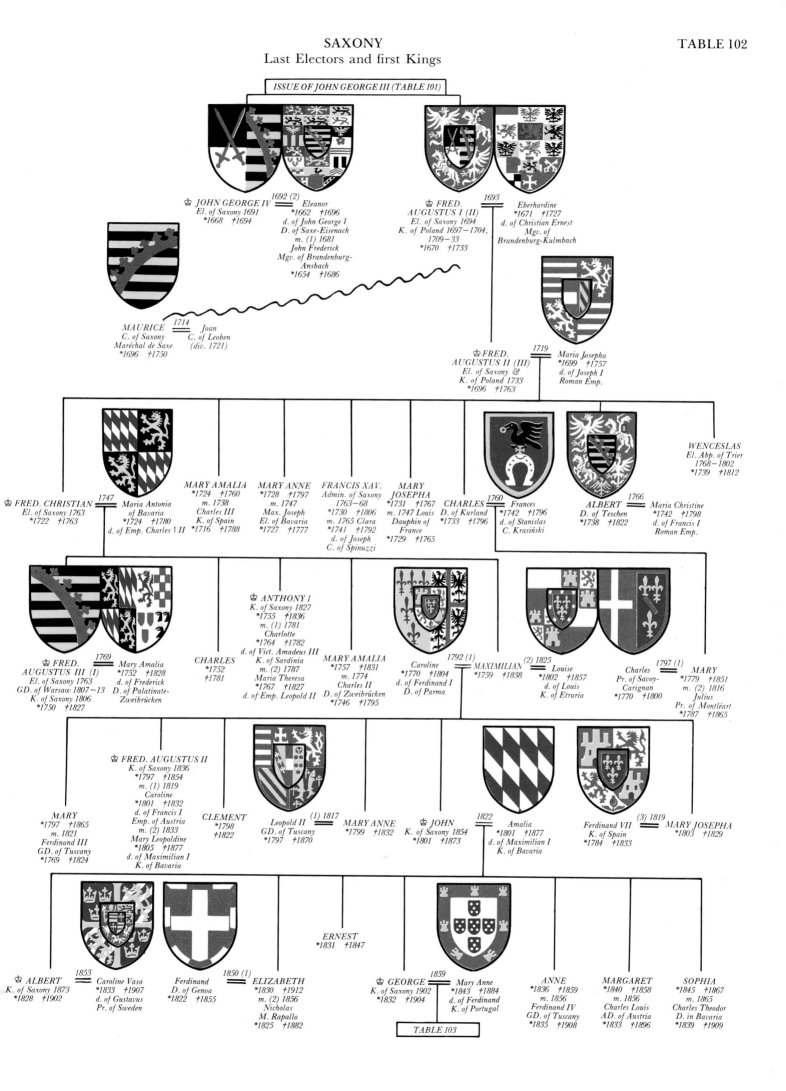

ISSUE OF JOHN GEORGE III (TABLE 101)

♔ JOHN GEORGE IV
El. of Saxony 1691
*1668 †1694

1692 (2)
═══ Eleanor
*1662 †1696
d. of John George I
D. of Saxe-Eisenach
m. (1) 1681
John Frederick
Mgv. of Brandenburg-
Ansbach
*1654 †1686

♔ FRED.
AUGUSTUS I (II)
El. of Saxony 1694
K. of Poland 1697–1704,
1709–33
*1670 †1733

1693
═══ Eberhardine
*1671 †1727
d. of Christian Ernest
Mgv. of
Brandenburg-Kulmbach

MAURICE
C. of Saxony
Maréchal de Saxe
*1696 †1750

1714
═══ Joan
C. of Leoben
(div. 1721)

♔ FRED.
AUGUSTUS II (III)
El. of Saxony &
K. of Poland 1733
*1696 †1763

1719
═══ Maria Josepha
*1699 †1757
d. of Joseph I
Roman Emp.

♔ FRED. CHRISTIAN
El. of Saxony 1763
*1722 †1763

1747
═══ Maria Antonia
of Bavaria
*1724 †1780
d. of Emp. Charles VII

MARY AMALIA
*1724 †1760
m. 1738
Charles III
K. of Spain
*1716 †1788

MARY ANNE
*1728 †1797
m. 1747
Max. Joseph
El. of Bavaria
*1727 †1777

FRANCIS XAV.
Admin. of Saxony
1763–68
*1730 †1806
m. 1765 Clara
*1741 †1792
d. of Joseph
C. of Spinuzzi

MARY
JOSEPHA
*1731 †1767
m. 1747 Louis
Dauphin of
France
*1729 †1765

CHARLES
D. of Kurland
*1733 †1796

1760
═══ Frances
*1742 †1796
d. of Stanislas
C. Krasiński

ALBERT
D. of Teschen
*1738 †1822

1766
═══ Maria Christine
*1742 †1798
d. of Francis I
Roman Emp.

WENCESLAS
El. Abp. of Trier
1768–1802
*1739 †1812

♔ FRED.
AUGUSTUS III (I)
El. of Saxony 1763
GD. of Warsaw 1807–13
K. of Saxony 1806
*1750 †1827

1769
═══ Mary Amalia
*1752 †1828
d. of Frederick
D. of Palatinate-
Zweibrücken

CHARLES
*1752
†1781

♔ ANTHONY I
K. of Saxony 1827
*1755 †1836
m. (1) 1781
Charlotte
*1764 †1782
d. of Vict. Amadeus III
K. of Sardinia
m. (2) 1787
Maria Theresa
*1767 †1827
d. of Emp. Leopold II

MARY AMALIA
*1757 †1831
m. 1774
Charles II
D. of Zweibrücken
*1746 †1795

Caroline
*1770 †1804
d. of Ferdinand I
D. of Parma

1792 (1)
═══ MAXIMILIAN
*1759 †1838

(2) 1825
═══ Louise
*1802 †1857
d. of Louis
K. of Etruria

Charles
Pr. of Savoy-
Carignan
*1770 †1800

1797 (1)
═══ MARY
*1779 †1851
m. (2) 1816
Julius
Pr. of Montléart
*1787 †1865

MARY
*1797 †1865
m. 1821
Ferdinand III
GD. of Tuscany
*1769 †1824

♔ FRED. AUGUSTUS II
K. of Saxony 1836
*1797 †1854
m. (1) 1819
Caroline
*1801 †1832
d. of Francis I
Emp. of Austria
m. (2) 1833
Mary Leopoldine
*1805 †1877
d. of Maximilian I
K. of Bavaria

CLEMENT
*1798
†1822

Leopold II
GD. of Tuscany
*1797 †1870

(1) 1817
═══

MARY ANNE
*1799 †1832

♔ JOHN
K. of Saxony 1854
*1801 †1873

1822
═══ Amalia
*1801 †1877
d. of Maximilian I
K. of Bavaria

Ferdinand VII
K. of Spain
*1784 †1833

(3) 1819
═══ MARY JOSEPHA
*1803 †1829

♔ ALBERT
K. of Saxony 1873
*1828 †1902

1853
═══ Caroline Vasa
*1833 †1907
d. of Gustavus
Pr. of Sweden

Ferdinand
D. of Genoa
*1822 †1855

1850 (1)
═══ ELIZABETH
*1830 †1912
m. (2) 1856
Nicholas
M. Rapallo
*1825 †1882

ERNEST
*1831 †1847

♔ GEORGE
K. of Saxony 1902
*1832 †1904

1859
═══ Mary Anne
*1843 †1884
d. of Ferdinand
K. of Portugal

ANNE
*1836 †1859
m. 1856
Ferdinand IV
GD. of Tuscany
*1835 †1908

MARGARET
*1840 †1858
m. 1856
Charles Louis
AD. of Austria
*1833 †1896

SOPHIA
*1845 †1867
m. 1865
Charles Theodor
D. in Bavaria
*1839 †1909

TABLE 103

until the decease in 1482 of their uncle, William III of Thuringia. In 1485 they executed a treaty of partition at Leipzig, which divided for ever the House of Wettin and its lands into two branches, called after them Ernestine and Albertine. Both lines continued to use the same basic arms, of which the essentials are the black lion rampant on gold of Meissen and the distinctive blazon of Saxony, which has a crancelin, or wreath of rue, over a black and gold barry background. Tradition, which is unlikely to be authentic, relates that the Emperor Barbarossa took a chaplet of rue from his own head and draped it across the shield of Duke Bernard of Ascania, which had hitherto consisted of black and gold bars only.

ERNESTINE SAXONY

Ernest, the elder brother, retained the Electorate and took Wittenberg, Thuringia and the provinces of Vogtland. Albert received the Margravate of Meissen; in the event his line was to achieve more success than the elder branch, but its story must wait. Towards the end of the rule of Elector Ernest there was born in his dominions a peasant who was to change the world. Martin Luther, though not of outstanding talents, was to launch the Reformation: it was on the door of the castle church at Wittenberg, capital of electoral Saxony, that he nailed in 1517 his famous ninety-five theses. This is no place to develop the story of the great Protestant movement, but it must be recorded that, much as Luther owed to the University of Wittenberg, his debt was even greater to the protection and patronage which he received from the Elector Frederick the Wise. In a very real sense Wittenberg was the cradle of the great Lutheran faith and of the tremendous movement which rippled outwards from the little town. Frederick loved peace, his home and his bible; his reward was to see his land devastated by the bitter 'Peasants' War'. His brother John the Steady and his nephew John Frederick I were both staunch supporters of the reformers. The latter was captured by the Emperor Charles V at Mühlberg (1547) and compelled to sign away his electoral rank to his cousin Maurice (of the Albertine line); with the title went many of his estates. The Ernestine branch was never again of high consequence in Germany.

Its fate was the usual one of subdivision, amalgamation and further partition. The existing lines all stem from Duke John of Saxe-Weimar, who died in 1605. Two main branches descend from him and are still extant today, those of Weimar and Gotha. In the former the principle of primogeniture was established in 1725 and the separate Duchies of Saxe-Weimar, Saxe-Eisenach and Saxe-Jena were united; in 1815 the rulers became grand-dukes. Charles Augustus, who reigned at Weimar from 1775 to 1828, was an enlightened and conspicuous patron of the arts; Goethe and Schiller both entered his service, and the rebirth of German literature virtually took place at his tiny court.

The Dukes of Saxe-Gotha were even more a prey to fractions. At the end of the seventeenth century there were minuscule duchies each with its own capital and court at Gotha, Coburg, Meiningen, Eisenberg, Römhild, Hildburghausen and Saalfeld. In 1826 there was a massive rearrangement of lands of the *Nexus Gothanus* which produced Dukes of Saxe-Meiningen and Hildburghausen, Saxe-Altenburg and Saxe-Coburg and Gotha.

By a series of felicitous marriages the third and most junior of these principalities has contrived to supply kings to Great Britain, Portugal, Bulgaria and Belgium (Table 42 and Chapter 9). The succession to the Duchy passed in 1893 to the heirs of the Prince Consort, husband of Queen Victoria.

Their second son Alfred, Duke of Edinburgh, was duke until his death in 1900 and was followed by his nephew Charles Edward (Table 42) who was deprived of his British dukedom of Albany in 1917.

ALBERTINE SAXONY

The Albertine line was less resolutely wedded to the Reformation than the Ernestine line. Margrave George (d. 1539) was a zealous Catholic, but his brother Henry was a Protestant. Maurice, the next heir, though a Lutheran, put policy and ambition before faith. With more adroitness than consistency he first allied with the Emperor (Charles V) and then attacked him. As has been noted, in 1547 he was given the electoral rank and some of the estates of his Ernestine cousin; but the booty was not enough and Maurice returned to the Protestant side. His brother, Augustus, was more devoted to the arts of peace. Coal-mining, introduced by Maurice, was encouraged, agriculture and commerce fostered. It seemed as if a prosperous future might lie before Saxony, but this was not to be.

The Elector John George I was married to a niece of the last Duke of Cleves and Jülich. While he had sufficient wisdom to refuse the Crown of Bohemia, he was none the less deeply involved in the Thirty Years' War, of which Saxony was one of the major battlefields. It is true that he acquired Lusatia from the Emperor in 1635, but his own homeland was devastated in the fighting and his alliance with the Catholic Empire allowed the leadership of reformed Germany to pass to Brandenburg. The last act of this rather ineffectual Prince was to bequeath independent duchies to his three younger sons, thus further weakening the impoverished Electorate of Saxony. Fortunately all three died out by 1759, and their states returned to the main line one by one.

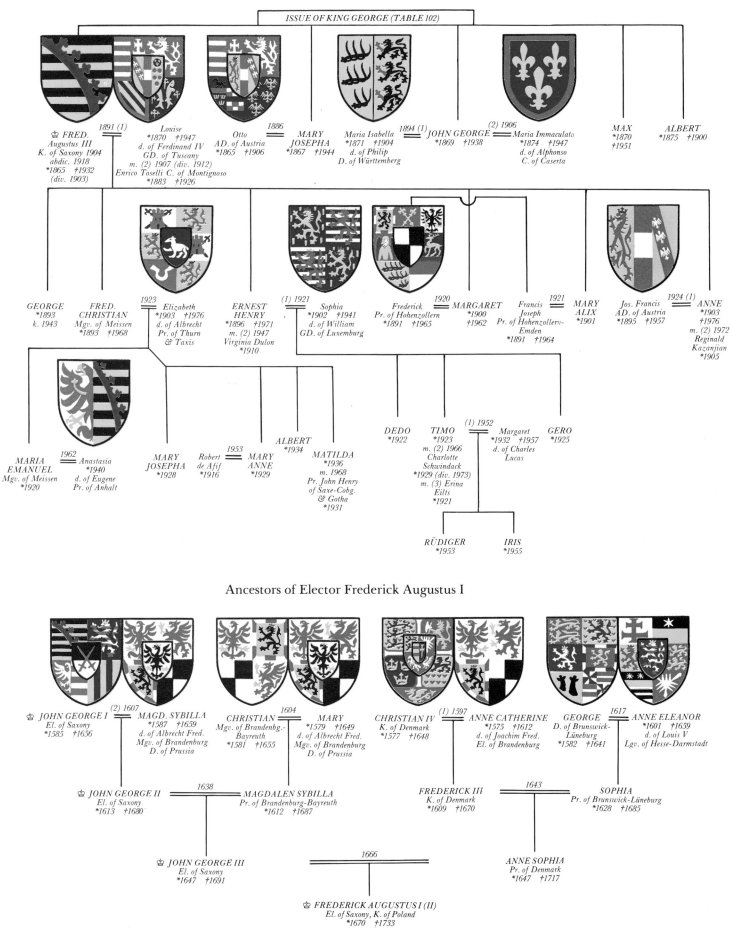

ISSUE OF KING GEORGE (TABLE 102)

👑 FRED. Augustus III
K. of Saxony 1904
abdic. 1918
*1865 †1932
(div. 1903)

═ 1891 (1)

Louise
*1870 †1947
d. of Ferdinand IV
GD. of Tuscany
m. (2) 1907 (div. 1912)
Enrico Toselli C. of Montignoso
*1883 †1926

Otto
AD. of Austria
*1865 †1906

═ 1886

MARY JOSEPHA
*1867 †1944

Maria Isabella
*1871 †1904
d. of Philip
D. of Württemberg

═ 1894 (1)

JOHN GEORGE
*1869 †1938

═ (2) 1906

Maria Immaculata
*1874 †1947
d. of Alphonso
C. of Caserta

MAX
*1870 †1951

ALBERT
*1875 †1900

GEORGE
*1893
k. 1943

FRED. CHRISTIAN
Mgv. of Meissen
*1893 †1968

═ 1923

Elizabeth
*1903 †1976
d. of Albrecht
Pr. of Thurn & Taxis

ERNEST HENRY
*1896 †1971
m. (2) 1947
Virginia Dulon
*1910

═ (1) 1921

Sophia
*1902 †1941
d. of William
GD. of Luxemburg

Frederick
Pr. of Hohenzollern
*1891 †1965

═ 1920

MARGARET
*1900 †1962

Francis Joseph
Pr. of Hohenzollern-Emden
*1891 †1964

═ 1921

MARY ALIX
*1901

Jos. Francis
AD. of Austria
*1895 †1957

═ 1924 (1)

ANNE
*1903 †1976
m. (2) 1972
Reginald Kazanjian
*1905

MARIA EMANUEL
Mgv. of Meissen
*1920

═ 1962

Anastasia
*1940
d. of Eugene
Pr. of Anhalt

MARY JOSEPHA
*1928

Robert de Afif

═ 1953

MARY ANNE
*1916

ALBERT
*1934

MATILDA
*1936
m. 1968
Pr. John Henry
of Saxe-Cobg. & Gotha
*1931

DEDO
*1922

TIMO
*1923
m. (2) 1966
Charlotte Schwindack
*1929 (div. 1973)
m. (3) Erina Eilts
*1921

═ (1) 1952

Margaret
*1932 †1957
d. of Charles Lucas

GERO
*1925

RÜDIGER
*1953

IRIS
*1955

Ancestors of Elector Frederick Augustus I

👑 JOHN GEORGE I
El. of Saxony
*1585 †1656

═ (2) 1607

MAGD. SYBILLA
*1587 †1659
d. of Albrecht Fred.
Mgv. of Brandenburg
D. of Prussia

CHRISTIAN
Mgv. of Brandenbg.-Bayreuth
*1581 †1655

═ 1604

MARY
*1579 †1649
d. of Albrecht Fred.
Mgv. of Brandenburg
D. of Prussia

CHRISTIAN IV
K. of Denmark
*1577 †1648

═ (1) 1597

ANNE CATHERINE
*1575 †1612
d. of Joachim Fred.
El. of Brandenburg

GEORGE
D. of Brunswick-Lüneburg
*1582 †1641

═ 1617

ANNE ELEANOR
*1601 †1659
d. of Louis V
Lgv. of Hesse-Darmstadt

👑 JOHN GEORGE II
El. of Saxony
*1613 †1680

═ 1638

MAGDALEN SYBILLA
Pr. of Brandenburg-Bayreuth
*1612 †1687

FREDERICK III
K. of Denmark
*1609 †1670

═ 1643

SOPHIA
Pr. of Brunswick-Lüneburg
*1628 †1685

👑 JOHN GEORGE III
El. of Saxony
*1647 †1691

═ 1666

ANNE SOPHIA
Pr. of Denmark
*1647 †1717

👑 FREDERICK AUGUSTUS I (II)
El. of Saxony, K. of Poland
*1670 †1733

Augustus the Strong (1670–1733), Elector of Saxony and King of Poland, with Frederick William I, King in Prussia, by Louis de Silvestre, c. 1730.

At the beginning of the eighteenth century the fortunes of Saxony took a new and disastrous turn. John George IV (Table 102) was the fourth consecutive Elector to bear this name. His arms show the crancelin of Saxony impaled with the crossed swords of the Marshalcy of the Empire which went with the Saxon Electorate. From this shield were derived the crossed swords on Dresden porcelain, which began to be made at this time; the manufacture of hard-paste china began at Meissen in about 1710. Frederick Augustus succeeded his brother in 1694 and embarked on larger ambitions. His ancestry (on Table 103) shows that in fact he was half of Brandenburg descent, mingled with other German strains. The more elaborate blazon of Saxony given for John George I shows the shield of the Marshalcy over quarterings for Saxony, Thuringia, Magdeburg

and Landsberg. In 1696 John Sobieski, King of Poland, died and Augustus the Strong, as he is sometimes known, put himself forward for election. In order to fortify his claims he announced his conversion to Catholicism. He was crowned at Cracow in 1697 but had considerable difficulty in establishing his position, which indeed he had to abandon between 1704 and 1709. His preoccupation with Poland left Saxony again at the mercy of warring armies.

Augustus begot by his mistress, Aurora von Königsmarck, the famous Maréchal de Saxe, one of the greatest soldiers of the age. Her family, blazing comet-like across Europe at this time, merits a brief digression. The grandfather was a Swedish general in the Thirty Years' War; her uncle directed the artillery which in 1687 blew up the Parthenon; one brother (Charles) arranged the murder of the richest English commoner of the day in Pall Mall, another disappeared mysteriously in Hanover under suspicion of being the lover of Sophia Dorothea of Zelle, wife of the future George I of England (Table 99).

Augustus the Strong was possibly meditating a partition of Poland when he died in 1733. Frederick Augustus II, his son and heir, had been brought up a Catholic and was married to a Hapsburg (Table 102). Moreover he was a very different man from his father; portly and indolent, little attracted by public business, he was inclined to leave great affairs to his ministers and devote his own attention to hunting. For most of his reign, Count von Brühl ruled in Saxony and the Czartoryski family in Poland. During the Seven Years' War (1756–63) the Elector-King withdrew to Poland, and Saxony itself was devastated by the various campaigns. When both Frederick Augustus II and his son, Frederick Christian, died in succession in 1763, Saxony was in a sorry condition. Leipzig had, however, been enriched by the glorious genius of the composer J. S. Bach.

Frederick Augustus III was more conscious of the interests of Saxony than his predecessors; he devoted himself to the reconstruction of the Electorate, possibly aware that Frederick the Great of Prussia coveted his domain. His mother had been Bavarian, and in 1777 he advanced claims to her inheritance. The indecisive manoeuvrings of the War of the Bavarian Succession left him richer by four million thalers, which he was able to use in buying back Saxon land alienated by his grandfather. In 1791, with great good sense, he declined the Crown of Poland. In 1806 he attached himself to Napoleon and assumed the title of King of Saxony. As a reward he was given in 1807 the Grand-Duchy of Warsaw, which the French Emperor had created from among his conquests. In the same year he founded the Order of the Crown of Rue: this surrounds the shield at the bottom of Table 101. Frederick Augustus I is usually numbered as the first King of Saxony. The last great battle of Napoleon's main reign was on Saxon soil at Leipzig (1813) and King Frederick Augustus was captured by the Allies. Prussia was anxious to absorb Saxony, but this desire was opposed at the Congress of Vienna by Britain and Austria. Eventually, Saxony emerged as a separate kingdom, but she had to cede a large northern area to her voracious neighbour.

In 1830 there were risings in Leipzig and Dresden which resulted in the appointment of Frederick Augustus II as co-ruler with his uncle (his father, Maximilian, had renounced the succession). Further revolts in 1848 were quelled by Prussian arms. King John was a scholarly man, who had translated the works of the poet Dante into German, but his reign saw Saxony increasingly drawn into the orbit of Prussia, which governed her foreign affairs and exercised control over her army. The history of the state was uneventful between 1870 and 1914, save for a steady rise in popular support for socialism. The short reign of King George (1902–4) witnessed a sensational scandal when his daughter-in-law, Louise of Tuscany, eloped with the Frenchman hired to teach her children; the errant Princess was given the title of Countess of Montignoso.

Frederick Augustus III (Table 103) was a field-marshal in the German army. In 1918, like other rulers in that country, he was compelled to abdicate, and Saxony became a mere province of the German Republic. His eldest son, another George, renounced all his royal rights in 1923 and became a Jesuit priest; he perished mysteriously by drowning during the Nazi regime. The second son, Prince Frederick Christian, who used the title Margrave of Meissen, died in 1968 and the heir to the throne of Saxony is his child, Maria Emanuel. His marriage to a Princess of Anhalt links the Wettin House of Saxony with the Ascanian dynasty which held the province before them (Table 101). As a result of World War II his realm is now a component part of East Germany.

The full blazon of the Kings of Saxony can be seen on Table 101, surrounded by the Order of the Crown of Rue. There are twelve main quarterings, in rows

The Maréchal de Saxe, illegitimate son of Augustus the Strong who entered the French service, by J. E. Leotard, c. 1750. He carries the baton of a Marshal of France.

of three: *1* Meissen, *2* Thuringia, *3* Palatinate of Thuringia; *4* Palatinate of Saxony, *5* and *8* red with an escutcheon of Saxony over all, *6* Lordship of Pleissen; *7* Vogtland, *8* see *5*, *9* County of Orlamünde; *10* Landsberg, *11* divided into three, above Upper Lusatia and below Altenburg (a rose) and Henneberg (a cock or hen), *12* Eisenberg.

Chapter 27

WÜRTTEMBERG AND BADEN

Württemberg, whose name was spelled in various ways until modern times, is a castle not far from Stuttgart. The area was part of the Duchy of Swabia until the middle of the thirteenth century. After the fall of the Hohenstaufen emperors, the local dynasts grew in power. Eberhard II (Table 104) largely increased his territory and made Stuttgart his capital. Perhaps fortunately, the family was not very prolific and division between heirs did not reach serious proportions. Eberhard V, the Bearded, married the daughter of the Count of Montbéliard (or Mömpelgard: between Besançon and Basle). Eberhard VI not only made his estates indivisible but was raised to the rank of duke in 1495. The basic arms of the County or Duchy are three stags' antlers of black on gold: later blazons insist that the two upper must have four, and the lowest three tines. Among the lordships acquired by successive counts were Urach (1260), Calw (1308) and part of the Duchy of Teck (1325). The arms of Teck are the bold black and gold pattern on Table 104. Later dukes and kings combined the horns of Württemberg with the black lions, each with one red paw, of Swabia. Around their shield is the ribbon of the Order of the Crown of Württemberg, founded in 1818.

Ulric VI enjoyed a long and eventful reign. His extravagance brought about a rising of the peasantry, nicknamed as 'Poor Conrads'; he embraced the Reformation; he was compelled to accept the overlordship of Austria for his Duchy – from which indeed he was briefly expelled; he finished as an ally of Charles V. His son Christopher was a more resolute reformer; his grandson Louis III died childless. The Duchy now passed to Frederick I, who had been governing the detached County of Mömpelgard on the west side of the Rhine: like many lordships in Bar this one had barbels in its shield, which constitutes the fourth quartering in the elaborate blazon

of King Frederick I at the head of Table 105.

Duke Frederick I succeeded in liberating himself from Austrian suzerainty in 1599. Württemberg suffered like most German states from the Thirty Years' War and from French invasions later in the seventeenth century. Duke Charles Alexander and his two older sons were Catholics, but the youngest of them, Frederick Eugene, was a Protestant.

Frederick, his eldest son (Table 105), came to terms with Napoleon in 1802 and was granted the title of elector and then that of king (1805); the alliance was cemented by the marriage of Frederick's daughter Catherine to Napoleon's brother, despite the existence of Jerome's American wife. King Frederick adroitly betrayed his benefactor in 1813

King William II of Württemberg (1848–1921) and his wife Charlotte.

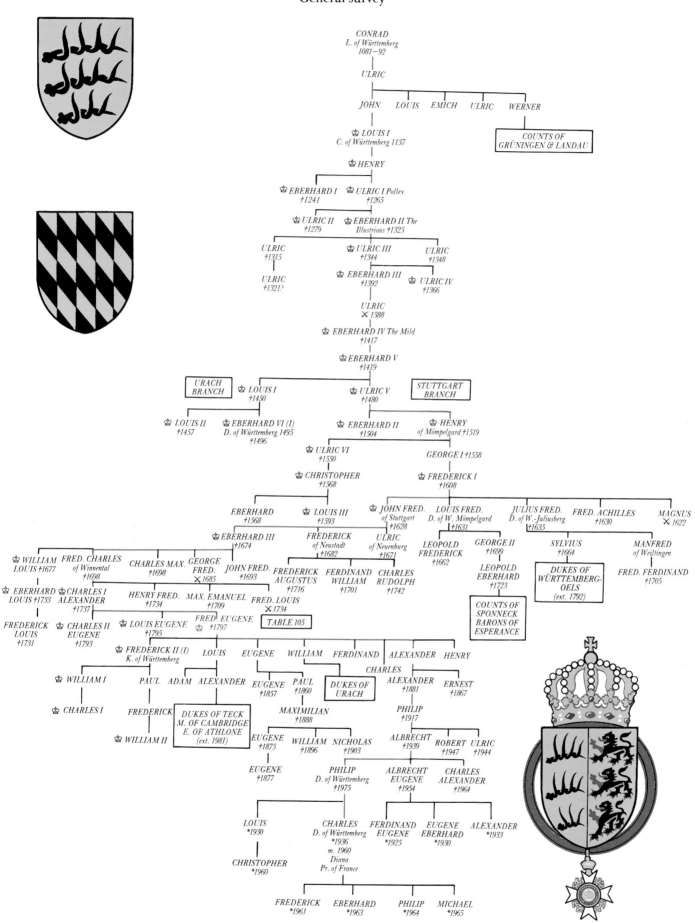

CONRAD
L. of Württemberg
1081–92

ULRIC

JOHN · LOUIS · EMICH · ULRIC · WERNER

COUNTS OF
GRÜNINGEN & LANDAU

♔ LOUIS I
C. of Württemberg 1137

♔ HENRY

♔ EBERHARD I †1241 · ♔ ULRIC I Pollex †1265

♔ ULRIC II †1279 · ♔ EBERHARD II The Illustrious †1325

ULRIC †1315 · ♔ ULRIC III †1344 · ULRIC †1348

ULRIC †1321? · ♔ EBERHARD III †1392 · ♔ ULRIC IV †1366

ULRIC ✕ 1388

♔ EBERHARD IV The Mild †1417

♔ EBERHARD V †1419

URACH BRANCH · ♔ LOUIS I †1450 · ♔ ULRIC V †1480 · STUTTGART BRANCH

♔ LOUIS II †1457 · ♔ EBERHARD VI (I) D. of Württemberg 1495 †1496 · ♔ EBERHARD II †1504 · ♔ HENRY of Mömpelgard †1519

♔ ULRIC VI †1550 · GEORGE I †1558

♔ CHRISTOPHER †1568 · ♔ FREDERICK I †1608

EBERHARD †1568 · ♔ LOUIS III †1593 · ♔ JOHN FRED. of Stuttgart †1628 · LOUIS FRED. D. of W. Mömpelgard †1631 · JULIUS FRED. D. of W.-Juliusberg †1635 · FRED. ACHILLES †1630 · MAGNUS ✕ 1622

♔ EBERHARD III †1674 · FREDERICK of Neustadt †1682 · ULRIC of Neuenburg †1671 · LEOPOLD FREDERICK †1662 · GEORGE II †1699 · SYLVIUS †1664 · MANFRED of Weiltingen

♔ WILLIAM LOUIS †1677 · FRED. CHARLES of Winnental †1698 · CHARLES MAX. †1698 · GEORGE FRED. ✕ 1685 · JOHN FRED. †1693 · FREDERICK AUGUSTUS †1716 · FERDINAND WILLIAM †1701 · CHARLES RUDOLPH †1742 · LEOPOLD EBERHARD †1723 · DUKES OF WÜRTTEMBERG-OELS (ext. 1792) · FRED. FERDINAND †1705

♔ EBERHARD LOUIS †1733 · ♔ CHARLES I ALEXANDER †1737 · HENRY FRED. †1734 · MAX. EMANUEL †1709 · FRED. LOUIS ✕ 1734 · TABLE 105 · COUNTS OF SPONNECK BARONS OF ESPERANCE

FREDERICK LOUIS †1731 · ♔ CHARLES II EUGENE †1793 · ♔ LOUIS EUGENE †1795 · FRED. EUGENE ♔ †1797

♔ FREDERICK II (I) K. of Württemberg · LOUIS · EUGENE · WILLIAM · FERDINAND · ALEXANDER · HENRY

♔ WILLIAM I · PAUL · ADAM · ALEXANDER · EUGENE †1857 · PAUL †1860 · DUKES OF URACH · CHARLES · ALEXANDER †1881 · ERNEST †1867

♔ CHARLES I · FREDERICK · DUKES OF TECK M. OF CAMBRIDGE E. OF ATHLONE (ext. 1981) · MAXIMILIAN †1888 · PHILIP †1917

♔ WILLIAM II · EUGENE †1875 · WILLIAM †1896 · NICHOLAS †1903 · ALBRECHT †1939 · ROBERT †1947 · ULRIC †1944

EUGENE †1877 · PHILIP D. of Württemberg †1975 · ALBRECHT EUGENE †1954 · CHARLES ALEXANDER †1964

LOUIS *1930 · CHARLES D. of Württemberg *1936 m. 1960 Diana Pr. of France · FERDINAND EUGENE *1925 · EUGENE EBERHARD *1930 · ALEXANDER *1933

CHRISTOPHER *1960

FREDERICK *1961 · EBERHARD *1963 · PHILIP *1964 · MICHAEL *1965

TABLE 105

WÜRTTEMBERG
Kings until the end of the monarchy

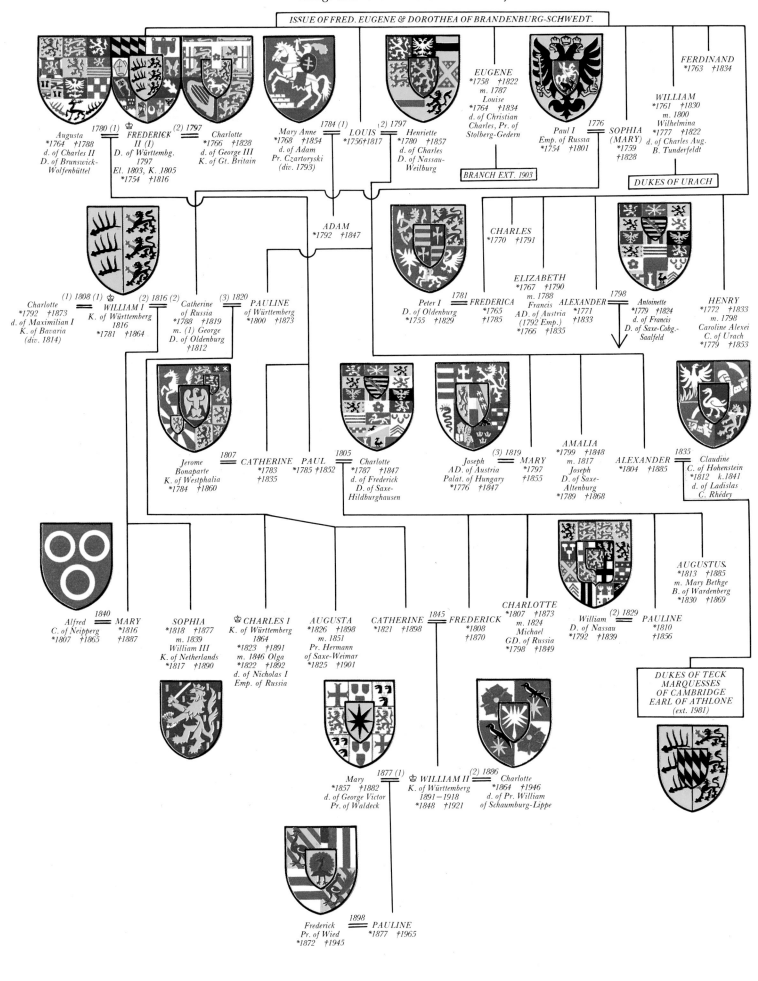

ISSUE OF FRED. EUGENE & DOROTHEA OF BRANDENBURG-SCHWEDT.

FERDINAND
*1763 †1834

WILLIAM
*1761 †1830
m. 1800
Wilhelmina
*1777 †1822
d. of Charles Aug.
B. Tunderfeldt

EUGENE
*1758 †1822
m. 1787
Louise
*1764 †1834
d. of Christian
Charles, Pr. of
Stolberg-Gedern

Augusta
*1764 †1788
d. of Charles II
D. of Brunswick-
Wolfenbüttel

1780 (1) FREDERICK *(2) 1797*
II (I)
D. of Württembg.
1797
El. 1803, K. 1805
*1754 †1816

Charlotte
*1766 †1828
d. of George III
K. of Gt. Britain

Mary Anne
*1768 †1854
d. of Adam
Pr. Czartoryski
(div. 1793)

1784 (1) LOUIS *(2) 1797*
*1756†1817

Henriette
*1780 †1857
d. of Charles
D. of Nassau-
Weilburg

Paul I 1776
Emp. of Russia
*1754 †1801

SOPHIA
(MARY)
*1759
†1828

BRANCH EXT. 1903

DUKES OF URACH

ADAM
*1792 †1847

CHARLES
*1770 †1791

Charlotte
*1792 †1873
d. of Maximilian I
K. of Bavaria
(div. 1814)

(1) 1808 (1) WILLIAM I *(2) 1816 (2)*
K. of Württemberg
1816
*1781 †1864

Catherine
of Russia
*1788 †1819
m. (1) George
D. of Oldenburg
†1812

(3) 1820 PAULINE
of Württemberg
*1800 †1873

Peter I 1781
D. of Oldenburg
*1755 †1829

FREDERICA
*1765
†1785

ELIZABETH
*1767 †1790
m. 1788
Francis
AD. of Austria
(1792 Emp.)
*1766 †1835

ALEXANDER 1798
*1771
†1833

Antoinette
*1779 †1824
d. of Francis
D. of Saxe-Cobg.-
Saalfeld

HENRY
*1772 †1833
m. 1798
Caroline Alexei
C. of Urach
*1779 †1853

Jerome
Bonaparte
K. of Westphalia
*1784 †1860

1807
CATHERINE
*1783
†1835

PAUL *1805*
*1785 †1852

Charlotte
*1787 †1847
d. of Frederick
D. of Saxe-
Hildburghausen

Joseph
AD. of Austria
Palat. of Hungary
*1776 †1847

(3) 1819
MARY
*1797
†1855

AMALIA
*1799 †1848
m. 1817
Joseph
D. of Saxe-
Altenburg
*1789 †1868

ALEXANDER
*1804 †1885

1835
Claudine
C. of Hohenstein
*1812 k.1841
d. of Ladislas
C. Rhédey

AUGUSTUS
*1813 †1885
m. Mary Bethge
B. of Wardenberg
*1830 †1869

Alfred *1840*
C. of Neipperg
*1807 †1865

MARY
*1816
†1887

SOPHIA
*1818 †1877
m. 1839
William III
K. of Netherlands
*1817 †1890

CHARLES I
K. of Württemberg
1864
*1823 †1891
m. 1846 Olga
*1822 †1892
d. of Nicholas I
Emp. of Russia

AUGUSTA
*1826 †1898
m. 1851
Pr. Hermann
of Saxe-Weimar
*1825 †1901

CATHERINE
*1821 †1898

1845
FREDERICK
*1808
†1870

CHARLOTTE
*1807 †1873
m. 1824
Michael
GD. of Russia
*1798 †1849

William *(2) 1829*
D. of Nassau
*1792 †1839

PAULINE
*1810
†1856

DUKES OF TECK
MARQUESSES
OF CAMBRIDGE
EARL OF ATHLONE
(ext. 1981)

Mary *1877 (1)*
*1857 †1882
d. of George Victor
Pr. of Waldeck

WILLIAM II *(2) 1886*
K. of Württemberg
1891—1918
*1848 †1921

Charlotte
*1864 †1946
d. of Pr. William
of Schaumburg-Lippe

Frederick *1898*
Pr. of Wied
*1872 †1945

PAULINE
*1877 †1965

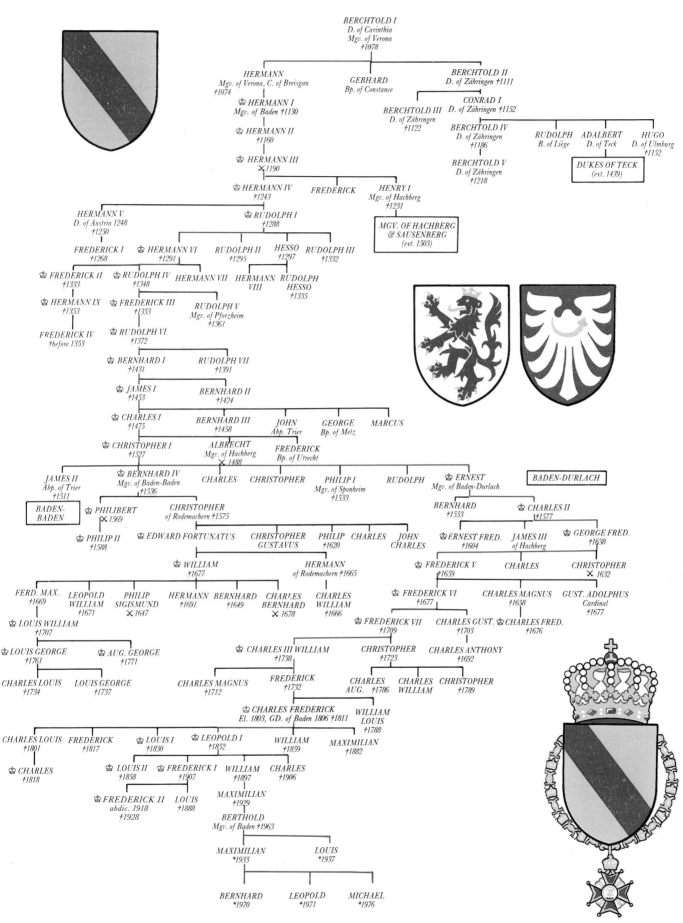

BERCHTOLD I
D. of Carinthia
Mgv. of Verona
†1078

HERMANN
Mgv. of Verona, C. of Breisgau
†1074

GEBHARD
Bp. of Constance

BERCHTOLD II
D. of Zähringen †1111

HERMANN I
Mgv. of Baden †1130

CONRAD I
D. of Zähringen †1152

BERCHTOLD III
D. of Zähringen
†1122

HERMANN II
†1160

BERCHTOLD IV
D. of Zähringen
†1186

RUDOLPH
B. of Liège

ADALBERT
D. of Teck

HUGO
D. of Ulmburg
†1152

HERMANN III
✕1190

BERCHTOLD V
D. of Zähringen
†1218

DUKES OF TECK
(ext. 1439)

HERMANN IV
†1243

FREDERICK

HENRY I
Mgv. of Hachberg
†1231

MGV. OF HACHBERG
& SAUSENBERG
(ext. 1503)

HERMANN V
D. of Austria 1248
†1250

RUDOLPH I
†1288

FREDERICK I
†1268

HERMANN VI
†1291

RUDOLPH II
†1295

HESSO
†1297

RUDOLPH III
†1332

FREDERICK II
†1333

RUDOLPH IV
†1348

HERMANN VII

HERMANN VIII

RUDOLPH HESSO
†1335

HERMANN IX
†1353

FREDERICK III
†1353

RUDOLPH V
Mgv. of Pforzheim
†1361

FREDERICK IV
†before 1353

RUDOLPH VI
†1372

BERNHARD I
†1431

RUDOLPH VII
†1391

JAMES I
†1453

BERNHARD II
†1424

CHARLES I
†1475

BERNHARD III
†1458

JOHN
Abp. Trier

GEORGE
Bp. of Metz

MARCUS

CHRISTOPHER I
†1527

ALBRECHT
Mgv. of Hachberg
✕1488

FREDERICK
Bp. of Utrecht

JAMES II
Abp. of Trier
†1511

BERNHARD IV
Mgv. of Baden-Baden
†1536

CHARLES

CHRISTOPHER

PHILIP I
Mgv. of Sponheim
†1533

RUDOLPH

ERNEST
Mgv. of Baden-Durlach

BADEN-DURLACH

BADEN-BADEN

PHILIBERT
✕1569

CHRISTOPHER
of Rodemachern †1575

BERNHARD
†1553

CHARLES II
†1577

PHILIP II
†1588

EDWARD FORTUNATUS

CHRISTOPHER
GUSTAVUS

PHILIP
†1620

CHARLES

JOHN
CHARLES

ERNEST FRED.
†1604

JAMES III
of Hachberg

GEORGE FRED.
†1638

WILLIAM
†1677

HERMANN
of Rodemachern †1665

FREDERICK V
†1659

CHARLES

CHRISTOPHER
✕1632

FERD. MAX.
†1669

LEOPOLD
WILLIAM
†1671

PHILIP
SIGISMUND
✕1647

HERMANN
†1691

BERNHARD
†1649

CHARLES
BERNHARD
✕1678

CHARLES
WILLIAM
†1666

FREDERICK VI
†1677

CHARLES MAGNUS
†1658

GUST. ADOLPHUS
Cardinal
†1677

LOUIS WILLIAM
†1707

FREDERICK VII
†1709

CHARLES GUST.
†1703

CHARLES FRED.
†1676

LOUIS GEORGE
†1761

AUG. GEORGE
†1771

CHARLES III WILLIAM
†1738

CHRISTOPHER
†1723

CHARLES ANTHONY
†1692

CHARLES LOUIS
†1734

LOUIS GEORGE
†1737

CHARLES MAGNUS
†1712

FREDERICK
†1732

CHARLES
AUG. †1786

CHARLES
WILLIAM

CHRISTOPHER
†1789

CHARLES FREDERICK
El. 1803, GD. of Baden 1806 †1811

WILLIAM
LOUIS
†1788

CHARLES LOUIS
†1801

FREDERICK
†1817

LOUIS I
†1830

LEOPOLD I
†1852

WILLIAM
†1859

MAXIMILIAN
†1882

CHARLES
†1818

LOUIS II
†1858

FREDERICK I
†1907

WILLIAM
†1897

CHARLES
†1906

FREDERICK II
abdic. 1918
†1928

LOUIS
†1888

MAXIMILIAN
†1929

BERTHOLD
Mgv. of Baden †1963

MAXIMILIAN
*1933

LOUIS
*1937

BERNHARD
*1970

LEOPOLD
*1971

MICHAEL
*1976

and succeeded in preserving his status and most of his dominions at the Treaty of Vienna. In 1871 Württemberg became part of the German Empire, reserving substantial powers for her own kings. The last King, William II, abdicated in 1918 and died in 1921. Two of his kinsmen made interesting alliances. Duke Alexander married morganatically Claudine Rhédey: his son Francis, Duke of Teck, married an English princess and Queen Mary of England was among their children. Duke William similarly married Wilhelmine Rhodis von Tunderfeldt and his children became Dukes of Urach (Chapter 13). The arms of Teck can be seen at the bottom of Table 105.

The death of William II without male issue caused the representation of the dynasty to pass to a collateral branch descended from Duke Alexander, a younger brother of Frederick, the first King. Duke Louis, elder son of Duke Philip, resigned his rights in 1959 on marrying a lady of lower rank. His younger brother Charles is the present Duke of Württemberg and has married a French princess (Table 104) and had four sons.

BADEN

The fiefs which gradually became the Grand-Duchy of Baden lie scattered in the shape of an 'L' between the Rhine and Württemberg, and formed part of the Duchy of Swabia. The family was founded by Berchtold I, Count of Zähringen (Table 106), who was nominated Duke of Carinthia. His son Berchtold II was disappointed of the Duchy of Swabia and consoled with the title of Duke of Zähringen. Hermann, his brother, acquired the County of Breisgau, and his son, Hermann I, adopted the title of Margrave of Baden, an area which had belonged to his mother. Baden is scarcely a frontier district and the title of margrave probably harked back to the Mark of Verona held by his grandfather. The early Margraves were successful in adding other properties to their domains, including Hachberg in about 1155 and Durlach in 1219. But at the end of the twelfth century a younger branch was invested with Hachberg and Sausenberg and held these lands until 1503. The arms of Hachberg were a red lion crowned with gold on a white field; those of Sausenberg a white eagle's wing on blue with a gold *kleestengel*. More

strikingly simple was the red bend on gold of Zähringen or Baden itself.

Christopher I reunited the two Margravates in 1503, but then redivided them among three of his sons: Bernhard was ancestor of Baden-Baden and Ernest of Baden-Durlach. Philip of Sponheim died without sons. Further partitions followed within the two branches, which were seldom at unity either in matters of religion or politics. The estates of both were broken up by a multitude of intervening lordships and episcopal fiefs. Hachberg, for example, was separated from Sausenberg by lands of the Bishopric of Strassburg, the Principality of Fürstenberg and less important secular properties, so that a map of Baden truly resembles a patchwork quilt. In 1715 the Order of Fidelity was founded by Margrave Charles III William: the collar can be seen on Table 106. In 1771 the extinction of the Baden-Baden line united the two Margravates once more; Charles Frederick in his long reign sought by every means to extend and link up his domains. His successes were crowned by the rank of elector in 1803, and of grand-duke in 1806 by grace of Napoleon.

Charles Frederick's first wife, Caroline of Hesse-Darmstadt, had borne three sons, but their male progeny seemed likely to die out. His second wife, Louisa Geyer von Geyersberg, was morganatic; her children were known as Counts of Hachberg. It has been suggested that the fate of the enigmatic Kaspar Hauser was in fact a by-product of this dynastic problem; but the mystery remains. The Great Powers at Vienna had blithely suggested that Baden should be allotted to Bavaria, if the Zähringens became extinct. With some spirit the Grand-Duke Charles issued a dynastic ordnance (*Hausgesetz*) in 1817, declaring that Leopold and his brothers were eligible for the succession. To gain support for his attitude, he also granted a liberal constitution to his subjects. Under Leopold I, who duly ascended the throne in 1830, and his wise and statesmanlike son, Frederick I, the democratic progress of Baden was an example to the other German states, until in 1870 it became part of the German Empire. Prince Max of Baden (d. 1929) was the last chancellor of that Empire in 1918. His grandson, also known as Max, is the present Margrave of Baden.

Chapter 28

BRABANT, THURINGIA, HESSE AND LORRAINE

In 843, at the Treaty of Verdun, the Empire of Charlemagne was divided among his grandchildren. This particular division was not final or definitive, but from this date separate entities exist, which can be distinguished as France and Germany (Chapter 15). The eldest of the three brothers, Lothair, received a less viable inheritance, which included the Low Countries and the left bank of the Rhine, Burgundy in its widest sense (Chapter 18) and north Italy. Within this narrow Kingdom lay Aachen (Aix-la-Chapelle) the capital of Charlemagne, Arles the capital of Burgundy, Monza (near Milan) the repository of the Iron Crown of the Lombard Kings, and Rome itself; within it also lay most of the battlefields and disputed territories of Europe for the next millenium.

This uneasy realm was again divided among the sons of Lothair and from the second of these, another Lothair, the name Lotharingia came to be given to the area lying south and west of the great bend in the Rhine. Ultimately the name contracted in French to Lorraine, which became one of the duchies of the German Kingdom, despite efforts of the French kings to assert their authority there. In the tenth century (959) the region was divided into two Duchies of Upper and Lower Lorraine. The latter was bestowed by the Emperor Otto II on Charles, a brother of the French King, and one of the last surviving male descendants of Charlemagne. His son was childless but one of his daughters married Lambert, Count of Louvain (Table 107), and one of his granddaughters married Gerard, Duke of Lorraine (Table 110). Another granddaughter married the Count of Boulogne, whose grandson Godfrey de Bouillon founded the Kingdom of Jerusalem.

Probably somewhere in Lorraine and around this date the story grew up of the Swan Knight which finds a mature expression in Wagner's *Lohengrin*.

Many of the descendants of the Counts of Louvain and Boulogne used the swan as a badge both in England and on the Continent. An Order of the Swan was founded in 1443 by Margrave Frederick II of Brandenburg (Table 91), whose ancestry led back to a daughter of the first Landgrave of Hesse (Table 108).

Upper Lorraine had been given to Frederick, Count of Bar, a member of the family of the Counts of Ardennes, who held it until the middle of the eleventh century when the Emperor Henry III awarded it to Gerard (Table 110), who was already the Count of Alsace. From his loins sprang the great House of Lorraine which in the eighteenth century took over the Hapsburg inheritance and still exists today in many branches. As will be seen later, his descendants succeeded in building up a relatively compact fief, to which the name of Lorraine has adhered. The fate of Lower Lorraine was very different. After the deaths of Duke Charles (994) and his son Otto (1016), which marked the end of the males of the Carolingian family, the Duchy was held by various local nobles, including the famous Godfrey de Bouillon, who abandoned his position here in order to lead the First Crusade. In 1100 the Emperor Henry IV gave Lower Lorraine to the Count of Limburg: in 1106 his son, Henry V, transferred it to Godfrey the Bearded, Count of Louvain, a descendant of Duke Charles (Table 107). The decision was resented by the Lords of Limburg, and the area was torn by war between the two families for most of the twelfth century. Henry I finally abandoned the style of Duke of Lower Lorraine in favour of that of Duke of Brabant. The most important towns in his domain were Brussels, Antwerp and Louvain.

Later tradition attributed to the Dukes of Lower Lorraine the same arms as those borne by the Hapsburgs (a white bar on red), still used by the city of

BRABANT, THURINGIA AND HESSE
General survey

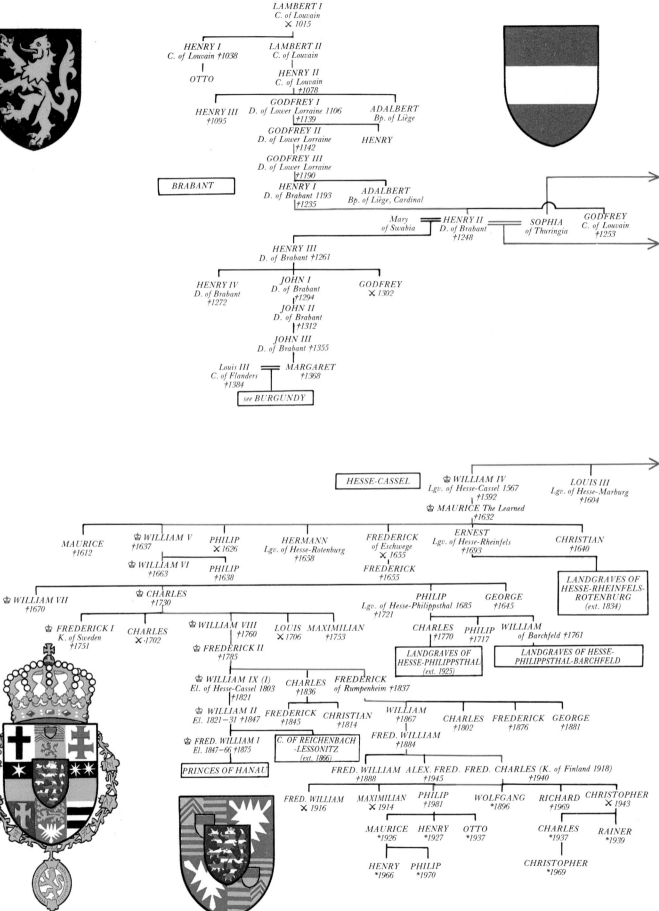

LAMBERT I
C. of Louvain
✕ 1015

HENRY I
C. of Louvain †1038

LAMBERT II
C. of Louvain

OTTO

HENRY II
C. of Louvain
†1078

HENRY III
†1095

GODFREY I
D. of Lower Lorraine 1106
†1139

ADALBERT
Bp. of Liège

GODFREY II
D. of Lower Lorraine
†1142

HENRY

GODFREY III
D. of Lower Lorraine
†1190

BRABANT

HENRY I
D. of Brabant 1193
†1235

ADALBERT
Bp. of Liège, Cardinal

Mary
of Swabia

HENRY II
D. of Brabant †1248

SOPHIA
of Thuringia

GODFREY
C. of Louvain
†1253

HENRY III
D. of Brabant †1261

HENRY IV
D. of Brabant
†1272

JOHN I
D. of Brabant
†1294

GODFREY
✕ 1302

JOHN II
D. of Brabant
†1312

JOHN III
D. of Brabant †1355

Louis III
C. of Flanders
†1384

MARGARET
†1368

see BURGUNDY

HESSE-CASSEL

♔ **WILLIAM IV**
Lgv. of Hesse-Cassel 1567
†1592

LOUIS III
Lgv. of Hesse-Marburg
†1604

♔ **MAURICE** The Learned
†1632

MAURICE
†1612

♔ **WILLIAM V**
†1637

PHILIP
✕ 1626

HERMANN
Lgv. of Hesse-Rotenburg
†1658

FREDERICK
of Eschwege
✕ 1655

ERNEST
Lgv. of Hesse-Rheinfels
†1693

CHRISTIAN
†1640

♔ **WILLIAM VI**
†1663

PHILIP
†1638

FREDERICK
†1655

♔ **WILLIAM VII**
†1670

♔ **CHARLES**
†1730

PHILIP
Lgv. of Hesse-Philippsthal 1685
†1721

GEORGE
†1645

LANDGRAVES OF
HESSE-RHEINFELS-
ROTENBURG
(ext. 1834)

♔ **FREDERICK I**
K. of Sweden
†1751

CHARLES
✕·1702

♔ **WILLIAM VIII**
†1760

LOUIS
✕1706

MAXIMILIAN
†1753

CHARLES
†1770

PHILIP
†1717

WILLIAM
of Barchfeld †1761

♔ **FREDERICK II**
†1785

LANDGRAVES OF
HESSE-PHILIPPSTHAL
(ext. 1925)

LANDGRAVES OF HESSE-
PHILIPPSTHAL-BARCHFELD

♔ **WILLIAM IX (I)**
El. of Hesse-Cassel 1803
†1821

CHARLES
†1836

FREDERICK
of Rumpenheim †1837

♔ **WILLIAM II**
El. 1821–31 †1847

FREDERICK
†1845

CHRISTIAN
†1814

WILLIAM
†1867

CHARLES
†1802

FREDERICK
†1876

GEORGE
†1881

♔ **FRED. WILLIAM I**
El. 1847–66 †1875

C. OF REICHENBACH
-LESSONITZ
(ext. 1866)

FRED. WILLIAM
†1884

PRINCES OF HANAU

FRED. WILLIAM
†1888

ALEX. FRED.
†1945

FRED. CHARLES (K. of Finland 1918)
†1940

FRED. WILLIAM
✕ 1916

MAXIMILIAN
✕ 1914

PHILIP
†1981

WOLFGANG
*1896

RICHARD
†1969

CHRISTOPHER
✕ 1943

MAURICE
*1926

HENRY
*1927

OTTO
*1937

CHARLES
*1937

RAINER
*1939

HENRY
*1966

PHILIP
*1970

CHRISTOPHER
*1969

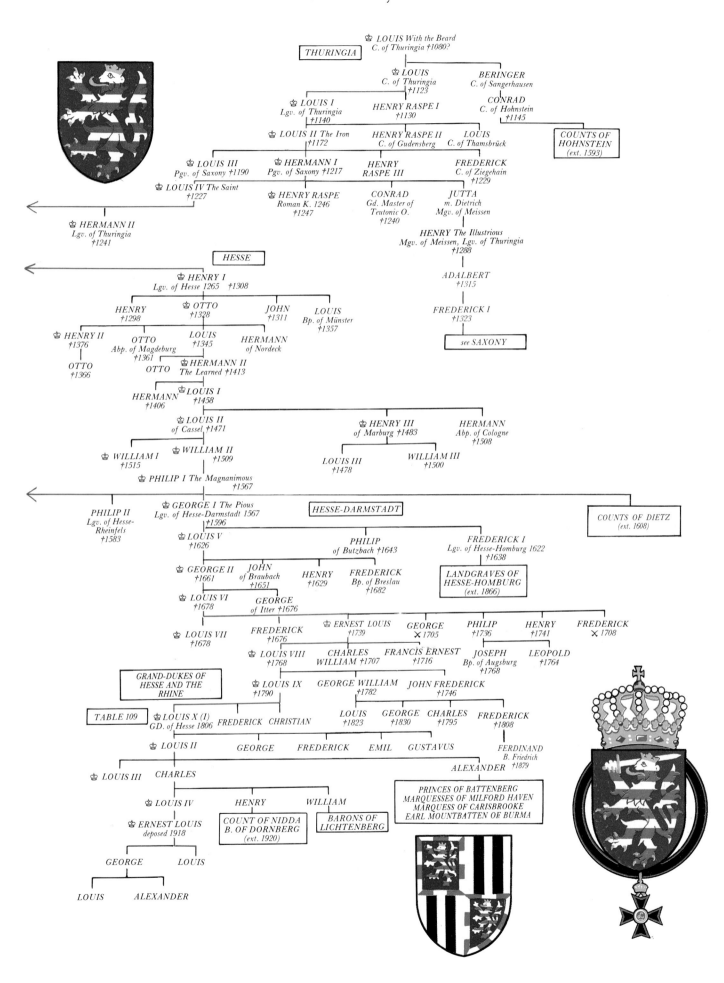

THURINGIA

♔ LOUIS With the Beard
C. of Thuringia †1080?

♔ LOUIS
C. of Thuringia
†1123

BERINGER
C. of Sangerhausen

♔ LOUIS I
Lgv. of Thuringia
†1140

HENRY RASPE I
†1130

CONRAD
C. of Hohnstein
†1145

♔ LOUIS II The Iron
†1172

HENRY RASPE II
C. of Gudensberg

LOUIS
C. of Thamsbrück

COUNTS OF
HOHNSTEIN
(ext. 1593)

♔ LOUIS III
Pgv. of Saxony †1190

♔ HERMANN I
Pgv. of Saxony †1217

HENRY
RASPE III

FREDERICK
C. of Ziegehain
†1229

♔ LOUIS IV The Saint
†1227

♔ HENRY RASPE
Roman K. 1246
†1247

CONRAD
Gd. Master of
Teutonic O.
†1240

JUTTA
m. Dietrich
Mgv. of Meissen

♔ HERMANN II
Lgv. of Thuringia
†1241

HENRY The Illustrious
Mgv. of Meissen, Lgv. of Thuringia
†1288

ADALBERT
†1315

HESSE

♔ HENRY I
Lgv. of Hesse 1265   †1308

FREDERICK I
†1323

HENRY
†1298

♔ OTTO
†1328

JOHN
†1311

LOUIS
Bp. of Münster
†1357

see SAXONY

♔ HENRY II
†1376

OTTO
Abp. of Magdeburg

LOUIS
†1345

HERMANN
of Nordeck

OTTO
†1361

OTTO
†1366

OTTO

♔ HERMANN II
The Learned †1413

HERMANN
†1406

♔ LOUIS I
†1458

♔ LOUIS II
of Cassel †1471

♔ HENRY III
of Marburg †1483

HERMANN
Abp. of Cologne
†1508

♔ WILLIAM I
†1515

♔ WILLIAM II
†1509

LOUIS III
†1478

WILLIAM III
†1500

♔ PHILIP I The Magnanimous
†1567

PHILIP II
Lgv. of Hesse-
Rheinfels
†1583

♔ GEORGE I The Pious
Lgv. of Hesse-Darmstadt 1567
†1596

HESSE-DARMSTADT

COUNTS OF DIETZ
(ext. 1608)

♔ LOUIS V
†1626

PHILIP
of Butzbach †1643

FREDERICK I
Lgv. of Hesse-Homburg 1622
†1638

♔ GEORGE II
†1661

JOHN
of Braubach
†1651

HENRY
†1629

FREDERICK
Bp. of Breslau
†1682

LANDGRAVES OF
HESSE-HOMBURG
(ext. 1866)

♔ LOUIS VI
†1678

GEORGE
of Itter †1676

♔ LOUIS VII
†1678

FREDERICK
†1676

♔ ERNEST LOUIS
†1739

GEORGE
✕ 1705

PHILIP
†1736

HENRY
†1741

FREDERICK
✕ 1708

♔ LOUIS VIII
†1768

CHARLES
WILLIAM †1707

FRANCIS ERNEST
†1716

JOSEPH
Bp. of Augsburg
†1768

LEOPOLD
†1764

GRAND-DUKES OF
HESSE AND THE
RHINE

♔ LOUIS IX
†1790

GEORGE WILLIAM
†1782

JOHN FREDERICK
†1746

TABLE 109

♔ LOUIS X (I)
GD. of Hesse 1806

FREDERICK   CHRISTIAN

LOUIS
†1823

GEORGE
†1830

CHARLES
†1795

FREDERICK
†1808

♔ LOUIS II

GEORGE   FREDERICK   EMIL   GUSTAVUS

FERDINAND
B. Friedrich
†1879

♔ LOUIS III

CHARLES

ALEXANDER

♔ LOUIS IV

HENRY

WILLIAM

PRINCES OF BATTENBERG
MARQUESSES OF MILFORD HAVEN
MARQUESS OF CARISBROOKE
EARL MOUNTBATTEN OF BURMA

♔ ERNEST LOUIS
deposed 1918

COUNT OF NIDDA
B. OF DORNBERG
(ext. 1920)

BARONS OF
LICHTENBERG

GEORGE   LOUIS

LOUIS   ALEXANDER

Louvain; but it is more certain that the Dukes of Brabant bore a gold lion rampant on a black shield (Table 107) and this blazon has been taken over by the modern Kingdom of Belgium (Chapter 9). The subsequent Dukes of Brabant were on the whole energetic and successful rulers, but they had to contend with the rising power of the towns and the rivalry of their nobility. John II had to accept a council of four nobles and ten townsfolk. His son, John III, granted a wide charter of liberties on the occasion of the wedding of his daughter to Wenceslas of Luxemburg (Table 87) and known therefrom as the *Joyeuse Entrée*. On the death of John III, without surviving male issue, the Duchy was disputed by the husbands of his two daughters. Margaret married the Count of Flanders: their daughter, another Margaret, married Philip the Bold, Duke of Burgundy. After various vicissitudes Brabant finally passed to Burgundy in 1430 (Chapter 18).

THURINGIA

In early medieval Germany Thuringia was a smallish area between Saxony and Franconia with the large Thuringian Forest along its southern frontier. There had originally been a distinct Thuringian people, but under the Saxon emperors the territory was amalgamated with Saxony. At the end of the eleventh century, Louis with the Beard began to build up an agglomeration of fiefs in the province: his mother seems to have been a kinswoman of the wife of the Emperor Conrad II. His grandson, Louis I, was appointed Landgrave of Thuringia in 1131 and also married the heiress of Gudensberg, an important part of Hesse. Louis II, the Iron, espoused a sister of the Emperor Frederick Barbarossa: the fortunes of the family were rising. Louis III and his brother Hermann I were in turn Counts Palatine of Saxony. Louis IV, the Saint, married the pious and ascetic St Elizabeth, a daughter of Andrew II of Hungary (Table 89); after his death she came under the influence of the bitter and fanatical Conrad of Marburg, a formidable persecutor of heresy.

Henry Raspe, who succeeded his nephew Hermann II in 1241, was the last of his line and was set up in 1246 as an anti-king against the Emperor Frederick II, only to die in the next year. The arms of the Landgraves of Thuringia were a lion crowned with gold and striped with white and red, all on a blue field. At Marburg are preserved in the University Museum some of the earliest surviving actual shields and they bear this beautiful blazon; the oldest is linked with the name of Conrad of Thuringia, Grand-Master of the Teutonic Order (d. 1240). The death of Henry Raspe led to discord between the husband of his niece, Henry, Duke of Brabant, and his sister's son, the Margrave of Meissen. Ultimately

John I (d. 1294), Duke of Brabant, at the battle of Worringen in 1288. His helmet carries a dragon crest. 15th-century MS.

the latter gained control of Thuringia, while Hesse was allotted in 1265 to Henry of Brabant who became the first Landgrave of Hesse. He divided his land into Upper Hesse (round Marburg) and Lower Hesse (round Cassel) for his sons Otto and John, but the division was not permanent.

A more lasting split came in the sixteenth century. Philip I, the Magnanimous, was an important figure in the German Reformation and adopted the faith of Luther. However, his later divorce (1540) and remarriage, coupled with the cynical advice tendered to him by the Protestant divines, scarcely lent lustre to the movement. He was also the founder of the University of Marburg. At his death he divided Hesse between his four sons. Fortunately the recipients of Hesse-Marburg and Hesse-Rheinfels did not found dynasties, but the lines of Hesse-Cassel and Hesse-Darmstadt still exist.

HESSE-CASSEL

The Landgraves of Hesse-Cassel (Table 107) in turn subdivided their estates from time to time; of the cadet branches Hesse-Philippsthal has proved the most enduring. William VI, succeeding his father at an early age, owed much to the regency of his mother, a vigorous princess who secured considerable territorial gains, notably the abbey of Hersfeld, at the Treaty of Westphalia (1648); he grew up a lover of the arts. His grandson Frederick was King of Sweden for over thirty years through marrying a Swedish princess. By the time of his death Hesse-Cassel had become well-known as a source of mercenary troops. Some 20,000 were hired by England from the Landgrave Frederick II to fight against America in the War of Independence. He founded in 1770 the Order of the Golden Lion.

William, his son, was involved in the Napoleonic Wars and became an elector in 1803. He was briefly allied to the French Emperor, but the latter suspected him of double-dealing. At the Congress of Vienna William I put forward an absurd claim to be styled King of the Chatti (an ancient Germanic tribe). Frustrated in this gambit, he clung to his new rank of elector, although the Holy Roman Empire itself had vanished. Alone of nineteenth-century German princes the rulers of Hesse-Cassel were thus known. The Elector William II was an unpopular ruler. His mistress, the Countess of Reichenbach, was detested, and his government was regarded as reactionary. In 1831 he withdrew from public life, nominating his son as regent. Frederick William I was not a noticeable improvement; he made a morganatic marriage but few other concessions to democracy. In 1850 the unpopularity of his administration and the discon-

Philip I of Hesse (1504–67) was an important supporter of Luther and early Protestantism. After H. Krell.

tent of his subjects almost provoked a war between Austria and Prussia which would have been premature for the latter. In 1866 the Elector joined Austria, was defeated and captured and his domains were added to those of Prussia (Chapter 23).

On the death of Frederick William I, the representation of Hesse-Cassel passed to his cousins, who ceased to use the title of elector. It is to be regretted that some of them were prepared to accept positions under the Nazi regime. On Table 107 can be seen the full blazon of Hesse-Cassel, surrounded by the collar of the Golden Lion; as in other German princely shields the striped lion of Hesse (originally Thuringia) is placed over a number of quarterings for minor fiefs.

The descendants of the morganatic marriage of Elector Frederick William received the title of Prince of Hanau. Their arms show in the first and fourth quarters the fiefs of Hanau and Rieneck, with Münzenberg in pretence, and in the second and third quarters, the nettle-leaf of Schaumburg. Over all is the barry lion of Hesse itself (Table 107).

HESSE-DARMSTADT

The inheritance of the Landgraves of Hesse-Darmstadt (Table 108) was diminished by setting up the tiny Landgraviate of Hesse-Homburg, which continued until 1866 when it was absorbed in Prussia. During the Thirty Years' War there was constant conflict with Hesse-Cassel which achieved little except the partition of Hesse-Marburg. The Landgrave Ernest Louis built the splendid palace at Darmstadt, striving like too many German princelings to match the glories of Versailles. Louis IX married Caroline of Zweibrücken-Birkenfeld, sometimes called the Great Landgravine: she was a woman of wide culture who even won the admiration of Frederick the Great of Prussia. Her son, Louis X, was a supporter of Napoleon and assumed the title of Grand-Duke of Hesse. In 1813 he prudently transferred to the Allies and as a result was recognized by the Congress of Vienna as Grand-Duke of Hesse and the Rhine (Table 109). Furthermore he founded the Order of Louis in 1807 and placed a sword in the right paw of the lion of Thuringia (Table 108).

In 1866 Hesse-Darmstadt fought against Prussia on the side of Austria, but succeeded in preserving her independence. There were close ties between the grand-dukes and the royal family of England: Louis IV married a daughter of Queen Victoria and Ernest Louis a daughter of the Duke of Edinburgh (Table 109). Nor was this all, for Prince Alexander of Hesse (1823–88) contracted a morganatic marriage with Countess Julia von Hauke who was created Princess of Battenberg in 1858. One of their sons became Prince of Bulgaria (Chapter 38); two others made

TABLE 109

HESSE AND THE RHINE
Grand-Dukes until the end of the monarchy

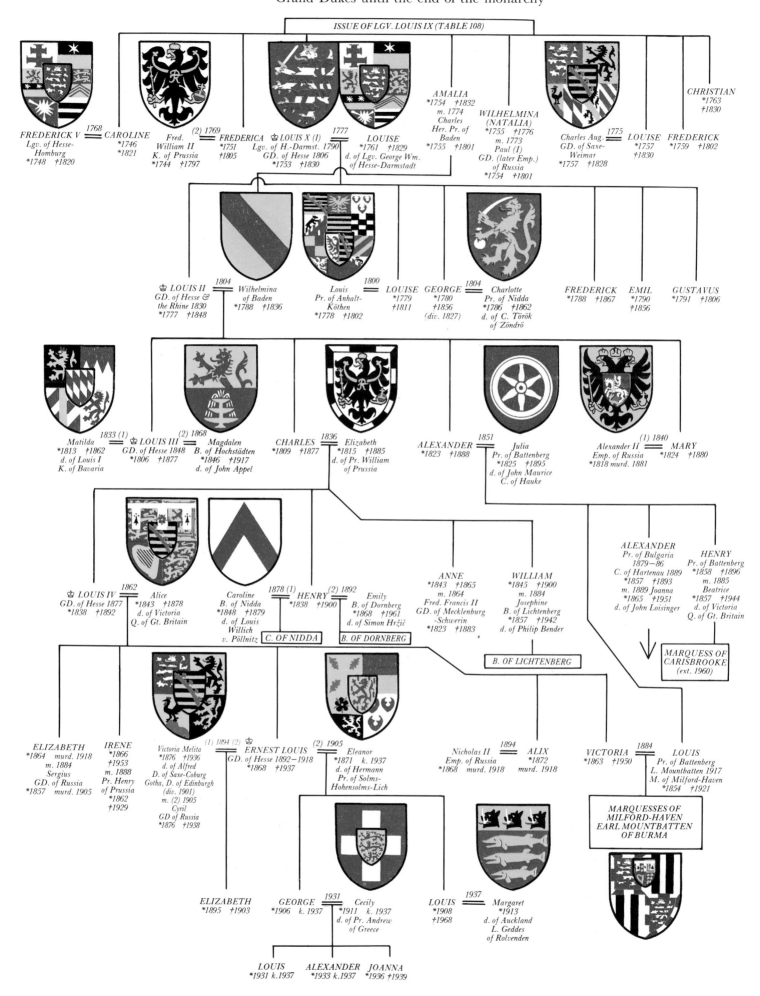

ISSUE OF LGV. LOUIS IX (TABLE 108)

FREDERICK V
Lgv. of Hesse-Homburg
*1748 †1820
— 1768 —
CAROLINE
*1746 †1821

Fred. William II
K. of Prussia
*1744 †1797
(2) 1769
FREDERICA
*1751 †1805

☗ **LOUIS X (I)**
Lgv. of H.-Darmst. 1790
GD. of Hesse 1806
*1753 †1830
— 1777 —
LOUISE
*1761 †1829
d. of Lgv. George Wm. of Hesse-Darmstadt

AMALIA
*1754 †1832
Charles Her. Pr. of Baden
*1755 †1801

WILHELMINA (NATALIA)
*1755 †1776
m. 1773
Paul (I) GD. (later Emp.) of Russia
*1754 †1801

Charles Aug.
GD. of Saxe-Weimar
*1757 †1828
— 1775 —
LOUISE
*1757 †1830

FREDERICK
*1759 †1802

CHRISTIAN
*1763 †1830

☗ **LOUIS II**
GD. of Hesse & the Rhine 1830
*1777 †1848
— 1804 —
Wilhelmina of Baden
*1788 †1836

Louis Pr. of Anhalt-Köthen
*1778 †1802
— 1800 —
LOUISE
*1779 †1811

GEORGE
*1780 †1856
(div. 1827)
— 1804 —
Charlotte Pr. of Nidda
*1786 †1862
d. of C. Török of Zöndrö

FREDERICK
*1788 †1867

EMIL
*1790 †1856

GUSTAVUS
*1791 †1806

Matilda
*1813 †1862
d. of Louis I K. of Bavaria
— 1833 (1) —
☗ **LOUIS III**
GD. of Hesse 1848
*1806 †1877
(2) 1868
Magdalen
B. of Hochstädten
*1846 †1917
d. of John Appel

CHARLES
*1809 †1877
— 1836 —
Elizabeth
*1815 †1885
d. of Pr. William of Prussia

ALEXANDER
*1823 †1888
— 1851 —
Julia
Pr. of Battenberg
*1825 †1895
d. of John Maurice C. of Hauke

Alexander II
Emp. of Russia
*1818 murd. 1881
— (1) 1840 —
MARY
*1824 †1880

☗ **LOUIS IV**
GD. of Hesse 1877
*1838 †1892
— 1862 —
Alice
*1843 †1878
d. of Victoria Q. of Gt. Britain

Caroline
B. of Nidda
*1848 †1879
d. of Louis Willich v. Pöllnitz
— 1878 (1) —
HENRY
*1838 †1900
(2) 1892
Emily
B. of Dornberg
*1868 †1961
d. of Simon Hržić

C. OF NIDDA

B. OF DORNBERG

ANNE
*1843 †1865
m. 1864
Fred. Francis II GD. of Mecklenburg-Schwerin
*1823 †1883

WILLIAM
*1845 †1900
m. 1884
Josephine B. of Lichtenberg
*1857 †1942
d. of Philip Bender

B. OF LICHTENBERG

ALEXANDER
Pr. of Bulgaria 1879—86
C. of Hartenau 1889
*1857 †1893
m. 1889 Joanna
*1865 †1951
d. of John Loisinger

HENRY
Pr. of Battenberg
*1858 †1896
m. 1885
Beatrice
*1857 †1944
d. of Victoria Q. of Gt. Britain

MARQUESS OF CARISBROOKE (ext. 1960)

ELIZABETH
*1864 murd. 1918
m. 1884
Sergius GD. of Russia
*1857 murd. 1905

IRENE
*1866 †1953
m. 1888
Pr. Henry of Prussia
*1862 †1929

Victoria Melita
*1876 †1936
d. of Alfred D. of Saxe-Coburg Gotha, D. of Edinburgh
(div. 1901)
m. (2) 1905 Cyril GD of Russia
*1876 †1938
— (1) 1894 (2) —
☗ **ERNEST LOUIS**
GD. of Hesse 1892—1918
*1868 †1937
(2) 1905
Eleanor
*1871 k. 1937
d. of Hermann Pr. of Solms-Hohensolms-Lich

Nicholas II
Emp. of Russia
*1868 murd. 1918
— 1894 —
ALIX
*1872 murd. 1918

VICTORIA
*1863 †1950
— 1884 —
LOUIS
Pr. of Battenberg
L. Mountbatten 1917
M. of Milford-Haven
*1854 †1921

**MARQUESSES OF MILFORD-HAVEN
EARL MOUNTBATTEN OF BURMA**

ELIZABETH
*1895 †1903

GEORGE
*1906 k. 1937
— 1931 —
Cecily
*1911 k. 1937
d. of Pr. Andrew of Greece

LOUIS
*1908 †1968
— 1937 —
Margaret
*1913
d. of Auckland L. Geddes of Rolvenden

LOUIS
*1931 k.1937

ALEXANDER
*1933 k.1937

JOANNA
*1936 †1939

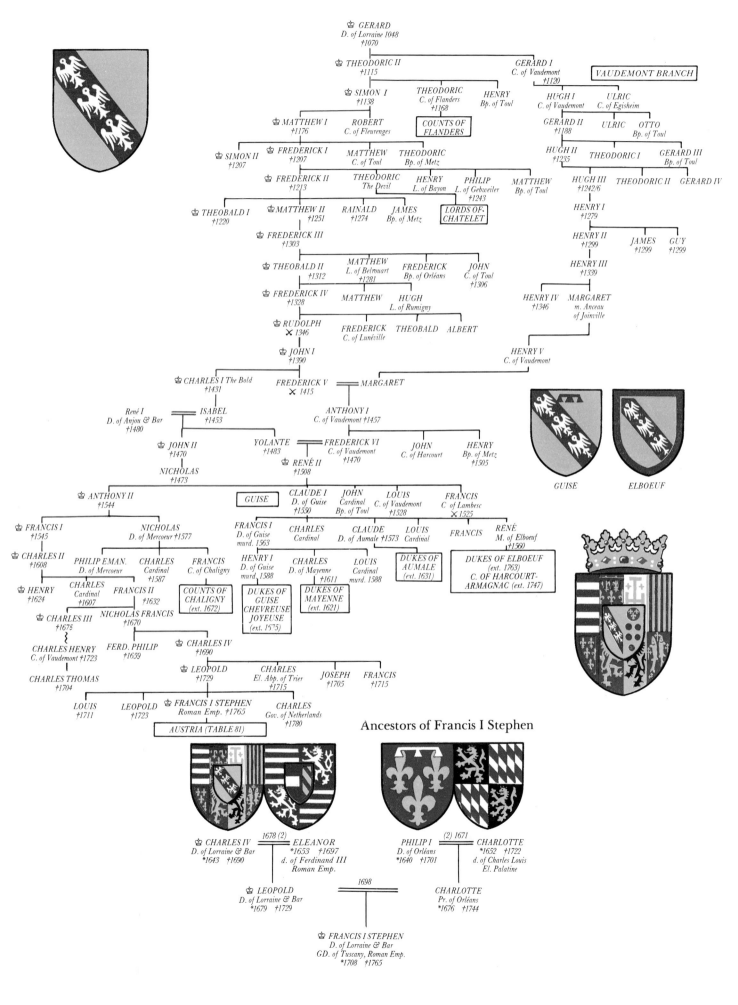

LORRAINE
General survey

♔ GERARD
D. of Lorraine 1048
†1070

♔ THEODORIC II
†1115

GERARD I
C. of Vaudemont
†1120

VAUDEMONT BRANCH

♔ SIMON I
†1138

THEODORIC
C. of Flanders
†1168

HENRY
Bp. of Toul

HUGH I
C. of Vaudemont

ULRIC
C. of Egisheim

♔ MATTHEW I
†1176

ROBERT
C. of Fleurenges

COUNTS OF
FLANDERS

GERARD II
†1188

ULRIC

OTTO
Bp. of Toul

♔ SIMON II
†1207

♔ FREDERICK I
†1207

MATTHEW
C. of Toul

THEODORIC
Bp. of Metz

HUGH II
†1235

THEODORIC I

GERARD III
Bp. of Toul

♔ FREDERICK II
†1213

THEODORIC
The Devil

HENRY
L. of Bayon

PHILIP
L. of Gebweiler
†1243

MATTHEW
Bp. of Toul

HUGH III
†1242/6

THEODORIC II

GERARD IV

♔ THEOBALD I
†1220

♔ MATTHEW II
†1251

RAINALD
†1274

JAMES
Bp. of Metz

LORDS OF
CHATELET

HENRY I
†1279

♔ FREDERICK III
†1303

HENRY II
†1299

JAMES
†1299

GUY
†1299

♔ THEOBALD II
†1312

MATTHEW
L. of Belmuart
†1281

FREDERICK
Bp. of Orléans

JOHN
C. of Toul
†1306

HENRY III
†1339

♔ FREDERICK IV
†1328

MATTHEW

HUGH
L. of Rumigny

HENRY IV
†1346

MARGARET
m. Anceau
of Joinville

♔ RUDOLPH
✕ 1346

FREDERICK
C. of Lunéville

THEOBALD

ALBERT

♔ JOHN I
†1390

HENRY V
C. of Vaudemont

♔ CHARLES I The Bold
†1431

FREDERICK V
✕ 1415

MARGARET

René I
D. of Anjou & Bar
†1480

ISABEL
†1453

ANTHONY I
C. of Vaudemont †1457

♔ JOHN II
†1470

YOLANTE
†1483

FREDERICK VI
C. of Vaudemont
†1470

JOHN
C. of Harcourt

HENRY
Bp. of Metz
†1505

NICHOLAS
†1473

♔ RENÉ II
†1508

GUISE

ELBOEUF

♔ ANTHONY II
†1544

GUISE

CLAUDE I
D. of Guise
†1550

JOHN
Cardinal
Bp. of Toul

LOUIS
C. of Vaudemont
†1528

FRANCIS
C of Lambesc
✕ 1525

♔ FRANCIS I
†1545

NICHOLAS
D. of Mercoeur †1577

FRANCIS I
D. of Guise
murd. 1563

CHARLES
Cardinal

CLAUDE
D. of Aumale †1573

LOUIS
Cardinal

FRANCIS

RENÉ
M. of Elboeuf
†1560

♔ CHARLES II
†1608

PHILIP EMAN.
D. of Mercoeur

CHARLES
Cardinal
†1587

FRANCIS
C. of Chaligny

HENRY I
D. of Guise
murd. 1588

CHARLES
D. of Mayenne
†1611

LOUIS
Cardinal
murd. 1588

DUKES OF
AUMALE
(ext. 1631)

DUKES OF ELBOEUF
(ext. 1763)
C. OF HARCOURT-
ARMAGNAC (ext. 1747)

♔ HENRY
†1624

CHARLES
Cardinal
†1607

FRANCIS II
†1632

COUNTS OF
CHALIGNY
(ext. 1672)

DUKES OF
GUISE
CHEVREUSE
JOYEUSE
(ext. 1575)

DUKES OF
MAYENNE
(ext. 1621)

♔ CHARLES III
†1675

NICHOLAS FRANCIS
†1670

CHARLES HENRY
C. of Vaudemont †1723

FERD. PHILIP
†1659

♔ CHARLES IV
†1690

CHARLES THOMAS
†1704

♔ LEOPOLD
†1729

CHARLES
El. Abp. of Trier
†1715

JOSEPH
†1705

FRANCIS
†1715

LOUIS
†1711

LEOPOLD
†1723

♔ FRANCIS I STEPHEN
Roman Emp. †1765

CHARLES
Gov. of Netherlands
†1780

AUSTRIA (TABLE 81)

Ancestors of Francis I Stephen

♔ CHARLES IV
D. of Lorraine & Bar
*1643 †1690

1678 (2)

ELEANOR
*1653 †1697
d. of Ferdinand III
Roman Emp.

PHILIP I
D. of Orléans
*1640 †1701

(2) 1671

CHARLOTTE
*1652 †1722
d. of Charles Louis
El. Palatine

♔ LEOPOLD
D. of Lorraine & Bar
*1679 †1729

1698

CHARLOTTE
Pr. of Orléans
*1676 †1744

♔ FRANCIS I STEPHEN
D. of Lorraine & Bar
GD. of Tuscany, Roman Emp.
*1708 †1765

GUISE

ELBOEUF

their homes and careers in England, where, in 1917, they changed their name to Mountbatten. Their coat-of-arms shows the lion of Hesse within a bordure gobony argent and azure quartered with the two pallets sable of the fief of Battenberg (Tables 108 and 109).

In 1918 the Grand-Duchy of Hesse and the Rhine was incorporated in the Republic of Germany. The last reigning Grand-Duke had only one son, named George, who was unhappily killed in a flying accident in 1937 together with his wife, his mother, and both his sons. His claims passed to his brother Louis who died childless in 1968. By a family compact, made in 1902 when it seemed that Ernest Louis might die without sons, it was arranged that the succession should pass to the elder branch of the family; the end of the junior line means Prince Philip of Hesse (Table 107) is heir to the claims not only of Hesse-Cassel but also of Hesse-Darmstadt, as well as being the direct male representative of Lambert, Count of Louvain, whose pedigree ascends to a certain Giselbert who died in 790.

LORRAINE

The Dukes of Brabant, and from them the family of Hesse, derived from the Dukes of Lower Lorraine. As has been seen, Upper Lorraine was given in 1048 to Gerard, Count of Alsace (Table 110). His younger son, Gerard, established the important cadet branch of the Counts of Vaudemont; his elder son, Theodoric, married the heiress of the Count of Flanders. In the next generation Theodoric's son, Simon, continued the line of the Dukes of Lorraine and his brother, Theodoric, that of the Counts of Flanders (destined in due course to pass to Burgundy). The Duchy of Lorraine was relatively compact, though broken up by the Bishoprics of Metz, Toul and Verdun; it had, however, powerful and jealous neighbours in the Counts of Champagne and the Counts of Bar. The earliest appearance of the arms of Lorraine is on the seal of Duke Simon II (d. 1207): these arms consist of three alerions of silver set on a red bend in a gold shield. An alerion was described by later heralds as an eagle without beak or claws. Legend attributed the blazon to a miraculous bow-shot by Godfrey de Bouillon (or another) which pierced the three birds with a single arrow; it is at least as possible that alerion is an anagram of Lor(r)aine.

The Dukes of Lorraine did not only perish in their own squabbles: Rudolph died at Crécy (1346) and his grandson, Frederick, at Agincourt. Frederick had made a good alliance with the heiress of his remote cousins, the Counts of Vaudemont. At the death of his elder brother, Charles the Bold, there was a disputed succession between René, Duke of Anjou, and Anthony, Count of Vaudemont; eventually it was arranged that René's daughter should marry Anthony's son, Frederick (or Ferri in the local form).

Thus René II inherited both the male descent of his father and the many pretensions of his maternal grandfather and so the beautiful and romantic shield of Lorraine began to take form. René I was a brilliant figure, already heir to Bar, patron of learning and literature, claimant to many titles – Naples, Hungary and Jerusalem, as well as Lorraine – and master for long of none, but loved by many of his subjects in Italy as well as France. Anthony II added two further quarters for Guelders and Jülich. The full arms of the Dukes of Lorraine can be seen over the name of Charles IV at the bottom of Table 110; the eight quarters stand for Hungary, Sicily, Jerusalem and Aragon, Anjou, Guelders, Jülich and Bar, with Lorraine over all. The barbels (fish) in the arms of Bar are canting.

Claude, the younger brother of Anthony II, established the House of Guise which played a great part in the politics of France in the second half of the sixteenth century, principally as leaders of the Catholic party. The Duke of Guise differenced the arms of Lorraine with a red label, and their younger branch, the Dukes of Elboeuf, did the same with a red bordure. Both can be seen on the right of Table 110. Anthony II of Lorraine's grandson, Charles II, had a long and eccentric reign in which he notably improved the finances and resources of his Duchy. His grandson, Charles III, was a more eccentric prince. Inadvisedly he became embroiled with Louis XIII of France and was deprived of many of his possessions; in 1634 Charles III abdicated and was succeeded by his brother, a bishop and a cardinal. But Charles tried to regain his Duchy and broke promises and treaties with equal abandon. Voltaire declared that he had spent his life losing his estates.

Charles IV, his nephew and son of the erstwhile cardinal, was barred by the French from Lorraine and accordingly entered the Austrian army where he achieved considerable military success and married a sister of the Emperor (Table 80). His son Leopold regained his Duchy at the Treaty of Ryswick in 1697 and devoted himself to increasing its prosperity. In 1736 Francis Stephen, Duke of Lorraine, married Maria Theresa, the heiress of the Hapsburgs. France, which had long coveted Lorraine, was reluctant to see that Duchy united with the Empire. An arrangement was produced whereby Francis Stephen should receive the Grand-Duchy of Tuscany (where the last Medici ruler had just died) and Lorraine should pass to Stanislas Leszczínski, the father-in-law of Louis XV and recently dethroned as King of Poland. The arms of Francis Stephen show those of his predecessors with Lorraine impaling Tuscany (Medici) over all. From this juncture the story of the Dukes of Lorraine is that of the Empire of Austria (Chapter 20), while their ancient Duchy became part of France at the death of Stanislas.

Chapter 29

MECKLENBURG AND OLDENBURG

In the north of Germany are two relatively impoverished states, those of Mecklenburg, lying southeast of Denmark and facing over the Baltic Sea, and Oldenburg, situated southwest of Denmark at the mouth of the Weser and looking over the North Sea. The destiny of Mecklenburg has been on the whole provincial and obscure; the House of Oldenburg has given kings and emperors to Denmark, Russia, Sweden, Greece and Norway.

MECKLENBURG

The area south of the Baltic was settled in about the sixth century after Christ by Slav peoples, of whom the Obodrites occupied the region now known as Mecklenburg. From the beginning of the tenth century various German rulers strove to convert and subdue them with scant success until the time of Henry the Lion, Duke of Saxony. In 1167 Pribislaw (Table 111) accepted Christianity and paid homage to Henry; in 1170 the Emperor Frederick Barbarossa made him a prince. His son Henry became Prince of Mecklenburg in 1180, after the fall of Henry the Lion (Chapter 26: Saxony). The first partition of the country took place among his four grandsons, but the elder branch was more enduring than the cadets. With the assistance of the Church, particularly of Cistercian monks, the colonization of waste lands was pushed forward. In 1348 the title of duke was recognized for the two branches of Schwerin and Stargard. Albrecht II (by descent of his mother) was King of Sweden (1363–89). The University of Rostock, the first in northern Germany, was founded in 1419; in 1471 all the family lands were united in the person of Duke Henry II. This followed the extinction of both the Wenden and Stargard branches.

The noteworthy feature of these dukes was their Slav origin. Only in Mecklenburg of all Germany were rulers drawn from this race. In 1540 the country accepted Lutheranism. Duke John Albrecht I tried to introduce primogeniture but in vain; there was a fresh division between his grandsons and a more decisive split one generation later. Frederick I founded the line of Mecklenburg-Schwerin and his brother in 1701 that of Mecklenburg-Strelitz. The

Albrecht VI of Mecklenburg (1488–1547) and his wife Anna of Brandenburg with their blazons. MS of 1526.

TABLE 111

MECKLENBURG
General survey

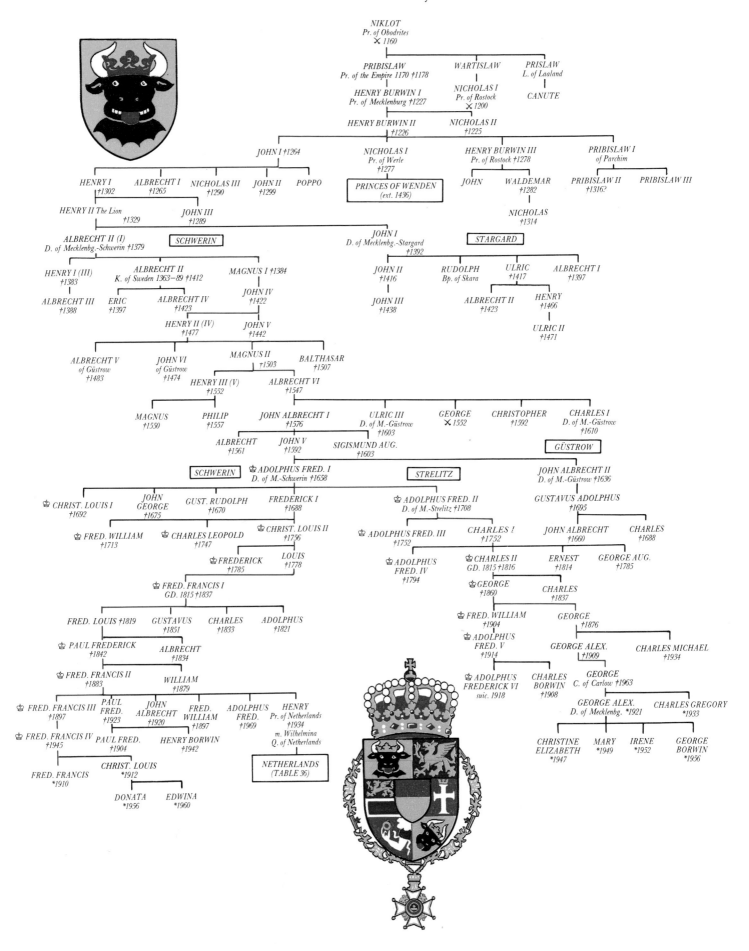

NIKLOT
Pr. of Obodrites
✕ 1160

PRIBISLAW
Pr. of the Empire 1170 †1178 — **WARTISLAW** — **PRISLAW**
L. of Laaland

HENRY BURWIN I
Pr. of Mecklenburg †1227 — **NICHOLAS I**
Pr. of Rostock
✕ 1200 — **CANUTE**

HENRY BURWIN II
†1226 — **NICHOLAS II**
†1225

JOHN I †1264 — **NICHOLAS I**
Pr. of Werle
†1277 — **HENRY BURWIN III**
Pr. of Rostock †1278 — **PRIBISLAW I**
of Parchim

HENRY I
†1302 — **ALBRECHT I**
†1265 — **NICHOLAS III**
†1290 — **JOHN II**
†1299 — **POPPO** | **PRINCES OF WENDEN**
(ext. 1436) | **JOHN** — **WALDEMAR**
†1282 | **PRIBISLAW II**
†1316? — **PRIBISLAW III**

HENRY II The Lion
†1329 — **JOHN III**
†1289

NICHOLAS
†1314

ALBRECHT II (I)
D. of Mecklenbg.-Schwerin †1379 | SCHWERIN — **JOHN I**
D. of Mecklenbg.-Stargard
†1392 | STARGARD

HENRY I (III)
†1383 — **ALBRECHT II**
K. of Sweden 1363−89 †1412 — **MAGNUS I** †1384 — **JOHN II**
†1416 — **RUDOLPH**
Bp. of Skara — **ULRIC**
†1417 — **ALBRECHT I**
†1397

ALBRECHT III
†1388 — **ERIC**
†1397 — **ALBRECHT IV**
†1423 — **JOHN IV**
†1422 — **JOHN III**
†1438 — **ALBRECHT II**
†1423 — **HENRY**
†1466

HENRY II (IV)
†1477 — **JOHN V**
†1442 — **ULRIC II**
†1471

ALBRECHT V
of Güstrow
†1483 — **JOHN VI**
of Güstrow
†1474 — **MAGNUS II**
†1503 — **BALTHASAR**
†1507

HENRY III (V)
†1552 — **ALBRECHT VI**
†1547

MAGNUS
†1550 — **PHILIP**
†1557 — **JOHN ALBRECHT I**
†1576 — **ULRIC III**
D. of M.-Güstrow
†1603 — **GEORGE**
✕ 1552 — **CHRISTOPHER**
†1592 — **CHARLES I**
D. of M.-Güstrow
†1610

ALBRECHT
†1561 — **JOHN V**
†1592 — **SIGISMUND AUG.**
†1603 | GÜSTROW

♕ **ADOLPHUS FRED. I**
D. of M.-Schwerin †1658 | SCHWERIN | STRELITZ — **JOHN ALBRECHT II**
D. of M.-Güstrow †1636

♕ **CHRIST. LOUIS I**
†1692 — **JOHN GEORGE**
†1675 — **GUST. RUDOLPH**
†1670 — **FREDERICK I**
†1688 — ♕ **ADOLPHUS FRED. II**
D. of M.-Strelitz †1708 — **GUSTAVUS ADOLPHUS**
†1695

♕ **FRED. WILLIAM**
†1713 — ♕ **CHARLES LEOPOLD**
†1747 — ♕ **CHRIST. LOUIS II**
†1756 — ♕ **ADOLPHUS FRED. III**
†1752 — **CHARLES !**
†1752 — **JOHN ALBRECHT**
†1660 — **CHARLES**
†1688

♕ **FREDERICK**
†1785 — **LOUIS**
†1778 — ♕ **ADOLPHUS FRED. IV**
†1794 — ♕ **CHARLES II**
GD. 1815 †1816 — **ERNEST**
†1814 — **GEORGE AUG.**
†1785

♕ **FRED. FRANCIS I**
GD. 1815 †1837 — ♕ **GEORGE**
†1860 — **CHARLES**
†1837

FRED. LOUIS †1819 — **GUSTAVUS**
†1851 — **CHARLES**
†1833 — **ADOLPHUS**
†1821 — ♕ **FRED. WILLIAM**
†1904 — **GEORGE**
†1876

♕ **PAUL FREDERICK**
†1842 — **ALBRECHT**
†1834 — ♕ **ADOLPHUS FRED. V**
†1914 — **GEORGE ALEX.**
†1909 — **CHARLES MICHAEL**
†1934

♕ **FRED. FRANCIS II**
†1883 — **WILLIAM**
†1879 — ♕ **ADOLPHUS FREDERICK VI**
suic. 1918 — **CHARLES BORWIN**
†1908 — **GEORGE**
C. of Carlow †1963

♕ **FRED. FRANCIS III**
†1897 — **PAUL FRED.**
†1923 — **JOHN ALBRECHT**
†1920 — **FRED. WILLIAM**
†1897 — **ADOLPHUS FRED.**
†1969 — **HENRY**
Pr. of Netherlands
†1934
m. Wilhelmina
Q. of Netherlands — **GEORGE ALEX.**
D. of Mecklenbg. *1921 — **CHARLES GREGORY**
*1933

♕ **FRED. FRANCIS IV**
†1945 — **PAUL FRED.**
†1904 — **HENRY BORWIN**
†1942 | **NETHERLANDS**
(TABLE 36) — **CHRISTINE ELIZABETH**
*1947 — **MARY**
*1949 — **IRENE**
*1952 — **GEORGE BORWIN**
*1956

FRED. FRANCIS
*1910 — **CHRIST. LOUIS**
*1912

DONATA
*1956 — **EDWINA**
*1960

TABLE 112

OLDENBURG
General survey

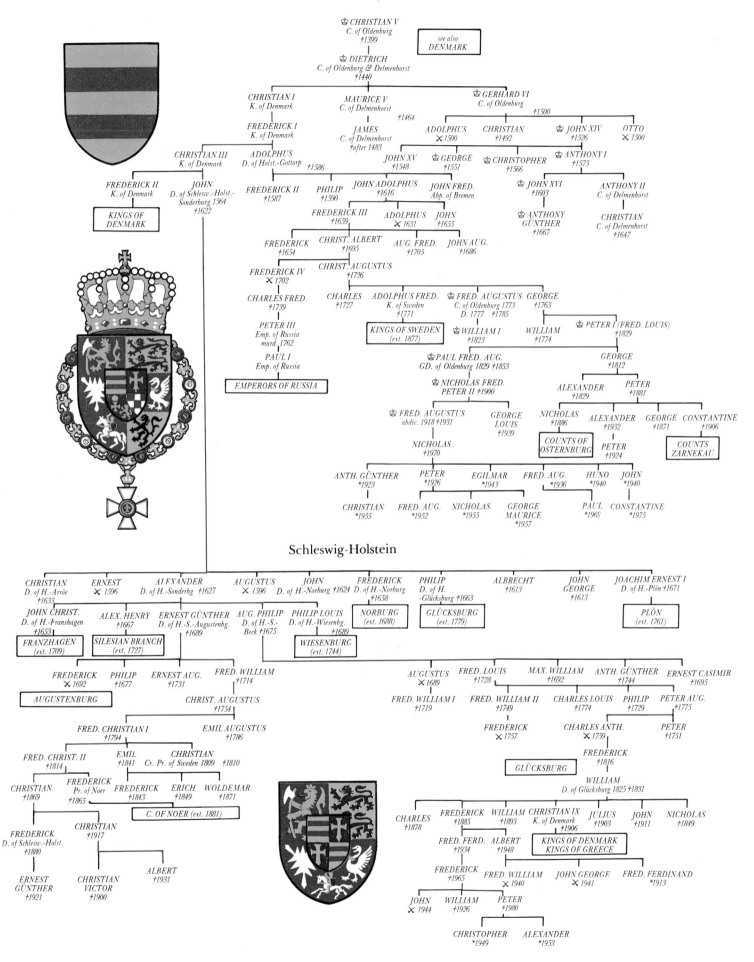

♔ *CHRISTIAN V*
C. of Oldenburg
†1399

see also
DENMARK

♔ *DIETRICH*
C. of Oldenburg & Delmenhorst
†1440

CHRISTIAN I
K. of Denmark

MAURICE V
C. of Delmenhorst

♔ *GERHARD VI*
C. of Oldenburg
†1500

†1464

FREDERICK I
K. of Denmark

JAMES
C. of Delmenhorst
†after 1483

ADOLPHUS
✕ *1500*

CHRISTIAN
†1492

♔ *JOHN XIV*
†1526

OTTO
✕ *1500*

CHRISTIAN III
K. of Denmark

ADOLPHUS
D. of Holst.-Gottorp

†1586

JOHN XV
†1548

♔ *GEORGE*
†1551

♔ *CHRISTOPHER*
†1566

♔ *ANTHONY I*
†1573

FREDERICK II
K. of Denmark

JOHN
D. of Schlesw.-Holst.-Sonderburg 1564
†1622

FREDERICK II
†1587

PHILIP
†1590

JOHN ADOLPHUS
†1616

JOHN FRED.
Abp. of Bremen

♔ *JOHN XVI*
†1603

ANTHONY II
C. of Delmenhorst

KINGS OF DENMARK

FREDERICK III
†1659

ADOLPHUS
✕ *1631*

JOHN
†1655

♔ *ANTHONY GÜNTHER*
†1667

CHRISTIAN
C. of Delmenhorst
†1647

FREDERICK
†1654

CHRIST. ALBERT
†1695

AUG. FRED.
†1705

JOHN AUG.
†1686

FREDERICK IV
✕ *1702*

CHRIST. AUGUSTUS
†1726

CHARLES FRED.
†1739

CHARLES
†1727

ADOLPHUS FRED.
K. of Sweden
†1771

♔ *FRED. AUGUSTUS*
C. of Oldenburg 1773
D. 1777 †1785

GEORGE
†1763

PETER III
Emp. of Russia
murd. 1762

KINGS OF SWEDEN
(ext. 1877)

♔ *WILLIAM I*
†1823

WILLIAM
†1774

♔ *PETER I (FRED. LOUIS)*
†1829

PAUL I
Emp. of Russia

♔ *PAUL FRED. AUG.*
GD. of Oldenburg 1829 †1853

GEORGE
†1812

EMPERORS OF RUSSIA

♔ *NICHOLAS FRED.*
PETER II †1900

ALEXANDER
†1829

PETER
†1881

♔ *FRED. AUGUSTUS*
abdic. 1918 †1931

GEORGE LOUIS
†1939

NICHOLAS
†1886

ALEXANDER
†1932

GEORGE
†1871

CONSTANTINE
†1906

NICHOLAS
†1970

COUNTS OF OSTERNBURG

PETER
†1924

COUNTS ZARNEKAU

ANTH. GÜNTHER
*1923

PETER
*1926

EGILMAR
*1943

FRED. AUG.
*1936

HUNO
*1940

JOHN
*1940

CHRISTIAN
*1955

FRED. AUG.
*1952

NICHOLAS
*1955

GEORGE MAURICE
*1957

PAUL
*1969

CONSTANTINE
*1975

Schleswig-Holstein

CHRISTIAN
D. of H.-Arröe
†1633

ERNEST
✕ *1596*

ALEXANDER
D. of H.-Sonderbg. †1627

AUGUSTUS
✕ *1596*

JOHN
D. of H.-Norburg †1624

FREDERICK
D. of H.-Norburg
†1658

PHILIP
D. of H.-Glücksburg †1663

ALBRECHT
†1613

JOHN GEORGE
†1613

JOACHIM ERNEST I
D. of H.-Plön †1671

JOHN CHRIST.
D. of H.-Franshagen
†1653

ALEX. HENRY
†1667

ERNEST GÜNTHER
D. of H.-S.-Augustenbg.
†1689

AUG. PHILIP
D. of H.-S.-Beck †1675

PHILIP LOUIS
D. of H.-Wiesenbg.
†1689

NORBURG
(ext. 1688)

GLÜCKSBURG
(ext. 1779)

PLÖN
(ext. 1761)

FRANZHAGEN
(ext. 1709)

SILESIAN BRANCH
(ext. 1727)

WIESENBURG
(ext. 1744)

FREDERICK
✕ *1692*

PHILIP
†1677

ERNEST AUG.
†1731

FRED. WILLIAM
†1714

AUGUSTUS
✕ *1689*

FRED. LOUIS
†1728

MAX. WILLIAM
†1692

ANTH. GÜNTHER
†1744

ERNEST CASIMIR
†1695

AUGUSTENBURG

CHRIST. AUGUSTUS
†1754

FRED. WILLIAM I
†1719

FRED. WILLIAM II
†1749

CHARLES LOUIS
†1774

PHILIP
†1729

PETER AUG.
†1775

FRED. CHRISTIAN I
†1794

EMIL AUGUSTUS
†1786

FREDERICK
✕ *1757*

CHARLES ANTH.
✕ *1759*

PETER
†1751

FRED. CHRIST. II
†1814

EMIL
†1841

CHRISTIAN
Cr. Pr. of Sweden 1809 †1810

FREDERICK
†1816

CHRISTIAN
†1869

FREDERICK
Pr. of Noer
†1865

FREDERICK
†1843

ERICH
†1849

WOLDEMAR
†1871

GLÜCKSBURG

WILLIAM
D. of Glücksburg 1825 †1831

FREDERICK
D. of Schlesw.-Holst.
†1880

CHRISTIAN
†1917

C. OF NOER *(ext. 1881)*

CHARLES
†1878

FREDERICK
†1885

WILLIAM
†1893

CHRISTIAN IX
K. of Denmark
†1906

JULIUS
†1903

JOHN
†1911

NICHOLAS
†1849

ERNEST GÜNTHER
†1921

CHRISTIAN VICTOR
†1900

ALBERT
†1931

FRED. FERD.
†1934

ALBERT
†1948

KINGS OF DENMARK
KINGS OF GREECE

FREDERICK
†1965

FRED. WILLIAM
✕ *1940*

JOHN GEORGE
✕ *1941*

FRED. FERDINAND
*1913

JOHN
✕ *1944*

WILLIAM
†1926

PETER
†1980

CHRISTOPHER
*1949

ALEXANDER
*1953

basic arms of Mecklenburg display a bull's head (Table 111), which is sometimes drawn with a ring in its mouth, but both branches used a more elaborate shield. In this are six quarterings, for Mecklenburg, Rostock, the principality of Schwerin, Ratzeburg, the County of Schwerin and Werle. Over all this the divided red and gold escutcheon of Stargard, a fief acquired by Henry II, the Lion, in 1304. It is more usual in German heraldry to have a family blazon in this position. For a brief spell during the Thirty Years' War Mecklenburg was handed over to the imperialist General Wallenstein (Waldstein).

After the division of 1701 both Duchies descended by primogeniture; in general they had a reputation for harsh treatment of the peasantry and the exploitation of aristocratic estates. By the Treaty of Vienna (1815) both branches were given the title of grand-duke. The direct male line of Strelitz came to an end with the suicide of Adolphus Frederick VI early in 1918. His cousin of Schwerin engineered the abdication of both thrones in November of that year. Duke Charles Michael of Strelitz adopted as his heir in 1928 the morganatic son of his brother hitherto known as Count of Carlow, thereafter styled Duke of Mecklenburg. The present head of the family, hereditary Grand-Duke Frederick Francis, has made a non-royal marriage which has proved to be childless, and his younger brother has only daughters. Their great uncle Henry was husband to Queen Wilhelmina of the Netherlands and father of Queen Juliana, who recently abdicated (Table 36).

OLDENBURG

The Counts of Oldenburg can be traced back to a certain Egilmar (d. 1108). They were originally vassals of Saxony, but became independent in 1180. Count Dietrich (Table 112) married the heiress of Delmenhorst and then the daughter of the ruler of Schleswig and Holstein. His son, by the second marriage, became Christian I of Denmark (Chapter 5): Delmenhorst and Oldenburg were assigned by Christian to younger brothers. Anthony I of Oldenburg became a Protestant. His grandson Anthony Günther, in 1647, finally incorporated Delmenhorst with his own County: when he died childless in 1667 both passed to Denmark. The succession problem was complicated and had been anticipated in 1649 by an arrangement that the two Counties should pass to the King of Denmark and the Duke of Holstein-Gottorp. Counter-claims were, however, advanced by Joachim Ernest, Duke of Plön, who belonged to the line of Holstein-Sonderburg (Table 112). In fact

Denmark gained control. In 1773 Christian VII of Denmark surrendered the two Counties of Oldenburg and Delmenhorst to the future Emperor Paul of Russia in return for the latter's rights in Holstein-Gottorp. Paul granted them to his cousin Frederick Augustus who in 1777 was advanced to be Duke of Oldenburg. This Duke's nephew, Peter I, acquired in 1802 the Bishopric of Lübeck on the Baltic, and in 1815 the Principality of Birkenfeld (miles away in the Rhineland) and the title of grand-duke (though this was not used until his heir's accession). His descendant, the Grand-Duke Frederick Augustus, like other German princes abdicated in 1918. By a family law of 1904 the descendants of Duke Frederick of Glücksburg (d. 1885) were recognized as eligible for the succession to Oldenburg.

The basic arms of Oldenburg were two red bars on gold. The more complicated escutcheon (Table 112) surrounded by the collar of the Order of Duke Peter Frederick Louis (founded 1838) shows quarterings reflecting his ancestry beneath an escutcheon combining Oldenburg, Delmenhorst, and their later lordships. The shield of the Dukes of Sonderburg at the bottom of the Table shows Norway, Schleswig, Holstein, Stormania and Ditmarschen with an escutcheon of Oldenburg and Delmenhorst over all.

The Dukes of Holstein-Sonderburg played their part in the infinitely complicated story of the Schleswig-Holstein succession. It is alleged that Lord Palmerston once stated that only three people had fully understood this problem: the Prince Consort (who was dead), a German professor (who had gone mad) and he himself, who had forgotten all about it. At bottom the issue arose in the Middle Ages when Schleswig was deemed part of Denmark and Holstein part of Germany (i.e. the Holy Roman Empire). Christian I, who figures at the top of Table 112, had proclaimed them inseparable, but since then other promises had been made and numerous claims advanced within a family of many branches. Differing rules of succession complicated an already labyrinthine problem (Chapter 5).

Duke Frederick of Augustenburg (d. 1880) advanced his claims in 1863 (just after the accession of Christian IX of Denmark) and was actually installed as Frederick VIII of Schleswig-Holstein by the Saxons and Hanoverians. His pretensions were abruptly ended at the defeat of Denmark by Austria and Prussia in 1864. His son, Ernest Günther, being childless, adopted his distant cousin John George of Glücksburg who was killed in action in 1941. This branch is therefore extinct today.

Chapter 30

HOLY ROMAN EMPIRE

The ghost of Charlemagne haunts a wide span of medieval history. This is not the place to discuss exactly what his coronation by Pope Leo III in Rome on Christmas Day 800 signified to the participants. It is enough that a new emperor appeared in the west in contrast to the dynamic continuity of the Byzantine Empire in the eastern Mediterranean, which continued the state established by Augustus down to 1453.

The Empire of Charlemagne comprised what we now call France and West Germany as well as the Low Countries, Switzerland, northern Italy and part of Spain. This burden was beyond the capacity of his successors; but in any case the Frankish or Germanic tradition was for division between the surviving sons of a parent. As has been seen (Chapters 15 and 28: first sections), the Treaty of Verdun in 843 arranged a partition into three which later events have made memorable. Germany fell to the share of Louis: but none of his three sons had legitimate issue, though one bastard grandson, Arnulf, became ruler of Germany. Meanwhile the style of emperor had passed to ever more limp and shadowy figures among the descendants of the great and vigorous Charlemagne. His triumph had been a personal one; nor indeed was the idea of empire consonant with the practice of subdivision of estates.

In 919 a new dynasty came to power in Germany with Henry the Fowler, Duke of Saxony. His son Otto I, the Great (936–73), was a capable and vigorous ruler who brought Germany to order and finally quashed the Hungarian menace (Chapter 22). In 962 he invaded Italy, entered Rome and was crowned emperor in St Peter's. He then proceeded to depose Pope John XII, who was scarcely an ornament to his high position. There can be no question that contemporaries looked back to the coronation of Charlemagne, but it is really from the sacring of Otto

that the story of the Holy Roman Empire begins: from this moment there is a series of rulers, under various titles and of differing powers, until the resignation of Francis II in 1806 (Table 81). But the successors of Otto I never had suzerainty over France or Spain, while their power in Italy steadily declined down the centuries. Otto I normally styled himself 'Imperator Augustus': it was probably his son, Otto II, who added the epithet 'Roman', as a weapon in his dispute with the Byzantine Emperor Basil II. The adjective 'Holy' was introduced by Barbarossa in 1157. Otto III, whose mother was a Greek princess, had lofty ideas of re-establishing the Roman Empire of classical times with a Christian tincture, but his early death (1002) put an end to them. His immediate successors were more concerned with being efficient rulers of Germany, though they journeyed to Rome to be crowned.

Henry III (Table 113), powerful and pious, was the second Emperor of the Salian House, which had succeeded the Saxon by the choice of the nobles. In 1046 he invaded Italy, purified the Papacy by deposing three rival Popes and installed a German Bishop of Rome (Clement II), who was devoted to the principles of reform which had developed in Burgundy and the Rhineland and are loosely known as the Cluniac movement. His early death was doubly unfortunate, for it exposed his son to a turbulent minority and to the growing ecclesiastical pressure of the reformed Papacy: from this sprang the destructive Investiture Contest. Henry IV was at one moment threatened by an anti-king, Rudolph of Swabia; more important, royal control of Germany was seriously weakened by civil war.

On the death of Henry V the Salian family became extinct; he had been married to Matilda, only daughter of Henry I of England, but it is idle to speculate what would have happened if they had

TABLE 113

HOLY ROMAN EMPIRE
General survey (until Frederick III)

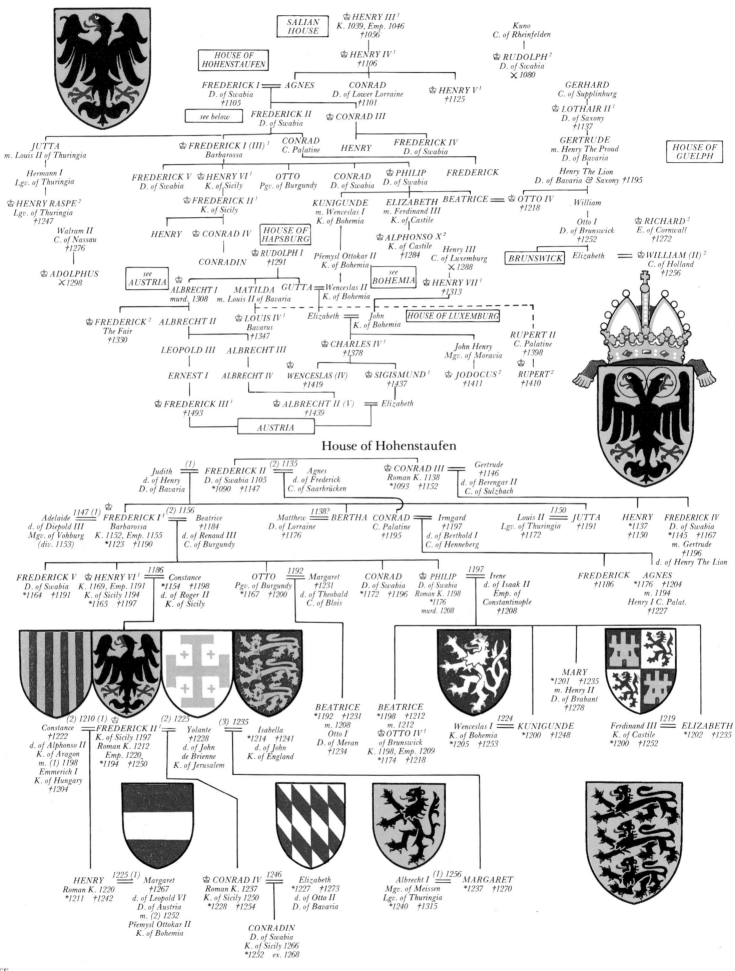

SALIAN HOUSE

♚ *HENRY III¹* K. 1039, Emp. 1046 †1056

Kuno C. of Rheinfelden

HOUSE OF HOHENSTAUFEN

♚ *HENRY IV¹* †1106

♚ *RUDOLPH²* D. of Swabia ✕1080

FREDERICK I — AGNES D. of Swabia †1105

CONRAD D. of Lower Lorraine †1101

♚ *HENRY V¹* †1125

GERHARD C. of Supplinburg

see below

FREDERICK II D. of Swabia

♚ *CONRAD III*

♚ *LOTHAIR II¹* D. of Saxony †1137

JUTTA m. Louis II of Thuringia

♚ *FREDERICK I (III)¹* Barbarossa

CONRAD C. Palatine

HENRY

FREDERICK IV D. of Swabia

GERTRUDE m. Henry The Proud D. of Bavaria

HOUSE OF GUELPH

Hermann I Lgv. of Thuringia

FREDERICK V D. of Swabia

♚ *HENRY VI¹* K. of Sicily

OTTO Pgv. of Burgundy

CONRAD D. of Swabia

♚ *PHILIP* D. of Swabia

FREDERICK

Henry The Lion D. of Bavaria & Saxony †1195

♚ *HENRY RASPE²* Lgv. of Thuringia †1247

♚ *FREDERICK II¹* K. of Sicily

KUNIGUNDE m. Wenceslas I K. of Bohemia

ELIZABETH m. Ferdinand III K. of Castile

BEATRICE — ♚ *OTTO IV* †1218

William

Walram II C. of Nassau †1276

HENRY

♚ *CONRAD IV*

HOUSE OF HAPSBURG

♚ *ALPHONSO X²* K. of Castile †1284

Henry III C. of Luxemburg ✕1288

Otto I D. of Brunswick †1252

♚ *RICHARD²* E. of Cornwall †1272

♚ *ADOLPHUS* ✕1298

CONRADIN

♚ *RUDOLPH I* †1291

Přemysl Ottokar II K. of Bohemia

BRUNSWICK

Elizabeth — ♚ *WILLIAM (II)²* C. of Holland †1256

see AUSTRIA

ALBRECHT I murd. 1308

MATILDA m. Louis II of Bavaria

GUTTA — Wenceslas II K. of Bohemia

see BOHEMIA

♚ *HENRY VII¹* †1313

♚ *FREDERICK²* The Fair †1330

ALBRECHT II

♚ *LOUIS IV¹* Bavarus †1347

Elizabeth — John K. of Bohemia

HOUSE OF LUXEMBURG

RUPERT II C. Palatine †1398

LEOPOLD III

ALBRECHT III

♚ *CHARLES IV¹* †1378

John Henry Mgv. of Moravia

ERNEST I

ALBRECHT IV

♚ *WENCESLAS (IV)* †1419

♚ *SIGISMUND¹* †1437

♚ *JODOCUS²* †1411

♚ *RUPERT²* †1410

♚ *FREDERICK III¹* †1493

♚ *ALBRECHT II (V)* — Elizabeth †1439

AUSTRIA

House of Hohenstaufen

Judith d. of Henry D. of Bavaria — *(1)* **FREDERICK II** D. of Swabia 1105 *1090 †1147 — *(2) 1135* Agnes d. of Frederick C. of Saarbrücken

♚ *CONRAD III* Roman K. 1138 *1093 †1152 — Gertrude †1146 d. of Berengar II C. of Sulzbach

Adelaide d. of Diepold III Mgv. of Vohburg (div. 1153) — *1147 (1)* ♚ **FREDERICK I¹** Barbarossa K. 1152, Emp. 1155 *1123 †1190 — *(2) 1156* Beatrice †1184 d. of Renaud III C. of Burgundy

Matthew D. of Lorraine †1176 — *1138?* BERTHA

CONRAD C. Palatine †1195 — Irmgard †1197 d. of Berthold I C. of Henneberg

Louis II Lgv. of Thuringia †1172 — *1150* JUTTA †1191

HENRY *1137 †1150

FREDERICK IV D. of Swabia *1145 †1167 m. Gertrude †1196 d. of Henry The Lion

FREDERICK V D. of Swabia *1164 †1191

♚ *HENRY VI¹* K. 1169, Emp. 1191 K. of Sicily 1194 *1165 †1197 — *1186* Constance *1154 †1198 d. of Roger II K. of Sicily

OTTO Pgv. of Burgundy *1167 †1200 — *1192* Margaret †1231 d. of Theobald C. of Blois

CONRAD D. of Swabia *1172 †1196

♚ *PHILIP* D. of Swabia Roman K. 1198 *1176 murd. 1208 — *1197* Irene d. of Isaak II Emp. of Constantinople †1208

FREDERICK †1186

AGNES *1176 †1204 m. 1194 Henry I C. Palat. †1227

Shields (coats of arms)

Constance †1222 d. of Alphonso II K. of Aragon m. (1) 1198 Emmerich I K. of Hungary †1204 — *(2) 1210 (1)* ♚ **FREDERICK II¹** K. of Sicily 1197 Roman K. 1212 Emp. 1220 *1194 †1250 — *(2) 1225* Yolante †1228 d. of John de Brienne K. of Jerusalem — *(3) 1235* Isabella *1214 †1241 d. of John K. of England

BEATRICE *1192 †1231 m. 1208 Otto I D. of Meran †1234

BEATRICE *1198 †1212 m. 1212 ♚ *OTTO IV¹* of Brunswick K. 1198, Emp. 1209 *1174 †1218

MARY *1201 †1235 m. Henry II D. of Brabant †1278

Wenceslas I K. of Bohemia *1205 †1253 — *1224* KUNIGUNDE *1200 †1248

Ferdinand III K. of Castile *1200 †1252 — *1219* ELIZABETH *1202 †1235

HENRY Roman K. 1220 *1211 †1242 — *1225 (1)* Margaret †1267 d. of Leopold VI D. of Austria m. (2) 1252 Přemysl Ottokar II K. of Bohemia

♚ *CONRAD IV* Roman K. 1237 K. of Sicily 1250 *1228 †1254 — *1246* Elizabeth *1227 †1273 d. of Otto II D. of Bavaria

Albrecht I Mgv. of Meissen Lgv. of Thuringia *1240 †1315 — *(1) 1256* MARGARET *1237 †1270

CONRADIN D. of Swabia K. of Sicily 1266 *1252 ex. 1268

NOTE
¹ Holy Roman Emperor
² Rival King

procreated. The German princes, no doubt partly as a protest against the hereditary principle, eschewed Frederick of Hohenstaufen and elected Lothair II, Duke of Saxony. Perhaps for similar reasons, on Lothair's death they avoided his son-in-law, the richest noble in Germany, and selected in 1138 Conrad III of Hohenstaufen who had already been put forward as an anti-king. His reign was unsuccessful (as was his participation in the Second Crusade of 1147); the feud between Guelph (or Welf) and Hohenstaufen (or Ghibelline) was growing; Conrad never achieved the journey to Rome to be crowned emperor, but lived and died as King of the Romans, the title by now given (somewhat anomalously) to the ruler of Germany before his coronation by the Pope as emperor.

For once united in desire for a robust king, the German princes turned to Frederick 'Barbarossa' (Table 113: lower half). Tall, handsome, auburn-bearded, he was a good soldier and well-educated; deservedly he has become a hero of German tradition. His long reign was devoted to the restoration of royal power in Germany after a century of strife and to an endeavour, only partially successful, to reassert imperial power in northern Italy where the great cities had made good their independence. In 1180 he broke the power of his most puissant subject, Henry the Lion, Duke of Saxony and Bavaria, partly because of the meagre help Henry had afforded him in Italy. From the redistribution of Henry's lands sprang many of the later German princely families (Chapter 26: Saxony, and Chapter 29: Mecklenburg). At the end of his life the venerable Emperor departed on the Third Crusade and was drowned in Cilicia on his way to the Holy Land. By the time of his death the eagle was the recognized insignia of the Empire; it first appeared as the top of a sceptre on the seal of Henry III. The early arms of the sovereigns of Germany are thus those shown at the top of Table 113, or at the head of this chapter.

Henry VI had made a marriage which proved to be sensational; his wife Constance was, in the event, sole heiress of the wealthy and cosmopolitan Kingdom of Sicily (which included southern Italy), founded in the late eleventh century by Norman adventurers of the de Hauteville family (Chapter 33). In his brief and dazzling reign this frail figure planned a consolidated Germano-Italian kingdom, an attack against Constantinople and, perhaps, a Europe paying homage to an august emperor of a new model. It was he who extorted submission from the captive Richard I of England. He himself had been elected King of the Romans in his father's lifetime, the first employment of this title for an heir-apparent. He now bribed the German princes into doing the same for his infant heir, Frederick II, and by lavish concessions of privileges sought their agreement to an hereditary kingdom of Germany. Then at the age of 31 he died abruptly with his exalted dreams unfulfilled.

The picture changed with startling rapidity. In Germany, the Duke of Swabia, brother of the dead Emperor, became king, but his right was bitterly contested by Otto IV of Saxony (great-grandson of Lothair and son of Henry the Lion) and Philip was never crowned emperor. Much of the work of the Hohenstaufen was undone in the ensuing civil war, and lay and ecclesiastical princes rejoiced in the opportunity to acquire privileges, lands and immunities. In Italy Pope Innocent III consolidated the position of the Papacy.

In 1220 Frederick II was crowned as emperor. He is one of the most remarkable figures of the Middle Ages. Short and unimposing, he was a patron of science and of poetry, a practical experimenter in both fields and author of a splendid book on falconry. In politics he was ambitious, in warfare skilful, in love active. His three wives came from the first families of Europe, but it was in fact a cherished bastard who carried on his regime in Sicily. In right of his second wife he was King of Jerusalem and, while excommunicate by the Pope, he organized a successful crusade. But for all his brilliant talent, his positive achievement was slender and his death was followed by a disastrous period for the Holy Roman Empire.

THE EMPIRE IN DISPUTE

After the death of Conrad IV, the anti-king William, Count of Holland, held the field for a while until he fell in an obscure battle. The doctrine of election had advanced swiftly; it was now recognized that only seven of the great princes had a right to participate. These were the three great ecclesiastical prelates of the Rhineland, the Archbishops of Mainz, Trier and Cologne, who were respectively Arch-Chancellors of Germany, Gaul and Italy, and four lay dynasts, the King of Bohemia (Imperial Cupbearer: Table 85), the Count Palatine of the Rhine (Imperial Seneschal: Table 96) the Duke of Saxony (Imperial Marshal: Table 101) and the Margrave of Brandenburg (Imperial Chamberlain: Table 91). In the earliest days there was some doubt about the relative claims of Bavaria and Bohemia, especially as the latter was somewhat outside Germany, but opinion swung against having two members of the Wittelsbach family. It must also be allowed that it was political influence rather than their courtly titles which marked out these particular princes. The death of Conradin, Duke of Swabia, brought the Hohenstaufen line to an end after a remarkable series of sovereigns. Three black lions on gold (Table 113) were the arms associated with the province and the dynasty.

In 1257 two candidates were advanced for election,

The Emperor Charles IV (1316–78) with the seven Electors – three archbishops and four laymen. MS c. 1370.

and each secured some of the seven votes; both were rich and neither was a German. Richard, Earl of Cornwall, was a brother of Henry III of England, though also a brother-in-law of Frederick II, while Alphonso X, the cultivated ruler of Castile, was a grandson of Philip of Swabia. Alphonso first used a nimbus round the single head of the eagle on his seal; a two-headed eagle was already becoming known as a symbol of empire, but it did not gain general acceptance until the time of the Emperor Sigismund. His arms are shown in the middle of Table 113 with the imperial crown; one of the earliest appearances of a bicephalous eagle is in the mid-thirteenth-century manuscript of the great English chronicler, Matthew Paris of St Albans. The origin of the two-headed eagle is still obscure. That it came from the East is tolerably certain, but the Byzantine emperors and their subjects knew nothing of heraldry in the Western sense. Only where their lands marched with heraldic neighbours was there some requirement for blazonry; then either the cross between the four 'B's or the two-headed eagle, which itself perhaps evolved from textiles, were called into play.

Neither Richard nor Alphonso were ever effective rulers of Germany, and on the death of the former the Electors made a new start. Still suspicious of a strong, local candidate, they chose an able but relatively obscure Swabian Count, Rudolph of Hapsburg (Table 76 and 113). He proved a competent ruler, but his interests were confined to Germany. His successor was Adolphus of Nassau, another nobleman not of the first rank, and for two centuries the Crown oscillated between the dynasties of Hapsburg, Wittelsbach and Luxemburg. Not surprisingly the emperors were constrained to play family politics and to use their reigns to enhance their kindred; a striking example is Rudolph of Hapsburg's acquisition of Austria for his sons (Chapter 19). Between the death of Frederick II (1250) and 1452, only Henry VII, Louis IV, Charles IV, Sigismund and Frederick III made the journey to Rome to receive the Imperial Crown. Thereafter the practice almost ceased and the title of 'Holy Roman Empire of the German people', which appeared in the reign of Frederick III, illustrated the new emphasis.

THE HAPSBURGS

In 1356 the Emperor Charles IV defined the processes of election and the number of electors in close detail in his famous Golden Bull; it is noteworthy that no mention is made of papal approval. From 1437 the Hapsburg family provided an unbroken series of rulers and the history of the

Empire is bound up with that of Austria, save for the brief reign (1742–5) of Charles Albrecht of Bavaria. But the character of the Empire continued to alter. The Reformation struck a deadly blow at any surviving idea of widespread dominion; henceforward Germany was fragmented in religion as well as in politics. The Thirty Years' War all but destroyed the authority of the Austrian Emperor within the bounds of Germany. And yet the Empire continued to exist, and furnished a ghostly semblance of unity for men of Teutonic speech. In the seventeenth century the number of the electors was increased; first, in 1648, a second electorate was allowed to the Wittelsbachs (Chapter 24), and then in 1692 Leopold I awarded a ninth to Brunswick-Lüneburg. But if the number of actual electors was small, that of the princes was much larger. In the middle of the seventeenth century there were 43 lay principalities and 33 ecclesiastical with a vote in the Diet; this number tended to grow rather than diminish as the Emperor rewarded good service. The rise of Liechtenstein (Chapter 12) may be taken as an example.

Many of the German princes had tiny domains and most of the large states were intermittently subjected to division. The total number of independent states, towns, bishoprics and abbeys, not all of which by any means had a direct vote in the Diet, was reckoned at 365 in 1715. Some imperial knights held land directly of the Emperor but owned little more than a couple of villages. This society was rigidly and severely stratified. Reigning Houses gave their children only to each other in marriage: noble family allied with noble family or knight with knight. Many religious houses and orders of chivalry were only open to those who could prove their *seize-quartiers*, that is show that all their great-great-grandparents were of noble birth. From time to time genuine affection would break through the schemes of planned alliances, and numerous morganatic marriages bear witness to this. Such a wedding was one in which the parties were truly married, but the wife did not enjoy the full status of her husband, nor did the children, though spared the stigma of illegitimacy, inherit his titles or estates. The issue of two such unions have played

some part in British life in the last hundred years, the families of Teck (Table 104) and Mountbatten or Battenberg (Table 109). It may be noted in passing that English law makes no provision whatsoever for such alliances (which are indeed mainly found in the Empire and Spain), a circumstance of some importance in 1936.

According to Goethe the Great Hall in Frankfurt (since 1424 the repository of the imperial insignia), decorated with portraits of the emperors, had but one space left when Francis II succeeded in 1792. The tempestuous career of Napoleon shook down the venerable, but by now decrepit, fabric of the Holy Roman Empire. His conquests swept across Germany and led to radical reorganization. In 1803 the rank of elector was conferred by Bonaparte on the rulers of Hesse-Cassel, Baden and Württemberg and on the Archbishop of Salzburg. All the ecclesiastical princes of Germany disappeared and their lands were annexed to secular states. In 1806 Francis abandoned the title of Holy Roman Emperor. In 1810 the traditional Hapsburg Emperor gave his daughter in marriage to the self-made Corsican ruler; it was with a deliberate sense of history that the Emperor Napoleon called his son the King of Rome.

In the resulting rearrangements in 1814–15 the map of Germany was greatly simplified. Over sixty princes, hitherto independent, lost their sovereignty, in particular those whose territory was entirely encircled by more powerful neighbours. They formed a new class of 'mediatized' princes; although they had forfeited independence and jurisdiction, their daughters were still eligible for marriage into reigning families. Thus in Table 103, the wife of Prince Frederick Christian of Saxony is the daughter of a 'mediatized' prince, Albrecht of Thurn and Taxis. The creation of a united Germany under the King of Prussia in 1870–71 still further reduced the number of semi-independent rulers; but the short-lived Empire of the Hohenzollerns had little to do with the now defunct Holy Roman Empire, which spanned the millenium between Charlemagne and Francis II, even if in its latest phase it was, according to Voltaire, neither holy nor Roman nor an empire.

Chapter 31

PORTUGAL

The story of Portugal as a separate state only begins at the end of the eleventh century. Before this point the territory north of the Douro was part of Leon, while the land south of that river was in Moorish hands. In 1093 King Alphonso VI of Castile married his illegitimate daughter Theresa to a French nobleman, Henry of Burgundy (Table 74), and granted him a fief round Oporto. From the Latin name of this harbour, Portus Cale, the area came to be known as the County of Portugal. Henry began to aim at independence, which was achieved by his son, Alphonso I (Table 115), who started to call himself king in 1139 and was recognized as such by Castile in 1143. After unsuccessful and unworthy efforts to expand his kingdom northwards into Galicia, Alphonso turned his attention southwards. In 1147, with the assistance of a body of English and Flemish crusaders sailing to the Holy Land, he captured Lisbon. In 1179 the Pope also approved his royal title; his long reign was the formative period in the history of Portugal. Alphonso's new territories were scantily populated and he made use of religious orders, especially the Cistercians.

Succeeding Kings of Portugal continued the work of colonization and gradually extended their boundaries down to Cape St Vincent. Sancho I is remembered as a builder of towns; the first meeting of the *Cortes* (or assembly) is recorded under Alphonso II. Alphonso III gained Portugal her modern territorial limits. He had spent some time in France where his first wife gave him a title to the County of Boulogne. But he returned to Portugal to dethrone his brother, Sancho II, who had made an unpopular marriage. Ironically Alphonso III proceeded to marry a daughter of the King of Castile while his first wife was alive.

During his reign the arms of Portugal crystallized into their present form. It has been conjectured that

they may originally have been a blue cross studded with silver nails. The seal of Alphonso I seems to show 12 small shields, each containing dots, arranged in a cruciform pattern. Sancho I has five shields crosswise, but with two on their sides; from then on there are considerable variations, and only gradually do all the shields become upright. In early examples the number of dots also varies. Alphonso III added a red border with gold castles, based no doubt on the arms of Castile, the dynasty to which his wife and his mother belonged. Later usage limited the number of castles to seven. Equally, later tradition, seeking meaning for heraldry, imagined that the five shields alluded to five Moorish kings defeated by Alphonso I and that the five discs referred to the five wounds of Christ. In popular speech these little shields (or escutcheons) with their five discs (or roundels) are known as 'quinas'.

King Denis is a noteworthy figure in the story of Portugal. He had been associated in the kingship by his father and made ruler of the Algarve, the southernmost area of the Kingdom. During his reign he added two tiny pieces of Castile to his country; he founded the Order of Christ (1319) to replace the disbanded Templars; he encouraged maritime trade and the growth of a fleet; he was a considerable poet and his works mark a stage in the evolution of the Portuguese language; to his own countrymen he is the 'Farmer king' because of his encouragement of agriculture. His wife, Isabel of Aragon, was a pious and charitable queen, later canonized; like many medieval rulers of Portugal her talented husband left several bastards. The oldest university in Portugal was founded in his reign at Lisbon in 1290, but transferred to Coimbra in 1308.

Alphonso IV was known as 'the Brave' from his courage in a great battle, fought in alliance with Castile, against the Moors at the river Salado in 1340. He

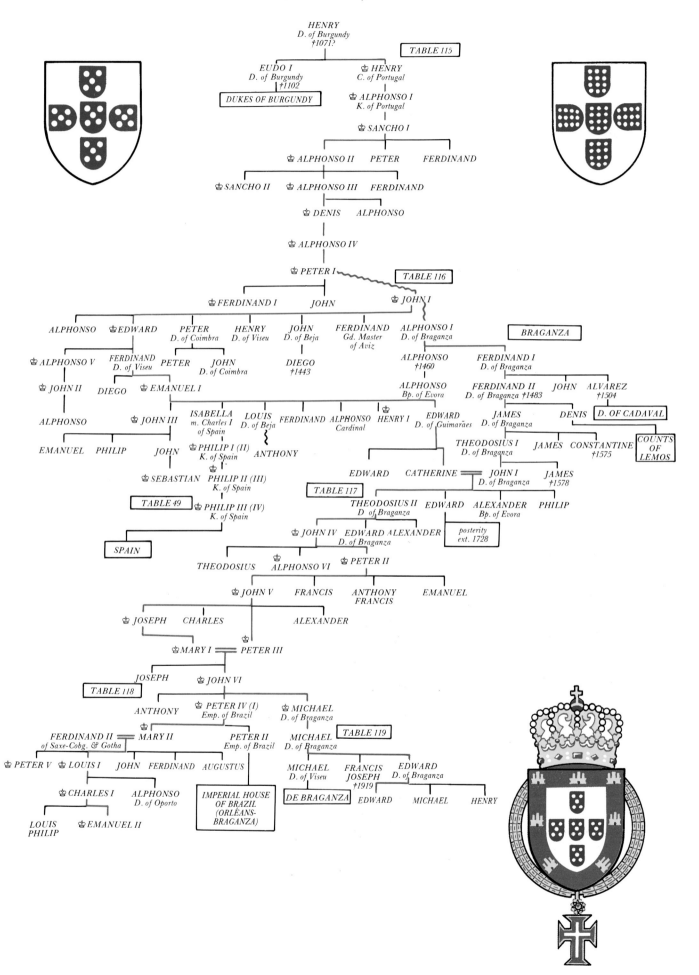

PORTUGAL
General survey

TABLE 115

HENRY
D. of Burgundy
†1071?

EUDO I
D. of Burgundy
†1102

♔ HENRY
C. of Portugal

DUKES OF BURGUNDY

♔ ALPHONSO I
K. of Portugal

♔ SANCHO I

♔ ALPHONSO II   PETER   FERDINAND

♔ SANCHO II   ♔ ALPHONSO III   FERDINAND

♔ DENIS   ALPHONSO

♔ ALPHONSO IV

♔ PETER I   TABLE 116

♔ FERDINAND I   JOHN   ♔ JOHN I

ALPHONSO   ♔ EDWARD   PETER   HENRY   JOHN   FERDINAND   ALPHONSO I   BRAGANZA
                        D. of Coimbra   D. of Viseu   D. of Beja   Gd. Master   D. of Braganza
                                                                of Aviz

♔ ALPHONSO V   FERDINAND   PETER   JOHN   DIEGO   ALPHONSO   FERDINAND I
                D. of Viseu   D. of Coimbra   †1443   †1460   D. of Braganza

♔ JOHN II   DIEGO   ♔ EMANUEL I   ALPHONSO   FERDINAND II   JOHN   ALVAREZ
                                        Bp. of Evora   D. of Braganza †1483   †1504

ALPHONSO   ♔ JOHN III   ISABELLA   LOUIS   FERDINAND   ALPHONSO   ♔ HENRY I   EDWARD   JAMES   DENIS   D. OF CADAVAL
                        m. Charles I   D. of Beja   Cardinal   D. of Guimarães   D. of Braganza
                        of Spain

EMANUEL   PHILIP   JOHN   ♔ PHILIP I (II)   ANTHONY   THEODOSIUS I   JAMES   CONSTANTINE   COUNTS
                            K. of Spain   D. of Braganza   †1575   OF LEMOS

♔ SEBASTIAN   PHILIP II (III)   EDWARD   CATHERINE   JOHN I   JAMES
                K. of Spain   D. of Braganza   †1578

TABLE 49   ♔ PHILIP III (IV)   TABLE 117   THEODOSIUS II   EDWARD   ALEXANDER   PHILIP
            K. of Spain   D. of Braganza   Bp. of Evora

SPAIN   ♔ JOHN IV   EDWARD ALEXANDER   posterity
                                D. of Braganza   ext. 1728

THEODOSIUS   ALPHONSO VI   ♔ PETER II

♔ JOHN V   FRANCIS   ANTHONY   EMANUEL
                        FRANCIS

♔ JOSEPH   CHARLES   ALEXANDER

♔ MARY I   PETER III

JOSEPH   ♔ JOHN VI

TABLE 118   ANTHONY   ♔ PETER IV (I)   ♔ MICHAEL
                        Emp. of Brazil   D. of Braganza

FERDINAND II   ♔ MARY II   PETER II   MICHAEL   TABLE 119
of Saxe-Cobg. & Gotha   Emp. of Brazil   D. of Braganza

♔ PETER V   ♔ LOUIS I   JOHN   FERDINAND   AUGUSTUS   MICHAEL   FRANCIS   EDWARD
                                                    D. of Viseu   JOSEPH   D. of Braganza
                                                            †1919

♔ CHARLES I   ALPHONSO   IMPERIAL HOUSE   DE BRAGANZA   EDWARD   MICHAEL   HENRY
            D. of Oporto   OF BRAZIL
                        (ORLÉANS-
LOUIS   ♔ EMANUEL II   BRAGANZA)
PHILIP

TABLE 115

PORTUGAL
Early Kings (House of Burgundy)

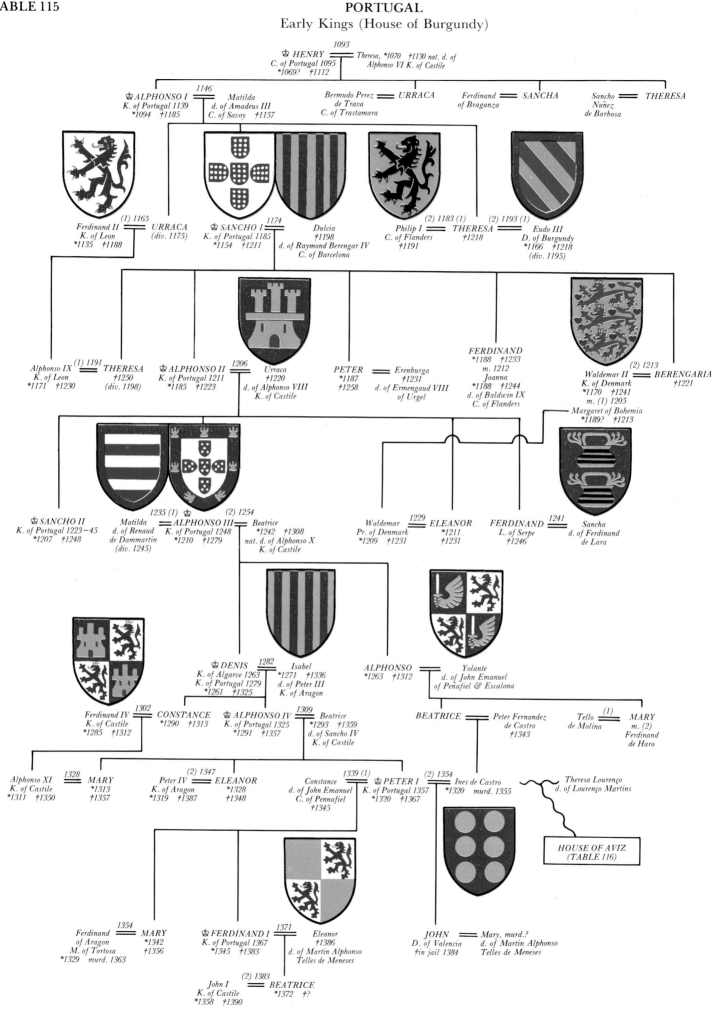

1093
☿ HENRY ═══ Theresa, *1070 †1130 nat. d. of
C. of Portugal 1095   Alphonso VI K. of Castile
*1069? †1112

1146
☿ ALPHONSO I ═══ Matilda
K. of Portugal 1139   d. of Amadeus III
*1094 †1185   C. of Savoy †1157

Bermudo Perez ═══ URRACA
de Trava
C. of Trastamara

Ferdinand ═══ SANCHA
of Braganza

Sancho ═══ THERESA
Nuñez
de Barbosa

(1) 1165
Ferdinand II ═══ URRACA
K. of Leon   (div. 1175)
*1135 †1188

1174
☿ SANCHO I ═══ Dulcia
K. of Portugal 1185   †1198
*1154 †1211   d. of Raymond Berengar IV
C. of Barcelona

(2) 1183 (1)
Philip I ═══ THERESA
C. of Flanders   †1218
†1191

(2) 1193 (1)
Eudo III
D. of Burgundy
*1166 †1218
(div. 1195)

(1) 1191
Alphonso IX ═══ THERESA
K. of Leon   †1250
*1171 †1230   (div. 1198)

1206
☿ ALPHONSO II ═══ Urraca
K. of Portugal 1211   *1220
*1185 †1223   d. of Alphonso VIII
K. of Castile

PETER ═══ Erenburga
*1187   †1231
†1258   d. of Ermengaud VIII
of Urgel

FERDINAND
*1188 †1233
m. 1212
Joanna
*1188 †1244
d. of Baldwin IX
C. of Flanders

(2) 1213
Waldemar II ═══ BERENGARIA
K. of Denmark   †1221
*1170 †1241
m. (1) 1205
Margaret of Bohemia
*1189? †1213

☿ SANCHO II
K. of Portugal 1223–45
*1207 †1248

Matilda
d. of Renaud
de Dammartin
(div. 1245)

1235 (1)   (2) 1254
☿ ALPHONSO III ═══ Beatrice
K. of Portugal 1248   *1242 †1308
*1210 †1279   nat. d. of Alphonso X
K. of Castile

1229
Waldemar ═══ ELEANOR
Pr. of Denmark   *1211
*1209 †1231   †1231

1241
FERDINAND ═══ Sancha
L. of Serpe   d. of Ferdinand
†1246   de Lara

1282
☿ DENIS ═══ Isabel
K. of Algarve 1263   *1271 †1336
K. of Portugal 1279   d. of Peter III
*1261 †1325   K. of Aragon

ALPHONSO ═══ Yolante
*1263 †1312   d. of John Emanuel
of Peñafiel & Escalona

BEATRICE ═══ Peter Fernandez
de Castro
†1343

Tello ═══ MARY
de Molina   m. (2)
Ferdinand
de Haro
(1)

1302
Ferdinand IV ═══ CONSTANCE
K. of Castile   *1290 †1313
*1285 †1312

1309
☿ ALPHONSO IV ═══ Beatrice
K. of Portugal 1325   *1293 †1359
*1291 †1357   d. of Sancho IV
K. of Castile

1328
Alphonso XI ═══ MARY
K. of Castile   *1313
*1311 †1350   †1357

(2) 1347
Peter IV ═══ ELEANOR
K. of Aragon   *1328
*1319 †1387   †1348

1339 (1)
Constance
d. of John Emanuel
C. of Pennafiel
†1345

☿ PETER I
K. of Portugal 1357
*1320 †1367

(2) 1354
Ines de Castro
*1320   murd. 1355

Theresa Lourenço
d. of Lourenço Martins

HOUSE OF AVIZ
(TABLE 116)

1354
Ferdinand ═══ MARY
of Aragon   *1342
M. of Tortosa   †1356
*1329 murd. 1363

1371
☿ FERDINAND I ═══ Eleanor
K. of Portugal 1367   †1386
*1345 †1383   d. of Martin Alphonso
Telles de Meneses

JOHN ═══ Mary, murd.?
D. of Valencia   d. of Martin Alphonso
†in jail 1384   Telles de Meneses

(2) 1383
John I ═══ BEATRICE
K. of Castile   *1372 †?
*1358 †1390

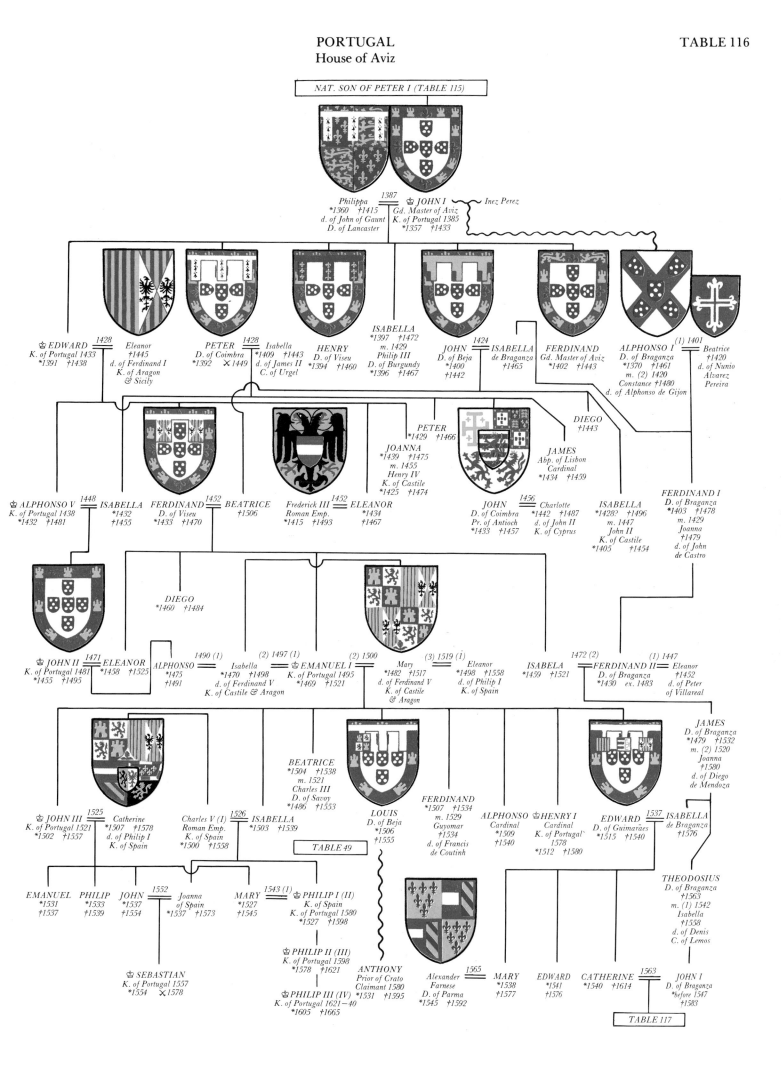

NAT. SON OF PETER I (TABLE 115)

Philippa \
*1360 †1415 \
d. of John of Gaunt \
D. of Lancaster

1387

♔ *JOHN I* \
Gd. Master of Aviz \
K. of Portugal 1385 \
*1357 †1433

Inez Perez

♔ *EDWARD* \
K. of Portugal 1433 \
*1391 †1438

1428

Eleanor \
†1445 \
d. of Ferdinand I \
K. of Aragon \
& Sicily

PETER \
D. of Coimbra \
*1392 ✕1449

1428

Isabella \
*1409 †1443 \
d. of James II \
C. of Urgel

HENRY \
D. of Viseu \
*1394 †1460

ISABELLA \
*1397 †1472 \
m. 1429 \
Philip III \
D. of Burgundy \
*1396 †1467

JOHN \
D. of Beja \
*1400 \
†1442

1424

ISABELLA \
de Braganza \
†1465

FERDINAND \
Gd. Master of Aviz \
*1402 †1443

ALPHONSO I \
D. of Braganza \
*1370 †1461 \
m. (2) 1420 \
Constance †1480 \
d. of Alphonso de Gijon

(1) 1401

Beatrice \
†1420 \
d. of Nunio \
Alvarez \
Pereira

PETER \
*1429 †1466

JOANNA \
*1439 †1475 \
m. 1455 \
Henry IV \
K. of Castile \
*1425 †1474

JAMES \
Abp. of Lisbon \
Cardinal \
*1434 †1459

DIEGO \
†1443

JOHN \
D. of Coimbra \
Pr. of Antioch \
*1433 †1457

1456

Charlotte \
*1442 †1487 \
m. 1447 \
d. of John II \
K. of Cyprus

ISABELLA \
*1428? †1496 \
m. 1447 \
John II \
K. of Castile \
*1405 †1454

FERDINAND I \
D. of Braganza \
*1403 †1478 \
m. 1429 \
Joanna \
†1479 \
d. of John \
de Castro

♔ *ALPHONSO V* \
K. of Portugal 1438 \
*1432 †1481

1448

ISABELLA \
*1432 \
†1455

FERDINAND \
D. of Viseu \
*1433 †1470

1452

BEATRICE \
†1506

Frederick III \
Roman Emp. \
*1415 †1493

1452

ELEANOR \
*1434 \
†1467

DIEGO \
*1460 †1484

♔ *JOHN II* \
K. of Portugal 1481 \
*1455 †1495

1471

ELEANOR \
*1458 †1525

ALPHONSO \
*1475 \
†1491

1490 (1)

Isabella \
*1470 †1498 \
d. of Ferdinand V \
K. of Castile & Aragon

(2) 1497 (1)

EMANUEL I \
K. of Portugal 1495 \
*1469 †1521

(2) 1500

Mary \
*1482 †1517 \
d. of Ferdinand V \
K. of Castile \
& Aragon

(3) 1519 (1)

Eleanor \
*1498 †1558 \
d. of Philip I \
K. of Spain

ISABELA \
*1459 †1521

1472 (2)

FERDINAND II \
D. of Braganza \
*1430 ex. 1483

(1) 1447

Eleanor \
d. of Peter \
of Villareal

JAMES \
D. of Braganza \
*1479 †1532 \
m. (2) 1520 \
Joanna \
†1580 \
d. of Diego \
de Mendoza

♔ *JOHN III* \
K. of Portugal 1521 \
*1502 †1557

1525

Catherine \
*1507 †1578 \
d. of Philip I \
K. of Spain

Charles V (I) \
Roman Emp. \
K. of Spain \
*1500 †1558

1526

ISABELLA \
*1503 †1539

TABLE 49

BEATRICE \
*1504 †1538 \
m. 1521 \
Charles III \
D. of Savoy \
*1486 †1553

LOUIS \
D. of Beja \
*1506 \
†1555

FERDINAND \
*1507 †1534 \
m. 1529 \
Guyomar \
†1534 \
d. of Francis \
de Coutinh

ALPHONSO \
Cardinal \
*1509 \
†1540

♔ *HENRY I* \
Cardinal \
K. of Portugal \
1578 \
*1512 †1580

EDWARD \
D. of Guimarães \
*1515 †1540

1537

ISABELLA \
de Braganza \
†1576

THEODOSIUS \
D. of Braganza \
†1563 \
m. (1) 1542 \
Isabella \
†1558 \
d. of Denis \
C. of Lemos

EMANUEL \
*1531 \
†1537

PHILIP \
*1533 \
†1539

JOHN \
*1537 \
†1554

1552

Joanna \
of Spain \
*1537 †1573

MARY \
*1527 \
†1545

1543 (1)

♔ *PHILIP I (II)* \
K. of Spain \
K. of Portugal 1580 \
*1527 †1598

♔ *SEBASTIAN* \
K. of Portugal 1557 \
*1554 ✕1578

♔ *PHILIP II (III)* \
K. of Portugal 1598 \
*1578 †1621

♔ *PHILIP III (IV)* \
K. of Portugal 1621−40 \
*1605 †1665

ANTHONY \
Prior of Crato \
Claimant 1580 \
*1531 †1595

*Alexander \
Farnese* \
D. of Parma \
*1545 †1592

1565

MARY \
*1538 \
†1577

EDWARD \
*1541 \
†1576

CATHERINE \
*1540 †1614

1563

JOHN I \
D. of Braganza \
*before 1547 \
†1583

TABLE 117

Pedigree of the Kings of Portugal from an early 16th–century MS. It rises from Alphonso III (1210–79) and his second wife Beatrice and shows his son Denis (1261–1325) and grandson Alphonso IV (1291–1357) with other children and many versions of the arms of Portugal.

codified the laws of Portugal. The King deeply disapproved of the infatuation of his heir, Peter, for Ines de Castro, a Galician lady-in-waiting of Peter's legal wife. In 1355 he was persuaded to agree to her murder, which was followed by a brief and bitter civil war. When Peter succeeded in 1357 he announced that he had been married to Ines and (at least in the account given by the sixteenth-century poet Camoens

in *The Lusiads*) disinterred her corpse, to which his nobles were constrained to pay allegiance. To emphasize her status he constructed the two lovely tombs for himself and his beloved which are one of the glories of the great abbey of Alcobaça. His short reign was devoted to the spread of inflexible justice, including floggings administered by the King himself.

Ferdinand I was a weak and wayward king. He coveted the throne of Castile during the dispute between Peter the Cruel and Henry of Trastamara. In 1373 he negotiated an alliance with England. Portuguese gratitude to England already went back to the capture of Lisbon in 1147: since 1373 the two countries have never been at war, a rare example of diplomatic constancy. He fell in love with Eleanor Telles de Meneses, although she had a husband, and eventually married her: the Queen was exceedingly unpopular, produced only a daughter and took a lover. After numerous proposals the Infanta Beatrice was married to John I of Castile, and Ferdinand promised them the succession.

The people of Portugal resented the idea of Castilian rule and put forward John (Table 116), illegitimate son of Peter I. In 1385 he was accepted as king and, with some English help, he inflicted, in the same year, a severe defeat on the Castilians at Aljubarrota: nearby, in thanksgiving, he founded the splendid abbey of Batalha (Battle), whose style shows some English influences. John I had been Grand-Master of the Order of Aviz before he became king. Accordingly, he added to his shield the fleurs-de-lys ends of the green cross which was the badge of the Order (Table 116). This distinction was maintained by his descendants down to John II who resumed the traditional form – though it should be emphasized that there were many variations in the number of castles on the border or roundels on the 'quinas' or escutcheons. Moreover, John I married a daughter of John of Gaunt; and it seems a fair assumption that the Portuguese derived from the English the elaborate labels which begin to be used as differences for the younger princes (or 'Infants' as they were formally known in Spain and Portugal). A less common distinction was that of Ferdinand, Grand-Master of Aviz, who changed some of the castles on the border to lions of England. Ferdinand, Duke of Viseu (d. 1470), is unusual in having only two pendants to his label. Alphonso, Duke of Braganza, progenitor of a future line of kings, placed the five 'quinas' on a red saltire. Two coats-of-arms, rather typical of Iberian heraldry, can be seen on Table 115: the cooking pots with emergent snakes of de Lara (which can be compared with Guzman on Table 48), and the dice-like arrangement of the roundels of de Castro which in northern Europe would normally be arranged 3, 2 and 1.

EXPANSION OF PORTUGAL

During the fifteenth century Portuguese sailors made an epic contribution to the exploration of the world. The guiding spirit of these voyages of discovery was Henry the Navigator, Duke of Viseu and the son of John I, who had a castle at Sagre (in the extreme south) and a burning desire to extend Christian geography. Senegal was reached in 1445; and before the death of Prince Henry, Cape Verde had been doubled and the slave trade had begun. Alphonso V was more concerned with direct conquest in Morocco, but John II was keenly interested in the search for a route to India. Under his patronage Bartholomew Diaz reached the Cape of Good Hope, and he planned the celebrated voyage of Vasco da Gama, who actually attained an Indian port in 1498. In 1519–22 the ship of Ferdinand Magellan circumnavigated the world, though its captain perished on the journey. Meanwhile a powerful trading empire had been established in India, with its capital at Goa. Westward, the discovery of Brazil was made in 1500; the definition of interests in the new world between Spain and Portugal made by Pope Alexander VI in 1494 left this land in the Portuguese sphere.

Alphonso V had been involved in the succession to Castile, which he tried to secure for his son, the future John II. His defeat at Toro by Ferdinand of Aragon in 1476 checked this scheme, though Alphonso continued to dream of its realization as he grew older, portly, bearded and bald. John II was a more practical monarch. Heavily built, red-faced and red-haired, he set about reorganizing his Kingdom and fostering discovery. His dangerously powerful subject (and brother-in-law), Ferdinand of Braganza, was beheaded in 1483. At home the supremacy of the Crown was established by numerous executions among the aristocracy; abroad, the navies of Portugal traversed the globe.

King Emanuel, often known as Manuel the Fortunate, had perhaps the most glorious reign in Portuguese history. He has lent his name to the vigorous and vivid 'Manueline' style, which distinguishes the architecture of the period with its exuberant, and often maritime, decoration. Not without justice did King Emanuel assume the title of 'Lord of the conquest, navigation and commerce of India, Ethiopia, Arabia and Persia'. In East Africa or Burma, and around the coasts of India, mouldering fortresses recall this great age of Portuguese dominance of the oceans. The King himself was thin, diligent and abstemious, fond of music, but conscious of his royalty. He used as a badge an armillary sphere, which later appeared in the arms of Brazil (Table 118) and is seen all over Portugal. A generation later (1572) this golden age was celebrated by Camoens in

King John I of Portugal (1357–1433) entertains John of Gaunt. Late 15th-century MS.

his famous poem, *The Lusiads*.

In fact the situation was difficult. The flood of wealth led to a catastrophic fall in prices, particularly of imports like pepper and spices. The population of the country, long engaged in wars against the Moors or Castile, was inadequate for the stupendous tasks which drained manpower to the unhealthy East. A liberal importation of African slaves led to intermarriage and permanently affected the make-up of the people. From his three marriages Emanuel begat nine sons; he can scarcely have supposed that within sixty years his dynasty would be extinct and his country in Spanish hands.

John III arranged a double marriage with the Emperor Charles V, but was forced to provide his sister with a huge dowry. He was of moderate ability only, and came under the influence of the Church in his later years. His third son, Prince John, was a frail creature, perhaps reflecting the concentration of inbred Portuguese and Castilian blood in his veins, and died young. The next King, Sebastian, the grandson of John III, was also frail, but combined this with excessive piety and reluctance to marry. Forgotten crusading ideas fired his imagination, and he was killed conducting an incompetent campaign in Morocco. He was succeeded by his venerable great-uncle, and sometime guardian, the Cardinal-Prince Henry, Archbishop of Lisbon. The new monarch announced his wish to marry, but the Pope was as slow to dispense him as were his subjects incredulous of the value of his intention. The question of succession was clearly of paramount importance. Louis, Duke of Beja, had left an illegitimate son, Anthony, Prior of Crato; John, Duke of Braganza was married to a daughter of the Duke of Guimarães; Philip II of Spain was both nephew and son-in-law of John III (Table 116). In the event the King of Spain obtained the throne in 1580 with only a modest display of force. For

TABLE 117

PORTUGAL
House of Braganza

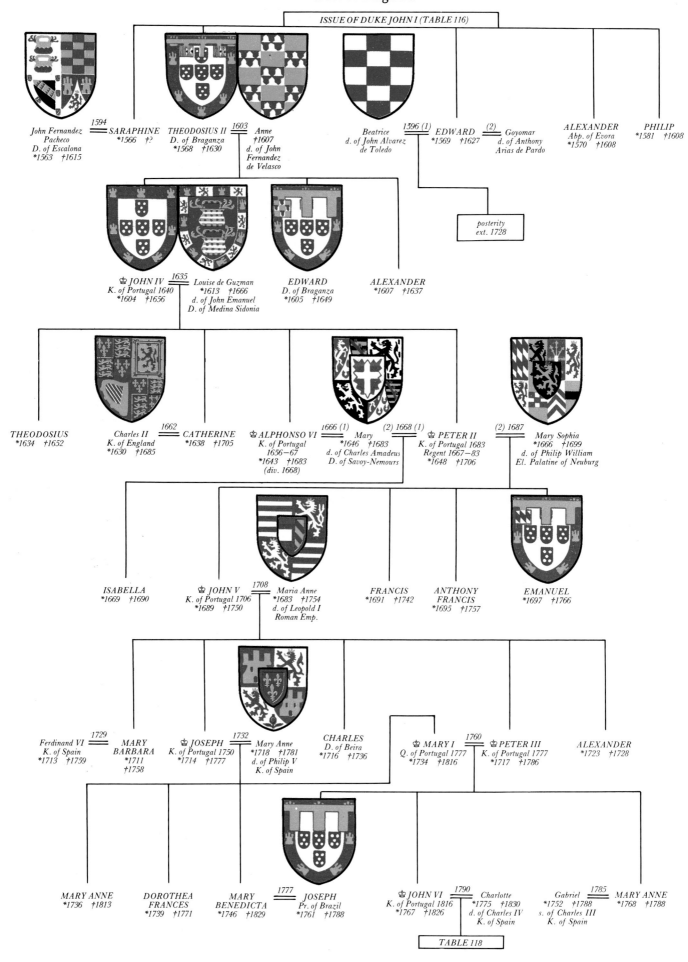

ISSUE OF DUKE JOHN I (TABLE 116)

John Fernandez
Pacheco
D. of Escalona
*1563 †1615
  1594
= SARAPHINE
*1566 †?

THEODOSIUS II
D. of Braganza
*1568 †1630
  1603
= Anne
†1607
d. of John
Fernandez
de Velasco

Beatrice
d. of John Alvarez
de Toledo
  1596 (1)
= EDWARD
*1569 †1627
(2) = Goyomar
d. of Anthony
Arias de Pardo

ALEXANDER
Abp. of Evora
*1570 †1608

PHILIP
*1581 †1608

posterity
ext. 1728

✠ JOHN IV
K. of Portugal 1640
*1604 †1656
  1635
= Louise de Guzman
*1613 †1666
d. of John Emanuel
D. of Medina Sidonia

EDWARD
D. of Braganza
*1605 †1649

ALEXANDER
*1607 †1637

THEODOSIUS
*1634 †1652

Charles II
K. of England
*1630 †1685
  1662
= CATHERINE
*1638 †1705

✠ ALPHONSO VI
K. of Portugal
1656–67
*1643 †1683
(div. 1668)
  1666 (1)
= Mary
*1646 †1683
d. of Charles Amadeus
D. of Savoy-Nemours
(2) 1668 (1) =
✠ PETER II
K. of Portugal 1683
Regent 1667–83
*1648 †1706
(2) 1687 = Mary Sophia
*1666 †1699
d. of Philip William
El. Palatine of Neuburg

ISABELLA
*1669 †1690

✠ JOHN V
K. of Portugal 1706
*1689 †1750
  1708
= Maria Anne
*1683 †1754
d. of Leopold I
Roman Emp.

FRANCIS
*1691 †1742

ANTHONY
FRANCIS
*1695 †1757

EMANUEL
*1697 †1766

Ferdinand VI
K. of Spain
*1713 †1759
  1729
= MARY
BARBARA
*1711
†1758

✠ JOSEPH
K. of Portugal 1750
*1714 †1777
  1732
= Mary Anne
*1718 †1781
d. of Philip V
K. of Spain

CHARLES
D. of Beira
*1716 †1736

✠ MARY I
Q. of Portugal 1777
*1734 †1816

✠ PETER III
K. of Portugal 1777
*1717 †1786

ALEXANDER
*1723 †1728

MARY ANNE
*1736 †1813

DOROTHEA
FRANCES
*1739 †1771

MARY
BENEDICTA
*1746 †1829

  1777
JOSEPH
Pr. of Brazil
*1761 †1788

✠ JOHN VI
K. of Portugal 1816
*1767 †1826
  1790
= Charlotte
*1775 †1830
d. of Charles IV
K. of Spain

Gabriel
*1752 †1788
s. of Charles III
K. of Spain
  1785
= MARY ANNE
*1768 †1788

TABLE 118

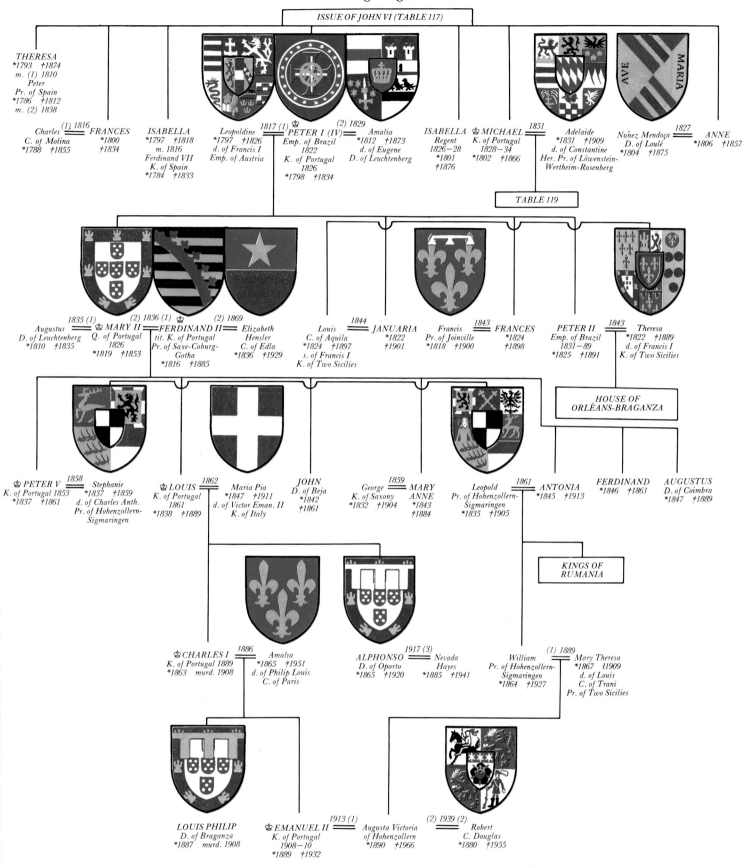

ISSUE OF JOHN VI (TABLE 117)

THERESA
*1793 †1874
m. (1) 1810
Peter
Pr. of Spain
*1786 †1812
m. (2) 1838

Charles —(1) 1816— FRANCES
C. of Molina   *1800
*1788 †1855   †1834

ISABELLA
*1797 †1818
m. 1816
Ferdinand VII
K. of Spain
*1784 †1833

Leopoldine
*1797 †1826
d. of Francis I
Emp. of Austria

—1817 (1)— ⚜ PETER I (IV) —(2) 1829—
Emp. of Brazil
1822
K. of Portugal
1826
*1798 †1834

Amalia
*1812 †1873
d. of Eugene
D. of Leuchtenberg

ISABELLA
Regent
1826–28
*1801
†1876

⚜ MICHAEL —1851—
K. of Portugal
1828–34
*1802 †1866

Adelaide
*1831 †1909
d. of Constantine
Her. Pr. of Löwenstein-
Wertheim-Rosenberg

Nuñez Mendoça —1827—
D. of Loulé
*1804 †1875

ANNE
*1806 †1857

TABLE 119

Augustus —1835 (1)—
D. of Leuchtenberg
*1810 †1835

⚜ MARY II —(2) 1836 (1)—
Q. of Portugal
1826
*1819 †1853

FERDINAND II —(2) 1869—
tit. K. of Portugal
Pr. of Saxe-Coburg-
Gotha
*1816 †1885

Elizabeth
Hensler
C. of Edla
*1836 †1929

Louis —1844—
C. of Aquila
*1824 †1897
s. of Francis I
K. of Two Sicilies

JANUARIA
*1822
†1901

Francis —1843—
Pr. of Joinville
*1818 †1900

FRANCES
*1824
†1898

PETER II
Emp. of Brazil
1831–89
*1825 †1891

Theresa —1843—
*1822 †1889
d. of Francis I
K. of Two Sicilies

HOUSE OF
ORLÉANS-BRAGANZA

⚜ PETER V —1858—
K. of Portugal 1853
*1837 †1861

Stephanie
*1837 †1859
d. of Charles Anth.
Pr. of Hohenzollern-
Sigmaringen

⚜ LOUIS —1862—
K. of Portugal
1861
*1838 †1889

Maria Pia
*1847 †1911
d. of Victor Eman. II
K. of Italy

JOHN
D. of Beja
*1842
†1861

George —1859—
K. of Saxony
*1832 †1904

MARY
ANNE
*1843
†1884

Leopold —1861—
Pr. of Hohenzollern-
Sigmaringen
*1835 †1905

ANTONIA
*1845 †1913

FERDINAND
*1846 †1861

AUGUSTUS
D. of Coimbra
*1847 †1889

KINGS OF
RUMANIA

⚜ CHARLES I —1886—
K. of Portugal 1889
*1863 murd. 1908

Amalia
*1865 †1951
d. of Philip Louis
C. of Paris

ALPHONSO —1917 (3)—
D. of Oporto
*1865 †1920

Nevada
Hayes
*1885 †1941

William —(1) 1889—
Pr. of Hohenzollern-
Sigmaringen
*1864 †1927

Mary Theresa
*1867 †1909
d. of Louis
C. of Trani
Pr. of Two Sicilies

LOUIS PHILIP
D. of Braganza
*1887 murd. 1908

⚜ EMANUEL II —1913 (1)—
K. of Portugal
1908–10
*1889 †1932

Augusta Victoria
of Hohenzollern
*1890 †1966

—(2) 1939 (2)—
Robert
C. Douglas
*1880 †1955

Chapter 32

SAVOY, SARDINIA AND ITALY

As late as 1849 it was possible for Prince Metternich, the Austrian statesman, to declare that Italy was a geographical expression (*ein geographisches Begriff*). By this he meant that the seemingly well-defined peninsula, with its long seaboard and the Alps to the north, enjoyed no historical cohesion or social bond of interest. Within a very few years political unity was in fact achieved under the auspices of the House of Savoy; for the first time since the collapse of the west Roman Empire, Italy was under a single ruler. The next three chapters survey some of this complex history. It should be emphasized that in the Middle Ages some of the great Italian cities, most notably Venice, established republics which are at best scantily represented in a volume devoted to royalty, and that Rome continued to be the seat of a secular power passing in relatively steady succession from one pope to the next. It is, however, with the Counts of Savoy that the story must begin.

SAVOY

The earliest known scion of the family is Humbert I, with the White Hands, in the middle of the eleventh century (Table 120). The territorial strength of the County lay in the nebulous domain of Burgundy and stretched from the river Rhône to the lake of Geneva. Gradually the influence of the counts began to reach over the Alps into the Lombard plain; the history of Savoy, in brief, is a shift of emphasis from the French to the Italian side of the valuable Alpine routes which its rulers controlled, namely the Mont Cenis and the two St Bernard passes. The reigning Kings of Italy in this century descend in direct male line from these early counts, a remarkable example of dynastic continuity. Humbert's son, Count Otto, married the heiress of an important area on the Italian foothills of the Alps (hence later called 'Piedmont').

Some generations later, Count Thomas I is a sig-nificant figure in the rise of the dynasty. He supported the Ghibelline (Hohenstaufen) emperors and was created Imperial Vicar, a position which he used to extend his lands on both sides of the Alps. Towards France he gained Bugey and Vaud, and to the east Carignan and other lordships. His influence reached down to the great ports of Savona and Genoa. One of his daughters wed the Count of Provence (Table 45), and their four daughters all married kings, including Henry III of England, who invited his wife's kinsmen to England. Boniface became Archbishop of Canterbury and Peter, Earl of Richmond, built a great palace on the strand of the Thames which has furnished the name of Savoy to that area of London. It is probable that Thomas I was already using the simple arms of Savoy – a silver cross on red; it is certainly found on the seal of his son Peter. At least by later tradition, the earlier counts had used a black eagle on a gold field: as they developed in power, the idea also grew up that they were descended from the German rulers of Saxony. Thomas I conferred Piedmont on his son Thomas II, whose grandson Philip married a Villehardouin heiress and thus acquired the title of Prince of Achaia.

It looked as though the state might suffer from fragmentation, but in the event Amadeus V firmly established his suzerainty both over the County of Piedmont and over his younger brother, Louis, Count of Vaud. Of his two sons, the elder was extravagant and the younger financially cautious. His grandson, Amadeus VI, the Green Count, was an amateur of crusading, chivalry and tournaments, at which he and the spectators wore green liveries. His crusading activities were altruistic in an age when the idealism of the movement had become tarnished. In about 1362 he founded the Order of the Annunciation, one of the most distinguished European orders of chivalry. The badge has always been worn from a

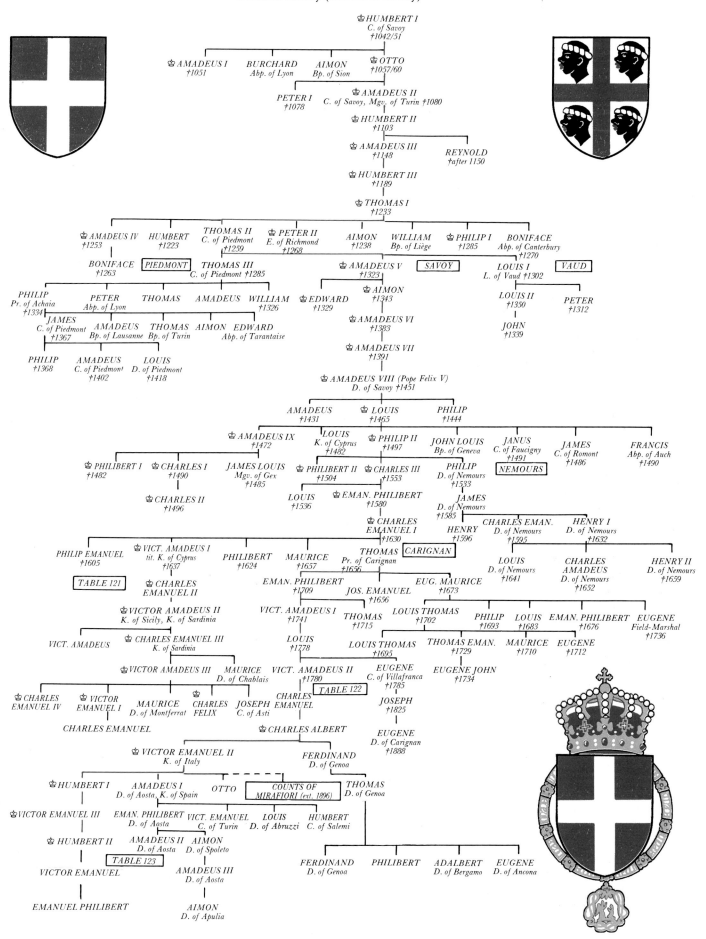

HUMBERT I
C. of Savoy
†1042/51

AMADEUS I †1051 BURCHARD Abp. of Lyon AIMON Bp. of Sion OTTO †1057/60

PETER I †1078 AMADEUS II C. of Savoy, Mgv. of Turin †1080

HUMBERT II †1103

AMADEUS III †1148 REYNOLD †after 1150

HUMBERT III †1189

THOMAS I †1233

AMADEUS IV †1253 HUMBERT †1223 THOMAS II C. of Piedmont †1259 PETER II E. of Richmond †1268 AIMON †1238 WILLIAM Bp. of Liège PHILIP I †1285 BONIFACE Abp. of Canterbury †1270

BONIFACE †1263 [PIEDMONT] THOMAS III C. of Piedmont †1285 AMADEUS V [SAVOY] LOUIS I L. of Vaud †1302 [VAUD]

PHILIP Pr. of Achaia †1334 PETER Abp. of Lyon THOMAS AMADEUS WILLIAM †1326 EDWARD †1329 AIMON †1343 LOUIS II †1350 PETER †1312

JAMES C. of Piedmont †1367 AMADEUS Bp. of Lausanne THOMAS Bp. of Turin AIMON EDWARD Abp. of Tarantaise AMADEUS VI †1383 JOHN †1339

PHILIP †1368 AMADEUS C. of Piedmont †1402 LOUIS D. of Piedmont †1418 AMADEUS VII †1391

AMADEUS VIII (Pope Felix V) D. of Savoy †1451

AMADEUS †1431 LOUIS †1465 PHILIP †1444

AMADEUS IX †1472 LOUIS K. of Cyprus †1482 PHILIP II †1497 JOHN LOUIS Bp. of Geneva JANUS C. of Faucigny †1491 JAMES C. of Romont †1486 FRANCIS Abp. of Auch †1490

PHILIBERT I †1482 CHARLES I †1490 JAMES LOUIS Mgv. of Gex †1485 PHILIBERT II †1504 CHARLES III †1553 PHILIP D. of Nemours †1533 [NEMOURS]

CHARLES II †1496 LOUIS †1536 EMAN. PHILIBERT †1580 JAMES D. of Nemours †1585 CHARLES EMAN. D. of Nemours †1595 HENRY I D. of Nemours †1632

CHARLES EMANUEL I †1630 HENRY †1596 LOUIS D. of Nemours †1641 CHARLES AMADEUS D. of Nemours †1652 HENRY II D. of Nemours †1659

PHILIP EMANUEL †1605 VICT. AMADEUS I tit. K. of Cyprus †1637 PHILIBERT †1624 MAURICE †1657 THOMAS Pr. of Carignan †1656 [CARIGNAN]

[TABLE 121] CHARLES EMANUEL II EMAN. PHILIBERT †1709 EUG. MAURICE †1673

VICTOR AMADEUS II K. of Sicily, K. of Sardinia JOS. EMANUEL †1656 LOUIS THOMAS †1702 PHILIP †1693 LOUIS †1683 EMAN. PHILIBERT †1676 EUGENE Field-Marshal †1736

VICT. AMADEUS I †1741 THOMAS †1715

VICT. AMADEUS CHARLES EMANUEL III K. of Sardinia LOUIS †1778 LOUIS THOMAS †1695 THOMAS EMAN. †1729 MAURICE †1710 EUGENE †1712

EUGENE JOHN †1734

VICTOR AMADEUS III MAURICE D. of Chablais VICT. AMADEUS II †1780 EUGENE C. of Villafranca †1785 [TABLE 122]

CHARLES EMANUEL IV VICTOR EMANUEL I MAURICE D. of Montferrat CHARLES FELIX JOSEPH C. of Asti CHARLES EMANUEL JOSEPH †1825

CHARLES EMANUEL CHARLES ALBERT EUGENE D. of Carignan †1888

VICTOR EMANUEL II K. of Italy FERDINAND D. of Genoa

HUMBERT I AMADEUS I D. of Aosta, K. of Spain OTTO [COUNTS OF MIRAFIORI (ext. 1896)] THOMAS D. of Genoa

VICTOR EMANUEL III EMAN. PHILIBERT D. of Aosta VICT. EMANUEL C. of Turin LOUIS D. of Abruzzi HUMBERT C. of Salemi

HUMBERT II AMADEUS II D. of Aosta AIMON D. of Spoleto [TABLE 123]

VICTOR EMANUEL AMADEUS III D. of Aosta FERDINAND D. of Genoa PHILIBERT ADALBERT D. of Bergamo EUGENE D. of Ancona

EMANUEL PHILIBERT AIMON D. of Apulia

TABLE 121

SARDINIA
Kings until extinction of the main line

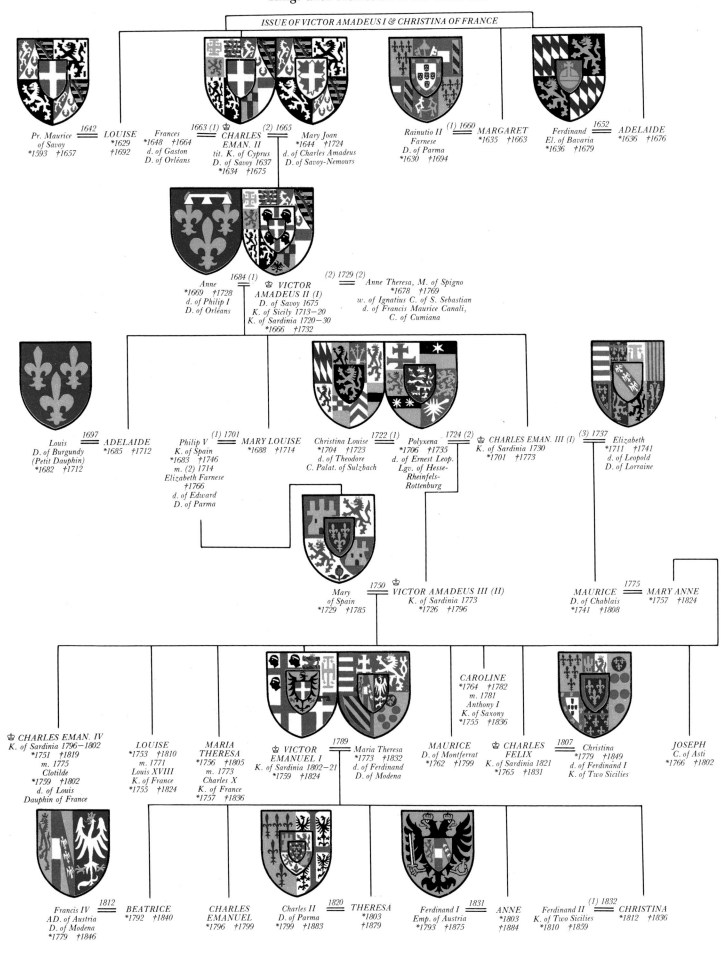

ISSUE OF VICTOR AMADEUS I & CHRISTINA OF FRANCE

Pr. Maurice ═══ 1642 ═══ LOUISE
of Savoy
*1593 †1657 — *1629 †1692

Frances ═══ 1663 (1) ♔ ═══ (2) 1665 ═══ Mary Joan
*1648 †1664 — CHARLES — *1644 †1724
d. of Gaston — EMAN. II — d. of Charles Amadeus
D. of Orléans — tit. K. of Cyprus — D. of Savoy-Nemours
D. of Savoy 1637
*1634 †1675

Rainutio II ═══ (1) 1660 ═══ MARGARET
Farnese — *1635 †1663
D. of Parma
*1630 †1694

Ferdinand ═══ 1652 ═══ ADELAIDE
El. of Bavaria — *1636 †1676
*1636 †1679

Anne ═══ 1684 (1) ♔ ═══ (2) 1729 (2) ═══ Anne Theresa, M. of Spigno
*1669 †1728 — VICTOR — *1678 †1769
d. of Philip I — AMADEUS II (I) — w. of Ignatius C. of S. Sebastian
D. of Orléans — D. of Savoy 1675 — d. of Francis Maurice Canali,
K. of Sicily 1713—20 — C. of Cumiana
K. of Sardinia 1720—30
*1666 †1732

Louis ═══ 1697 ═══ ADELAIDE
D. of Burgundy — *1685 †1712
(Petit Dauphin)
*1682 †1712

Philip V ═══ (1) 1701 ═══ MARY LOUISE
K. of Spain — *1688 †1714
*1683 †1746
m. (2) 1714
Elizabeth Farnese
†1766
d. of Edward
D. of Parma

Christina Louise ═══ 1722 (1) ═══ Polyxena ═══ 1724 (2) ♔ CHARLES EMAN. III (I) ═══ (3) 1737 ═══ Elizabeth
*1704 †1723 — *1706 †1735 — K. of Sardinia 1730 — *1711 †1741
d. of Theodore — d. of Ernest Leop. — *1701 †1773 — d. of Leopold
C. Palat. of Sulzbach — Lgv. of Hesse- — D. of Lorraine
Rheinfels-
Rottenburg

Mary ═══ 1750 ♔ ═══ VICTOR AMADEUS III (II)
of Spain — K. of Sardinia 1773
*1729 †1785 — *1726 †1796

MAURICE ═══ 1775 ═══ MARY ANNE
D. of Chablais — *1757 †1824
*1741 †1808

♔ CHARLES EMAN. IV
K. of Sardinia 1796—1802
*1751 †1819
m. 1775
Clotilde
*1759 †1802
d. of Louis
Dauphin of France

LOUISE
*1753 †1810
m. 1771
Louis XVIII
K. of France
*1755 †1824

MARIA
THERESA
*1756 †1805
m. 1773
Charles X
K. of France
*1757 †1836

♔ VICTOR ═══ 1789 ═══ Maria Theresa
EMANUEL I — *1773 †1832
K. of Sardinia 1802—21 — d. of Ferdinand
*1759 †1824 — D. of Modena

CAROLINE
*1764 †1782
m. 1781
Anthony I
K. of Saxony
*1755 †1836

MAURICE
D. of Montferrat
*1762 †1799

♔ CHARLES
FELIX
K. of Sardinia 1821
*1765 †1831

Christina ═══ 1807
*1779 †1849
d. of Ferdinand I
K. of Two Sicilies

JOSEPH
C. of Asti
*1766 †1802

Francis IV ═══ 1812 ═══ BEATRICE
AD. of Austria — *1792 †1840
D. of Modena
*1779 †1846

CHARLES
EMANUEL
*1796 †1799

Charles II ═══ 1820 ═══ THERESA
D. of Parma — *1803
*1799 †1883 — †1879

Ferdinand I ═══ 1831 ═══ ANNE
Emp. of Austria — *1803
*1793 †1875 — †1884

Ferdinand II ═══ (1) 1832 ═══ CHRISTINA
K. of Two Sicilies — *1812 †1836
*1810 †1859

collar (Table 120: base) and not from a ribbon. In 1388 Amadeus VII acquired Nice, on the Mediterranean. Amadeus VIII enjoyed a remarkable career. He reigned from 1391 to 1434 with signal success, extending his domains in Italy and receiving in 1416 the title of duke from the Emperor. On the extinction of the Counts of Piedmont in 1418 he added their lands to his own. But in 1434, after promulgating a famous code of laws for his people, he retired to a hermitage by the side of the lake of Geneva. In 1439, though still a layman, he was elected pope (as Felix V) by the remnants of the Council of Basel: he was never recognized by the whole Church and abdicated as pope in 1449 to receive a cardinal's hat.

Duke Louis married Anne of Lusignan, daughter of John I of Cyprus, acquiring thereby a claim to the thrones of Cyprus and Jerusalem; his son Louis married her younger sister. A series of brief reigns and minorities checked the progress of the Duchy. Philibert II was commemorated by his widow in the wonderful church of Brou, near Bourg-en-Bresse. His brother Charles III reigned longer but without much good fortune. Adherence to the Emperor Charles V led to frequent invasions by French forces. Geneva and Vaud were lost to Switzerland. At his death his duchy was in French occupation and his only son had entered the imperial service. The future of the Duchy seemed dim. Happily, Emanuel Philibert was a soldier of talent and a statesman of resource. He won the great victory of St Quentin (1557) for the Empire over France, a battle which effectually marked the end of a century of French intervention in Italy. The consequent Treaty of Cateau Cambrésis gave him possession of most of his father's duchy; it was no doubt hoped that Savoy might become a useful buffer state between France and the Hapsburgs. His rule was autocratic but crowned with success. Gradually he recovered the fortresses which had been assigned to the Great Powers. He gained Tende from the French by exchange for a small fief nearer France; he built up a useful army; he altogether refashioned the destiny of Savoy, but did so perhaps as a state looking towards the Lombard plain.

Charles Emanuel I continued the process and acquired in 1601 the important enclave of Saluzzo, for which he ceded Bresse and Bugey to France. Two of his sons founded branches which were to carry on the dynasty, Victor Amadeus as Duke of Savoy and Thomas as Prince of Carignan. A line of cousins had become Dukes of Nemours, but their activities were principally in France. Victor Amadeus was married to a daughter of Henry IV of France, who acted as regent for her infant son, Charles Emanuel II (Table 121); despite the efforts of both, Savoy continued to suffer in the Franco-Spanish conflicts of the seventeenth century. Matters changed under Victor

Amadeus II, partly because the Carignan branch had produced one of the ablest generals of the age, the celebrated Prince Eugene of Savoy (d. 1736). The Duke changed sides adroitly and in 1706 Prince Eugene, who had entered the imperial service, defeated the French severely outside Turin. At the Treaty of Utrecht (1713), Savoy was well-treated; she gained Montferrat on her eastern boundary and was also allotted the island of Sicily from which her ruler took the title of king. In 1720, however, the Powers arranged an exchange of islands and Victor Amadeus II became King of Sardinia.

His pedigree (Table 123) shows a mild preponderance of French blood, allowing the Houses of Lorraine and Savoy-Nemours to come under that heading; only Savoy and Medici can be reckoned Italian. The arms of Sardinia were a cross between four Moors' heads (Table 120) and they were incorporated with those of Savoy by Victor Amadeus II (Table 121). The elaborate arms of Savoy, as used by Charles Emanuel II, show four main quarterings. The first has itself four quarters for Jerusalem, Lusignan, Armenia and Cyprus (this last hidden), which represent the Cypriot marriage of Duke Louis; the second has a triple coat for Saxony, and reflects the spurious belief that the Savoyards sprang from Saxon stock; in the third, Chablais and Aosta, and in the fourth, Geneva and Montferrat are impaled. Over all is the plain cross of Savoy. Victor Amadeus II, as well as interposing Sardinia between the main shield and Savoy, added at the base of the shield the eagle allegedly borne by the earliest counts. This eagle can be seen again on the blazon of Victor Emanuel I. The Dukes of Savoy-Nemours differenced the cross of Savoy with an indented bordure (Table 123).

UNION OF ITALY

The island of Sardinia had suffered a confused history. It had been part of the Byzantine Empire, governed by native princelings, invaded by Saracens and disputed between the rising commercial powers of Genoa and Pisa. In 1175 the Emperor divided the island between them. The Emperor Frederick II (Chapter 30) tried to make it a kingdom for his handsome bastard Enzio; Pope Boniface VIII awarded the island to Aragon, though the Spaniards had to fight long and hard to establish their rule. In the division of spoils at the close of the War of the Spanish Succession it was allotted to Austria, and then, in exchange for Sicily, in 1720 it came to Savoy.

Charles Emanuel III was another competent soldier, who played his part in the wars of the eighteenth century, adding morsel after morsel to the dominions of Savoy. But Victor Amadeus III, his son, was a less robust character, who sought to oppose the French Revolution and saw his country overrun by

TABLE 122

SARDINIA AND UNITED ITALY
Kings until the end of the monarchy

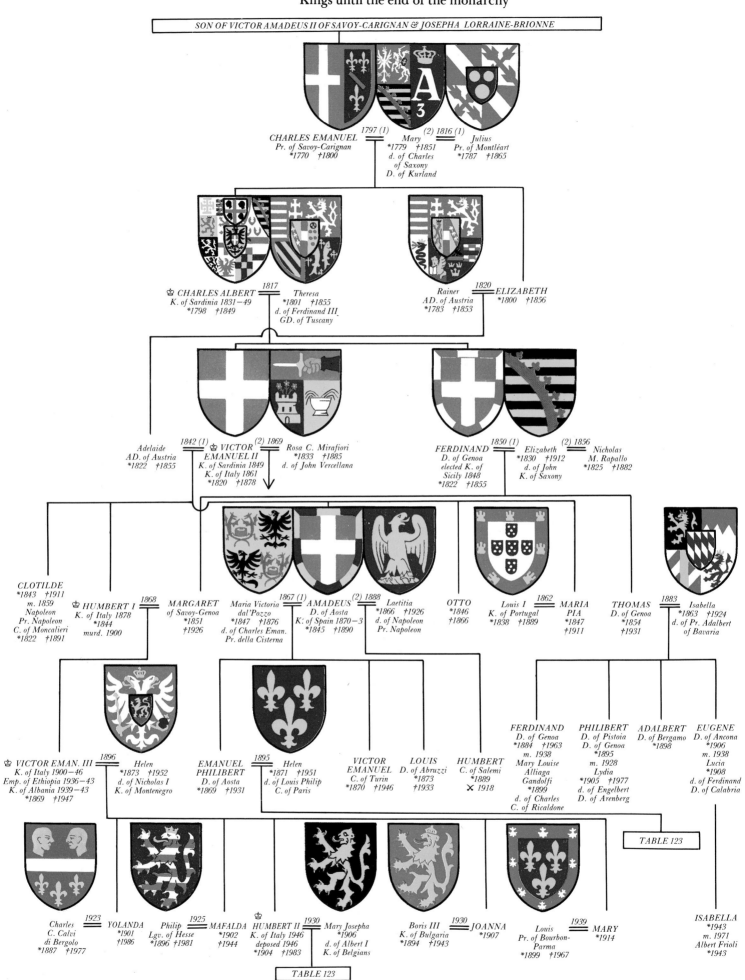

SON OF VICTOR AMADEUS II OF SAVOY-CARIGNAN & JOSEPHA LORRAINE-BRIONNE

CHARLES EMANUEL   1797 (1)   Mary   (2) 1816 (1)   Julius
Pr. of Savoy-Carignan   *1779 †1851   Pr. of Montléart
*1770 †1800   d. of Charles   *1787 †1865
                             of Saxony
                             D. of Kurland

♔ CHARLES ALBERT   1817   Theresa   Rainer   1820   ELIZABETH
K. of Sardinia 1831−49   *1801 †1855   AD. of Austria   *1800 †1856
*1798 †1849   d. of Ferdinand III   *1783 †1853
                          GD. of Tuscany

Adelaide   1842 (1)   ♔ VICTOR   (2) 1869   Rosa C. Mirafiori   FERDINAND   1850 (1)   Elizabeth   (2) 1856   Nicholas
AD. of Austria   EMANUEL II   *1833 †1885   D. of Genoa   *1830 †1912   M. Rapallo
*1822 †1855   K. of Sardinia 1849 d. of John Vercellana elected K. of   d. of John   *1825 †1882
                      K. of Italy 1861   Sicily 1848   K. of Saxony
                      *1820 †1878   *1822 †1855

CLOTILDE   ♔ HUMBERT I   1868   MARGARET   Maria Victoria   1867 (1)   AMADEUS   (2) 1888   Laetitia   OTTO   Louis I   1862   MARIA   THOMAS   1883   Isabella
*1843 †1911   K. of Italy 1878   of Savoy-Genoa dal'Pozzo   D. of Aosta   *1866 †1926 *1846   K. of Portugal   PIA   D. of Genoa   *1863 †1924
m. 1859   *1844   *1851   *1847 †1876   K: of Spain 1870−3 d. of Napoleon †1866   *1838 †1889   *1847   *1854 †1931   d. of Pr. Adalbert
Napoleon   murd. 1900   †1926   d. of Charles Eman.   *1845 †1890   Pr. Napoleon   †1911   of Bavaria
Pr. Napoleon   Pr. della Cisterna
C. of Moncalieri
*1822 †1891

♔ VICTOR EMAN. III   1896   Helen   EMANUEL   1895   Helen   VICTOR   LOUIS   HUMBERT   FERDINAND   PHILIBERT   ADALBERT   EUGENE
K. of Italy 1900−46   *1873 †1952   PHILIBERT   *1871 †1951   EMANUEL   D. of Abruzzi C. of Salemi   D. of Genoa   D. of Pistoia   D. of Bergamo D. of Ancona
Emp. of Ethiopia 1936−43   d. of Nicholas I D. of Aosta   d. of Louis Philip C. of Turin   *1873   *1889   *1884 †1963   *1895   *1898   *1906
K. of Albania 1939−43   K. of Montenegro *1869 †1931   C. of Paris   *1870 †1946   †1933   ✕ 1918   m. 1938   m. 1928   m. 1938
*1869 †1947   Mary Louise   Lydia   Lucia
                                                                                                                            Alliaga   *1905 †1977   *1908
                                                                                                                            Gandolfi   d. of Engelbert   d. of Ferdinand
                                                                                                                            *1899   D. of Arenberg   D. of Calabria
                                                                                                                            d. of Charles
                                                                                                                            C. of Ricaldone

                                                                                                                                                                          TABLE 123

Charles   1923   YOLANDA   Philip   1925   MAFALDA   ♔ HUMBERT II   1930   Mary Josepha   Boris III   1930   JOANNA   Louis   1939   MARY   ISABELLA
C. Calvi   *1901   Lgv. of Hesse   *1902   K. of Italy 1946   *1906   K. of Bulgaria   *1907   Pr. of Bourbon-   *1914   *1943
di Bergolo   †1986   *1896 †1981   †1944   deposed 1946   d. of Albert I   *1894 †1943   Parma   m. 1971
*1887 †1977   *1904 †1983   K. of Belgians   *1899 †1967   Albert Frioli
                                                                                                                                                                            *1943

TABLE 123

TABLE 123

ITALY
House of Savoy since World War II

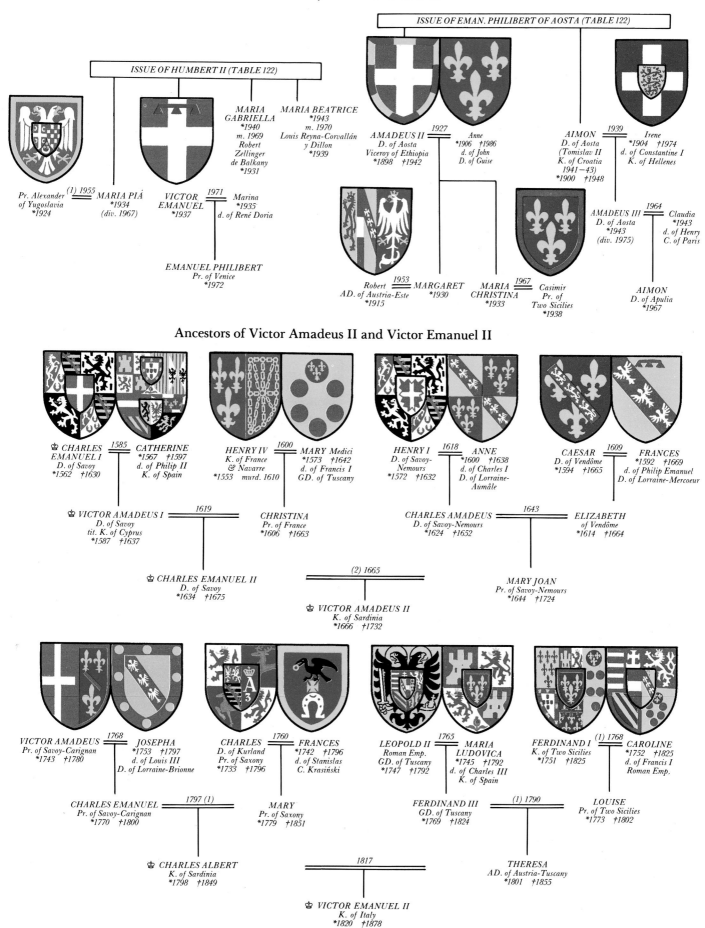

ISSUE OF EMAN. PHILIBERT OF AOSTA (TABLE 122)

ISSUE OF HUMBERT II (TABLE 122)

MARIA
GABRIELLA
*1940
m. 1969
Robert
Zellinger
de Balkany
*1931

MARIA BEATRICE
*1943
m. 1970
Louis Reyna-Corvallán
y Dillon
*1939

AMADEUS II
D. of Aosta
Viceroy of Ethiopia
*1898 †1942

1927 Anne
*1906 †1986
d. of John
D. of Guise

AIMON
D. of Aosta
(Tomislav II
K. of Croatia
1941–43)
*1900 †1948

1939 Irene
*1904 †1974
d. of Constantine I
K. of Hellenes

Pr. Alexander
of Yugoslavia
*1924

(1) 1955 MARIA PIÁ
*1934
(div. 1967)

VICTOR
EMANUEL
*1937

1971 Marina
*1935
d. of René Doria

AMADEUS III
D. of Aosta
*1943
(div. 1975)

1964 Claudia
*1943
d. of Henry
C. of Paris

EMANUEL PHILIBERT
Pr. of Venice
*1972

Robert
AD. of Austria-Este
*1915

1953 MARGARET
*1930

MARIA
CHRISTINA
*1933

1967 Casimir
Pr. of
Two Sicilies
*1938

AIMON
D. of Apulia
*1967

Ancestors of Victor Amadeus II and Victor Emanuel II

♛ CHARLES
EMANUEL I
D. of Savoy
*1562 †1630

1585 CATHERINE
*1567 †1597
d. of Philip II
K. of Spain

HENRY IV
K. of France
& Navarre
*1553 murd. 1610

1600 MARY Medici
*1573 †1642
d. of Francis I
GD. of Tuscany

HENRY I
D. of Savoy-
Nemours
*1572 †1632

1618 ANNE
*1600 †1638
d. of Charles I
D. of Lorraine-
Aumâle

CAESAR
D. of Vendôme
*1594 †1665

1609 FRANCES
*1592 †1669
d. of Philip Emanuel
D. of Lorraine-Mercoeur

♛ VICTOR AMADEUS I
D. of Savoy
tit. K. of Cyprus
*1587 †1637

1619 CHRISTINA
Pr. of France
*1606 †1663

CHARLES AMADEUS
D. of Savoy-Nemours
*1624 †1652

1643 ELIZABETH
of Vendôme
*1614 †1664

♛ CHARLES EMANUEL II
D. of Savoy
*1634 †1675

(2) 1665

MARY JOAN
Pr. of Savoy-Nemours
*1644 †1724

♛ VICTOR AMADEUS II
K. of Sardinia
*1666 †1732

VICTOR AMADEUS
Pr. of Savoy-Carignan
*1743 †1780

1768 JOSEPHA
*1753 †1797
d. of Louis III
D. of Lorraine-Brionne

CHARLES
D. of Kurland
Pr. of Saxony
*1733 †1796

1760 FRANCES
*1742 †1796
d. of Stanislas
C. Krasiński

LEOPOLD II
Roman Emp.
GD. of Tuscany
*1747 †1792

1765 MARIA
LUDOVICA
*1745 †1792
d. of Charles III
K. of Spain

FERDINAND I
K. of Two Sicilies
*1751 †1825

(1) 1768 CAROLINE
*1752 †1825
d. of Francis I
Roman Emp.

CHARLES EMANUEL
Pr. of Savoy-Carignan
*1770 †1800

1797 (1) MARY
Pr. of Saxony
*1779 †1851

FERDINAND III
GD. of Tuscany
*1769 †1824

(1) 1790 LOUISE
Pr. of Two Sicilies
*1773 †1802

♛ CHARLES ALBERT
K. of Sardinia
*1798 †1849

1817 THERESA
AD. of Austria-Tuscany
*1801 †1855

♛ VICTOR EMANUEL II
K. of Italy
*1820 †1878

NOTE
Arms shown for Victor Emanuel (*1937)
are those he used as Prince of Venice.

French armies. Three of his sons reigned after him, two of them abdicating in favour of a brother; the Treaty of Vienna (1815) increased the kingdom of Victor Emanuel by adding Genoa, whose red cross on white figures in his arms. The death without issue of Charles Felix in 1831 marked the end of the main branch of Savoy. The Crown of Sardinia now passed to Charles Albert of Savoy-Carignan, Count of Soissons (Table 122). It may be added that Victor Emanuel I inherited in 1807 (through his great-grandmother Anne of Orléans) the Jacobite claim to the throne of England: at his death this passed to his eldest daughter and the Dukes of Modena, and thence to the Kings of Bavaria (Table 97).

The convulsive changes in established boundaries, which were the aftermath of the Napoleonic campaigns, left a legacy of unrest in Italy. Despite the restoration of Hapsburg and Bourbon, despite the extinction of the ancient Republic of Venice, men began to dream again of Italian freedom and unity. Some of these dreamers believed that their only hope lay with the House of Savoy, an Italian dynasty with a well-trained army; others, like Joseph Mazzini who founded the Association of Italian Youth in 1831, were republican at heart; yet others had visions of a liberal pope. Charles Albert, the first king of the new line, was a cautious and slow-moving man. His elaborate arms (Table 122) show quarterings for Cyprus and Jerusalem, for the alleged Saxon descent, for Aosta, Genoa, Chablais and Piedmont and fourthly for Geneva and Montferrat. Two superimposed escutcheons stand for Sardinia and for Savoy ancient and modern; the eagle below and the cross above. Rightly, he doubted if his army was a match for the Austrian hosts, so firmly dominating the Lombard plain. In the year of the revolutions, risings broke out all over Italy. Almost hesitantly he led his troops against Austria, to be defeated at Custozza (1848) and Novara (1849). In the latter year he abdicated and died.

Victor Emanuel II, his son, was destined to be more fortunate. His ancestry (Table 123) shows a wide variety of strains: on the maternal side Bourbon and Hapsburg dominate, but his paternal forebears display a cadet branch of Lorraine and the wilder heraldic fancies of Kurland. The rapid triumph of Savoy was mainly due to the brilliant statesmanship of Cavour and to the refusal of Pope Pius IX to advance the unity of Italy. The virtuosity of Cavour lay in attracting the support of both France and Britain for the cause of Italian freedom. With calculated daring he aligned Savoy beside both in the Crimean War against Russia. In 1858 he made an agreement with Napoleon III to yield Nice and French Savoy; now he awaited any attack by Austria, and to his satisfaction one came in 1859. At Magenta and Sol-

Charles Albert of Savoy (1798–1849), King of Sardinia and ancestor of the Kings of Italy, by H. Vernet, 1834.

ferino, two sanguinary battles which contributed a violent colour and the foundation of the Red Cross movement to the sum of civilization, France and Savoy shattered the Hapsburg armies. Yet at the hour of triumph Napoleon made a peace with Austria which gave Lombardy only, not Venetia, to his ally. Cavour briefly resigned, but risings in Parma, Modena and Florence in favour of Savoy changed the picture. Cavour accepted their incorporation in the Kingdom of Sardinia, and honoured his earlier pledge by ceding to France both Nice and that part of Savoy which was the cradle of the dynasty. An effective kingdom of North Italy was now established.

It was at this juncture, and indubitably with the connivance of Cavour, that Garibaldi and his thousand red-shirted followers sailed for Sicily. In the summer of 1860 they liberated that island and crossed to the mainland to attack Naples. By the end of a fantastic year, all Italy except the environs of Rome and the provinces of Venice had demanded union with the Kingdom of Sardinia. The rise of Prussia did the rest: Austria ceded Venetia in 1866, the Papacy could no longer command French support after 1870. Florence became the capital of Italy in 1866; Rome replaced it in 1871. But the Papacy did not acquiesce and the Pontiff became the 'prisoner of the Vatican' in protest at the loss of his temporalities: Catholic clergy were forbidden to participate in the government of the new Kingdom. As King of Italy Victor Emanuel II assumed the plain and simple arms of

UNIFICATION OF ITALY

- Kingdom of Sardinia in 1815
- Territory gained 1859
- Territory gained May 1860
- Territory gained November 1860
- Territory lost to France 1860
- Territory gained 1866
- Territory gained 1870
- - - - - International frontier 1914

Savoy. His son, Amadeus, was briefly King of Spain (Chapter 11).

Hideous problems confronted the new monarchy. There were wide differences between the north and south; the country was overpopulated; its finances were precarious; its neighbour France was hostile. In 1882 Italy joined Germany and Austria in the Triple Alliance. An early venture in colonialism led to a disastrous defeat at Adowa in Ethiopia (1896); none the less colonies were achieved in Eritrea and Somaliland. In 1911 war with Turkey added Libya, Cyrenaica and the Dodecanese. When war broke out in 1914, Italy held back, and eventually joined England, France and Russia. Her armies were routed by an Austrian force at Caporetto and had to be rescued by the troops of her allies. At Versailles Italy was disappointed by her reception and her rewards; in particular she gained less than she had hoped in Dalmatia and in Turkey.

Victor Emanuel III had succeeded his father, Humbert I, the victim of an anarchist assassin, as long ago as 1900. He now found himself the ruler of a tired and disillusioned people. When in 1922 the ex-socialist Mussolini marched on Rome at the head of his blackshirt band, the tiny King entrusted him with the government of Italy. Within a few years a shadowy democracy was transformed into blunt dictatorship, and the word Fascist began its career as a term of abuse. None the less, many Italians supported the Duce. He achieved a reconciliation with the Papacy

(1929) which instituted the minuscule Vatican state; he gave a battered, and still young nation a sense of pride; he brought many overt signs of efficiency where these had been lacking. But a punctual railway service does not entirely compensate for gross bullying, a sombre curtailment of liberty and an outrageous foreign policy. In 1935 Ethiopia and in 1939 Albania were wantonly attacked and occupied; these tinsel titles were added to the more honourable styles of Victor Emmanuel III.

The increasing involvement of Fascism with Nazi Germany forced on Italy an unprofitable participation in the Second World War, which yielded a sorry tale of military disaster. In 1946 the old King abdicated in favour of his son, but the reign of the latter lasted only two months before Italy became a republic. King Humbert II never actually abdicated before his death in 1983.

The cadet members of the family, such as the Dukes of Aosta or Genoa (Table 122), differenced the basic arms of Savoy with a parti-coloured border. Amadeus II, Duke of Aosta (Table 123), was Viceroy of Ethiopia and died in captivity after losing a stern but honourable campaign. The Crown Prince (Table 123) bears the title of Duke of Naples; but hitherto the heir to the rulers of Savoy has for generations been known as the Prince of Piedmont. The arms of Count Calvi di Bergolo, the ex-king's brother-in-law, with their two hairless heads, are a play upon the Italian word *calvo* (bald).

[245]

Chapter 33

THE TWO SICILIES

During the ninth and tenth centuries the coasts of western Europe were ravaged by invaders from Scandinavia, the Vikings or Northmen. In 911 a group of these men led by a certain Rollo settled in France at the mouth of the Seine, and swiftly gave the locality their own name – Normandy. Here the pagan barbarians acquired a veneer of Christianity and French speech and manners, but their restless instinct was not sublimated. In 1066 Duke William conquered England (Chapter 2); even before this, Norman adventurers were to be found on every battlefield in Europe from Spain to Constantinople. Nowhere was their success more brilliant than in south Italy. At the beginning of the eleventh century the mainland was a confused welter of Lombard princes and Byzantine outposts, while Sicily was in Muslim hands. From about 1017 little bands of tough Norman soldiers began to appear, and from about 1034 the numerous sons, mostly of great stature and bellicosity, of a minor Norman noble, Tancred de Hauteville, became prominent. William made himself Count of Apulia, and in 1059 the lordship of his half-brother Robert was recognized by the Papacy, which also conferred Sicily upon him. The conquest of this island was mainly carried out by the youngest brother, Roger I (Table 124).

SICILY

Roger II united the island and the mainland dominions of his family and was granted the title of King of Sicily by the Pope in 1130. He made his capital in Palermo and exercised a firm, but tolerant and polyglot monarchy where Saracen and Greek, Christian and Jew could live and trade together. Commerce and hostility with the Eastern Empire alternated; but Sicily owes its glittering silks and mosaics to Byzantine influence. It was an age of high prosperity for the island. In 1189 the death of

William II, the Good, left his aunt Constance, wife of Henry VI, as his heiress. The Sicilians preferred Tancred, Count of Lecce, but the German Emperor subdued him in a ferocious campaign (Chapter 30). There is fairly good evidence in Sicily that the de Hauteville rulers used a coat-of-arms which consisted of a bend of red and white checkered pattern on a blue field. But, rather curiously, this blazon does not seem to have been embodied in the achievements of any of their descendants or successors.

The frail physique of Henry VI did not allow him time to fulfil his vaulting ambitions of a new empire. Frederick II, his only child, was more Italian than German, and preferred the warmth and culture of Palermo to the chiller politics of a Germany wasted by civil war. Learning and science flourished at his Sicilian capital. In youth, on receiving the Empire, Frederick had pledged himself to resign Sicily. His long effort to avoid doing so plunged him into hostility with the Papacy, which was resolute against the union of Germany (with its loose control over north Italy) and the south Italian kingdom. The Popes, who were the temporal rulers of central Italy, envisaged themselves as crushed by such a nutcracker combination. The two greatest powers in Christendom, the spiritual and the secular, were locked in unedifying conflict. Heavy taxation was laid upon Sicily and Apulia to support Frederick's endless wars, but he died with his aims unachieved. He was himself a poet; and the birth of Italian vernacular literature, destined to reach so exalted a level with Dante at the close of the century, took place at his court.

The Papacy was resolved that no Hohenstaufen should continue to reign in Sicily and south Italy. In fact Manfred, a bastard of Frederick II, succeeded by 1258 in establishing himself there. The Pope hawked the throne of Sicily round Europe. Henry III of England, by an act of gross folly, accepted it for his second

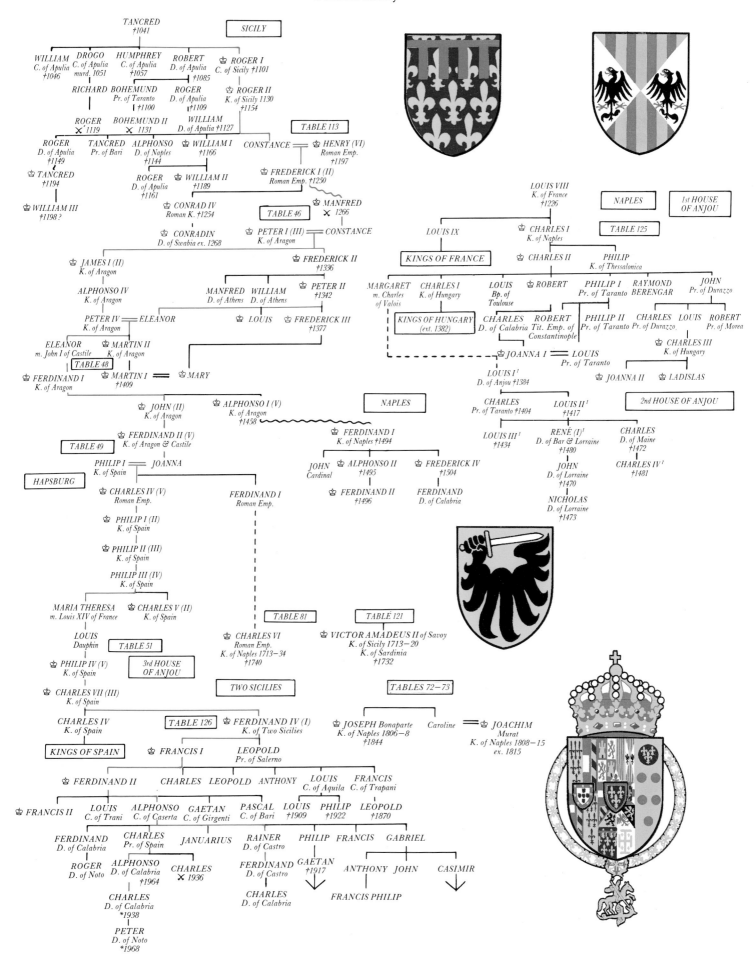

SICILY

TANCRED †1041

WILLIAM C. of Apulia †1046 — DROGO C. of Apulia murd. 1051 — HUMPHREY C. of Apulia †1057 — ROBERT D. of Apulia †1085 — ROGER I C. of Sicily †1101

RICHARD — BOHEMUND Pr. of Taranto †1100 — ROGER D. of Apulia †1109 — ROGER II K. of Sicily 1130 †1154

ROGER ✕ 1119 — BOHEMUND II ✕ 1131 — WILLIAM D. of Apulia †1127

TABLE 113

ROGER D. of Apulia †1149 — TANCRED Pr. of Bari — ALPHONSO D. of Naples †1144 — WILLIAM I †1166 — CONSTANCE — HENRY (VI) Roman Emp. †1197

TANCRED †1194 — ROGER D. of Apulia †1161 — WILLIAM II †1189 — FREDERICK I (II) Roman Emp. †1250

WILLIAM III †1198? — CONRAD IV Roman K. †1254 — MANFRED ✕ 1266

TABLE 46

CONRADIN D. of Swabia ex. 1268 — PETER I (III) K. of Aragon — CONSTANCE

FREDERICK II †1336

JAMES I (II) K. of Aragon

ALPHONSO IV K. of Aragon — MANFRED D. of Athens — WILLIAM D. of Athens — PETER II †1342

PETER IV — ELEANOR — LOUIS — FREDERICK III †1377
K. of Aragon

ELEANOR m. John I of Castile — MARTIN II K. of Aragon

TABLE 48

FERDINAND I K. of Aragon — MARTIN I †1409 — MARY

JOHN (II) K. of Aragon — ALPHONSO I (V) K. of Aragon †1458

FERDINAND II (V) K. of Aragon & Castile

TABLE 49

PHILIP I K. of Spain — JOANNA

HAPSBURG

CHARLES IV (V) Roman Emp.

PHILIP I (II) K. of Spain

PHILIP II (III) K. of Spain

PHILIP III (IV) K. of Spain

MARIA THERESA m. Louis XIV of France — CHARLES V (II) K. of Spain

LOUIS Dauphin — TABLE 51

PHILIP IV (V) K. of Spain

3rd HOUSE OF ANJOU

CHARLES VII (III) K. of Spain

TWO SICILIES

CHARLES IV K. of Spain — TABLE 126 — FERDINAND IV (I) K. of Two Sicilies

KINGS OF SPAIN — FRANCIS I — LEOPOLD Pr. of Salerno

FERDINAND II — CHARLES — LEOPOLD — ANTHONY — LOUIS C. of Aquila — FRANCIS C. of Trapani

FRANCIS II — LOUIS C. of Trani — ALPHONSO C. of Caserta — GAETAN C. of Girgenti — PASCAL C. of Bari — LOUIS †1909 — PHILIP †1922 — LEOPOLD †1870

FERDINAND D. of Calabria — CHARLES Pr. of Spain — JANUARIUS — RAINER D. of Castro — PHILIP — FRANCIS — GABRIEL

ROGER D. of Noto — ALPHONSO D. of Calabria †1964 — CHARLES ✕ 1936 — FERDINAND D. of Castro — GAETAN †1917 — ANTHONY — JOHN — CASIMIR

CHARLES D. of Calabria *1938 — CHARLES D. of Calabria — FRANCIS PHILIP

PETER D. of Noto *1968

NAPLES — 1st HOUSE OF ANJOU

LOUIS VIII K. of France †1226

TABLE 125

LOUIS IX — CHARLES I K. of Naples

KINGS OF FRANCE — CHARLES II — PHILIP K. of Thessalonica

MARGARET m. Charles of Valois — CHARLES I K. of Hungary — LOUIS Bp. of Toulouse — ROBERT — PHILIP I Pr. of Taranto — RAYMOND BERENGAR — JOHN Pr. of Durazzo

KINGS OF HUNGARY (ext. 1382) — CHARLES D. of Calabria — ROBERT Tit. Emp. of Constantinople — PHILIP II Pr. of Taranto — CHARLES Pr. of Durazzo — LOUIS Pr. of Morea — ROBERT

JOANNA I — LOUIS Pr. of Taranto — CHARLES III K. of Hungary

LOUIS I¹ D. of Anjou †1384 — JOANNA II — LADISLAS

2nd HOUSE OF ANJOU

CHARLES Pr. of Taranto †1404 — LOUIS II¹ †1417

LOUIS III¹ †1434 — RENÉ (I)¹ D. of Bar & Lorraine †1480 — CHARLES D. of Maine †1472

JOHN D. of Lorraine †1470 — CHARLES IV¹ †1481

NICHOLAS D. of Lorraine †1473

NAPLES

FERDINAND I K. of Naples †1494

JOHN Cardinal — ALPHONSO II †1495 — FREDERICK IV †1504

FERDINAND II †1496 — FERDINAND D. of Calabria

FERDINAND I Roman Emp.

TABLE 81

CHARLES VI Roman Emp. K. of Naples 1713–34 †1740

TABLE 121

VICTOR AMADEUS II of Savoy K. of Sicily 1713–20 K. of Sardinia †1732

TABLES 72–73

JOSEPH Bonaparte K. of Naples 1806–8 †1844 — Caroline — JOACHIM Murat K. of Naples 1808–15 ex. 1815

NOTE
¹ Titular King of Naples

son, Edmund Crouchback (Table 3), but was quite unable to fulfil his contract. Eventually, in 1265, Pope Clement IV reached agreement with a more resolute character, Charles of Anjou, brother of St Louis of France and Count of Provence in right of his wife. Able and ruthless, Charles defeated and slew Manfred in 1266 and routed the youthful Conradin, last sprig of the Hohenstaufen tree, at Tagliacozzo in 1268. Conradin and many of his kindred were executed or imprisoned. Charles I (Table 125) was undisputed master of Sicily. His rule was harsh and his ambition considerable, aiming ultimately, in the tradition of his Norman and German precursors, at the Eastern Empire. But in 1282 a rising against him broke out in Sicily (the Sicilian Vespers), which enlisted Aragonese support and elected Peter of Aragon (Table 124) as king.

Prolonged war followed. Imprudently, the Papacy committed itself to this local squabble and sought to depose Peter from Aragon in favour of a French prince. In 1295 King James of Aragon agreed to give up Sicily, but the inhabitants elected his younger brother Frederick. In 1301 the Treaty of Caltabellotta allowed Frederick to reign for his lifetime with the style of King of Trinacria: in fact he and his descendants reigned for four centuries and called themselves Kings of Sicily. The House of Anjou on the mainland also termed themselves Kings of Sicily, though for convenience they will here be called Kings of Naples. When the two were reunited under Spanish rule in the early sixteenth century, the realm was known as the Two Sicilies. Until Napoleonic times the only formal 'King of Naples' was Philip II of Spain, so created in the lifetime of his father to honour his marriage to Mary of England.

Independence was of small profit to Sicily. Her wealth and civilization declined under the Aragonese rulers, and there were intermittent wars with Naples. Frederick II had flouted the treaty by associating his son with himself. Only in 1372, after Naples had launched half a dozen vain assaults, was peace finally made. It was then laid down that Sicily should be subject to Naples, but this condition never materialized. When Frederick III died in 1377, Sicily was claimed by Peter IV of Aragon, who was his brother-in-law. In 1380, however, Peter assigned his rights to his son Martin, and his grandson Martin was married to the heiress Mary, who had been abducted and handed over to Aragon; the boy thus became King Martin I and he proved to be a successful and popular ruler. When Martin I died in 1409, he was rather anomalously succeeded by his father who was already King of Aragon. The father thus became Martin II. From this moment Sicily was united to the Crown of Aragon and was ruled by viceroys sent from Spain until 1713. The island then passed briefly to Savoy (1713–20) (Chapter 32), and to Austria (1720–35) before becoming part of the Bourbon Kingdom of the Two Sicilies. The arms of Sicily (Table 124) reflect the long connection with Aragon. By their side is the shield of the first House of Anjou.

NAPLES

Charles of Anjou (Table 125) had conquered southern Italy with ruthless efficiency. He had purchased in 1276–7 a claim to the Crown of Jerusalem and impaled the arms of the Holy City beside his own French coat with its red label of four points. The revolt of Sicily deprived him of half his dominions, and his heirs spent much time and money essaying reconquest in vain. His own son was captured in 1284 and when Charles I died in 1285 a regency was briefly exercised by his grandson. Charles II was soon released by Aragon, and his eldest son, another Charles, departed to follow his destiny in Hungary (Chapter 22). In 1302 Charles II recognized Frederick II as King of Trinacria and the separation of Sicily and mainland was confirmed: Charles' daughter Eleanor was then married to Frederick.

Robert of Naples was a scholarly king; he numbered Petrarch among his friends. He regarded himself as the leader of the Guelph (or anti-Hohenstaufen) partly in Italy. The Pope had made him Vicar of Romagna and he was gradually extending his influence in northern Italy. When the Emperor Henry VII (of Luxemburg, Table 113) invaded Italy and was crowned at Rome in 1312, Robert was his enemy and sent troops to Rome. Old-fashioned in his concept of empire, Henry proclaimed Robert to be deposed and marched south towards Naples, only to perish of fever on the way; this was probably a fortunate escape for Robert, since he was no warrior and Henry was in alliance with Frederick of Sicily. If Robert had been a vigorous and active ruler he could now have extended his power north of Rome and perhaps become in some fashion King of Italy: instead he squandered his resources on profitless attacks on Sicily. He lost ground in Romagna and, though he gained control of Genoa in 1318, he scarcely deserves his nickname of 'the Wise'. At home his financial demands stirred up the hostility of a discontented baronage.

Charles, Duke of Calabria, son of King Robert, had predeceased his father, and in 1343 the throne came to his daughter. The arms of Calabria, a wing holding a sword, can be seen on the right of Table 124. Joanna had already been married to her cousin Andrew of Hungary, whose arms impale Hungary and Anjou; they were ill-suited and the lively and voluptuous queen disliked her husband. In 1345 the dour Andrew was murdered, possibly at the instigation of Catherine, Princess of Taranto, whose son

King Robert of Naples (1277–1343), enthroned before a panel of French fleurs-de-lys, is confronted by a mourning figure symbolising Italy. Early 14th-century MS.

Robert, the titular Emperor of Constantinople, was deemed to be Joanna's lover. In 1346 the volatile Queen married Louis, Robert's younger brother. Meanwhile King Louis of Hungary, Andrew's elder brother, was planning revenge: in 1348 he invaded Naples and executed Charles of Durazzo whom he suspected of his brother's murder. Joanna and her husband fled, but were soon restored since the nobility of Naples had small taste for Magyar rule. Two terrible plagues distressed the Kingdom, the Black Death and the mercenary companies left behind by the Hungarian King.

Despite her four husbands and lively career, Joanna I was childless (Table 124). When she adopted her distant French kinsman, Louis, Duke of Anjou, her local cousin and nephew by marriage, Charles of Durazzo, rebelled and murdered her. He then became king as Charles III; his arms combine Hungary, Jerusalem and Anjou. Charles III reigned long enough to defeat an assault by Louis of Anjou who died in 1384; but Charles himself perished in 1386. Naples was torn by the contest of his son Ladislas and Louis II of Anjou, in which the former eventually triumphed. Unfortunately the French royal house did not forget that they had a claim on Naples; Charles IV of Anjou bequeathed his titular kingdom to Louis XI of France in 1481. Ladislas was followed by his sister Joanna II, an even more lascivious queen

than her earlier namesake. But neither wedlock nor intrigue brought her children and after hesitating between Aragon and Anjou, she finally bequeathed Naples to Alphonso V of Aragon who succeeded in 1435. Sicily was thus once more joined with Naples under the Crown of Aragon; the reunion was brief (Table 124).

When Alphonso died in 1458 he left Sicily and Aragon to his brother John, but Naples to his bastard, Ferdinand (Table 124). The latter discovered that his authority over Naples was precarious and he had to wage a series of campaigns to enforce his rights. By about 1464 he had brought his Kingdom under control; his policy was one of alliance with the Papacy and Milan against Florence, until Lorenzo dei Medici in person negotiated a peace with him in 1480. Thereafter he was more alarmed by the threat of French interference; when he died, in 1494, his fears were realized. As soon as Ferdinand was dead, the deformed and lecherous Charles VIII of France invaded Italy. Ferdinand II and his uncle Frederick were driven out and, although both reigned briefly, their realm was battered by the Franco-Spanish conflict. Louis XII of France also reached Naples, but

[249]

TABLE 125

NAPLES
First House of Anjou

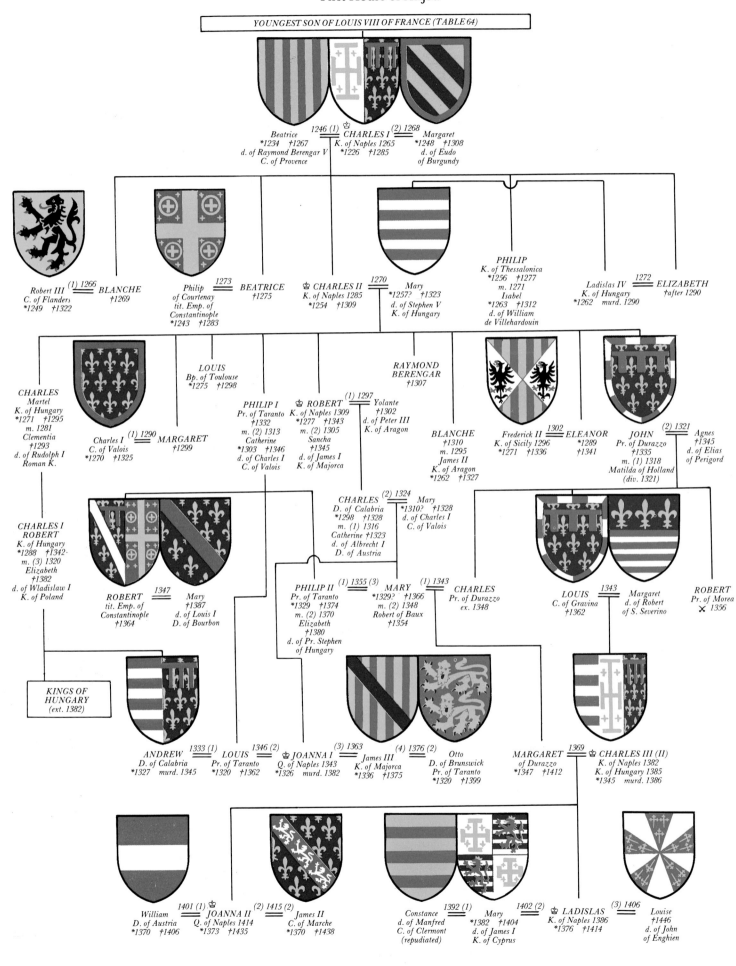

YOUNGEST SON OF LOUIS VIII OF FRANCE (TABLE 64)

Beatrice   *1246 (1)* ⚜ CHARLES I   *(2) 1268*   Margaret
*1234 †1267   K. of Naples 1265   *1248 †1308
d. of Raymond Berengar V   *1226 †1285   d. of Eudo
C. of Provence   of Burgundy

Robert III *(1) 1266*   BLANCHE
C. of Flanders   †1269
*1249 †1322

Philip   *1273*   BEATRICE
of Courtenay   †1275
tit. Emp. of
Constantinople
*1243 †1283

⚜ CHARLES II   *1270*   Mary
K. of Naples 1285   *1257? †1323
*1254 †1309   d. of Stephen V
     K. of Hungary

PHILIP
K. of Thessalonica
*1256 †1277
m. 1271
Isabel
*1263 †1312
d. of William
de Villehardouin

Ladislas IV   *1272*   ELIZABETH
K. of Hungary   †after 1290
*1262   murd. 1290

CHARLES
Martel
K. of Hungary
*1271 †1295
m. 1281
Clementia
†1293
d. of Rudolph I
Roman K.

LOUIS
Bp. of Toulouse
*1275 †1298

Charles I *(1) 1290*   MARGARET
C. of Valois   †1299
*1270 †1325

PHILIP I
Pr. of Taranto
†1332
m. (2) 1313
Catherine
*1303 †1346
d. of Charles I
C. of Valois

⚜ ROBERT   *(1) 1297*   Yolante
K. of Naples 1309   †1302
*1277 †1343   d. of Peter III
m. (2) 1305   K. of Aragon
Sancha
†1345
d. of James I
K. of Majorca

RAYMOND
BERENGAR
†1307

BLANCHE
*1310
m. 1295
James II
K. of Aragon
*1262 †1327

Frederick II   *1302*   ELEANOR
K. of Sicily 1296   *1289
*1271 †1336   †1341

JOHN   *(2) 1321*   Agnes
Pr. of Durazzo   †1345
†1335   d. of Elias
m. (1) 1318   of Perigord
Matilda of Holland
(div. 1321)

CHARLES I
ROBERT
K. of Hungary
*1288 †1342·
m. (3) 1320
Elizabeth
†1382
d. of Wladislaw I
K. of Poland

CHARLES   *(2) 1324*   Mary
D. of Calabria   *1310? †1328
*1298 †1328   d. of Charles I
m. (1) 1316   C. of Valois
Catherine †1323
d. of Albrecht I
D. of Austria

ROBERT   *1347*   Mary
tit. Emp. of   †1387
Constantinople   d. of Louis I
†1364   D. of Bourbon

PHILIP II   *(1) 1355 (3)*   MARY   *(1) 1343*
Pr. of Taranto   *1329? †1366
*1329 †1374   m. (2) 1348
m. (2) 1370   Robert of Baux
Elizabeth   †1354
†1380
d. of Pr. Stephen
of Hungary

CHARLES
Pr. of Durazzo
ex. 1348

LOUIS   *1343*   Margaret
C. of Gravina   d. of Robert
†1362   of S. Severino

ROBERT
Pr. of Morea
✕ 1356

*KINGS OF
HUNGARY
(ext. 1382)*

ANDREW   *1333 (1)*   LOUIS   *1346 (2)* ⚜ JOANNA I   *(3) 1363*   James III   *(4) 1376 (2)*   Otto
D. of Calabria   Pr. of Taranto   Q. of Naples 1343   K. of Majorca   D. of Brunswick
*1327 murd. 1345   *1320 †1362   *1326 murd. 1382   *1336 †1375   Pr. of Taranto
     *1320 †1399

MARGARET   *1369* ⚜ CHARLES III (II)
of Durazzo   K. of Naples 1382
*1347 †1412   K. of Hungary 1385
     *1345 murd. 1386

William   *1401 (1)* ⚜ JOANNA II   *(2) 1415 (2)*   James II
D. of Austria   Q. of Naples 1414   C. of Marche
*1370 †1406   *1373 †1435   *1370 †1438

Constance   *1392 (1)*   Mary   *1402 (2)* ⚜ LADISLAS   *(3) 1406*   Louise
d. of Manfred   *1382 †1404   K. of Naples 1386   †1446
C. of Clermont   d. of James I   *1376 †1414   d. of John
(repudiated)   K. of Cyprus   of Enghien

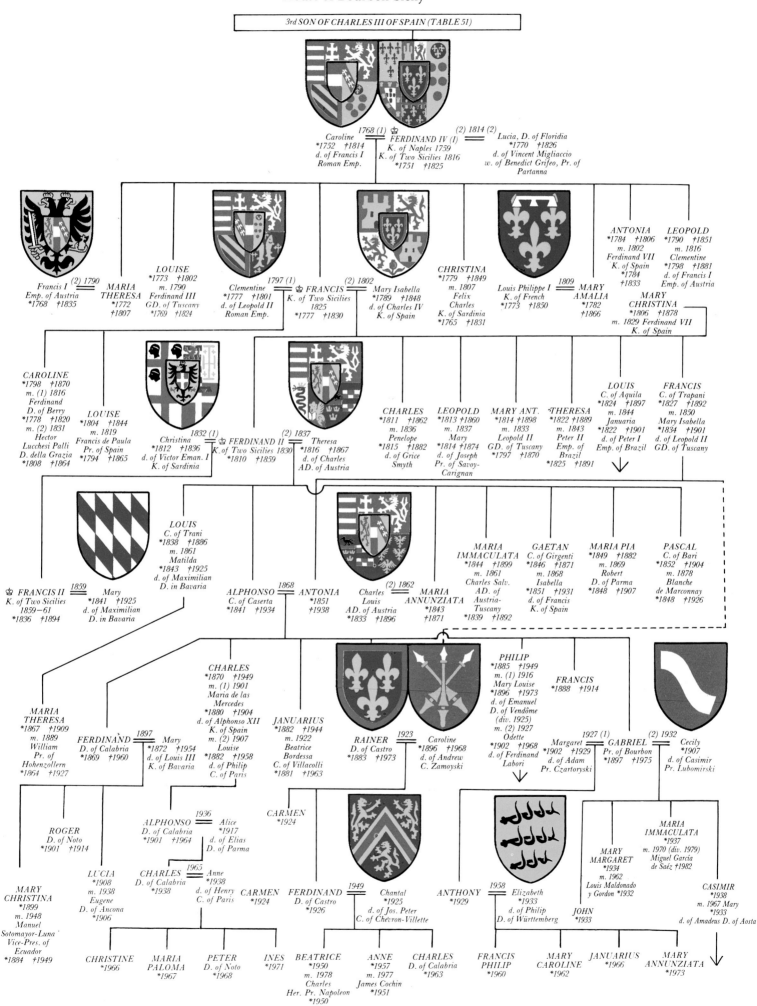

3rd SON OF CHARLES III OF SPAIN (TABLE 51)

Caroline
*1752 †1814
d. of Francis I
Roman Emp.

1768 (1) FERDINAND IV (1)
K. of Naples 1759
K. of Two Sicilies 1816
*1751 †1825

(2) 1814 (2) Lucia, D. of Floridia
*1770 †1826
d. of Vincent Migliaccio
w. of Benedict Grifeo, Pr. of
Partanna

Francis I (2) 1790
Emp. of Austria
*1768 †1835

MARIA
THERESA
*1772
†1807

LOUISE
*1773 †1802
m. 1790
Ferdinand III
GD. of Tuscany
*1769 †1824

Clementine
*1777 †1801
d. of Leopold II
Roman Emp.

1797 (1) FRANCIS (2) 1802
K. of Two Sicilies
1825
*1777 †1830

Mary Isabella
*1789 †1848
d. of Charles IV
K. of Spain

CHRISTINA
*1779 †1849
m. 1807
Felix
Charles
K. of Sardinia
*1765 †1831

Louis Philippe I
K. of French
*1773 †1850

1809 MARY
AMALIA
*1782
†1866

ANTONIA
*1784 †1806
m. 1802
Ferdinand VII
K. of Spain
*1784
†1833

LEOPOLD
*1790 †1851
m. 1816
Clementine
*1798 †1881
d. of Francis I
Emp. of Austria

MARY
CHRISTINA
*1806 †1878
m. 1829 Ferdinand VII
K. of Spain

CAROLINE
*1798 †1870
m. (1) 1816
Ferdinand
D. of Berry
*1778 †1820
m. (2) 1831
Hector
Lucchesi Palli
D. della Grazia
*1808 †1864

LOUISE
*1804 †1844
m. 1819
Francis de Paula
Pr. of Spain
*1794 †1865

Christina
*1812 †1836
d. of Victor Eman. I
K. of Sardinia

1832 (1) FERDINAND II (2) 1837
K. of Two Sicilies 1830
*1810 †1859

Theresa
*1816 †1867
d. of Charles
AD. of Austria

CHARLES
*1811 †1862
m. 1836
Penelope
*1815 †1882
d. of Grice
Smyth

LEOPOLD
*1813 †1860
m. 1837
Mary
*1814 †1874
d. of Joseph
Pr. of Savoy-
Carignan

MARY ANT.
*1814 †1898
m. 1833
Leopold II
GD. of Tuscany
*1797 †1870

THERESA
*1822 †1889
m. 1843
Peter II
Emp. of
Brazil
*1825 †1891

LOUIS
C. of Aquila
*1824 †1897
m. 1844
Januaria
*1822 †1901
d. of Peter I
Emp. of Brazil

FRANCIS
C. of Trapani
*1827 †1892
m. 1850
Mary Isabella
*1834 †1901
d. of Leopold II
GD. of Tuscany

LOUIS
C. of Trani
*1838 †1886
m. 1861
Matilda
*1843 †1925
d. of Maximilian
D. in Bavaria

FRANCIS II 1859
K. of Two Sicilies
1859–61
*1836 †1894

Mary
*1841 †1925
d. of Maximilian
D. in Bavaria

ALPHONSO 1868 ANTONIA
C. of Caserta   *1851
*1841 †1934   †1938

Charles
Louis
AD. of Austria
*1833 †1896

(2) 1862 MARIA
ANNUNZIATA
*1843
†1871

MARIA
IMMACULATA
*1844 †1899
m. 1861
Charles Salv.
AD. of
Austria-
Tuscany
*1839 †1892

GAETAN
C. of Girgenti
*1846 †1871
m. 1868
Isabella
*1851 †1931
d. of Francis
K. of Spain

MARIA PIA
*1849 †1882
m. 1869
Robert
D. of Parma
*1848 †1907

PASCAL
C. of Bari
*1852 †1904
m. 1878
Blanche
de Marconnay
*1848 †1926

MARIA
THERESA
*1867 †1909
m. 1889
William
Pr. of
Hohenzollern
*1864 †1927

CHARLES
*1870 †1949
m. (1) 1901
Maria de las
Mercedes
*1880 †1904
d. of Alphonso XII
K. of Spain
m. (2) 1907
Louise
*1882 †1958
d. of Philip
C. of Paris

FERDINAND 1897 Mary
D. of Calabria *1872 †1954
*1869 †1960   d. of Louis III
K. of Bavaria

JANUARIUS
*1882 †1944
m. 1922
Beatrice
Bordessa
C. of Villacolli
*1881 †1963

RAINER 1923
D. of Castro
*1883 †1973

Caroline
*1896 †1968
d. of Andrew
C. Zamoyski

PHILIP
*1885 †1949
m. (1) 1916
Mary Louise
*1896 †1973
d. of Emanuel
D. of Vendôme
(div. 1925)
m. (2) 1927
Odette
*1902 †1968
d. of Ferdinand
Labori

FRANCIS
*1888 †1914

Margaret
*1902 †1929
d. of Adam
Pr. Czartoryski

1927 (1) GABRIEL (2) 1932
Pr. of Bourbon
*1897 †1975

Cecily
*1907
d. of Casimir
Pr. Lubomirski

ROGER
D. of Noto
*1901 †1914

ALPHONSO 1936 Alice
D. of Calabria *1917
*1901 †1964   d. of Elias
D. of Parma

CARMEN
*1924

CARMEN
*1924

MARIA
IMMACULATA
*1937
m. 1970 (div. 1979)
Miguel García
de Saéz *1982

MARY
MARGARET
*1934
m. 1962
Louis Maldonado
y Gordon *1932

CASIMIR
*1938
m. 1967 Mary
*1933
d. of Amadeus D. of Aosta

MARY
CHRISTINA
*1899
m. 1948
Manuel
Sotomayor-Luna
Vice-Pres. of
Ecuador
*1884 †1949

LUCIA
*1908
m. 1938
Eugene
D. of Ancona
*1906

CHARLES 1965 Anne
D. of Calabria *1938
*1938   d. of Henry
C. of Paris

FERDINAND 1949 Chantal
D. of Castro   *1925
*1926   d. of Jos. Peter
C. of Chèvron-Villette

ANTHONY
*1929

1958 Elizabeth
*1933
d. of Philip
D. of Württemberg

JOHN
*1933

CHRISTINE
*1966

MARIA
PALOMA
*1967

PETER
D. of Noto
*1968

INES
*1971

BEATRICE
*1950
m. 1978
Charles
Her. Pr. Napoleon
*1950

ANNE
*1957
m. 1977
James Cochin
*1951

CHARLES
D. of Calabria
*1963

FRANCIS
PHILIP
*1960

MARY
CAROLINE
*1962

JANUARIUS
*1966

MARY
ANNUNZIATA
*1973

by 1502 the Kingdom was in Spanish hands. Henceforward the Kingdom of the Two Sicilies was governed by viceroys appointed from Spain; their government was punctuated by revolts of the oppressed Italian populace.

TWO SICILIES

Charles II of Spain ranked as Charles V of the Two Sicilies (Table 124). His death in 1700 led to the War of the Spanish Succession. In 1707 an Austrian army conquered Naples, though Sicily held out for Philip V of Spain. In 1713 the Treaty of Utrecht assigned Sicily to Savoy, and Naples to the Emperor Charles VI, but in 1720 Sicily also went to Austria in exchange for Sardinia. However, Philip V of Spain had married as his second wife the ambitious Elizabeth Farnese (Table 130), who yearned to advance the fortunes of her children. For her eldest son, Charles, she procured in 1731 her family Duchy of Parma; but in 1733 an alliance was made between Spain, France and Savoy to the detriment of Austria. In 1734 Charles invaded Naples and Sicily, conquering both without difficulty; thereon his kindly father resigned all rights in his favour, and he became Charles VII, independent ruler of the Two Sicilies. Parma passed to his brother Philip (Chapter 34).

Charles was small and suffered from bad teeth; his nose and his piety were alike conspicuous. But he was a conscientious and careful king, welcome to his subjects as the end of absentee rule. He improved the army, built lavishly and encouraged the excavation of Herculaneum; his most ostentatious work was the vast royal palace of Caserta. In 1759 his older half-brother, Ferdinand VI, died; the monarch of the Two Sicilies was now Charles III of Spain. Scrupulously he took nothing with him from Naples, and transferred that throne to his third son Ferdinand; his eldest boy, Philip Anthony, was an imbecile, his second became the heir of Spain (Table 51). Elizabeth Farnese was still alive to welcome him back to Madrid.

Ferdinand IV (Table 126) was ill-educated and little concerned with the business of government. He was easily led by his Austrian wife, a favourite sister of Mary Antoinette, but was only interested himself in hunting and practical jokes; he had a small head, coarse hands and a protruding lower jaw. The principal minister was Acton, an English emigré of good family (grandfather of the historian), and the Neapolitan court rejoiced in the presence of the English minister, Sir William Hamilton, his remarkable wife, Emma, and in due course her admirer, Lord Nelson. The King of Naples was hostile to the French Revolution after the execution of Louis XVI. In 1799 the French invaded Naples and set up the Parthenopaean Republic; Ferdinand fled to Palermo, but was restored by Nelson's fleet. But in 1806 Napoleon's brother, Joseph Bonaparte, was installed as King of Naples, only to be replaced by Joachim Murat, his brother-in-law, in 1808 (Tables 72–3). In 1816 Ferdinand formally assumed the style of King of the Two Sicilies by uniting their separate constitutions: technically he had hitherto been Ferdinand III of Sicily and IV of Naples.

His full arms are elaborate and are shown on Table 124 surrounded by the collar of the Constantinian Order of St George; this decoration, allegedly derived from the Eastern Empire, was brought from Parma by Charles VII. The shield is divided vertically into three with a small escutcheon of Anjou modern over all: in the first section Farnese is quartered with Austria-Burgundy with Portugal over all; in the second, the Hapsburg-Spain quarterings are displayed over Anjou ancient and Jerusalem; in the third, Tuscany. The restoration of Ferdinand I (as he now became) was followed by popular risings both in Sicily and in Naples. A democratic constitution was introduced but functioned poorly. In 1821 the King was returned to his own realm under the protection of Austrian bayonets, which remained in Naples until 1827. After the death of his Austrian Queen he made a morganatic marriage with his former mistress.

Francis I was a debauchee of limited capacity, whose administration was a byword for corruption and the sale of offices. His son, Ferdinand II, was not a noticeable improvement; some early signs of liberalism were replaced by savage repression of a series of risings, particularly in Sicily. His subjects nicknamed him 'Bomba' (after he had bombarded several towns); Mr Gladstone, with greater orotundity, declared that his regime was 'the negation of God erected into a system of government'. In 1859 the King died, just when the alliance of France and Savoy was subverting Austrian dominance in north Italy. Victor Emanuel of Savoy twice offered Francis II plans for dividing Italy between them; they were twice rejected. Nemesis was at hand in the person of Garibaldi who landed at Marsala in Sicily on 11 May 1860. By July he was master of the island, and in August landed on the mainland; a month later he was in Naples. In February 1861 Victor Emanuel was proclaimed King of Italy at Turin. Francis II moved to Rome and never renounced his rights; these were inherited in turn by his half-brother, the Count of Caserta, and by his half-nephews Ferdinand, Duke of Calabria, and Rainer, Duke of Castro. Their intervening brother, Charles, gave up his rights on joining the Spanish royal family, though his descendants have asserted them. The mother of the Duchess of Castro was a daughter of the Count of Trapani; the marriage of Prince Ferdinand (though non-royal) has been accepted by the family as valid.

Chapter 34

TUSCANY, MODENA, MILAN, MANTUA AND PARMA

If southeast Italy at least enjoyed some unity under the Kingdom of Naples, the reverse was the case north of Rome. Here in the Middle Ages authority was dispersed among a number of states, each usually based on a flourishing town, which grew steadily more independent of any imperial control. Already by the twelfth century the greater cities of the Lombard plain, especially Milan, had established 'communes', that is corporations controlling the urban area and the surrounding countryside and arrogating to themselves the rights of justice, coinage, tolls and administration which had belonged to the Crown or its agents. Initially their government was democratic or oligarchic but only Venice kept republican forms to the end; elsewhere local dynasties thrust upward in the later Middle Ages, and first usurped power, then assumed titles. In almost all cases they combined a measure of tyranny with patronage of the visual arts. In the towns there were constant and bitter disputes, between Guelph and Ghibelline (in broad terms the papal and imperial parties) or even between two factions of Guelphs. Between city states there was vigorous commercial rivalry and not infrequent war.

TUSCANY

Florence had formed part of the County of Tuscany, bequeathed to the Papacy by Countess Matilda in 1114. From this point various cities quickly asserted their independence – Pisa, Lucca, Siena and Florence itself. Nominally ruled by twelve guilds the city was passionately political; Dante was exiled for his membership of the 'white' Guelphs. The contrast between her brilliant painting and bloodthirsty local feuds is a curious commentary on human nature; her international position rested largely on the development of banking within her walls. In this business John dei Medici (Table 127) made a vast fortune. His son Cosimo, known as Pater Patriae, was the dominant figure in a society still in form republican; with no title, he suppressed his enemies and lived in regal style. It was the age of the sculptor Donatello and his peers but Cosimo was also a genuine lover of literature.

His grandson, Lorenzo the Magnificent, survived a violent conspiracy in 1478 by the Pazzi, a rival family in the world of banking, who were also linked with the Papacy of Sixtus IV, during which his brother Giuliano was killed in the cathedral itself. Lorenzo reigned over Florence in splendour by manipulating the machinery of government, at which he was more adept than in the actual business of banking. He was an active scholar, leading the learned men who surrounded him, and a writer of significance. One son and one nephew became pope; Leo X continued gloriously in Rome the family tradition of art patronage, with the painter Raphael as a leading beneficiary. Clement VII was responsible for the Medici chapel in Florence with the superb monuments by Michelangelo commemorating his kinsmen, Giuliano, Duke of Nemours (d. 1516) and Lorenzo, Duke of Urbino (d. 1519). The Medici arms were originally a number of red balls (*palle*), sometimes eight, sometimes less, on a gold field. In the time of Cosimo the number settled at six. In 1465 Louis XI of France granted that the uppermost ball should bear the lilies of France.

Alexander, an illegitimate son of Lorenzo, Duke of Urbino, was the first Medici actually to use the title of duke: he was murdered by his distant cousin Lorenzo, a companion in his debauches, himself slain in 1548. The government of Florence now fell to Cosimo, the son of a famous mercenary belonging to the younger branch of the family. He enlarged the territory of Florence by acquiring Siena and was made grandduke by the Pope, but his successors, though mainly interested in the arts, were undistinguished as rulers.

TABLE 127

TUSCANY
General survey

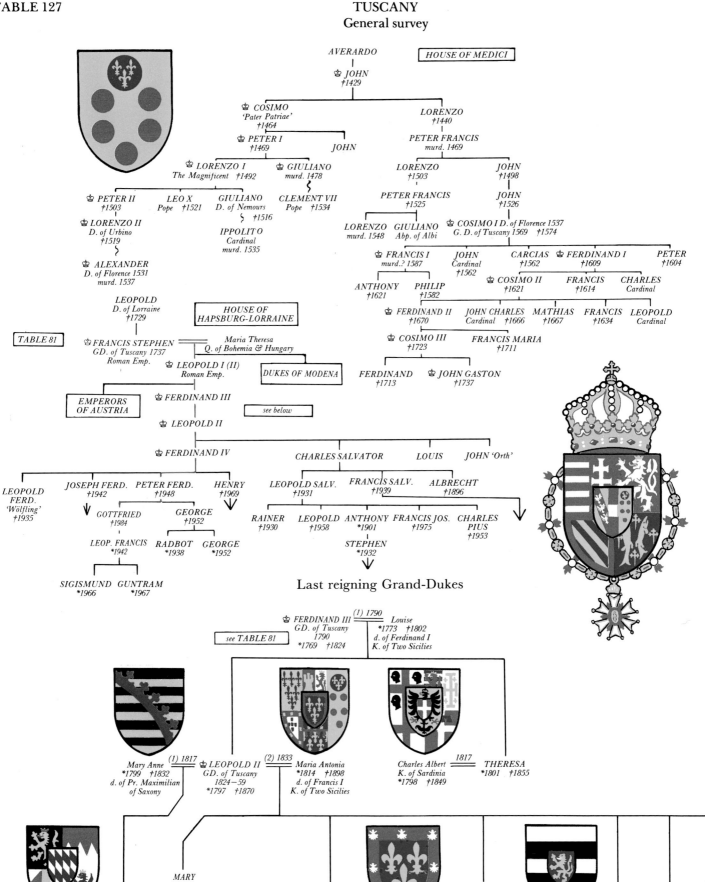

HOUSE OF MEDICI

AVERARDO

👑 JOHN
†1429

👑 COSIMO
'Pater Patriae'
†1464

LORENZO
†1440

PETER FRANCIS
murd. 1469

👑 PETER I
†1469

JOHN

LORENZO
†1503

JOHN
†1498

👑 LORENZO I
The Magnificent †1492

👑 GIULIANO
murd. 1478

PETER FRANCIS
†1525

JOHN
†1526

👑 PETER II
†1503

LEO X
Pope †1521

GIULIANO
D. of Nemours
†1516

CLEMENT VII
Pope †1534

LORENZO
murd. 1548

GIULIANO
Abp. of Albi

👑 COSIMO I D. of Florence 1537
G. D. of Tuscany 1569 †1574

👑 LORENZO II
D. of Urbino
†1519

IPPOLITO
Cardinal
murd. 1535

👑 FRANCIS I
murd.? 1587

JOHN
Cardinal
†1562

CARCIAS
†1562

👑 FERDINAND I
†1609

PETER
†1604

👑 ALEXANDER
D. of Florence 1531
murd. 1537

ANTHONY
†1621

PHILIP
†1582

👑 COSIMO II
†1621

FRANCIS
†1614

CHARLES
Cardinal

LEOPOLD
D. of Lorraine
†1729

HOUSE OF
HAPSBURG-LORRAINE

👑 FERDINAND II
†1670

JOHN CHARLES
Cardinal †1666

MATHIAS
†1667

FRANCIS
†1634

LEOPOLD
Cardinal

TABLE 81

👑 FRANCIS STEPHEN
GD. of Tuscany 1737
Roman Emp.

Maria Theresa
Q. of Bohemia & Hungary

👑 COSIMO III
†1723

FRANCIS MARIA
†1711

👑 LEOPOLD I (II)
Roman Emp.

DUKES OF MODENA

FERDINAND
†1713

👑 JOHN GASTON
†1737

EMPERORS
OF AUSTRIA

👑 FERDINAND III

see below

👑 LEOPOLD II

👑 FERDINAND IV

CHARLES SALVATOR

LOUIS

JOHN 'Orth'

LEOPOLD
FERD.
'Wölfling'
†1935

JOSEPH FERD.
†1942

PETER FERD.
†1948

HENRY
†1969

LEOPOLD SALV.
†1931

FRANCIS SALV.
†1939

ALBRECHT
†1896

GOTTFRIED
†1984

GEORGE
†1952

RAINER
†1930

LEOPOLD
†1958

ANTHONY
*1901

FRANCIS JOS.
†1975

CHARLES
PIUS
†1953

LEOP. FRANCIS
*1942

RADBOT
*1938

GEORGE
*1952

STEPHEN
*1932

SIGISMUND
*1966

GUNTRAM
*1967

Last reigning Grand-Dukes

👑 FERDINAND III
GD. of Tuscany
1790
*1769   †1824

(1) 1790

Louise
*1773 †1802
d. of Ferdinand I
K. of Two Sicilies

see TABLE 81

Mary Anne
*1799 †1832
d. of Pr. Maximilian
of Saxony

(1) 1817

👑 LEOPOLD II
GD. of Tuscany
1824–59
*1797 †1870

(2) 1833

Maria Antonia
*1814 †1898
d. of Francis I
K. of Two Sicilies

Charles Albert
K. of Sardinia
*1798 †1849

1817

THERESA
*1801 †1855

Luitpold
Pr. Regent
of Bavaria
*1821 †1912

1844

AUGUSTA
*1825
†1864

MARY
ISABELLA
*1834 †1901
m. 1850
Francis
C. of Trapani
Pr. of Bourbon-
Sicily
*1827 †1892

Anne
*1836 †1859
d. of John
K. of Saxony

1856 (1)

👑 FERDINAND IV
GD. of Tuscany
1859–60
*1835 †1908

(2) 1868

Alix
*1849 †1935
d. of Charles III
D. of Parma

CHARLES
SALVATOR
*1839 †1892
m. 1861
Maria Immaculata
*1844 †1899
d. of Ferdinand II
K. of Two Sicilies

Charles
Pr. of Isenburg
*1838
†1899

1865

MARY
LOUISE
*1845
†1917

LOUIS
*1847
†1915

JOHN
'Orth'
*1852
†1891 ?

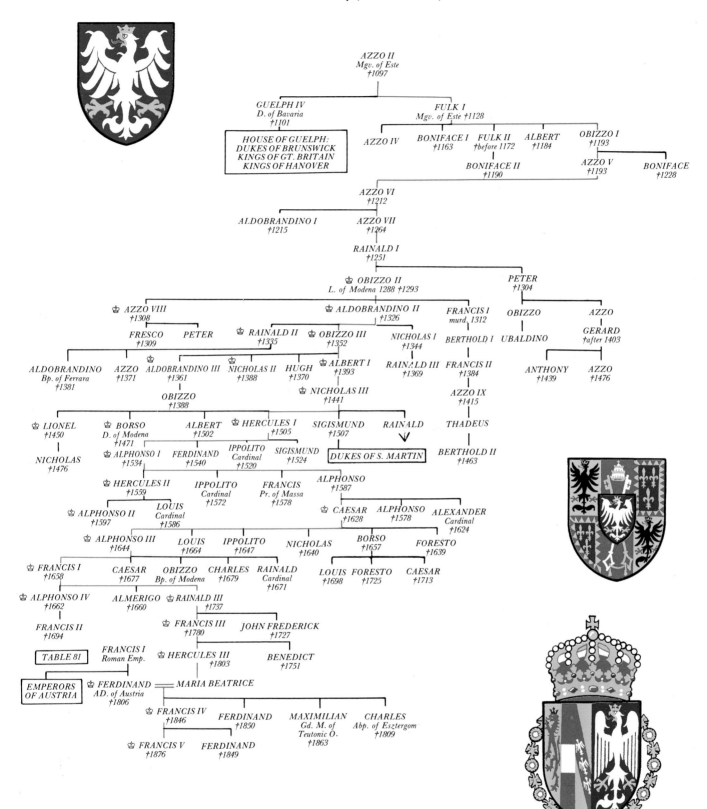

AZZO II
Mgv. of Este
†1097

GUELPH IV
D. of Bavaria
†1101

HOUSE OF GUELPH:
DUKES OF BRUNSWICK
KINGS OF GT. BRITAIN
KINGS OF HANOVER

FULK I
Mgv. of Este †1128

AZZO IV

BONIFACE I
†1163

FULK II
†before 1172

ALBERT
†1184

OBIZZO I
†1193

AZZO V
†1193

BONIFACE
†1228

BONIFACE II
†1190

AZZO VI
†1212

ALDOBRANDINO I
†1215

AZZO VII
†1264

RAINALD I
†1251

OBIZZO II
L. of Modena 1288 †1293

PETER
†1304

AZZO VIII
†1308

ALDOBRANDINO II
†1326

FRANCIS I
murd. 1312

OBIZZO

AZZO

FRESCO
†1309

PETER

RAINALD II
†1335

OBIZZO III
†1352

NICHOLAS I
†1344

BERTHOLD I

UBALDINO

GERARD
†after 1403

ALDOBRANDINO
Bp. of Ferrara
†1381

AZZO
†1371

ALDOBRANDINO III
†1361

NICHOLAS II
†1388

HUGH
†1370

ALBERT I
†1393

RAINALD III
†1369

FRANCIS II
†1384

ANTHONY
†1439

AZZO
†1476

OBIZZO
†1388

NICHOLAS III
†1441

AZZO IX
†1415

LIONEL
†1450

BORSO
D. of Modena
†1471

ALBERT
†1502

HERCULES I
†1505

SIGISMUND
†1507

RAINALD

THADEUS

NICHOLAS
†1476

ALPHONSO I
†1534

FERDINAND
†1540

IPPOLITO
Cardinal
†1520

SIGISMUND
†1524

DUKES OF S. MARTIN

BERTHOLD II
†1463

HERCULES II
†1559

IPPOLITO
Cardinal
†1572

FRANCIS
Pr. of Massa
†1578

ALPHONSO
†1587

ALPHONSO II
†1597

LOUIS
Cardinal
†1586

CAESAR
†1628

ALPHONSO
†1578

ALEXANDER
Cardinal
†1624

ALPHONSO III
†1644

LOUIS
†1664

IPPOLITO
†1647

NICHOLAS
†1640

BORSO
†1657

FORESTO
†1639

FRANCIS I
†1658

CAESAR
†1677

OBIZZO
Bp. of Modena

CHARLES
†1679

RAINALD
Cardinal
†1671

LOUIS
†1698

FORESTO
†1725

CAESAR
†1713

ALPHONSO IV
†1662

ALMERIGO
†1660

RAINALD III
†1737

FRANCIS II
†1694

FRANCIS III
†1780

JOHN FREDERICK
†1727

TABLE 81

FRANCIS I
Roman Emp.

HERCULES III
†1803

BENEDICT
†1751

EMPERORS
OF AUSTRIA

FERDINAND
AD. of Austria
†1806

MARIA BEATRICE

FRANCIS IV
†1846

FERDINAND
†1850

MAXIMILIAN
Gd. M. of
Teutonic O.
†1863

CHARLES
Abp. of Esztergom
†1809

FRANCIS V
†1876

FERDINAND
†1849

Francis I was a notable libertine and Cosimo III a pious glutton; John Gaston was childless and already worn out by sexual excess when he became grand-duke, only to spend most of his time in bed. The question of who should succeed him was vigorously debated by the Great Powers while he lived. At first his duchy was to go to Charles of Spain (later King of Naples); then it was allotted to Francis of Lorraine, the husband of the Empress Maria Theresa (Chapter 28). From him it passed to his second son, Leopold, who (on becoming emperor in 1790) gave it to his second son, Ferdinand III. Leopold was an accomplished and successful ruler who restored prosperity to his dominions.

During the Napoleonic Wars Tuscany was first in the Kingdom of Etruria, and then in part given as a principality to Napoleon's sister Elisa Baciocchi (Tables 72–3). Ferdinand III and Leopold II were both blameless and liberal rulers. In 1847 Lucca was added to the Grand-Duchy. In 1859 partisans of unity compelled Leopold to resign in favour of his son, but in the next year the provisional government voted for union with Savoy. The arms used by the Hapsburg Grand-Dukes showed a small shield of Lorraine, Austria and Tuscany (Medici) over quarterings for Hungary, Bohemia, Burgundy and Bar (Table 127). The Order of St Joseph, whose collar surrounds the shield, was founded in 1807 by Ferdinand III, while he was still Grand-Duke of Würzburg – a Napoleonic appointment. The badge was therefore modelled on that of the Legion of Honour.

MODENA

The little town of Este, halfway between Padua and Ferrara, has given its name to a family which sired great dynasties in Germany and Italy. Azzo II (Table 128) married the heiress of the German Guelph; from this union descended the powerful Henry the Lion, the Emperor Otto IV, and more remotely the Electors of Hanover and Kings of Great Britain (1714–1837), a male line still extant in the person of the Duke of Brunswick (Table 99). By a second marriage Azzo started the Italian House of Este which only died out in 1803; another son became Count of Maine in France.

Azzo VI became Lord of Ferrara in 1208, but there was strong local rivalry and not until the end of the life of Azzo VII was the family hold secure. Obizzo II acquired Modena in 1288 and Reggio a year later. His son Azzo VIII lost both and a confused period of family disputes followed. Nicholas III was a more capable ruler and gathered Ferrara, Modena, Reggio and Parma under his sway. He was also made standard-bearer of the Roman Church. His eldest son, Lionel, was a notable patron of the arts, and his next-born, Borso, obtained the title of Duke of Modena and

Ferrara from the Emperor Frederick III. In addition he was given the Lordship of Rovigo, and began to use the imperial eagle on his shield. The original arms of Este are a silver eagle with a gold crown on a blue field. By 1508 a more complicated blazon had built up with the imperial eagle in the first and fourth quarters and in the second and third France within an indented bordure (granted by Charles VIII and later associated with Ferrara); between the quarters was a pale with the papal keys (from 1474) and the tiara (1508) for the Gonfaloniership; over all the eagle of Este. The family continued to use the papal insignia whether they held the office or not.

Hercules I began the greatest age of the Duchy. One of his daughters, Beatrice, married the Duke of Milan and was a lovely and learned light of the high Renaissance; another, Isabel, married the Marquis of Mantua and maintained an equally brilliant court there, frequented by Castiglione, Raphael and Mantegna. His son, Alphonso I, espoused the famous Lucretia Borgia, natural daughter of Pope Alexander VI. Alphonso's military reputation was high, especially in the use of artillery, and he had to fight hard against papal armies. Hercules II married a daughter of Louis XII of France and built the Villa d'Este at Tivoli. Ariosto was a servant of Alphonso I; Tasso was encouraged by Alphonso II. The latter prince was a great builder of canals, residing mainly at Ferrara. His death brought the main line to an end. He named his cousin Caesar as his heir; but the Papacy incorporated Ferrara into the states of the Church, and Caesar only inherited Modena, to which he prudently removed the celebrated Este library.

The rulers of the younger branch played a less splendid part in the world of art and counted for less in European politics. Alphonso III retired to a monastery in 1629. Alphonso IV was the father of Mary, second wife of James II of England and mother of the Old Pretender. Rainald III made an intriguing match with his infinitely distant cousin, Charlotte of Brunswick-Lüneburg. Hercules III, the last of his line, was driven from his Duchy by the French revolutionary armies, and saw it become part of the Cisalpine Republic. His only daughter married the Archduke Ferdinand of Austria. In 1814 their son Francis IV was restored to the Duchy, which was ruled as an outpost of Austria. In 1859 the people of Modena voted for union with Savoy and in the following year Francis V was deposed.

The Emperor Francis Joseph conferred the name and arms of Austria-Este on his heir, the Archduke Francis Ferdinand (Table 82), and, after the death of the latter, on the Archduke Robert, second son of the (future) Emperor Charles. Their arms show Este impaled by a threefold shield of Hapsburg-Austria-Lorraine. At the foot of Table 128 their shield is sur-

rounded by the collar of the order of the Eagle of Este, founded by Francis V in 1855.

MILAN

The great city of Milan, noted for its weavers, armourers and goldsmiths, early attained commercial pre-eminence in the Lombard plain. Destroyed by Barbarossa in 1162, it was rebuilt five years later. For a time the town was controlled by the Della Torre family, but in 1277 Archbishop Otto Visconti defeated them in battle, suspended half a dozen of them in iron cages and took possession of his see. From then Milan was controlled by members of that family. The lovers of legend have made merry with the dramatic Visconti arms (Table 129), some attributing them to the badge of a Saracen slain on crusade, others to a monster devouring the heir of Milan; it may possibly be a play on *Anguis*, the Latin for both a serpent and the Visconti castle of Angleria. To Matthew Visconti was given the position of Imperial Vicar and henceforward he quartered the German eagle. The Emperor Albrecht gave a crown to the serpent. The arms thus combined were taken over by the Sforza family when they succeeded to Milan. Matthew also considerably extended the domains of Milan by adding Pavia, Piacenza, Bergamo and other lordships. Luchino added Parma, but was murdered by his wife. John, in addition to being archbishop and cardinal, added Bologna and the valuable port of Genoa. In negotiations with Venice he employed the poet Petrarch as his emissary.

John Galeazzo I reunited the state which his father and uncle (after murdering their brother Matthew) had ruled jointly from Pavia and Milan. He started the cathedral at Milan, one of the most remarkable monuments of Christian Europe; he obtained the title of duke from the Emperor. Fair-haired and without scruple or remorse, he aimed at the creation of a potent north Italian state. Up to a point he succeeded, but the tough and maritime Venetian Republic blocked the east and the affluent and artistic Floren-

tine Republic barred the south. The great mercenary leaders (*condottieri*) battened upon the wars between the three, and grew rich. Philip Maria did his best to mature his father's plans, after his mad brother had been killed, but made little headway. His only daughter, who was illegitimate, had been married to a leading *condottiere*, Francis Sforza, himself a bastard. For almost a century the Sforza family strove to preserve their heritage, but north Italy was becoming a battleground for the larger ambitions of France and Austria. Twice the Milanese were conquered by France; twice the Sforzas were restored. The death of Francis II (1535) ended the dynasty, and Milan passed to the Hapsburgs and thence to the Spanish Crown. At the Peace of Utrecht (1713) it was transferred to Austria who retained it until the union of Italy in 1860.

MANTUA

Mantua occupies a strategic position between two great lakes. In classical times it was the birthplace of Virgil; in the Middle Ages it became a redoubtable fortress. At a later date it produced Sordello (commemorated by Dante and Browning), a noted and errant troubadour. In 1328 Louis Gonzaga (Table 129), a prominent Guelph, became captain of the town, and thereafter the fortunes of Mantua were bound up with this family. Their original arms were a simple barry pattern of gold and black; in 1433 the Emperor Sigismund nominated John Francis to be Marquess of Mantua and also gave him new arms of a red cross between four imperial eagles (Table 129). The court of Mantua now began to take its part in the Renaissance. Louis III married a Hohenzollern, and his grandson John Francis II the beautiful and

[257]

TABLE 129

MILAN
General survey

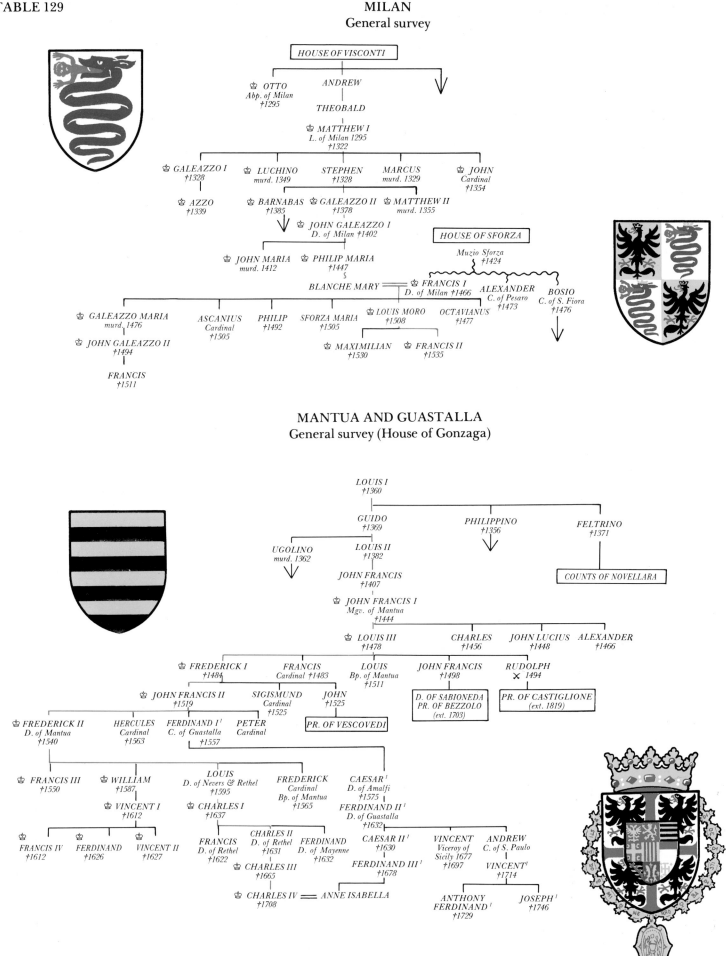

HOUSE OF VISCONTI

♔ OTTO
Abp. of Milan
†1295

ANDREW

THEOBALD

♔ MATTHEW I
L. of Milan 1295
†1322

♔ GALEAZZO I
†1328

♔ LUCHINO
murd. 1349

STEPHEN
†1328

MARCUS
murd. 1329

♔ JOHN
Cardinal
†1354

♔ AZZO
†1339

♔ BARNABAS
†1385

♔ GALEAZZO II
†1378

♔ MATTHEW II
murd. 1355

♔ JOHN GALEAZZO I
D. of Milan †1402

HOUSE OF SFORZA

Muzio Sforza
†1424

♔ JOHN MARIA
murd. 1412

♔ PHILIP MARIA
†1447

BLANCHE MARY ═══ ♔ FRANCIS I
D. of Milan †1466

ALEXANDER
C. of Pesaro
†1473

BOSIO
C. of S. Fiora
†1476

♔ GALEAZZO MARIA
murd. 1476

ASCANIUS
Cardinal
†1505

PHILIP
†1492

SFORZA MARIA
†1505

♔ LOUIS MORO
†1508

OCTAVIANUS
†1477

♔ JOHN GALEAZZO II
†1494

♔ MAXIMILIAN
†1530

♔ FRANCIS II
†1535

FRANCIS
†1511

MANTUA AND GUASTALLA
General survey (House of Gonzaga)

LOUIS I
†1360

GUIDO
†1369

PHILIPPINO
†1356

FELTRINO
†1371

UGOLINO
murd. 1362

LOUIS II
†1382

COUNTS OF NOVELLARA

JOHN FRANCIS
†1407

♔ JOHN FRANCIS I
Mgv. of Mantua
†1444

♔ LOUIS III
†1478

CHARLES
†1456

JOHN LUCIUS
†1448

ALEXANDER
†1466

♔ FREDERICK I
†1484

FRANCIS
Cardinal †1483

LOUIS
Bp. of Mantua
†1511

JOHN FRANCIS
†1498

RUDOLPH
✗ 1494

♔ JOHN FRANCIS II
†1519

SIGISMUND
Cardinal
†1525

JOHN
†1525

D. OF SABIONEDA
PR. OF BEZZOLO
(ext. 1703)

PR. OF CASTIGLIONE
(ext. 1819)

PR. OF VESCOVEDI

♔ FREDERICK II
D. of Mantua
†1540

HERCULES
Cardinal
†1563

FERDINAND I¹
C. of Guastalla
†1557

PETER
Cardinal

♔ FRANCIS III
†1550

♔ WILLIAM
†1587

LOUIS
D. of Nevers & Rethel
†1595

FREDERICK
Cardinal
Bp. of Mantua
†1565

CAESAR¹
D. of Amalfi
†1575

♔ VINCENT I
†1612

♔ CHARLES I
†1637

FERDINAND II¹
D. of Guastalla
†1632

♔
FRANCIS IV
†1612

♔
FERDINAND
†1626

VINCENT II
†1627

FRANCIS
D. of Rethel
†1622

CHARLES II
D. of Rethel
†1631

FERDINAND
D. of Mayenne
†1632

CAESAR II¹
†1630

VINCENT
Viceroy of
Sicily 1677
†1697

ANDREW
C. of S. Paulo

♔ CHARLES III
†1665

FERDINAND III¹
†1678

VINCENT¹
†1714

♔ CHARLES IV ═══ ANNE ISABELLA
†1708

ANTHONY
FERDINAND¹
†1729

JOSEPH¹
†1746

NOTE
¹ Ruler in Guastalla

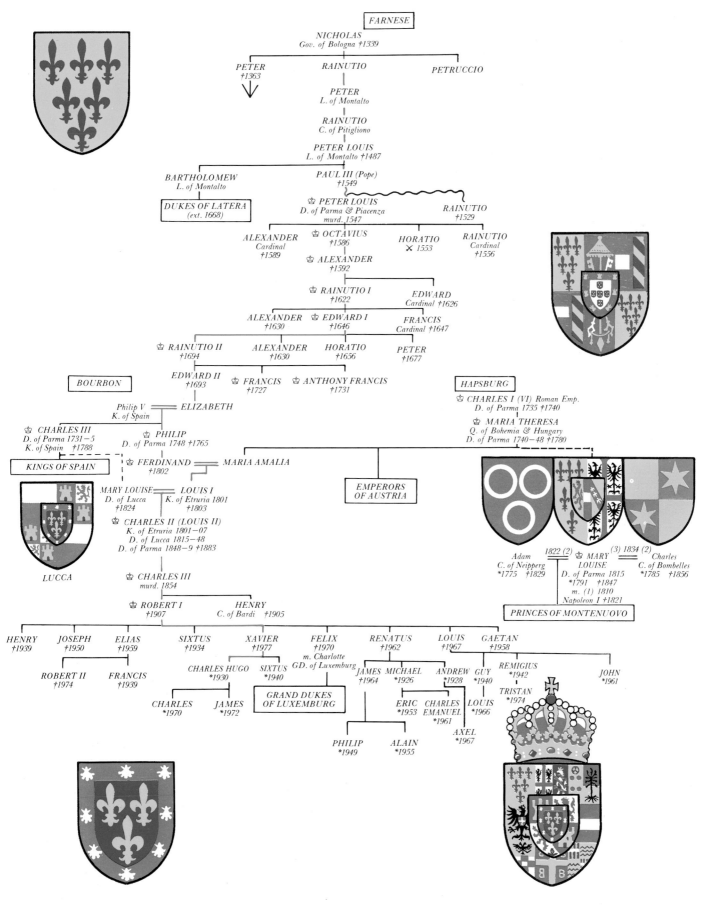

FARNESE

NICHOLAS
Gov. of Bologna †1339

PETER †1363 — RAINUTIO — PETRUCCIO

PETER
L. of Montalto

RAINUTIO
C. of Pitigliono

PETER LOUIS
L. of Montalto †1487

BARTHOLOMEW
L. of Montalto
DUKES OF LATERA (ext. 1668)

PAUL III (Pope) †1549

PETER LOUIS
D. of Parma & Piacenza
murd. 1547 — RAINUTIO †1529

ALEXANDER
Cardinal †1589 — OCTAVIUS †1586 — HORATIO ✕ 1553 — RAINUTIO Cardinal †1556

ALEXANDER †1592

RAINUTIO I †1622 — EDWARD Cardinal †1626

ALEXANDER †1630 — EDWARD I †1646 — FRANCIS Cardinal †1647

RAINUTIO II †1694 — ALEXANDER †1630 — HORATIO †1656 — PETER †1677

EDWARD II †1693 — FRANCIS †1727 — ANTHONY FRANCIS †1731

BOURBON

Philip V K. of Spain === ELIZABETH

CHARLES III
D. of Parma 1731–5
K. of Spain †1788

PHILIP
D. of Parma 1748 †1765

KINGS OF SPAIN

FERDINAND †1802 === MARIA AMALIA

MARY LOUISE
D. of Lucca †1824 === LOUIS I
K. of Etruria 1801 †1803

CHARLES II (LOUIS II)
K. of Etruria 1801–07
D. of Lucca 1815–48
D. of Parma 1848–9 †1883

LUCCA

CHARLES III
murd. 1854

ROBERT I †1907 — HENRY
C. of Bardi †1905

HAPSBURG

CHARLES I (VI) Roman Emp.
D. of Parma 1735 †1740

MARIA THERESA
Q. of Bohemia & Hungary
D. of Parma 1740–48 †1780

EMPERORS OF AUSTRIA

Adam
C. of Neipperg
*1775 †1829 — 1822 (2) MARY LOUISE
D. of Parma 1815
*1791 †1847
m. (1) 1810
Napoleon I †1821 — (3) 1834 (2) Charles
C. of Bombelles
*1785 †1856

PRINCES OF MONTENUOVO

HENRY †1939 — JOSEPH †1950 — ELIAS †1959 — SIXTUS †1934 — XAVIER †1977 — FELIX †1970 m. Charlotte GD. of Luxemburg — RENATUS †1962 — LOUIS †1967 — GAETAN †1958

ROBERT II †1974 — FRANCIS †1939

CHARLES HUGO *1930 — SIXTUS *1940

GRAND DUKES OF LUXEMBURG

JAMES †1964 — MICHAEL *1926 — ANDREW *1928 — GUY *1940 — REMIGIUS *1942 — JOHN *1961

TRISTAN *1974

CHARLES *1970 — JAMES *1972

ERIC *1953 — CHARLES EMANUEL *1961 — LOUIS *1966

AXEL *1967

PHILIP *1949 — ALAIN *1955

talented Isabella d'Este, whose apartments are still one of the glories of the palace.

Frederick II built the enchanting Palazzo del Te on the outskirts of the town, designed by his favourite artist, Giulio Romano. He obtained the title of Duke of Mantua in 1530 and conferred the County of Guastalla on his younger brother in 1538: the cadet line continued here until 1746, becoming dukes on the way. Frederick was succeeded by his eldest son, Francis III, but his third son, Louis, married a French heiress and became Duke of Nevers. On the extinction of the main line in 1627, Charles of Nevers laid claim to Mantua, which was promptly sacked and looted by the imperial forces. Although Charles made good his right, the fortunes of the city never recovered. Charles IV supported France in the War of the Spanish Succession, at the conclusion of which his Duchy was divided between Savoy and Austria. The full arms, surrounded by the Order of the Holy Sacrament, show Gonzaga surmounted by an escutcheon with nine coats for various fiefs, namely: the Eastern Empire, Lombardy, old Gonzaga; Byzantium, Aragon, Montferrat; Saxony, Bar and Jerusalem. The more pretentious of these blazons refer back to the alliance of Frederick II with the heiress of Montferrat; the arrangement, with the family arms below the fiefs, is the reverse of normal.

PARMA

Parma was disputed in the Middle Ages between a number of families of which that of Correggio was the most important. In 1346 it was acquired by the Visconti of Milan, but from 1512 to 1545 it was in the hands of the Papacy.

The family of Farnese (Table 130) came from near Orvieto in the Patrimony of St Peter. The lovely Giulia Farnese attracted the concupiscent eye of Pope Alexander VI. Her brother was made a cardinal, and later became pope himself, as Paul III; his morals were no more austere than those of his benefactor, and one of his first cares was to provide for his numerous bastards. Peter Louis Farnese, a brutal man of pleasure, was given various lordships near Rome, and then in 1545 made Duke of Parma and Piacenza. Two years later he was murdered in Piacenza, which was seized by the imperialists. Of his children, Cardinal Alexander finished the great Farnese palace in Rome; Horatio inherited the properties near Rome; while Octavius, after marrying Margaret, natural daughter of the Emperor Charles V, regained Parma, and eventually Piacenza. Alexander, Duke of Parma, his son, was one of the greatest soldiers of the sixteenth century. He married a Portuguese princess, and served as Governor of the Netherlands (1578–90) with considerable distinction. Had the Armada been successful he would have led the invasion of England; but these preoccupations left him little time for his own duchy.

The original Farnese arms were probably a gold field strewn with blue fleurs-de-lys, but the number was reduced to six. Alexander and the later Dukes, who were of little consequence, quartered these arms with those of Hapsburg-Burgundy (in allusion to his mother) with a pale of the papal crossed keys and ceremonial pavilion or *ombrellino* (compare Modena). The Farnese were appointed standard-bearers to the See of St Peter from 1546 to 1641. The escutcheon of Portugal refers to the wife of the great Duke of Parma (Table 116), through whom he had a claim to that Kingdom.

The death of Duke Anthony Francis in 1731 left Parma to the machinations of the able Queen Elizabeth of Spain (Chapter 11) and it was conferred in succession on two of her sons. Charles removed the best of the art collections to Naples before Philip succeeded. In 1796 Parma was overrun by the revolutionary armies of France. In 1801 a substitute Kingdom of Etruria south of the Apennines was fabricated for Louis the son of the dethroned Duke. Then in 1815 Parma, Piacenza and Guastalla were united into a duchy to support Mary Louise of Austria, the wife of Napoleon, himself exiled to St Helena. Here she lapsed into comfortable adultery with the one-eyed General von Neipperg and married him morganatically after Napoleon's death. A dim woman, she knew (it was said) neither how to be an empress, nor a wife, nor a mother. At her death, late in 1847, Parma passed to Charles II, who had filled in time as Duke of Lucca. His shield as Duke of Lucca (1815–48) displays the bi-coloured arms of that city quartered with Spain and an escutcheon of Bourbon over all. He resigned in 1849; his son was assassinated in 1854; his grandson was overthrown in 1860 (at only twelve years old) and Parma became part of the Kingdom of Italy. The dispossessed Duke, Robert I, had an extensive family; three of his sons succeeded in turn to his pretensions. Another, Prince Sixtus, made a significant effort to end the First World War by negotiation in 1917. Prince Felix was the father of the present Grand-Duke of Luxemburg (Table 39). Prince Xavier inherited the leadership of the Spanish Carlists (Chapter 11), but on the death of his nephew, Duke Robert II, also became the titular Duke of Parma. His son, Prince Charles Hugo, is the present head of the Bourbon-Parma family and is married to a Dutch princess (Table 36).

The arms of the last Dukes of Parma display a quartered shield of Farnese (for Parma), Hapsburg-Austria-Lorraine, Gonzaga (for Guastalla) and Tuscany surmounted by Bourbon-Spain, with the lilies of France differenced for this branch by a red bordure with eight white scallop shells.

[260]

Chapter 35

POLAND

The early history of the Poles is obscure, but they are found occupying the area between the rivers Oder and Vistula; the name, appropriately enough, seems to mean 'the dwellers of the plain'. In the same way the area to the north, Pomerania, derives its name from being 'along the coast'. As will be seen, the boundaries of medieval Poland varied greatly from generation to generation, but reached their widest extent after the union with Lithuania under Wladislaw II, the first Jagellon king (Table 131).

In the tenth century the eastward expansion of Germany brought the Ottonian kings into contact with Poland, which was converted to Christianity under Mieszko I. This ruler married a Bohemian princess and belonged to a family which traced its origin to a semi-legendary Piast, who should have lived in the ninth century. His son, Boleslaw I, established the independence of the Polish Church and probably gained the title of king from Otto III in 1000. The marriage of a niece of Otto to Boleslaw's heir introduced into the Polish dynasty a strain of Byzantine blood, but Boleslaw's death was followed by a period of discord and dispute. The survival of Casimir I (head of Table 132) achieved some sort of order in Church and state. Accordingly, his son, Boleslaw II, the Bold, was able to have himself crowned king and pursue an expansionist policy. But his execution in 1079 of Archbishop Stanislas of Cracow (who subsequently became one of Poland's national saints) seems to have led to his own exile.

His brother Wladislaw I was a feeble ruler who made no claim to the title of king and was compelled to share his realm with two of his sons; more importantly he was inactive on the eastern frontier at a time when Russia was expanding. Boleslaw III, Wrymouth, was able to vindicate his freedom from German control, and by acquiring Pomerania gained an important access to the sea. Before his death he arranged a careful division of his domains among his numerous sons. The scheme, which has been criticized by later historians, was designed to obviate discord and to establish one definitely senior prince, the holder of the capital of Cracow.

Unhappily his intentions were not fulfilled. An age of political partition set in. The 'seniorate' did survive, but with minimal authority, save for control of the capital, which was growing in wealth and influence, and the province of 'Little Poland'. But Great Poland, to the northwest, was generally in different hands, while Silesia remained in the possession of the eldest line for some five hundred years. Eventually Cracow was seized by Casimir II, the youngest (and probably posthumous) son of Boleslaw III, to whom his father had bequeathed nothing, but after his death there was further confusion. This was the more unfortunate as Poland was confronted by difficult and ruthless neighbours. Conrad, Duke of Mazovia (Table 133), invited the aid of the Teutonic Knights, the great German crusading order, against the heathen Prussians; by the end of the thirteenth century the Order had occupied Pomerania and cut Poland off from the Baltic. On the eastern frontier, the country was threatened by the Mongol hordes. Batu, with his great general Subuday, had advanced through Russia and defeated a Polish army at Liegnitz in 1241. The Poles were commanded by Duke Henry II of Silesia, a great-grandson of Wladislaw II (Table 132). Although Poland was not actually occupied by the Tartars, the condition of disintegration was acute.

The seal of Boleslaw V (Table 133) shows an eagle on the shield of a mounted warrior, and it is clear that by this time the arms of the country were becoming recognizable as a white eagle with gold *kleestengel*, beak and claws on a red field; at the beginning of the fourteenth century a gold crown was added (top of

TABLE 131

POLAND AND LITHUANIA
General survey

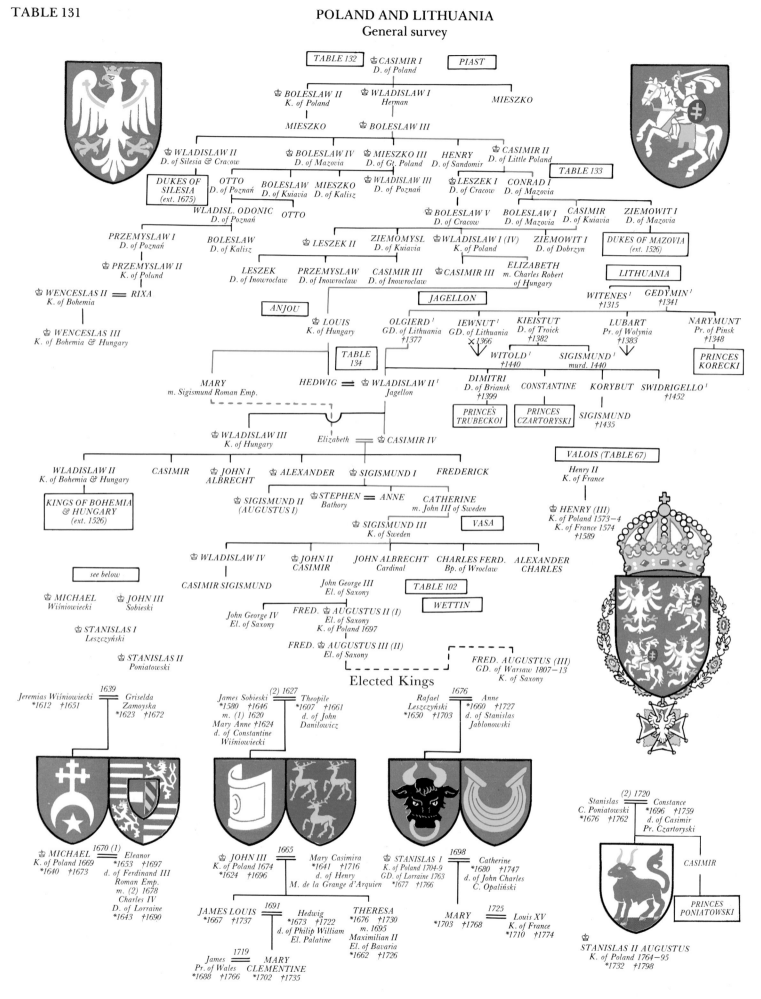

Elected Kings

NOTE
Arms of elected kings were placed in pretence of the arms of the Kingdom
[1] Grand-Duke of Lithuania

TABLE 132

POLAND
House of Piast (elder branch)

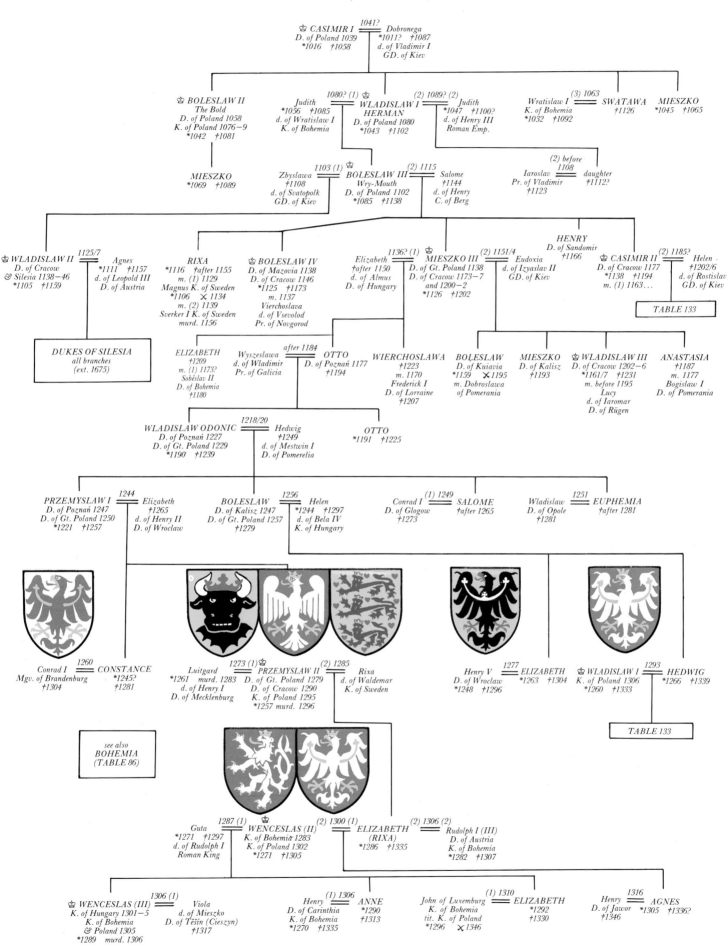

♛ CASIMIR I — 1041? — Dobronega
D. of Poland 1039 — *1011? †1087
*1016 †1058 — d. of Vladimir I
GD. of Kiev

♛ BOLESLAW II
The Bold
D. of Poland 1058
K. of Poland 1076−9
*1042 †1081

Judith — 1080? (1) — ♛ WLADISLAW I — (2) 1089? (2) — Judith
*1056 †1085 — HERMAN — *1047 †1100?
d. of Wratislaw I — D. of Poland 1080 — d. of Henry III
K. of Bohemia — *1043 †1102 — Roman Emp.

Wratislaw I — (3) 1063 — SWATAWA
K. of Bohemia — †1126
*1032 †1092

MIESZKO
*1045 †1065

(2) before
1108
Iaroslav — daughter
Pr. of Vladimir — †1112?
†1123

MIESZKO
*1069 †1089

Zbyslawa — 1103 (1) — ♛ BOLESLAW III — (2) 1115 — Salome
†1108 — Wry-Mouth — †1144
d. of Svatopolk — D. of Poland 1102 — d. of Henry
GD. of Kiev — *1085 †1138 — C. of Berg

♛ WLADISLAW II — 1125/7 — Agnes
D. of Cracow — *1111 †1157
& Silesia 1138−46 — d. of Leopold III
*1105 †1159 — D. of Austria

RIXA
*1116 †after 1155
m. (1) 1129
Magnus K. of Sweden
*1106 ✕ 1134
m. (2) 1139
Sverker I K. of Sweden
murd. 1156

♛ BOLESLAW IV
D. of Mazovia 1138
D. of Cracow 1146
*1125 †1173
m. 1137
Vierchoslava
d. of Vsevolod
Pr. of Novgorod

Elizabeth — 1136? (1) — ♛ MIESZKO III — (2) 1151/4 — Eudoxia
†after 1150 — D. of Gt. Poland 1138 — d. of Izyaslav II
d. of Almus — D. of Cracow 1173−7 — GD. of Kiev
D. of Hungary — and 1200−2
*1126 †1202

HENRY
D. of Sandomir
†1166

CASIMIR II — (2) 1185? — Helen
D. of Cracow 1177 — †1202/6
*1138 †1194 — d. of Rostislav
m. (1) 1163... — GD. of Kiev

TABLE 133

DUKES OF SILESIA
all branches
(ext. 1675)

ELIZABETH
†1209
m. (1) 1173?
Sobéslav II
D. of Bohemia
†1180

Wyszeslawa — after 1184 — OTTO
d. of Wladimir — D. of Poznań 1177
Pr. of Galicia — †1194

WIERCHOSLAWA
†1223
m. 1170
Frederick I
D. of Lorraine
†1207

BOLESLAW
D. of Kuiavia
*1159 ✕ 1195
m. Dobroslawa
of Pomerania

MIESZKO
D. of Kalisz
†1193

♛ WLADISLAW III
D. of Cracow 1202−6
*1161/7 †1231
m. before 1195
Lucy
d. of Iaromar
D. of Rügen

ANASTASIA
†1187
m. 1177
Bogislaw I
D. of Pomerania

WLADISLAW ODONIC — 1218/20 — Hedwig
D. of Poznań 1227 — †1249
D. of Gt. Poland 1229 — d. of Mestwin I
*1190 †1239 — D. of Pomerelia

OTTO
*1191 †1225

PRZEMYSLAW I — 1244 — Elizabeth
D. of Poznań 1247 — †1265
D. of Gt. Poland 1250 — d. of Henry II
*1221 †1257 — D. of Wroclaw

BOLESLAW — 1256 — Helen
D. of Kalisz 1247 — *1244 †1297
D. of Gt. Poland 1257 — d. of Bela IV
†1279 — K. of Hungary

Conrad I — (1) 1249 — SALOME
D. of Glogow — †after 1265
†1273

Wladislaw — 1251 — EUPHEMIA
D. of Opole — †after 1281
†1281

Conrad I — 1260 — CONSTANCE
Mgv. of Brandenburg — *1245?
†1304 — †1281

Luitgard — 1273 (1) — ♛ PRZEMYSLAW II — (2) 1285 — Rixa
*1261 murd. 1283 — D. of Gt. Poland 1279 — d. of Waldemar
d. of Henry I — D. of Cracow 1290 — K. of Sweden
D. of Mecklenburg — K. of Poland 1295
*1257 murd. 1296

Henry V — 1277 — ELIZABETH
D. of Wroclaw — *1263 †1304
*1248 †1296

♛ WLADISLAW I — 1293 — HEDWIG
K. of Poland 1306 — *1266 †1339
*1260 †1333

TABLE 133

see also
BOHEMIA
(TABLE 86)

Guta — 1287 (1) — ♛ WENCESLAS (II) — (2) 1300 (1) — ELIZABETH — (2) 1306 (2) — Rudolph I (III)
*1271 †1297 — K. of Bohemia 1283 — (RIXA) — D. of Austria
d. of Rudolph I — K. of Poland 1302 — *1286 †1335 — K. of Bohemia
Roman King — *1271 †1305 — *1282 †1307

♛ WENCESLAS (III) — 1306 (1) — Viola
K. of Hungary 1301−5 — d. of Mieszko
K. of Bohemia — D. of Těšín (Cieszyn)
& Poland 1305 — †1317
*1289 murd. 1306

Henry — (1) 1306 — ANNE
D. of Carinthia — *1290
K. of Bohemia — †1313
*1270 †1335

John of Luxemburg — (1) 1310 — ELIZABETH
K. of Bohemia — *1292
tit. K. of Poland — †1330
*1296 ✕ 1346

Henry — 1316 — AGNES
D. of Jawor — *1305 †1336?
†1346

Table 131). Przemyslaw II (Table 132) built up a brief union of northern provinces and was actually crowned king by the Archbishop of Gniezno, but he was assassinated shortly afterwards and enjoyed little real authority. His only daughter married Wenceslas of Bohemia and it seemed likely that Poland, or at least a great part of it, might become part of an empire centred upon Prague; this dream ended, however, with the murder of Wenceslas III in 1306. These two Kings impaled the two-tailed lion of Bohemia with the eagle of Poland.

Events now turned in favour of the Polish dynasty. Wladislaw IV (Table 133), Duke of Cracow, had been driven into exile by Wenceslas II, but opinion in Poland began to rally to his side. Gradually he garnered together the various provinces and in 1320 felt able to resume the royal title (and add a crown to his coat-of-arms). Finally, in 1331 he inflicted a severe defeat on the Teutonic Knights at Plowce. By this date Silesia, though still ruled by princes of the Piast family, was moving more definitely into the orbit of Bohemia and the Empire. None the less Wladislaw I, as he became, had begun the revival of Poland, which was carried on by his son. Casimir III, the Great, was the most distinguished of Polish medieval kings; he had served a fruitful apprenticeship at the end of his father's reign. A series of matrimonial alliances with Hungary, Bavaria and Pomerania strengthened his international position. An appeal to the Papacy against the Teutonic Knights led to a legal action at the hitherto unknown town of Warsaw. Domestic reforms increased the prosperity of his country. He won the important provinces of Galicia to the southeast and regained control of Mazovia to the north. The towns flourished; the laws were codified; protection was accorded to the Jews who came to Poland, in flight from persecutions in the west. Cracow was beautified and became the seat of a university.

UNION WITH LITHUANIA

Casimir had no sons and had appointed as heir his nephew, Louis of Hungary. The arms of the latter show Hungary ancient and Anjou, Poland, Hungary modern, and Dalmatia. The new King had already ruled in Hungary with great distinction, but he had many problems there and was also embroiled in Italy. In 1374 Louis issued at Koszyce a famous charter of rights which in particular gave privileges to the landed minor nobility, a class known collectively as the *szlachta*. He had intended that his elder daughter Mary should inherit Poland, but on his death (1382) she was chosen by the Hungarians. For two years there was a period of dispute about the succession, though Hedwig, younger daughter of King Louis I, was generally recognized as the heir and was crowned 'king' in 1384; finally in 1386 she was married to Jagellon, the Grand-Duke of Lithuania.

This was a remarkable and dramatic match, little to the taste of Hedwig who preferred her earlier betrothed, William of Hapsburg. Jagellon was a heathen; his state had become important in the thirteenth century and had expanded down the valleys of the rivers Dniester and Dnieper to reach the Black Sea. Now he promised the Polish nobles that he and his family would become Catholic and that Poland would be the leading partner in the union of the two realms. The arms of Lithuania (top of Table 131) displayed a fully caparisoned knight, with a gold patriarchal cross on his blue buckler; these were now quartered with those of Poland (Table 133: bottom). At his baptism, early in 1386, Jagellon took the Christian name of Wladislaw; he and his wife were joint sovereigns. A new power had arisen in eastern Europe; nobody was more disconcerted than the Teutonic Knights, who had striven for two centuries to convert the Lithuanians by violence, and whose very *raison d'être* seemed to vanish. Hedwig, it is pleasant to record, came to esteem and work with her husband; before her death she advised him to marry one of her cousins, Anne of Cilly. Not, however, until his fourth marriage, did Wladislaw II beget an heir. In the meantime he had won a sensational victory over the Teutonic Knights at Tannenburg (known in Polish history as Grünewald) in 1410. This triumph was a significant co-operation between Poland and Lithuania, for in 1401 Wladislaw had transferred the latter to his cousin Witold (Table 131). In the documents of the period the Polish nobility, who for heraldic purposes were organized in clans with common arms, affiliated to themselves the families of the Lithuanian boyars. Forty-seven families were thus linked and solidarity between the two peoples was enhanced.

Two sons of Wladislaw II succeeded him (Table 134). Wladislaw III became briefly King of Hungary and was slain fighting the Turks at Varna; Casimir IV had already been Grand-Duke of Lithuania and by 1445 had reunited the two portions of his heritage. After a long war with the Teutonic knights, he imposed on them the Peace of Thorn (1466) by which Poland acquired Marienburg and Dantzig and access to the sea. In 1471 he was able to vindicate the claims of his son to the throne of Bohemia, to which the younger Wladislaw later added Hungary. During Casimir's reign the Polish assembly or *Sejm* steadily increased its powers. The nobility had negotiated this with Jagellon before he came to the throne; by the death of his grandson the monarchy was clearly seen to be elective. Nevertheless three sons were chosen in succession to Casimir IV, partly no doubt in tribute to the splendour of his reign; they were not all however the equals of their father. John Albrecht engaged in an elaborate but unprofitable attack upon the Turks in Bukovina. Alexander, who had been ruler of Lithuania, finally united the two in 1501, but conceded to the *Sejm* the famous privilege of *Nihil Novi*, prohibiting any change without their leave. Sigismund I, a handsome and devout prince, had a longer and more peaceful reign, during which the first wave of the Reformation reached Poland and began to undermine Catholic dominance. In 1525, when the Teutonic Order was secularized, Sigismund succeeded in demanding homage from the first Duke of Prussia (Chapter 23: Prussia); he was able to bring Mazovia, with its capital of Warsaw, under his direct rule on the death of the last Piast Duke (Table 131) in 1526. He was less successful in trying to create an efficient military system, each proposal being sabotaged by the independent spirit and hatred of taxation expressed by either nobility or gentry.

For the first part of the reign of Sigismund II Augustus, Calvinism spread widely in Poland; but from about 1565 the Counter-Reformation took over, and the Catholicism of the nation was re-established. Livonia was acquired, and in 1569 the Union of Lublin welded all provinces into an indissoluble entity, under an elected sovereign. When Sigismund II died, without issue, in 1572, the new realm was put to the test. The Jagellon dynasty had served Poland well, but without placing the country on a solid administrative foundation on which future kings could build. Poland was in fact a crowned republic, in which the king held too little control.

ROYAL ELECTIONS

Fifty thousand nobility and gentry gathered at Warsaw to choose a new king. Neighbouring candidates, such as John III of Sweden, were eschewed in favour of Henry of Valois, the best-loved son of the Queen of France (Tables 131 and 67). Scarcely crowned, Henry learned of his elder brother's death: promptly and furtively he returned to France. During the anarchy which followed, a Tartar horde devastated eastern Poland. The next choice was Stephen Bathory (Table 134), a Hungarian noble who had been Prince of Transylvania since 1571; a small body of Senators put forward the Emperor Maximilian II, who eased the situation by dying soon afterwards. Stephen proved an admirable king; tall, with a neat beard and heavy moustache, he acted vigorously to assert the royal power and to create an army equipped with artillery, but his reign was too short for his purposes to be fulfilled. Like all the elected Kings of Poland who followed and like Henry of Valois before him, he placed his personal arms on an escutcheon over the quartered shield of Poland and Lithuania.

Again there was an interregnum. This time the candidature of Sigismund, son of the King of Sweden, and nephew of Stephen Bathory's widow, prevailed over that of an Austrian archduke. The new King was pious and morose, an uncongenial ruler for the jovial, if lamentably short-sighted, Polish gentry. The *szlachta* showed increasing self-interest in declining to vote taxes and in establishing the disastrous principle of the *liberum veto* by which a single dissentient could block any proposal or end a sitting of the *Sejm*. In 1596 Sigismund established the Uniate Church, wherein a large body of his Orthodox subjects accepted the supremacy of Rome. But much of his reign was taken up with vain endeavours to establish his own succession to the throne of Sweden (Chapter 7); against this may be set his skill in evading Polish involvement in the destructive Thirty Years' War. His efforts at internal reform achieved little.

His son Wladislaw IV was elected without difficulty. He made some headway against Sweden, Russia, and Turkey but became involved in the turbulent affairs of the Cossacks on his southern frontier. Shortly after his sudden death they destroyed a Polish army. His brother, John II Casimir, was elected, though not without some rivalry from another brother, the Bishop of Wroclaw (Breslau). By 1651 he had suppressed the Cossacks; but Poland was soon invaded from the north by Sweden and from the east by Russia. In 1667 she had to cede to Russia the city of Kiev and all land east of the Dnieper. In 1668 the unhappy King resigned his crown and retired to France.

On this occasion the choice of the electors fell upon a native nobleman, Michael Wiśniowiecki, whose appearance suggested a Tartar ancestry. His arms (Table 131) were very Polish in character; there are many examples of crosses mounted on either crescents or horseshoes. They were placed over Poland and Lithuania once he became king. His father had been a famous warrior, but Michael was spineless. Against the increasing Turkish menace, the only military successes were gained by the Chief General, John Sobieski. At the next election in 1674 this great commander was preferred, after a brief contest, to Charles of Lorraine.

John III Sobieski was an enormous man with striking good looks, who varied heroism with indolence, altruism with impetuosity. He was devoted to his French wife, whom he had loved from a distance through her earlier marriage to a Zamoyski, and who undoubtedly spurred on his ambition. He had two basic aims, the repulse of the Ottoman Empire and the establishment of an hereditary monarchy in Poland. To a considerable extent he achieved the former by his great victory at Vienna in 1683, wrought in rare accord with his former rival, Charles

TABLE 133

POLAND
House of Piast (younger branch and House of Anjou)

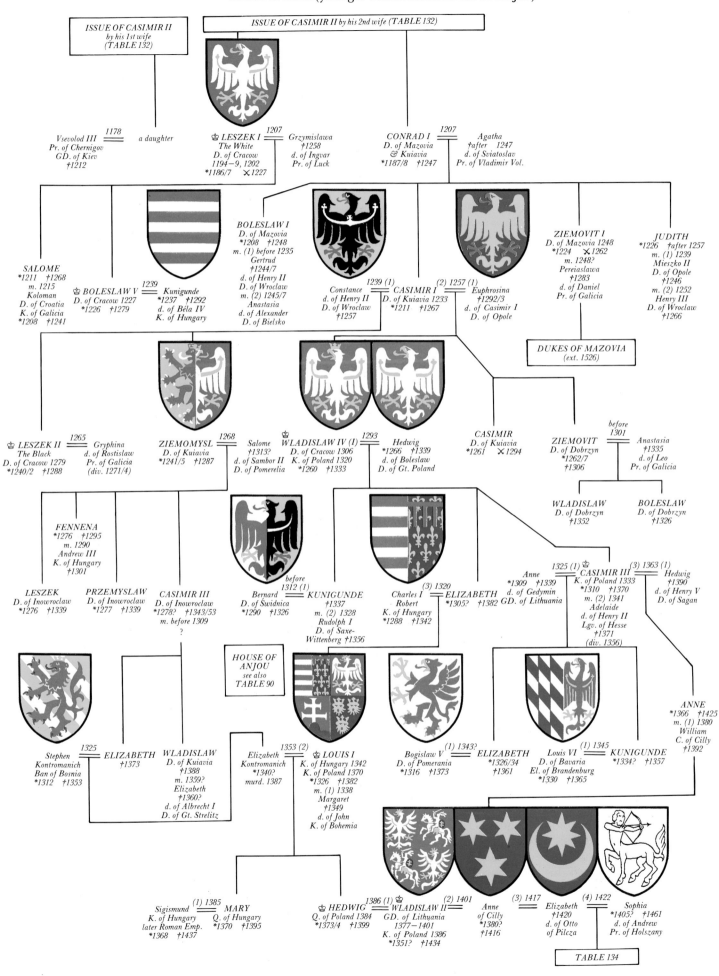

ISSUE OF CASIMIR II
by his 1st wife
(TABLE 132)

ISSUE OF CASIMIR II by his 2nd wife (TABLE 132)

Vsevolod III | 1178 | a daughter
Pr. of Chernigov
GD. of Kiev
†1212

♚ LESZEK I | 1207 | Grzymislawa
The White | †1258
D. of Cracow | d. of Ingvar
1194—9, 1202 | Pr. of Luck
*1186/7 ✕1227

CONRAD I | 1207 | Agatha
D. of Mazovia | †after 1247
& Kuiavia | d. of Sviatoslav
*1187/8 †1247 | Pr. of Vladimir Vol.

BOLESLAW I
D. of Mazovia
*1208 †1248
m. (1) before 1235
Gertrud
†1244/7
d. of Henry II
D. of Wroclaw
m. (2) 1245/7
Anastasia
d. of Alexander
D. of Bielsko

ZIEMOVIT I
D. of Mazovia 1248
*1224 ✕1262
m. 1248?
Pereiaslawa
†1283
d. of Daniel
Pr. of Galicia

JUDITH
*1226 †after 1257
m. (1) 1239
Mieszko II
D. of Opole
†1246
m. (2) 1252
Henry III
D. of Wroclaw
†1266

SALOME
*1211 †1268
m. 1215
Koloman
K. of Galicia
*1208 †1241

♚ BOLESLAW V | 1239 | Kunigunde
D. of Cracow 1227 | *1237 †1292
*1226 †1279 | d. of Béla IV
| K. of Hungary

Constance | 1239 (1) | CASIMIR I | (2) 1257 (1) | Euphrosina
d. of Henry II | | D. of Kuiavia 1233 | †1292/3
D. of Wroclaw | | *1211 †1267 | d. of Casimir I
†1257 | | | D. of Opole

DUKES OF MAZOVIA
(ext. 1526)

♚ LESZEK II | 1265 | Gryphina
The Black | d. of Rostislav
D. of Cracow 1279 | Pr. of Galicia
*1240/2 †1288 | (div. 1271/4)

ZIEMOMYSL | 1268 | Salome
D. of Kuiavia | †1313?
*1241/5 †1287 | d. of Sambor II
| D. of Pomerelia

♚ WLADISLAW IV (I) | 1293 | Hedwig
D. of Cracow 1306 | *1266 †1339
K. of Poland 1320 | d. of Boleslaw
*1260 †1333 | D. of Gt. Poland

CASIMIR | before 1301
D. of Kuiavia | ZIEMOVIT | Anastasia
*1261 ✕1294 | D. of Dobrzyn | †1335
| *1262/7 | d. of Leo
| †1306 | Pr. of Galicia

WLADISLAW
D. of Dobrzyn
†1352

BOLESLAW
D. of Dobrzyn
†1326

FENNENA
*1276 †1295
m. 1290
Andrew III
K. of Hungary
†1301

LESZEK
D. of Inowroclaw
*1276 †1339

PRZEMYSLAW
D. of Inowroclaw
*1277 †1339

CASIMIR III
D. of Inowroclaw
*1278? †1343/53
m. before 1309
?

Bernard | before 1312 (1) | KUNIGUNDE
D. of Świdnica | †1337
*1290 †1326 | m. (2) 1328
| Rudolph I
| D. of Saxe-
| Wittenberg †1356

Charles I | (3) 1320 | ELIZABETH
Robert | *1305? †1382
K. of Hungary |
*1288 †1342

Anne | 1325 (1) ♚ | CASIMIR III | (3) 1363 (1) | Hedwig
*1309 †1339 | | K. of Poland 1333 | †1390
d. of Gedymin | | *1310 †1370 | d. of Henry V
GD. of Lithuania | | m. (2) 1341 | D. of Sagan
	Adelaide
	d. of Henry II
	Lgv. of Hesse
	†1371
	(div. 1356)

HOUSE OF
ANJOU
see also
TABLE 90

ANNE
*1366 †1425
m. (1) 1380
William
C. of Cilly
†1392

Stephen | 1325 | ELIZABETH
Kontromanich | †1373
Ban of Bosnia |
*1312 †1353 |

WLADISLAW
D. of Kuiavia
†1388
m. 1359?
Elizabeth
†1360?
d. of Albrecht I
D. of Gt. Strelitz

Elizabeth
Kontromanich
*1340?
murd. 1387

LOUIS I | 1353 (2) ♚
K. of Hungary 1342
K. of Poland 1370
*1326 †1382
m. (1) 1338
Margaret
†1349
d. of John
K. of Bohemia

Bogislaw V | (1) 1343? | ELIZABETH
D. of Pomerania | *1326/34
*1316 †1373 | †1361

Louis VI | (1) 1345 | KUNIGUNDE
D. of Bavaria | *1334? †1357
El. of Brandenburg |
*1330 †1365 |

Sigismund | (1) 1385 | MARY
K. of Hungary | Q. of Hungary
later Roman Emp. | *1370 †1395
*1368 †1437

♚ HEDWIG | 1386 (1) ♚ | WLADISLAW II | (2) 1401 | Anne | (3) 1417 | Elizabeth | (4) 1422 | Sophia
Q. of Poland 1384 | | GD. of Lithuania | of Cilly | | †1420 | | *1405? †1461
*1373/4 †1399 | | 1377—1401 | *1380? | | d. of Otto | | d. of Andrew
| | K. of Poland 1386 | †1416 | | of Pilcza | | Pr. of Holszany
| | *1351? †1434 | | | | |

TABLE 134

TABLE 134

POLAND
House of Jagellon and House of Vasa

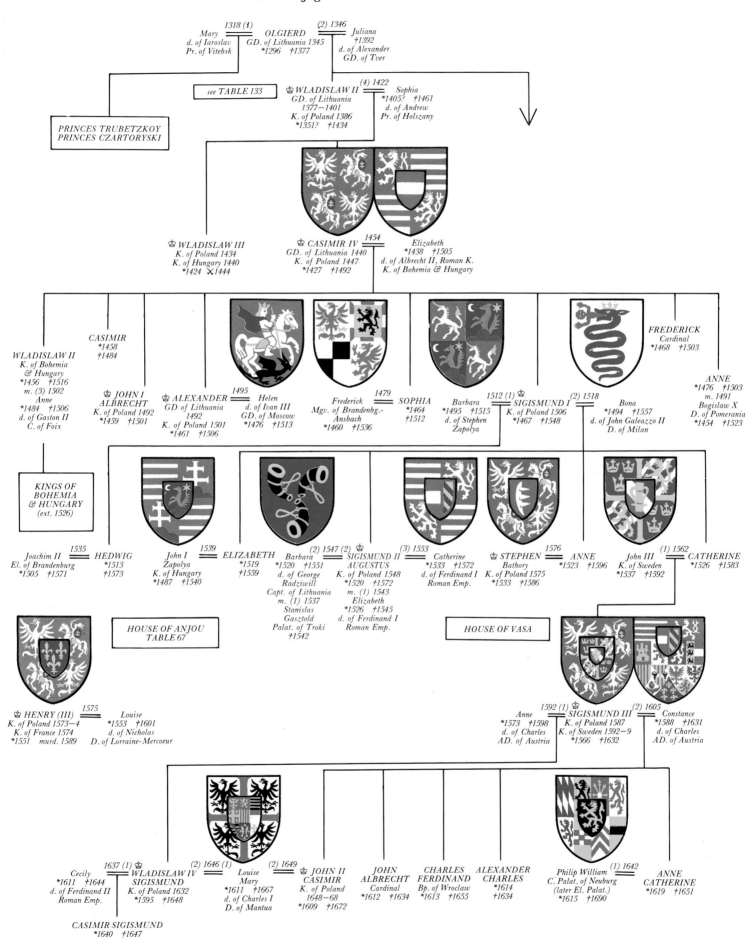

1318 (1) Mary
d. of Iaroslav
Pr. of Vitebsk

OLGIERD
GD. of Lithuania 1345
*1296 †1377

(2) 1346 Juliana
†1392
d. of Alexander
GD. of Tver

see TABLE 133

PRINCES TRUBETZKOY
PRINCES CZARTORYSKI

♔ WLADISLAW II
GD. of Lithuania
1377−1401
K. of Poland 1386
*1351? †1434

(4) 1422 Sophia
*1405? †1461
d. of Andrew
Pr. of Holszany

♔ WLADISLAW III
K. of Poland 1434
K. of Hungary 1440
*1424 ✕1444

♔ CASIMIR IV
GD. of Lithuania 1440
K. of Poland 1447
*1427 †1492

1454 Elizabeth
*1438 †1505
d. of Albrecht II, Roman K.
K. of Bohemia & Hungary

WLADISLAW II
K. of Bohemia
& Hungary
*1456 †1516
m. (3) 1502
Anne
*1484 †1506
d. of Gaston II
C. of Foix

CASIMIR
*1458
†1484

♔ JOHN I
ALBRECHT
K. of Poland 1492
*1459 †1501

♔ ALEXANDER
GD of Lithuania
1492
K. of Poland 1501
*1461 †1506

1495 Helen
d. of Ivan III
GD. of Moscow
*1476 †1513

Frederick
Mgv. of Brandenbg.-
Ansbach
*1460 †1536

1479 SOPHIA
*1464
†1512

Barbara
*1495 †1515
d. of Stephen
Zapolya

1512 (1) ♔ SIGISMUND I
K. of Poland 1506
*1467 †1548

(2) 1518 Bona
*1494 †1557
d. of John Galeazzo II
D. of Milan

FREDERICK
Cardinal
*1468 †1503

ANNE
*1476 †1503
m. 1491
Bogislaw X
D. of Pomerania
*1454 †1523

KINGS OF
BOHEMIA
& HUNGARY
(ext. 1526)

Joachim II
El. of Brandenburg
*1505 †1571

1535 HEDWIG
*1513
†1573

John I
Zapolya
K. of Hungary
*1487 †1540

1539 ELIZABETH
*1519
†1559

Barbara
*1520 †1551
d. of George
Radziwill
Capt. of Lithuania
m. (1) 1537
Stanislas
Gasztold
Palat. of Troki
†1542

(2) 1547 (2) ♔ SIGISMUND II
AUGUSTUS
K. of Poland 1548
*1520 †1572
m. (1) 1543
Elizabeth
*1526 †1545
d. of Ferdinand I
Roman Emp.

(3) 1553 Catherine
*1533 †1572
d. of Ferdinand I
Roman Emp.

1576 ♔ STEPHEN
Bathory
K. of Poland 1575
*1533 †1586

ANNE
*1523 †1596

John III
K. of Sweden
*1537 †1592

(1) 1562 CATHERINE
*1526 †1583

HOUSE OF ANJOU
TABLE 67

HOUSE OF VASA

♔ HENRY (III)
K. of Poland 1573−4
K. of France 1574
*1551 murd. 1589

1575 Louise
*1553 †1601
d. of Nicholas
D. of Lorraine-Mercoeur

Anne
*1573 †1598
d. of Charles
AD. of Austria

1592 (1) SIGISMUND III
K. of Poland 1587
K. of Sweden 1592−9
*1566 †1632

(2) 1605 Constance
*1588 †1631
d. of Charles
AD. of Austria

Cecily
*1611 †1644
d. of Ferdinand II
Roman Emp.

1637 (1) ♔ WLADISLAW IV
SIGISMUND
K. of Poland 1632
*1595 †1648

(2) 1646 (1) Louise
Mary
*1611 †1667
d. of Charles I
D. of Mantua

(2) 1649 ♔ JOHN II
CASIMIR
K. of Poland
1648−68
*1609 †1672

JOHN
ALBRECHT
Cardinal
*1612 †1634

CHARLES
FERDINAND
Bp. of Wroclaw
*1613 †1655

ALEXANDER
CHARLES
*1614
†1634

Philip William
C. Palat. of Neuburg
(later El. Palat.)
*1615 †1690

(1) 1642 ANNE
CATHERINE
*1619 †1651

CASIMIR SIGISMUND
*1640 †1647

of Lorraine (Chapter 20: first section); in the latter he failed to compass his ends. He found his son unsatisfactory and their relations were bad. By the time of his death, it can now be seen, the age of Polish greatness was emphatically over. The wide territories of the Jagellons had been eroded by Sweden, Prussia, Russia and Turkey. The corrupting and selfish power of the *szlachta* had vitiated the promise of medieval Poland as a European Power. The Sobieski blazon of a shield or buckler is derived from membership of the Janina clan; other families still existing today such as Kaszowski and Suchodolski have the same blazon, also with a red background.

Ten names were advanced after the death of John III, ranging from his own son to a nephew of the Pope. At a crucial moment the Elector Frederick Augustus of Saxony (Table 102) announced his conversion to Catholicism; he was elected in 1697. It cannot be pretended that Augustus II was a satisfactory king. Before and after his timely change of faith he was a lecher on a prodigious scale, a spendthrift, vain and ambitious only for himself (Chapter 26: Albertine Saxony). His profligate habits failed to endear him to his new subjects; his policies only brought them harm, not least by involving Poland in the wars between Russia and Sweden. In 1704, and in the face of Swedish attack, a group of Polish nobles repudiated Augustus II and elected Stanislas Leszczyński, the Palatine (or governor) of Poznan. In 1706 Augustus II was forced to resign and he did not recover the Polish throne until 1709, after the Russian defeat of Charles XII of Sweden at Poltava; from now on the Muscovite neighbour was a greater peril to Poland than Turk or Scandinavian. Before he died, it seems that Augustus was contemplating a plan to divide Poland; this was to prove a wicked political legacy for his adopted country.

Augustus III followed his father in Saxony and Poland and reigned for 30 years. He did not accede to Poland without difficulty, for Stanislas Leszczyński was again proclaimed in 1733; the situation was not resolved until 1735, when Stanislas retired from Poland and accepted the Duchy of Lorraine (Chapter 28: Lorraine), where he was able to realize his undoubted talents in the beautification of Nancy. Stanislas owed his comfortable exile to the marriage of his daughter to Louis XV of France. Augustus III was stout and idle; affairs in Saxony were left to the sycophant Count von Brühl, but in Poland the best positions and the greatest influence were in the hands of the Czartoryski family, sprung originally from the Grand-Dukes of Lithuania (Table 131). They had

ideas of constitutional reform, but met with opposition from the Potocki clan, who looked to Prussia rather than Moscow for assistance. Augustus died just at the end of the Seven Years' War, having taken refuge in Poland during that emergency.

Next year (1764) Stanislas II Poniatowski was elected king. He had three qualifications: he was kin to the potent Czartoryski family; he had been the lover of Catherine of Russia, and his modest qualities convinced the watchful and relentless Frederick of Prussia that chaos would continue in Poland. The black eagles were gathering to despoil the white. In 1772 they swooped; the Prussian and the Russian were followed more doubtfully by the Austrian. By the first partition Poland lost about twenty-five per cent of her territory. In 1788 a great revisionist movement began its work and a new constitution was produced in 1791. Royal power was increased; the *liberum veto* was abolished; the army grew in strength; but it was all too late. In 1793 Russian troops invaded, only to be followed by those of Prussia; each power seized a further large slice of Poland. Two years later, and with Austrian co-operation, the horrid process was completed and Poland ceased to exist. The King's nephew, Joseph Poniatowski, distinguished himself in battle and later became a Napoleonic marshal; a national rising led by Kosciuszko was ruthlessly smashed. Whatever the shortcomings of the Poles, the conduct of their neighbours was atrocious by any standards.

The later history of Poland is little concerned with dynasties. Napoleon established a short-lived and territorially meagre Grand-Duchy of Warsaw. After Waterloo the Russian Czar Alexander I had himself crowned in Warsaw, but his successors were less sympathetic. Only after the Prussian, Russian and Austrian empires had crumbled into defeat in 1918 was a new republic of Poland born into the twentieth century. Here again it had to face the opportunism of a German warlord, who had all too clearly studied the career of Frederick of Prussia.

The arms of the Kings of Poland, that is Poland quartered with Lithuania, are shown on Table 131 surrounded by the collar of the Order of the White Eagle, which was established by King Augustus II. The later elective kings all placed their family shield in pretence.

As has been mentioned above, the Catholic faith has long been the dominant religion of the Poles. This fact received a new emphasis with the election of Pope John Paul II in 1978, the first non-Italian Pope to occupy the Vatican since 1523.

Chapter 36

RUSSIA

The existence of Russia as a Great Power is of very recent date compared to most of the dynasties and realms which have already been discussed. The vast area of flattish land between the Crimea and the White Sea has an involved, if not long, history, and only came under one ruler as late as the eighteenth century. Much of this great space was settled by Slav peoples, though with a liberal mixture of Bulgars, Alans, Huns, and others, by the end of the tenth century. More than a hundred years before, a dynasty of 'Rus' under the semi-historical Rurik had settled at Novgorod, on Lake Volkhov. There is fairly wide agreement now that these Rus – who gave their name to the country – were Scandinavian adventurers, akin to the Varangians who penetrated to Constantinople. Igor, the son of Rurik, moved to Kiev.

A landmark in their history came in 988. Vladimir, Prince of Kiev, was dissatisfied with the religion of his forebears: he made careful enquiry into the faiths of the Arabs, the Jews, the Romans and the Christians of Constantinople. The splendour of the Byzantine liturgy enthralled him, and by a momentous decision he opted for the Orthodox Church. Given his somewhat lax sexual habits, his later canonization must be regarded as fortunate. From one of his many sons, Yaroslav I (Table 135), stem most of the later rulers of Russia. Little idea of unity prevailed among the princelings of this era, though the possession of Kiev gave a certain seniority. Vladimir Monomakh and Rostislav I were notable rulers of Kiev, but there were a great number of other lesser areas controlled by agnates of the House of Rurik who transferred to more important localities as they became vacant. Andrew I, Grand-Duke of Vladimir (Table 136), sacked Kiev and shifted the centre of gravity northwards to his own province, east of Moscow. Novgorod, an important commercial centre, Smolensk,

Halich (later Galicia), Ryazan and Chernigov were among the other more important lordships.

In the first half of the thirteenth century came the Tartar invasions which cut a great swathe across the south of Russia. Kiev was ravaged in 1240; two years later Batu Khan made his capital on the Volga: his successors were known as the Commanders of the Golden Horde, and levied tribute from the miscellaneous rulers of the House of Rurik, each of whom had to journey to Sarai to receive investiture. Only to the westward could Russia gain glory. Alexander Nevski, Prince of Novgorod (d. 1263), won two sensational battles, the first against the Swedes (1240) and the second on the frozen surface of Lake Peipus against the Teutonic knights. His youngest son, Daniel, founded the principality of Moscow; here, in 1325, the first Russian Metropolitan was to fix his see.

RISE OF MOSCOW

From this moment Moscow was of ever-increasing importance. Yuri (George) III contrived the murder of his cousin Michael (1318) and obtained from the Tartars the senior title of Grand-Duke (or Grand Prince) of Vladimir. His younger brother Ivan Kalita (of the Purse) became Grand Prince in 1328, but preferred to reign from Moscow and collect revenue from the other princes. Dimitri IV won a great battle against the Horde on the Don, and was thereafter known as Donskoi. The blow was not decisive, for the Golden Horde revived; but at this date the growing power of Lithuania on the west was a more serious threat to Russia, particularly after the union with Poland in 1386 (Chapter 35: Union with Lithuania). Basil I, Dimitri's son, married a Lithuanian princess; it is in his reign that a mounted figure first appears as the arms of the rulers of Moscow, which may easily be based on the arms of his wife. His grandson, Ivan

[269]

III, married a Byzantine princess; the horseman is now seen destroying a monster. Later generations were to associate this cavalier with St George and the dragon; but it is quite possible it is an importation from Constantinople of a much older iconographic motif of the emperor, as champion of Christianity, striking down evil.

Ivan III was a hunchback of evil appearance but he was the founder of Moscow's greatness. In 1478 he absorbed Novgorod; he extended his boundaries until they touched the Arctic and the Urals; he rejected the suzerainty of the Golden Horde; he adopted the title of gospodar or czar, a style hitherto applied by Slavs to the Emperor of the East. It is at this moment that the two-headed eagle begins to appear

as a Russian emblem. No doubt his marriage contributed to all this; if Constantinople had been the second Rome, a growing tradition was henceforward to claim Moscow as the third.

Basil III continued the work of his father, though his acquisitions of Pskov and Ryazan were less extensive. His court began to assume elements of grandeur; the nobility (the boyars) were consulted less than in former times when the prince had only been the first among equals. Since his first wife was childless, Basil secured a divorce which outraged the stricter ecclesiastics. From his second union came Ivan IV, known as the Terrible (Table 137), who was only three when his father died.

For a while the boyars reacted violently to the

[270]

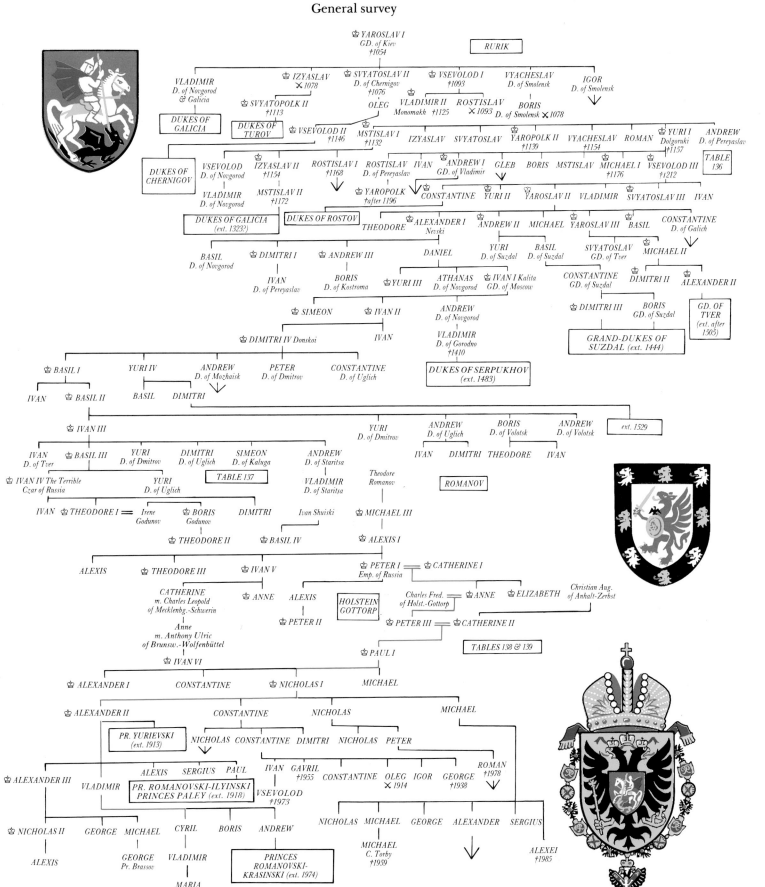

disappearance of authority. When Ivan came of age, he was formally crowned as czar – the first coronation in Russian history – and took up the family policy. Great areas in the Volga basin were annexed, including Kazan and Astrakhan. But the death of his first wife, who belonged to the Romanov family, and a serious illness seem to have warped his never stable character. He began a reign of terror and recruited a special corps of armed officials to carry out his savage decrees, the dreaded *Oprichnina* whose badge was a dog's head and a broom on their saddles. In 1581 he murdered his eldest son in a spasm of fury. It was in his reign that ships from England, seeking the Northwest Passage, first reached Russian ports. The Czar died, regretted by none, in 1584. His first marriage had been happy; but after the mysterious death of his third wife, he moved from one unsatisfactory alliance to another, despite the Orthodox custom only allowing three wives. He even solicited by proxy the hand of an English noblewoman, Lady Mary Hastings.

Theodore (Feodor) I suffered from rickets and an extreme addiction to religion. He came under the influence of his brother-in-law, Boris Godunov, who established the patriarchate of Moscow. He is also credited with establishing serfdom, but in fact he merely confirmed a long existing process, attaching the peasant to the soil. On Theodore's death Boris seemed the obvious successor, but his reign was unhappy and he could not control his fellow boyars. Moreover, rumours began to circulate that Dimitri, the half-brother of Theodore, who apparently perished in a brawl in 1591, was not dead. His reign is commemorated in the eponymous opera by Moussorgsky. When Boris died in 1605 his son Theodore II was soon killed and a false Dimitri (conceivably a natural son of Ivan IV) reigned for some months. But in 1606 he was overthrown in favour of Prince Basil Shuiski, a cadet of the House of Rurik, of insignificant appearance and small ability. The advent of another Dimitri drove Basil IV to abdicate; the principal sponsor of the pretender was Wladislaw, son of Sigismund III of Poland. From 1610 to 1612 the Poles controlled Moscow, but eventually a popular rising drove them out. In 1613 a national assembly was collected at the capital, and after some deliberation it chose Michael Romanov to be czar. The title czar is no more and no less than a Slavic form of the Latin *Caesar*.

THE HOUSE OF ROMANOV

The young ruler found his realm in sorry disarray. He made peace with Sweden and Poland and restored internal order; in the process the serfs were tied more closely to the estates of their owners. As an indication of his desire for firmer government, Michael III adopted the Byzantine title of autocrat. From 1618

until 1633 he shared the task of government with his father, Theodore, who had been forced into a monastery by Boris Godunov, and now, under his religious name of Philaret, was Patriarch of Moscow. Alexis I was unanimously elected on the death of Michael, and proved a sensible and normal ruler. His reign witnessed an influx of western advisers to give technical help and a great codification of the laws. Against this must be set a series of popular disorders, of which the most serious were a rising in 1670–71 in the Volga basin and a great schism in the Orthodox Church which led to the excommunication of the 'Old Believers'. After a war with Poland, Alexis added to his domains in 1667 a large part of Little Russia (or Ukraine), including the historic city of Kiev.

Before his death Alexis proclaimed his eldest surviving son, Theodore, as his heir, but the boy was puny and died aged twenty. After a brief crisis, Ivan V and his half-brother, Peter, were proclaimed joint sovereigns, with their sister Sophia as regent. Peter was exiled to a village, until at seventeen he staged a coup which disposed of the Regent and Ivan V. The new Czar was remarkable physically, for he was nearly 2.5m (8ft) and of enormous strength. He was scantily educated, delighted in carpentry and manual work, and possessed a dynamic will. Peter cared little for luxury but passionately believed in his country and its destiny, while lacking any talents for winning popularity. In 1697, after the death of his brother, he embarked on an unprecedented journey to western Europe, mainly to Holland and England, in order to inform himself about the civilization which Russia sorely needed.

For all his bouts of intoxication and his cruelty, his achievement was as titanic as his stature. Within the country he attacked the reactionary features of domestic life; the universal beard was prohibited, the seclusion of women and the wealth of the clergy diminished, even the alphabet was shorn of eight letters. He also had the foresight to begin the imperial collection of Russian archaeological remains. In every sphere the higher standards and techniques of Europe were introduced into a country still oriental in much of its lineage and habits. A minor reform was the appearance of a system of heraldry, though it was more personal than hereditary. Fuller organization only came under the Emperor Paul I (1796–1801). From the time of Ivan IV, the horseman arms of the Grand-Duchy of Moscow had been placed on a two-headed (Byzantine) eagle with a crown between the heads. Michael III increased the crowns to three, and Alexis I added an orb and sceptre to the eagle. But the blazons shown for his wife, and the wives of his sons (Table 137), were only granted to their respective families in the reign of Peter the Great. The personal

TABLE 136

RUSSIA
Grand-Dukes of Vladimir and Moscow (House of Rurik)

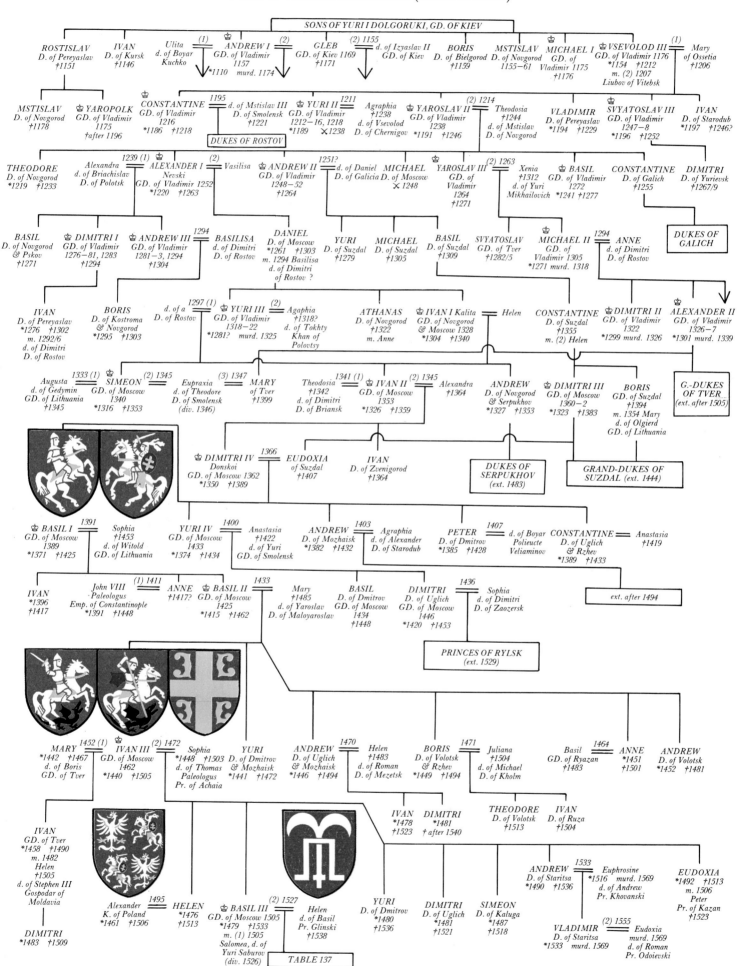

SONS OF YURI I DOLGORUKI, GD. OF KIEV

ROSTISLAV D. of Pereyaslav †1151

IVAN D. of Kursk †1146

Ulita d. of Boyar Kuchko — (1) — ANDREW I GD. of Vladimir 1157 *1110 murd. 1174 — (2) — GLEB GD. of Kiev 1169 †1171

(2) 1155 — d. of Izyaslav II GD. of Kiev

BORIS D. of Bielgorod †1159

MSTISLAV D. of Novgorod 1155–61

MICHAEL I GD. of Vladimir 1175 †1176

VSEVOLOD III GD. of Vladimir 1176 *1154 †1212 m. (2) 1207 Liubov of Vitebsk

(1) — Mary of Ossetia †1206

MSTISLAV D. of Novgorod †1178

YAROPOLK GD. of Vladimir 1175 †after 1196

CONSTANTINE GD. of Vladimir 1216 *1186 †1218 — 1195 — d. of Mstislav III D. of Smolensk †1221

YURI II GD. of Vladimir 1212–16, 1218 *1189 ✗1238 — 1211 — Agraphia †1238 d. of Vsevolod D. of Chernigov

YAROSLAV II GD. of Vladimir 1238 *1191 †1246 — (2) 1214 — Theodosia †1244 d. of Mstislav D. of Novgorod

VLADIMIR D. of Pereyaslav *1194 †1229

SVYATOSLAV III GD. of Vladimir 1247–8 *1196 †1252

IVAN D. of Starodub *1197 †1246?

DUKES OF ROSTOV

THEODORE D. of Novgorod *1219 †1233

Alexandra d. of Briachislav D. of Polotsk — 1239 (1) — ALEXANDER I Nevski GD. of Vladimir 1252 *1220 †1263 — (2) — Vasilisa

ANDREW II GD. of Vladimir 1248–52 †1264 — 1251? — d. of Daniel D. of Galicia

MICHAEL D. of Moscow ✗1248

YAROSLAV III GD. of Vladimir 1264 †1271 — (2) 1263 — Xenia †1312 d. of Yuri Mikhailovich

BASIL GD. of Vladimir 1272 *1241 †1277

CONSTANTINE D. of Galich †1255

DIMITRI D. of Yurievsk †1267/9

DUKES OF GALICH

BASIL D. of Novgorod & Pskov †1271

DIMITRI I GD. of Vladimir 1276–81, 1283 †1294

ANDREW III GD. of Vladimir 1281–3, 1294 †1304

BASILISA d. of Dimitri D. of Rostov — 1294

DANIEL D. of Moscow *1261 †1303 m. 1294 Basilisa d. of Dimitri of Rostov ?

YURI D. of Suzdal †1279

MICHAEL D. of Suzdal †1305

BASIL D. of Suzdal †1309

SVYATOSLAV GD. of Tver †1282/5

MICHAEL II GD. of Vladimir 1305 *1271 murd. 1318

ANNE d. of Dimitri D. of Rostov — 1294

ALEXANDER II GD. of Vladimir 1326–7 *1301 murd. 1339

IVAN D. of Pereyaslav *1276 †1302 m. 1292/6 d. of Dimitri D. of Rostov

BORIS D. of Kostroma & Novgorod *1295 †1303

d. of a D. of Rostov — 1297 (1) — YURI III GD. of Vladimir 1318–22 *1281? murd. 1325 — (2) — Agaphia †1318? d. of Tokhty Khan of Polovtsy

ATHANAS D. of Novgorod †1322 m. Anne

IVAN I Kalita GD. of Novgorod & Moscow 1328 *1304 †1340 — Helen

CONSTANTINE D. of Suzdal †1355 m. (2) Helen

DIMITRI II GD. of Vladimir 1322 *1299 murd. 1326

G.-DUKES OF TVER (ext. after 1505)

Augusta d. of Gedymin GD. of Lithuania †1345 — 1333 (1) — SIMEON GD. of Moscow 1340 *1316 †1353 — (2) 1345 — Eupraxia d. of Theodore D. of Smolensk (div. 1346) — (3) 1347 — MARY of Tver †1399

Theodosia †1342 d. of Dimitri D. of Briansk — 1341 (1) — IVAN II GD. of Moscow 1353 *1326 †1359 — (2) 1345 — Alexandra †1364

ANDREW D. of Novgorod & Serpukhov *1327 †1353

DIMITRI III GD. of Moscow 1360–2 *1323 †1383

BORIS GD. of Suzdal †1394 m. 1354 Mary d. of Olgierd GD. of Lithuania

DIMITRI IV Donskoi GD. of Moscow 1362 *1350 †1389 — 1366 — EUDOXIA of Suzdal †1407

IVAN D. of Zvenigorod †1364

DUKES OF SERPUKHOV (ext. 1483)

GRAND-DUKES OF SUZDAL (ext. 1444)

BASIL I GD. of Moscow 1389 *1371 †1425 — 1391 — Sophia †1453 d. of Witold GD. of Lithuania

YURI IV GD. of Moscow 1433 *1374 †1434 — 1400 — Anastasia †1422 d. of Yuri GD. of Smolensk

ANDREW D. of Mozhaisk *1382 †1432 — 1403 — Agraphia d. of Alexander D. of Starodub

PETER D. of Dmitrov *1385 †1428 — 1407 — d. of Boyar Polieucte Veliaminov

CONSTANTINE D. of Uglich & Rzhev *1389 †1433 — Anastasia †1419

IVAN *1396 †1417

John VIII Paleologus Emp. of Constantinople *1391 †1448 — (1) 1411 — ANNE †1417? — BASIL II GD. of Moscow 1425 *1415 †1462 — 1433

Mary †1485 d. of Yaroslav D. of Maloyaroslav

BASIL D. of Dmitrov GD. of Moscow 1434 †1448

DIMITRI D. of Uglich GD. of Moscow 1446 *1420 †1453 — 1436 — Sophia d. of Dimitri D. of Zaozersk

ext. after 1494

PRINCES OF RYLSK (ext. 1529)

MARY *1442 †1467 d. of Boris GD. of Tver — 1452 (1) — IVAN III GD. of Moscow 1462 *1440 †1505 — (2) 1472 — Sophia *1448 †1503 d. of Thomas Paleologus Pr. of Achaia

YURI D. of Dmitrov & Mozhaisk *1441 †1472

ANDREW D. of Uglich & Mozhaisk *1446 †1494 — 1470 — Helen †1483 d. of Roman D. of Mezetsk

BORIS D. of Volotsk & Rzhev *1449 †1494 — 1471 — Juliana †1504 d. of Michael D. of Kholm

Basil GD. of Ryazan †1483 — 1464 — ANNE *1451 †1501

ANDREW D. of Volotsk *1452 †1481

IVAN GD. of Tver *1458 †1490 m. 1482 Helen †1505 d. of Stephen III Gospodar of Moldavia

IVAN *1478 †1523

DIMITRI *1481 †after 1540

THEODORE D. of Volotsk †1513

IVAN D. of Ruza †1504

ANDREW D. of Staritsa *1490 †1536 — 1533 — Euphrosine *1516 murd. 1569 d. of Andrew Pr. Khovanski

EUDOXIA *1492 †1513 m. 1506 Peter Pr. of Kazan †1523

Alexander K. of Poland *1461 †1506 — 1495 — HELEN *1476 †1513

BASIL III GD. of Moscow 1505 *1479 †1533 m. (1) 1505 Salomea, d. of Yuri Saburov (div. 1526) — (2) 1527 — Helen d. of Basil Pr. Glinski †1538

YURI D. of Dmitrov *1480 †1536

DIMITRI D. of Uglich *1481 †1521

SIMEON D. of Kaluga *1487 †1518

VLADIMIR D. of Staritsa *1533 murd. 1569 — (2) 1555 — Eudoxia murd. 1569 d. of Roman Pr. Odoievski

DIMITRI *1483 †1509

TABLE 137

TABLE 137

RUSSIA
Accession of the House of Romanov

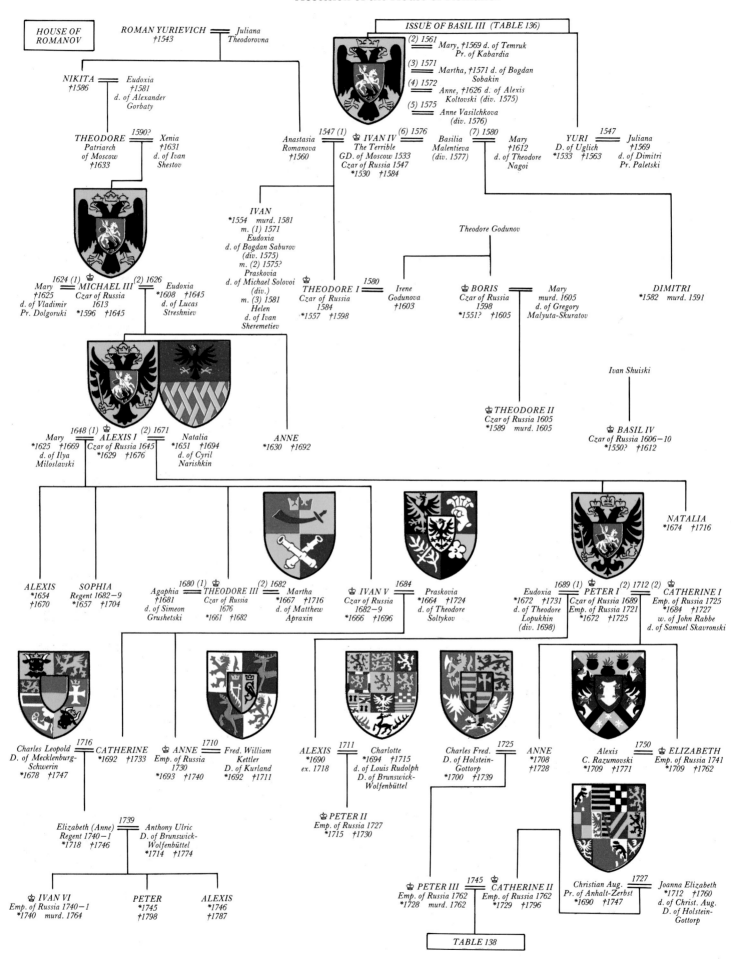

HOUSE OF ROMANOV

ROMAN YURIEVICH †1543 = Juliana Theodorovna

ISSUE OF BASIL III (TABLE 136)

NIKITA †1586 = Eudoxia †1581 d. of Alexander Gorbaty

(2) 1561 — Mary, †1569 d. of Temruk Pr. of Kabardia
(3) 1571 — Martha, †1571 d. of Bogdan Sobakin
(4) 1572 — Anne, †1626 d. of Alexis Koltovski (div. 1575)
(5) 1575 — Anne Vasilchkova (div. 1576)

THEODORE Patriarch of Moscow †1633 — 1590? Xenia †1631 d. of Ivan Shestov

Anastasia Romanova †1560 — 1547 (1) IVAN IV The Terrible GD. of Moscow 1533 Czar of Russia 1547 *1530 †1584 — (6) 1576 Basilia Malentieva (div. 1577) — (7) 1580 Mary †1612 d. of Theodore Nagoi

YURI D. of Uglich *1533 †1563 — 1547 Juliana †1569 d. of Dimitri Pr. Paletski

IVAN *1554 murd. 1581 m. (1) 1571 Eudoxia d. of Bogdan Saburov (div. 1575) m. (2) 1575? Praskovia d. of Michael Solovoi (div.) m. (3) 1581 Helen d. of Ivan Sheremetiev

Theodore Godunov

Mary †1625 d. of Vladimir Pr. Dolgoruki — 1624 (1) MICHAEL III Czar of Russia 1613 *1596 †1645 — (2) 1626 Eudoxia *1608 †1645 d. of Lucas Streshniev

THEODORE I Czar of Russia 1584 *1557 †1598 — 1580 Irene Godunova †1603

BORIS Czar of Russia 1598 *1551? †1605 — Mary murd. 1605 d. of Gregory Malyuta-Skuratov

DIMITRI *1582 murd. 1591

Ivan Shuiski

Mary *1625 †1669 d. of Ilya Miloslavski — 1648 (1) ALEXIS I Czar of Russia 1645 *1629 †1676 — (2) 1671 Natalia *1651 †1694 d. of Cyril Narishkin

ANNE *1630 †1692

THEODORE II Czar of Russia 1605 *1589 murd. 1605

BASIL IV Czar of Russia 1606–10 *1550? †1612

ALEXIS *1654 †1670

SOPHIA Regent 1682–9 *1657 †1704

Agaphia †1681 d. of Simeon Grushetski — 1680 (1) THEODORE III Czar of Russia 1676 *1661 †1682 — (2) 1682 Martha *1667 †1716 d. of Matthew Apraxin

IVAN V Czar of Russia 1682–9 *1666 †1696 — 1684 Praskovia *1664 †1724 d. of Theodore Soltykov

Eudoxia *1672 †1731 d. of Theodore Lopukhin (div. 1698) — 1689 (1) PETER I Czar of Russia 1689 Emp. of Russia 1721 *1672 †1725 — (2) 1712 (2) CATHERINE I Emp. of Russia 1725 *1684 †1727 w. of John Rabbe d. of Samuel Skavronski

NATALIA *1674 †1716

Charles Leopold D. of Mecklenburg-Schwerin *1678 †1747 — 1716 CATHERINE *1692 †1733

ANNE Emp. of Russia 1730 *1693 †1740 — 1710 Fred. William Kettler D. of Kurland *1692 †1711

ALEXIS *1690 ex. 1718 — 1711 Charlotte *1694 †1715 d. of Louis Rudolph D. of Brunswick-Wolfenbüttel

Charles Fred. D. of Holstein-Gottorp *1700 †1739 — 1725 ANNE *1708 †1728

Alexis C. Razumovski *1709 †1771 — 1750 ELIZABETH Emp. of Russia 1741 *1709 †1762

Elizabeth (Anne) Regent 1740–1 *1718 †1746 — 1739 Anthony Ulric D. of Brunswick-Wolfenbüttel *1714 †1774

PETER II Emp. of Russia 1727 *1715 †1730

IVAN VI Emp. of Russia 1740–1 *1740 murd. 1764

PETER *1745 †1798

ALEXIS *1746 †1787

PETER III Emp. of Russia 1762 *1728 murd. 1762 — 1745 CATHERINE II Emp. of Russia 1762 *1729 †1796

Christian Aug. Pr. of Anhalt-Zerbst *1690 †1747 — 1727 Joanna Elizabeth *1712 †1760 d. of Christ. Aug. D. of Holstein-Gottorp

TABLE 138

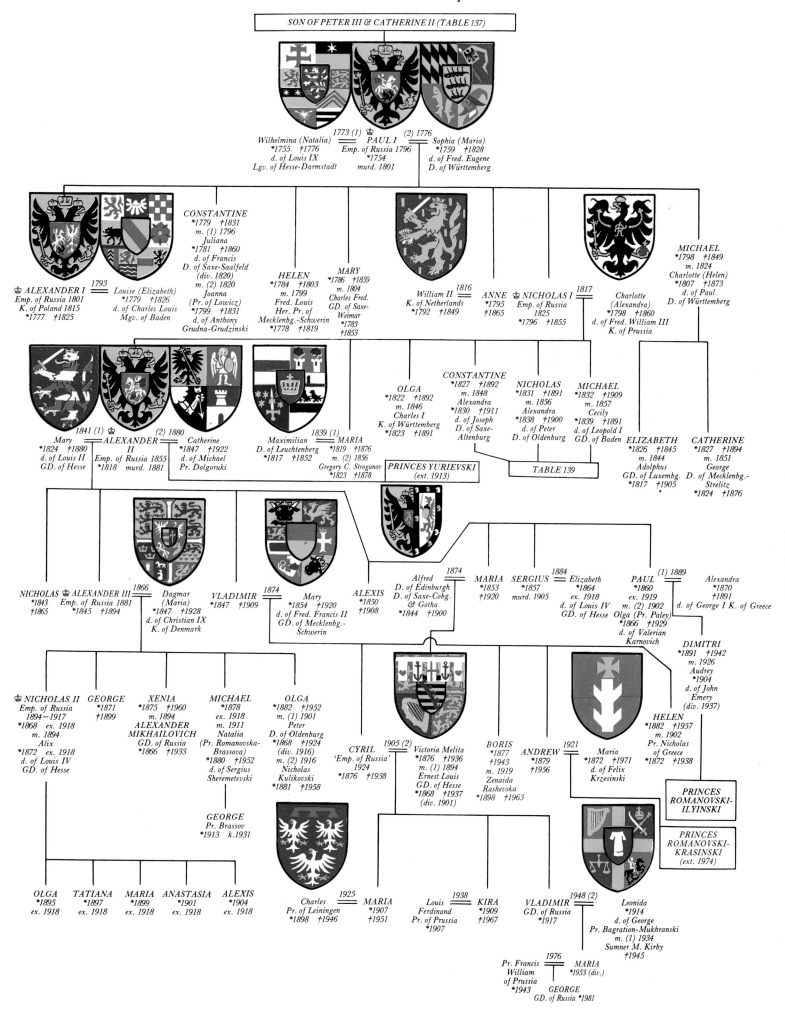

SON OF PETER III & CATHERINE II (TABLE 137)

Wilhelmina (Natalia) *1755 †1776 d. of Louis IX Lgv. of Hesse-Darmstadt — 1773 (1) — PAUL I Emp. of Russia 1796 *1754 murd. 1801 — (2) 1776 — Sophia (Maria) *1759 †1828 d. of Fred. Eugene D. of Württemberg

CONSTANTINE *1779 †1831 m. (1) 1796 Juliana *1781 †1860 d. of Francis D. of Saxe-Saalfeld (div. 1820) m. (2) 1820 Joanna (Pr. of Lowicz) *1799 †1831 d. of Anthony Grudna-Grudzinski

ALEXANDER I Emp. of Russia 1801 K. of Poland 1815 *1777 †1825 — 1793 — Louise (Elizabeth) *1779 †1826 d. of Charles Louis Mgv. of Baden

HELEN *1784 †1803 m. 1799 Fred. Louis Her. Pr. of Mecklenbg.-Schwerin *1778 †1819

MARY *1786 †1859 m. 1804 Charles Fred. GD. of Saxe-Weimar *1783 †1853

William II K. of Netherlands *1792 †1849 — 1816 — ANNE *1795 †1865

NICHOLAS I Emp. of Russia 1825 *1796 †1855 — 1817 — Charlotte (Alexandra) *1798 †1860 d. of Fred. William III K. of Prussia

MICHAEL *1798 †1849 m. 1824 Charlotte (Helen) *1807 †1873 d. of Paul D. of Württemberg

Mary *1824 †1880 d. of Louis II GD. of Hesse — 1841 (1) — ALEXANDER II Emp. of Russia 1855 *1818 murd. 1881 — (2) 1880 — Catherine *1847 †1922 d. of Michael Pr. Dolgoruki

Maximilian D. of Leuchtenberg *1817 †1852 — 1839 (1) — MARIA *1819 †1876 m. (2) 1856 Gregory C. Stroganov *1823 †1878

PRINCES YURIEVSKI (ext. 1913)

OLGA *1822 †1892 m. 1846 Charles I K. of Württemberg *1823 †1891

CONSTANTINE *1827 †1892 m. 1848 Alexandra *1830 †1911 d. of Joseph D. of Saxe-Altenburg

NICHOLAS *1831 †1891 m. 1856 Alexandra *1838 †1900 d. of Peter D. of Oldenburg

MICHAEL *1832 †1909 m. 1857 Cecily *1839 †1891 d. of Leopold I GD. of Baden

TABLE 139

ELIZABETH *1826 †1845 m. 1844 Adolphus GD. of Luxembg. *1817 †1905

CATHERINE *1827 †1894 m. 1851 George D. of Mecklenbg.-Strelitz *1824 †1876

NICHOLAS *1843 †1865

ALEXANDER III Emp. of Russia 1881 *1845 †1894 — 1866 — Dagmar (Maria) *1847 †1928 d. of Christian IX K. of Denmark

VLADIMIR *1847 †1909 — 1874 — Mary *1854 †1920 d. of Fred. Francis II GD. of Mecklenbg.-Schwerin

ALEXIS *1850 †1908

Alfred D. of Edinburgh D. of Saxe-Cobg. & Gotha — 1874 — MARIA *1853 †1920

SERGIUS *1857 murd. 1905 — 1884 — Elizabeth ex. 1918 d. of Louis IV GD. of Hesse

PAUL *1860 †1919 m. (2) 1902 Olga (Pr. Paley) *1866 †1929 d. of Valerian Karnovich — (1) 1889 — Alexandra *1870 †1891 d. of George I K. of Greece

NICHOLAS II Emp. of Russia 1894–1917 *1868 ex. 1918 m. 1894 Alix *1872 ex. 1918 d. of Louis IV GD. of Hesse

GEORGE *1871 †1899

XENIA *1875 †1960 m. 1894 ALEXANDER MIKHAILOVICH GD. of Russia *1866 †1933

MICHAEL *1878 ex. 1918 m. 1911 Natalia (Pr. Romanovska-Brassova) *1880 †1952

OLGA *1882 †1952 m. (1) 1901 Peter D. of Oldenburg *1868 †1924 (div. 1916) m. (2) 1916 Nicholas Kulikovski *1881 †1958

CYRIL 'Emp. of Russia' 1924 *1876 †1938 — 1905 (2) — Victoria Melita *1876 †1936 m. (1) 1894 Ernest Louis GD. of Hesse *1868 †1937 (div. 1901)

BORIS *1877 †1943 m. 1919 Zenaida Rashevska *1898 †1963

ANDREW *1879 †1956 — 1921 — Maria *1872 †1971 d. of Felix Krzesinski

DIMITRI *1891 †1942 m. 1926 Audrey *1904 d. of John Emery (div. 1937)

HELEN *1882 †1957 m. 1902 Pr. Nicholas of Greece *1872 †1938

PRINCES ROMANOVSKI-ILYINSKI

PRINCES ROMANOVSKI-KRASINSKI (ext. 1974)

GEORGE Pr. Brassov *1913 k.1931

OLGA *1895 ex. 1918

TATIANA *1897 ex. 1918

MARIA *1899 ex. 1918

ANASTASIA *1901 ex. 1918

ALEXIS *1904 ex. 1918

Charles Pr. of Leiningen *1898 †1946 — 1925 — MARIA *1907 †1951

Louis Ferdinand Pr. of Prussia *1907 — 1938 — KIRA *1909 †1967

VLADIMIR GD. of Russia *1917 — 1948 (2) — Leonida *1914 d. of George Pr. Bagration-Mukhranski m. (1) 1934 Sumner M. Kirby †1945

Pr. Francis William of Prussia *1943 — 1976 — MARIA *1953 (div.)

GEORGE GD. of Russia *1981

arms of the Romanov family can be seen on Table 135 and show a griffin with sword and shield within a black border charged with gold and silver lions' heads. In 1698 Peter founded the Order of St Andrew, whose insignia surround the Russian eagle (Table 135). In 1721 he adopted the western title of emperor in addition to that of czar. It may be doubted whether the average boyar regarded a blazon as compensation for his beard.

His travels had impressed on Peter the need for an outlet to the sea. In 1709 his army destroyed that of Charles XII at Poltava and broke the myth of Swedish invincibility; but already in 1703 the Emperor had founded his new capital of St Petersburg. Not only did this barren site amid the lakes and pine forests burgeon into a romantically beautiful city, it was a symbol of Peter's westward vision. By the time of his death, this truly remarkable man had provided Russia with a civil administration, an army, a navy and a sea on which his fleet could sail. The ancestry of Peter the Great, which is displayed on Table 140, reveals that he was of pure Russian stock. This is in marked contrast to the ascending pedigrees of most of his descendants, where German blood tends to predominate.

Peter had taken powers to nominate his own successor, but did not exercise them. In consequence he was followed arbitrarily by his widow, his grandson, his niece and his daughter. None of them proved an outstanding ruler; too much influence came to rest in the hands of the Guard regiments, which often determined the succession. Peter himself had condemned to a cruel death his only son, for participating in a conspiracy; he had also divorced his first wife. Catherine I, the daughter of a Lithuanian peasant, became the mistress of two of Peter's generals and was passed on to their sovereign who eventually married her. At the end of his life only she could control his formidable outbursts of rage; as a ruler she was brief, frivolous and extravagant. At her demise the claims of Peter II could no longer be overlooked, but the hapless prince died of smallpox on what should have been his wedding day. A group of nobles now offered the Crown to Anne, Duchess of Kurland, daughter of Ivan V, on condition that she accepted the governance of a Grand Council and moved the capital back to Moscow. Anne accepted the condition, but annulled it as soon as she was firmly on the throne. She was an autocratic and unpleasant sovereign, resenting her long, dull years at Kurland; so frail had been her father that doubts were widely expressed as to her share of Romanov blood. The port of Azov on the Black Sea was captured during her reign.

Anne did appoint an heir, her great-nephew Ivan VI, whose major handicap was his age of two months. The prospect of a regency by his mother alarmed many, including the surviving daughter of Peter the Great. Elizabeth, though not born in wedlock, was an obvious rival to Ivan VI and was likely to be sent to a nunnery. Throwing herself on the mercy of the Preobrazhenski Guards (named from the village of her father's exile), she was swiftly raised to the throne in 1741. Her German cousins were all imprisoned, some of them for very long periods. Indeed it was under Elizabeth that French became to a large extent the court language of Russia.

The Empress was pretty, with a good figure, and a great taste for music and dancing. After other liaisons she made a morganatic marriage with Count Alexis Razumovski. As her heir she called to Russia the only remaining descendant of Peter the Great, the orphan child of her sister, had him converted to the Orthodox faith, and styled him Grand-Duke Peter. He was then married to his second cousin Sophie of Anhalt-Zerbst, who at her Orthodox baptism was named Catherine. Peter was short, ill-educated and said to look like a monkey; his intellect was limited, his morals loose and his main passion was the drilling of soldiers. Catherine was good-looking, well-read and an excellent judge of men; she never pretended to care for Peter, and some uncertainty hangs over the origin of her son Paul, born after nine years of wedlock.

CATHERINE THE GREAT

Peter III cherished a childlike adulation of Frederick the Great of Prussia; his first act was to throw away the Russian position in the Seven Years' War – its first European conflict – by offering Prussia an easy peace. He then freed the nobility of their duty to perform service under the Crown. Only six months after his accession another revolution of the palace guards proclaimed Catherine Empress and Peter deposed; he perished a few weeks later in custody, after a drunken brawl. Thus began the extraordinary reign of this obscure German princess, which lasted 34 years. In a sense she was haunted, if not by the fate of her husband, at least by the insecurity of her position. Her son was alive; so was Ivan VI in his fortress; she was enchained by her debt to the guards and to the gentry who officered them. Thus she could not give full play to her lively intelligence and liberal views; she ranks among the enlightened despots of her generation, but in Russia the stress was as much on despotism as on enlightenment. She was sensual but frugal; her acknowledged lovers were mostly of a large stature, and were not few in number.

Great territorial accessions marked her reign through the annexation of the Crimea (1783) and the partitions of Poland (Chapter 35). South Russia was reorganized by Prince Potemkin, one of her favourites. A Black Sea fleet was formed: the port of

Sevastopol was founded. Meanwhile the administration of the Empire was refashioned; the ten provinces of Peter I were broken down to 50 provincial governments. In her old age the Empress, perhaps forgetful of her own accession, was profoundly shocked by the decapitation of Louis XVI of France. In all, she was probably not an originator, but a talented controller of the course of events.

Paul I (Table 138) had waited a long time in the wings; his brief appearance was dramatic. His wayward fancy fastened upon Napoleon much the same admiration as his father had bestowed upon Frederick. Many of his mother's acts were reversed; but in 1797 he prudently established succession by primogeniture. In 1798 he was elected Grand-Master of the Order of St John by some knights evicted from Malta. But his behaviour was unstable and capricious, his cruelty all too apparent. In 1801 a number of conspirators entered the palace, perhaps seeking only his abdication, and strangled him.

Alexander I at once cancelled many of his father's more oppressive edicts, such as the bans on foreign travel and foreign books. He had been educated under the direction of his grandmother and was sympathetic to reform. The political horizon abroad was dominated by the rise of Napoleon, but at home the new Emperor embarked on a considerable programme of education and also tried to check the sale of serfs. In 1805 he was defeated by Napoleon at Austerlitz, and again in 1807 at Eylau and Friedland; he then came to terms with Napoleon at Tilsit. At the same time he completed the conquest of Finland from Sweden, and shortly afterwards won Bessarabia from the Turks; to gratify the Finns he adopted the title of Grand-Duke of Finland. Meanwhile his relations with France deteriorated; in 1812 Napoleon launched his great attack on Russia. The eminent general Kutuzov held Napoleon at Borodino, but was obliged to abandon Moscow, which Napoleon occupied for a mere month. The horrors of the French retreat through an early winter are notorious. In 1813 Russia and Prussia defeated Bonaparte at Leipzig. The negotiations at Vienna were briefly interrupted by the Hundred Days and Waterloo, but then continued to remodel Europe.

Alexander saw himself as the saviour of Europe; he went on to envisage a league of Austria, Prussia and Russia, the three Powers which dominated eastern Europe. This 'Holy Alliance' soon proved to be reactionary and to be dominated by Metternich, the principal statesman of the Hapsburg Empire; against it was set the liberalism of the West in Europe and America associated with the name of Canning. The domestic policy of Alexander, after Waterloo, made few concessions to reform but did encourage some commercial revival after the wreckage of the wars.

Catherine the Great of Russia (1729–96) with her husband Peter III, whom she deposed, and her child, the future Paul I, by R. Mathieu, 1756.

On the whole he became more autocratic as he grew older; but his subjects, who had travelled in the West, were increasingly interested in the problems of liberty and began to form secret societies.

On the death of Alexander I his next brother, Constantine, because he had made a morganatic marriage, renounced the succession. The Crown passed to Nicholas I, not without a period of confusion; he had been trained as a soldier, and was regarded as a natural conservative. Not much was done to dispel this image. A rebellion in Poland was harshly suppressed in 1831, and the very use of the Polish

TABLE 139

RUSSIA
The Imperial House and the Revolution

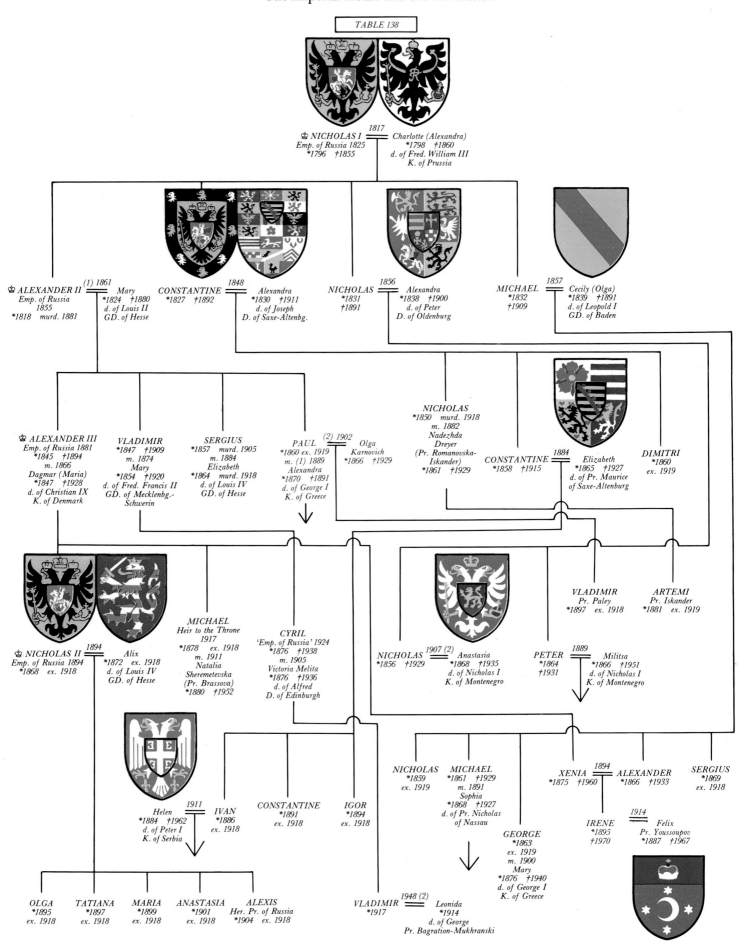

TABLE 138

♔ NICHOLAS I ══ 1817 Charlotte (Alexandra)
Emp. of Russia 1825 *1798 †1860
*1796 †1855 d. of Fred. William III
K. of Prussia

♔ ALEXANDER II ══ (1) 1861 Mary   CONSTANTINE ══ 1848 Alexandra   NICHOLAS ══ 1856 Alexandra   MICHAEL ══ 1857 Cecily (Olga)
Emp. of Russia *1824 †1880   *1827 †1892   *1830 †1911   *1831   *1838 †1900   *1832   *1839 †1891
1855   d. of Louis II   d. of Joseph   †1891   d. of Peter   †1909   d. of Leopold I
*1818 murd. 1881   GD. of Hesse   D. of Saxe-Altenbg.   D. of Oldenburg   GD. of Baden

NICHOLAS
*1850 murd. 1918
m. 1882
Nadezhda
Dreyer
(Pr. Romanovska-
Iskander)
*1861 †1929

♔ ALEXANDER III   VLADIMIR   SERGIUS   PAUL ══ (2) 1902 Olga   CONSTANTINE ══ 1884 Elizabeth   DIMITRI
Emp. of Russia 1881   *1847 †1909   *1857 murd. 1905   *1860 ex. 1919   Karnovich   *1858 †1915   *1865 †1927   *1860
*1845 †1894   m. 1874   m. 1884   m. (1) 1889   *1866 †1929   d. of Pr. Maurice   ex. 1919
m. 1866   Mary   Elizabeth   Alexandra   of Saxe-Altenburg
Dagmar (Maria)   *1854 †1920   *1864 murd. 1918   *1870 †1891
*1847 †1928   d. of Fred. Francis II   d. of Louis IV   d. of George I
d. of Christian IX   GD. of Mecklenbg.-   GD. of Hesse   K. of Greece
K. of Denmark   Schwerin

♔ NICHOLAS II ══ 1894 Alix   MICHAEL   CYRIL   NICHOLAS ══ 1907 (2) Anastasia   PETER ══ 1889 Militsa   VLADIMIR   ARTEMI
Emp. of Russia 1894   *1872 ex. 1918   Heir to the Throne   'Emp. of Russia' 1924   *1856 †1929   *1868 †1935   *1864   *1866 †1951   Pr. Paley   Pr. Iskander
*1868 ex. 1918   d. of Louis IV   1917   *1876 †1938   d. of Nicholas I   †1931   d. of Nicholas I   *1897 ex. 1918   *1881 ex. 1919
      GD. of Hesse   *1878 ex. 1918   m. 1905   K. of Montenegro   K. of Montenegro
                     m. 1911   Victoria Melita
                     Natalia   *1876 †1936
                     Sheremetevska   d. of Alfred
                     (Pr. Brassova)   D. of Edinburgh
                     *1880 †1952

Helen ══ 1911 IVAN   CONSTANTINE   IGOR   NICHOLAS   MICHAEL   XENIA ══ 1894 ALEXANDER   SERGIUS
*1884 †1962   *1886   *1891   *1894   *1859   *1861 †1929   *1875 †1960   *1866 †1933   *1869
d. of Peter I   ex. 1918   ex. 1918   ex. 1918   ex. 1919   m. 1891   ex. 1918
K. of Serbia   Sophia
                            *1868 †1927
                            d. of Pr. Nicholas
                            of Nassau

IRENE ══ 1914 Felix
*1895   Pr. Youssoupov
†1970   *1887 †1967

GEORGE
*1863
ex. 1919
m. 1900
Mary
*1876 †1940
d. of George I
K. of Greece

OLGA   TATIANA   MARIA   ANASTASIA   ALEXIS   VLADIMIR ══ 1948 (2) Leonida
*1895   *1897   *1899   *1901   Her. Pr. of Russia   *1917   *1914
ex. 1918   ex. 1918   ex. 1918   ex. 1918   *1904 ex. 1918   d. of George
                                  Pr. Bagration-Mukhranski

TABLE 140

RUSSIA
Ancestors of Peter I, Alexander I and Nicholas II

THEODORE
Patriarch of Moscow
†1633

1590?

XENIA
†1631
d. of Ivan
Shestov

LUCAS
Streshniev
†1650

ANNE
d. of Constantine
Volkonski

PULUKHT
Narishkin
†1634

?

LEONTI
Leontiev

PRASKOVIA
d. of Ivan
Rayevski
†1641

♛ *MICHAEL III*
Czar of Russia
*1596 †1645

(2) 1626

EUDOXIA
Streshniev
*1608 †1645

CYRIL
Narishkin
*1623 †1691

?

ANNE
Leontiev
†1706

♛ *ALEXIS I*
Czar of Russia
*1629 †1676

(2) 1671

NATALIA
Narishkin
*1651 †1694

♛ *PETER I*
Emp. of Russia
*1672 †1725

CHARLES FRED.
D. of Holstein-Gottorp
*1700 †1739

1725

ANNE
*1708 †1728
d. of Peter I
Emp. of Russia

CHRISTIAN AUG.
Pr. of Anhalt-
Zerbst
*1690 †1747

1727

JOANNA
*1712 †1760
d. of Christ. Aug.
D. of Holstein-
Gottorp

*CHARLES I
ALEXANDER*
D. of Württemberg
*1684 †1737

1727

MARY AUGUSTA
d. of Anselm Francis
Pr. of Thurn & Taxis
*1706 †1756

*FRED.
WILLIAM*
Mgv. of Brandenbg.-
Schwedt
*1700 †1771

1734

SOPHIA
*1719 †1765
d. of Fred. William I
K. in Prussia

♛ *PETER III*
Emp. of Russia
*1728 murd. 1762

1745

♛ *CATHERINE II*
Emp. of Russia
*1729 †1796

FREDERICK EUGENE
D. of Württemberg
*1732 †1797

1753

DOROTHEA
Pr. of Brandenbg.-Schwedt
*1736 †1798

♛ *PAUL I*
Emp. of Russia
*1754 murd. 1801

(2) 1776

SOPHIA (MARIA)
Pr. of Württemberg
*1759 †1828

♛ *ALEXANDER I*
Emp. of Russia
*1777 †1825

♛ *NICHOLAS I*
Emp. of Russia
*1796 †1855

1817

*CHARLOTTE
(ALEXANDRA)*
*1798 †1860
d. of Fred. William III
K. of Prussia

LOUIS II
GD. of Hesse
& the Rhine
*1777 †1848

1804

WILHELMINA
*1788 †1836
d. of Charles Louis
Her. Pr. of Baden

WILLIAM
D. of Holstein-
Sonderburg-
Glücksburg
*1785 †1831

1810

LOUISE
*1789 †1867
d. of Charles
Lgv. of Hesse-
Cassel

WILLIAM
Lgv. of Hesse-
Cassel-
Rumpenheim
*1787 †1867

1810

CHARLOTTE
*1789 †1864
d. of Frederick
Her. Pr. of Denmark

♛ *ALEXANDER II*
Emp. of Russia
*1818 murd. 1881

(1) 1841

MARY
Pr. of Hesse
*1824 †1880

CHRISTIAN IX
K. of Denmark
*1818 †1906

1842

LOUISE
Pr. of Hesse-Cassel
*1817 †1898

♛ *ALEXANDER III*
Emp. of Russia
*1845 †1894

1866

DAGMAR (MARIA)
Pr. of Denmark
*1847 †1928

♛ *NICHOLAS II*
Emp. of Russia
*1868 ex. 1918

language was forbidden. In 1848 he showed his hand more clearly by sending a Russian army into Hungary to put down the insurrection there against the Hapsburgs. His armies made steady progress in the Caucasus; his diplomacy sought to dominate the Ottoman Empire and make Russia protector of the Balkans. In this field he encountered the rival aims of Britain and France. The Crimean War, one of the most futile struggles known to history, had begun before his death. The ancestry of Nicholas I, and equally of his elder brother Alexander I (Table 140), shows scant traces of Russian blood. Thanks to the policy of exogamic marriages, introduced by Peter the Great, the predominant strains are German, with Holstein and Prussia most evident. Alexander I was actually crowned as King of Poland (Chapter 35) and bore the blazons of Moscow and Poland over the Russian eagle (Table 138). His successors were less sympathetic to the Poles.

Alexander II, the eldest son of Nicholas I, came to the throne without difficulty. His first aim was to stop the war; he then announced his sympathy with the serfs. A considerable measure of emancipation was introduced in 1861, and was followed by large-scale legal reforms three years later. The press was liberated in St Petersburg; the universities were allowed a measure of freedom; regular budgets were introduced. On the other hand, a rising in Poland in 1863 was brutally repressed; the extensive secret police was ubiquitous; the ugly weapons of assassination and the sombre name of nihilism became part of Russian public life at all levels. The rich springs of Russian literature, associated with names like Turgenev, Dostoyevsky and Tolstoy, bubbled forth in his reign, but scarcely in his favour. Russian ambitions in the Balkans reached a high water mark in 1878 at the Treaty of San Stefano (Chapter 38) only to be cast down by the Treaty of Berlin. In 1881 Alexander II was killed by a bomb explosion.

Alexander III was a reactionary. His policy was one of nationalism, orthodoxy and autocracy. Minorities, who did not speak Russian or subscribe to the doctrines of the Eastern Church, were persecuted, including the Jews. At the beginning of his reign he supported the League of the Three Emperors (Germany, Austria and Russia), but gradually he came to suspect Germany and move towards France, with whom a military alliance was concluded in 1894. Huge areas of Asia were added to his dominions.

NICHOLAS II

Nicholas II was a simple, honest character who bore a striking facial resemblance to his first cousin, George V of England (their mothers were sisters). Pious, devoted to his wife, innocent of political sense, he was sadly ill-equipped to face the crises of his reign.

He believed in autocracy, but was reluctant to impose it. In 1904–5 Russia was catastrophically defeated in the Far East by Japan. In 1905, after a series of riots, which included the fragmentation by bomb of the Grand-Duke Sergius, a Duma, or parliamentary assembly, was granted by the Czar. It was a body with strictly limited powers, but it was gradually gaining experience until 1914, despite a mutual mistrust between Duma and government.

The savage ultimatum launched by Austria on Serbia, after the wanton murder of Francis Ferdinand in his own province of Bosnia, drew Russia to the defence of the tiny Kingdom in the Balkans, where for a century she had been posing as the protector of the Slavs. The massive and irreversible process of Russian mobilization was set on foot. Inexorably the Powers were plunged into war, for which Holy Russia was ill-trained and ill-equipped. The lack of incisive quality in the Czar became more apparent; in his anxiety for his late-born, much-loved, haemophiliac son, he leaned upon the strange gifts of the near-charlatan Rasputin. Revolution broke out in 1917; Nicholas abdicated in favour of his brother, but Michael declined the doubtful Crown unless offered by a popular assembly. It was the last act of Imperial Russia. In October the Bolsheviks seized power. Almost the first action of the new regime was to bring the war to an end.

For the doom-burdened dynasty of Romanov the end was drastic. The Czar and his family (Table 138) were taken to Yekaterinburg (now Sverdlovsk), and despite rumours to the contrary, it seems likely that they were all executed there in July 1918. Table 139 shows the ruthlessness with which their kinsfolk were eliminated by the Soviets, who were admittedly under pressure from military invasions in support of the fallen family. The ancestry of the weak but virtuous Nicholas II (Table 140) shows a spread of Germanic families; three lines of Hesse are represented and two of Denmark, to which his paternal line also pertained. Younger members of the family used the eagle of Russia, within a border derived from the original arms of Romanov (see Grand-Duke Constantine on Table 139). It should be noted that in 1856 the mounted horseman in the ancestral arms of the Czars of Moscow was turned to face the right (instead of looking left, contrary to western heraldic usage).

Today there is no emperor and autocrat of all the Russias. The claimant is the Grand-Duke Vladimir, first cousin of the last Czar. He has made an interesting marriage with a member of the ancient family of Bagration, sometime rulers of Georgia, which was annexed to Russia by Alexander I. The harp in the arms of Bagration (Table 138) asserts their descent from King David.

Chapter 37

GREECE

The name of Greece conjures up pictures of the Athens of Pericles and the splendour of the Acropolis, the heroic resistance to Persia or the tragedies of the Peloponnesian war. But the Hellas of that age was never united and preferred, on the whole, democratic forms of government to crowned monarchies. After the classical age the Greek peninsula was in turn part of the Macedonian, Roman and Byzantine empires; it enjoyed neither independence nor importance. At the end of the sixth century the Balkans were ravaged by Slav invaders. In the middle of the fifteenth century they became part of the Turkish (Ottoman) Empire and they thus remained until about a hundred and fifty years ago. But through all these vicissitudes the people of Greece clung to three things: their language, the Christian (Orthodox) religion and the memory of their glorious past.

One of the by-products of the French Revolution was a growth of nationalism among the European peoples subject to Turkish rule. The banner of revolt was raised in the Peloponnese in 1821, and the Greek insurgents were joined by many sympathizers, including the English poet Lord Byron. In 1827 a combined British, French and Russian naval force annihilated the Turkish fleet at Navarino. In 1832 the Great Powers established an independent state and chose Otto of Wittelsbach to be its first king (Table 141). The new Greece was of limited size, for its northern boundary ran from the Gulf of Arta to the Gulf of Volos. Otto was not a successful king; he brought numbers of Germans with him and tried to rule autocratically. The most memorable of his entourage was the Bavarian brewer Fuchs, whose name and products the Greeks have altered to Fix. In 1862 Otto abdicated; he was, as it happened, childless.

The Greeks wanted to have Alfred, Duke of Edinburgh, the son of Queen Victoria, but the Powers selected Prince William of Denmark, who became constitutional ruler of Greece as King George I of the Hellenes. Five of his descendants have since ruled. Great Britain handed over the Ionian Islands to inaugurate the new reign. The arms of Greece were a short cross, and the blue and white colours were copied from those of the Bavarian royal family (Table 96), which can be seen on the small shield of Otto I

King George I of Greece (1845–1913), who founded the Greek royal family.

TABLE 141

GREECE
General survey

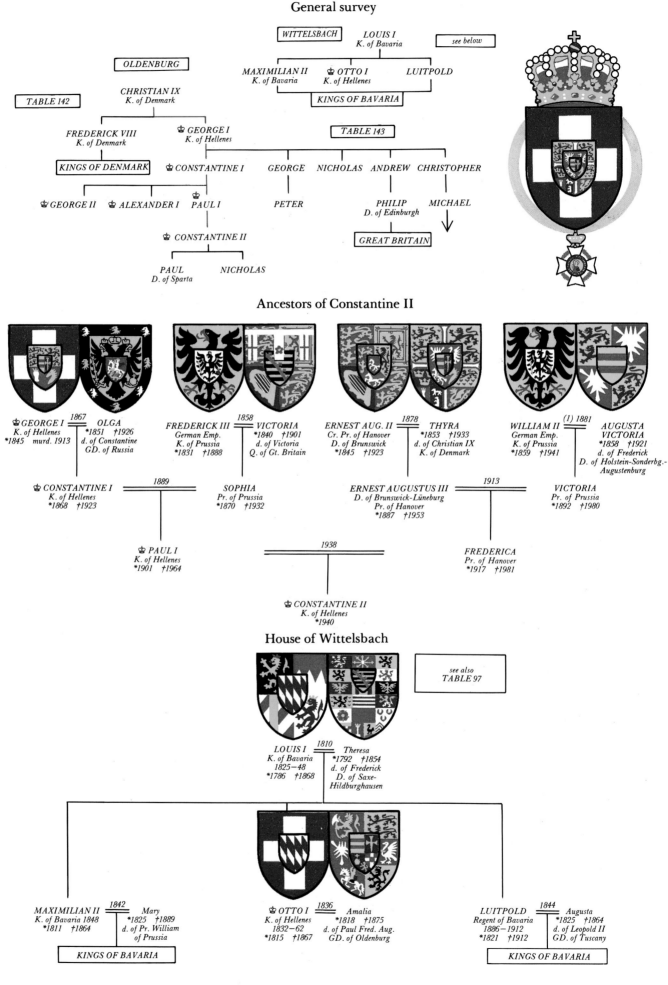

WITTELSBACH

LOUIS I
K. of Bavaria

see below

OLDENBURG

MAXIMILIAN II
K. of Bavaria

♔ OTTO I
K. of Hellenes

LUITPOLD

KINGS OF BAVARIA

CHRISTIAN IX
K. of Denmark

TABLE 142

FREDERICK VIII
K. of Denmark

♔ GEORGE I
K. of Hellenes

TABLE 143

KINGS OF DENMARK

♔ CONSTANTINE I

GEORGE

NICHOLAS

ANDREW

CHRISTOPHER

♔ GEORGE II

♔ ALEXANDER I

♔ PAUL I

PETER

PHILIP
D. of Edinburgh

MICHAEL

♔ CONSTANTINE II

GREAT BRITAIN

PAUL
D. of Sparta

NICHOLAS

Ancestors of Constantine II

♔ GEORGE I
K. of Hellenes
*1845 murd. 1913

1867

OLGA
*1851 †1926
d. of Constantine
GD. of Russia

FREDERICK III
German Emp.
K. of Prussia
*1831 †1888

1858

VICTORIA
*1840 †1901
d. of Victoria
Q. of Gt. Britain

ERNEST AUG. II
Cr. Pr. of Hanover
D. of Brunswick
*1845 †1923

1878

THYRA
*1853 †1933
d. of Christian IX
K. of Denmark

WILLIAM II
German Emp.
K. of Prussia
*1859 †1941

(1) 1881

AUGUSTA
VICTORIA
*1858 †1921
d. of Frederick
D. of Holstein-Sonderbg.-
Augustenburg

♔ CONSTANTINE I
K. of Hellenes
*1868 †1923

1889

SOPHIA
Pr. of Prussia
*1870 †1932

ERNEST AUGUSTUS III
D. of Brunswick-Lüneburg
Pr. of Hanover
*1887 †1953

1913

VICTORIA
Pr. of Prussia
*1892 †1980

♔ PAUL I
K. of Hellenes
*1901 †1964

1938

FREDERICA
Pr. of Hanover
*1917 †1981

♔ CONSTANTINE II
K. of Hellenes
*1940

House of Wittelsbach

see also
TABLE 97

LOUIS I
K. of Bavaria
1825–48
*1786 †1868

1810

Theresa
*1792 †1854
d. of Frederick
D. of Saxe-
Hildburghausen

MAXIMILIAN II
K. of Bavaria 1848
*1811 †1864

1842

Mary
*1825 †1889
d. of Pr. William
of Prussia

KINGS OF BAVARIA

♔ OTTO I
K. of Hellenes
1832–62
*1815 †1867

1836

Amalia
*1818 †1875
d. of Paul Fred. Aug.
GD. of Oldenburg

LUITPOLD
Regent of Bavaria
1886–1912
*1821 †1912

1844

Augusta
*1825 †1864
d. of Leopold II
GD. of Tuscany

KINGS OF BAVARIA

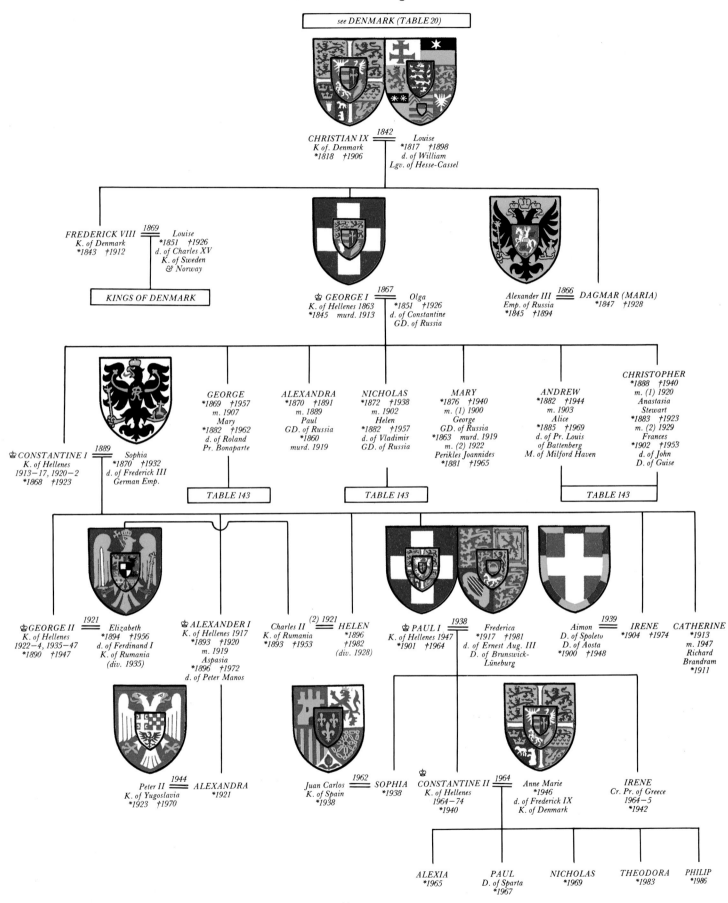

see DENMARK (TABLE 20)

CHRISTIAN IX ══1842══ Louise
K of Denmark   *1817 †1898
*1818 †1906   d. of William
   Lgv. of Hesse-Cassel

FREDERICK VIII ══1869══ Louise
K. of Denmark   *1851 †1926
*1843 †1912   d. of Charles XV
   K. of Sweden
   & Norway

KINGS OF DENMARK

♔ GEORGE I ══1867══ Olga
K. of Hellenes 1863   *1851 †1926
*1845 murd. 1913   d. of Constantine
   GD. of Russia

Alexander III ══1866══ DAGMAR (MARIA)
Emp. of Russia   *1847 †1928
*1845 †1894

♔ CONSTANTINE I ══1889══ Sophia
K. of Hellenes   *1870 †1932
1913–17, 1920–2   d. of Frederick III
*1868 †1923   German Emp.

GEORGE
*1869 †1957
m. 1907
Mary
*1882 †1962
d. of Roland
Pr. Bonaparte

ALEXANDRA
*1870 †1891
m. 1889
Paul
GD. of Russia
*1860
murd. 1919

NICHOLAS
*1872 †1938
m. 1902
Helen
*1882 †1957
d. of Vladimir
GD. of Russia

MARY
*1876 †1940
m. (1) 1900
George
GD. of Russia
*1863 murd. 1919
m. (2) 1922
Perikles Joannides
*1881 †1965

ANDREW
*1882 †1944
m. 1903
Alice
*1885 †1969
d. of Pr. Louis
of Battenberg
M. of Milford Haven

CHRISTOPHER
*1888 †1940
m. (1) 1920
Anastasia
Stewart
*1883 †1923
m. (2) 1929
Frances
*1902 †1953
d. of John
D. of Guise

TABLE 143   TABLE 143   TABLE 143

♔ GEORGE II ══1921══ Elizabeth
K. of Hellenes   *1894 †1956
1922–4, 1935–47   d. of Ferdinand I
*1890 †1947   K. of Rumania
   (div. 1935)

♔ ALEXANDER I
K. of Hellenes 1917
*1893 †1920
m. 1919
Aspasia
*1896 †1972
d. of Peter Manos

Charles II ══(2) 1921══ HELEN
K. of Rumania   *1896
*1893 †1953   †1982
   (div. 1928)

♔ PAUL I ══1938══ Frederica
K. of Hellenes 1947   *1917 †1981
*1901 †1964   d. of Ernest Aug. III
   D. of Brunswick-
   Lüneburg

Aimon ══1939══ IRENE
D. of Spoleto   *1904 †1974
D. of Aosta
*1900 †1948

CATHERINE
*1913
m. 1947
Richard
Brandram
*1911

Peter II ══1944══ ALEXANDRA
K. of Yugoslavia   *1921
*1923 †1970

Juan Carlos ══1962══ SOPHIA
K. of Spain   *1938
*1938

♔ CONSTANTINE II ══1964══ Anne Marie
K. of Hellenes   *1946
1964–74   d. of Frederick IX
*1940   K. of Denmark

IRENE
Cr. Pr. of Greece
1964–5
*1942

ALEXIA
*1965

PAUL
D. of Sparta
*1967

NICHOLAS
*1969

THEODORA
*1983

PHILIP
*1986

TABLE 143

GREECE
Collateral branches (sons of George I)

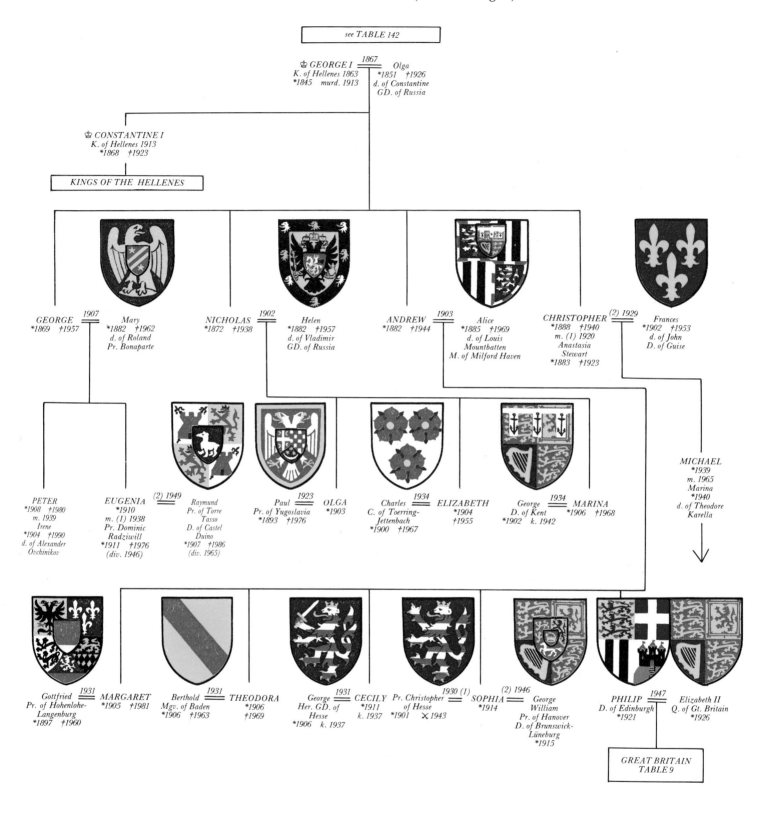

♔ *GEORGE I* ══1867══ *Olga*
K. of Hellenes 1863 *1851 †1926
*1845 murd. 1913 d. of Constantine
GD. of Russia

♔ *CONSTANTINE I*
K. of Hellenes 1913
*1868 †1923

KINGS OF THE HELLENES

GEORGE ══1907══ *Mary*
*1869 †1957 *1882 †1962
d. of Roland
Pr. Bonaparte

NICHOLAS ══1902══ *Helen*
*1872 †1938 *1882 †1957
d. of Vladimir
GD. of Russia

ANDREW ══1903══ *Alice*
*1882 †1944 *1885 †1969
d. of Louis
Mountbatten
M. of Milford Haven

CHRISTOPHER ══(2) 1929══ *Frances*
*1888 †1940 *1902 †1953
m. (1) 1920 d. of John
Anastasia D. of Guise
Stewart
*1883 †1923

MICHAEL
*1939
m. 1965
Marina
*1940
d. of Theodore
Karella

PETER
*1908 †1980
m. 1939
Irene
*1904 †1990
d. of Alexander
Ovchinikov

EUGENIA ══(2) 1949══ *Raymund*
*1910 Pr. of Torre
m. (1) 1938 Tasso
Pr. Dominic D. of Castel
Radziwill Duino
*1911 †1976 *1907 †1986
(div. 1946) (div. 1965)

Paul ══1923══ *OLGA*
Pr. of Yugoslavia *1903
*1893 †1976

Charles ══1934══ *ELIZABETH*
C. of Toerring- *1904
Jettenbach †1955
*1900 †1967

George ══1934══ *MARINA*
D. of Kent *1906 †1968
*1902 k. 1942

Gottfried ══1931══ *MARGARET*
Pr. of Hohenlohe- *1905 †1981
Langenburg
*1897 †1960

Berthold ══1931══ *THEODORA*
Mgv. of Baden *1906
*1906 †1963 †1969

George ══1931══ *CECILY*
Her. GD. of *1911
Hesse k. 1937
*1906 k. 1937

Pr. Christopher ══1930 (1)══ *SOPHIA* ══(2) 1946══ *George*
of Hesse *1914 William
*1901 ✕1943 Pr. of Hanover
D. of Brunswick-
Lüneburg
*1915

PHILIP ══1947══ *Elizabeth II*
D. of Edinburgh Q. of Gt. Britain
*1921 *1926

**GREAT BRITAIN
TABLE 9**

(Table 141). King George kept the cross but replaced the escutcheon of Wittelsbach with the blazon of the House of Denmark (Table 142). His long reign gave stability to Greece and witnessed a wide extension of her frontiers. In 1881 the Plain of Thessaly was added and in 1912–13 Greece, with her allies Serbia and Bulgaria, engaged in war with Turkey, triumphed and then fell out over the spoils. As a result Greece gained Crete and a large area of Macedonia including the important city and port of Salonika. Tragically, the venerable King was assassinated here by an idiot in the fiftieth year of his reign. It was the first of many misfortunes to his dynasty.

His son Constantine I had married a Prussian wife and been impressed by the glitter of German military might. The interests of his realm lay with the Allied Powers however; and in 1917 he left the country, nominating his second son Alexander as his successor. By the Treaty of Sèvres (1920) Greece was awarded almost all of Turkey in Europe (except Constantinople itself) and a considerable slice of Asia Minor round Smyrna. Unhappily in 1920 Alexander I was bitten by a pet monkey and died. In the election which followed the voters decided, against general expectation, in favour of King Constantine, who thus reigned again from 1920 to 1922, and excluded the distinguished statesman Venizelos. The victorious Allied Powers had not reckoned with the revival of Turkey under Mustafa Kemal; the Greeks were disastrously defeated in Asia Minor at the river Sakharia. In 1922 King Constantine left Greece a second time; on this occasion he abdicated in favour of his eldest son, and died soon after. The political scene was exceedingly disturbed and violent. The government, which was created after an uprising in Chios, actually executed five ministers and a general, blamed for the Sakharia disaster. At the end of 1923 King George II was advised to leave and in 1924 a plebiscite proclaimed Greece a republic. Grave social problems beset the new regime, since the small and barren state of Greece had to accept a large influx of refugees from Turkey and try to incorporate them into her meagre economy.

For eleven uneasy years the Republic endured, with a waxing revival of monarchic sentiment. At the end of 1935 another plebiscite restored King George II, who endeavoured to establish a constitutional monarchy. A sudden series of deaths among the better known politicians brought to power General Metaxas; and in 1936 he established a dictatorship. His authoritarian rule was resented, but he gave Greece heroic leadership when she was wantonly attacked by Italy in 1940. The Greeks held their own against the Fascist forces, but, even with British help, could not hold up the German attack in 1941 and the King and government went into exile. At the end of the war Greece was torn by civil war, launched by the Communists, but a plebiscite at the end of 1946 endorsed the return of George II. His Kingdom was augmented by the Dodecanese Islands, including Rhodes, which were ceded by Italy to Greece after the war. When he died, childless, in 1947 he was succeeded by King Paul, the third son of Constantine I to reign. Like his father, Paul had a German wife, Princess Frederica of Hanover.

On the death of King Paul in 1964, his son became Constantine II and married his distant cousin Princess Anne Mary of Denmark. As Table 141 demonstrates, the ancestry of the dethroned King is predominantly German, with a strong streak of Hohenzollern blood. The Order of the Redeemer beneath his shield was founded by Otto I in 1834 and adapted by George I in 1863. The difficult path of the Greek monarchy is not yet terminated. In 1967 elements of the army set up a military regime, the 'rule of the colonels'; at the end of that year the young King attempted a countermove which failed, and he was compelled to flee his realm. But though the increasingly harsh government of the officers crumbled into failure in 1974, the people of Greece voted at the end of that year against the monarchy. Accordingly the King and his heir, the Diadoch Paul, are still in exile. In the light of the many swings of opinion during this century, the idea of restoration cannot be eliminated but it would be a brave prophet who would predict the time and circumstances.

The younger descendants of King George I (Table 143) show a variety of alliances. One of the King's sons married a Bonaparte princess and another a Bourbon, an unusual combination. Two alliances linked Greece with England: Prince Nicholas was the father of Marina, Duchess of Kent, and Prince Andrew of the Duke of Edinburgh. The future sovereigns of the United Kingdom are, therefore, likely to stem back in the male line through George I of Greece to the royal House of Denmark.

Chapter 38

YUGOSLAVIA, SERBIA, MONTENEGRO, RUMANIA AND BULGARIA

The history of the Balkan peninsula is exceedingly complicated. It was part of the Roman Empire, whose frontier in general lay along the Danube, though Dacia (roughly the modern Rumania) was occupied between AD 106 and 271. Most of the Balkans was part of the Byzantine Empire, which continued the eastern section of the classical Roman Empire, though independent states arose from time to time, particularly after the sack of Constantinople by the Fourth Crusade in 1204. These were ruled by indigenous dynasties. Then, from the fourteenth century the domination of the Ottoman Turks spread into Europe, by-passing Constantinople itself until 1453, and extending up to the Danube valley and into Hungary. Twice Vienna was besieged. Meanwhile the racial confusion within the peninsula was considerable. Indeed the gastronomic term 'Macédoine' for a mixed dish of fruit or vegetables derives from this confusion.

In the course of the nineteenth century, there were a series of nationalist uprisings against Turkish rule, which are discussed in detail below. Montenegro was never conquered by the Turks; but by the end of the century discrete Christian states had emerged in differing degrees for Greece (see Chapter 37), Serbia, Bulgaria and Rumania. The fate of the Ottoman Empire, the 'sick man of Europe', was a preoccupation of the chanceries of the Western Powers; to the east, Russia was ever eager to gain control of Constantinople and with it an access to the warm waters of the Mediterranean. In 1877, in furtherance of these ambitions, Russia assisted the Bulgarians against the Turks and strove, by the Treaty of San Stefano, to set up a much enlarged Bulgar state (which would, of course, have owed a great debt to its ally). The other Great Powers were not prepared to accept this, and the settlement was revised and re-written to the detriment of Bulgaria by the treaty of

Berlin in 1878 (to a large extent the work of Disraeli and Bismarck). Thereafter the Austro-Hungarian Empire gradually extended its influence southwards.

In 1912 four of the Balkan states, Greece, Serbia, Montenegro and Bulgaria, united in an assault on the now much-reduced Turkish Empire. They achieved an unexpected degree of success in the first Balkan War. But the victors fell out among themselves and again the Western Powers intervened. In the second Balkan War of 1913, Rumania joined Greece and Serbia in curtailing the ambitions of Bulgaria, but their profits were affected by the decision of the Powers to constitute a separate and independent state of Albania. True to form, a German princeling was installed rather than any native ruler. These plans had scarcely reached fruition when the First World War erupted.

SLAV SETTLEMENTS

In the course of the sixth century, tribes of Slavs from the north invaded the Balkan peninsula. They penetrated deeply into Greece (Chapter 37) but did not break the continuity of the Greek language; they settled with their own speech in much of the territory which now comprises Bulgaria and Yugoslavia, at first as subjects of the Byzantine Empire centred upon Constantinople. In the eighth century another barbarian folk, the Bulgars, crossed the Danube and established themselves south of the river. Although of Asiatic origin, akin to the Huns, they adopted the Slavic speech of their subjects; despite negotiations with the Roman Church they also adopted the Orthodox religion of their neighbours in the reign of Boris I (864). During the tenth century they prospered and became the most powerful state in the central Balkans. This 'first Bulgarian Empire' stretched from the Black Sea to the Adriatic, under two able rulers, Czars Simeon and Samuel, but it was

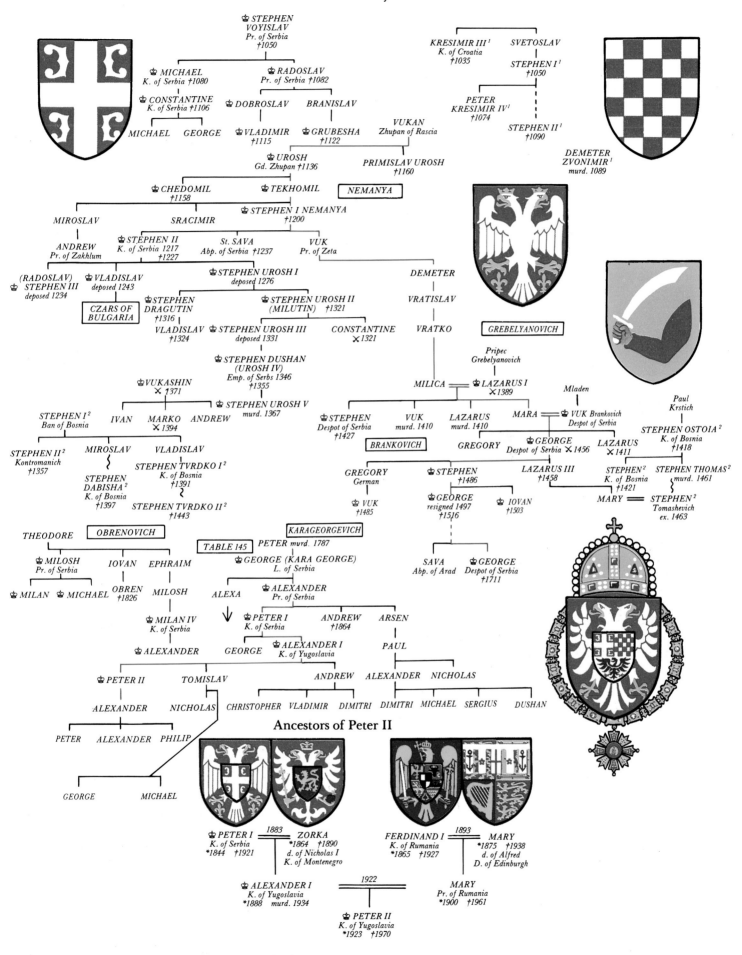

STEPHEN VOYISLAV — Pr. of Serbia †1050

KRESIMIR III[1] K. of Croatia †1035 — SVETOSLAV — STEPHEN I[1] †1050

MICHAEL K. of Serbia †1080 — RADOSLAV Pr. of Serbia †1082

CONSTANTINE K. of Serbia †1106 — DOBROSLAV — BRANISLAV

PETER KRESIMIR IV[1] †1074 — STEPHEN II[1] †1090

MICHAEL — GEORGE — VLADIMIR †1115 — GRUBESHA †1122 — VUKAN Zhupan of Rascia

DEMETER ZVONIMIR[1] murd. 1089

UROSH Gd. Zhupan †1136 — PRIMISLAV UROSH †1160

CHEDOMIL †1158 — TEKHOMIL — NEMANYA

MIROSLAV — SRACIMIR — STEPHEN I NEMANYA †1200

ANDREW Pr. of Zakhlum

STEPHEN II K. of Serbia 1217 †1227 — St. SAVA Abp. of Serbia †1237 — VUK Pr. of Zeta

(RADOSLAV) STEPHEN III deposed 1234 — VLADISLAV deposed 1243 — STEPHEN UROSH I deposed 1276 — DEMETER

CZARS OF BULGARIA

STEPHEN DRAGUTIN †1316 — STEPHEN UROSH II (MILUTIN) †1321 — CONSTANTINE ×1321 — VRATISLAV

VLADISLAV †1324 — STEPHEN UROSH III deposed 1331 — VRATKO

GREBELYANOVICH

STEPHEN DUSHAN (UROSH IV) Emp. of Serbs 1346 †1355

VUKASHIN ×1371 — STEPHEN UROSH V murd. 1367

Pripec Grebelyanovich

STEPHEN I[2] Ban of Bosnia — IVAN — MARKO ×1394 — ANDREW — MILICA == LAZARUS I ×1389 — Mladen — Paul Krstich

STEPHEN II[2] Kontromanich †1357 — MIROSLAV — VLADISLAV

STEPHEN Despot of Serbia †1427 — VUK murd. 1410 — LAZARUS murd. 1410 — MARA == VUK Brankovich Despot of Serbia — STEPHEN OSTOIA[2] K. of Bosnia †1418

STEPHEN DABISHA[2] K. of Bosnia †1397 — STEPHEN TVRDKO I[2] K. of Bosnia †1391

BRANKOVICH — GREGORY — GEORGE Despot of Serbia ×1456 — LAZARUS ×1411

STEPHEN TVRDKO II[2] †1443

GREGORY German — STEPHEN †1486 — LAZARUS III †1458 — STEPHEN[2] K. of Bosnia †1421 — STEPHEN THOMAS[2] murd. 1461

VUK †1485 — GEORGE resigned 1497 †1516 — IOVAN †1503 — MARY == STEPHEN[2] Tomashevich ex. 1463

OBRENOVICH

THEODORE — KARAGEORGEVICH — PETER murd. 1787

TABLE 145

MILOSH Pr. of Serbia — IOVAN — EPHRAIM — GEORGE (KARA GEORGE) L. of Serbia

SAVA Abp. of Arad — GEORGE Despot of Serbia †1711

MILAN — MICHAEL — OBREN †1826 — MILOSH — ALEXA — ALEXANDER Pr. of Serbia

MILAN IV K. of Serbia — PETER I K. of Serbia — ANDREW †1864 — ARSEN

ALEXANDER — GEORGE — ALEXANDER I K. of Yugoslavia — PAUL

PETER II — TOMISLAV — ANDREW — ALEXANDER — NICHOLAS

ALEXANDER — NICHOLAS — CHRISTOPHER — VLADIMIR — DIMITRI — DIMITRI — MICHAEL — SERGIUS — DUSHAN

PETER — ALEXANDER — PHILIP

GEORGE — MICHAEL

Ancestors of Peter II

PETER I K. of Serbia *1844 †1921 — 1883 — ZORKA *1864 †1890 d. of Nicholas I K. of Montenegro

FERDINAND I K. of Rumania *1865 †1927 — 1893 — MARY *1875 †1938 d. of Alfred D. of Edinburgh

ALEXANDER I K. of Yugoslavia *1888 murd. 1934 — 1922 — MARY Pr. of Rumania *1900 †1961

PETER II K. of Yugoslavia *1923 †1970

NOTE
[1] King of Croatia
[2] Ruler of Bosnia

TABLE 145

YUGOSLAVIA
Houses of Obrenovich and Karageorgievich

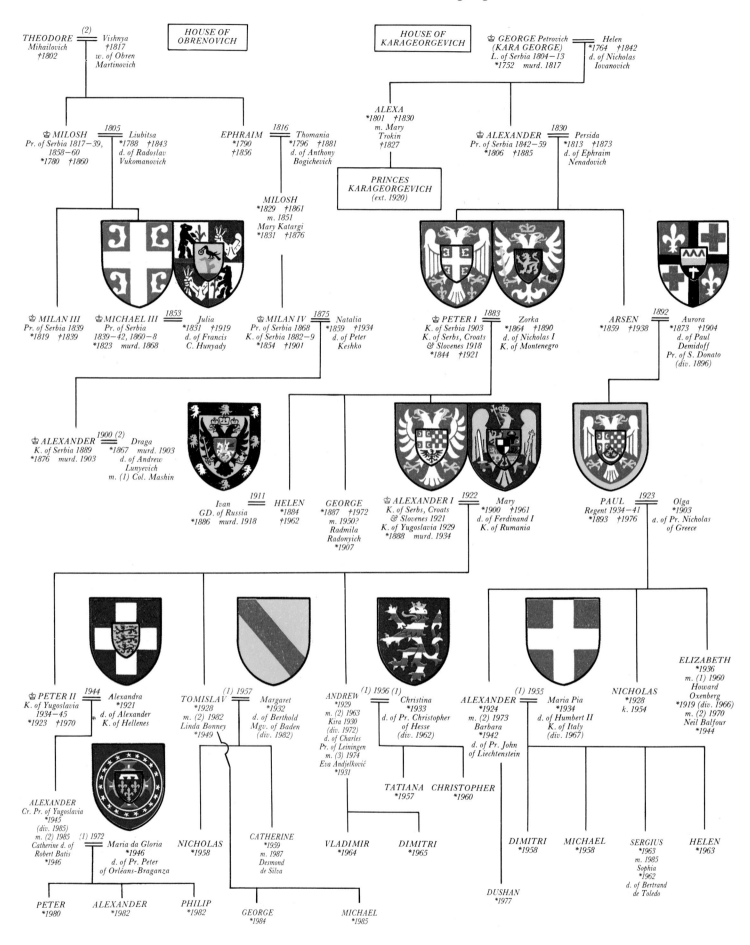

HOUSE OF OBRENOVICH	**HOUSE OF KARAGEORGEVICH**

THEODORE Mihailovich †1802 — (2) — *Vishnya* †1817 w. of Obren Martinovich

♛ *GEORGE Petrovich (KARA GEORGE)* L. of Serbia 1804–13 *1752 murd. 1817 — *Helen* *1764 †1842 d. of Nicholas Iovanovich

♛ *MILOSH* Pr. of Serbia 1817–39, 1858–60 *1780 †1860 — 1805 — *Liubitsa* *1788 †1843 d. of Radoslav Vukomanovich

EPHRAIM *1790 †1856 — 1816 — *Thomania* *1796 †1881 d. of Anthony Bogichevich

ALEXA *1801 †1830 m. Mary Trokin †1827

♛ *ALEXANDER* Pr. of Serbia 1842–59 *1806 †1885 — 1830 — *Persida* *1813 †1873 d. of Ephraim Nenadovich

PRINCES KARAGEORGEVICH (ext. 1920)

MILOSH *1829 †1861 m. 1851 Mary Katargi *1831 †1876

♛ *MILAN III* Pr. of Serbia 1839 *1819 †1839

♛ *MICHAEL III* Pr. of Serbia 1839–42, 1860–8 *1823 murd. 1868 — 1853 — *Julia* *1831 †1919 d. of Francis C. Hunyady

♛ *MILAN IV* Pr. of Serbia 1868 K. of Serbia 1882–9 *1854 †1901 — 1875 — *Natalia* *1859 †1934 d. of Peter Keshko

♛ *PETER I* K. of Serbia 1903 K. of Serbs, Croats & Slovenes 1918 *1844 †1921 — 1883 — *Zorka* *1864 †1890 d. of Nicholas I K. of Montenegro

ARSEN *1859 †1938 — 1892 — *Aurora* *1873 †1904 d. of Paul Demidoff Pr. of S. Donato (div. 1896)

♛ *ALEXANDER* K. of Serbia 1889 *1876 murd. 1903 — 1900 (2) — *Draga* *1867 murd. 1903 d. of Andrew Lunyevich m. (1) Col. Mashin

Ivan GD. of Russia *1886 murd. 1918

HELEN *1884 †1962 — 1911

GEORGE *1887 †1972 m. 1950? Radmila Radonyich *1907

♛ *ALEXANDER I* K. of Serbs, Croats & Slovenes 1921 K. of Yugoslavia 1929 *1888 murd. 1934 — 1922 — *Mary* *1900 †1961 d. of Ferdinand I K. of Rumania

PAUL Regent 1934–41 *1893 †1976 — 1923 — *Olga* *1903 d. of Pr. Nicholas of Greece

ELIZABETH *1936 m. (1) 1960 Howard Oxenberg *1919 (div. 1966) m. (2) 1970 Neil Balfour *1944

♛ *PETER II* K. of Yugoslavia 1934–45 *1923 †1970 — 1944 — *Alexandra* *1921 d. of Alexander K. of Hellenes

TOMISLAV *1928 m. (2) 1982 Linda Bonney *1949 — (1) 1957 — *Margaret* *1932 d. of Berthold Mgv. of Baden (div. 1982)

ANDREW *1929 m. (2) 1963 Kira 1930 (div. 1972) d. of Charles Pr. of Leiningen m. (3) 1974 Eva Andjelković *1931 — (1) 1956 (1) — *Christina* *1933 d. of Pr. Christopher of Hesse (div. 1962)

ALEXANDER *1924 m. (2) 1973 Barbara *1942 d. of Pr. John of Liechtenstein — (1) 1955 — *Maria Pia* *1934 d. of Humbert II K. of Italy (div. 1967)

NICHOLAS *1928 k. 1954

ALEXANDER Cr. Pr. of Yugoslavia *1945 (div. 1985) m. (2) 1985 Catherine d. of Robert Batis *1946 — (1) 1972 — *Maria da Gloria* *1946 d. of Pr. Peter of Orléans-Braganza

NICHOLAS *1958

CATHERINE *1959 m. 1987 Desmond de Silva

TATIANA *1957

CHRISTOPHER *1960

DIMITRI *1958

MICHAEL *1958

SERGIUS *1963 m. 1985 Sophia *1962 d. of Bertrand de Toledo

HELEN *1963

VLADIMIR *1964

DIMITRI *1965

DUSHAN *1977

PETER *1980

ALEXANDER *1982

PHILIP *1982

GEORGE *1984

MICHAEL *1985

violently overthrown by the great Byzantine Emperor, Basil II, in 1014.

The end of the twelfth century, however, witnessed a period of weakness in the Byzantine Empire and two independent states arose to its north. In 1186 began the 'second Bulgarian Empire' under John Asen I (Table 149), while towards the Adriatic developed a separate kingdom of Serbia under Stephen I Nemanya (Table 144). The Bulgarian Empire reached its apogee under John Asen II, with a splendid capital at Trnovo, but a period of confusion and disorder followed his death, in which a somewhat sinister role was played by his granddaughter, the Byzantine Princess Mary Laskaris (Table 149). The House of Asen died out, and Bulgaria was ruled by a Serbian prince, Constantine (who adopted the name of Asen and married Mary Laskaris). They were succeeded by rulers of the family of Terteres.

MEDIEVAL SERBIA

The heart of medieval Serbia was the valley of the river Morava. Across the Dinaric Alps and the river Sava was the land of Croatia, but its links tended to be closer with Hungary. Each tribe was governed by a Zhupan, and from time to time one of these would assert supremacy over his neighbours and claim the style of prince of Serbia. The area formed part of the first Bulgarian Empire, but thereafter resumed a fitful allegiance to Constantinople. In 1185 Stephen Nemanya (Table 144) proclaimed himself independent King of Serbia and founded a famous dynasty. He himself retired to end his days as a monk on Mount Athos, but his eldest son Stephen II was solemnly crowned by another son, St Sava, the patron saint of the Kingdom, and during his lifetime its archbishop. Thereafter almost all the rulers bear the name of Stephen, the Greek word for crown.

The expansion of Serbia under the Nemanya family brought the Kingdom into contact with Hungary in the north and Bulgaria to the southeast. Its most powerful phase began under Stephen Urosh II and in 1330 the Bulgarians were decisively defeated by Stephen Urosh III in a great battle at Köstendil. The new Bulgar dynasty, that of Shishman (Table 149), was dominated by the power and policy of Serbia.

The golden age of medieval Serbia was the reign of Stephen Dushan (1331–55). It began with a savage deed, for he is reputed to have strangled his father who had fallen under the influence of a Greek wife. Dushan's dominions spread from the Danube in the north to the Gulf of Corinth in the south. But if territorial extension was mainly at the expense of the Byzantine Emperors, it was none the less the culture of Constantinople which enriched the Serbian Kingdom; in particular this age produced a wonderful series of churches decorated with frescoes of extremely high quality. Dushan (the epithet may mean 'strangler' or 'victorious') was a tall man and a great leader of men; in 1346 he assumed the title of 'Emperor of the Greeks and Serbians', and was actually attacking Constantinople when he died, still young, in 1355. At this time an ominous element entered Balkan politics with the arrival of the Ottoman Turks, who made their headquarters at Adrianople (Edirne) in 1367.

Dushan's heir was dethroned by one of his subjects. Bosnia became independent under Stephen Tvrdko (Table 144); and in 1389 the forces of Slav Christendom were catastrophically defeated at Kossovo Polje by Sultan Murat I. Prince Lazarus fell in the battle, but the Sultan was assassinated shortly after it, and the victory was not followed up. The heirs of Lazarus ruled for a while as vassals of the Turks, but in 1459 Serbia was formally annexed to the Turkish Empire. Marko Kraljevich (son of King Vukashin), the hero of so many Serbian ballads and folk-tales, probably fought on the Turkish side. For four centuries the Serbian people existed under Ottoman rule, though they preserved their traditions, their speech and their religion.

MONTENEGRO

On the east side of the Adriatic, opposite to the heel of Italy, is an enclave of Albanian people. Distinct from the Slavs in race and language, they accepted Turkish rule and the Moslem religion and only achieved political independence in the twentieth century, since when they have pursued a path of their own. North of Albania lies the wild and mountainous area, known in the Middle Ages as Zeta and more lately as Crnagora or Montenegro: both mean Black Mountain. Hither some Serbian refugees fled after Kossovo and here the flag of Slav freedom was kept flying all through the centuries when Turkish dominion devoured the rest of the Balkans. In the dark year of 1389, a local dynasty of Balsha (Table 146) had for two generations ruled over Zeta. They were followed by the family of Crnoyevich, who were distant kinsmen. Stephen the Black was an ally of the great Albanian hero Skanderbeg in his battles against the Turks; Ivan moved his capital to the remote, upland town of Cetinje: there George IV in 1493 established the first printing press to use the Cyrillic alphabet. Campaigns against Turkish attack had become almost incessant and the principle was established at this time that in Montenegro a small invading army is defeated while a large one perishes from hunger.

In 1516 George V, who had many interests in Venice, resolved to live there; he handed over power to the local bishop (Vladika) and retired to the

TABLE 146

MONTENEGRO
General survey

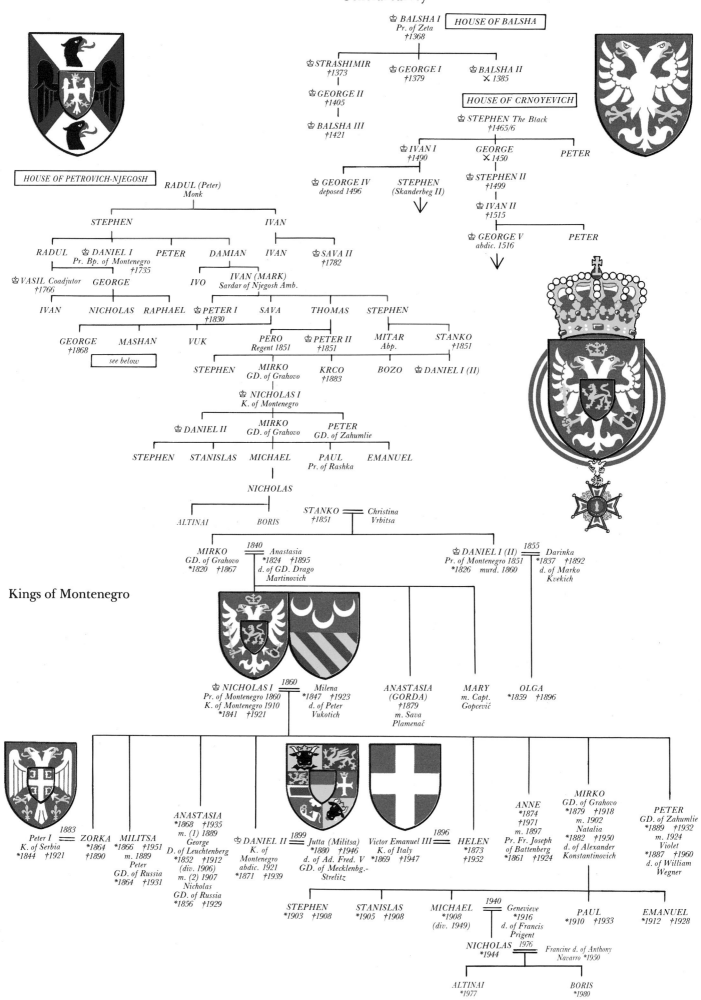

HOUSE OF BALSHA

♕ *BALSHA I*
Pr. of Zeta
†1368

♕ *STRASHIMIR*
†1373

♕ *GEORGE I*
†1379

♕ *BALSHA II*
✕ 1385

♕ *GEORGE II*
†1405

♕ *BALSHA III*
†1421

HOUSE OF CRNOYEVICH

♕ *STEPHEN The Black*
†1465/6

♕ *IVAN I*
†1490

GEORGE
✕ 1450

PETER

♕ *GEORGE IV*
deposed 1496

STEPHEN
(Skanderbeg II)

♕ *STEPHEN II*
†1499

♕ *IVAN II*
†1515

♕ *GEORGE V*
abdic. 1516

PETER

HOUSE OF PETROVICH-NJEGOSH

RADUL (Peter)
Monk

STEPHEN

IVAN

RADUL

♕ *DANIEL I*
Pr. Bp. of Montenegro
†1735

PETER

DAMIAN

IVAN

♕ *SAVA II*
†1782

♕ *VASIL* Coadjutor
†1766

GEORGE

IVO

IVAN (MARK)
Sardar of Njegosh Amb.

IVAN   *NICHOLAS*   *RAPHAEL*

♕ *PETER I*
†1830

SAVA

THOMAS

STEPHEN

GEORGE
†1868

MASHAN

see below

VUK

PERO
Regent 1851

♕ *PETER II*
†1851

MITAR
Abp.

STANKO
†1851

STEPHEN

MIRKO
GD. of Grahovo

KRCO
†1883

BOZO

♕ *DANIEL I (II)*

♕ *NICHOLAS I*
K. of Montenegro

♕ *DANIEL II*

MIRKO
GD. of Grahovo

PETER
GD. of Zahumlie

STEPHEN   *STANISLAS*   *MICHAEL*   *PAUL*
Pr. of Rashka

EMANUEL

NICHOLAS

ALTINAI   *BORIS*

STANKO ═══ *Christina*
†1851   *Vrbitsa*

MIRKO   1840   *Anastasia*
GD. of Grahovo   *1824 †1895
*1820 †1867   d. of GD. Drago
              Martinovich

♕ *DANIEL I (II)*   1855   *Darinka*
Pr. of Montenegro 1851   *1837 †1892
*1826 murd. 1860   d. of Marko
                  Kvekich

Kings of Montenegro

♕ *NICHOLAS I*   1860   *Milena*
Pr. of Montenegro 1860   *1847 †1923
K. of Montenegro 1910   d. of Peter
*1841 †1921   Vukotich

*ANASTASIA
(GORDA)*
*1879
m. Sava
Plamenać

MARY
m. Capt.
Gopcević

OLGA
*1859 †1896

Peter I ═══ *ZORKA*
K. of Serbia   *1864
*1844 †1921   †1890

MILITSA
*1866 †1951
m. 1889
Peter
GD. of Russia
*1864 †1931

ANASTASIA
*1868 †1935
m. (1) 1889
George
D. of Leuchtenberg
*1852 †1912
(div. 1906)
m. (2) 1907
Nicholas
GD. of Russia
*1856 †1929

1883

♕ *DANIEL II*   1899   *Jutta (Militsa)*
K. of   *1880 †1946
Montenegro   d. of Ad. Fred. V
abdic. 1921   GD. of Mecklenbg.-
*1871 †1939   Strelitz

Victor Emanuel III   1896   *HELEN*
K. of Italy   *1873
*1869 †1947   †1952

ANNE
*1874
†1971
m. 1897
Pr. Fr. Joseph
of Battenberg
*1861 †1924

MIRKO
GD. of Grahovo
*1879 †1918
m. 1902
Natalia
*1882 †1950
d. of Alexander
Konstantinovich

PETER
GD. of Zahumlie
*1889 †1932
m. 1924
Violet
*1887 †1960
d. of William
Wegner

STEPHEN
*1903 †1908

STANISLAS
*1905 †1908

MICHAEL   1940   *Genevieve*
*1908   *1916
(div. 1949)   d. of Francis
              Prigent

PAUL
*1910 †1933

EMANUEL
*1912 †1928

NICHOLAS   1976   *Francine* d. of Anthony
*1944   Navarro *1950

ALTINAI
*1977

BORIS
*1980

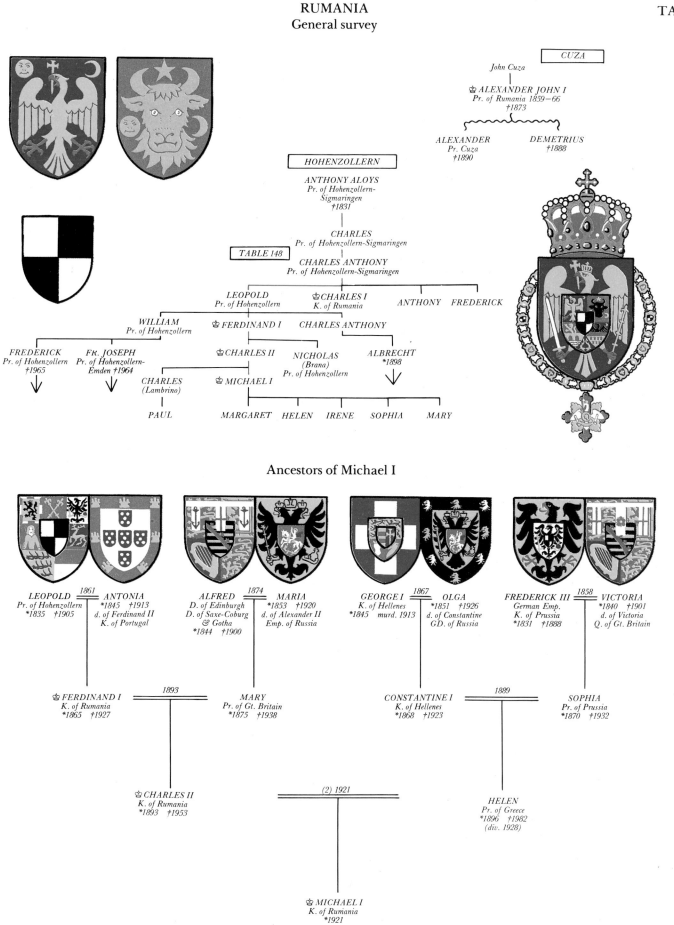

RUMANIA — General survey

CUZA

John Cuza

♕ *ALEXANDER JOHN I*
Pr. of Rumania 1859—66
†1873

ALEXANDER
Pr. Cuza
†1890

DEMETRIUS
†1888

HOHENZOLLERN

ANTHONY ALOYS
Pr. of Hohenzollern-
Sigmaringen
†1831

CHARLES
Pr. of Hohenzollern-Sigmaringen

TABLE 148

CHARLES ANTHONY
Pr. of Hohenzollern-Sigmaringen

LEOPOLD
Pr. of Hohenzollern

♕ *CHARLES I*
K. of Rumania

ANTHONY   *FREDERICK*

WILLIAM
Pr. of Hohenzollern

♕ *FERDINAND I*

CHARLES ANTHONY

FREDERICK
Pr. of Hohenzollern
†1965

FR. JOSEPH
Pr. of Hohenzollern-
Emden †1964

♕ *CHARLES II*

NICHOLAS
(Brana)
Pr. of Hohenzollern

ALBRECHT
*1898

CHARLES
(Lambrino)

♕ *MICHAEL I*

PAUL

MARGARET   *HELEN*   *IRENE*   *SOPHIA*   *MARY*

Ancestors of Michael I

| LEOPOLD
Pr. of Hohenzollern
*1835 †1905 | 1861 | ANTONIA
*1845 †1913
d. of Ferdinand II
K. of Portugal | ALFRED
D. of Edinburgh
D. of Saxe-Coburg
& Gotha
*1844 †1900 | 1874 | MARIA
*1853 †1920
d. of Alexander II
Emp. of Russia | GEORGE I
K. of Hellenes
*1845 murd. 1913 | 1867 | OLGA
*1851 †1926
d. of Constantine
GD. of Russia | FREDERICK III
German Emp.
K. of Prussia
*1831 †1888 | 1858 | VICTORIA
*1840 †1901
d. of Victoria
Q. of Gt. Britain |

♕ *FERDINAND I*
K. of Rumania
*1865 †1927

1893

MARY
Pr. of Gt. Britain
*1875 †1938

CONSTANTINE I
K. of Hellenes
*1868 †1923

1889

SOPHIA
Pr. of Prussia
*1870 †1932

♕ *CHARLES II*
K. of Rumania
*1893 †1953

(2) 1921

HELEN
Pr. of Greece
*1896 †1982
(div. 1928)

♕ *MICHAEL I*
K. of Rumania
*1921

canals, being of less heroic stature than Ivan I, whose return – like that of Arthur or Barbarossa or Marko Kraljevich – is still expected by his people. For 180 years successive bishops were elected, ruled and died; intermittent Turkish assaults were repulsed. Then, in 1696, Daniel Petrovich from Njegosh established that the bishop, though celibate himself, might nominate a successor from his own family. Under his sway occurred in 1703 the Montenegrin Vespers, a celebrated massacre of Moslems. The dynastic arms of the Petrovich-Njegosh can be seen at the top of Table 146 on the left. Successive bachelor prelates reigned with varying degrees of achievement, always resisting the attacks of the Turks. Peter I also repelled Napoleon and thereby made some increase of territory. He was followed in turn by Peter II, a valiant giant over 2m (6 ft) tall, and by Daniel II, the second Vladika of that name. But in 1851 this Bishop secularized his office and proceeded to marry. He thus became Prince Daniel I of Montenegro. He issued a new code of laws and instituted a regular army. His brother Mirko, called the 'Sword of Montenegro', won a resounding victory over the Turks at Grahovo and used that as a title. He was the father of Nicholas I, the next Prince.

Nicholas I had a long and striking life. Tall and good-looking, he was also a poet and an accomplished diplomat. In 1876 he declared war on Turkey, but (like Bulgaria) was deprived by the Treaty of Berlin of the larger gains promised at San Stefano: none the less he won access to the sea. In 1900 he took the style of royal highness and in 1910 that of king: it will be seen (Table 146: lower half) that his daughters made a striking series of dynastic marriages with Russia, Italy and Serbia. His armies took part in the first Balkan War (1912–13) and on the Allied side against Germany; but in 1918 his little kingdom was incorporated in Yugoslavia, and the old King died, protesting, in sorrow and in exile. The medieval arms of the province of Zeta comprised a two-headed eagle on a red field; to this Nicholas added the crown, orb and sceptre of royalty and an escutcheon of his family arms. The shield is encircled by the Order of Peter I.

MODERN SERBIA

Despite the long centuries of Turkish occupation the sense of Slav nationality continued to exist, and was fostered by news of the French Revolution. In 1804 a rising in Serbia brought to leadership a powerful, black-haired breeder of pigs named George (Table 145), who led an independence movement for nine years, and was recognized as supreme chief. In 1817 another insurrection was led by Milosh Obrenovich (he took the name from his stepfather), who was recognized by the Turks as prince and who caused the murder of Black (Kara) George. The next cen-

tury of Serbian history was rendered even more complex by the rivalry between these two families.

In 1830 the Sultan recognized the principality as hereditary in the Obrenovich family, though Milosh was still under Turkish suzerainty. The new Prince reigned tyrannically – though indeed Serbia was hardly ready for any other form of government – and in 1839 was constrained to abdicate in favour of his son, Milan III. On the sudden death of the latter, Michael (his brother) succeeded, but his efforts at modernization brought him in turn to abdication in 1842. The country now turned to Alexander, the son of Kara George, who successfully kept his realm neutral during the Crimean War and gained thereby a guarantee of independence from the Great Powers. But his policy seemed to some to lean too much towards Austria and in 1859 he was compelled to resign, in favour of the now aged Milosh.

When Milosh died, Michael again became prince and ruled with more circumspection. He attempted a revision of the tax laws and established a regular army. In 1867 the Turkish garrisons were withdrawn. In the next year Michael was assassinated by plotters possibly linked with the Karageorgevich family, and was followed by his cousin Milan IV. Milan led Serbia against Turkey in 1876, and was rewarded at the Treaty of Berlin with large extensions of territory in Macedonia; in 1882 his complete independence from Turkey was underlined by the adoption of the title of king.

However, Milan had begun to show pro-Austrian sympathies and accepted without rancour the Austrian occupation of Bosnia and Hercegovina in 1878. It must be remembered that at this time Serbia was bounded on the north by the river Sava and that this Hapsburg expansion was a severe blow to Serbian aspirations. His profligate behaviour alienated the sympathies of his subjects, and he cut a poor figure beside prince Nicholas of Montenegro as a leader of Slav ambitions. In 1885 he launched a futile and ill-prepared attack on Bulgaria and was only saved by Austrian diplomacy. Suddenly at the age of 35 he abdicated in favour of his son (1889) and withdrew to the pleasures of Vienna, though he returned in 1897 to become a surprisingly efficient commander of the army.

His son, King Alexander, declared himself of age in 1893. His tragedy was a marriage with a domineering and unpopular widow, who was known to be barren. In 1903 he and his wife were murdered by a group of officers in a singularly barbarous manner. The assassins then proceeded to summon Peter Karageorgevich from his exile. The new ruler was a brave and blameless man: he had even translated Mill's *On Liberty* into Serbian; he was married to a daughter of the romantic Prince of Montenegro; but

THE BALKANS IN THE NINETEENTH CENTURY

•••••• *Borders proposed by Treaty of San Stefano in March 1878*
– – – – *Borders established by Congress of Berlin in June-July 1878*
▓ *Ottoman Empire in 1878 (after Congress of Berlin)*
▬▬ *Borders in 1914*

| 0 | 50 | 100 | 150 miles |
| 50 | 100 | 200 km | |

the horror of his predecessor's death tarnished the early part of his reign. It was a sad blow to Slav hopes when in 1908 Austria annexed to her Empire the provinces of Bosnia and Hercegovina which she had administered since 1878.

In 1912 the Christian states in the Balkans resolved to attack Turkey. To the surprise of Europe the armies of Bulgaria, Serbia, Montenegro and Greece defeated the Ottoman forces on all sides; Turkey in Europe was reduced to a small area round Constantinople. But the Bulgarians were ill-content with their gains: as we shall see, they still yearned for the larger

TABLE 148

RUMANIA
House of Hohenzollern

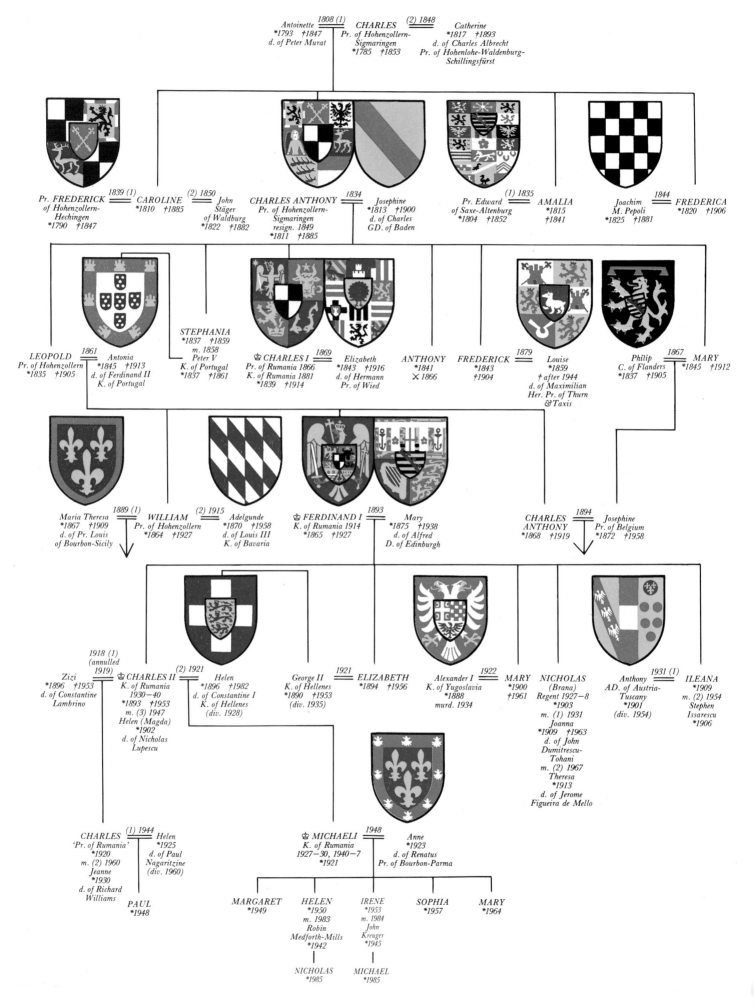

Antoinette *1793 †1847 d. of Peter Murat — 1808 (1) — CHARLES Pr. of Hohenzollern-Sigmaringen *1785 †1853 — (2) 1848 — Catherine *1817 †1893 d. of Charles Albrecht Pr. of Hohenlohe-Waldenburg-Schillingsfürst

Pr. FREDERICK of Hohenzollern-Hechingen *1790 †1847 — 1839 (1) — CAROLINE *1810 †1885 — (2) 1850 — John Stäger of Waldburg *1822 †1882

CHARLES ANTHONY Pr. of Hohenzollern-Sigmaringen resign. 1849 *1811 †1885 — 1834 — Josephine *1813 †1900 d. of Charles GD. of Baden

Pr. Edward of Saxe-Altenburg *1804 †1852 — (1) 1835 — AMALIA *1815 †1841

Joachim M. Pepoli *1825 †1881 — 1844 — FREDERICA *1820 †1906

LEOPOLD Pr. of Hohenzollern *1835 †1905 — 1861 — Antonia *1845 †1913 d. of Ferdinand II K. of Portugal

STEPHANIA *1837 †1859 m. 1858 Peter V K. of Portugal *1837 †1861

♛ CHARLES I Pr. of Rumania 1866 K. of Rumania 1881 *1839 †1914 — 1869 — Elizabeth *1843 †1916 d. of Hermann Pr. of Wied

ANTHONY *1841 ✕ 1866

FREDERICK *1843 †1904 — 1879 — Louise *1859 † after 1944 d. of Maximilian Her. Pr. of Thurn &Taxis

Philip C. of Flanders *1837 †1905 — 1867 — MARY *1845 †1912

Maria Theresa *1867 †1909 d. of Pr. Louis of Bourbon-Sicily — 1889 (1) — WILLIAM Pr. of Hohenzollern *1864 †1927 — (2) 1915 — Adelgunde *1870 †1958 d. of Louis III K. of Bavaria

♛ FERDINAND I K. of Rumania 1914 *1865 †1927 — 1893 — Mary *1875 †1938 d. of Alfred D. of Edinburgh

CHARLES ANTHONY *1868 †1919 — 1894 — Josephine Pr. of Belgium *1872 †1958

Zizi *1896 †1953 d. of Constantine Lambrino — 1918 (1) (annulled 1919) — ♛ CHARLES II K. of Rumania 1930–40 *1893 †1953 m. (3) 1947 Helen (Magda) *1902 d. of Nicholas Lupescu — (2) 1921 — Helen *1896 †1982 d. of Constantine I K. of Hellenes (div. 1928)

George II K. of Hellenes *1890 †1953 (div. 1935) — 1921 — ELIZABETH *1894 †1956

Alexander I K. of Yugoslavia *1888 murd. 1934 — 1922 — MARY *1900 †1961

NICHOLAS (Brana) Regent 1927–8 *1903 m. (1) 1931 Joanna *1909 †1963 d. of John Dumitrescu-Tohani m. (2) 1967 Theresa *1913 d. of Jerome Figueira de Mello

Anthony AD. of Austria-Tuscany *1901 (div. 1954) — 1931 (1) — ILEANA *1909 m. (2) 1954 Stephen Issarescu *1906

CHARLES 'Pr. of Rumania' *1920 m. (2) 1960 Jeanne *1930 d. of Richard Williams — (1) 1944 — Helen *1925 d. of Paul Nagaritzine (div. 1960)

PAUL *1948

♛ MICHAEL I K. of Rumania 1927–30, 1940–7 *1921 — 1948 — Anne *1923 d. of Renatus Pr. of Bourbon-Parma

MARGARET *1949

HELEN *1950 m. 1983 Robin Medforth-Mills *1942

NICHOLAS *1985

IRENE *1953 m. 1984 John Kreuger *1945

MICHAEL *1985

SOPHIA *1957

MARY *1964

General survey

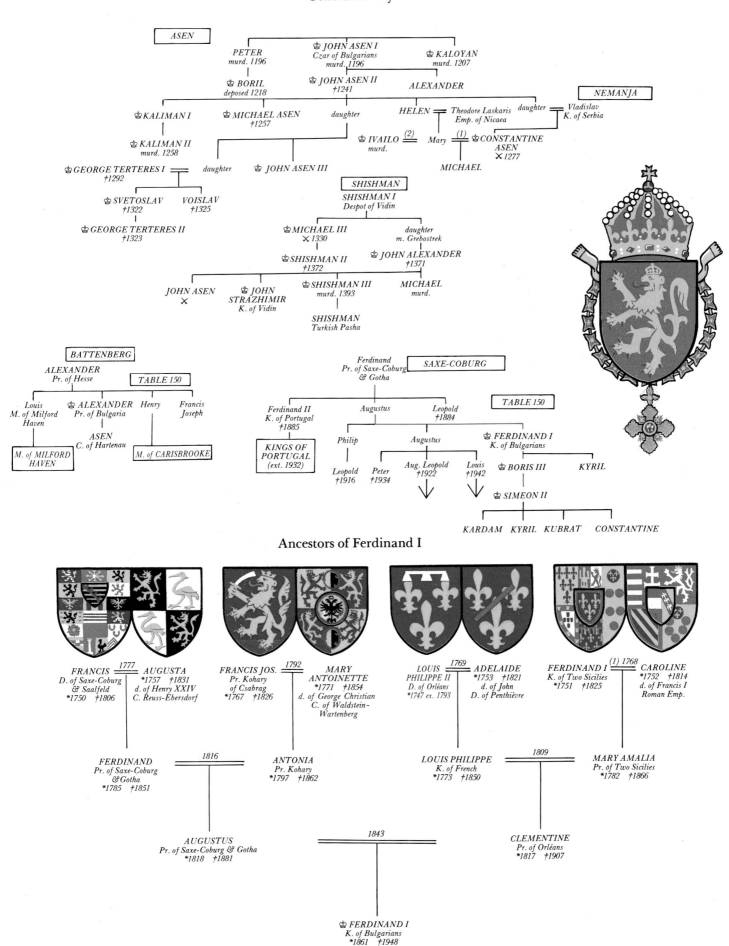

ASEN

PETER
murd. 1196

♔ JOHN ASEN I
Czar of Bulgarians
murd. 1196

♔ KALOYAN
murd. 1207

♔ BORIL
deposed 1218

♔ JOHN ASEN II
†1241

ALEXANDER

NEMANJA

♔ KALIMAN I

♔ MICHAEL ASEN
†1257

daughter

HELEN ══ Theodore Laskaris
Emp. of Nicaea

daughter ══ Vladislav
K. of Serbia

♔ KALIMAN II
murd. 1258

♔ IVAILO (2)
murd.

Mary (1) ♔ CONSTANTINE
ASEN
✕ 1277

♔ GEORGE TERTERES I ══ daughter
†1292

♔ JOHN ASEN III

MICHAEL

♔ SVETOSLAV
†1322

VOISLAV
†1325

SHISHMAN

SHISHMAN I
Despot of Vidin

♔ GEORGE TERTERES II
†1323

♔ MICHAEL III
✕ 1330

daughter
m. Grebostrek

♔ SHISHMAN II
†1372

♔ JOHN ALEXANDER
†1371

JOHN ASEN
✕

♔ JOHN
STRAZHIMIR
K. of Vidin

♔ SHISHMAN III
murd. 1393

MICHAEL
murd.

SHISHMAN
Turkish Pasha

BATTENBERG

ALEXANDER
Pr. of Hesse

TABLE 150

Ferdinand
Pr. of Saxe-Coburg
& Gotha

SAXE-COBURG

Louis
M. of Milford
Haven

♔ ALEXANDER
Pr. of Bulgaria

Henry

Francis
Joseph

Ferdinand II
K. of Portugal
†1885

Augustus

Leopold
†1884

TABLE 150

M. of MILFORD
HAVEN

ASEN
C. of Hartenau

M. of CARISBROOKE

Philip

Augustus

♔ FERDINAND I
K. of Bulgarians

KINGS OF
PORTUGAL
(ext. 1932)

Leopold
†1916

Peter
†1934

Aug. Leopold
†1922

Louis
†1942

♔ BORIS III

KYRIL

♔ SIMEON II

KARDAM   KYRIL   KUBRAT   CONSTANTINE

Ancestors of Ferdinand I

FRANCIS ──1777── AUGUSTA
D. of Saxe-Coburg   *1757 †1831
& Saalfeld   d. of Henry XXIV
*1750 †1806   C. Reuss-Ebersdorf

FRANCIS JOS. ──1792── MARY
Pr. Kohary   ANTOINETTE
of Csabrag   *1771 †1854
*1767 †1826   d. of George Christian
                       C. of Waldstein-
                       Wartenberg

LOUIS ──1769── ADELAIDE
PHILIPPE II   *1753 †1821
D. of Orléans d. of John
*1747 ex. 1793 D. of Penthièvre

FERDINAND I (1) 1768 CAROLINE
K. of Two Sicilies   *1752 †1814
*1751 †1825   d. of Francis I
                       Roman Emp.

FERDINAND ──1816── ANTONIA
Pr. of Saxe-Coburg   Pr. Kohary
& Gotha   *1797 †1862
*1785 †1851

LOUIS PHILIPPE ──1809── MARY AMALIA
K. of French   Pr. of Two Sicilies
*1773 †1850   *1782 †1866

AUGUSTUS
Pr. of Saxe-Coburg & Gotha
*1818 †1881

──1843──

CLEMENTINE
Pr. of Orléans
*1817 †1907

♔ FERDINAND I
K. of Bulgarians
*1861 †1948

Alexander I (1888–1934), King of Yugoslavia, reviews a group of patriot fighters.

boundaries of San Stefano. Rashly, they attacked their recent allies: in the second Balkan war (1913) they were soundly defeated by Greece and Serbia with aid on this occasion from Rumania. It was towards an area already familiar with war that the heir to the Austrian Empire journeyed in 1914. On 28 June he was shot dead at Sarajevo in Bosnia by a fanatical Bosnian student. Sarajevo was, of course, in Austrian territory; none the less on 23 July a devastating ultimatum was issued by Austria to Serbia, a series of demands which would have ended Serbian freedom. Russia manifested her sympathy for Serbia, Germany her alliance with Austria, France her solidarity with Russia and by August the First World War had begun.

YUGOSLAVIA

During the First World War Serbia was overrun by the far more numerous armies of the Austro-Hungarian Empire; after the victory of the Allies, a new state was constituted in 1918 with Peter as first King of the Serbs, Croats and Slovenes. The elderly King had disinherited his eldest son George in 1909 on account of his private life, and Alexander, the second son, acted as regent for his father. His Kingdom included Croatia (the land north of the river Sava), Bosnia and Hercegovina, Slovenia and almost all Dalmatia, historic Serbia and the hitherto independent Montenegro. In 1929 the name was changed to Yugoslavia, that is South Slavia. Unhappily the union was an uneasy one. In the north the Croats and Slovenes had traditions looking towards Vienna, were mainly Catholic and used the Roman alphabet; in the south the Serbs and Bosnians were Orthodox

or Moslem, had more or less recent memories of Turkish rule and used the Cyrillic script.

In 1929 King Alexander, a wise and statesmanlike man, felt obliged to abolish the constitution and to rule arbitrarily. Before he could achieve his aims he was assassinated in Marseilles by an exiled Croat. His son became king, as Peter II; his cousin Paul became regent. Prince Paul was a distinguished connoisseur of art, but did not check the drift of Yugoslavia into economic dependence on the rising power of Nazi Germany. In 1941 Germany demanded passage for her forces through Yugoslavia; Paul and the government were inclined to yield, but a military group carried out a *coup d'état*, exiled Paul and proclaimed Peter II of age. In response to this heroic gesture of independence, Hitler attacked the country with savage success and the young King fled.

As can be seen on Table 144, his ancestry is half Balkan and half from the established reigning families of Europe. His shield is surrounded by the collar of the Order of St Lazarus, an exclusive decoration held only by the King himself and by his heir apparent. The extinction of the family of Obrenovich left King Peter II as the undisputed claimant to the throne of Yugoslavia. On the other hand, the success of the Communist guerrilla movement led by Marshal Tito (Josip Broz) has established a viable, left-wing state whose linked republics have to some extent eliminated ancient racial rivalries.

The old arms of Serbia (Table 144) were based on those attributed to the Byzantine Empire (Chapter 30: Empire in Dispute). Though the four charges round the cross are nowadays described as 'flints', they were probably in origin the letter 'C' (the Cyrillic capital 'S' for Serbia). The early Kings of Croatia used a shield of white and red checks. In medieval times the blazon of the Nemanya dynasty was an eagle with two fleurs-de-lys at its feet. The Obrenovich princes used the old arms of Serbia (Table 145), but Peter I (Karageorgevich) employed the Nemanya arms with Serbia set on them. His son, King Alexander I, dropped the fleurs-de-lys from the Nemanya arms and added a more elaborate escutcheon with the arms of Serbia, Croatia and the blue eagle of Carniola. This last was an heraldic gesture of protest against the division in 1918 of the Duchy of Carniola between Italy and his own Kingdom. His cousin Prince Paul differenced the main arms with a gold border, but has on the escutcheon the arms of Serbia, Croatia and Slovenia. Paul's mother was descended from the blacksmith of Peter the Great, whose issue were created princes by Tuscany.

BULGARIA

As has been seen, the second Bulgarian Empire came under Serbian domination and then passed into Turkish power. For long centuries Bulgaria was a relatively well-ordered province of the Ottoman Empire. In 1875 a rising against alien misgovernment began in Bosnia and spread to Bulgaria. The Turks reacted strongly, and the insurgents were suppressed with great brutality. The 'Bulgarian atrocities' supplied Mr Gladstone with a rousing theme in Britain, but it also turned the attention of the Great Powers to the Balkans. Russia invaded and defeated Turkey and by the Treaty of San Stefano (March 1878) proposed to set up an extensive Bulgarian state, under Russian protection, which would have included the bulk of Macedonia and reached the Aegean coast. The other Powers deeply mistrusted this enlargement of Russian influence; at Berlin (June 1878) the earlier treaty was superseded. A limited Bulgaria was granted autonomy but the southern section (Eastern Roumelia) remained under direct Turkish rule. In 1879 Prince Alexander of Battenberg (Table 150) was offered the throne; he was a nephew of the Czar, but not a member of a reigning family since his father's marriage had been morganatic.

In 1885 a rising in Eastern Roumelia dislodged the Turkish pasha and the conspirators begged Alexander to reign there also. With hesitation he did so, and became ruler of a united Bulgaria (though still of far smaller dimensions than the haunting, dream state of San Stefano). Stirred by envy King Milan of Serbia attacked Bulgaria, but Alexander led his subjects to a dramatic victory at Slivnitza. Unluckily for himself, the Prince had by now alienated Russian sympathy and he was dethroned by a plot in 1886. Adopting the title of Count of Hartenau, he retired to Austria and married a beautiful opera singer. His arms (Table 150) as Prince of Bulgaria show quarterings from Bulgaria and Eastern Roumelia separated by a cross, with a differenced version of Hesse over all. His brother, who entered the British navy and became Lord Milford Haven, quartered Hesse (this time within a bordure) with the black pallets of Battenberg. Alexander's good looks and valour, however, were not matched by his political capacity and experience.

Some difficulty was experienced in finding a new prince. The Bulgarian title was offered from Denmark to the Caucasus and even to the King of Rumania, but was eventually accepted by Prince Ferdinand of Saxe-Coburg and Gotha (Table 42) who became Prince of Bulgaria in 1887. As can be seen in Table 149, he was of varied descent; his father's lineage was German and Hungarian (Francis Joseph, Prince Kohary, was the last of that family), but his mother's blood was mainly Bourbon, and Ferdinand married a Catholic princess. He gave his first-born the historic Bulgarian name of Boris, but

the infant was baptized in the Roman faith. This produced controversy, and the child was converted to the Orthodox religion at the age of two, an event which delighted the populace.

Ferdinand was an accomplished and wily statesman and in 1908 he proclaimed Bulgaria independent of all Turkish suzerainty and himself adopted the title of king (czar); this step was gradually accepted by Turkey and by the older monarchies of Europe. In 1909 he founded the Order of Saints Cyril and Methodius (the original Byzantine apostles of the Slavs), which surrounds the traditional arms of Bulgaria, a gold, crowned lion on a purple background (Table 149).

Not all his subtleties – he was often called 'the Fox' – preserved Bulgaria from an unhappy destiny in the wars of the twentieth century. In 1912 he joined the other Christian states of the Balkans in the assault on the Ottoman Empire; Bulgaria contributed most in men and blood to the victory which was won, and hoped to gain most. The insistence of the Great Powers on creating an independent Albania under Prince William of Wied, who never really exercised his authority, disturbed the designs of the victorious Balkan states. In foolhardy fashion Bulgaria attacked her recent allies. Greece and Serbia were joined by Rumania in throwing back the assault. The final Treaty of Bucharest (1913) showed scant gains to Ferdinand and his followers. Once again the aspirations of Bulgaria had been shattered; it was not perhaps surprising that she sought fresh opportunities for revenge and expansion by joining the Central Powers late in 1915.

The defeat of Germany and her allies brought only discomfiture to Bulgaria. The tiny access to the Aegean, secured in 1913, was forfeited to Greece by the Treaty of Neuilly. Ferdinand abdicated in favour of his son, whose style of Boris III recalled the glories of the first Bulgarian Empire. The new Czar, whose main private interest was in railway trains, had to cope with a long series of involved, and often violent, political situations. Gradually he established himself, and was successful in cultivating better relations with Yugoslavia and in suppressing clandestine Macedonian activity. In foreign affairs he was committed to Nazi Germany, which assisted him in regaining the southern Dobruja (lost to Rumania in 1913). Boris III died mysteriously on a visit to Hitler in 1943 and a regency, headed by his brother Kyril, was formed in favour of his six-year-old son Simeon. However, in 1945 Kyril was shot by Communists and in 1946 the royal family was expelled after a referendum . King Simeon II has lived mainly in Spain and married a Spanish woman. The names of his children are a reminder of the first great period of Bulgarian history.

[297]

TABLE 150

BULGARIA
Houses of Hesse and Saxe-Coburg

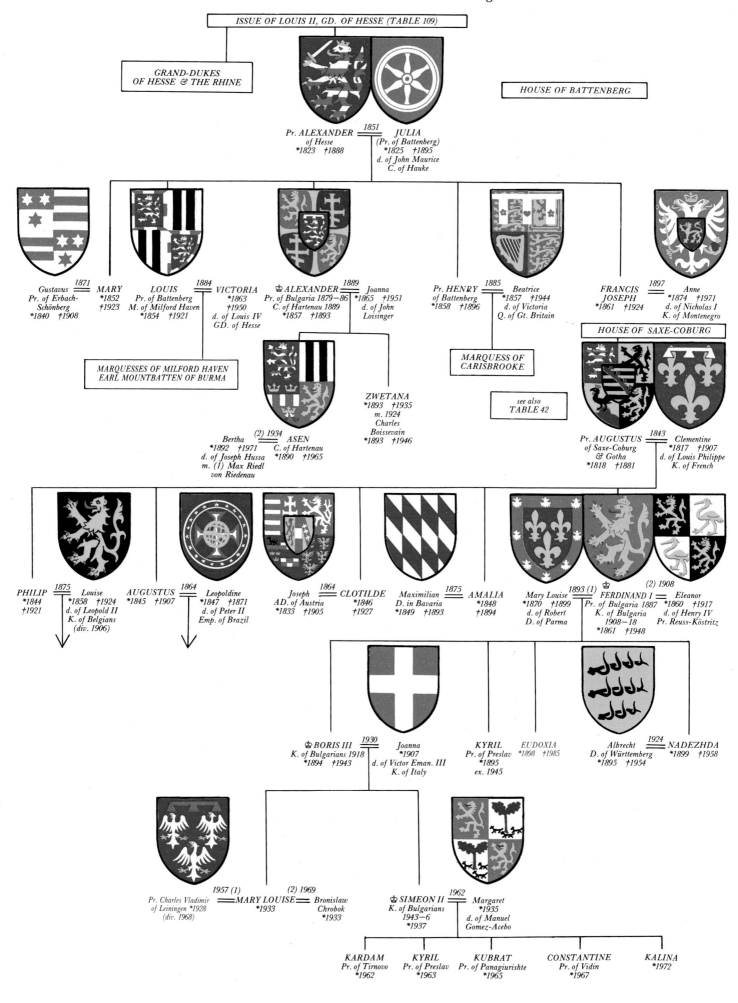

ISSUE OF LOUIS II, GD. OF HESSE (TABLE 109)

GRAND-DUKES
OF HESSE & THE RHINE

HOUSE OF BATTENBERG

Pr. ALEXANDER ══1851══ JULIA
of Hesse (Pr. of Battenberg)
*1823 †1888 *1825 †1895
d. of John Maurice
C. of Hauke

Gustavus ══1871══ MARY
Pr. of Erbach- *1852
Schönberg †1923
*1840 †1908

LOUIS ══1884══ VICTORIA
Pr. of Battenberg *1863
M. of Milford Haven d. of Louis IV
*1854 †1921 GD. of Hesse

ALEXANDER ══1889══ Joanna
Pr. of Bulgaria 1879—86 *1865 †1951
C. of Hartenau 1889 d. of John
*1857 †1893 Loisinger

Pr. HENRY ══1885══ Beatrice
of Battenberg *1857 †1944
*1858 †1896 d. of Victoria
Q. of Gt. Britain

FRANCIS ══1897══ Anne
JOSEPH *1874 †1971
*1861 †1924 d. of Nicholas I
K. of Montenegro

HOUSE OF SAXE-COBURG

MARQUESSES OF MILFORD HAVEN
EARL MOUNTBATTEN OF BURMA

ZWETANA
*1893 †1935
m. 1924
Charles
Boissevain
*1893 †1946

MARQUESS OF
CARISBROOKE

see also
TABLE 42

Bertha ══(2) 1934══ ASEN
*1892 †1971 C. of Hartenau
d. of Joseph Hussa *1890 †1965
m. (1) Max Riedl
von Riedenau

Pr. AUGUSTUS ══1843══ Clementine
of Saxe-Coburg *1817 †1907
& Gotha d. of Louis Philippe
*1818 †1881 K. of French

PHILIP ══1875══ Louise
*1844 *1858 †1924
†1921 d. of Leopold II
K. of Belgians
(div. 1906)

AUGUSTUS ══1864══ Leopoldine
*1845 †1907 *1847 †1871
d. of Peter II
Emp. of Brazil

Joseph ══1864══ CLOTILDE
AD. of Austria *1846
*1833 †1905 †1927

Maximilian ══1875══ AMALIA
D. in Bavaria *1848
*1849 †1893 †1894

Mary Louise ══1893 (1)══ FERDINAND I ══(2) 1908══ Eleanor
*1870 †1899 Pr. of Bulgaria 1887 *1860 †1917
d. of Robert K. of Bulgaria d. of Henry IV
D. of Parma 1908—18 Pr. Reuss-Köstritz
*1861 †1948

BORIS III ══1930══ Joanna
K. of Bulgarians 1918 *1907
*1894 †1943 d. of Victor Eman. III
K. of Italy

KYRIL EUDOXIA
Pr. of Preslav *1898 †1985
*1895
ex. 1945

Albrecht ══1924══ NADEZHDA
D. of Württemberg *1899 †1958
*1895 †1954

Pr. Charles Vladimir ══1957 (1)══ MARY LOUISE ══(2) 1969══ Bronislaw
of Leiningen *1928 *1933 Chrobok
(div. 1968) *1933

SIMEON II ══1962══ Margaret
K. of Bulgarians *1935
1943—6 d. of Manuel
*1937 Gomez-Acebo

KARDAM
Pr. of Tirnovo
*1962

KYRIL
Pr. of Preslav
*1963

KUBRAT
Pr. of Panagiurishte
*1965

CONSTANTINE
Pr. of Vidin
*1967

KALINA
*1972

RUMANIA

Rumania, the Dacia of the classical period, has had a rather different history from her neighbours. She has retained a form of the Latin language, though a majority of the population has in recent years adhered to the Orthodox Church. In medieval times two distinct provinces appeared: Wallachia, drawing its name from Vlach settlers, was the land north of the Danube and south of the Carpathians, while Moldavia lay east of those mountains and west of the river Pruth. Between the rivers Pruth and Dniester was the province of Bessarabia, linked historically with Moldavia, but long coveted by Russia.

By the end of the fourteenth century the whole area had passed into Turkish control, though efforts towards independence did not cease. In particular, Michael the Brave (1593–1601) briefly united Wallachia, Moldavia and Transylvania (west of the Carpathians) and bequeathed a vision of a great and free Rumania. The sixteenth century also saw a brilliant period of church decoration, mainly with broad eaves and exterior frescoes. During the succeeding centuries the Turks made considerable use of Greek families from Constantinople (Phanariots) in the administration of the country.

In 1812 Russia won Bessarabia from the Turks; nationalism was growing north of the Danube but the proximity of the Muscovite Empire was always a factor. After the Crimean War the Treaty of Paris (1856) united Wallachia and Moldavia, to which Bessarabia was restored, and a native leader, Alexander Cuza, was chosen as 'vojvod', a Slav word originally meaning general, but later governor or even prince; in 1859 the name Rumania was introduced. In a few years Cuza ran into political and economic difficulties; in 1866 Charles of Hohenzollern-Sigmaringen was chosen as prince. He belonged to a branch of the great Hohenzollern family (Table 91), senior to that of Prussia, but separated from it since the thirteenth century. But his grandmother was a niece of Joachim Murat (Table 148) which made him acceptable to Napoleon III. His wife, Elizabeth of Wied, was a talented authoress under the *nom de plume* of Carmen Sylva (and an aunt of the transient Prince of Albania in 1914).

Charles I led his armies in alliance with the Russians against the Turks in 1877, and Rumanian troops displayed great valour in the assault on Plevna. By the Treaty of Berlin Rumania acquired complete emancipation from Turkish control, but she had to yield part of Bessarabia to Russia; in return she gained the less profitable district of Dobruja (just south of the mouths of the Danube), which embittered her relations with Bulgaria. In 1881 Charles was crowned king: his crown was made of Turkish cannon captured at Plevna, and can be seen on Table

147. The ancient arms of Wallachia displayed an eagle with a cross in its beak and a sun and moon above. The Kings of Rumania removed the two last, but added to the eagle the crown, sceptre and sword indicative of regal power. On the breast of the eagle was placed an escutcheon with four quarters representing Wallachia, Moldavia, the Banat of Severin and Oltenia and Transylvania, with the two dolphins of Dobruja in base. Over this a smaller shield carried the white and black quarters of Hohenzollern. Around this complicated blazon is the Order of Charles I, founded in 1906. The ancient arms of Moldavia, also shown on Table 147, were an aurochs' head between full moon, star and crescent moon.

Rumania took no part in the first Balkan War (1912) against Turkey, but intervened against Bulgaria in the second (1913) and gained the southern Dobruja. At the outbreak of the First World War, Charles I was on the whole pro-German, but he died in 1914. He was succeeded by his nephew Ferdinand (whose elder brother William continued the princely line of Hohenzollern), already married to a British princess. In 1916 Rumania joined the Allies and, though initially defeated, acquired extensive provinces, especially in Transylvania, from Austria-Hungary by the Treaty of the Trianon; she also regained Bessarabia from Russia. In 1922 Ferdinand was ceremoniously re-crowned as King of the greater Rumania thus created.

King Ferdinand died in 1927. His son Charles was a wayward prince who had contracted a morganatic alliance in 1918 (from which one son resulted); in 1925 he renounced all rights to the throne. Accordingly in 1927 his son by Princess Helen of Greece succeeded as Michael I, under a regency. Three years later Carol (as he was widely known) returned to the country and became Charles II. His name was already associated with that of Magda (or Helen) Lupescu, and his rule moved steadily into a royal dictatorship. In 1940 he was deposed, and Michael became king again; real power was in the hands of the pro-Axis dictator, General Antonescu. Considerable Rumanian forces went to aid the Nazis on the Russian front. The end of the war saw Bessarabia once again in Russian hands and part of Dobruja returned to Bulgaria.

In 1947 King Michael was constrained to abdicate, and his country proceeded to become a Communist republic. His ancestry (Table 147) shows that he had two descents from the Russian dynasty, but also two from Queen Victoria; his mother's mother (Queen Sophia of Greece) belonged to the junior branch of the Hohenzollern family, which had attained the Crown of Prussia; thus the elder and younger lines are linked in the persons of the exiled King of Rumania and his children.

INDEX

Figures in bold refer to Table numbers, all others to page numbers. Page numbers in italics refer to the black-and-white illustrations, which are either pictures of people or drawings of coats-of-arms at the head of each chapter. An asterisk indicates a heraldic term, which is usually explained on the first page referred to. Individuals are indexed under their family or country name, and a Table reference for an individual indicates that there is an illustration of the person's arms on that Table, although the person may also be found on other Tables referred to under the general, family or country heading.

[301]

[303]

LIST OF TABLES

[307]